ESSENTIALS OF MARKETING RESEARCH

FOURTH EDITION

TONY PROCTOR PhD
Professor in Marketing,
Chester Business School

FT Prentice Hall
FINANCIAL TIMES

An imprint of **Pearson Education**
Harlow, England • London • New York • Boston • San Francisco • Toronto
Sydney • Tokyo • Singapore • Hong Kong • Seoul • Taipei • New Delhi
Cape Town • Madrid • Mexico City • Amsterdam • Munich • Paris • Milan

Pearson Education Limited
Edinburgh Gate
Harlow
Essex CM20 2JE
England

and Associated Companies throughout the world

Visit us on the World Wide Web at:
www.pearsoned.co.uk

First published 1997
Second edition 2000
Third edition 2003
Fourth edition published 2005

ISBN-13: 978-0-273-69494-6
ISBN-10: 0-273-69494-4

British Library Cataloguing-in-Publication Data
A catalogue record for this book is available from the British Library

Library of Congress Cataloging-in-Publication Data
Proctor, Tony
    Essentials of marketing research / Tony Proctor.— 4th ed.
      p. cm.
    Includes bibliographical references and index.
    ISBN 0-273-69494-4 (alk. paper)
     1. Marketing research. I. Title.

    HF5415.2.P736 2005
    658.8'3—dc22

    2005048453

10 9 8 7 6 5 4 3 2
10 09 08 07 06

Typeset in 10/12.5pt Palatino by 35
Printed by Ashford Colour Press Ltd., Gosport

The publisher's policy is to use paper manufactured from sustainable forests.

Essentials of Marketing Research

Brief contents

Full contents

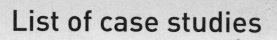

List of case studies

Further case studies

Preface

'Marketing research' has often been called 'market research', and there has been much confusion about what these terms actually mean. Indeed, some writers have been so worried about the terminology that they have called their books 'research for marketing decisions' to overcome the problems. The term marketing research, of which market research is but one element, encompasses the full range of research and evaluation activities undertaken by marketing professionals to guide them in decision making, and it is marketing research that I address in this book.

There have been vast changes in marketing research, largely as a result of the development of information technology. Marketing research is, to some extent, a quantitative subject and although many of the techniques have been around for many years, using them was hindered by the lack of powerful and readily available computational aids. It is sobering to remember that in the mid-1960s the slide rule was the main calculating tool, mainframe computers were in their infancy and the mechanical Burroughs' comptometers had only just given way to more sophisticated electronic ones. Now the problem is not so much lack of computing power as the need to acquire the skills necessary to select from and use the many sophisticated analytical methods that are available.

SCOPE AND COVERAGE

This book looks at the traditional approach to marketing research and the traditional tools of analysis. It also discusses new developments – particularly in the areas of qualitative data analysis and marketing decisions support systems. I have tried to make the book into a teaching/study book designed primarily for undergraduates but of interest to MBA and other postgraduate or post-experience students wanting to get some idea of the subject matter. In writing such a book, getting the balance right between different topics and the depth at which each is covered is constrained by the length of the book. Because it is designed as a teaching book, I have devoted much of the available space to case studies, illustrations and questions.

The various chapters address different topics in marketing research:

- Chapter 1 looks at the nature of, and the need for, marketing research. An overview is given of the process of marketing research and the chapter concludes by looking at the role of agencies and at ethical issues.

- Chapter 2 pays attention to planning the research project and in particular to the use of PERT analysis to guide the management of the project.

- Chapter 3 examines the uses and limitations of secondary data, indicating when secondary data may be useful in research and giving details of useful internal and external sources of data.

- Chapter 4 examines the process of sampling. Attention is given to all aspects of sampling, including the sampling frame, sampling unit selection, sampling method, the sample size and the sampling plan.

- Methods and applications of surveys are dealt with in Chapter 5. Sources of error, methods of data collection, dealing with non-response, panel/syndicated marketing research and omnibus surveys are among the topics discussed.

- Chapter 6 covers measurement, scales and attitude measurement. The process of measurement is discussed along with levels and variations in measurement. The chapter also looks at the nature of attitudes and their measurement.

- Chapter 7 looks at questionnaire construction and development. Particular attention is given to question content, question phrasing, kinds of response format, question sequence, question layout, pretesting and revising. Validity, reliability and sensitivity are also considered.

- Qualitative research methods are outlined in Chapter 8. Focus group discussions, individual depth interviews and projective techniques are considered.

- Chapter 9 looks first at observation as a research method and then at experimentation. Details of many different experimental designs are given. The chapter also looks at test marketing, both in the marketplace and under simulated conditions.

- Chapter 10 examines data interpretation and the various tools of quantitative data analysis. A wide range of statistical methods is examined. It is presupposed that the reader is familiar with statistics at an introductory level.

- Chapter 11 presents an aspect of marketing research that is not usually discussed in a textbook of this kind. Qualitative data analysis is an important dimension of marketing research. The chapter looks at a variety of tools and methods that can assist in the analysis of qualitative data.

- Chapter 12 discusses reports and their presentation. Emphasis is placed on the use of information technology to help prepare and present good reports.

- Chapter 13 looks at a variety of examples of applied marketing research, including product research, segmentation research, competition research and promotion research.

- Business-to-business marketing research, services research and research for internal marketing are the subject matter of Chapter 14.

- Global marketing research is the subject matter of Chapter 15.

- Chapter 16 discusses marketing decision support systems. Among the most interesting developments here are applications of neural network software as expert systems.

NEW TO THIS EDITION

This edition recognises that the Internet is becoming more and more important as a source for information. Chapter 3 provides more information on how the Internet can provide more information and how it can be used advantageously in the course of research. In particular, the focus of attention is directed towards the availability of Internet databases which can provide very relevant information for marketers.

In addition, all chapters have been re-examined, revised and updated as appropriate. The list of references in the book has also been extended considerably and the questions at the end of each chapter have been modified and reduced in number. New cases studies have replaced some of the older cases. These include case studies 1.2 Spirit of Magellan Enterprises, 2.2 *Cheri*, 11.3 Renault Clio, 13.1 Tourism in Bukhara, among others.

ADDED BENEFITS

In addition the book also features:

- further case studies to promote thought on how marketing research as an entity can be applied in practice

- a glossary to reinforce key terms

- a full bibliography offering additional references.

LEARNING RESOURCES

Visit www.pearsoned.co.uk/proctor_emr to access an Instructor's Manual and PowerPoint slides.

AUTHOR'S ACKNOWLEDGEMENTS

My thanks are due to Jim Blythe for the case studies that he has contributed. In addition, I extend thanks to Lucy, Carol and Zoë for their contributions. The following reviewers provided useful feedback for this edition:

Nigel Culkin, University of Hertfordshire
Jouan de Kervenoael, Lancaster University
Rod Harradwe, Teeside Business School
Kathy Mouat, Napier University
Jane Hemsley-Brown, University of Surrey
Richard West, University of Westminster

I would also like to thank the editorial team at Pearson for making this 4th edition a reality. Thanks to Thomas Sigel, Senior Acquisitions Editor; Peter Hooper, Editorial Assistant; Anita Atkinson, Senior Desk Editor; Helen Baxter, Copy Editor.

Tony Proctor
Spring 2005

Acknowledgements

We are grateful to the following for permission to reproduce copyright material:

Figures 2.3, 2.4, 2.5, 2.6 and 16.8 featuring Microsoft's Windows ™ browser bar, screen shots reprinted by permission from Microsoft Corporation; Table 4.1 from 'The "Marketing Research Services Classification' of Social Class,' in *National Readership Survey*, JINCARS 1981, National Readership Surveys Ltd; unnumbered table on pp. 118–19 from http://www.caci.co.uk/acorn/acornmap.asp, 22 April 2005, © 2005 CACI Limited, Acorn is a registered trade mark of CACI Limited; Figure 11.3 a screen shot from NUD*IST, Version 6, *Work Interactions Project*, NUD*IST is developed by QSR Pty Ltd; Figure 16.2 a screen shot from SNAP software, Mercator Research Group Ltd; Table 16.13 from Kotler, Philip, *Marketing Management*, 11th edition, © 2003, p. 499, reprinted by permission of Pearson Education, Inc., Upper Saddle River, NJ.

The American Marketing Association for a definition of 'Marketing Research'; Editions Rebondir for extracts adapted from 'Small business ideas and studying the local market' published in *Rebondir* no. 12 1996; The Market Research Society for the following extracts; 'How a spoonful of research helps the medicine go down' by Tracey Sanderson April 1996, 'With growing demands for data, will purity prove only theoretical?' by Peter Mouncey May 1996, 'Quality will mark the route to deeper client relationships' by Bryan Bates March 1996, Extracts adapted from *Research Plus* 'Homelink' September 1993, 'Get a helping of the sugar-free chips game' by Sue White September 1993, 'The launch went fine – then the devil's in the dealing' by Andrew Scott April 1996, 'In Europe's complex market, check the price is right' by A.J. Bowditch April 1996, 'The cascade theory that shows practical gains' by Peter Gorle October 1995, 'Now business research is every agency's research' by D. Jamieson October 1995, 'The world shrinks, maybe, but there's still the need to travel' by M. Goodyear May 1996, 'Why we won't keep taking pills' by A. Branthwaite and J. Bruggemann April 1996, 'Now that India's got GATT, a massive market beckons' by Sue Bunn April 1996, and 'The markets are emerging – and research is hard on their heels' by Mia Bartonova January 1996; Marketing Week for extracts adapted from *Marketing Week* 'Research needs more creativity' by Clare Nutall 29th April 1996, 'Working on site' 26th April 1996, 'Commercial TV audiences rise' by Paul McCann 26th April 1996, 'The data game' by David Reed 3rd May 1996, 'PepsiCo needs new strategy for iced tea' by Jon Rees 16th April 1996, and 'Poster watch' 26th April

1996; Rene Spindler for an extract adapted from her MSc dissertation, Odense University 1991; Zoe Cooper for an extract adapted from her MBA dissertation, Keele University; Carol Fry for extracts adapted from her MBA dissertation, Keele University; Marketing for extracts adapted from 'Research propels innovation', and 'Avon ads praise the real woman' by Ruth Nicholas published in *Marketing* 27th January 1994, and 'Eastern Promise is worth all the pain of red tape' by Bob Tyrell published in *Marketing* 3rd February 1994; Business Opportunity World for an extract adapted from 'Safety letterbox' published in *Business Opportunity World* May 1996; Lucy Double for an extract adapted from her MBA dissertation, Keele University 1991; Marketing News for an extract adapted from 'Delphi technique can work for new product development' by Gianni Bolongaro published in *Marketing News* 3rd January 1994; MapInfo Limited for extracts from their website www.mapinfo.co.uk/products/spftware.cfm and company literature; South Africa Tourism Board for an extract adapted from *South Africa: a World in One Country*, 1996; International Wrist Watch for an extract adapted from 'The French Connection' published in *International Wrist Watch* 1995, Issue 31; Rushuang Xiong for an extract adapted from an MBA dissertation, Keele University 1994; Mercator Research Group Limited for 'SNAP'; Emerald Group Publishing Limited for an extract adapted from 'Forecasting: the key to managerial decision-making' by D. Waddell and A.S. Sohal published in *Management Decision*, 32(1) 1994 © MCB University Press Limited; and The Lake Lucerne Navigation Company, Switzerland, 2005, for information in 'Lake Lucerne Navigation Company (SGV)'.

We are grateful to the Financial Times Limited for permission to reprint the following material:

'Potential benefits of market research', from Marketing wake-up, © *Financial Times*, 3 June 1997; Golden nuggets on a long and winding road, © *Financial Times*, 3 December 1997; Data loss, © *Financial Times*, 23 January 1997; Opinion polling faces new scrutiny, © *Financial Times*, 21 March 1997; Baby boomers get the message, © *Financial Times*, 26 May 1997; Shoppers under the microscope, © *Financial Times*, 5 December 1997; Caught in the neighbours' tangled web, © *Financial Times*, 15 August 1997; Public puts faith in brand names, © *Financial Times*, 13 October 1997; Soft drinks switch to PET leaves industry struggling, © *Financial Times*, 22 October 1997; 'Newspapers are a source of information about competitiors', from 'Nike' part of the Lex column, © *Financial Times*, 20 December 1997; 'Electronic revolution in the retailing world', from Pressures in the marketplace, © *Financial Times*, 3 September 1997; British divided into four types, © *Financial Times*, 5 September 1997; Deceptive appearance, © *Financial Times*, 3 February 1997; Orchestras aim to pass the baton, © *Financial Times*, 26 May 1997; The decline of frills, © *Financial Times*, 28 April 1997; Noteworthy response, © *Financial Times*, 26 October 2004; Moving images, © *Financial Times*, 19 October 2004; Going below the surface, © *Financial Times*, 28 September 2004; Desmond sizes up shopping, © *Financial Times*, 19 October 2004; Is fizzing up its look enough?, © *Financial Times*, 26 October 2004; Now interacting with lots of new partners, © *Financial Times*, 12 October 2004.

We are grateful to the following for permission to use copyright material:

Why researchers are so jittery from *The Financial Times Limited*, 3 March 1997, © Winston Fletcher; The future lies abroad from *The Financial Times Limited*, 30 June 1997, © Sir Martin Sorrell; One strike and you're down from *The Financial Times Limited*, 5 October 2004, © Richard Gillis; They might as well be men . . . from *The Financial Times Limited*, 5 October 2004, © Jasmine Montgomery.

In some instances we have been unable to trace the owners of copyright material, and we would appreciate any information that would enable us to do so.

1 Nature of marketing research

Objectives

After reading this chapter, you should be able to:

- define marketing research, understand the philosophy of science and understand how marketing research relates to marketing decision making and planning

- appreciate the major divisions of marketing research and how it is part of marketing strategy

- recognise the role played by marketing research agencies and the kind of services they provide

- understand the ethical issues involved in marketing research

- understand how the Internet can be used in marketing research

- appreciate the need for creativity in marketing research

- appreciate problems created by non-response in marketing research.

Keywords

agencies
conclusive research
creativity
customer research
epistemology
ethics
in-house research
market research

ontology
performance research
preliminary research
primary research
quantitative research
research proposal
risk reduction
secondary research

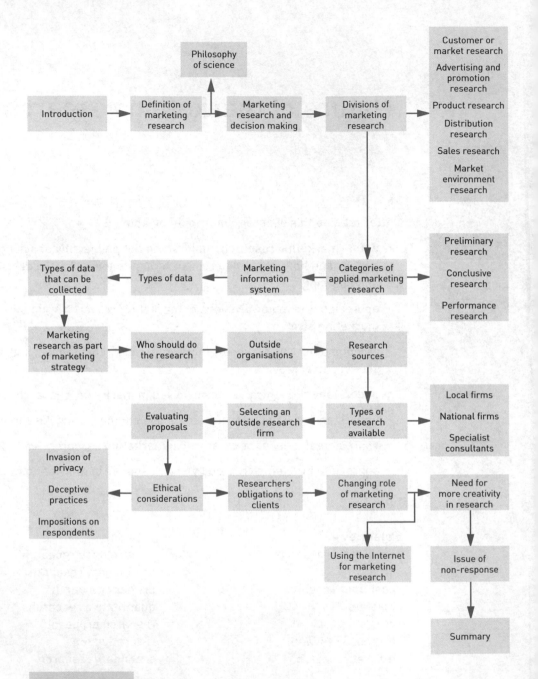

Plan of Chapter 1

INTRODUCTION

Marketing research aims to take some of the risk out of marketing decisions by providing information that can form part or the entire basis of decision making. It is applicable to all aspects of marketing-mix decisions and should be an integral part of the process of formulating marketing strategy. Marketing research can help in a variety of studies and makes use of both primary and secondary data sources. It can be conducted either in-house by a firm's own staff or by outside marketing research companies that specialise in marketing research activities. Outside research companies, or **agencies**, offer a wide range of services, ranging from off-the-peg studies to tailor-made studies to meet the needs of individual clients. As is the case with many other services involving obtaining information from firms and members of the public, ethical considerations are an important issue. In a rapidly changing environment, the need to come up with new ideas is also extremely important and priority needs to be given to introducing creativity into marketing research.

MARKETING RESEARCH: A DEFINITION

Peter Chisnall (1992)[1] points out that although the term '**market research**' is now largely used as a synonym for 'marketing research' there was originally a distinct difference between the scope of the activities they covered. Some confusion has been caused by the term 'market research' being rather freely used to describe the full range of activities properly covered by marketing research. Chisnall (1992) notes, however, that market or marketing research is essentially about the disciplined collection and evaluation of specific data in order to help suppliers to understand their customer needs better. Moreover, since decision making necessarily involves some element of risk, the collection and evaluation of such data should be used to reduce and control, to some degree, the parameters of risk surrounding particular marketing proposals.

MARKETING RESEARCH AS DEFINED BY THE AMERICAN MARKETING ASSOCIATION

Marketing research is the function that links the consumer, customer and public to the marketer through information – information used to identify and define marketing opportunities and problems; generate, refine, and evaluate marketing actions; monitor marketing performance; and improve understanding of marketing as a process. Marketing research specifies the information required to address these issues; designs the method for collecting information; manages and implements the data-collection process; analyses the results; and communicates the findings and their implications.

Source: AMA[2]

Any definition of marketing research has to take account of the changing role of research in modern marketing. Marketing research connects the consumer, the customer and the public to the marketer through the medium of information. This information is used to distinguish and define marketing opportunities and threats or problems. It is also used to create, improve and assess marketing actions and to monitor marketing performance. It also helps to improve understanding of marketing as a process. Marketing research identifies the information required to address these issues. It comprises methods for collecting data, analysis of data collected and their interpretation and communication of the findings and their implications. It takes account of experience, the present situation and the likely future so that marketing executives can make sound decisions.

This definition of marketing research underlines the role of research in all phases of marketing, assisting and guiding the marketing efforts of the organisation (see Figure 1.1). Marketing research involves more than studies of specific problems or specific situations, for it prevents problems arising in the first place. There is a need for marketing research to be at the centre of decision making.[3, 4] It is a fact-finding and forecasting function that is used by all phases of marketing and even by other functional aspects of an organisation.

PHILOSOPHY OF SCIENCE

All academic research is said to be grounded in a philosophical perspective. Easterby-Smith et al.[5] provide a useful summary as to why a philosophical perspective on any research study is important. For example, it can help to clarify research design in terms of its overall configuration, what kind of evidence is gathered and from where, and how this can be interpreted to provide answers to the question(s) asked. It can help recognise those designs that are likely to work and those that will not, and highlight limitations of particular approaches. It can help the researcher identify research designs that may be outside his/her past experiences.

There continues however to be a great deal of debate among academic researchers around the most appropriate philosophical position from which methods of research should be derived. In this instance, the competing *schools of thought* are often described as *positivist* and *phenomenological*. These schools of thought are perhaps best viewed as extremes on a continuum. Each school has its own set of assumptions and a range of methodological implications associated with its position. However, there is a danger of oversimplification if this distinction is taken too literally. It is important to recognise that rarely does any piece of research work fit neatly into a particular school of thought. Rather a piece of research tends to subscribe to a particular school of thought.

The researcher's methodological, epistemological and ontological premises can be termed a paradigm or interpretive framework that encompasses a set of beliefs that guide the research action. This comprises:

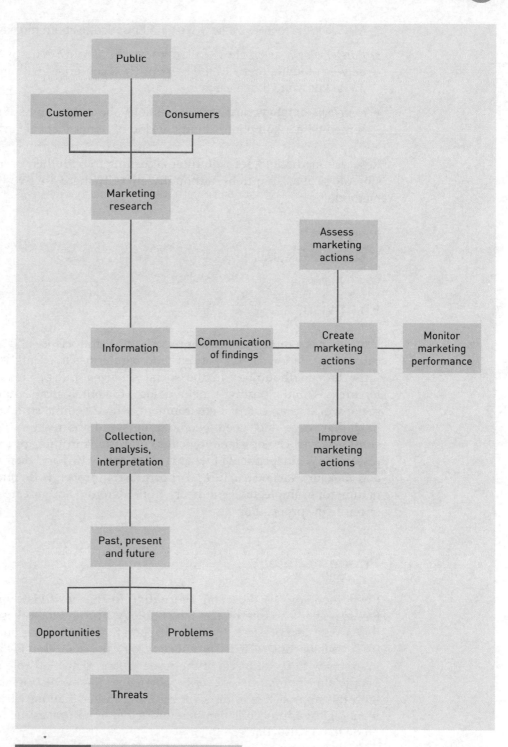

FIGURE 1.1   Role of marketing research

- *Methodology*: focuses on how we gain knowledge about the world.

- *Epistemology*: asks: How do we know the world? What is the relationship between the inquirer and the known? (It is concerned with how things can be made known to the researcher.)

- *Ontology*: **ontology** raises basic questions about the nature of reality. (It is concerned with assumptions about the kind of things there are in the world.)

Research methodologies will differ according to both their ontological and epistemological assumptions, although generally there are two types of research methodology:

- positivist

- phenomenological.

Positivism

Positivism is a more dominant approach in natural science and is concerned with causal explanation such as patterns and regularities in events. As such, this is an important methodology in the social sciences and particularly in business research. Within a positivist methodology, the ontological assumptions view the social world as an external environment, where definite structures affect people in similar ways, and where people understand and react to these structures in similar ways. The epistemological assumptions in this approach are that the researcher is independent of what is being researched and their role is to observe and measure social structures. A positivist approach is therefore deductive in nature; for example, taking a theory from literature and researching it to confirm or refute the proposition.

Phenomenology

Phenomenology is the main alternative to the positivist approach in social research and is an interpretive methodology. The ontological assumption here is that people are not passive in simply responding to structures but instead reality is itself socially constructed. The epistemological assumption is that the researcher interacts with the subjects of the research and that their role is to understand people's interpretation of events rather than the events themselves. The focus with this approach is to discover meaning rather than measurement. A phenomenological approach is therefore inductive in nature, as the investigation will guide the construction of a theory.

To understand fully the traditions of each school of thought, and its theoretical basis, is a significant field of study in its own right and is beyond the scope of this book. (To gain a fuller appreciation of the theoretical foundations of each school of thought see: Allison et al;[6] Bekesi;[7] and Embree.[8])

It is important that the research study and its findings are fully accepted by its target audience, if it is to have any actionable value. A positivist approach will help to overcome some of these reservations given that its approach is widely adopted in this environment as a means of research. Allison et al. argue that positivism and phenomenology are in fact *complementary* rather than incompatible and that there are many similarities between the two schools of thought. Hannabuss,[9] citing the work of Gummesson,[10] provides a useful summary of the differences between a positivistic and hermeneutic approach. The positivistic approach stresses rules by which we can explore and explain phenomena objectively, defining valid knowledge and inquiry in scientific terms. It focuses on description and explanation. There exist clear distinctions between facts and values, rationality and logic, statistical techniques and detachment, and explicit theories and hypotheses.

Academics agree that there is no one research method that is the most appropriate for all research problems. Each research study has its own distinctiveness, assumptions, bias and degrees of usefulness. It is generally argued that the choice of research design imposes intellectual and practical constraints on a researcher in terms of **reliability, validity** and generalisability.[11]

MARKETING RESEARCH AND DECISION MAKING

There are elements of uncertainty and risk attached to all business decisions and **risk reduction** is the main difficulty involved in the choices that are made. Common sense suggests that the availability of good information reduces the risk. After all, having perfect information all the time would make the job of exercising choice much easier since there would be no risk in making marketing decisions. Correct answers to such questions as how much to spend on advertising and what message should be contained in the advertising would always be known.

The first step in the decision-making process is the identification of needed information. Incorrect specification of requirements will provide only useless information, so it is necessary to ensure that the specification is correct. Poor or misleading information not only costs time and money but also generates confusion, chaos and badly informed decisions. One must determine what information is needed to make a particular decision. Next, consideration has to be given to whether the information can be obtained within a reasonable time and at a reasonable cost, and whether one can afford to spend both the time and the money to obtain it.

Information used in the right way can be a powerful aid to marketing. A competitive advantage can be achieved with the help of accurate, relevant information since it helps marketers make better decisions. Inaccurate, irrelevant information is both misleading and dangerous in the extreme.

POTENTIAL BENEFITS OF MARKET RESEARCH

Plastics chemist Graham West thought marketing was an expensive exercise in woolly thinking.

He is the managing director of Belgrade Insulations, a plastics and vacuum-forming company based in Wellingborough. In 1991 a Department of Trade and Industry official called to talk about the department's Marketing Initiative to help smaller businesses write a marketing plan. As a result of changes partly inspired by the programme, West says: 'I realised I had been lacking direction for years. We had been simply unable to look for markets where we could apply the company's skills.' A recent study by the Marketing Council and Warwick Business School looked at companies, including Belgrade Insulations, that had taken part in the DTI scheme. It found that some simple marketing tasks had fostered significant sales growth.

John Stubbs, chief executive of the Marketing Council, thinks the findings should encourage personal business advisers at Business Links, the government-led support service, to think hard about how to help sharpen marketing skills.

West had been running his own company for 20 years without a thought of marketing. In 1991 the building industry, to which he supplied a variety of products including lids for cold water tanks, 'stopped dead'. Worse, Belgrade Insulations was dependent for at least 60% of its sales – and 'far more' of its profits – on a single customer. The company had a healthy balance sheet, with no borrowing, but turnover seemed to have plateaued at about £3m – producing pre-tax profits of about £230,000.

West hired a sales development manager. But he already had a sales executive. 'All I had done was put another man in the field with a scattergun approach. We had to look outside the building industry, but we did not know where.'

So West was receptive when he heard about the DTI scheme. A marketing consultant was allocated to him and spent part of two or three weeks producing a report. The government paid half the consultant's fee. 'He was very sharp. He could see our problems and didn't talk down to us. But he probably went too far. There was such an enormous list of things to do.' More pertinently, the report assumed marketing knowledge. 'It didn't quite get us off the ground.'

Shortly after, attracted by cheap training, he took part in the Investors in People scheme, one of whose consultants had a marketing background. Building on the DTI report, West says: 'We sat down and identified the company's strengths and weaknesses and what we could bring to the table that our competitors could not – which was actually very little.'

The car components industry looked relatively promising – and, unlike the building trade, was still ticking over, in spite of the recession. A telephone survey was conducted, and West followed up every inquiry, however small – 'odds and ends, orders no one else wanted'.

At the same time, West decided that he needed to bolster research and development capabilities and hired a pattern maker who could concentrate on developing prototypes from the new customers' requests. Some sizeable orders materialised.

'I have to say we lost money on the majority, but we had gone up a very steep learning curve. The ideas were tumbling out.' Now the company could produce a prototype in a week or less – rather than the month or two it had previously taken.

Eighteen months ago West brought in a full-time marketing man with a brief to hunt out growth industries where the company's skills – including its sharper research and development capabilities – could be used. In addition to car components, Belgrade Insulations is now selling to the leisure industry, to heating and ventilation companies and to the general engineering sector. It has recently focused on waste disposal as another growth area where it is working with customers to fashion new products. 'We can charge whatever is the going rate, we are not beholden to one customer.' The company to which West was once selling 60% of his goods now accounts for less than 25% of sales, and he hopes that will reduce further as expansion continues elsewhere.

In the year to August 1996 pre-tax profits rose to about £500,000 on sales of £4.8m and he is aiming for sales of £7m by 1999. Belgrade Insulation's financial strength, its R&D skills and, as West puts it, the 'team effort' have played a crucial role in its development. But it was some simple marketing, he reckons, that really awoke the business.

Source: Campbell[12] (reprinted with permission)

DIVISIONS OF MARKETING RESEARCH

Marketing research has developed a number of broad divisions covering the range of problems and decisions with which executives have to deal. These are indicated in Figure 1.2.

Customer or market research

Customer or **market research** can produce quantitative facts about particular markets and market segments, for example, the size of the market in terms of both unit sales and value. When these data are collected over time, it allows one to identify trends and helps to predict future sales. It can also provide information on where customers are located, their spending patterns, their earnings and their creditworthiness. It can also explain why customers prefer one brand to another and what price they are willing to pay. Market research can also provide information about market share of all the firms operating in a market or market segment.

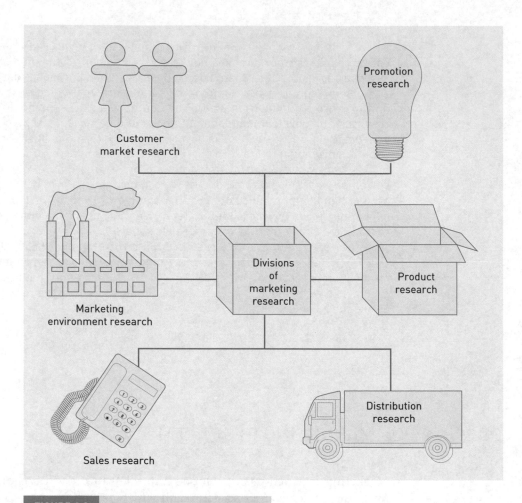

FIGURE 1.2   Divisions of marketing research

CUSTOMER MARKET RESEARCH PROVIDES INFORMATION ON:

- market and market segment sizes
- trends in the market that can be used for forecasting
- brand shares
- customer characteristics and motivations
- competitors' brands shares

Advertising and promotion research

Advertising research measures the success of advertising campaigns in relationship to their objectives. It also helps users of advertising in selecting the most appropriate promotional media and methods that are likely to produce the most effective results. Advertising research can provide information on which medium is most likely to reach the target audience for specific campaigns. It also provides information about what messages are most likely to appeal to the target audience. Research also helps in the process of evaluating in advance the likely impact of a campaign by testing out advertisements on a limited scale. Through **tracking** studies the effectiveness of a campaign can be monitored at all stages of its implementation.

PROMOTIONAL RESEARCH PROVIDES INFORMATION ON:

- the most suitable method of promotion
- the most suitable copy and campaign material
- the most suitable media to use
- the effectiveness of the communications in achieving objectives

Product research

Product research helps to find additional uses for existing and potential products or services. It also helps, in the case of new product ideas, to test out the product **concept** with potential users and purchasers before the expensive process of product development. If a product concept is found to be sound and is then developed, product research can test the product out on potential users before the launch. This latter information can be used to remove any apparent design faults in a product. Product research helps to provide an effective assessment of the strengths and weaknesses of a product or service in comparison with competitors' products or services. Research also provides information on the appropriate packaging of a product, helping to design it in such a way as to promote the image of the product (or service).

PRODUCT RESEARCH PROVIDES INFORMATION ON:

- opportunities for new product development
- product design requirements
- comparative performance *vis-à-vis* competitors' offerings
- packaging

Distribution research

Research helps to find the best channels of distribution for a product and helps in the selection of distribution channel members. With regard to physical distribution, research indicates the best sites for warehouse and retail locations.

DISTRIBUTION RESEARCH PROVIDES INFORMATION ON:

- suitable distribution methods
- appropriateness of channel members
- best location for warehouses and retail outlets

Sales research

Sales research helps to assess and measure the effectiveness of different methods or techniques of selling. It helps to ensure that sales patches are roughly equivalent in size so that sales staff are not unfairly discriminated against when it comes to setting sales targets. Sales research provides information on the suitability of remuneration methods and levels for motivating the salesforce. Research is also concerned with sales training and can provide extensive feedback on the quality of sales presentations made by sales staff.

SALES RESEARCH PROVIDES INFORMATION ON:

- effectiveness of sales methods and techniques
- establishing sales territories
- the adequacy of remuneration methods
- sales training requirements

Marketing environment research

This division of marketing research examines the political, economic, social and technological influences that may impact on a firm's marketing operations.

In the case of the political aspect of the environment, changes in government can affect trading conditions and these need to be anticipated on a worldwide basis. Clearly, the economic climate within which a business operates exerts an effect. These effects may be temporary or more permanent. Attention has to be given to such influences when planning, and research helps to assess the impact of political and economic factors.

Social influences can also have a substantial impact on some businesses. Population explosions or declines directly influence the demand for certain goods. Research provides information on which factors are relevant and how they impinge on the organisation's activities.

Technological influences can have a sudden and dramatic impact on the fortunes of a business. A sudden technological breakthrough can make currently successful products and processes obsolete in a very short space of time. Research can monitor technological progress and provide advance notice of new developments.

MARKET ENVIRONMENT RESEARCH PROVIDES INFORMATION ON:

- political influences
- economic influences
- social influences
- technological influences

CATEGORIES OF APPLIED MARKETING RESEARCH

Preliminary research

Preliminary research is often necessary before a final statement and definition of a problem can be agreed on. For example, someone may come up with the idea for a new service. Preliminary research may concern such matters as: whether the market for such a service is regional or national; who would use the service; and what substitute services people use. Answers to these kinds of question can help to define the nature and scope of more complete research.

A review of earlier research may be helpful. It is possible, for example, that the suggestion put forward as an idea for a new service has been previously researched. There may even be already published sources of information that can provide pertinent information. Government publications might mention the service, for example, or some trade publication may have mentioned it and even considered its use.

Conclusive research

Conjectures or hypotheses are developed in the preliminary search and in the course of defining the marketing problem. **Conclusive research** is carried out to produce evidence to support these hypotheses. In conducting conclusive research, a thorough search of already published data is made. Fieldwork may also be conducted.

Performance research

Performance research is concerned with assessing how well recommended marketing actions are being carried out and what benefits in terms of the objectives set are being realised. Performance research monitors the effectiveness of marketing management. It questions the definition of the problem that has directed the work to date. It makes one review whether a new study is desirable because certain questions remain unsatisfactorily resolved.

Marketing research provides information for marketing decision making and problem solving and it may thus be regarded as part of the marketing information system. In the last chapter in the book, we look in detail at the marketing information system. However, because of its relationship to marketing research we introduce the subject in this chapter.

SMALL BUSINESS IDEAS AND STUDYING THE LOCAL MARKET

When you have got some idea of the national market for your idea and some insights into the most suitable openings that relate to the activities in which you are interested, the next step is to study possibilities in the local market.

You need to immerse yourself in the environment. Start by making a tour of the streets in the town and the town's commercial centres. Note the neighbouring kinds of business, particularly those that offer similar or complementary kinds of products or services to those you want to offer. Take note of the kind of clientele they attract.

This study will give you a better understanding of the neighbourhood. You can then find out from your local Chamber of Commerce how long certain kinds of businesses on particular streets have been there – a good indicator of your own particular chances of long-term survival. You may also find out what kind of businesses have been unsuccessful either in general or in particular areas and, more to the point, why this has been the case.

Source: *Rebondir*[13]

MARKETING INFORMATION SYSTEMS

Marketing information systems have been around for a long time – conceptually there is nothing particularly new about them. The original ones were paper-based systems in which summarised information was stored in large banks of filing cabinets. In comparison with current notions of information systems, the early paper-based systems were relatively inefficient. With the advent of computers, particularly desktop computers, the opportunity developed for marketing information systems to become more sophisticated and efficient.

A marketing information system is a way of systematically gathering and giving helpful marketing information to the right people on a continuous basis and at the right time. Since information needs, sources and costs alter with time, a review of any information system is desirable from time to time. Such a review should specify individual people's information requirements, at what times information is required and where it can be found.

Marketing managers use many different types of information and there are many ways of putting together a marketing information system. The required information can be classified in a number of different ways. One way of classifying the information is:

- internal information

- external information

- position information

- decision information

- forecast information.

Internal information is made up of sales reports, sales analyses and cost analyses related to sales. Most of the raw data already exist within the organisation and need to be processed or analysed so that they become helpful information. An information system facilitates this process.

External information refers to the size and structure of the market (or potential market) and to trends, opportunities and threats in the environment. It also includes information on competitors and customers, both existing and potential. Employees, customers and distributors contribute this form of marketing information.

Position information is created by combining internal and external information. For example, one might combine the enterprise's sales and the overall sales of the enterprise and its competitors in the market to calculate market share. In a similar fashion, internal strengths and weaknesses can be compared to those of competitors to find competitive advantage and unique selling points, and to ascertain whether any competitive advantage is sustainable.

Decision information results from various analyses which can involve mathematical and statistical **treatment** of data.

Forecast information can be based on either subjective opinions, ascertained by survey, or on statistical analysis of trends.

Some of this information can be obtained cheaply, while other forms take time to gather and analyse. There is a tradeoff between the value of information and its cost – in terms of both time and money. Executives must know which information affects which decisions and which information is essential.

TYPES OF DATA

Research can be categorised into primary and secondary and into qualitative and quantitative. **Primary research** is usually carried out for the specific use of a client company or even by the company itself. **Secondary research** makes use of research already carried out by someone else for some other purpose.

Quantitative research produces numbers and figures – such as numbers and percentages of consumers who are aware of particular products or services. Qualitative research, contrariwise, provides data on why people buy – what motivates them to buy – or their impressions of products, services or advertisements. Both forms of research produce information on markets, competitors, distributors and customers. For example, reports provide information on markets, their size, structure, key producers and distributors, their market share, trends and prices. They also provide information on behaviour, attitudes and intentions.

In the case of consumer goods, retail audits measure market sales, week by week or day by day, competitor's sales, market shares, prices, special offers and stock levels. Customer surveys use structured questionnaires to assess, among other things, customer attitudes, levels of awareness, intentions to purchase and actual purchases. Qualitative research techniques, such as focus groups and in-depth interviews, obtain data on customers' opinions, motivations, perceptions and reactions to marketing-mix variables and changes in the variables – for example, price changes. Customer reactions to the marketing-mix variables can be observed and assessed by simulated test markets and real test markets. Consumer panels provide information on customer lifestyles, media habits and consumption patterns.

In the case of industrial or business goods, many of the same kinds of data are sought after, as in the case of consumer research. Research methods vary slightly but there are many commonalities between the two.

Types of data that can be collected

When looking at consumer markets, it can be observed that various factors influence the way people purchase goods and services. These factors can be classified as cultural factors, personal characteristics and psychological variables. For example, people tend to belong to certain social groupings and are influenced by the motivations and values of the group to which they belong. Social status, family and friends all influence people's buying decisions. Culture influences what people do and what they buy. Personal factors include age, income, job, lifestyle, personality and self-concept. Changes in any of these factors may exert an influence on purchasing behaviour. Income and lifestyle, for instance, affect both the buying process and the eventual choice of goods people make. Finally, psychological factors influence individual buying behaviour and how people respond to promotional methods. Psychological factors include perception, motivation, attitudes and learning.

MEASURING CUSTOMER LOYALTY

Measuring customer loyalty is not only a means of identifying a target audience for marketing programmes, but it also facilitates assessing the performance of implemented advertising and promotion strategies. In order to measure customer loyalty, information is required on, for example, the frequency of purchase, the value of purchase and its contribution to total revenue. In assessing the impact of a marketing campaign, the difference in these factors has to be weighed against the cost of their implementation.

This information is already available to a retailer through its EPOS scanning terminal. More specific customer information can also be obtained by issuing shoppers with a card and PIN number. Purchase information can then be recorded each time customers pay at the checkout. This kind of information is quantitative in nature and not qualitative. It will show the trend in consumer behaviour, but it cannot explain it. Explanations can only be obtained through consumer surveys and interviews.

Source: Samways and Whittcome[14]

PSYCHOLOGICAL FACTORS INFLUENCE INDIVIDUALS' RESPONSES

- People *perceive* advertisements in a particular way.
- People *see* only a few of the hundreds of advertisements they encounter each day.
- People only *remember* some of the advertisements.
- People hold particular attitudes and *learn* new ones.
- People *learn* about new products and new benefits.

Marketers need to become familiar with people's perceptions, values, attitudes, beliefs, the way they learn and their needs and wants. Through using this information, marketers can influence customers' buying behaviour. Marketers must also know how social, personal and psychological factors can influence customers' buying behaviour so that they can use this information to good effect in the marketing of products and services.

MARKETING RESEARCH AS PART OF MARKETING STRATEGY

Marketing strategy involves implementing well-thought-out plans. The plans themselves should involve a sequence of soundly informed and executed steps. Much of the information used as a basis for the planning can be provided by marketing research. Here is a simplified list of the steps involved in planning:

1 Establish company goals and assess how the firm has departed from these goals in the past.

2 Decide on products or services that best contribute to the likely attainment of these goals.

3 Establish the minimum market share required for specific products or services to produce a satisfactory profit and return on investment.

4 Determine a pricing strategy that will best lead to the required profit and return on investment.

5 Forecast sales demand over the planning horizon.

6 Decide on the best distribution channels to produce continuous satisfactory sales and profits.

7 Decide on the best promotional strategy to produce the desired sales and profits.

8 Anticipate problems that may arise as these decisions are implemented and set out contingency plans to meet any of the anticipated problems.

Marketing research has a role to perform in all the key decisions that affect the direction an organisation takes.

DECIDING WHO SHOULD DO THE RESEARCH

A firm's own research staff alone may undertake research, it may be given to an outside agency to perform or some combination of these two options may be chosen. Where both an outside agency and internal personnel undertake research on the same problem, consultation between the outside agency and internal personnel is essential. Handing over a complex study completely to an outside firm can be fraught with problems. Having said that, however, allowing internal personnel to have too much of an input may prevent new and useful insights emerging. The **research proposal** should identify who should do what.

Where company personnel are used in the research, even though a competent agency has been hired, there are several advantages to be gained. Using people from departments that will be affected by the study will help 'sell' the results.

Using company personnel can also direct and redirect the progress of the study into the most useful and profitable areas. Using people from departments other than marketing will educate them about the ways and benefits of marketing research.

ASSISTANCE FROM OUTSIDE RESEARCH ORGANISATIONS

In recent years, there has been a trend towards using outside suppliers. This has probably occurred because of the more complex and sophisticated research techniques that have recently been developed and the fact that people in organisations do not usually have the necessary skills for these techniques. Computerisation has produced ways of finding and analysing information that could not have been dreamed of only a few years ago. While computers have been adopted almost universally, their use for marketing research has developed as a specialised field of knowledge and few firms have developed this expertise for themselves. Companies are also reducing their middle and top management staff. For financial reasons, many companies believe that an outside research firm can perform market research better and more cheaply than the companies' own personnel. Because of the wealth of information now available to clients on a continuing basis from agencies that specialise in gathering, analysing and reporting information, it is too costly and time-consuming for any single company to attempt to collect such information itself. The use of outside firms is desirable when confidentiality is of paramount importance. This is important where knowing the company and its products has an effect on the responses given by subjects participating in the research.

Research sources

Outside research firms specialise in one or more forms of research assistance and relatively few firms can offer all methods with equal expertise. The specialised research assistance that can be given is as follows:

- mail surveys
- personal interview studies
- telephone studies
- panels
- omnibus studies
- sampling
- focus groups.

Specialisation in overall marketing measurements might include the following:

- test marketing
- scanner test marketing
- controlled test marketing
- simulated test marketing.

There are also research firms that specialise in the problems of market segmentation, customer/prospect databases, advertising media studies and audience studies.

Types of research available

A number of types of marketing research are offered by specialist agencies:

- *Custom-designed studies*: designed to meet the specific needs of the buyer.
- *Syndicated studies*: ongoing surveys conducted continuously or periodically, using the same basic data that are reported separately to multiple clients. The reports can be adjusted to meet client needs.
- *Standardised studies*: based on a method of doing things (usually a unique method) such as **copy testing**, simulated test marketing or setting up a consumer panel or an omnibus study. Special equipment or facilities may be an inbuilt part of the service.

Outside agencies, offering research, may be categorised according to their type and location.

Local firms offering special types of assistance

These firms may specialise in interviewing, mall intercepts, telephone research etc. They may take on special local assignments for large, nationwide research companies. Such firms often offer facilities for focus and other types of research groups and may handle research other than their specialities.

National research firms

Agencies of this kind may be able to do almost all forms of marketing research. The companies often offer consulting in marketing and even general management. They also may offer computer-based information for use in databases, marketing strategy decisions and the like.

Consultants in various specialities

These firms may consult and advise about packaging, advertising and personnel problems. They also may offer to do some research relating to their specialities.

These firms may have a major field of interest, such as engineering or electronics. The research offered by consultants can include necessary outside studies, both marketing and technical.

Selecting an outside research firm

In the case of selecting an ongoing research service, the buyer must think not only of the dependability of the research method offered, but also about whether the research firm is likely to stay in business. For services with standardised procedures, the crucial element is whether the concept of the procedure selected can produce the information deemed necessary. Quality of work is important but the probability is that a research firm would not still be in business if the quality of its work were poor.

In selecting an outside agency, account should be taken of the degree to which an in-depth knowledge of the employing company and its field is required and the agency's skill in the type of study to be undertaken. An outside agency often needs some weeks of training or instruction about the company and its marketing problems before it can understand what the client requires.

STEPS IN CHOOSING A RESEARCH FIRM

1 Check sources for finding names of research companies.

2 Compile a list of firms and decide on two or three that appear to be the most promising.

3 Contact the research firm in writing, giving as full a description as possible of the problem.

4 Arrange an interview with the research firm, preferably in its office.

5 Find out more about the research supplier and about its previous clients.

6 Explore how the research firm prefers to work with clients.

7 Ask for a written proposal.

8 Come to a clear understanding that further discussions may change the proposal in some ways.

9 Agree about who will be the prime contacts between client and researcher.

10 Make it clear to a firm submitting a proposal that proposals from other firms are also being considered when this is the case.

EVALUATING PROPOSALS

In evaluating proposals one should consider the factors shown in the box.

FACTORS TO CONSIDER WHEN EVALUATING PROPOSALS

1 Whether the proposal shows an understanding of the problem and its marketing implications.

2 The nature of the organisation undertaking the research and the skills the researchers possess.

3 Whether the total price is reasonable and acceptable. Whether there are large price differences among different proposals and, if so, whether they signal different assumptions by different firms.

4 Whether the proposal contains a procedure for changes if they are required and whether this procedure is acceptable to the client.

ETHICAL CONSIDERATIONS IN MARKETING RESEARCH

Coinciding with the rise of consumerism and equal rights legislation, people have become more assertive of their rights, especially in the marketplace. An increased concern for privacy, a reluctance to be used as guinea pigs for new products and an increased reluctance to accept research claims for new products in advertisements characterise the new outlook of many consumers.

In applying the term '**ethics**' to marketing research, it is assumed that ethics involves the assessment of an action in terms of that action being morally right or wrong. Each society possesses standards to which it expects its members to adhere. Sometimes, these standards are quite precise and there is little dispute about their meaning. At other times, however, the standards are quite general and can be interpreted in different ways. The area of greatest concern is marketing researchers' treatment of participants. The abuses that arise in this area tend to fall into three broad categories: invasion of privacy, deceptive practices and impositions (see Figure 1.3).

Invasion of privacy

Invasion of privacy is not an issue that is unique to marketing research. It also occurs in many other aspects of business and has heightened people's sensitivity

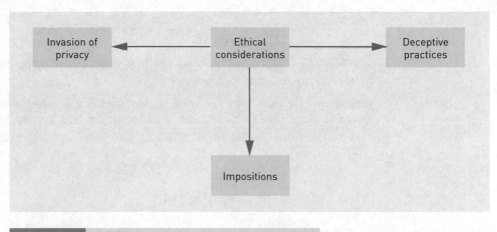

Ethical considerations in marketing research

to the privacy issue. However, actually defining when a person's privacy is invaded may be difficult. For example, is observing the actions of a shopper in a supermarket an invasion of his privacy? Is questioning a person about her income, product use or future purchase plans an invasion of privacy?

Up to the present, it has been felt that observing a person's public actions (e.g. shopping in a supermarket) does not infringe on privacy. It is also maintained that information willingly provided by respondents in a survey does not constitute an invasion of privacy, since the person's participation implies consent. However, questions are currently being raised about whether many respondents in surveys appreciate when they are in situations where they must provide information (as is the case in government **census** studies) and when they are in situations where they have a real choice of whether to provide information. Since there is no widely acceptable definition of privacy, the invasion of privacy issue is of considerable concern for marketing researchers.

Deceptive practices

It is a deceptive practice when a researcher misrepresents the purpose of the research, its sponsorship, its promises of anonymity, the amount of time required to participate in the research or inducement for participating in it. Perhaps the most notorious deception is obtaining a sales pitch under the guise of marketing research.

An operational definition of deception in marketing research may be difficult to make with absolute precision. A code of ethics should clarify what actions might be considered acceptable practice.

A CODE OF ETHICS – IS THERE A BREACH OF ETHICS INVOLVED?

- A potential telephone respondent is told that the questioning will only take a few minutes, when it takes 20 minutes.

- Return envelopes in an 'anonymous' mail survey are coded so that respondents and non-respondents can readily be identified in order to save money when sending out second requests.

Impositions on respondents

Here we are looking at actions by researchers that show a lack of concern for the participants. Under this heading are such actions as contacting respondents at inconvenient times, wasting participants' time because of inappropriate research and poorly prepared interviews.

ETHICAL CONSIDERATIONS IN TASTE TESTING WITH DRUGS

The Market Research Society makes no reference to the testing of medicines in its Code of Conduct. Butterworth's *Law of Food and Drugs* details the requirements for clinical trials of the efficacy of products, but does not provide any definition of requirements for the testing of other aspects of pharmaceutical products such as flavour acceptability. Indeed, there are no real guidelines for taste testing pharmaceuticals. The responsibility for designing safe consumer research resides with the agency doing the work. Moreover, providing an agency takes sufficient steps to ensure the safety of the research protocol, responsibility for the safety of the actual product and product ingredients lies with the manufacturer.

Increasingly, over-the-counter medicines are becoming more important to pharmaceutical firms. Manufacturers can increase sales and market share by improving the appeal of their products to consumers. There is an increase in research activities into the reformulation of products to achieve better taste characteristics and subsequent testing with consumers to investigate preference or prove claims made about taste. Nevertheless, this type of research produces ethical concerns since many of the products tested contain active drugs. However, the issues involved in showing that one product is preferred to another in terms of taste are completely different from clinical trial issues.

Reading Scientific Services Ltd (RSSL) is a multidisciplinary scientific consultancy providing research and analytical services to the food, drink, consumer goods, chemical and healthcare industries. It has expertise in both routine and investigative pharmaceutical analysis including sensory evaluation and consumer research. When conducting consumer research on pharmaceutical products the dose each respondent receives has to be limited. In practice this means controlling the amount and number of products tasted. Pre-screening of product prototypes is essential in order to ensure the selection of the best samples to research with consumers. Sensory evaluation, making use of trained panels, is an efficient way of pre-screening. Panellists are selected for their taste sensitivity and are trained to describe and measure flavour and mouthfeel characteristics. Results of the sensory evaluation are used to make sure that only prototypes that seem to have the required range of flavour and mouthfeel characteristics are taken forward to the stage of consumer research. Moreover, because sensory evaluation gives an objective and precise description of the flavour and mouthfeel characteristics of each product, the task of consumer research is simplified to preference judgements and opinions about key product characteristics. At the same time the dose administered can be kept to a minimum.

Nonetheless, consumers must give their 'informed consent' to take part in such research and interviewers must explicitly inform respondents of any restrictions or exclusions. Respondents must also read and sign a consent form which states the restrictions and tells consumers of the nature of the research. If appropriate, a GP supervises the tasting sessions.

Source: Sanderson[15]

Ethics is also involved in the type of marketing research carried out and/or whether it is carried out in an ethically correct manner. When the research involves the testing of products that might have potentially dangerous side effects on consumers, considerable care has to be taken to ensure that procedures adopted are ethically acceptable and that they are not open to criticism.

RESEARCHERS' OBLIGATIONS TO CLIENTS

As well as ethical obligations to respondents, researchers also have obligations to their clients. Among the obligations are:

- *Methods used and results obtained must be accurately represented*. Researchers must use effective research procedures in obtaining and analysing data. There is also an obligation to tell clients when they make ill-advised research requests. The researcher must also inform the client of any critical weakness or limitation in collected data, especially those that could lead to major errors if the information is acted on without reservation.

- *Client's identity and information obtained must be held in confidence*. Any actual or prospective client approaching or using a research firm has the right to expect that what is revealed to that firm as part of this relationship is confidential.

Research should not be undertaken for competition if such research will jeopardise the confidential nature of the client–researcher relationship.

ICC/ESOMAR Code

This is a professional code of practice for market researchers, published by the European Society for Opinion and Marketing Research. It is based on the following eight principles:

1 Personal data have to be processed fairly and lawfully.

2 Personal data have to be obtained only for lawful purposes and should not be processed in any manner that is incompatible with such purposes.

3 Personal data have to be adequate, relevant and not excessive in relationship to the purpose for which they are being used.

4 Personal data have to be accurate and up to date where this is appropriate.

5 Personal data should not be kept on file any longer than is necessary for the purpose for which they were acquired.

6 Personal data have to be processed in accordance with the requirements of the Data Protection Act (see following section).

7 Appropriate technical and organisational measures have to be in place to prevent unauthorised or unlawful processing of personal data and to protect them against accidental loss, destruction or damage.

8 Personal data should not be transferred anywhere outside the European Economic Area unless there are preventative measures in place to ensure the rights and freedoms of data subjects in relation to the processing of personal data.

Data Protection Act

In 1999 the Data Protection Act 1998 was extended. The definition of data now includes all manual and electronic records – including video recordings and group discussions. Under the new provisions there is now specific reference to sensitive personal data: information carried regarding racial or ethnic origin; political opinions; religious or other similar beliefs; physical or mental health; sex life; and criminal convictions or proceedings. Conditions are laid down under which sensitive personal data may be lawfully processed. The 1984 Act set out a system of registration for all users of personal data covered by the Act: data user's name and address; description of personal data held; purpose for which the data are held; description of sources from which the data are derived; description of people to whom the data may be disclosed; names of places outside the UK to where the data may be sent; and an address for the receipt of requests from data subjects who wish to have access to the data. The 1998 Act introduced a new system of notification. It should be noted that it is against the law to hold or use any data in a way that is inconsistent with the registered entry. Registered entries are valid for specific periods and changes have to be recorded officially.

The Act is concerned with individuals, not corporate bodies, and does not refer to the processing of data by manual means. (Useful guides to the Data Protection Act are available from the Data Protection Registrar, Springfield House, Water Lane, Wilmslow, Cheshire SK9 5AX.)

TRENDS IN MARKETING RESEARCH

- A movement away from probability sampling towards quota sampling, along with a fall in sample sizes.

- Because of cost and time pressures, less use of the integrated survey model of qualitative, pilot and full survey in projects.

- More qualitative research as a 'stand-alone' method in a wider number of applications.

- Growing use of databases for sampling.

Source: Mouncey[16]

CHANGING ROLE OF MARKETING RESEARCH

Organisations are dynamic entities existing within a continuous state of flux and trying to adapt to the requirements of rapidly changing environments. This very much applies to marketing research organisations whether they are in-house departments or agencies. The last 25 years have witnessed vast changes in the way in which information is handled in organisations of all types and sizes. Alongside this revolution in information management the role of marketing research has undergone substantial change. The change is not complete and it is impossible to say that the role of marketing research is now a fixed, static entity: its role is certain to change further in the future.

Adapting to the changing conditions of the business environment means dealing with new problems and decisions that may not previously have arisen. This accentuates the need for creativity in marketing research to enable new ways of researching new problem situations.

CHANGING ROLE OF MARKET RESEARCH

In the years ahead, successful research suppliers will need to develop close co-operation with their research clients. It is likely that much of the day-to-day work formerly carried out by **in-house** market **research** departments will be outsourced to specialist research agencies. This will entail agencies having to have a much better understanding of their clients' problems and the manner in which research survey data can contribute towards the solution of such problems. Researchers are not primarily data gatherers, although data gathering is essential and the work must be properly organised and controlled. The specialist skill of researchers, however, is being able to spot how research can help resolve a problem and help a firm make better decisions. It is the skill and creativity that is part of knowing how to get worthwhile information, how to help clients understand what data are telling them and what decisions they should consider making as a result.

Substantial changes have occurred in the market research business over the past decade. In particular there has been considerable change in the way research is bought and sold and the manner in which research is conducted. During the 1980s there was a slimming down in the size of market research departments and research suppliers often found themselves dealing with brand and marketing management, rather than in-house market research managers. For a long time, research suppliers had bemoaned the fact that they seldom dealt directly with executives who used research data they supplied. The change in circumstances meant that researchers had to deal directly with brand and marketing managers and help them make the best use of research.

Unfortunately, things have not worked out as well as might have been anticipated. There have been practical difficulties, such as research needs not being anticipated early enough within research users' companies. Research suppliers have also had to acknowledge that brand and marketing managers make use of information of which market research data are only a part. Executives are not research specialists and do not have the same depth of interest in the research process. In practice, market research data are now bought more as a component input to a company's overall activity rather than to meet specific client needs for a particular project.

Data-collection methods are likely to change in the future, with an increasing use of computer assisted techniques, email and the Internet as a means of communicating with customers, retailers and consumers. The trend of the last ten years, in which many market research departments have been abolished or combined with marketing departments, is also likely to be reversed. The unique skills of the specialist market researcher will come to be better understood and appreciated. It is unlikely that large in-house market research departments will develop again, but the establishment of small, high-level specialist teams of researchers within medium-sized and major companies is likely. Such teams will have a specialist role to play in the development of research briefs that will enable information to be made available as and when it is required. They will also contribute significantly to the way information is used within a marketing organisation.

Source: Bates[17]

USING THE INTERNET FOR MARKETING RESEARCH

The Internet has remarkable potential as a tool for marketing research. It enables primary marketing research to become much less expensive to conduct than by using traditional media. Such research can, however, only really be exploratory. In using the Internet for collecting data and information, the scope of the **sampling frame** is restricted to those members of the Internet community who agree to respond. It has to be borne in mind that the demographics of users of the Internet are different from the general population. Results from Internet marketing research should not usually be generalised to the entire population. However, as more and more households gain access to the Internet this is a problem that may resolve itself in due course.

Web page self-completion forms facilitate the assessing of attitudes, wants and values of an organisation's customers. For example, a firm might use a self-completion form to learn about its customers' demographics and product preferences. The firm might employ such data as a basis for segmenting its market.

The Internet might be used during product/service development. A company can quickly assess globally customers' thoughts about product changes or new products before any research and development investments are made. In the same way, firms can gain much information through monitoring discussion groups made up of members of the firm's customer base. Executives can use this information to learn not only of the perceived strengths and weaknesses of their own products or services, but also of those of their competitors.

NEED FOR MORE CREATIVITY IN RESEARCH

We live in a world that is undergoing continuous and rapid change. Situations are regularly encountered that have not previously arisen. Technology, competition, changes in social values, new expectations of customers, economic upheaval and all the other kinds of changes that can occur in the business environment produce new problems for management. Solutions to such problems often require insight that traditional, well-used problem-solving techniques are unable to provide. Under such circumstances, the need for creative problem solving assumes a greater importance than ever before. Developments in world markets, shorter production cycles, the need to find new ways to resource the exploitation of opportunities and the scarcity and cost of basic resources are just a few of the new challenges for the modern-day executive. In order to respond to such challenges there is a need to think creatively.

Research findings have provided support for the argument that there is a direct link between creative thinking and organisational efficiency and effectiveness.[18] In particular, creativity helps to improve the value of solutions to persistent organisational problems. It has also been found that **creativity** helps to encourage profitable innovations, rekindles employee motivation and improves personal skills and team performance. All these can contribute towards a continuous flow of ideas for new products and services and, by improving work processes, provide the platform on which an organisation can develop its competitive advantage.

There are few aspects of organisational activity where the need for creativity does not make itself felt. While the need for new ideas often predominates problem tasks, old ideas, too, need to be re-examined. After all, creativity is the process of revealing, selecting, swapping around and combining our store of facts, ideas and skills. Rickards[19] has described creativity as an 'escape from mental stuckness', an operational definition that is very much in keeping with its role in decision making and problem solving.

CREATIVE RESEARCH

One of the key reasons for the lack of genuine innovation in the 1990s is that researchers keep asking the same questions and using the same processes, with the result that predictable responses are obtained from consumers. Since there are nowadays so many 'expert' consumers, a new creative focus is required to encourage new kinds of consumer responses to be made. It is necessary to inject creativity into research, making use of both environmental stimuli and people, for it is these elements that make creative research more effective. It is essential, however, that researchers should be familiar with and confident in the use of creativity techniques.

A step in the right direction is to introduce a high level of interaction into consumer workshops in order to interpret the sensory experiences of the consumer. It is often the case that what consumers say and actually do conflict with one another. Knowing this and observing it may help us to intuitively read between the lines and make research more efficient and meaningful.

Source: Nuttall[20]

The need for creativity in research is no less than in any other area of marketing or management. If research is to provide useful information for helping organisations to gain a competitive advantage, it needs to be imaginative and capable of bringing forth equally new ideas, insights and viewpoints from respondents.

NON-RESPONSE AS AN ISSUE IN MARKETING RESEARCH EFFECTIVENESS

In a society where people are becoming more and more cynical towards marketing research, non-response is becoming an issue that is relevant to the effectiveness of marketing research. Answers to questions posed in surveys, for example, may differ considerably between those who respond and those who do not. In busy shopping malls, those who spend time helping the researcher fill in questionnaires may have very different ideas and concerns to those who walk rapidly by and refuse to cooperate. Moreover, in the case of business-to-business research, the non-respondent may be an organisation of major significance whose exclusion results in the research having little meaning. While training of interviewers, extra incentives and even patience can sometimes overcome potential non-response, pressure of time, apathy, scepticism and greater feelings of rights to privacy all contribute to the potential problems posed by non-response.

SUMMARY

This chapter has explored how marketing research can take some of the risk out of marketing decision making by providing information that can contribute to sound marketing decision making. This may be achieved in all elements of the marketing mix and, through involvement in problem formulation and solution finding, marketing research becomes an integral part of the process of formulating marketing strategy. Marketing research can perform a variety of studies and makes use of both primary and secondary data sources. It can be applied either in-house or by marketing research companies that specialise in this form of consultancy. The latter offer a wide range of services from off-the-peg studies to tailor-made studies to meet the needs of individual clients. Like many other services involving the generation of confidential information and reports, ethical considerations are an important issue and need to be fully explored. New ways of asking questions pose challenges for marketing researchers and the introduction of creativity into marketing research is paramount.

QUESTIONS

1 Discuss how marketing research helps reduce the risk in marketing decision making.

2 Design a marketing information system for an SME marketing a soft drink. How would you incorporate marketing research data into such a system?

3 Discuss how marketing research is part of marketing strategy.

4 Why is there a need for more creativity in marketing research?

CASE STUDY 1.1: LAMPELICHTER AG, ESSEN

All manufacturers of lamps are frantically trying to maintain and protect their share in a shrinking market. Each manufacturer has a large number of production facilities across Europe and the profitability of the companies is determined by production loading. In this industry, economies of scale play a major role and the overcapacity of the manufacturers ensuing from the shrinking market has brought about aggressive price competition. This has been reflected in lower unit selling prices and reduced margins and has put further emphasis on achieving economies of scale. Currently, lamp manufacturing is not a profitable industry. Companies are fighting for market share and high exit barriers prevent withdrawal. However, whenever the upturn occurs, those firms that survive the recession will be in a good position to take advantage of future growth and new markets.

Recently, Philips has entered the Polish market both to access the emerging ex-Comecon markets and to obtain a lower cost base to aid its price competitiveness in established European markets. Similarly, GE has invested heavily in Hungary and Osram has expanded its distribution into the former East Germany and purchased the North American operations of GTE, which has retrenched its business activities to the core of telecommunications. The acquisition of GTE's share of the North American market was critical to Osram to prevent it being marginalised as a European producer. The North America move countered GE's expansion into Europe. GE has also acquired controlling interests in manufacturing sites in Italy, Japan and China. Philips and Osram are also investing in joint ventures in China and the Far East.

As manufacturers have moved into areas of lower cost production, the unit selling price of the manufacturers since 1993 has fallen in real terms – a trend that is expected to continue. However, while the unit production cost of the product has fallen, the distribution and sales cost associated with it have risen.

Lampelichter employs around 100 personnel and was established in 1970. As one of the leading independent suppliers of replacement lamps to independent electrical retailers in Germany, the firm undertakes marketing and distribution but has no manufacturing capacity. It has a single warehousing and office facility in Essen and uses carriers to deliver its consignments to customers. In 1993, 65% of its annual sales were under its own label brand. In 1995 the firm was looking towards a sales revenue target of DM30m. In 1994 the firm's sales revenues were made up as follows:

- light bulbs 74%

- plugs, sockets and other accessories 10%

- security, task lighting, etc. 12%

- torches, batteries, etc. 4%.

In Europe generally, the independent electrical retailers have chosen to reduce stockholding, thereby holding stock back at their suppliers. This has produced an increase in the number of orders placed but a reduction in the average order value. Unless suppliers can break the trend of falling selling prices coupled with rising sales and distribution costs, the long-term net margin position of the suppliers in the independent market will continue to worsen. The lamp supply industry is especially seasonal – November's turnover is approximately twice that of June. The period September to March is critical to the success of the organisation, but the resources available to allow it to take advantage of the season are carried throughout the year. This makes it a high fixed cost organisation that actually budgets to lose money in the spring and summer periods.

Lampelichter differs from the majority of its competitors. It markets its products on a national basis rather than the more usual local or regional basis adopted by the competition. Competition comprises manufacturers (competing directly for major accounts), national electrical wholesalers, local electrical wholesalers, special lamp distributors, appliance and accessory distributors. Within the company's organisational structure there are board representatives for sales, marketing, finance and operations. Approximately 60% of company manpower is directly related to the sales/sales support roles. The remaining 40% is taken up in staffing the following departments: data processing, accounts and finance, quality assurance, warehousing and transport.

The sales budget in 1995 split the total revenue targets as shown in Table 1.1.

Lampelichter considers that it has committed and talented management and employees, a good reputation in the trade, excellent goodwill and significant customer loyalty. It also has a substantial field salesforce, its own branded product range, consistent attractive barcoded own-brand packaging and excellent supplier relationships with all major lamp suppliers. The firm is a financially strong private company with limited borrowings. It has high stock inventory coupled with an extensive product range. Furthermore, it has expertise in fragile products. The firm has a market-led culture (with the object of being customer led).

TABLE 1.1	Lampelichter sales budget, 1995	

Distribution channel	1995 target	1994 target
Independent electrical retailer	60%	65%
Commercial user	32%	25%
Onward distributor	8%	10%

Lampelichter's historic customer base is in decline and the firm is reluctant to accept added-value products. Within the company, there is a lack of internal performance standards. Profitability is declining and there is under-utilisation of assets. Compared with competition the firm is a relatively high-fixed-cost operation. Moreover, delivery performance is poorer than that of competitors. Under-manning of the salesforce is causing ineffective sales management. The salesforce is also an ageing one in terms of selling skills and professionalism and exhibits an absence of any customer segmentation and associated objectives and strategies. The company has a weak planning structure and skills base and a poor training culture.

There is a range of possible opportunities in the marketplace. These include: range extension into complementary non-lamp products; supply chain integration; and new markets. However, the firm faces: increased competition from lower cost distributors; increased competition from manufacturers on direct contracts with large users; increased seasonality of the core business; falling real costs of lamps; centralisation of supplier power with fewer own-brands suppliers; and fewer independent retailers.

Following discussion between the top management of the company and a European management consultancy organisation, the consultancy firm recommended that Lampelichter should commission marketing research to explore the various avenues open to it.

Question

What kind of marketing research information do you think Lampelichter should try to obtain?

CASE STUDY 1.2: SPIRIT OF MAGELLAN ENTERPRISES

Spirit of Magellan Enterprises in Winchester, England, is well known for providing its customers with out of the ordinary guided holidays abroad. The company prides itself on its ability to retain customers year after year and its ability to offer them something different and interesting every year. With the help of keen contacts abroad, the firm produces competitive offerings for the would-be holiday traveller. Recently, South America and Russia have been among the destinations that have attracted some holidaymakers and in response to this, the firm has developed a number of tours.

Spirit of Magellan Enterprises produces an annual detailed and well-illustrated brochure, which it sends in the post to all previous customers. It also makes the content of its brochure available through its website to all enquirers. The website is regularly updated with new destinations and tours as they become available.

Tours can last from 8 days to 21 days, although the majority are no longer than 14 days. Here is an example of one itinerary on offer:

Ukrainian experience

Day 1   Early morning flight from London Gatwick to Kiev. On arrival, transfer to the MV *Marshal Orenschenko*

Day 2   Morning sightseeing tour of Kiev. Afternoon at leisure

Day 3   Sail along the River Dnieper

Day 4   Arrive in Zaporizhya and enjoy a tour of the city

Day 5   Cruise to Odessa. Free time to see the sights. Optional opera or ballet performance in the evening

Day 6   Sail across the Black Sea to Sevastapol. Free time in the late afternoon and evening for sightseeing

Day 7   Day excursion to the Crimean resort of Yalta, visiting the Livadia Palace, the former summer residence of the Romanovs. Rest of the day at leisure

Day 8   A tour of Sevastopol in the morning. Afternoon at leisure

Day 9   Cruise to Kherson. Sightseeing at leisure

Day 10   Arrive late afternoon for sightseeing in Dnipropetrovsk

Day 11   Cruise back to Kiev

Day 12   Arrive Kiev early morning. Return flight to London Gatwick

Question

How might marketing research aid such a company in both choice of tours and the itinerary that goes along with such tours?

CASE STUDY 1.3: ROSINE AND VERA

France retains its international reputation as a centre for the avant garde. Paris has always been a magnet for experimental writers, artists and musicians. Paris has also been the home of haute couture. Original haute couture garments, as opposed to imitation ones and adaptations, are original one-off creations designed by the 23 couture houses listed with the *Féderation Française de la Couture*. Very high prices put haute couture beyond the reach of most pockets yet it still remains the lifeblood and focus of the French fashion industry. Most couture houses are on or near the rue de Faubourg-St-Honoré. Houses include Chanel, Christian Lacroix, Guy Laroche, Nina Ricci, Yves St Laurent and Christian Dior to name just a few. Comme des Garçons produces avant garde quirky clothes for both men and women. In the nearby rue Jean-Jacques Rousseau, the eccentric but celebrated designer Jean-Paul Gaultier has a shop at Les Halles shopping centre, as does Agnès B, whose clothes combine the very latest chic with comfort. In the same centre there are also inexpensive outlets selling copies of new designs. The rue de Rosiers in the Marais is full of new designers.

Rosine graduated with a first class honours degree in fashion and business management in Manchester, England, in 1994. From the very beginning she was keen to run her own business. While on the degree course she had become friendly with a woman the same age as herself, Vera, who, in addition to working from home and producing cheap garments mainly for children, had recently acquired space in a small production unit in the Ancoats district of the city. Vera was technically proficient while Rosine had flair and imagination as well as a good training in how to work in business. From 1991–95 Rosine and Vera built up a small business using various contacts they had made in the trade and occasional breakthroughs with boutiques in downtown areas throughout the UK.

The real breakthrough into London, however, came in 1999 when Vera and Rosine designs were worn by a leading UK female rock band, The Witches, on *Top of the Pops*. Almost overnight their £60,000 turnover business increased tenfold and they were hard pressed to find workers who could produce the garments in the quantities required to satisfy the demand. Apart from relocating their business premises to London, Rosine and Vera registered their partnership as a limited company taking on the name Pique Dame, which until then had been the brand name or label of their creations.

By the year 2004, the image of Pique Dame had changed slightly, although the emphasis was very much on the avante garde. The firm now supplied many export markets with some 30% of output going to US markets. New labels had been introduced and among these Narcissus and Femme Fatale had proved highly successful. Narcissus appealed to the 15–20 year olds wanting to accentuate their youthfulness with an accent on dark colours and ragged appearance. In contrast, Femme Fatale had been aimed in the main at the 30–40-year-old market where the emphasis was on sophistication and the creation of an alluring air of mystery, excitement and even danger.

Two big challenges now faced Rosine and Vera. The first was how to market their designs to women in the over-20-under-30-year age range and what they should do for the large untapped market of the over-40s. Indeed, they even wondered whether they should restrict their portfolio of offerings to the under-40s. Rosine felt that the 20–30-year-old woman had characteristics that set her apart from other groups of women. She saw such women as being uncertain of what they really wanted, easily influenced by peer and social pressures and in need of constant reassurance. As Rosine put it: 'Women in their 20s are full of hope and expectations but they are unsure of what they really want so it is difficult for anyone to meet such women's expectations.' Moreover, she thought that many women in this age group were experimenters wanting to try out new ideas on almost a daily basis. It was difficult to create a fashion in a market where fads abounded.

In the autumn of 2004 the firm acquired retail premises on the rue de Rosiers in the Marais district of Paris. The decision had now to be made about how to position the firm in people's minds in world markets and how to set about promoting this image.

Question

What role might marketing research play in helping the firm to promote its image?

 ## CASE STUDY 1.4: THE ENGLISH BEAR COMPANY

The English Bear Company was founded in 1991 by Alise Crossick, 29, and her husband Jonty, 28. They now have ten shops in cities including Bath, Cambridge and London and have recently opened in Tokyo. Their annual turnover is £4m.

Jonty: 'Alise and I met at Cambridge in 1988 when we were both impecunious students. We knew we wanted to be in business on our own and that whatever we did, we would have to start with nothing. Designing and selling T-shirts was the obvious choice because it didn't need any capital, only an understanding supplier. The bear idea grew out of that. Our most popular T-shirt featured a bear which Alise had drawn, yet she'd never actually made one when we decided to launch the bear company.

'Being a typical Antipodean, she just got on with it: advertised for bear-makers, and then sat down with a bear manual. Most of the applicants patiently watched her demonstrate, and then showed her how it could be done 100% better.

'We always wanted to create a company that would communicate something from the heart, something magical. I think the bears do that because they express fun and cuddles. We make them out of distressed mohair which makes them look old and loved. Our customers don't want something pristine, they're looking for character.

'We initially made mistakes in identifying our customers. Our first outlet was a kiosk in Whiteley's which we thought was perfect as it gave us a start in London. The rent was so cheap that we didn't bother to carry out market research. It wasn't until we opened in Cambridge that we realised the tourist trade was much more lucrative.

'Our sites are now picked with greater care. It's about 50% strategic choice, 30% gut feeling and 20% scientific data.'

Alise: 'It was never just about selling bears, our vision was the whole concept of people wearing bear clothes, eating bear marmalade and drinking bear tea.

'When people love bears, they personify them and become absorbed in the lifestyle. We get young businessmen coming into our shops who look like they want to quickly buy a bear and run out again. The next minute they're captivated and umming and ahhing over which face they like the best. Occasionally we get people bringing old bears in for repairs, like the chap who rushed in with something his dog had half-eaten.

'There's not enough people in retail trying to help their customers, it's all take, take, take. We put our hearts into the business and believe passionately in the products. If you put enough energy and care into something it should work.

'We're not in business to suffer so we only work with people we like. Bears bring out the best in people because they cross gender and race and represent unconditional love. If we weren't working together I wouldn't find it so worthwhile. We generate so much love between us that it makes it wonderful for everyone around.'

Source: Lafferty[21]

Questions

1 Discuss how the English Bear Company may have used marketing research beneficially.

2 How might marketing research still prove a useful tool to the company?

CASE STUDY 1.5: 21ST-CENTURY MARKET RESEARCH

Market research is coming out of the closet. Direct marketing firms have emerged to service the new phenomenon of relationship marketing – lifestyle databases underpinning the mailings of the firms to provide a direct interface between research and practice.

Direct marketing company databases hold a mass of fine detail on customers' purchasing habits. Advances in computer technology have given firms the ability to combine databases to give a fuller picture of customer purchasing habits without ever having to approach a respondent with a questionnaire – the information is directly available. Researchers no longer need to reassure respondents about anonymity, either; instead they offer rewards to consumers in exchange for giving personal information to the researchers.

Data mining is the new catchword for market researchers. Using what used to be considered as secondary sources of information, the researchers analyse direct marketing company records to build up an in-depth picture of the lifestyles of millions of consumers. New ways of segmenting markets based on lifestyles and attitudes are being discovered and ways of translating market research into market action are working more quickly and effectively. Because of the speed of analysing such research, market researchers are able to offer high-quality tailored research packages to small firms which previously could not have afforded professional market research.

Another area in which market research is being revolutionised is through the Internet. On one Web-based project, 160 out of 400 respondents replied to an email survey within three hours – formerly, this many responses would have taken days to obtain or even weeks using normal postal services. An additional advantage is that such surveys cost around one-third the price of telephone surveys. Currently most of this research is being conducted in the United States, where more people are connected to the Net than is the case in Europe, but eventually Web-based research is expected to outperform all other methods of conducting surveys.

The relatively new activity of category management (CM) has also thrown up new challenges for market researchers. The Institute of Grocery Distribution defines CM as: 'The strategic management of product groups through trade partnerships which aim to maximise sales and profits by satisfying consumer needs.' In practice, what this means is that manufacturers and retailers need to cooperate in managing certain product categories, rather than concentrating solely on brands. For example, Van den Bergh Foods (manufacturers of margarine and other fats) saw a need to establish retailer-specific market research programmes to develop an understanding of consumers' motivations to buy margarine. The research programme involved 1200 interviews conducted as customers left the stores, 1300 interviews at the margarine display fixtures in the stores, 200 **depth interviews**, 76 accompanied shopping trips and 36 hours of video observation. The research was carried out in seven major retail chains. Marked differences between the different retailers were found, so Van den Bergh was able to conclude that marketing, merchandising and even pricing might need to be varied between retailers to take account of differences in consumer motivation between store chains.

Ultimately, it seems that such research would be more efficiently carried out if the retailers themselves participated in the costs and shared the benefits – this would, of course, require agreements between the retailers to share information. Such agreements do not present a problem if an independent market research company, of course, carries out the work but the result for the market researchers is that they may find themselves forced into a tight brief that allows little room for creativity.

Increasingly, the business community is becoming more information oriented. In a constantly changing world, the need for up-to-date and accurate information is more important than ever before, and market researchers are using (and seeking) new tools for collecting and analysing that information.

(Case contributed by Jim Blythe)

Questions

1 What might be the limitations of using Web-based research in the UK?

2 What are the advantages and disadvantages of research for category management purposes?

3 How might the disadvantages of category management research be reduced?

4 What ethical problems might arise from the combination of direct mail databases to generate detailed information about consumers?

5 How might creative approaches to Web research increase **response rates**?

REFERENCES AND NOTES

1   Chisnall, P (1992) *Marketing Research* (4th edn), Maidenhead: McGraw-Hill, 5–6.

2   AMA (1987) New marketing research definition approved, *Marketing News*, 21, January.

3   Cowan, D (1994) Good information, *Journal of the Market Research Society*, 36(2), 105–14.

4   Freeling, A (1994) Marketing is in a crisis – can marketing research help? *Journal of the Market Research Society*, 36, 97–104.

5   Easterby-Smith, M, Thorpe, R and Lowe, A (1991) *Management Research: An introduction*, London: Sage, 21.

6   Allison, B, O'Sullivan, T, Owen, A, Rice, J, Rothwell, A and Saunders, C (1996) *Research Skills for Students: Transferable and learning skills*, London: Kogan Page.

7   Bekesi, J (1997) Gruppe Phänomenologie. Society for the Advancement of the Critical Development of Phenomenology and its Impulses, http://gph.freezope.org.

8   Embree, L (1997) What is phenomenology? Center for Advanced Research in Phenomenology, http://www.phenomenologycenter.org/phenom.htm.

9   Hannabuss, S (1995) Approaches to research, *Aslib Proceedings*, 47(1), 3.

10 Gummesson, E (1990) *Qualitative Methods in Management Research*, London: Sage.

11 Cresswell, J W (1994) *Research Design: Qualitative and quantitative approaches*, London: Sage.

12 Campbell, S (1997) Marketing wake-up, *Financial Times*, 3 June.

13 *Rebondir* (1996) 12, 35.

14 Samways, A and Whittcome, K (1994) UK brand strategies, a *Financial Times* management report, 60.

15 Sanderson, T (1996) How a spoonful of research helps the medicine go down, *Research Plus*, April, 6–8.

16 Mouncey, P (1996) With growing demands for data, will purity prove only theoretical? *Research Plus*, May, 9.

17 Bates, B (1996) Quality will mark the route to deeper client relationships, *Research Plus*, March, 9, 14.

18 Raudsepp, T (1987) Establishing a creative climate, *Training and Development Journal*, April, 50–53.

19 Rickards, T (1988) *Creativity and Innovation: A transatlantic perspective*, Manchester: Manchester Business School (Creativity and Innovation Yearbook).

20 Nuttall, C (1996) Research needs more creativity, *Marketing Week*, 29 April, 32.

21 Lafferty, F (1997) The English Bear Company, *Financial Times*, 28 April.

 ## FURTHER READING

Aschenbaum, A A (1993) The future challenge to market research, *Marketing Research: A magazine of management and application*, 5(2), 12–18.

Bogda, P and Meyers, G C (1991) Grab a partner for more effective research, *Marketing News*, 7 January, 2ff.

Brown, S (1996) Art or science? Fifty years of marketing debate, *Journal of Marketing Management*, 12(4), 243–67.

Jackson, P (1994) *Buying Market Research*, London: Kogan Page.

Piercy, N and Evans, M (1993) *Managing Marketing Information*, London: Croom Helm.

Weinman, C (1991) It's not an 'art', but marketing research can be creative, *Marketing News*, 25(8), 9, 24.

West, C (1995) Marketing research, in Baker, M J (ed.) *Companion Encyclopaedia of Marketing*, London: Routledge.

2 Planning the research project

Objectives

After reading this chapter, you should be able to:

* understand how marketing research helps in allaying uncertainty

* appreciate the cost and value of marketing research

* appreciate the need to plan, schedule and control a marketing research project, probably with the aid of computer-based PERT in this process.

Keywords

PERT	research proposal
problem definition	research schedule
research control	uncertainty
research limitations	value of research
research plan	

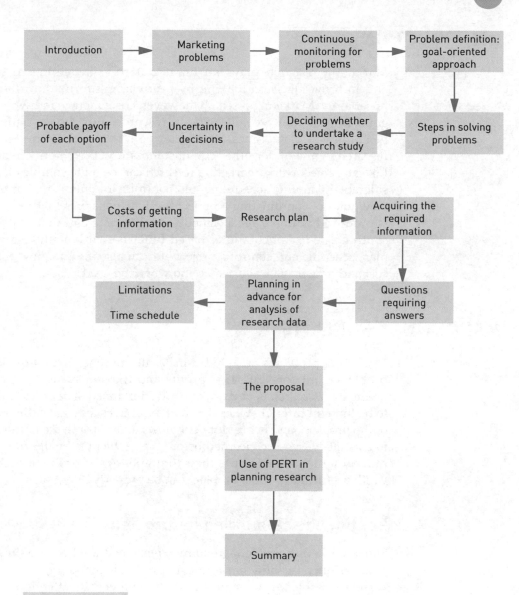

Plan of Chapter 2

INTRODUCTION

Marketing research plays an important role in helping to solve problems and improve decision making by producing information that helps to allay uncertainty. Marketing research, however, costs money and while the benefits of good information are self-evident, research must be cost-effective if it is to be employed. Sometimes, it may not be worthwhile to undertake marketing research, while under other circumstances it will be highly beneficial to do so. Like all project work, marketing research can be quite complex and requires considerable planning, scheduling and control. Not only is this important from the viewpoint of coordinating a project but it also ensures that research information is produced within a prespecified period of time and that costs are kept under control. The use of computer-based PERT network methods not only helps to plan, schedule and control a project but can also indicate how further savings in cost and time may be effected as and when the need arises.

MARKETING PROBLEMS

Marketing problems arise in business all the time. Some are vitally important problems and concern sales, profits and the general welfare of the business. Before any research is undertaken, a well-planned statement of the problem has to be thought through. Since different executives may have different perspectives of the problem, and hence different views about its precise nature, there is a need to consult everyone concerned before the problem is finally fully specified. Each individual must contribute their thoughts to the problem definition before a valid, useful study of the problem can be properly undertaken.

Continuous monitoring for problems

Some marketing problems require extensive study because they seem likely to uncover the possibility of producing profitable marketing opportunities or, conversely, sizeable losses. Some will require immediate attention while others may be less urgent.

A PROBLEM THAT REQUIRES A THOROUGH STUDY

A firm produces a wide range of food products for the consumer market. It believes that its jellies are of a superior quality and taste, but sales are below what the firm might have expected. The fault may lie with the price or the packaging, but the firm does not really have any precise ideas. It is even wondering whether it should drop out of the jellies market entirely. If this last action is seriously contemplated, the firm needs to know how this would affect its other product lines and, in particular, what effect this would have on distributors' readiness to stock the firm's other products.

A systematic approach to **problem definition** can help to direct marketing research staff in their efforts to obtain relevant information. It is also informative to all those people in the organisation who will be affected by the findings and recommendations.

MANY PARTIES MAY BE INVOLVED IN HELPING TO DEFINE A MARKETING PROBLEM AND IT HAS TO BE APPROACHED IN A SYSTEMATIC MANNER

A firm manufactures high-quality crystal glassware and wants to expand and become more profitable. It is considering manufacturing and distributing a line of lower-quality, lower-price products. It is unsure, however, whether it has the manufacturing and marketing experience to make such a venture successful.

In defining such a problem we have to adopt a systematic approach. The first step is to find out what the firm needs to know. Certainly, the firm needs a complete knowledge of the market. What competitive lines are being sold? Are competitors' lines profitable? Is there room for another line? How strong are brand names? How strong would the firm's brand name be in this lower-price line? Should the firm even use its brand name for this product? Can current distribution channels handle the new line? How strong are lines coming in from other countries?

The definition of the marketing problem must cover these questions together with additional questions posed by other involved parties.

Problem definition must take into account the situation of the company and its ability to take sound action. Poorly thought-out marketing decisions can cause major problems, sometimes with disastrous consequences. Many things can go wrong and many opportunities can be missed. The marketers in the firm need to anticipate and prevent as many of these as possible and in each case the first action should be a precise definition of the problem.

SWISS WATCH INDUSTRY – MISSING AN OPPORTUNITY THROUGH INCORRECT PERCEPTION OF THE PROBLEM

The Swiss watch industry chose to ignore the application of a new technology even though it had created the technology in the first place. Although the Swiss watch industry invented the quartz movement it did not initially make use of the invention because it felt that this invention would have strong negative effects on its existing product markets.[1] The Swiss argued that anyone else could make the quartz movement, whereas only the Swiss themselves had the skills to make the clockwork components required for automatic and mechanical movements.

With the benefit of hindsight we can appreciate that the Swiss were right in their thinking but wrong in their strategy. Watchmakers in Japan and Hong Kong

▶

immediately adopted the quartz movement and, in one year, the sales of Swiss watches dropped by some 25%.

Swiss watch manufacturers became entrapped because the executives in the firms did not really understand the nature of the market. They did not appreciate or understand customer wants and needs. The Swiss Swatch company rescued the Swiss watch industry by providing a bulk outlet for quartz movements so that prices could be brought down. The firm also recognised that telling the time was no longer the most important thing in a watch. The Swatch was not selling 'an indicator of the time' as much as fun and costume jewellery.

From the very beginning of awareness and consideration of a marketing problem, research should be an integral part of the problem-solving approach.

EXAMPLE OF A MARKETING DECISION – A NEW PRODUCT FOR A MANUFACTURER

Marketing research can find information that helps to answer the following questions:

- Does an obvious need for the product exist?
- Has the company sufficient financial resources to design, manufacture and push the product through the early sales growth years?
- What will be the best design to adopt?
- What will be the best price level(s) for the market or market segments?
- How should the firm choose between volume, price and profit?
- What will be the probable market life for the product?
- What level of quality will be required?
- Who are the competitors, who is about to enter the market and how strong are actual and potential competitors?
- What will be required in the way of promotion? What will it cost?
- How will this new product affect current lines?

Problem definition: goal-oriented approach

Rickards[2] suggests a useful way in which to approach problem definition is the technique known as goal orientation. Essentially, the method employs identifying needs, obstacles and constraints in the search for an adequate definition of the problem. The procedure, along with an illustration, is given in Table 2.1.

(See also Proctor[3] for an extensive coverage of problem-definition techniques.)

TABLE 2.1	Problem definition: goal orientation

• Write down description of problem. Then ask:	• *Problem*: sales/profits of main product are stagnating
• What do we need to accomplish (needs)?	• *Need*: increased sales and profits
• What are the obstacles?	• *Obstacles*: competition intense so increase in market share unlikely; market saturated; home market in recession
• What constraints must we accept in order to solve the problem?	• *Constraints*: lack of funds for internal new product development
• Redefine the problem, bearing the above in mind.	• *Problem redefinition*: possible avenues to explore: new markets, market segments, diversification, licensing, joint ventures, integrative strategies

Steps in solving problems

It is usually possible to solve problems in more than one way. For example, a new range of furniture may be produced for sale in the domestic market, the domestic market and Europe or for worldwide distribution. A decision has to be taken as to which of these options is the best strategy to adopt. The decision here reflects the nature of the problem and, in such a problem statement, there are three possible options.

The problem statement illustrates the important point that the various options need to be identified and set out. Information then has to be obtained that is pertinent to each of the identified courses of action so that an objective evaluation can then be made about the course of action to follow. There may be some disagreement about the nature of the options and it is therefore of paramount importance that these disagreements are resolved as soon as possible. Before the final definition of the marketing problem, those involved in the decision must also agree on the nature and quality of the information needed to make a sound decision.

DECIDING WHETHER TO UNDERTAKE A RESEARCH STUDY

Whether marketing research makes organisations more profitable is open to question for there are other factors to consider. Profits are associated not just with increased revenues but also result from controlling or even cutting costs – to name but two sources! Many of these factors may have nothing to do with marketing research. However, in theory decision making based on good information should be better than decision making made on the basis of no information or poor information. Of course, in practice, this may not hold true. Even information that is thought to be good may not necessarily be useful. People's attitudes and opinions do not always match with their actions so that information collected can sometimes be misleading. For example, people may say that they will buy a new car in the next year and that they will buy a specific model. Many factors can then intervene in the meanwhile that will mean that the intended actions are not followed through.

The above, however, is a negative picture and it is argued that in many instances, hopefully the majority, marketing research will lead to better information that will, in turn, lead to better decisions. The better decisions may, in turn, lead to increased revenues or lower costs and hence to more profits. For example, group discussions may indicate the need for additional features that can be built into a product. The additional features will enhance the product's competitive advantage in the marketplace which, in turn, will enhance its sales. The additional cost of including the features may involve a price increase to the customer but the overall effect is an increase in profits associated with the product.

It is arguably better to make decisions based on objective data than purely subjective feelings – and better still to use both in decision making. Better research and better management judgment, for example, might have prevented the disaster when the Sinclair C5 car was introduced in the UK some years ago.[4] Similar comments also apply in the case of the Swiss watch industry and its failure to exploit the opportunities presented by the quartz movement.

UNCERTAINTY IN DECISIONS

Marketing decisions are made under conditions of **uncertainty**. We can never be sure whether a new product will be successful or whether an advertising campaign will be effective in terms of meeting its objectives. In fact, in marketing there is very little of which we can be certain.

MARKETING RESEARCH HELPS TO DISPEL UNCERTAINTY

A producer of gourmet foods encounters uncertainty when contemplating a new product containing large percentages of saturated fat and cholesterol. How strong is consumer awareness of these dangers to health? Are people likely to become rapidly more health conscious? Marketing research would be very advisable for this new product.

Probable payoff of each option

Attention to the probable payoff of each new product, service or other option should be considered. The greatest potential payoff, other things being equal, is the determining factor in exercising choice. We should attempt to estimate the probable payoff of each option before we specify the necessity of researching material that is relevant to that option. Past product successes or failures can give clues about what might happen.

The cost of getting information should be weighed against possible sales and profits that may result from implementing a proposed course of action. Hence, the nature and amount of marketing research to be undertaken must be strictly controlled by cost and profit considerations. In many cases the cost of research is small compared with the possible benefits to be derived from adopting a course of action. The profits associated with the introduction of new products can run into many millions of pounds whereas the cost of marketing research may be measured in thousands of pounds. However, there may be instances where marketing research is relatively costly in relation to expected benefits. In such cases, decision trees like the one in Figure 2.1, including the options of 'with' or 'without' research, can be set up to estimate the **value of** undertaking **research**.

Sometimes, for competition reasons, it may be considered undesirable to undertake research since this may provide advance warning to the competition of what the firm is intending to do. While not undertaking research is a risky strategy, it is possible that signalling one's possible intentions to competitors may be even riskier.

Figure 2.1 shows the use of a decision tree to evaluate whether it is worthwhile undertaking research. We can see at a glance (see pp. 504–05) that the expected payoff from using research is £30,000 whereas if research is not used the payoff is

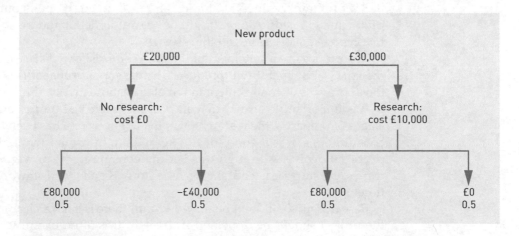

FIGURE 2.1   Value of marketing research

only £20,000. This Bayesian approach to evaluating the possible value of information assumes that the same kind of decision will be made many times and that it is possible to attach subjective probabilities to the various outcomes.

Costs of getting information

Using the maximum or minimum payoff projections, management should decide how much it could spend on research. There also has to be an estimate of the time that can be spent on adequate research. Marketing management is always keen to move ahead since a new product or a new service is exciting, especially when the future of the product appears bright. New lines and new markets stimulate the imagination. Taking time for adequate marketing research is difficult in such circumstances, but it is necessary. Failure to provide adequate time can lead to inadequate research, poor decisions – and regret and recriminations.

RESEARCH PLAN

Some preliminary steps are required before the preparation of a **research plan** (see Figure 2.2). If these steps are not followed, the research study may be unsatisfactory or even useless. Early discussion with those who need and will use the findings of a study usually produces better research. It can help to determine the cost/benefit of research or even whether the study is needed at all. Attention can be placed on what the organisation can afford to spend on marketing research in the light of the potential usefulness of the findings.

A plan is a blueprint for the design, execution and monitoring of a study. While it is a preliminary document and can be changed, it spells out the company's problem and needs. A plan has to be set out in detail and be shown to all those involved in the decision and the research.

The proposal is a statement of the plan comprising a discussion of the need for the study and what it will produce. The **research proposal** is often used to gain the approval and commitment to the plan of those involved in the project.

It is important to ensure that all possible interested parties are involved at all stages of preparing the research plan. Even if everyone has been involved in early consultations, it is a good idea to keep them informed while the plan and the proposal evolve. Although this is time-consuming, it prevents key personnel expressing surprise later at the way the study is going and showing strong opposition to it.

Researchers should not begin work until there is such a clear statement of why the project should be done and its benefit. It is often useful to hypothesise the findings likely to result from the study.[5] An indication of what these different findings may mean to the sponsors of the research may be productive. Such a

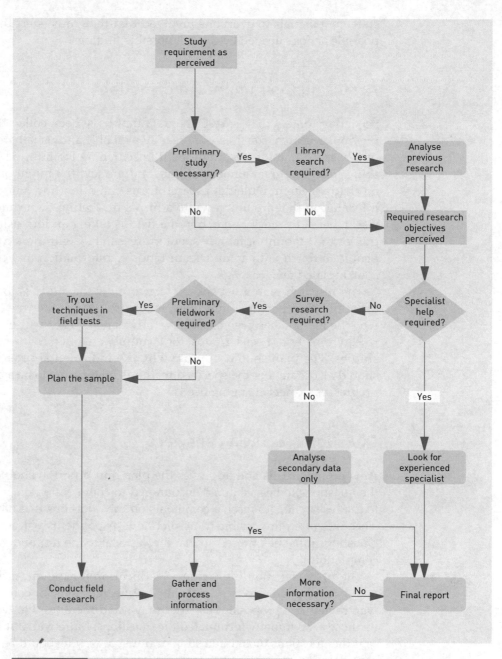

FIGURE 2.2 Stages of a marketing research project

statement signals to everyone involved that they must start thinking about the possible actions needed because of possible findings.

Acquiring the required information

Secondary data – that is, research data that have been collected as the result of previous research exercises – are readily available and usually relatively cheap to purchase. In many cases, time spent in searching for information in secondary sources saves a great amount of time and money that might otherwise be spent on field research. Outside research firms can often find sources of secondary information that are unknown to a firm's marketing department and 'internal researchers'. Primary research in the field is taking an increasingly smaller portion of the amount of money spent on research. Computers can put marketing people in touch with amounts and kinds of information that could not even be contemplated ten years ago.

The research plan must specify exactly how the study is to be done – postal questionnaire, personal interview, focus groups or other method – and justify why the method has been chosen. A study may require the use of several types of research method. Focus groups, for example, are often followed by quantitative studies. The plan should indicate why the indicated approach is necessary. It should also state that the specified methods might have to be altered as the study progresses to meet changing needs.

Questions requiring answers

Anyone who reads and approves the plan and proposal should be informed of the questions to be asked and encouraged to comment on them. It can be helpful to the researchers to receive comments on the questions that have been prepared since it is often impossible to predict how respondents will interpret questions. Questions must be phrased so that they appeal to the respondents and encourage completion.

The proposal should provide a justification for the questions that are to be asked. It is a good idea to provide alternative questions for consideration by those who review the proposal. The latter may see difficulties that were not perceived by those who initially formulated the questions. Moreover, if it is possible to present the questions in an interesting or unusual way it should be given favourable consideration.

Planning in advance for analysis of research data

How one analyses research data depends on how the research data were collected and the type of data they are. The method used for analysing data obtained from experiments and observational studies will be different to that involved in analysing survey data. The preparation of questionnaires requires careful consideration about how the data will be analysed and this has to be taken into account when setting out the format of questions.

Limitations

Any study will have limitations in terms of the applicability of its findings. The proposal should indicate **research limitations** by explaining what the proposed study can do and what it cannot. Such an explanation may prevent undeserved criticism at a later date and prevent any feeling of disappointment with the usefulness of the research.

Time schedule

The time schedule for research must be clearly established from the outset. Timing should be a part of the proposal and discussed at meetings concerning the proposal. If management wants to move more quickly, it must adopt a different research method.

The **research schedule** must be agreeable to all parties and, once established, the schedule must be followed as closely as possible. Some departments in the firm will be waiting for and depending on the findings of the research and a delayed study can be costly. Delays can prevent these departments from going ahead on other projects that may be even more important to the firm. Everyone has to realise that some schedules may have to be changed. New and unexpected findings may have to be pursued, perhaps producing a change in research technique. A proposal should allow for such possibilities, even though the importance of staying with the original schedule is recognised.

ITEMS FOR INCLUSION IN A RESEARCH PROJECT MARKET PLAN

Research reasons and objectives

- Establish motivation for research project.
- Establish purpose of research project.
- Determine budget for research project.
- Define research problem.
- Find and review previous research on research topic.
- Determine current opinion.
- Determine previous recommendations.
- Determine research questions.

Method/analysis for research

- Select data collection method.
- Select analysis method.
- Select supplier/field service.
- Choose facility location(s).
- Prepare focus group materials.
- Supervise recruiting.
- Supervise/conduct sessions.
- Review sessions.

Data analysis and interpretation

- Choose appropriate analysis.
- Run analysis.
- Interpret results.
- Choose report format.
- Highlight findings.

Report: write up research method and management

- Present overview.
- Review literature.
- Design and execute.
- Describe population; sampling frame; sampling method/size.
- Detail collection method.
- Report completion rate.
- Explain data processing.

Report: write up analysis and interpretation

- Present data.
- Present data manipulations.
- Present interpretations.
- Summary/conclusion.
- Review significant findings.
- State major discovery.
- Report study limitations.

- Prepare tables.
- Prepare illustrative graphs.
- List references.
- Write abstract.
- Edit report.
- Revise report.
- Print report.

Research project: presentation to management
- Highlight findings.
- Prepare slides/overheads.
- Rehearse presentation.
- Present report.

THE PROPOSAL

The producers of the proposal and plan should take into account how the findings and recommendations should be presented and to whom. These details impinge on how collected information is subsequently organised and best presented as charts, tables, slides or in other ways. A study that will be presented solely to top management may require important differences in method of presentation and details. Some thought has to be given to the types of personality that will examine the proposal. This means assessing the extent to which the proposal will have to 'prove itself' to certain management members and what will be needed to convince them to accept the proposal.

RESEARCH PROPOSAL

1 Clear statement of the marketing problem or problems to be investigated.
2 Contributory factors and constraints related to the problem.
3 Definition of the product/service to be investigated.
4 Definition of the survey population to be sampled.
5 Major areas of measurement – consumption, beliefs about products, expectations, attitudes, motivations, classifications of buyers etc.
6 Methodology to be adopted (types of data, method of sampling, research instruments etc.).

7 Expected degree of accuracy of research findings.

8 Cost and time involved in conducting the research.

9 Conditions applying to research.

10 Previous experience of researchers.

USE OF PERT IN PLANNING RESEARCH

A marketing research plan is a form of project and as such may be thought of as a combination of interrelated activities that have to be carried out in a certain order so that the entire task is completed. There is a logical sequence to the interrelated activities in the sense that some of them cannot start until others are completed. Projects and planning activities have become extremely complex and require systematic and effective management techniques to help optimise the efficiency of executing such activities. Efficiency amounts to bringing about the greatest reduction in the time to complete the scheduled activities while taking into account the economic feasibility of using available resources.

A network analysis tool such as **PERT** (project evaluation and review technique) can assist planning, scheduling and **research control**. This tool provides help to monitor and organise resources in order to enable a project or activity to be completed on time and within budget limits. Projects and planning activities are complex entities that often have extensive duration times, involve many different and interrelated costs, and comprise work of a distinctive, unique, non-repetitive nature. It is customary to model projects and planning activities as networks to capture the nature of the interrelationships and the sequencing of their various component parts.

PERT is a three-part technique:

1 *Planning*: incorporates an in-depth analysis of the project or planning task and the construction of the network to describe it.

2 *Scheduling*: involves the analysis of the project or exercise to determine completion time, critical activities and the start and finish times for each activity.

3 *Controlling*: includes using the network and the schedule to keep track of progress and making any revisions necessary to keep the project or exercise on schedule and within budget.

The planning stage involves three parts:

1 identifying and sequencing all activities

2 drawing the network to represent the exercise

3 estimating activity times and costs.

Once the network has been constructed and the expected times decided it becomes possible both to determine the minimum completion time for the exercise and to schedule each activity. This stage is handled well by a computer program.

At some stage in the project, it may be thought desirable to shorten the completion time. This can usually be achieved by allocating additional resources to critical activities. A minimum duration for the project or exercise will exist and further expenditure will not be able to reduce completion time below this minimum. It also has to be realised that the efficient allocation of resources requires further analysis of the project or exercise, examining time/cost tradeoffs in order to obtain the greatest time reduction per amount of money expended.

Computers have made a significant impact on the process of project management and planning, and specialised software packages – more specifically, packages that run on desktop computers – have been developed. In applying the PERT technique, the networks produced are often large and require many revisions for replanning and updating. Making such revisions by hand can be time-consuming, confusing and costly. The process is much accelerated by the use of appropriate computer software, making changes and comparisons much easier. There are many relevant software packages available, some specifically designed for use with the desktop computer. A useful guide to have when selecting a package is that provided by Smith and Gupta.[6]

An example of a sophisticated project management computer software package is Time Line for Windows.[7] It possesses convenient graphing tools that make it easy to build and revise schedules and to assign and coordinate resources, dependencies and due dates across multiple projects and planning exercises. Multiple views also allow us to see many aspects of a complex model simultaneously. There are six types of view permissible:

- the overview

- the Gantt view

- the PERT view

- the time-scaled PERT view

- the resource view

- the cross-tabulation view.

The package also includes Guide Line software that enables the user to generate project and planning schedules just by answering a series of questions. The Guide Maker add-on enables the user to create custom guides for any business situation. Guide Line is based on the idea that most projects and planning exercises have been done before. Once the user has specified project or planning exercise requirements, it produces task lists, resource allocations and time estimates for the project or exercise.

Information about projects is stored in a database and it is taking various views of the database, coupled with appropriate graphical representations, that enables detailed and informative analysis to take place. (See Figures 2.3–2.6.)

Figure 2.3 shows the standard cross-tabulation view of a marketing research plan. Two views or windows on the data are being displayed simultaneously. Moreover, the two views are synchronised to examine the same set of records. The two windows can be expanded or contracted to show more or fewer fields and further records can be viewed by panning down through the records to ones that are not currently displayed on the screen. The cross-tabulation view or windows allow the user to examine the tasks that have to be completed in their logical sequence and to see how the costs will arise over time and affect cash-flow requirements.

Figure 2.4 shows the standard resource view of the data along with availability and cost of each person involved in the exercise.

Figure 2.5 shows the standard Gantt view of the data. Here again two windows on the database are simultaneously displayed. The right-hand window shows graphically how elements of the plan take up time slots. The left-hand window identifies both the nature of the task involved and the nature of the human resource requirement to carry out the task. Once again, the user displays more or fewer fields in each window and pans through the data to examine as yet undisplayed records.

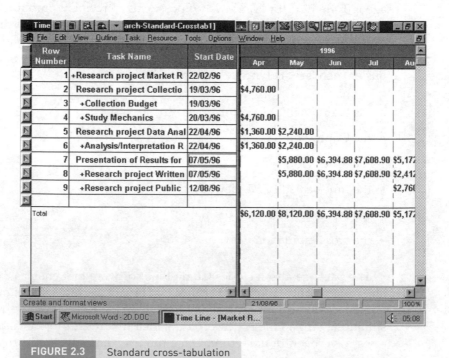

FIGURE 2.3　Standard cross-tabulation

Source: Screenshot reprinted by permission from Microsoft Corporation

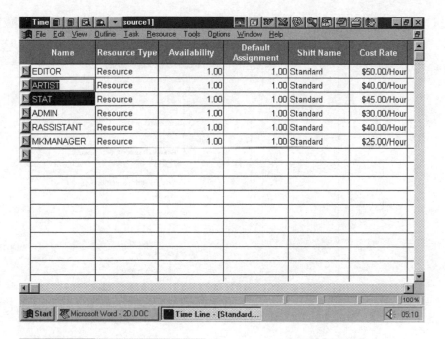

FIGURE 2.4   Standard resource

Source: Screenshot reprinted by permission from Microsoft Corporation

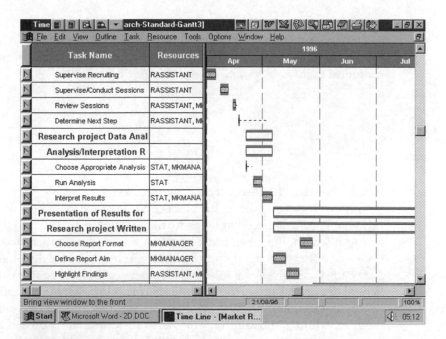

FIGURE 2.5   Standard Gantt view of data

Source: Screenshot reprinted by permission from Microsoft Corporation

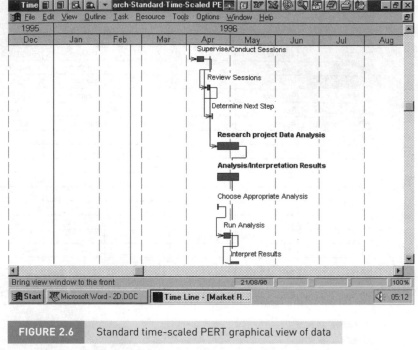

FIGURE 2.6   Standard time-scaled PERT graphical view of data

Source: Screenshot reprinted by permission from Microsoft Corporation

Figure 2.6 shows the standard time-scaled PERT graphical view of the data for the marketing plan. As above, different parts of the data can be viewed in this graphical manner by panning vertically or horizontally.

SUMMARY

In this chapter it has been argued that marketing research performs a key role in helping to solve marketing problems and improve decisions. It achieves this by producing information that helps to allay uncertainty. The cost and value of marketing research, however, must be taken into account when deciding how much time and effort to expend on this activity. While the benefits of good information speak for themselves, the research has to be cost-effective if it is to be used at all. Where the costs outweigh the benefits it is not desirable to undertake research. Marketing research projects are complex entities and require considerable planning, scheduling and control. This helps to coordinate a project and ensures that research information is produced within the specified period and cost specifications. Computer-based PERT network methods help to plan, schedule and control a project and facilitate savings in the cost and time required to complete the project.

QUESTIONS

1 Small firms may think undertaking marketing research is too expensive and not worth their while. How might you persuade them otherwise? Under what circumstances might there be some truth in their viewpoint?

2 Construct a research proposal that has as its purpose identifying new product and market opportunities for a small computer software development company currently employing 30 staff and achieving an annual sales turnover of £8 million.

3 Discuss the basic methods of collecting marketing research information and outline the circumstances under which each of the identified methods might most appropriately be used.

4 Why is it important to indicate at the research planning stage how one is going to analyse the data?

5 What is meant by the limitations of a study? Why are they important?

CASE STUDY 2.1: NEW SHOE COMPANY

The New Shoe Company, based in the English Midlands, is experiencing a fall in profits. The company measures profits in terms of the annual pre-tax return on capital employed earned by the company.

The sales director says that falling profitability is a reflection of the current slump in the market. Total demand in the marketplace is much less than it was 12 months ago and the company has struggled to maintain its market share at the previous level as competition has intensified. Competition from European manufacturers has been sharpened by changes in EU trading regulations and Spanish manufacturers, in particular, have taken advantage of their lower cost structure to make inroads into the British market. At the same time, the New Shoe Company has failed to take full advantage of opportunities in Europe. It has not fully developed its market niching strategy where it can gain a competitive advantage. The sales director blames the firm's lack of competitiveness on the poor performance of the R&D team and the inability of the manufacturing departments to control costs.

The technical director claims that the firm's products are competitive with any that are produced worldwide. Indeed, in her view, the firm's products are by far the best available at the price offered. She points to the lack of marketing effort expended by the firm in the past year, pointing to the necessity to keep the firm's name before the public at all times, especially when competition is increasing in strength. At the same time she recognises that marketing effort requires financing and that this was not adequately provided during the period in question.

The production director points out that the company has been able to lower its manufacturing costs substantially through the introduction of new technology into the manufacturing process. However, he points out the accounting practices adopted by the firm distort the true picture. Profitability, in his view, has improved, although this is not truly reflected in the company's management accounts.

The finance director feels that the drop in profitability is attributable to recent acquisitions the firm has made. Ventures into retailing have not been as profitable as had first been supposed. This might to some extent have been reflective of bad timing on behalf of the company, given the current recession, in making such acquisitions.

The managing director points out that there clearly is a problem and that perhaps one should pay particular attention to what competitors are doing and how the firm is responding from a marketing viewpoint.

Questions

1 Given the limited information in this case, what do you think could be the real problem or problems in this example?

2 Depending on the real nature of the problem identified, how might marketing research help in this case?

CASE STUDY 2.2: *CHERI-ROSE*

The editor of *Cheri-Rose*, a women's fashion magazine, has approached you about undertaking some research on behalf of the magazine. The magazine has not been successful in attracting handbag manufacturers as advertisers. On the occasions when it has approached the manufacturers it has been told that ladies' outfitters are a rapidly declining segment of the handbag market and since *Cheri-Rose* appeals primarily to women who buy from those particular outlets the handbag manufacturers argue that the magazine is not a good vehicle for their advertising.

The editor thinks that a survey of women's outfitters will show that these kinds of outlet are not, in fact, declining in terms of their importance as outlets for women's accessories – including handbags.

Question

Draft a suitable research proposal for a study that will produce information that is pertinent to the editor's problem.

CASE STUDY 2.3: WHY RESEARCHERS ARE SO JITTERY

With a general election looming, Britain's market research wizards are on tenter-hooks. The latest issue of the UK's Market Research Society magazine is titled *1997: Year of Decision for MR*, and the lead article starts by asking whether 1997 will be a year of 'further embarrassment'. The second article is titled: 'Laying the ghost of the nightmare of '92', a reference to the way UK opinion polls were all at sea with their predictions of the 1992 UK election result.

Having celebrated their society's 50th birthday last year with much braggadocio, researchers now have a hangover. This being election year, the opinion polls are on trial again, and if researchers get things wrong – which hardly seems possible, but then it did not seem possible last time – their credibility will be in smithereens.

Inevitably, the entire market research business will be seen as guilty by associ-ation and market research is now pretty big business. With £7bn in turnover and steady, compound growth of 8–10% a year, the UK research business has done extremely well of late. Moreover, the Association of Market Survey Organisations (Amso) forecasts growth of 15–20% this year.

Research is a nice little export earner, too. As with other marketing activities, Britain is a world leader. According to Amso, about 20% of UK market research turnover comes from international surveys and international work is growing faster than domestic.

Today there are few manufacturing companies, media houses, government departments, public bodies, academic institutions or even retailers in Britain that do not integrate research into their decision-making processes. For many years, retailers were market research Cinderellas. They believed they could learn from their store traffic everything they wanted to know. As a result, they felt they did not need to ask any questions. But retailers now account for some 5% of total research expenditure and their share is growing steadily.

However, not everything is rosy. Although other market researchers strive to distance themselves from the political pollsters, they know they share their prob-lems, and many of those problems are fundamental. On one hand, some members of the public manifestly enjoy taking part in research surveys and focus groups. The paid interviewers know who they are and return to them repeatedly. This leads to bogus results.

On the other hand, more people are becoming refuseniks. In Britain the indus-try now conducts well over 15 million interviews per year and 100 million questionnaires are mailed out by database companies. Although there are no pub-lished figures, most experienced researchers will confirm that refusal rates are rising steadily.

Even in flagship studies like the National Readership Survey, response rates are now just over 60% after eight or more calls on respondents. (When the survey started in 1954 they reached 85% after six calls.) So 40% of the NRS universe is nowadays uncanvassed. Political polls suffer similarly high non-response rates, which was one of the reasons for the 1992 debacle.

More worryingly, a welter of evidence shows that a growing proportion of the public is now playing games with market researchers. They understand the processes (which are hardly rocket science) and consciously manipulate their responses. Like voters in by-elections, they deliberately send messages to companies and political parties, using the researchers as conduits. It takes only a small percentage of such respondents to invalidate results. None too soon, the research industry has started to investigate these problems. Several of the key papers at last month's Amso annual conference addressed the increasingly uncertain relationship between market researchers and their raw material – the public.

It is by no means clear what, if anything, can be done, and that is why so much hangs on the election pollsters' accuracy this time round. Polls capture the headlines. Polls have also captured politicians. Nobody pays more attention to surveys than politicians. Contrary to conventional wisdom, market research is a far more potent influence in modern politics than advertising. Politicians read, mark, learn and inwardly digest the voters' views on everything from abortion to traffic crossings. And the pollsters revel in their influence.

Behind the Oval Office, the new sell-and-tell potboiler by President Bill Clinton's former chief electoral strategist, Dick Morris, shows Clinton messily awash with market research findings in the run-up to last year's election. Indeed, Clinton often felt himself drowning in them.

The pollsters tried to control his every waking moment. They told him to become a father figure with a powerful red tie and dictated how he should spend his holidays. 'Can I golf?' the president asked the pollsters, his tone dripping sarcasm. 'Maybe if I wear a baseball cap?' He was told: 'No, sir, go rafting.'

In compensation, market research has given political leaders, both in western and ex-communist democracies, new power over their parties. In Britain, former prime minister Margaret Thatcher was able to march on with confidence during the Falklands War because she tracked public opinion throughout. Neil Kinnock, the former Labour leader, was able to defeat Militant extremists because he knew that the vast majority of the electorate, and the vast majority of Labour voters, supported him. The ability of the present Labour leader, Tony Blair, to ride roughshod over Labour's historic articles of faith has, again, been built on firmly researched foundations. When zealous and partisan supporters claim 'the party'll never buy that,' the leader, research data in hip pocket, can nowadays ignore them with insouciance.

All this emphasises the present symbiosis between market research and politics. It will last as long as the politicians continue to have faith in the researchers' wizardry. The politicians influence a great deal of business, both directly, via government departments, and indirectly, via publicity and the media.

So the researchers wait – and worry – for 1992 was not their only cock-up. They also bombed in 1970. And in the 13 elections between 1945 and 1987, some 40% of pollsters' forecasts were inaccurate by more than plus or minus 2% – a small margin, but usually sufficient to swing the result, which is all that matters.

Most of the time the researchers' findings cannot be verified. They cannot be proved right or wrong. Except at elections. That is why market researchers are now so jumpy. Their outlook is far from bleak, but it is distinctly unsettled.

Source: Fletcher[8] (reprinted with permission)

Question

If most of the time the researchers' findings cannot be verified, how does this affect the true value of market research?

CASE STUDY 2.4: TRACKING THE RAILWAYS

Since the British railway system was privatised in 1996, the new rail companies have been plagued with problems. Poor rolling stock, delayed trains, disaffected passengers, and poor coordination between the different companies regarding timetabling and through ticketing have all contributed to the feeling of malaise that plagues the industry.

Some of the directors of the companies have been less than sympathetic towards their customers – one director went so far as to suggest that the 40,000 complaints a year his company was getting were being written during people's working time and that he was considering writing to their bosses about it. Another director said that the non-functioning toilets on his trains were 'a detail' that would have to wait. The same director raised fares by 5%, justifying this on the grounds that he was acting within the terms of his operating contract – apparently ignoring the moral obligation he has to his customers. The reason for these attitudes could be that the rail companies have only been given a seven-year franchise – a period of time hardly conducive to making major long-term investments in capital goods such as rolling stock and locomotives. The temptation to take a short-term view is clearly a strong one.

Equally problematically, each company seems to be trying to establish its own brand, and even competing with other companies, at a time when the industry needs to present a united front in order to stave off competition from road transport.

One of the problems facing the train operating companies – or TOCs – is that branding may not be very effective when approaching customers who prefer to be called passengers and only want to get from A to B in the most efficient way possible. Design company Wolff Olins found that the most popular layout for the Heathrow Express was the most practical one rather than the most luxurious, and Virgin Trains reports that the poor image of its rail services has damaged the previously invulnerable Virgin brand.

Some commentators believe that the TOCs need to segment their market more clearly and respond better to customer needs. 'People must be very careful to distinguish superficial marketing from true marketing,' says Fiona McAnena of the Added Value Company. Both Great North Eastern Railway and Great Western Trains have modelled themselves on British Airways; market research showed that people wanted a more personal approach and GNER has taken these findings on board to the extent of asking staff to seek out opportunities to add a personal touch.

Market research has not always worked for the railways, however. When the Gatwick Express was being redesigned, customers were asked how the service could be improved. They were unable to come up with anything beyond the obvious, whereas the researchers were hoping that they would be able to suggest radical changes to the service. The researchers responded by setting up a panel (a think tank) of advertisers, researchers and psychologists in the hope that they would be able to second-guess the consumers. So far the results of this panel have not been divulged.

In the longer term, the TOCs will need to work out the problem of short-termism. This will probably require a change of heart on the part of government, allowing longer franchises to be granted – the Catch-22 is that the government is unlikely to do so until standards improve. In the meantime, the TOCs and the passengers (or customers) will need to make the best of a difficult situation.

Questions

1 Why might the Gatwick Express research have failed?

2 How would you plan a research programme to identify the needs of the different market segments for rail transport?

3 What are the problems inherent in running a research programme for the railways?

4 Given the negative attitudes of some rail bosses towards their customers, what might be the problems of presenting the findings of the research?

5 How might market research help in effecting a reconciliation between the TOCs and their passengers?

 REFERENCES AND NOTES

1   De Bono, E (1992) in Peters, T, *Liberation Management*, London: Macmillan, 635.

2   Rickards, T (1974) *Problem Solving through Creative Analysis*, Aldershot: Gower.

3   Proctor, T (1999) *Creative Problem Solving for Managers*, London: Routledge.

4   Marks, A P (1990) The Sinclair 5 – why did it fail? *Management Decision*, 28(4), 9–14.

5   Kerlinger, F (1973) *Foundations of Behavioral Research*, New York: Holt, Rinehart & Winston, Chapter 2.

6   Smith, L A and Gupta, S (1985) Project management software in P & IM, *P & IM Review and APICS News*, June, 66–68.

7   Time Line 6 for Windows, Symantec Corporation, 10201 Torre Avenue, Cupertino, CA 95014, USA.

8   Fletcher, W (1997) Why researchers are so jittery, *Financial Times*, 3 March.

FURTHER READING

Andreasen, A (1983) Cost-conscious marketing research, *Harvard Business Review*, 61, 4.

Butler, P (1994) Marketing problems: from analysis to decision, *Marketing Intelligence and Planning*, 12(2), 4–13.

Chapman, R G (1989) Problem definition in marketing research studies, *Journal of Services Marketing*, 3(3), 51–59.

Markland, R E (1983) *Topics in Management Science*, New York: Wiley.

McCullough, D (1999) Why marketing research is a waste of money (and what you can do about it), *Marcom Today*, November.

Robson, C (2002) *Real World Research* (2nd edn), Oxford: Blackwell.

Taha, H A (1992) *Operations Research: An introduction* (5th edn), New York: Macmillan, Chapter 13.

Zemke, R (1978) How market research techniques can pay off for trainers, *Training*, 15(12).

3   Secondary data

Objectives

After reading this chapter, you should be able to:

- appreciate the various sources of secondary data

- understand how to start systematically to collect these data.

Keywords

abstracts	indexes
bibliographies	internal data
CD-ROM	libraries
database	online
external data	secondary data
government statistics	

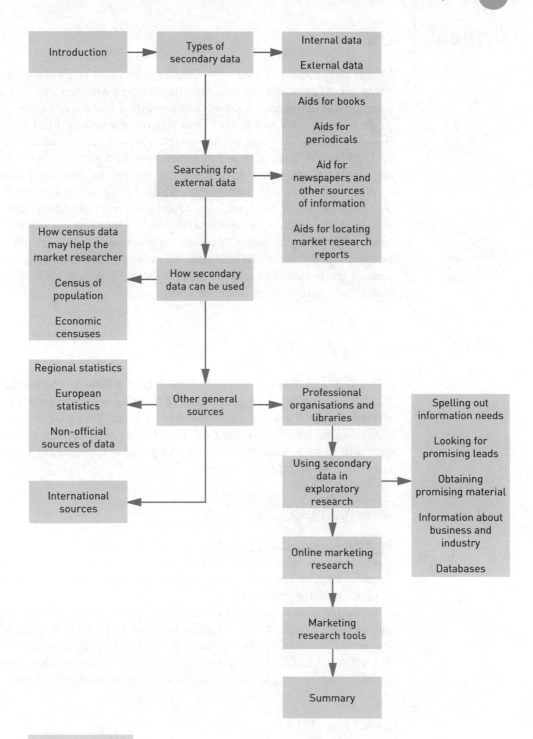

Plan of Chapter 3

INTRODUCTION

In this chapter, we review the various sources of secondary data. Information helps an organisation to solve its marketing problems and to make marketing decisions. A distinction between information and data has to be made. Data comprise unorganised news, facts and figures about any kind of topic you could possibly name. Information, by comparison, is quite different from data. It is a body of facts that is organised around a specific topic or subject. It comprises facts organised and presented to help solve a problem or develop a plan.

When we read about something that has happened, for example, new products that have been launched, we have been looking at **secondary data**. Actually being involved in launching a new product and noting our experience in this connection amounts to generating and collecting primary data. When doing research we never collect primary data if someone else has already collected the material, since it is a waste of time and effort. We should always start, therefore, by examining secondary sources of information.

TYPES OF SECONDARY DATA

There is a large amount of secondary data available to the marketing researcher. While only a very small proportion of existing secondary data may be useful in any one project, marketing researchers should know where to obtain relevant data and should be familiar with procedures to reduce the amount of time required to search for data. A starting point is to separate secondary data into either *internal* or *external* sources.

Internal data

Internal secondary data are produced by an organisation in its day-to-day operations. Data on sales, advertising expenditures, inventory records, salespersons' reports, distribution costs and prices are just some examples of the type of internal data that are produced.

In many instances, internal data are gathered in a relatively unorganised manner and people in the organisation may have little knowledge of what data are actually available. The growth of marketing information systems alongside the trend towards the computerisation of all records in a business has done and can do much to simplify the organisation and accessibility of internal data.

External data

External data are data that come from a wide variety of sources outside an organisation. So numerous are the various forms of external data that in order to

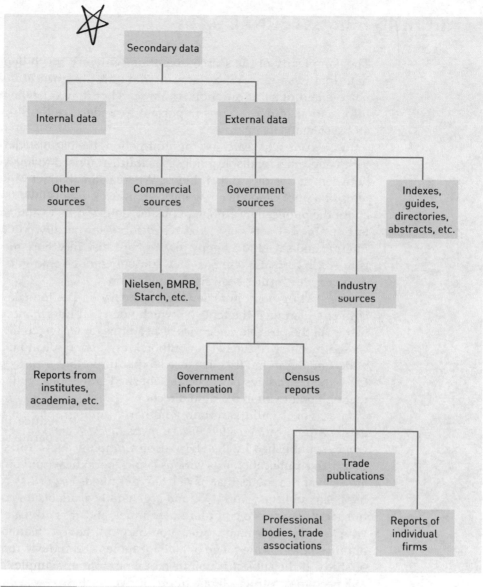

FIGURE 3.1   Secondary sources of information

use them effectively a researcher needs to be skilled in the use of **indexes**, **abstracts** and directories to locate relevant material. Without the use of these aids much time and effort is invariably wasted and much relevant information may be overlooked. (See Figure 3.1 for the interlinkage of these two types of data.)

SEARCHING FOR EXTERNAL DATA

The complexity of the search operation will very much depend on the type of data that is sought. Where specific data are sought, the search may be quite narrow and of short duration. The researcher may often be unaware of specific information sources so it is important to undertake the search in an organised and systematic manner.

In the course of searching for information, the use of indexes, abstracts, directories and other available guides is helpful. You need to appreciate the difference between an abstract and an index. Whereas an abstract presents the basic contents of a publication in a few lines, an index presents only the minimum of data about the publication: author, publisher, date of publication and so on. Today collections of abstracts may be searched for electronically on **CD-ROM** disks or the Internet and saved to a floppy disk or hard disk file. Since the stored information is in ASCII format, these files may subsequently be read into word processors or databases for further analysis or exploration.

The starting point in reviewing secondary data is to make sure that you have correctly identified the topic on which you need information. This first involves listing all the possible categories or headings under which the topic might be discussed by other researchers or authors. It is a good idea to make the topics fairly wide ranging in the first instance so that important aspects are not overlooked. Once these headings have been established, attention can then be turned to aids that will point you in the right direction.

First, you should ascertain whether a bibliography on the subject already exists. A publication called *Bibliographies Index: A cumulative bibliography of bibliographies*, published by the HH Wilson Company, New York, is a useful starting point. This publication lists various books, periodicals and other publications that are relevant to topics that have been identified. *The British National Bibliography* has been published since 1950 and is generally available for consultation in public **libraries**. There are cumulative volumes and it is advisable to use the index which will list terms or topics you may not have considered. Most academic libraries have a wide range of **bibliographies** and indexes that cover major fields of study. If the subject is unique a bibliography may not exist. In this case, you will need to construct a bibliography for yourself.

ABSTRACT AVAILABLE ON CD-ROM – PERMITTING ELECTRONIC SEARCHES OF THOUSANDS OF ABSTRACTS

Access No:	01075313 ProQuest ABI/INFORM (R) Research
Title:	Breaking away
Authors:	Selwyn, Padi
Journal:	*Successful Meetings* [SMM] ISSN: 0148–4052
	Vol: 44 Iss: 9 Date: Aug 1995 pp: 79–83

Reprint:	Contact UMI for article reprint (order no. 9753.02) Restrictions may apply
Subjects:	Business community; Meetings; Planning; Creativity; Success
Geo Places:	US
Codes:	9190 (United States); 2310 (Planning); 2200 (Managerial skills)
Abstract:	A 1993 Porter/Novelli survey of 100 Fortune 500 executives revealed that creativity is the most important element for business success. Six tips to help meetings planners to enhance their own and others' creativity are offered: 1. Open your mind. 2. Diversify. 3. Clear your mind for each day. 4. Stop looking for the right answer. 5. Discover your creative rhythm. 6. Health makes wealth.

Specific sources of information include books, periodicals, newspapers, government information, directories, and statistics and information stored for use with a computer. Many different aids can help you find information that is most appropriate to your needs. However, remember that the availability and comprehensiveness of these aids varies from country to country. For example, while there is a vast amount of aids available in the USA for such purposes their relevance to the needs of researchers in, say, Europe is not always guaranteed.

Aids for books

Every library keeps a *card catalogue* file on what it contains and this should usually be the starting point for most library research. Most catalogue systems present information on books in at least two ways: an author–title section for those looking for works of a particular author, and a subject section for those looking for information on a specific subject. Where books are not held by a library, interlibrary loan facilities usually exist. Many UK libraries possess facilities to enable researchers to examine a **database** on a CD-ROM. *Boston Spa* details the 500,000 books in the British Library's national interlibrary loan collection. Another database, *Bookbank*, also provides details of books published in Britain. *Books in Print* (UK and USA) enables researchers to identify all books that have been published and that are currently in print. Equivalent systems operate in most other countries. The interlibrary loan facility may operate on a reciprocal basis between a number of regional and/or local libraries. Alternatively, the British Library at Boston Spa in Yorkshire operates a service for books and periodical articles. Researchers may find it useful to visit the British Library Centre at Boston Spa but it should be noted that advanced notice of a visit is appreciated.

Aids for periodicals

The large number of periodicals and their variety of articles mean that the researcher has to rely on indexes in searching for appropriate data. Most of these indexes are to be found in the reference areas of libraries.

Ulrich's *International Periodicals Directory* (New York: Bowker) is a good place to start because it lists subject specialisms and publication details of journals that are currently available. In the case of specifically British journals, *Current British Journals: A subject guide to periodicals* is helpful. Other indexing services list all the material published in specified periodicals and are produced on a regular basis with annual accumulations. They are arranged by subject matter and author but do not give detailed information on the contents of the article.

Abstracting services provide the same information as indexes and also a summary or abstract of the article that provides enough detail for the researcher to know if it is relevant. A rapidly increasing number of indexes and abstracts are now available as databases on CD-ROM disks. These include:

- ABI-Inform: business and management

- Bookbank: British books in print

- PSYCLIT: psychological abstracts

- UK Official Publications: parliamentary, non-parliamentary and non-TSO publications

- indexes and abstracts are also becoming available on the Internet.

Aid for newspapers and other sources of information

For some researchers the material sought will be contained in newspapers, national census reports or other statistical databases. Most universities, for example, have access to a retrieval system for the national census.

National Online Management Information System (NOMIS) is a computerised employment information system developed at Durham University on behalf of the Department of Employment. It has been in national use since 1982 and permits access to official statistics on employment, vacancies and population, together with facilities to compare and analyse data on a wide range of areas from local to national levels. The information is available at a wide range of geographical levels and some data analysis facilities, such as graphs and percentages, are available within the system itself. Among the data that NOMIS can provide are:

- census of population data to ward level

- census of employment total since 1971 – specifically employment by industrial classification for local travel-to-work areas

- annual population projections

- National Health Service migration datasets.

Such data are available for many scales of study, including the following:

- wards
- travel-to-work areas
- local authority districts
- parliamentary constituencies
- regions.

When searching for UK **government statistics**, researchers should start with the free *Government Statistics, a Brief Guide to Sources* or the *Guide to Official Statistics*, which can be bought from The Stationery Office (formerly HMSO).

THE UK MARKET FOR FITTED BATHROOMS: THE USE OF SECONDARY DATA AND ITS LIMITATIONS

At first the idea was to concentrate on the market for fitted bathrooms, but as this market in the UK is still in its infancy the market structure is very fragmented, so it is difficult to obtain information about this segment. Because of this problem the research concentrated on the British market for baths and sanitaryware. The objectives of the research were to provide the reader with a general understanding of:

- market structure
- distribution system
- buyer behaviour of private customers.

Using the Aslib directory, a list of eight libraries that could be of help was drawn up. Four of these were in London: London Business School, Overseas Trade Library, London Commercial Library and British Library – the science and business department. Two libraries were in Manchester: Manchester Business School and the Central Library commercial section. One library was in Birmingham – Birmingham Central Library – and the other was the British Library in Boston Spa.

Being based in the north of England, I started in the local area and visited the two libraries in Manchester and the one in Birmingham. The result was quite good in terms of identifying the available material as there were several good publications about available market reports, newspaper articles and magazines. The search words used during this part of the desk research were:

- bath(s)
- showers
- sanitaryware
- en-suite bathroom
- bathroom

- ceramics
- toilet
- WC

The initial desk research was followed by a three-day stay in London. The material obtained in London comprised market analyses made by professional companies and articles from magazines. On average the reports were one to two years old. All the reports more or less followed the same structure:

1 introduction

2 market size

3 demand composition: the customers

4 distribution: concentrating on the merchants

5 manufacturers

6 prospects and recent developments.

The information in reports was to a large extent a replication of the same facts and figures. This at least suggested that the data were reliable. However, the major problem was that none of the reports looked into the distribution system in depth nor did they describe the consumer buying behaviour in a systematic way.

Source: Spindler[1]

Aids for locating market research reports and other marketing information

There are many thousands of reports available and they can be located through several sources, for example, *Market Search*,[2] *Reports Index*[3] and *Findex*.[4] Information on organisations providing marketing information and **online** data can be found in *The UK Marketing Source Book*[5] and *The Source Book*.[6] Database source books include: *On-Line Business Source Book*,[7] *On-Line Business and Company Databases*[8] and *Directory of On-Line Databases*.[9]

GOLDEN NUGGETS ON A LONG AND WINDING ROAD

Getting lost on the information superhighway? Online business information services can provide the shortcuts to show business users where they need to go.

The Internet is a goldmine of information, but searching for that elusive nugget often yields nothing but frustration.

Online business information services provide better and quicker ways of finding information on the Internet – albeit at a price. And through the Internet, these companies can reach a global market of information seekers and offer new products.

Business information has been available online for many years. Initially, access was only via proprietary terminals and private networks, on Reuters and Lexis-Nexis, for example. But the growth of the personal computer has led most services to move to PC-based access with a Windows-based interface design to make searching for information easier.

Many information services use agency distributors, including big online networks such as CompuServe, to extend their reach around the globe. But in the Internet age, these traditional delivery channels are costly and old-fashioned. So providers of business information are adapting their proprietary services to allow access from the Web.

'The Internet allows us to serve our existing market with new products,' says Gerard Buckley, marketing director with Dun & Bradstreet, a leading US business information provider. The company opened its global information database to the Internet in July.

Web surfers can search free of charge the D&B GlobalSeek database, which has details on more than 45 million companies in 200 countries. They also can buy a synopsis of the business operations of a particular company. The report is purchased by credit card directly from the Web for $5 (£2.95). D&B's existing contract subscribers can also buy reports on the Web using the password they use to access the traditional proprietary service.

FT Information, the business information division of Pearson, publisher of the *Financial Times*, recently announced a new Internet-based product: FT Discovery for the Web. It provides users with news alerts and international business information including news, company information and market intelligence. The product is designed to appeal to smaller businesses and is thus offered at a fixed price – £99 a month for each user – and can be accessed using a standard Web browser and Internet connection.

Dialog, which claims to be the world's oldest and largest online information service, celebrated its 25th anniversary this year by launching an Internet-based service. Called Dialog Web, the service is accessed via a standard Web browser using the same command language adopted for the proprietary Dialog service. Dialog comprises more than 470 databases from a broad range of disciplines, including business news, patents and trademarks, science and technology, as well as consumer news. It is the flagship product of Dialog Corporation, formed last month from the merger of MAID, a fast-growing UK information provider, and Knight-Ridder Information, the online division of US newspaper publisher Knight-Ridder and previous owner of Dialog.

KRI's information empire comprises more than 900 databases, 9 terabytes of data and 160,000 customers. The smaller MAID has 4700 corporate subscribers – a single subscription may, however, cover hundreds of users. Its core product is Profound, which offers around 100 million pages of information from more than 5000 content publishers, including market research reports, business news, company statistics, brokerage research and stock market prices. Profound uses MAID's proprietary InfoSort data-indexing technology that allows fast, accurate searching

▶

across all the databases. The service was launched in 1995, initially just as a dial-up service. But in mid-1996, MAID added access via the Internet.

At the end of 1996 an intranet version of Profound was launched that can be custom designed for an organisation at a fixed price and offers the security advantage of an intranet. The intranet (a private network) system also uses the InfoSort technology to allow each company to define its information needs and index information in predetermined categories. This facility aims to overcome the information overload problem common to online information services and ensure that only information relevant to the company is provided on its intranet. British Telecom plans to use the intranet version of Profound to offer large business customers a complete managed intranet service, including customised information.

Financial analysts were surprised when loss-making MAID, whose 1996 sales were just £21m, announced in August its plan to buy the much larger KRI, with revenues last year of almost $290m. KRI's parent Knight-Ridder justified the sale by saying it wanted to focus resources on expanding its newspaper empire.

Online information services have proved a thorn in the side of many media groups because of their heavy upfront development costs. The Internet creates further uncertainty in the online market, and the big consumer-oriented services, such as CompuServe, have lost subscribers because of the Internet's growth.

Analysts say business-oriented online services are not as vulnerable because of their sophisticated search engines and high-value data. However, much of the bread-and-butter information they offer, such as company results, and magazine and newspaper articles, can often be found for free on the Web. This is, however, assuming users have the patience to search for it. The rapid rise of the Web browser as a standard, easy-to-use interface has left online service providers wondering whether they should continue to sink money into developing and supporting proprietary software.

CompuServe, for example, announced in October it would make many of its databases and technical forums available to Web surfers on a pay-as-you-go basis, as well as continuing with its traditional proprietary service. Gerard Buckley, of Dun & Bradstreet, believes proprietary services still have the edge because of the effort that has gone into optimising the software used to acess the service. But their longer term future looks less certain.

'There will always be people who will need value-added (proprietary) software, but increasingly we are moving to the Internet,' he says.

Source: Nairn[10] (reprinted with permission)

HOW SECONDARY DATA CAN BE USED

Secondary data can be useful in one or more of three ways in marketing research: in exploratory work, as a news source or in marketing decisions. When secondary data are used as part of an exploratory study, they are often associated with long-range considerations of a firm, such as whether to think seriously about developing a completely new product or service. A manufacturer of leather goods, for example, might want to consider the feasibility of establishing a chain of leatherware shops. The first step in the research process would involve a great deal of secondary research.

There is one secondary source – the census – that is both so extensive and intensive that it cuts across all three categories. There are also some other general sources that can apply to one or more of the three categories.

The census

The census is the largest single source of secondary data. The range and amount of information available from the census is too great to describe in depth here. The material covers both population and business. First, we consider how census data may help the marketing researcher, and then we list the major types of information available in the census.

How census data may help the marketing researcher

- Studying the growth trends of production data over a period of years can help a manufacturer to identify new product lines or additions to a product line.

- Census data may help in determining business location. Studying demographic data for an area before deciding to open a retailer outlet in that particular area is a case in point. Furthermore, a firm may establish sales territories for its sales staff based on census of population data.

All countries will have censuses of one type or another. Here we choose illustrations from the UK.

Census of population

Conducted every ten years, the census of population provides details on the nature of the population. It covers demographics such as sex, age, ethnicity, family size, marital status, occupation, income and education.

Economic censuses

Economic censuses include the census of production and the census of distribution.

The census of production, taken every five years, provides data on shipments (in both units and money terms) of thousands of manufactured products. Shown by Standard Industry Classification (SIC) numbers and descriptions, these data can pinpoint exactly where particular items are produced.

The census of distribution provides basic information on the structure of retail areas of distribution. Since 1976 it has been superseded by annual sample enquiries.

OTHER GENERAL SOURCES

Other sources of secondary data include national and local government (Table 3.1) and chambers of commerce. For business and professional markets, another possibility is trade, business or professional associations.

In the UK, a very useful government publication, published by TSO, is the *Guide to Official Statistics*: this covers all official and significant non-official sources of statistics, both regular and occasional, published during the last ten years. It attempts to give the user a broad indication of whether the statistics required have been compiled and, if so, whether they have been published. It does not contain statistics but it does indicate where to find them.

TABLE 3.1	Useful UK government sources of information
Abstract of Regional Statistics	Economic and social regional statistics for UK
Agricultural Statistics: England and Wales (annually)	
Annual Abstract of Statistics	Data on housing, manufactured goods, population, etc.
Annual Estimates of the Population of England and Wales and of Local Authority Areas (annually)	
Bill of Entry Service	Customs and Excise data
Business Monitor	Information on different UK industries – provides performance indicators and trends against which one can compare one's own performance. Helps to determine size of market
Department of Employment Gazette (monthly)	
Digest of Energy Statistics (annually)	

Digest of Health Statistics for England and Wales (annually)	
Economic Trends	Monthly review of the economic situation
Family Expenditure Survey Reports (annually)	Trends in expenditure on consumer products – indicates changes in patterns of expenditure
Financial Statistics (monthly)	UK monetary and financial statistics
Food Survey	Trends in expenditure on food
General Household Survey	A continuous sample survey providing a picture of changing social conditions in many aspects of everyday life
Highway Statistics (annually)	
Housing and Construction Statistics (quarterly)	
Key Data	Overview of statistics produced by government, at a modest cost
Monthly Bulletin of Construction Statistics	
Monthly Digest of Statistics	Data on housing, manufactured goods, population, etc.
National Income and Expenditure Blue Book (annually)	
Overseas trade statistics of the UK (monthly)	
Passenger Transport in Great Britain (annually)	
Social Trends	Annual collection of social statistics – population, households, education, health, housing, environment, leisure, etc. Useful for indicating changes in expenditure

DATA LOSS

Next week, *Social Trends*, the annual snapshot of life in the UK, will be published, significant parts of its data drawn from the General Household Survey. The edition due in two years' time will not be as good, for the Office of National Statistics has just announced that this year's GHS, a survey of more than 10,000 households a year, is to be suspended. It is a suspension, furthermore, that sounds worryingly like a death knell. The survey will be resumed the following year, its users have been told, 'if this is appropriate'.

This is a short-sighted and damaging decision. The GHS is a prime source of continuous survey data since 1971. Its value lies in an unbroken series embracing income, housing, family composition, health, employment status, education, disability, use of social services, informal care and much else. It provides a window into the growing world of self-employment, the effects of widening inequality and the growth and impact of lone parenthood, while providing measures of social integration and exclusion. It is used in government, in academia and in market research.

Over the past five years it has been the most used of the wealth of datasets held in the Economic and Social Research Council's archive. While other surveys duplicate some of the GHS's coverage, none provides its ability to combine such disparate elements of British life over time in measures that can inform public policy.

Its suspension, to save £500,000, follows a cut in ONS's £100m budget. It goes on hold while a rapid and wide-ranging review is held of future social survey needs. Such a review, to avoid unneeded duplication and ensure value for money, is sensible.

It is not sensible for the ONS to have to act first and consider afterwards. At a time when reform of welfare policies is centre stage, it cannot be right to suspend the survey that can inform those policies and measure their outcomes. The ONS should be given the chance to think again, even if that means a temporary budget reprieve.

Source: *Financial Times*[11] (reprinted with permission)

Regional statistics

The Office for National Statistics also publishes a useful booklet entitled *Government Statistics: A brief guide to sources*. This publication lists the government ministries and departments responsible for gathering specific economic and social data, such as annual statistics in retail trades, classified list of manufacturing businesses.

INTERNATIONAL SOURCES

International data can be obtained from the International Chamber of Commerce, 14/15 Belgrave Square, London SW1X 8PS, United Kingdom.

The Organisation for Economic Cooperation and Development provides data, information and charts about member countries and reports are available online.

European Sources

The European Commission offers online material and free publications. The latter are obtainable from the Publications Centre. The Information Centre for members of the European Information Network offers a helpline and specialist publications and provides a forum for discussion through regular meetings.

The *Eurostat Catalogue*[12] appears annually and comprises monographs, collections, CD-ROMs and computer output products published by Eurostat. The catalogue provides a summary of each available publication or statistical document. Where statistics in printed form are also available as computer output products on magnetic tape, disks or online, this is also indicated. The organisations disseminating the information are also given. The useful sources of information listed are shown in Table 3.2.

TABLE 3.2	European statistical sources
Atlas GIS for Windows and DOS, Eurostat Edition	Displays socioeconomic data on city, region and country of Europe on maps. Displaying data on maps pinpoints patterns and relationships between data elements. *REGIO* statistics include population, births, deaths, employment, gross value added and GDP as well as NUTS boundaries covering three levels of the EU regions
Basic Statistics of the Community	Gives all the main statistics on the EU and provides comparisons of a number of European countries. Covers general statistics, economy and finance, population and social conditions, forestry and fisheries, external trade, services and transport and the environment
Europe in Figures	The publication presents figures on the most important aspects of the EU. It uses diagrams, tables, maps, illustrations and text to summarise the process of European integration, its achievements and the important facts about the Union today. It is essential for understanding current and future developments in Europe
European Official Statistics: A guide to databases	Almost 100 publicly accessible databases within the field of official statistics are listed. The information contained in these databases covers virtually all economic and social sectors
European Official Statistics: Sources of information	Lists the addresses of about 250 bodies: statistical offices of international and supranational organisations; national statistics institutes; regional statistics institutes; and national ministries and central banks that publish information

▶

TABLE 3.2   European statistical sources (*continued*)

Eurostat-CD	Contains economic and social statistics, regional data, external trade data at product level and the nomenclatures used to classify the different data
Eurostat Yearbook	The contents are organised into five chapters: the people; the land and environment; the national economy; trade and industry; and the Union
Eurostat – Your Partner for European Statistics: A guide to the Statistical Office of the European Communities	The guide shows where to obtain statistical information about the EU – the sort of facts that are needed to be really well informed about the EU
Facts through Figures	Illustrates the life of people in Europe under five headings: the environment; men and women; education and employment; the economy; and day-to-day life
Portrait of the Islands	This provides information on all inhabited islands of the EU
Portrait of the Regions	Some 200 regions, comprising the entire territory of the EU, feature in this publication in the form of maps and illustrations in colour, general and harmonised statistical tables, commentaries and analyses on territory, strengths and weaknesses of a region, changes in population, employment and unemployment and structure of the economy
Regions: Statistical Yearbook	Gives the latest statistics relating to economic and social factors in the regions of the EU
Reports on ACP Countries	Various: e.g. Bulgaria, Hungary, Poland

Eurostat data are stored in different databases, for example *New Cronos, COMEXT, REGIO, GISCO, EUROFARM, IOT and EUROCRON*. Data are offered on magnetic tapes, on diskettes, on paper and, in some cases, online:

- *New Cronos* contains around 55 million statistical data covering every sector of the economy. The data may be monthly, quarterly, half-yearly or yearly depending on the statistical field covered.

- *COMEXT* exists on CD-ROM and contains statistics on trade between the member states of the Union and their trade with some 300 non-member countries.

- *REGIO* contains socioeconomic information on the various regions of the European Union. These are classified in line with a specific system called nomenclature of territorial units for statistics (NUTS). The subjects covered by *REGIO* are demography, economic accounts, unemployment, labour force sample survey, industry, agriculture and transport. The entire database of approximately 100 tables is available on magnetic tape, diskette or printout.

- *GISCO* is the Geographic Information System of the Commission of the European Communities. Geographical data files provide a digital backcloth to many types of cartographic applications and spatial analyses. Eurostat holds several completely integrated subsets of data.

- *EUROFARM* is a database containing the results, in tabular form, of the Union surveys on the structure of agricultural holdings.

- *IOT* contains the input–output tables of Eurostat that appear every five years.

- *EUROCRON* contains the latest data for the main macroeconomic indicators in the major statistical sectors.

Further information on the databases is available from the European Commission, rue de la Loi 200, B-1049 Brussels, Belgium, or at 2 rue Mercier, L-2985 Luxembourg.

NON-OFFICIAL SOURCES OF DATA

There are also many non-government sources of data published by a variety of bodies: trade associations, banks, academic institutions, the trade and professional press, newspapers, and surveys produced by commercial research organisations. Some of these are shown in Table 3.3.

TABLE 3.3	Useful sources of information provided by commercial organisations
ADMAP (monthly)	Covers all advertising media with regular analyses of advertising expenditures by product categories and media
BLA Group: Market Assessment (bi-monthly)	Home, office and leisure sectors in the UK

TABLE 3.3	Useful sources of information provided by commercial organisations (*continued*)
British Rate and Data (BRAD)	Detailed information on newspapers, magazines, television and other advertising media
Euromonitor: Market Research Europe (bi-monthly)	Studies of specific markets
Euromonitor: Market Research Great Britain (monthly)	Studies of specific markets
Financial Times: Business Information Service	Business intelligence service: national and international commerce and industry data. Brand shares, advertising expenditure, production, imports and exports
Keynotes Reports	Consumer and industrial market sizes and trends
Kompass Directory	Provides information on firms in different industries and also geographically. Available for the UK, Europe and elsewhere. Useful for identifying competitors
Kompass On-line	Provides company names and addresses for thousands of firms throughout Europe, along with other pertinent information about the companies
Marketing in Europe (monthly)	Specific aspects of markets
Market Research Society Yearbook	Mainly useful for providing comprehensive lists of organisations providing market research services in Britain
Media Expenditure Analysis (MEAL)	Advertising expenditure across media types
Mintel Market Intelligence Reports (monthly)	Reports on consumer products
Retail Business (monthly)	Specific aspects of markets
Retail Intelligence (Mintel) (quarterly)	Special studies of various market sectors

An interesting new partnership has formed between the Office for National Statistics (ONS) and Taylor Nelson Sofres. These two bodies are the largest gatherers and analysers of data in the UK in their respective sectors – public and private. The ONS's mission is to improve decision making in business by providing quality statistics. Taylor Nelson Sofres, as the UK's largest market research firm, has set the standard for market data analysis for more than 20 years. These two organisations have joined forces to produce *UK Markets*, published by Taylor Nelson Sofres from data provided by the ONS. The data relate to 4800 products taken from 28,500 statistical returns made by the ONS under the Products of the European Community (PRODCOM) inquiry. The returns provide 90% coverage of UK manufacturers' sales – the remaining 10% is estimated. The aggregated UK product sales totals are passed to Taylor Nelson Sofres, which processes the data further, adding derived tables, analysis, commentary and charts.

UK MARKETS: A JOINT VENTURE BETWEEN THE OFFICE FOR NATIONAL STATISTICS AND TAYLOR NELSON SOFRES

UK Markets is a series of 91 annual and 34 quarterly reports on UK manufacturers' sales, export/import and net supply. Data are provided for every manufacturing sector of the UK on:

- total manufacturers' sales for each of 4800 products
- export/import totals in terms of both value and volume, inside and outside the EU
- the value of net supply to the UK market
- import and export ratios, inside and outside the EU
- average values of the product for each category
- trend data for up to the last five periods, both as actual figures and indices
- analysis and interpretation, with user-friendly commentaries, charts and graphs.

The data and analyses in each report enable a firm to:

- compare its own performance with that of the total market
- assess market share in every category
- compare unit sales with the industry and market norms
- monitor trends and more accurately forecast the future
- measure share of exports
- measure share of the UK market held by imports.

UK Markets is available in three formats: hard copy, CD-ROM and Intelligent fax.

PROFESSIONAL ORGANISATIONS AND LIBRARIES

Various professional organisations and libraries are also useful sources of data. Professional organisations that are particularly useful in the UK include:

- Association of Market Survey Organisations
- Institute of Management
- Market Research Society
- Confederation of British Industry
- Chartered Institute of Marketing
- Institute of Practitioners in Advertising
- Advertising Association.

Main libraries in major UK cities, such as Manchester, have substantial commercial libraries attached and these provide large quantities of relevant data. The following specialist libraries are also of interest.

British Library

There is an extensive collection of international market research reports. The library has trade directories, exhibition catalogues, trade journals and other trade literature, including stockbroker reports. There are also CD-ROMs available including the *Financial Times*, *F & S Index*, *Quest Economics*, *European Business ASAP*, and *FAME*. Other publications available include *Market Research Locator* (index of published market research).

British Library-Lloyds TSB Business Line

British Library-Lloyds TSB Business Line is an enquiry service that is partially funded through sponsorship from Lloyds TSB. The information provided may be used to gain new clients, find new suppliers, or contribute to either the business plan or marketing strategy. The service provides the following information:

- company information – contact details, names of key personnel and shareholders, turnover figure
- market information – market size, names of major players
- product information – suppliers of particular products or services, name of the company that manufactures a product with a specific trade name.

Other library and library-type sources include:

- *City Business Library, Brewers Hall Gardens, London EC2* City Business Library has an extensive range of business information, trade directories, journals and market survey reports. It also has a collection of company annual reports, company financial summary reports, UK economic reports and CD-ROMs.

- *Datamonitor, http://www.datamonitor.com/* This includes reports on international business and consumer markets. There are also databases, built up with over ten years of historical data from many countries. Data are collected through industry panel research and through consumer research.

- *Department of Trade and Industry, Export Market Intelligence Centre (EMIC), Ashdown House, 123 Victoria Street, London* Information available includes UK and foreign statistics on trade, production, prices, employment, population, etc. Foreign trade and telephone directories, overseas market surveys, development plans and overseas mail order catalogues are also available.

- *Euromonitor, http://www.euromonitor.com/* Euromonitor concentrates on global consumer goods and services sectors. This site enables viewing of the contents listings for market reports. There is coverage of more than 300 markets (consumer, industrial and service sectors) and countries worldwide. The source concentrates on global market intelligence, tracking international trends in both consumer and industrial markets.

- *Libraries attached to London, Manchester and Warwick Business Schools* For example, the London Business School Library, at 25 Taunton Place, London NW1, has many market research reports along with electronic databases, thousands of books, serial titles and international/historic company annual reports.

- *National Statistics Library (NSILS), 1 Drummond Gate, Pimlico, London SW1 2QQ* This is the Office for National Statistics and provides access and assistance to anyone who requires official statistics for research. The library maintains a collection of international statistical data published by major organisations such as the UN, Eurostat and individual national statistical institutions.

- *Science Reference Library, Chancery Lane, London WC2*

- *Statistics and Market Intelligence Library, 1 Victoria Street, London SW1*

- *Trade Partners UK Information Centre, Export Market Information Centre (EMIC)/ Trade Partners UK, Kingsgate House, 66–74 Victoria Street, London SW1E 6SW* Here there is an extensive electronic collection of statistical, marketing and contact information. This includes:

  - electronic resources: a large range of statistical, contact, marketing and aid-funded project information available on CD-ROMs and via Internet terminals
  - CD-ROM databases: information on CDs falls into three main categories: statistical, contact and marketing information.

Academic researchers also publish research findings on various aspects of the marketing process, often within specific industry sectors, at an even lower cost.

Government departments collect, analyse and publish a vast array of facts, figures, surveys and reports. Newspapers, trade journals and trade associations regularly publish surveys and market reports for as little as the cover price. The burden of scanning the press, wandering through libraries and searching among mountains of journals can be reduced with database search facilities. Both CD-ROM databases and online databases can search newspapers, magazines and journals for keywords. Some databases cover books, research reports and dissertations. Other online services, such as the Internet, are a great source of marketing intelligence. However, much of the information required by marketing researchers is only available from commercial providers that charge for access, for example, Infoplus[13] and Dialog.[14]

Secondary sources are cheaper and faster, whether the researcher needs a complete market report or just a key fact, figure or name. However, the accuracy and reliability of the secondary source must also be considered.

USING SECONDARY DATA IN EXPLORATORY RESEARCH

Exploratory research provides a broad understanding of an industry, a service or an area in which a firm wants to expand its limited knowledge. Three steps are involved:

1 spelling out information needs

2 looking for promising leads by title or apparent content

3 getting hold of promising published material.

One often has to choose between print format and computer format when choosing how to capture the data. Although readily available print sources are usually inexpensive, checking out print sources takes considerable time. Use of online sources, by comparison, is much quicker and can often provide information that is more pertinent. However, it costs money to obtain data in this way and the novice or even the person with computer experience is likely to need some expert assistance.

Spelling out information needs

Marketing research begins with a statement of the problem. A statement of the marketing problem indicates the nature of the marketing decisions to be made. In turn, this leads to a statement of the kind of information that is required to reach these decisions. The nature of the information requirement always has to be specified. Failure to do this will make the search for secondary information unfocused and indefinite.

Looking for promising leads

Libraries are the best source for printed material. Libraries include the public library, the college or university library and the specialist library. The public library is often a good starting point. Even in a small town, the public library may have commercial directories and other sources of data. Even better is the college, university or business school library, if there is one readily available – in the larger ones, online searches may be possible. In major cities, there is probably an excellent commercial library. The commercial library in a large city usually has not only good materials, but good general facilities as well.

An investigator will also want to see if there is a specialist library nearby. Typically found in industrial and commercial areas, these are usually privately maintained (by a business or an association) and carry considerable depth of material within some specialised topic, such as advertising or direct-mail selling. A good public library may give information on specialist libraries that may be prepared to make their services available.

When visiting a library you should arrive armed with a complete knowledge of the business problem. When talking with the library staff about the problem, it will soon become clear whether they know how to help. If the person at the desk cannot help, they will generally refer you to someone else. Your enquiry may also indicate that there are specialists in other library systems that can be of help.

Obtaining promising material

The economy

In order to have an understanding of the economic climate, since all marketing effort operates within this framework, the marketer or marketing researcher must have a continuing and current understanding of the state of the economy. Several newspapers and periodicals can be used for this purpose – for example, the *Financial Times* and the *Economist*. Libraries retain numbers of the major publications and these can be easily accessed.

Particular fields of business

Keeping up to date with knowledge about a particular field of business makes it a necessity to read trade papers covering the field on a regular basis. These also can be helpful in getting a general feel of a particular business or industry field that the firm is considering entering.

Consumer geographics, demographics and psychographics

The term *geographics*, in terms of consumers, means where people live. The word *demographics* concerns the statistics of an area's population, such as number of households along with their composition, income, sex, age, education and occupation. Combining geographics and demographics has coined the word *geodemographics*, which is simply a demographic description of those within specific geographic areas. The data are sometimes presented as descriptions of localities; in other cases the marketer predefines the characteristics of what are considered their best customers or prospects and obtains a list of where such people live.

Psychologists use the term *psychographics* to mean the personality characteristics of an individual. Now that its usage has been adapted to marketing research, its meaning has been expanded. It is used to describe people not only in terms of their personality characteristics, but also in terms of their interests and lifestyles as a reflection of these characteristics.

Lifestyle databases and geodemographic information

Data on sales and purchases underpin many databases and this is usually overlaid with a considerable amount of profile data. This is known as *biographics* – the fusion of profile and data on sales and purchases. As a result of associating people's names, addresses, purchasing behaviour and lifestyles and placing it all together on a single record we can obtain an idea of someone's lifestyle. We can also create data fusion by linking such data with a geographic information system database. Linking purchasing behaviour data with lifestyle, geodemographics and panel data helps to produce patterns of purchasing in various regions.

Information sources for statistics

The census and private sources provide statistics about consumers. Since the census provides details about where and who consumers are – specific geography by characteristics such as age, sex, ethnicity, size and nature of the living unit, type of dwelling and rental or value of dwelling unit – it has many immediate marketing applications. A firm can use local data to tailor neighbourhood promotions. A bank can make use of local data to obtain a demographic picture of the neighbourhoods surrounding its various locations. With this information, it can single out neighbourhoods most closely matching its profiles of typical purchasers of personal loans, mutual funds and other banking services. It can effectively target its advertising and direct mail efforts.

Information about business and industry

General categorisation of business and industry using the SIC

Grouping by kind of business is just as important for business and industry as demographics is for consumers. One of the best and most commonly used methods of classifying business and industry by type is the Standard Industrial Classification (SIC), which lists all types of business and assigns classification numbers to each.

The categorisation of the SIC is formulated so that no industry is missed. Only with knowledge of the SIC number is it possible to search most sources for material relevant to the particular marketing problem. A full explanation of how to use the SIC classification is provided in Chaper 14.

Directories

The *Yellow Pages* of the telephone directory is a good source of company names by type of business. In the UK, even local public libraries usually have most of the *Yellow Pages* for the entire country. A limitation of the use of the *Yellow Pages* should, however, be borne in mind. There is no quality control of the companies listed: a listed firm might be a one-man operation handled on a part-time basis. Many other business directories may also be found on library shelves in the reference section. For example, the *Kompass Directories* provide useful information on businesses and their products.

Databases

Searching databases is a good way to seek out published information. Online vendors of bibliographic databases include BRS (BRS Information Technologies), Dialog (Dialog Information Services, Inc.), NEXIS (Mead Data Central, Inc.) and Dow Jones/Text-Search Services. These services give access to computer-readable databases. Dialog is the distributor of more than 350 databases. A typical database may have one million or more records, each consisting of an abstract of a published article containing one or two paragraphs that give the major points of the article along with bibliographic information.

ONLINE MARKETING RESEARCH

Widespread use of the Internet has given rise to the online Internet marketing research firm and a shift in focus towards measurement and analysis of e-commerce Internet business activity. Research firms now offer e-business analysis in addition to traditional quantitative and qualitative research methods.

MARKETING RESEARCH TOOLS

The BRMB International offers the target group index (TGI). People are recruited to fill in an extensive questionnaire concerning their reading and shopping habits and their lifestyles. This allows media companies to use TGI data to produce a snapshot of the person who buys a particular magazine or newspaper and target promotions and advertising accordingly. CACI International has developed e-types – the first classification of online consumers and their behavioural habits. The e-types classification provides information such as how long consumers stay on one site, how frequently they purchase, what products they are buying, etc. Use of the Internet for research purposes greatly reduces data collection costs and it tends to be quicker. Virtual focus groups are employed to conduct marketing research using the Internet.

SUMMARY

The chapter has considered the various sources of secondary data and suggested systematic ways of searching for appropriate data or information relevant to a marketing problem. Attention has been drawn to both government and commercial sources of data and to libraries, bibliographies, indexes and abstracts as important aids in the search for information process. Detailed information has been presented about many secondary information sources.

QUESTIONS

1 What role do secondary as opposed to primary data play in the marketing research process? Discuss.

2 Indicate some of the main UK and European government published statistics and reports and outline how they might be useful to marketers.

3 How might generalist or specialist UK libraries be useful to market researchers? Indicate some of the establishments and the relevant information they might contain.

4 Academic institutions undertake research and produce publications in a variety of fields. To what extent might the information that is produced be useful to marketing management?

5 How might online marketing databases and online marketing research assist in the process of marketing decision making?

CASE STUDY 3.1: MONTRES D'OCCASION

The jewellery quarter in Birmingham is one of the last surviving British examples of the transition from an essentially domestic to an industrialised economy. Three centuries of industrial innovation, growth and decay can be traced in its streets and buildings. It typifies the essential character of entrepreneurial activity in Victorian Birmingham and it throws out a challenge to any ability to plan for the future. Working in precious metal in Birmingham dates from at least the 14th century, but the industry did not attain national importance until the second half of the 18th century.

Charles is contemplating taking up the lease on workshop/retail premises in the jewellery quarter of Birmingham at Hockley. He wants to refurbish and repair second-hand wristwatches under the French name for second-hand watches, 'Montres d'Occasion'. Birmingham is the UK's second largest city with over one million inhabitants and its jewellery quarter has a national and some say even international reputation for the breadth and variety of jewellery goods and services it can offer.

In the jewellery quarter many businesses are engaged in buying, selling and repairing jewellery items, including watches. Charles' interest in the idea stems from his own experience as an amateur horologist and the skills he developed at college in working with gold and silver. He has been an avid collector of wristwatches for the past 20 years and has a comprehensive collection of more than 500 wristwatches of different kinds. These range from modern-day quartz Swatches to First World War officers' wristwatches. He plans to offer many of these watches for sale as part of his opening stock. Naturally, there are three or four favourite ones that he plans to keep for himself.

Charles visited Hockley to get some idea of the kind of place he would be working in if he did decide to go ahead with the venture. Now he wants to obtain more detailed information that will help him make a sensible decision.

Question

What difficulties might Charles encounter in doing this?

CASE STUDY 3.2: THE WEB

You first need an understanding of what the Internet is and what it is not. You have to be conversant with the concept of networking – building relationships around common interests. The World Wide Web is the part of the Internet that is likely to be of particular interest to marketers, because it brings together sound, vision, text and direct communication with individuals: in other words, multimedia. At least 100,000 companies around the world launched websites during 1995–96.

Firms can design and run a website themselves. The big investors include companies with international brands, such as drinks manufacturers, which recognise that the Web is a cost-effective global communication tool. Another website is the Yell International directory site for *Yellow Pages*. Other companies include Rank Xerox, whose site has already generated sales worth nearly £200,000. Rank Xerox markets colour laser printers and multifunctional faxes – which means it needs to target early adopters. Research showed the firm that these are exactly the sort of people who are likely to be using the Internet. The Glaxo Wellcome site invites you to choose from the following options:

- *Science*: browse a selection of information relevant to those involved in pharmacology, or find out about scientific research at Glaxo Wellcome.

- *Healthcare*: take a look at this collection of informative reports relating to disease and disease management issues.

- *News*: keep yourself up to date with our latest developments.

Perhaps one of the faults with many sites is that they try to be all things to all people. Many website launches promote the fact that a company's information is being presented to 20 or 30 million people worldwide, as if it were some kind of global television broadcast. However, the Web is different to TV and press communication. It is 'narrowcasting' in the sense that the audience is self-selecting: the audience chooses to visit the site and, once in, the user chooses what information they want to look at.

Running a site is time-consuming if it is to be done properly and it is imperative to keep information up to date. Virgin Atlantic fell foul of a US court for failing to update its fare information.

Source: Working on site[15]

Question

Discuss the possibility of using a website to provide secondary marketing information. What kind of difficulties are there in doing this?

CASE STUDY 3.3: SALARIES

In 1996 the James Market Research Organisation was trying to put together a list of published figures relating to people's earnings. It was looking for information for the occupations shown in Table 3.4.

TABLE 3.4	Lining up occupations with earnings

Army
Private
Colonel

Prison service
Prison officer
Principal officer

Police
Constable
Superintendent

Health
Nurse
General practitioner
Dentist
Consultant

Education
Teachers
(primary/secondary)
Head teacher (secondary)
University lecturer
Professor

Council workers
Road sweeper
Office cleaner
Filing clerk
Senior officer
Chief executive

Retail
Sales assistant
Storekeeper

Transport
Tyre/exhaust fitter
Car mechanic
Airline stewardess
Airline captain

Media
Reporter (national)
National TV reporter

▶

TABLE 3.4   Lining up occupations with earnings (*continued*)

Advertising
Product manager
Marketing manager
Marketing director

Civil service
Graduate civil servant
Permanent Secretary

Fire service
Firefighter
Senior divisional officer

Construction
Labourer
Carpenter/joiner
Civil engineer
Architect

Food and restaurants
Barman
Chef

Football players
Premier League
Third Division

Computing
Programmer
Computing manager

Accountancy
Accountant
Chief accountant

Lawyers
Solicitor
Criminal QC
High Court judge

PoliticiansD
Member of Parliament
Prime Minister

Miscellaneous
Hairdresser
Receptionist
Postman
Social worker
Librarian

Questions

1 Indicate likely data sources for each one of the figures.

2 What will the figures in each case actually represent?

3 In each case, do you think that the figures will represent a true picture of actual earnings? Why or why not?

CASE STUDY 3.4: POWERUP ELECTRICITY PLC

The deregulation of the UK electricity supply industry in 1988 allowed new suppliers to enter the energy market and compete with the traditional (although now privatised) electricity supply companies. PowerUp Electricity plc is a subsidiary of a French utility company and was formed specifically to take advantage of the new competitive environment.

For the French company, the UK was an unknown territory. Having seen some of the mistakes made by French utility companies during the privatisation of water supplies in Britain, the parent company's management were nervous about making the same errors, so they decided to carry out a major market research exercise in order to ascertain the likely acceptability of PowerUp plc. The company's target market was home owners with family incomes in excess of £25,000 a year; an analysis of the French utility company's own records showed that these households (or at least, their French equivalents) had the lowest rate of default on credit, were relatively large consumers of electricity and were usually prompt payers. PowerUp needed to identify these customers, establish ways of reaching them and (more importantly) find out what would attract them to switch electricity suppliers.

In the first instance, the firm's researchers set out to find out how many such households exist within the UK. This proved straightforward enough; government statistics supplied the answer, at 2.2 million households. This was more than enough to make entering the market worthwhile; PowerUp could go to the next stage.

ACORN statistics were bought in to find out where the households were located, but then the work of surveying the households began. The researchers decided to opt for a quota sample, using the ACORN classifications to establish the quotas. This meant that considerable travel was involved, but since the survey was intended to establish parameters for a national company, this was only to be expected – PowerUp certainly did not want to skimp on research that might save the company millions in the long term.

Unfortunately, although the ACORN data were extremely reliable for judging the type of housing and the lifestyles of the inhabitants, they did not prove a successful predictor of income. For this the firm needed another source of data, which it was able to buy in from a specialist mailing list supplier. By combining details from the mailing list with those supplied by ACORN, PowerUp's researchers were able to generate a more refined mailing list of customers within the target market and use this to run a questionnaire-based survey to determine their needs.

Furthermore, some doubt was expressed at board level as to whether the figures for France could be applied to the UK – the directors were not naive enough to believe that credit ratings in the UK could be calculated in exactly the same way as they were in France or that UK consumers would have the same consumption profiles as their French equivalents, even if other details such as income and home ownership were similar. Apart from any other considerations, the rate of home ownership in the UK is much higher than that in France, which would alone be enough to distort the comparisons.

Overall, the directors felt that the research as conducted so far was inconclusive to say the least, and downright inaccurate to say the worst. Their feeling was that the UK should be considered as a completely separate market, with its own rules and parameters; very little could be carried over from experience of the French market, and indeed it might be dangerous to attempt to do so.

(Case contributed by Jim Blythe)

Questions

1 How might PowerUp have used secondary sources to check the comparability of the French target market with the British target market?

2 What other sources of secondary data might PowerUp have used to find out about its target market?

3 What information needs did the secondary research reveal?

4 What sources are available for PowerUp to find out how to promote the product to the target market?

5 Why did PowerUp need to use primary research at all?

REFERENCES AND NOTES

1 Spindler, R (1991) unpublished MSc dissertation, Odense University.

2 *Market Search*, Arlington Publications, 25 New Bond Street, London W1Y 9HD.

3 *Reports Index*, Business Surveys Ltd, Osmington Drive, Broadmayne, Dorset DT2 8ED.

4 *Findex*, available through Euromonitor, 87 Turnmill Street, London EC1 5QU.

5 *UK Marketing Source Book*, NTC Publications, Farm Road, Henley-on-Thames, Oxfordshire RG9 1EJ.

6 *The Source Book*, Keynote Publications, 72 Oldfield Road, Hampton, Middlesex TW12 2HQ.

7 *On-Line Business Source Book*, Headland Press, Henry Smith's Terrace, Headland, Cleveland TS24 0PD.

8 *On-Line Business and Company Databases*, ASLIB, 20 Old Street, London EC1V 9AP.

9 *Directory of On-Line Databases*, Gale Research International, PO Box 699, North Way, Andover, Hampshire SP10 5YE.

10 Nairn, G (1997) Golden nuggets on a long and winding road, *Financial Times*, 3 December.

11 *Financial Times*, 23 January 1997.

12 *Eurostat Catalogue: Publications and Electronic Services*, Office for the Official Publications of the European Communities, L-2985 Luxembourg.

13 Infoplus, PO Box 12, Sunbury-on-Thames, Middlesex TW16 7UD.

14 Dialog, Plaza Suite, 114 Jermyn Street, London SW1Y 6HJ.

15 Working on site (1996) *Marketing Week*, 26 April, 51ff.

FURTHER READING

Abdel-Ghany, M and Sharpe, D L (1997) Consumption patterns among the young-old and old-old, *Journal of Consumer Affairs*, 31(1), Summer, 90–112.

Abraham, M and Lodish, L (1990) Getting the most out of advertising and promotion, *Harvard Business Review*, 68(3), 50–63.

Baker, K (1989) Using geodemographics in market research, *Journal of the Market Research Society*, 31, 37–44.

Blattberg, R and Deighton, J (1991) Interactive marketing: exploiting the age of addressability, *Sloan Management Review*, 33(1), 5–14.

Blattberg, R and Hoch, S (1990) Database models and managerial intuition: 50% model + 50% manager, *Management Science*, 36(8), 887–99.

Crouch, S (1985) *Marketing Research for Managers*, London: Pan.

Government Statistics: A brief guide to sources, London: Office for National Statistics.

Jackson, P (1994) *Desk Research*, London: Kogan Page.

Larson, E (1992) Watching Americans watch TV, *The Atlantic Monthly*, March.

Levitas, R and Guy, W (eds) (1996) *Interpreting Official Statistics*, London: Routledge.

Mayer, M (1990) Scanning the future, *Forbes*, 15 October.

Marketing Pocket Book, published annually by The Advertising Association in conjunction with NTC Publications, Farm Road, Henley-on-Thames, Oxfordshire RG9 1EJ. See also the *Lifestyle Pocket Book*, the *Media Pocket Book* and the *Regional Marketing Pocket Book*.

4 Sampling

Objectives

After reading this chapter, you should be able to:

- appreciate the key elements involved in devising a sampling plan

- understand the important features of both probability and non-probability samples

- understand the major types and primary practical uses of both probability and non-probability sampling

- understand the primary approaches for determining sample size

- appreciate the nature of the sources of sampling and non-sampling error and how to minimise them.

Keywords

ACORN	population
call-backs	probability sample
census	quota sample
cluster sample	random sample
convenience sample	response error
frame	sample
judgement sample	social classification
non-probability sample	stratified sample
non-response error	universe

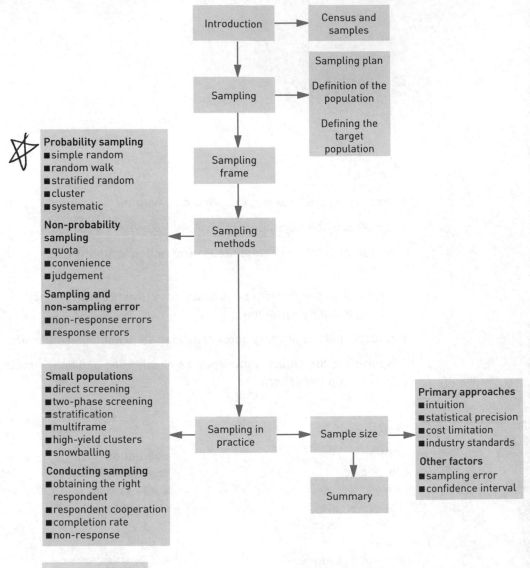

Plan of Chapter 4

INTRODUCTION

Once the researcher has decided how primary data are to be collected, the next task is to obtain a sample of respondents that is representative of the target population of interest. This chapter discusses the major sampling techniques and how they are used in marketing research. The techniques can be divided into probability and non-probability methods. In **probability sampling** each element of the population has a known non-zero chance of being selected. In such cases it is possible to compute sampling variation and project the results to the entire population. In the case of **non-probability sampling**, the chance of selection of a particular population element is known and, strictly speaking, results cannot be projected to the entire population. Although sampling can be technically rigorous, the need to be so does depend on the particular application.

This chapter discusses the key elements involved in devising a sampling plan and explores the importance of properly defining the target population of interest. It illustrates the important features of both probability and non-probability samples and describes the major types and primary practical uses of both probability and non-probability sampling. The chapter outlines the primary approaches to determining sample size, defines the concept of sampling and non-sampling error and explains the nature of the factors contributing **response** and **non-response errors**. Finally, it suggests how response rates can be improved and discusses ways of remedying non-response errors.

CENSUS AND SAMPLES

When we want to uncover information about the attitudes, ideas, beliefs and habits of a population, one way is to ask every member of it to participate in our study. Such an approach is called taking a **census**.

A census

A census is a count of people, houses, business firms or other items of interest taken at a particular time. Governments of different countries often take censuses of population and production every ten years. A census of the population, for example, tries to count everyone in the country at a specific time. A questionnaire is sent to every household asking how many persons are living there at the designated time and asking for information about gender, age and other details.

Census data are used for market research and changes in the data are indispensable in forecasting trends in demand for goods and services. Almost every country now conducts a census of some kind, usually at intervals of five or ten years. The information obtained ranges from basic data on the size, ages and locations of a country's population to information on migration, family composition, income and standard of living. Censuses can vary in their accuracy; questions have to be skilfully framed to obtain objective answers or at least to minimise the degree of inaccuracy.

SAMPLING

- Marketing research of a whole population is impractical.
- Sampling allows us to obtain valid data on a representative section of a population from which we can draw valid conclusions about the whole population.
- Random and quota sampling methods are usually applied in marketing research.

SAMPLING

Some so-called census information is in fact obtained by sampling. Computer-assisted statistical procedures make it possible to obtain useful information about many characteristics of the population by questioning only a selected **sample** of persons. Samples cost only a fraction of what it would cost to interrogate everyone.

To sample something is to examine a small portion of it, usually for the purpose of judging the nature or quality of the whole. In statistics, a collection of elements that have one or more specified characteristics is called a **population**. A sample, then, is some portion of a population. Because many populations of interest are too large to work with directly, techniques of statistical sampling have been devised to obtain samples taken from larger populations.

Unless a sample is chosen by a random mechanism, however, the results that are obtained from a study are likely to be biased in some direction. It is for this reason that methods of random sampling have been devised. A random sample can be chosen, for example, by throwing dice. Most commonly, however, when a list of names exists from which a sample can be chosen, the actual technique is to use random numbers generated by a computer. The list is numbered, and the computer provides a string of numbers from this list in such a way that various batches of entries in the list have an equal chance of being drawn.

Suppose that a market survey is being taken. A sample group is chosen from the population in the above manner, and the individuals who make up the sample are then interviewed. For example, an individual may be asked about washing powder brand choice. The arithmetic mean of the total answers provided by the individuals yields the proportion preferring one brand or the other. Any statistical population asked this question will also have an average response to it. The responses of the individuals in the population vary about this average response. The variability of the response is described by a quantity called the population variance. The arithmetic mean varies from one sample to the next, but it varies about the average response. In addition, the bigger the sample relative to the population size, the more accurate is the estimate determined by sampling.

Some situations permit the population to be split into a few very homogenous groups or strata. The sample may then consist of a **random sample** taken within each stratum. Such a sample is called a **stratified** random **sample**.

Thus far we have assumed that a list, or **sampling frame**, is available. This is not true, however, in all cases. For example, no list exists of the pony population of Dartmoor. Thus the important topic of estimating the size of some populations must be handled differently. Areas are usually chosen at random.

THE BASIC NOTION OF A RANDOM SAMPLE

If the population is (1,2,3), there are three possible two-member samples:

(1,2), (2,3), and (1,3).

Each of them has a one in three chance of being drawn. This is called random sampling.

Key elements in devising a sampling plan

Surveys attempt to find things out about a population. For marketing research purposes populations may consist of people or firms. A population for a survey comprises all the persons or companies to which you would like to direct questions. It would be highly advantageous to contact all members of a population and ask them to answer all the questions we want to put. If this could be done we could produce very accurate results. However, only seldom is it possible to contact or gain a response from all the members of a population. The exception is in the case of industrial market research where it may be possible to contact all the firms that make up a particular population because the population may be very small (see Figure 4.1).

Usually, large populations are encountered in marketing research and it is impractical or too expensive to contact all the members. In such cases we have to take a sample from the population – but we must ensure that the sample we choose represents the population as a whole.

There are three decisions to be taken in drawing up a sampling plan:

- *Who is to be surveyed?* This defines the target population. Once this has been done the next step is to develop a sampling frame: that is a way of giving everyone in the target population a known chance of inclusion in the sample.

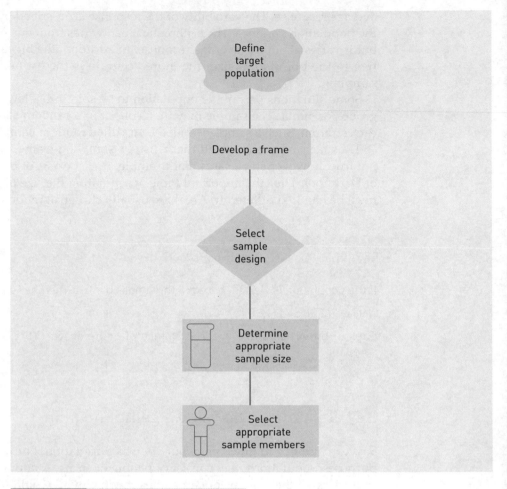

FIGURE 4.1   Steps in developing a sample

- *How many people/companies should be surveyed?* Large samples give better results than smaller ones. However, samples of less than 1% of a population can often provide good, reliable information provided that the sampling procedure is creditable.

- *How should the respondents be chosen?* Probability samples allow the calculation of confidence limits for sampling error. Thus in taking probability samples we can attach probabilities to any point estimates that are made. Cost and time often make it impractical to collect data through probability samples. Researchers often use non-probability samples – particularly **quota samples**. Strictly speaking, sampling errors cannot be measured in such cases.

SAMPLING PLAN

- Who is to be surveyed?
- How many people/companies should be surveyed?
- How should respondents be chosen?

Definition of the population

The population is the total group to be studied, the target population (sometimes referred to as the **universe**). It is the grand total of what is being measured: people, stores, homes or whatever. But since most samples in marketing research are of people, homes or stores, the term population, as we use it here, typically refers to one of these. If the purpose of the study has been well defined, the population is also well delineated. This is crucial if the study is to be significant and practical for the guidance of marketing management.

Importance of properly defining target population

A sample should reflect the characteristics of the population of interest to the study – that is, the target population. It is essential to define the target population precisely since failure to do so is likely to lead to the ineffective solving of a research problem.

A population needs to be defined in terms of elements, units and time. The population for a new TV quiz programme, for example, may be defined as:

- males or females
- aged between eight and eighty
- who have watched an existing quiz TV programme in the past 30 days in their own homes.

POPULATION FOR A NEW TV QUIZ PROGRAMME

Elements: males or females, aged between eight and eighty, who have watched
an existing quiz programme in the past 30 days
Units: household
Time: January 1997

The elements that constitute the population are referred to as sampling units. In the new TV quiz programme example, households are designated as the sampling units. It is easier to select households, the place where the programmes are watched, than to interview everyone who qualifies as a member of the population. In some situations, population elements and the sampling unit will be the same, while in others they will be different.

It is up to the marketing researchers to provide explicit instructions to the field workers about the qualifications of the target population. This is achieved with the help of a list of screening questions that can be used to qualify respondents. Screening questions specifically define who should be included in the sample and who should be excluded. Most marketing research surveys exclude certain individuals for a variety of reasons. For example, in the case of a TV sports programme, if a member of a household works for a TV company, then they are excluded. This is usually the first question asked and the interview is terminated at this point if this is the case. These individuals may be excluded for security reasons since they may work for competitors and the researchers would not want them to find out what the study is about.

SAMPLING FRAME

Obtaining a sample involves selecting some elements from the target population. In order to do this, it is assumed that it is possible to identify the target population of interest. A sampling frame is simply a list that identifies the target population. It can be a list of names and telephone numbers, as in telephone surveys, an area map of housing or a list of addresses purchased from a mailing-list supplier. It could also be a database. The frame defines the sampling unit, the unit used in the design of the sample. The frame, and therefore the sampling unit, may take the form of households, students, retail stores of a particular defined type (nature and size, for instance), businesses or transactions.

Although lists or other geographic breakdowns can be found, the list rarely matches the target population exactly. For instance, a list of residents of a given district naturally does not include new arrivals or households living in dwellings built since the list was compiled. Lists are rarely up to date and often contain duplication, such as households with more than one telephone number or individuals whose names appear on two or more lists.[1]

No sampling frame is perfect. For example, the listing in a telephone book omits unlisted numbers and is outdated on the day of publication because of moves in and out of the area it covers (for implications, see McKenzie).[2] Good research planning requires knowledge of the shortcomings of the sampling frame in order to make adjustments in the sampling design. The sampling frame or list that is used defines what may be termed the operational or working population. The difference between the operational population and the target population is usually referred to as the sampling gap. This gap appears in most marketing research studies and efforts should be applied to try to minimise the gap since its presence increases the potential for misleading results. This can sometimes be done by combining two or more lists, taking care to remove one set of the names that appear on both lists.

SAMPLING FRAME OPTIMISATION

- Target population – Operational population = Sample gap
- Combine lists to minimise sample gap

Sometimes no sampling frame is available. As a rather extreme example, suppose that for some reason it is desirable to conduct a study of those who are overweight. No such list exists. But it is possible to use screening as a method of locating such people. A general frame of individuals can be used, and **filter questions** (with standards of overweight set up in advance) can be used, asking age, height and weight to determine those who qualify.

One frame that might be used is the telephone directory. The typical approach is to randomly select a number from the alphabetical list – say 578343 – and then to add a predetermined number, say +3, to this. The number actually used in the frame then becomes 578346. The logic seems reasonable – but the list should include unlisted as well as listed numbers.

Another possibility for a frame is the mailing list. Depending on the needs for the particular study, it is possible to obtain, on the consumer side, lists as varied as camera club members, computer owners, home owners (by value of home), prime investors (by nature of interest) and magazine subscribers (for many magazines). On the business and professional side, we can find lists of small-town businesspeople, personnel executives, retailers and plumbers.

An obvious sampling frame is the self-accumulated list: a list already in the hands of the marketing firm. It may include the names and addresses of those who have made purchases, have had deliveries made, used credit cards or registered at trade shows.

SAMPLING METHODS

There are two major types of sampling methods: probability sampling and non-probability sampling (see Figure 4.2).

Probability samples comprise samples in which the elements being included have a known chance of being selected. A probability sample enables sampling error to be estimated. This, in simple terms, is the difference between the sample value and the true value of the population being surveyed. A sampling error can

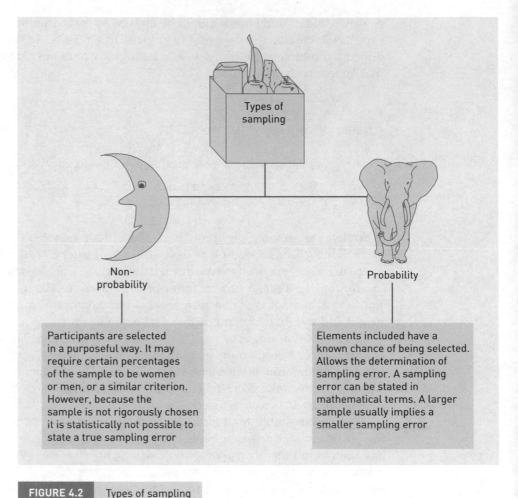

Non-probability

Participants are selected in a purposeful way. It may require certain percentages of the sample to be women or men, or a similar criterion. However, because the sample is not rigorously chosen it is statistically not possible to state a true sampling error

Probability

Elements included have a known chance of being selected. Allows the determination of sampling error. A sampling error can be stated in mathematical terms. A larger sample usually implies a smaller sampling error

FIGURE 4.2   Types of sampling

be stated in mathematical terms: usually plus or minus a certain percentage. A larger sample usually implies a smaller sampling error.

Non-probability samples are ones in which participants are selected in a purposeful way. The selection may require certain percentages of the sample to be women or men, housewives under 30 or a similar criterion. This type of selection is an effort to reach a cross-section of the elements being sampled. However, because the sample is not rigorously chosen it is statistically impossible to state a true sampling error.

Today, most samples chosen for applied research are non-probability samples. If carefully done – with quotas, for example, of persons to be studied – the findings are usually valid. A true probability sample, because of the stringent requirements, is likely to be far too expensive and too time-consuming for most uses. The sampling method chosen for any particular study, therefore, must be explained carefully, with the reasons for its acceptability and likelihood of supplying accurate data.

The research plan may not require that the whole country be sampled. Cost and time factors may lead to the decision to cover only part of a country. Past experience for the products or services being studied may indicate that the selected areas are representative of the nation with respect to what is being studied. However, the more specific the description of those to be studied, the larger the sample must be.

The major problem with the quota method of sampling is that the interviewers are allowed discretion in choosing the individual respondents within the quota categories. This discretion introduces a possible source of bias, because the resulting sample can largely omit some types of people, such as those who are difficult to contact.

A much better approach is the probability method of sampling, in which specific respondents are chosen by random selection methods. The result of this method is that no type of individual is systematically omitted from the sample and the likely amount of error in the resulting data can be calculated.

Statistical laws have established that no matter how large the population being studied (from a small city to a whole country), the size of the sample is the main factor that determines the expected range of error in a probability sample. Most current polls use samples ranging in size from 1000 to 2000 individuals. Many polling organisations have adopted probability methods in selecting their samples, but the less reputable polls still use quota methods or even non-scientific haphazard methods of sample selection – and the quality of their findings suffers accordingly.

Forms of probability sampling

There are five forms of probability sampling:

1 simple random

2 random walk

3 stratified random

4 cluster

5 systematic.

The following are illustrative of the kind of sampling approach that might be taken (and see Figure 4.3).

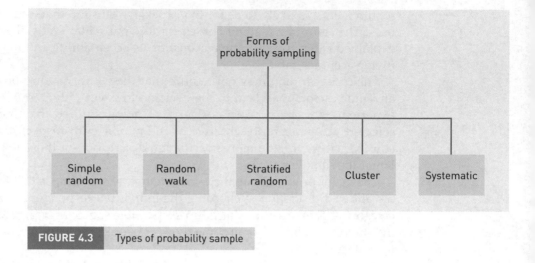

Types of probability sample

Simple random sampling

In this case all members of the population have a known and equal chance of being included in the sample. For example, the names of every firm in a given population could be written on slips of paper and the slips deposited in a box. The box could then be shaken so that all the slips of paper become thoroughly mixed up. A blindfolded person drawing successive slips of paper from the box would be taking a random sample of the population.

Simple random sampling works well when we are dealing with relatively small populations. For large-scale consumer populations, however, the method is not appropriate since it is difficult to obtain a list of all the people in a given population!

Random walk sampling

This form of sampling is used extensively in market research as a cheap approximation to true random sampling. The sample involves conducting random walks in small areas. These areas are usually wards within constituencies. First, a random sample of constituencies is drawn from a list of constituencies and then within each of the randomly selected constituencies a random selection of wards is chosen. Next, selected random starting points within these areas (wards) are chosen and interviewers are given fixed routes to follow and instructions to obey. The instructions specify the interval of households to contact (for example, every seventh house) and the action to take at each street junction (turn alternatively left or right). Special instructions are given about blocks of flats and what to do when non-residential buildings are encountered. Although the resulting sample is not truly random it is usually treated as if it were.

| TABLE 4.1 | Market Research Services classification of social class |

Grade	% of population	Status	Head of household's occupation
A	3	Upper middle class	Higher managerial, administrative or professional
B	13	Middle class	Intermediate managerial, administrative or professional
C1	23	Lower middle class	Supervisory or clerical junior managerial, administrative or professional
C2	32	Skilled working class	Skilled manual workers
D	19	Working class	Semi- and unskilled manual workers
E	10	Those at lowest level of subsistence	State pensioners or widows; casual or lowest grade workers

Source: JICNARS[3]

Stratified random sampling

This approach is more suitable for sampling large consumer populations. It entails dividing the population into mutually exclusive groups and drawing random samples from each group. For example, the population might be divided into six groups, A, B, C1, C2, D and E, reflecting the social background of the people involved (see Table 4.1). Random samples are then drawn from each group. Again, however, there still remains the problem of obtaining suitable lists of people who make up the population and the various groups within it. Stratified sampling may be used in industrial marketing research where it is possible to identify a population of firms. A stratified sample is usually adopted to make sure that minority groups are adequately represented.

The ABCDE classification conceived by Market Research Services Ltd has been the system most frequently used as a method of **social classification** for marketing purposes. Its failure to capture the complexity of class differences has led to new systems such as SAGACITY and **ACORN**.

Cluster sampling

In this case the universe and the frame are defined and classified into homogeneous segments. Random samples are then chosen from each segment. The method offers a sharpening of sampling, virtually guaranteeing that the use of these cells of units – done in two dimensions or more – will provide a cross-section of each.

Cluster sampling is a suitable approach to sampling large consumer populations. Here the population is divided into mutually exclusive groups and the researcher draws a sample of the groups to interview. This time we are not interested in a person's social class but in where they live or some other characteristic. Assuming that residence is the key factor and that the objective is to interview household heads, then the first step is to divide up the locality under study into individual areas of housing. A random or stratified sample of the areas identified is then taken and interviews are held with every household head within each sampled area.

This is a 'single-stage' **cluster sample** since only a sample of the blocks or areas of housing is taken. A 'two-stage' cluster sample might involve undertaking the same number of interviews but making sure that a large number of blocks are covered but that only a sample of households in each block is interviewed. For example, if an area comprises three high-rise tower blocks of flats, we might randomly select one of the three blocks and interview all household heads within that block.

Systematic sampling

In the systematic sampling method, the sampling units are chosen from the sampling frame at a uniform interval at a specified rate. For example, we might use the residential telephone directory. Perhaps the book has 400 pages in it, with an average, after a check of perhaps ten widely dispersed pages, of 400 listings per page, for an estimated total of 160,000 listings (400 × 400). The particular study requires a list of 2000 for sampling purposes. (For simplicity at this point, we forget the number of completions required.) This means that every 80th listing (160,000/2000) should be drawn.

So that the method is a true probability method, where every sampling unit has an equal chance of coming into the sample, there also must be a random starting point. So if we are using every 80th listing, we must select a random starting number of between 1 and 79.

Forms of non-probability sampling

There are three forms of non-probability sampling (see Figure 4.4):

1 quota

2 convenience

3 **judgement**.

Quota sampling

In the case of quota sampling, the researcher starts with the knowledge of how the universe is divided by strata. The investigators are instructed simply to fill the cells, so that the sample obtained is indeed representative in terms of the cells. The procedures used in quota sampling make the choice of respondents the

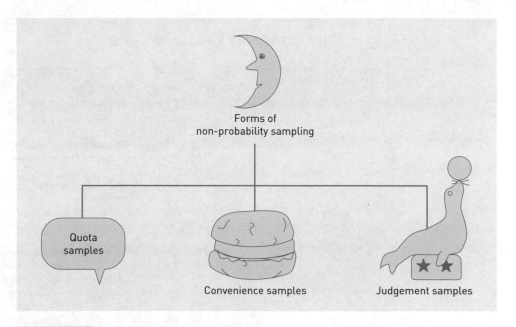

FIGURE 4.4   Types of non-probability sample

responsibility of the interviewers. Unfortunately, this can lead to substantial bias that cannot be objectively measured. Wide use of quota sampling has been made in marketing research since it is relatively cost-effective compared with other methods. However, with the development of random sampling techniques, researchers have become more critical of the drawbacks of this method. Properly applied the method can be successful because it is possible to introduce representativeness by stratifying the quota sample by objective and known population characteristics such as age, sex, family status and socioeconomic group. Quota samples may be accurately constructed using classifications such as ACORN. This is because such classifications are based on objective distributions of statistical variations in demographic, housing and occupational factors.

The first step is to estimate the sizes of the various subclasses or strata in the population. This is usually done through reference to some outside source, for example, census of population data. The relevant strata to the study have to be specified. For instance, a person's age may be something that a researcher thinks is relevant to a particular study. As a consequence, age will have to be taken into account when drawing up the sample. For example, if it is found that in the population 25% of people are aged between 25 and 30, then the aim should be to make sure that 25% of the people in the sample fit into this age band. There are similar requirements for other age bands reflecting the proportions with which they appear in the population under study. Other factors as well as age might also be considered.

SELECTED ACORN TYPES AND GROUPS

Category	Group	Type
Wealthy Achievers	Wealthy Executives	01 – Affluent mature professionals, large houses 02 – Affluent working families with mortgages 03 – Villages with wealthy commuters 04 – Well-off managers, larger houses
	Affluent Greys	05 – Older affluent professionals 06 – Farming communities 07 – Old people, detached houses 08 – Mature couples, smaller detached houses
	Flourishing Families	09 – Larger families, prosperous suburbs 10 – Well-off working families with mortgages 11 – Well-off managers, detached houses 12 – Large families and houses in rural areas
Urban Prosperity	Prosperous Professionals	13 – Well-off professionals, larger houses and converted flats 14 – Older professionals in detached houses and apartments
	Educated Urbanites	15 – Affluent urban professionals, flats 16 – Prosperous young professionals, flats 17 – Young educated workers, flats 18 – Multi-ethnic young, converted flats 19 – Suburban privately renting professionals
	Aspiring Singles	20 – Student flats and cosmopolitan sharers 21 – Singles and sharers, multi-ethnic areas 22 – Low-income singles, small rented flats 23 – Student terraces
Comfortably Off	Starting Out	24 – Young couples, flats and terraces 25 – White-collar singles/sharers, terraces
	Secure Families	26 – Younger white-collar couples with mortgages 27 – Middle-income, home-owning areas 28 – Working families with mortgages 29 – Mature families in suburban semis 30 – Established home-owning workers 31 – Home-owning Asian family areas
	Settled Suburbia	32 – Retired home owners 33 – Middle-income, older couples 34 – Lower-income people, semis
	Prudent Pensioners	35 – Elderly singles, purpose-built flats 36 – Older people, flats

Category	Group	Type
Moderate Means	Asian Communities	37 – Crowded Asian terraces 38 – Low-income Asian families
	Post Industrial Families	39 – Skilled older family terraces 40 – Young family workers
	Blue Collar Roots	41 – Skilled workers, semis and terraces 42 – Home owning, terraces 43 – Older rented terraces
Hard Pressed	Struggling Families	44 – Low-income larger families, semis 45 – Older people, low income, small semis 46 – Low income, routine jobs, unemployment 47 – Low-rise terraced estates of poorly-off workers 48 – Low incomes, high unemployment, single parents 49 – Large families, many children, poorly educated
	Burdened Singles	50 – Council flats, single elderly people 51 – Council terraces, unemployment, many singles 52 – Council flats, single parents, unemployment
	High Rise Hardship	53 – Old people in high-rise flats 54 – Singles and single parents, high-rise estates
	Inner City Adversity	55 – Multi-ethnic purpose-built estates 56 – Multi-ethnic, crowded flats

Source: CACI[4]

Convenience sampling

In convenience sampling, there is no sample design. It is similar to an interviewer questioning people as they meet them on the street or in shopping precincts. Choice of the respondent is left entirely to the interviewer. Some methods, such as this, also allow potential respondents to decide for themselves whether or not to respond.

The researcher takes the most accessible population members from which to obtain information. This happens, for example, when a firm producing a proto-type new domestic appliance gets some of its employees to test out the product in their own homes. Such a sample provides useful information to the researcher as long as the sample seems to be reasonably representative of the population being studied. However, asking a **convenience sample** of students about their reading habits might not be appropriate if you are interested in the reading habits of the population as a whole – i.e. all ages and occupations.

Judgement sampling

This type of sampling relies on sound judgement or expertise. It depends on selecting elements that are believed to be typical or representative of the population in such a way that errors of judgement in the selection will cancel each other out. **Judgement samples** tend to be used more often in industrial market research than in consumer market research. In industrial market research a firm may get 50% of its business from ten large purchasers and the remaining 50% from 300 smaller firms. A judgement sample might therefore comprise five of the large purchasers (50%) and 150 of the remainder (50%). Judgement would be exercised to ensure that the firms chosen in the sample represented the subgrouping.

Sampling and non-sampling error

The quality of the data in a particular survey is a function of what is termed the *total survey error*. Total survey error reflects the difference between the overall population's true mean value of the characteristic of interest and its mean observed value obtained from the particular sample of respondents. What is of interest is what causes the information obtained from a sample of respondents to differ from that of the entire population. Total survey error is composed of **random sampling error** and non-sampling error.

Random sampling error occurs because the selected sample is not a perfect representation of the overall population. It represents how accurately the chosen sample's true mean value reflects that of the population. Random sampling error can be controlled by employing an appropriate statistical design and by increasing the sample size.

Non-sampling error represents the extent to which the mean observed value (on the characteristic of interest) for the respondents of a particular sample disagrees with the mean true value for the particular sample of respondents. The size of the non-sampling error depends on two factors: **non-response errors** and **response errors**. Non-response errors occur because not all those included in the sample do, in fact, respond. Moreover, the mean true value of those who do not respond may be different from the entire sample's true mean value. Response error, by way of contrast, occurs when respondents give *inaccurate* answers.

Non-response errors

Very few studies ever achieve a 100% response success rate. The problem of non-response error occurs because those who agree to participate in the study are in some respects different from those who decline to participate. Usually, the higher the response rate the lower the probability of non-response error effects. Nevertheless, response rates are not always a good indicator of non-response error. First, response rates do not reflect whether the respondents are good representatives of the target sample. Second, an increase in response does not always lead to a reduction in the non-response error. Third, the notion of response rate is ambiguous since the number of eligible respondents used in the calculation of response rates frequently differs across studies. Unfortunately, the extent of the difference between respondents and non-respondents can seldom be directly determined (see Hahlo[5] for a discussion of non-response errors).

NON-RESPONSE ERRORS

- Low response rates: those not responding differ in some way from those who do
- Unrepresentative sample

RESPONSE ERRORS

- Wanting to give an answer that pleases the researcher
- Faulty memory, fatigue or nature of the questions
- Lack of knowledge/familiarity with subject matter
- Wanting to give socially acceptable answers
- Interviewer influence

Response errors

People may give an inaccurate response either intentionally or unintentionally simply because they are being interviewed. For example, respondents may deliberately not report their duly considered answer because they want to help or please the researcher. This is often encountered in new product tests. In another instance, even though the respondent intends to respond accurately, response error arises because of faulty memory, fatigue, question format or even question content. It also arises when people have little or no experience with the survey topic, for example, asking a low-income respondent about comparatively expensive goods.

Interviewers can influence respondents' answers, incorrectly record respondents' answers and even falsify respondents' answers. People may also be influenced by their attitude to the organisation conducting the study. Last, the wish to give socially acceptable answers to sensitive or potentially embarrassing questions can also lead to response errors.

A variety of factors can cause errors in survey results. The onus is on the researcher to:

- determine whether respondents have enough information about the topic on which to base their opinions

- word and/or pose the questions carefully

- avoid biases in wording that suggest a socially desirable answer or lead respondents to agree with one side of an issue

- pretest questions in pilot studies to ensure their clarity and impartiality

- train interviewers to avoid influencing respondents' answers.

SAMPLING IN PRACTICE

So far we have examined some of the methods of applying sampling in a study. We now consider the choice of a sampling method.

Required precision is a factor in influencing the choice of sampling method. Getting a clear-cut answer about the most likely effect of a proposed price reduction on market share demands a sampling design where precision of results can be measured – some kind of probability sample. However, an exploratory study that is trying to obtain some rough idea about which price-reduction method is most promising for further development and testing can use a non-probability sample. It would not be cost-effective to spend additional money on a more precise sample. The availability of an appropriate sampling frame is another factor. Drawing a sample without a frame can be difficult and expensive.

Some factors specific to the study may dictate the form of data collection to be used, such as personal interviews in shopping precincts, postal questionnaire or telephone study. If the study requires the placement of a product with people for in-home trial, the telephone and postal methods (except in combination with other methods) are not feasible. These methods also cannot be used for testing television advertisements. However, if the study intends to measure the number of people reached by a particular radio or television advertisement, the telephone procedure, with its easy access and low unit cost, may be the right method. On the other hand , if the study is aimed at measuring the readership of a publication, then a meeting between interviewer and respondent is essential to show and go through the publication. Finally, the cost of collecting the information has to match with the value of the study to the sponsor.

Sampling small populations

The sampling methods just mentioned are standard procedures to adopt when sampling populations that occur reasonably often. Sometimes, however, the population sought is not that easy to find. Special sampling methods may be required in these cases. A good illustration is to be found by a researcher who is interested in ascertaining attitudes and other information about prescription drug brands used by only a very small number of patients. There are likely to be few of them and, without special sampling methods, it will be too difficult and expensive to study them.

There are six techniques that can be applied in such a case:

1 direct screening

2 two-phase screening

3 stratification

4 multiframe sampling

5 selection of high-yield clusters

6 multiplicity sampling (also known as 'snowballing').

There is also a seventh approach that could involve using data from an existing database.

Direct screening

Here, people are approached, on the telephone or in a shopping precinct, to ascertain whether they meet the requirements for being part of the sample and, if so, they are subsequently questioned. The method has the drawback that if the incidence is too low it will mean a lot of non-productive interview time, progress will be slow and costs will be high.

Two-phase screening

In this case, one survey is followed by a second among those who qualify. The first contact defines the qualifiers. The second produces the responses sought from those who qualify.

THREE APPROACHES TO TWO-WAY SCREENING

Cluster sampling

Where users of barbecues are to be questioned, clusters of neighbourhoods where barbecues are likely to be common can be identified. Either by telephone interviewing (using clusters by postal code, perhaps) or by personal interviewing within clusters, those having barbecues can be located efficiently.

Omnibus study

A continuing study, it is done either personally or by telephone. It makes it possible to ask a screening question and have the research firm **follow up** with those who

▶

qualify. It is an inexpensive way to accumulate lists of those who qualify. However, there are limitations. If the study requires follow-ups, in-home placement of a product, exposure of a television commercial, or the like, the research firm may not be able to do this at reasonable cost, if at all.

Panels

The panel typically is a national list of families that have agreed to participate in mail and telephone studies, and the sponsoring research firm tries to make sure that the total panel represents national and regional demographics. The screening and follow-up can be over the telephone or by post.

Stratification

Stratification entails sorting out those with specific demographic characteristics from selected small geographic areas where there seem to be concentrations of specific groups of people with certain characteristics. Using census data it may be possible to do this for postal code areas.

Multiframe sampling

A list of the desired rare population is seldom complete or even available. So the answer, both in terms of costs and a good sample, is to work with two frames.

High-yield clusters

This is almost trial and error. It is useful in residential telephone surveys where the costs of an initial qualifying call are inexpensive. Let us say that a random-digit dialling system is intended to produce a sample of residences only. Such a system is almost certain to produce non-residence numbers as well. To minimise the proportion of non-residence numbers, clusters of perhaps 100 numbers are set up. Within each cluster, a ten-digit number is randomly chosen.

Multiplicity sampling (snowballing)

Members of the rare population are located by screening within each individually designated enumeration unit. A respondent who qualifies for the sample is asked to provide the names of others who also presumably qualify. A network of contacts is produced which might include all households containing parents or their children. Each network of households then becomes the sampling unit, from which information about the other members of the network can be obtained.

A major drawback to this method is that there is no way of checking to be sure that the sample is representative of the population of interest.

Conducting sampling

Here, we consider the problems associated with obtaining the right respondent, gaining the respondent's cooperation, the completion rate and handling the problems of people being too busy to cooperate and not answering (in telephone surveys).

Obtaining the right respondent

We should firmly establish in the minds of researchers the qualifications for being a respondent in a study. If a telephone survey requires a specific person in a household, the questioning procedure should establish the position of the person answering the call and not allow the interviewer to assume that any voice on the phone belongs to the desired person. If a heavy user of instant puddings is required, the questions and questioning procedures must be objective and thorough. The interpretation of the term 'heavy' is not something that should be left to either interviewer or respondent. There should be strict guidelines about classifying respondents into heavy, medium or light users, for example, so that this objective definition can be used in deciding who qualifies for questioning.

In a shopping precinct study where interviewers stop shoppers to question them, investigators can be given instructions about the ratio of men and women to interview. However, there can be special problems in shopping precinct interviews. The Monday shopper is likely to be different from the Saturday shopper and the morning shopper is different from the afternoon or evening shopper. The interviewing should be scheduled to represent all the varying categories.

When carrying out consumer telephone surveys, it is essential to make use of a recording form to ensure that the prescribed steps are properly carried out. This ensures that the consumer telephone sample is carried out as planned. The same kind of attention is required with a sample of business respondents. In a telephone survey where executives are the target sample, it is often difficult to get past the secretary or the assistant to the executive. A personal visit to the office often presents the same problem. Making a telephone call or sending a letter ahead of time, to see if a specific time can be set for that telephone call or personal visit, can help to resolve the problem. The nature of the questioning can be outlined. This not only gives the secretary a chance to clear it with the boss, but gives the executive time to obtain materials and documents ready for the interview. However, advance notice may also cause problems. It is often difficult for the potential respondent to arrange time ahead. Moreover, the advance call may provide the person with the means of postponing or refusing the interview outright.

Respondent cooperation

A large proportion of the public often refuses to participate in market surveys. Non-participation rises with interview length and varies with subject matter. This presents the possibility of a serious sampling problem.

Completion rate

The completion rate is the proportion of those in the potential sample who actually participate in the research. The sampling is ineffective if too few candidates end up being questioned or observed. We would expect at least 50 to 60% of those designated as potential respondents to participate. The problem is that non-respondents are often different in some way from those who participate. The way in which this problem is tackled depends on how both the first contact with the person and the follow-up contacts are made.

In consumer telephone surveys, the timing of the call may be a critical factor. If the study involves working mothers, the hours of dinner preparation and serving should be avoided in order to gain cooperation. Evenings and weekends provide a better opportunity to secure interviews where the male household head is to be questioned. However, evening calls to retired people may be unproductive since some senior citizens retire early and will not be pleased if prevented from doing so or if awakened from their sleep.

Achieving a 50% response rate on the first call is good going. **Call-backs** are a necessity, as are specific plans and record keeping to ensure that the call-back plan is properly carried through. Where a postal survey is involved, records should be kept for each individual showing the original date of posting. After a set number of days without a response, a second letter or even a telephone call is made. In the case of telephone and personal interview studies, you need to have some idea about why there is a non-response. It may be that there is no one at home (or no answer to the telephone), or the qualified respondent is not available. In the former case, the call-back is made on a random basis, following a predetermined plan that may schedule the follow-up attempt at a time when someone is there. It may be a different day, a different hour. If the non-response is because the qualified person is not available, there should be a procedure in which the individual who is at home can suggest a good time to make the call.

When a person is busy or there is no answer

One of the major reasons for no answers is the increasing proportion of couples who both work, and the proportion is greater among high-income groups and in towns. At evenings and weekends young couples may form a dining-out or a shopping team. Weather is also a consideration: in the good weather during the summer months, people spend less time in the house and more outdoors, while in the cold season, the reverse is true. Call-backs are the solution but they have to be planned systematically.

In the case of telephone studies, interviews should be conducted only between 9 a.m. and 9 p.m. Interviewers should be thoroughly trained, and an emphasis should be put on making the interviewing experience pleasant and appealing to the respondent so that further cooperation is encouraged. The respondent should be told the topic at the start of the questioning and the questionnaire should be kept to a reasonable length.

SAMPLE SIZE

Primary approaches for determining sample size

Marketing researchers use at least four different methods of determining sample size. Sample size determination can be based on:

1 intuition

2 statistical precision

3 cost limitations

4 industry standards.

Intuition

This is the most unsatisfactory method of determining sample size. It uses informed intuition as the basis for determining how many units to sample. The method of determining sample size is completely arbitrary and does not consider the likely precision of the survey results or the cost of obtaining them.

Statistical precision

The size of a sample affects the quality of the research data and it is not simply a question of applying some arbitrary percentage to a specific population. The sample size that needs to be taken should reflect the basic characteristics of the population, the type of information required and the costs entailed. The larger the sample size, the greater its precision or reliability, but practical constraints of time, staff and other costs intervene.

When computing the size of a sample, the size of the non-response factor should be borne in mind. If, for example, a final sample of 3500 is planned and the non-response is estimated at 30% then it would be advisable to increase the original factor to 5000. Such a correction will help to obtain the number of responses required but it will not correct the bias that arises from non-response errors – the fact that those who do not respond may have significantly different opinions from those who do respond.

The error of a sample varies inversely with the square root of the sample size. A sample of 9000 is more accurate than a sample of 1000. After a certain sample size has been reached, additional large increases in size do not significantly improve the statistical precision of a given sample. Costs, however, certainly *do* increase with larger samples.

The precision of the survey is a function of the sample size (although see Chisnall[6]). Precision is related to the square of the number in the sample. That is, the accuracy of results increases proportionately to the square of the sample size. If the sample size is doubled, let us say from 500 to 1000, accuracy rises only to the square root of the doubled sample size (2), or a bit less than half (1.4). While technically the rationale applies only to probability sampling, it is usually used as a guide in planning the size of non-probability samples as well. By sampling precision we do not mean how accurate the results are, for accuracy depends on too many factors: how good the questions are, whether or not the interviewer (if there is one) affects the results, etc. What is referred to here is the degree to which data on a simultaneously replicated study parallel those of another study or how similar the results of two simultaneous studies are.

Sampling error   Sampling error is the difference between a survey result and its parameter (a known statistic of the universe) – that is, the difference between the true value of a parameter of a population and that estimated from a sample. The error occurs because the value has been calculated from a sample rather than from the whole parent population.

Confidence interval   The confidence interval is an interval within which a parameter of a parent population is calculated (on the basis of sample data) to have a stated probability of lying. Generally, the researcher settles for a 95% probability – meaning that there are 95 or more chances in 100 that the reported figure falls within the range of a stated numerical value from the parameter.

For simplicity and because it answers almost all needs, our discussion here is limited to a discussion of percentages. But another measure of the confidence interval might be in terms of means. The confidence interval can be calculated only when the study has used probability sampling to obtain the results.

Overall precision required   Once the overall precision (range of the confidence interval) has been defined for the particular study, it is possible to make some tentative decisions on sample size. We say tentative only because there are still other aspects to be considered. In principle this approach can be used only with probability sampling, since there is no way of knowing whether a non-probability sample produces a sample similar to one based on selection probabilities. Practically, however, it is often used as a guide in determining the sample size of non-probability samples. As the sample size is quadrupled the confidence interval is cut in two. The confidence interval decreases as the expected percentage of results moves away from 50% (either plus or minus). This has some practical implications. First, increasing the required accuracy places a heavy premium on the price of the survey because of the effect it has on sample size requirements. Second, if the expected result cannot be predicted, 50% is the correct percentage to use. That is where the greatest error margin is experienced. So if results cannot be predicted in advance, sample size planning should be on the conservative side: in this case, the larger, more expensive side.

Cost limitations

This method determines sample size on the basis of the budget allocated to the project. It first involves subtracting from the available budget all non-sampling-related costs (for example, the fixed cost of designing the survey, questionnaire preparation, data analysis and report generation) and second dividing this amount by the estimated cost per sampling unit to arrive at the desired sample size. The approach is unsatisfactory because it emphasises cost to the exclusion of all other factors, especially precision.

Industry standards

These refer to those rules of thumb, developed from experience, that have become standard industry guidelines for determining how large a sample to draw. Conventional guidelines on sample size vary with the type of marketing research study as well as with the number of cells included in the study. The conventional approach to determining sample size is frequently used in non-probability designs, especially in quota samples. In quota samples, for example, the minimum number of respondents per cell is usually 50. A cell of 1000–1500 is usually considered as a reasonable sample for a national (probability) market study. Also, 200–300 per cell is the convention for a typical concept or product test.

Other factors

Deciding on sample size is not simply a statistical matter. The actual decision is a judgement call by marketing management or top management, depending on the importance of the particular problem. In any case, the decision will not be based on such points as sampling size: it will centre on costs versus value.

SUMMARY

This chapter has introduced the idea of sampling, contrasting it with a census. The key elements involved in devising a sampling plan have been discussed and the importance of properly defining the target population of interest has been emphasised. Illustrations of the important features of both probability and non-probability samples have been given and the major types and primary practical uses of both probability and non-probability sampling have been outlined. The primary approaches for determining sample size have been discussed and the concept of sampling and non-sampling error has been considered. The nature of the factors contributing to response and non-response errors has been described and suggestions made as to how response rates can be improved and non-response errors minimised. Particular attention has been given to sampling methods that are most appropriate for small populations. Attention has also been paid to the management of the sampling process and the determination of sample size.

QUESTIONS

1 What are the major arguments for undertaking research using sample data?

2 What are the key elements involved in developing a sample plan?

3 Why is no sampling frame perfect? What can you do to compensate for this?

4 Differentiate between probability and non-probability sampling.

5 Indicate the main sources of sampling and non-sampling errors in survey research.

6 What are the essential components of ensuring that the sampling process is well managed?

CASE STUDY 4.1: RESEARCH CONSULTANTS

Research Consultants has been commissioned to determine the following: Why do people select one estate agent over another? Do customers know or care if an estate agent is a member of a particular institute or professional body? And what additional services would customers like to receive from estate agents?

Research Consultants underbid four other research firms to obtain the contract and in fact their bid was some 50% of the next lowest bid. The main reason that Research Consultants was able to do this was because of the sampling methodology it selected. In its proposal the company said that university students would be used to gather the survey data. The company said that it would randomly select 20 universities from across the UK and contact the head of the business or management department at each college. The head would be asked to submit a list of ten students who would be interested in earning some extra money and then a senior consultant in the company would contact the students individually. The company's aim was to identify five students at each institute who would ultimately complete ten interviews each. When the students were contacted by the senior consultant they were told that they would be given £5 for each completed interview. The only requirement about who would be interviewed was that it must be someone who had had some experience of dealing with an estate agent in the previous 12 months. In fact, the consultant said that probably the easiest thing to do was for students to visit local pubs during the lunch hour and go from table to table asking for people who might be interested in being interviewed.

Questions

1 How would you describe this method of sampling?

2 What problems do you see arising from this approach?

3 Suggest a much better sampling method.

CASE STUDY 4.2: JEROME'S DEPARTMENT STORE

Jerome's customers are in the middle and upper middle income bracket and the store bases its reputation on having good, serviceable and not-too-fashionable clothing. The store also sells popular lines of cosmetics. Like all good department stores, the firm has a variety of departments ranging from china and jewellery to soft furnishings. At one time the firm also sold major electrical appliances but competition became too cut-throat and the firm decided to withdraw from that market.

In the last 12 months the store has experienced a slowing down of sales of clothes. Management felt that perhaps this was because it was not really very fashion conscious in what it had to offer. As a result a decision was taken to have a market research study conducted to ascertain whether the store should stock more designer clothing in the men's, women's and children's departments.

It was intended that the survey interviews were going to be conducted in the consumers' homes and would last more than one hour and a half. Jerome planned to show respondents a number of potential lines that could be added, including examples of clothing and information about the clothes designers. The cost of the proposed survey was of some concern to management. As a result, management was particularly concerned about the number of interviews that should be taken since this would obviously influence the total cost of the exercise.

Question

How should Jerome proceed with respect to the market research survey? Specifically, what approach should it take to sampling?

CASE STUDY 4.3: MCBAIN'S FAST FOOD RESTAURANT

McBain's is considering opening a fast food restaurant in Liverpool and, as part of the viability study, it wants to assess people's attitudes to a new fast food restaurant. There are to be 200 completed interviews and as far as possible the sample should be as follows:

Gender   50% should be male
            50% should be female

Age   40% between 16 and 24
            40% between 25 and 50
            10% to be under 16
            10% to be over 50

Occupation   20% to be students
             80% to be non-students

The interviews are to be conducted at the St Johns shopping precinct.

Question

Indicate how such a quota sample might be achieved.

 ## CASE STUDY 4.4: STUDENT RESEARCH PROJECTS

A marketing lecturer set his students the task of thinking up an idea for a new product, then researching the market for it. The students were allowed to use any research methods that seemed appropriate, but all were expected to carry out secondary research before designing their primary research programmes. Most of the groups of students found that thinking up the product idea was fun, but the research was more like hard work – that said, they did appreciate the opportunity to put some of their own ideas to work.

Altogether, there were 42 ideas for new products; some of these were not technically feasible, or would be unlikely to be profitable, but some of the ideas seemed viable. In any case, the assignment was about research, not about the technical design of products, so the feasibility or otherwise of the products was irrelevant.

The students carried out the necessary secondary research, then designed their own primary research programmes. Most used questionnaire-based surveys, a few used focus groups, and a small number used depth interviews, observation, experimentation or other techniques.

The students were left to their own devices somewhat; the idea was to allow them to learn from their mistakes and find out for themselves what the pitfalls of market research are. In most cases, students managed to produce fairly good results, but quite obviously some of them had serious difficulties.

The questionnaire surveys turned out to be the ones that caused the most difficulty; apart from the problems of designing the questionnaire, many of the students had made basic sampling errors. Here are some examples, taken from the students' written-up assignments:

- 'We conducted a random sample of shoppers by stopping people in the High Street on Saturday morning.' (new type of shopping basket)

- 'In order to find out the views of young people, we asked for volunteers and interviewed 23 students from the university.' (radio station)

- 'We surveyed 10 women and 10 men. The women were 20% more likely to like the product than were the men, and people over 60 were 10% more likely to like the product. Overall, 40% of the respondents liked the product.' (gardening tool)

- 'Telephone interviews with 100 respondents revealed that 32% of those interviewed would buy the roof sealer. Unfortunately, a further eight people who were interviewed later turned out to be grown-up children of the household rather than the home owner.' (emergency roof-sealing tarpaulin)

- 'The main problem we had with the interviews was that most people were too busy to stop and talk to us. Eventually, we managed to complete 70 useable questionnaires, however.' (banking services)

- 'Having obtained the permission of the crèche to conduct our research, we gave the questionnaire to the mothers when they arrived to collect their children. The following day we collected the questionnaires; unfortunately only about half were returned. However, these were enough to enable us to draw some conclusions.'

The focus groups were rather better, but even here some problems became apparent:

- 'Our group consisted of six boys and two girls, aged between 18 and 20. We showed them the model of the product and asked them to comment on it; at first they seemed to find it difficult to say much, but after some prompting they began to discuss it more freely.' (car vacuum cleaner)

- 'When we showed them the product most of them seemed puzzled. We had six housewives in the group, all of them from a coffee-morning group of friends.' (safety device for lawnmowers)

- 'Our group often strayed from the subject. We had a representative sample consisting of three teenagers (one male, two female), two middle-aged people, and three old-age pensioners.' (carpet cleaning device)

Although the students were able (in most cases) to work out what had gone wrong, they did not always know what to do to put matters right. This meant that the lecturer needed to spend considerable time with them to correct misconceptions and to help them understand the issues raised by the research; despite that, all those concerned, both lecturer and students, felt that the exercise had been a useful introduction to market research.

(Case contributed by Jim Blythe)

Questions

1 In each of the above cases, say what you think is wrong with the sampling.

2 For each of the above cases, say what you think the students *should* have done instead of what they actually did.

3 For each of the above cases, say what additional research you could do to correct the sampling errors or minimise their effect.

4 How can sampling errors such as these be avoided in future?

5 Is it possible to obtain a perfect sample?

REFERENCES AND NOTES

1 Semon, T T (1994) A good sample of accounts may not always be a good sample of your customers, *Marketing News*, 28(9), 8–11.

2 McKenzie, J (1988) Study of characteristics of ex-directory telephone owners, *Market Research Newsletter*, December.

3 JICNARS (1981) *National Readership Survey*, London: JICNARS.

4 CACI (2005) http://www.caci.co.uk/acorn/acornmap.asp, 22 April.

5 Hahlo, G (1992) Examining the validity of re-interviewing respondents for quantitative surveys, *Journal of the Market Research Society*, 34, 99–118.

6 Chisnall, P M (2001) *Marketing Research* (6th edn), Maidenhead: McGraw-Hill, 89–90.

FURTHER READING

Adcock, C J (1997) Sample size determination – a review, *Statistician*, 46(2), 261–83.

Bailar, B A (1997) Does sampling work? *Business Economics*, 32(1), January, 47–53.

Bolton, R N (1994) Covering the market, *Marketing Research: A magazine of management and application*, 6(3), 30–35.

Butcher B (1994) Sampling methods – an overview and review, *Survey Methods Centre Newsletter*, 15, 4–8.

Cowan, C D (1991) Using multiple sample frames to improve survey coverage, quality and costs, *Marketing Research: A magazine of management and application*, 3(4), 66–69.

Dent, T (1992) How to design for a more reliable customer sample, *Business Marketing*, 17(2), 73–76.

Dutka, S and Frankel, L R (1988) *Techniques for the Cost-efficient Sampling of Small or Rare Populations*, New York: Audits & Surveys.

Hague, P N (1985) *The Industrial Market Research Handbook* (2nd edn), London: Kogan Page.

Hoinville, G, Jowell, R and Assoc. (eds) (1978) *Survey Research Practice*, Oxford: Heinemann, Chapter 4.

Kress, G (1988) *Marketing Research* (3rd edn), Upper Saddle River, NJ: Prentice-Hall, Chapters 8–9.

Marsh, C and Scarborough, C (1990) Testing nine hypotheses about quota sampling, *Journal of the Market Research Society*, 32, October, 485–506.

Rowland, M L and Forthofer, R N (1993) Adjusting for non-response bias in a health examination survey, *Public Health Reports*, 108(3), May–June, 380–86.

Semon, T T (1994) Save a few bucks on sample size, risk millions in opportunity loss, *Marketing News*, 28(1), 19.

Watson, M A (1992) Researching minorities, *Journal of the Market Research Society*, 34(4), 337–44.

5 Surveys

Objectives

After reading this chapter, you should be able to:

- appreciate the various approaches to collecting primary data through surveys: postal surveys, personal interviews, telephone surveys, completely self-administered surveys, panels and omnibus studies

- understand the criteria used for selecting the data-collection method best suited to the specific marketing research problem on hand

- understand that, when using surveys to help answer a marketing problem, relevance, accuracy, timeliness and cost must be taken into account

- appreciate the merits of different survey methods.

Keywords

bias	panels
interactive research	questionnaire
interviews	syndicated research
omnibus surveys	telephone surveys
opinions	

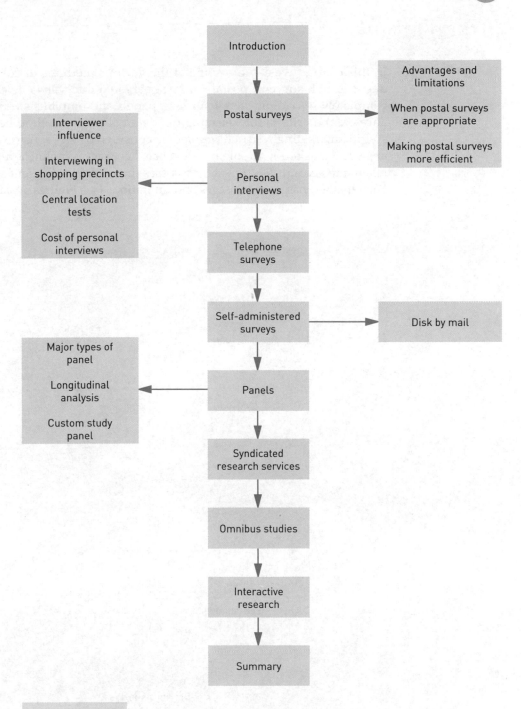

Plan of Chapter 5

INTRODUCTION

In this chapter we explore some of the various methods of collecting primary data through surveys: postal surveys, personal interviews, telephone surveys, completely self-administered surveys, panels and omnibus studies. The importance of, and criteria for, selecting the data-collection method best suited to the specific marketing research problem is considered. When using surveys to help answer a marketing problem, relevance, accuracy, timeliness and cost must be taken into account. The chapter discusses the merits of different survey methods. Each method has its advantages and limitations (see Figures 5.1 and 5.2).

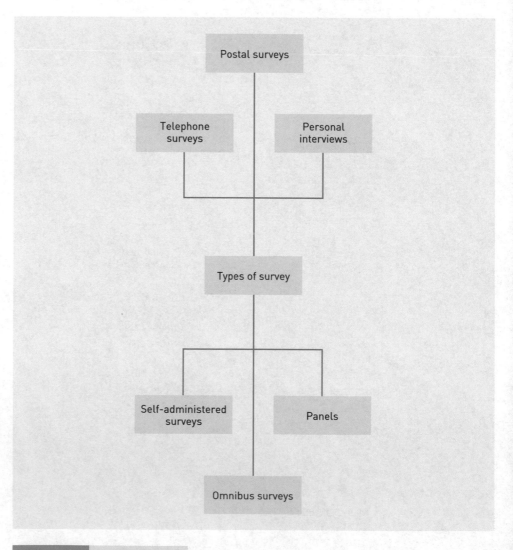

FIGURE 5.1   Survey methods

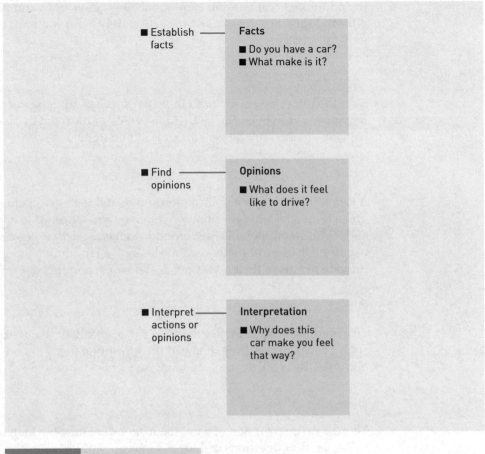

FIGURE 5.2   What surveys can do

POSTAL SURVEYS

In the case of postal surveys a **questionnaire** is sent to a potential respondent and the person writes in the replies and posts it back.

Advantages and limitations

Low cost per response

The costs of a postal survey are low. However, it is assumed that the user is an expert in postal surveys and understands how to get a high rate of return. On this assumption, the costs per return are low compared with most other survey methods. It is the going-in cost that is high; once the basic costs have been paid, the additional cost per unit is minimal. Once envelopes and paper costs are paid, although postage costs rise proportionately with numbers, printing costs rise only minimally.

No interviewer bias or cost

Since no interviewers are used in postal surveys, interviewer **bias** is absent in the responses. Moreover, the lack of interviewers means that one of the largest cost elements in the interviewer survey is eliminated.

Questionnaire scope

It is possible to request information about, and get answers to, a breadth of topics. The lack of a face-to-face situation removes any reticence to reveal personal habits and feelings. Women freely respond to subjects such as personal hygiene and the use of birth control methods and devices. Men, under the guise of anonymity, provide details of their investments, net worth and income.

Questionnaire length

Provided the subject matter interests the respondent, the person responding will spend considerable time filling in the questionnaire. This means that there is an opportunity to ask a reasonably long sequence of questions.

Respondent interaction

There is no interruption of what the respondent may be doing in order to respond to the series of questions and the person can reply whenever it is convenient to do so. There is an opportunity for a considered response, since the respondent is under no pressure to make an immediate reply. The postal survey makes it easy to present exhibits, such as advertisements and product models.

Sampling problems

Unlike many other survey methods, the sampling frame is either a good list or a not-so-good list. As a result, the adequacy of the postal survey is dependent on the quality of the postal list. In reality, few sampling frames for postal surveys – telephone books, city directories, industrial directories or purchased postal lists – are complete or current.

Response problems

The response rate is low, unless the researcher/marketer knows how to get good responses to a postal study. A problem with a low response rate is that those who respond are not necessarily similar to those who do not. The results, therefore, may be misleading. Experience often indicates that people who reply to a survey are those who are most interested or those with extreme feelings or **opinions** about the survey's subject matter. It is essential to compare the reactions of those who respond immediately and those who respond only on follow-up. Moreover, it can be dangerous to depend on the findings of a postal survey.

ADVANTAGES AND LIMITATIONS OF POSTAL SURVEYS

Advantages

- low cost
- no interviewer bias
- questionnaire length

Limitations

- questionnaire scope
- respondent interaction
- sampling problems
- response rate problems
- lack of control over respondents
- wrong respondents – wrong information

Another response problem concerns the market definition for the particular product or service. Partial illiteracy is a feature of many populations in the west. It is also greater among households with lower incomes. If the product or service is one whose market extends into the lower income levels, people simply cannot or will not respond, leading to a non-measurement of that segment of the market.

Lack of control over respondent

Since the recipient of a postal questionnaire can see and examine all the questions before answering any, there is no control over the sequence in which the questions are exposed. This lack of control limits the scope of questions in the postal questionnaire. For instance, we cannot ask for unaided recall of advertising slogans for household goods and then ask about the names of household goods recalled showing a list. Such a list would help people connect household goods' names with advertising messages.

Wrong respondents, wrong information

Another limitation of the postal survey is that the questionnaire may be answered by someone other than the addressee. For the executive or professional, it might be the secretary. For a specific member of a household, it might be someone else in that household. These self-substitutions can rarely be detected. The postal questionnaire recipient may also consult others before responding to the questionnaire.

When postal surveys are appropriate

The postal survey is also used to get information from people who are difficult to interview in person: those insulated from personal contact by a 'gatekeeper' (doorman, security guard, receptionist, secretary), including groups such as management, professionals (lawyers, physicians) and those living in exclusive quarters.

The postal survey may be able to handle difficult questionnaire content. If the topic concerns delicate or personal topics – such as birth control, sexual behaviour or personal finances – the postal questionnaire may be the best way of eliciting desired information.

In the case of an industrial survey, a question about sales or purchases of a particular item will almost certainly require the checking of records, if an accurate response is to be obtained. The postal questionnaire, once again, may serve such a purpose well, but the rate of response will probably fall if records must be consulted.

Making postal surveys more efficient

Notifying people in advance increases the rate of return in a survey and should be communicated to recipients a few days ahead of the postal questionnaire. The simplest approach is to make use of a personally addressed advance postcard, which alerts the recipient that a questionnaire will soon be on its way. There is a tendency to ignore post sent to 'the occupant' or job title in a place of business, so efforts should be made to personalise the approach. Where a long questionnaire is to be used, advance notice by telephone may be worthwhile.

The cover letter must motivate the recipient to complete and return the questionnaire. It must look interesting and important and seem short so that the recipient need spend little time in finding out the message. The purpose of the study should be described briefly and the benefits to the recipient should be highlighted. Sometimes the recipient can be offered a small token of appreciation for participation and this is generally included in the posted materials. It is important to retain the impression of quality, so a good-quality return envelope should be used.

Follow-ups are intended to increase the proportion of respondents, thereby ensuring a more representative survey. However, the researcher should ensure that enthusiastic respondents do not reply twice. Most often this can be handled by keying, a method of identifying those who respond to the first posting, and approaching only the non-respondents in the follow-up procedure.

PERSONAL INTERVIEWS

In personal **interviews**, respondent and interviewer speak face to face. At one time it was a very popular way of conducting surveys, particularly in-home interviews for consumer products. Today, the in-home personal interview is no longer a popular research method. It is expensive and generates a low response rate unless a great deal of time is spent in making call-backs. Fewer people are at home when interviewers are most likely to want to call.

Personal interviews now are largely conducted in shopping precincts. Shopping precincts are now a way of life in metropolitan areas, as is personal interviewing in these locations. Personal interviews are also conducted at business and professional locations.

Interviewer influence

The interviewer is the chief factor in the value of the obtained data. The accuracy of the data obtained is influenced by the manner in which the questions are put to the respondents and the skill with which follow-up and probing questions are handled. The interviewer must act in a neutral way to avoid exerting a bias on the replies.

ADVANTAGES AND LIMITATIONS OF PERSONAL INTERVIEWS IN SHOPPING MALLS

Advantages

- low cost
- little of the investigator's time is wasted
- procedures are standardised and specific
- monitoring of the interviewers
- possible to use illustrative materials during the course of the interview

Limitations

- time pressure – people in a hurry can be difficult to question
- interviewer may be tempted to seek out those shoppers who do not appear to be in such a hurry
- per-interview cost is the highest of any survey method
- refusal rate is high, running anywhere from 5% to 30%

A good interviewer should be able to establish rapport with others. They also need to be trained and training should cover the role and nature of marketing research, what surveys are and how they are conducted, and the role and importance of the interviewer. Training for a specific study is also necessary. An example of training for a specific study is given in the following box.

TRAINING FOR A SPECIFIC STUDY

Interviewing instructions are provided with regard to:

- introduction to the particular study
- interviewer timing requirements (dates and hours of work assignments)
- general purpose of the study
- the process of interviewing
- selection of prospective respondents
- specific procedures for the initial contact and for securing cooperation

Interviewing in shopping precincts

The process is easy and fast and it can be set up and carried out in a hurry. The approach makes it easy to spread the geographic distribution of respondents without having to take steps such as paying for interviewer travel. Compared with most other methods, the approach is generally low cost. Little of the investigator's time is wasted, procedures are standardised and specific, and there is monitoring of the interviewees. All these augur well for efficiency. Whatever the form of personal interview, one major advantage of interview surveys is that it is possible to use illustrative materials, such as advertisements or illustrations of the product, during the course of the interview.

Interviews in shopping precincts are not based on a probability sample. Usually it is a quota sample and the interviewer is given instructions about the proportions they are expected to get by demographics (such as gender and age). There are problems with sampling with personal interviews in shopping precincts. On weekdays there may be greater proportions of the elderly and teenagers and if, in the case of a shopping centre, it has a number of entrances, those shoppers coming in from the parking lot will typically be of a higher income level than those entering from the bus stop entrance. The strategic placement of interviewers to cover key thoroughfares is therefore critically important.

Many shopping precinct interviews have to be conducted quickly. Shopping precinct shoppers are there to shop and to get back to their homes or offices. They can be difficult people to question. They don't have time and it is not the right point in their activities to interrupt them. So even when the interviewer gets their attention, they are under pressure to speed up the questioning – which does not make for high-quality interviewing. There is also the problem that the interviewer may be tempted to seek out those shoppers who do not appear to be in such a hurry – they may be the ones who are shopping at leisure and are not in a hurry to get anywhere.

Central location tests

These involve personal interviews in which respondents are first contacted and personal details taken by phone. Interested respondents are then invited to attend at a central location in their district at specified times to participate in research. People are scheduled in groups or 'waves' to enable multiple interviews to take place simultaneously. These tests are used to establish acceptance or reaction to new products or to identify taste preferences in foods. Usually, one offers the participant a gift or payment as recompense for their help.

Cost of personal interviews

The per-interview cost of personal interviewing is the highest of any survey method. A considerable amount of non-productive time has to be paid for. The refusal rate is high, running anywhere from 5% to 30%. Moreover, more non-productive time is spent returning for **recall** interviews where in-home or business interviews are sought. Indeed, if the potential respondent is in a business or profession, the time spent on the interview is often excessive. If an appointment has not been arranged in advance, many hours may be spent in a waiting room hoping for a session.

TELEPHONE SURVEYS

If the study is one requiring a broad geographic sample, national or regional, the telephone survey may be ideal. **Telephone surveys** can also be used as an efficient follow-up method in connection with another basic method of data collection. Telephone surveys involve a team of interviewers working from a central location, with workstations provided along with outgoing telephone lines for each.

Today, almost all telephone interviewing is computer controlled. The interviewer works with a computer. In a consumer survey, when the interviewer gets an answer to a call, they check to make sure that it is a household and then ask to speak to the desired respondent. Then the interviewer uses the computer. Each question is shown on the monitor in sequence and the interviewer reads the question exactly as it appears on screen. Since most questions designed for telephone surveys are short-answer questions, where the respondent's replies are limited to a choice of possibilities, these are also shown on the screen. All the responses go immediately into the computer for later analysis.

Telephone interviews have many advantages. There is a compulsion to answer the telephone, regardless of what a person happens to be doing at the time: the ringing sound compels action. Some 95% of households have telephones and the business telephone coverage is practically 100%. In the telephone method, efficient call-backs are the rule; they are made at times when the desired respondent is more likely to be at home. A very high response rate is not unusual in the case of telephone interviewing. As no travel time is needed for the interviewer to make contact with the respondent, it is wasteful neither of interview time nor costly travel expenses. As a result, the amount of time needed for the study and interviewing costs are reduced.

ADVANTAGES AND LIMITATIONS OF TELEPHONE INTERVIEWS

Advantages

- compulsion to answer the telephone
- efficient call-backs
- high response rate
- no travel
- question modification possible

Limitations

- list of telephone numbers outdated
- demanding nature of the telephone ring may announce an unwanted sales pitch
- limit to the length of the typical telephone interview
- no way to provide visual aids

With a computerised interviewing program, it is generally possible to modify the questions during the survey process. Sometimes, the order in which a list of possible answers is given to respondents can affect their response. The first item on the list usually gets more responses than it should and the last position on the list may also bias replies (**order bias**). The first and last positions are the most likely to be affected. Computerised interviewing can be programmed to provide for equal average position, eliminating any such bias.

TELEPOST: AN ADJUNCT TO PERSONAL INTERVIEWS

The aim of the research was to gather information that would ultimately help to define an effective marketing strategy for the sponsoring firm's market offering supplied as either a product or service, or as some combination of both. The research studied both the actions and reactions to the market offering as well as the degree of sophistication, in sales and marketing, of the companies interviewed.

The first stage of the research process was conducted using personal interviews, primarily because of their high degree of flexibility. The method used is termed as a guided or focused interview that, while allowing the respondent to talk freely around each topic, successfully covers the topics of crucial context in a more or less systematic way. The number of respondents was small and only partially representative of the population of interest. However, it was especially effective with busy business executives and was ideal for this research as the respondents were chosen as experienced and authoritative executives from the field of sales and marketing in industrial and business-to-business marketing. Thirty names and addresses were located. Of the companies chosen, some were named by the sponsoring firm as ones that they wanted to interview. Others were located in *Key British Enterprises – British Business Rankings* (Dun & Bradstreet International).

The Telepost combination technique was the method used for the second stage of the research. This method is very effective in obtaining a high-quality response in complex markets. A sample frame was developed that was supportive of the personal interviews and that widened the sample base. The information gathered from the personal interviews allowed the sponsoring firm to produce revised documentation on the market offering. This second document was used and sent out as the material for the Telepost survey. A questionnaire, to be administered by telephone, was prepared to cover what had been established in the personal interviews, as the key dimensions. Letters were then sent to named respondents within the sample frame, informing them that they would be contacted by telephone and providing details of the nature of the interview and requesting that they read the revised documentation before the interview.

The telephone interviews therefore provided a quantification, extension and **verification** of the findings of the personal interviews.

Source: Cooper[1]

Despite all its strong points, telephone interviewing does have limitations. Unless special steps are taken, the list of telephone numbers used in a survey will be outdated on the day of publication, with omissions of new listings and inclusion of outdated ones. Although the demanding nature of the telephone ring is an advantage it can all too often signal an unwanted sales pitch and the owner may not answer the call. There is also a limit to the length of the typical telephone interview and usually it cannot run for more than about 15 minutes. Moreover, there is no way to provide visual aids, such as advertisements or other display materials.

SELF-ADMINISTERED SURVEYS

These kinds of study are often conducted by service firms such as restaurants, motels or hotels, and occasionally by health and financial institutions or even retail stores. In these cases questionnaires are left in convenient places for the potential respondent to pick up, fill in and return either in a convenient depository or by a prepaid return envelope.

Disk by mail

This is a comparatively new approach in which a computer disk with a self-administered questionnaire programmed on it is mailed to respondents. Respondents answer the questions on screen and return the completed disk. Often, a screening phone call is required to ensure that the respondent has the necessary equipment to use the disk.

PANELS

Panels are continuing groups that respond to questioning from time to time. A panel can be made up of persons, households or business firms. A panel may exist, for questioning purposes, for as little as a week or as long as a year or more. The panel may be set up by telephone, postal or personal interview. Some research firms offer the use of their ongoing panels to provide syndicated information available to all subscribers, while other research companies make their panels available for custom use. The user can specify the demographics or even require specific category or brand users.

Syndicated panel services measure such things as buying volume by brand and television viewing and use consumer diaries or electronic devices to obtain the desired data. The consumer diary is a form on which the consumer records their purchases or some other form of behaviour. An electronic device attached to the television set may monitor television tuning. With retail store panels, the data-collection method may be through the use of either scanners or physical audits.

CABLE TV HAS THE MOST VIEWERS

According to the first *Cable Audience Measurement Survey*, published this week, the main cable-exclusive channels reach over half of all people. Moreover, research shows that more TV is watched in cable homes than non-cable households. In total, cable and satellite channels achieve a combined average weekly reach of 93.6% of all cable home individuals.

Target audiences are relatively well satisfied with cable-exclusive channels according to research findings. The Box achieves a higher viewing share than MTV among 10–15 year olds: 1.8% compared with 1.5% for MTV and 0.8% for VH-1.

The survey also shows that cable householders make extensive use of technology: 34% have a games console and 29% have a computer compared with the national average of 24%, according to TGI.

The findings are based on diary research commissioned by the Cable Research Group. Research was conducted in January among 997 adults and 315 children by research company RSMB.

Source: McCann[2]

Major types of panel

The major ongoing panels are divided into panels used for syndicated offerings and those used for custom studies. The panel method has some great advantages, several of which are unique.

Longitudinal analysis

A custom panel or a syndicated panel enables us to monitor the reactions or behaviour of the same person, household or business respondent over a period of time. The panel approach makes it possible to get a continuing series of reports from the same people.

Where one-off studies are used, the researcher may encounter people who are not consistent users of the brand in question. Researchers might then question them about their inconsistent patterns of purchase. However, the panel method gives an opportunity to ask the question at the time the purchase behaviour has changed and to obtain a current and immediate reply rather than one that is dependent on memory.

PURCHASE OF A BRAND BY EXPOSURE TO EARLY ADVERTISING
(Measured in first wave)

	End of first month	End of second month
Total panel members	(6000)	(6000)
Total exposed to early advertising	(600)	(600)
Purchases by total sample	9.6%	10.8%
Purchases by those exposed to early advertising	15%	18%
Purchases by those not exposed to early advertising	9%	10%

Suppose you wanted to ascertain the impact of advertising on purchases. The introduction of a new product in the market might use an advertising blitz concentrated in the first month. On two successive one-shot surveys, done at the end of the first month and again a month later, questions about advertising recall and brand purchase could be asked, with results showing that brand advertising recall for the test product dropped from 10% to 5% in the two sweeps, while brand purchases went from 9.6% to 10.8%.

People would be unlikely to recall whether they were exposed to the blitz advertising, even though they could recall brand purchase within the week. The panel results among 6000 customers are shown in the table. The data show clearly that blitz advertising had a continued impact.

Panels cost less than a comparable series of parallel but separate samples. There is only a one-time basic sampling cost, be it households or stores, and continuing cooperation may also be high. The sample is the most serious limitation of the panel. With consumer panels, annual loss of members can be substantial. Some panel members soon lose interest and others are sometimes so self-conscious about their participation that their behaviour is affected.

NIELSEN HOMESCAN GROCERY CONSUMER PANEL

Typical of the kind of data provided by this panel are the following. The reports produced refer to the research purchaser's specific products.

For the information purchaser's particular brand, up-to-date data are provided on such things as total households buying the brand, penetration, brand volume, market share, percentage of the volume on offer, average price, purchase occasions per buyer, market volume per buyer. A demographic analysis is provided for all buyers broken down by social class, household size, age of housewife and region. For example, the report might identify the percentage of a firm's plastic products sold to different sizes of households.

A trend report is also produced showing consumer expenditure on specific product items, such as the firm's plastic bags and plastic bags in total. It might also show sales trends through different types of outlet, for example, ASDA, Boots, Gateway, etc.

Custom study panel

The postal panel can be specific for two types of small segments of the population: one is demographic and the other is behavioural. The research firm may already have information in its files identifying such households of people. If this is not the case, most research firms offering custom panel use provide postal screening. Alternatively, most of these firms will make a fast telephone survey to locate those who qualify.

A postal panel does have some definite drawbacks. It is usually self-administered, so the questionnaire is filled in by the respondent without supervision and can clearly be seen in its entirety before any questions are answered. Where careful sequencing through the questioning steps is required to obtain reliable information, the postal panel, like the postal questionnaire, can produce misleading findings. Moreover, as is the case with all postal questionnaires, it is unlikely that a person's response to an **open-ended question** will be very deep. No opportunity exists for an interviewer to probe to get a full and meaningful reply. An inherent disadvantage of the custom panel is the time it takes for results. It is at least as slow as the outgoing and returning post. Another disadvantage is that the typical custom panel has no way of showing its members television commercials and so has no way of getting reactions to these.

SYNDICATED RESEARCH SERVICES

Most **syndicated research** services are owned by the research companies that run them and, in the main, are continuous panels. The main problem for people wanting to make use of these services lies in identifying which services are available and who provides them. The *Market Research Society Yearbook* contains a list of providers of these services. In effect, **syndicated research services** are off-the-peg research studies.

Syndicated service firms collect and distribute information for many different users. The firms specialise in making available secondary information and other services at a lower price than it would cost a user of the information if the user had to conduct the study itself. An example of a syndicated service firm is AC Nielsen. Syndicated research firms can provide excellent information. For example, a producer of consumer package goods – inexpensive items that are branded, packaged and sold via self-service in grocery stores, mass-merchandise outlets and other retail stores – may subscribe to Nielsen's retail research services in order to get a variety of information about its brands and their comparative competitive performance with other brands. The manufacturer receives much valuable information, including:

- industry volume
- sales trends
- sales by package size
- competitors' sales
- local or regional sales

- inventory figures
- market share information
- distribution and out-of-stock figures.

The costs of conducting the research are shared among the entire client base.

LIFESTYLE MARKETING

Many brands are sponsoring questions on surveys about the use of competing brands. Companies such as Procter & Gamble, Imperial Tobacco, Guinness and Premier Beverages have all taken the exclusive rights for a year on answers by consumers about their branded products. Information on specific buying behaviour remains the strongest element of lifestyle data.

There is currently very little interest in attitudinal questions. Clients are looking for specific information on potential buyers or buyers of competitors' products. There is less interest in attitudinal data than four or five years ago. This view is expressed at CMT, which runs the National Shoppers' Survey and markets a lifestyle database called Behaviour Bank. The managing director of the firm says that it tends not to get too involved in attitudinal questions over and above what they already ask, such as reasons for purchase. Questions that are very important concern whether the consumer buys on price, promotion or brand name or whether the consumer simply rotates products. The power of the grocery multiples and electrical goods chains has helped to stimulate the market for lifestyle data and manufacturers need to be able to understand what share of customers they have and what is stimulating purchase.

Geodemographic profile providers have been motivated to respond to the recent upsurge in interest in lifestyle data. CACI indicates that its base is in census data and that this is still very much needed, for example in retail planning. The advantage geodemographics still has over lifestyle is that it is based on data on every individual in the country whereas the closest that lifestyle can get is data for households from the MIC database, formed by pooling CMT and NDL's surveys. CACI, however, is among a number of suppliers that have developed and launched systems that draw on both sets of data. CensusLifestyle combines CACI's ACORN geodemographics with lifestyle data licensed from ICD. This enables bias to be taken out of lifestyle data. One new product to flow from this fusion of data is PayCheck, which enables marketers to predict the likely income for every postcode, something that has always been difficult to achieve in the UK.

In an effort to expand use of targeting and profiling beyond direct marketing and store planning, some suppliers are now combining market research products with lifestyle and census information. Taylor Nielsen AGB, for instance, is marketing 'SmartBase' that bridges the gap between market research and database marketing. By licensing data on 13 million households from MIC and linking it to the AGB SuperPanel, SmartBase combines both breadth and depth of information. MIC has information on 60% of households and has a match to 7000 of the households on the SuperPanel. A similarly complex process has been used by Equifax Europe to build its Dimensions database, which incorporates census, lifestyle and market research from MORI and other data sources.

Source: Reed[3]

OMNIBUS STUDIES

An omnibus study (or survey) is an ongoing study through which a buyer can ask a limited number of questions at a very reasonable cost, because the general overhead costs of fielding the study are shared by a number of clients. Omnibus studies are often scheduled on a weekly, monthly or quarterly basis. Some are conducted through personal interviews but most omnibus services collect data by telephone interviews, so it is impossible to show display materials such as advertisements or products.

Omnibus studies assist in finding small segments of the population and the costs of locating a sufficient number of such respondents are low. If the incidence is too low to produce a sufficient number in one survey, the questions are retained in subsequent ones at a modest cost. Most omnibus services offer follow-up probes of those giving specific replies. These probes are usually conducted on a follow-up basis rather than at the time of original questioning (unless there are only a few questions) so as not to delay completion of fieldwork for the standard service.

Omnibus research is a hybrid between off-the-peg research, where data have already been collected and the researcher simply purchases whatever is available, and primary research, where the researcher collects data first hand. The term describes regular research surveys undertaken with a certain frequency and definite method, which use a set number of respondents and sampling points.

Omnibus research is particularly suitable for fairly robust data – for example, the usage and purchase of products – but it is less useful for attitudinal and opinion studies. Typical **omnibus surveys** might last for 40 minutes or more and during that time the respondent might be asked about six or more entirely different topics. The superficiality of some questions can prevent respondents from gaining the amount of concentration necessary to pursue any particular topic in depth. The *Market Research Society Newsletter* provides a list of organisations offering omnibus services.

Most consumer omnibus surveys reach at least 1000 adults per wave. This provides a substantial sample size for most purposes of analysis. It is also possible to increase the sample size by running questions over several waves of the omnibus. In the case of the more specialist omnibus survey, the sample size is much smaller (often around 100–200 respondents per wave) and they tend to be conducted less frequently.

Omnibus surveys employ one of three sampling designs. The most common approach uses a random location – with quotas set for age and working status within gender – although there are surveys utilising pre-selected and quota sampling. The standard output of most omnibuses is computer tables, although many suppliers provide data in various formats.

INTERACTIVE RESEARCH

In **interactive research** the participant interacts, via a computer connection, to questions or other stimuli presented on a screen or by some other means. The process may provide a response by means of a keyboard, a computer mouse or a touch-sensitive screen.

There is no interviewer with most interactive research systems and this helps to remove potential problems associated with such matters as the cost of interviewers, the need for supervision and potential biasing influence. There is no risk of the influence of inflection or accent, nor is there any limitation on delicate subject matter, often present with an interviewer.

As responses are automatically entered into the system, there is no need for the expensive process of the individual **coding** of each answer and all interactive systems ask the questions in the same form and order. Most interactive research systems provide questionnaire skip patterns, so that subsidiary questions are always asked when they should be asked and skipped when they should not be asked. As with all computer-based systems, these interactive methods provide rapid reporting of results. The responses are barely in the system before the summary tables are produced.

Interactive methods have their limitations. Only a reasonably straightforward series of questions can be asked; a complicated questionnaire cannot be handled through this medium. Moreover, since the method is almost a self-administered exercise, no opportunity exists for asking open-ended questions.

 ## SUMMARY

This chapter has explored some of the various methods of collecting primary data through surveys: postal surveys, personal interviews, telephone surveys, completely self-administered surveys, panels and omnibus studies. The importance of, and criteria for, selecting the data-collection method best suited to the specific marketing research problem have been considered. When using surveys to help answer a marketing problem, relevance, accuracy, timeliness and cost have to be taken into account. The chapter has discussed the merits of different survey methods, since each method has its own advantages and limitations. Attention has also been given to the use of panels, syndicated research services, omnibus studies and interactive research.

QUESTIONS

1 What are the main ways of conducting surveys? Discuss their appropriateness for different kinds of research problems and explain their advantages and disadvantages.

2 What is a consumer panel? Indicate the main types of consumer panel and their purpose.

3 How do syndicated research services differ from other kinds of marketing research services? What kinds of information do they collect?

4 What are omnibus studies? Explain their usefulness in practice.

5 Indicate what is meant by interactive research. What are its advantages and limitations?

CASE STUDY 5.1: CENTRAL TRAINING COLLEGE (1)

The Central Training College is the headquarters of a training group that is part of a consultation, recruitment and training company. One of the recruiting divisions of the company carries out the recruitment of permanent and temporary sales, construction, finance and management personnel, as well as office personnel. The Central Training College offers a wide range of general office courses as well as more specialised courses such as languages, business administration and desktop publishing. The consultation, recruitment and training company has been developing its activities in training and recruitment through organic and acquisitional growth. It has been proposed to move into the London market in time to take advantage of any improvements in industry growth. The most cost-effective method is thought to be to develop the property in central London already owned by the firm – the Central Training College – rather than pay for new premises.

At the moment, graduates of the college are left to find their own employment contacts or they are referred to a suitable employment agency. No financial gain is received by the college from this arrangement. If there were a recruitment agency that was part of the same company operating in the college, all students would be referred to it rather than to rival firms' recruitment agencies. This would increase the potential turnover per student. (Turnover refers to the money received through tuition and placement fees.)

A consultant was called in to advise on the viability of opening a recruitment agency in central London. On the basis of initial discussions the consultant produced the following research proposal.

Research proposal

Summary of brief

1 To determine the viability of opening a recruitment agency in central London.

2 To determine if the Central Training College would be a good location.

3 To find out if the name Central Recruitment would be acceptable.

Proposed research objectives

1 Investigate current and future demand for recruitment agencies.

2 Investigate actual intentions to use the service.

3 Discover if the name of the recruitment agency is an important factor in the purchase decision.

4 Investigate student and business attitudes to the provision of such a service.

5 Obtain demographic details of both students and businesses interested in the service.

Proposed research design

Conduct two surveys, one of the students at the college and the other of the employers. Students to be interviewed face to face and the employers to be contacted through the post.

Source: Fry[4]

Question

Evaluate the research proposal.

CASE STUDY 5.2: CONSUMER PRODUCTS

Phil Rice, marketing manager of Consumer Products, wants to gather as much information as he can about purchasers of aluminium wrapping foil and plastic wrapping bags. This covers both his own firm's products and those of competitors.

Competitive products include retailers' own brands and this makes up a substantial proportion of sales in the market.

Phil would like to have information on such things as the total households buying his firm's brand, the penetration of the market, the brand volume, the market share, the average price, the purchase occasions per buyer and the market volume per buyer, all by different demographic characteristics of consumers – i.e. broken down by social class, household size, age of housewife and region. For example, he would like to know such things as the percentage of the firm's wrapping foil sold to different sizes of households. He also needs to have a good idea of trends, including, for instance, consumer expenditure on specific product items such as the firm's aluminium foil sales by region. Information on sales through different types of retail outlets is also desirable.

In addition to such things as usage rates, purchase patterns and their relationship to consumer characteristics, he also wants to know what customers think about the various brands already on the market.

Question

What might be the best way for Phil Rice to obtain such data? Explain your answer.

CASE STUDY 5.3: LIPTONJUICE (1)

In March 1994 Britvic felt that all its research indicated that it was onto another winning brand in the iced tea drink, Liptonjuice, a joint venture between Unilever, the maker, PepsiCo, and its part-owned distributor, Britvic. It was expected that the product would achieve a sales volume of £20m in its first year and the producers mistakenly saw the British tradition of tea drinking as an advantage. Liptonjuice, it was believed, would play on the public's love of tea in combination with an increasing preference for more varied soft drinks. Despite initial optimism, the brand's future is now in serious jeopardy since PepsiCo and Britvic have said they will no longer distribute the brand. Unilever now has to go it alone or find a new partner. It was first launched in March 1994 and subsequently relaunched after radical changes to give a cleaner, more refreshing taste, better suited to British palates. But all this has been to no purpose.

PepsiCo might consider introducing its own iced tea as part of its Radical Fruit range. The range – minus an iced tea – is already available in Spain. The feeling as far as the UK market is concerned is that the British take a singular view of tea: it is something to be drunk hot, at any time of the day. Moreover, it was felt that even a multimillion pound advertising campaign that had been used to back Liptonjuice had failed to persuade the British to change their minds (see Figure 5.3).

However, tea drinkers in other European countries take their tea without milk and, as in the case of the USA, at specific times of the day. For Europeans and

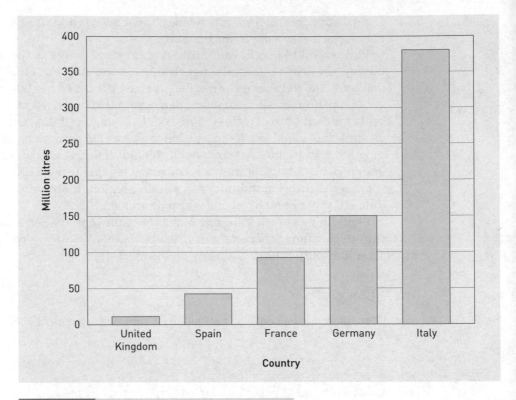

FIGURE 5.3   Iced tea consumption in Europe, 1995

Americans the idea of drinking cold tea, without milk, as just another drink is far more acceptable, since the associations with hot, milky tea are not as strong. It has also been easier to position the product as a sports drink in Europe and to sell it through sports clubs.

In 1995, iced tea was the fastest growing soft drink in Italy.

Coca-Cola has its own iced tea in the USA and Europe, where it is called Nestea. Liptonjuice was launched in Spain in 1994, a year after Nestea's Spanish debut but sales have been disappointing, as in the UK. PepsiCo's Radical Fruit range has, however, been a success in Spain.

Source: Rees[5]

Questions

1 Britvic's original enthusiasm based on research seems to have been misguided. Discuss the kinds of thing that might have gone wrong.

2 Do you think that survey research might have a role to play in guiding any of the companies still interested in marketing iced tea to European countries, including the UK? Explain your answer.

CASE STUDY 5.4: OPINION POLLING FACES NEW SCRUTINY

FT

'The general election will determine which techniques will be used for opinion polling in future, although the diversity of current practices may make it more difficult for the polling industry as a whole to win credibility,' Mr John Curtice, a reader in politics at Strathclyde University, said yesterday.

He said that because pollsters had changed their methodologies in different ways after getting the 1992 election wrong, this election would be a test of which of the various methods now in use was most accurate.

The polling industry was as diverse in its methodologies as it had ever been, in contrast to the last election, when there was a broad consensus about how polling should be conducted, Mr Curtice said.

He told the Market Research Society conference in Birmingham that the election would provide an opportunity to assess the relative merits of telephone and face-to-face polling and of sampling on a random basis or by setting certain quotas for the types of people to be questioned.

A study following the debacle of 1992 said the surveys did not identify hidden Tories and that the controls in quota sampling were not enough to counter the possibility that people questioned in a quota poll were more likely to be Labour than the population in general.

The polls' failure in 1992 to reflect the Tory victory has allowed the Conservative party to cast doubt on the credibility of the overwhelming Labour lead, which most have shown for many months.

Among changes brought in since 1992, NOP and Mori have altered how they weight the quotas they set, by making more use of government surveys, such as the Labour Force Survey.

ICM and Gallup have both switched to using a form of random sampling rather than quota sampling and to telephone polling instead of face-to-face interviews. Pollsters have also adjusted how they weight figures depending on how people say they voted in the last election.

Source: Smith[6] (reprinted with permission)

Question

Discuss the problems associated with quota sampling in surveys. How might such problems be solved?

CASE STUDY 5.5: VOLVO CAR UK

Volvo Car UK is the British marketing arm of the Volvo company, the Swedish manufacturer of high-quality, reliable cars. Volvo cars have a reputation for being solid, extremely safe, reliable, long-lasting and comfortable; they also hold their value well. For many drivers (and fleet operators) this makes Volvo the ideal prestige company car.

In terms of its long-term corporate strategy, Volvo aims to become 'the most desired and successful speciality car brand and the most customer-focused organisation in the world, achieving exemplary standards and support which will match or exceed customer expectations'. The problem for Volvo lies in deciding who is the customer – is it the extensive dealer network, which sells the cars, is it the corporations and fleet operators, which specify Volvo as company cars, or is it the world's motorists, who ultimately buy the cars?

Volvo believes that one of its major markets in the UK is the corporate customer; 70% of sales of Volvos in the UK are to corporations. Ultimately, these sales are to corporate employees who would like to choose Volvo as their company car. To meet the needs of these customers, Volvo runs two programmes; first, the Corporate Account Relationship Experience (CARE), which is aimed at corporate customers and fleet operators, and, second, the One Customer One Relationship (Oncore) programme, which is a dealer programme designed to satisfy the drivers of the cars. CARE is aimed at encouraging corporate customers and fleet operators to specify Volvo, but once the cars are sold and the drivers take possession of them, the Oncore programme takes over. Oncore is concerned with the relationship between the dealers (some of which are directly owned by Volvo, but most of which are independent businesses) and the drivers.

Volvo deals directly with the largest corporate customers, but dealers are involved both before and after sales with all the organisations that run fleets of Volvos. Some dealerships have in-house corporate specialists who have the expertise to understand the needs of fleet operators; typically, these dealerships are located in large cities where there are plenty of potential corporate customers.

Market research has shown that drivers of company Volvos are involved in six relationships that Volvo has input into. These relationships are as follows:

1 Volvo and its corporate customers

2 Corporate customers and their employees

3 Corporate customers and Volvo dealers

4 Volvo and Volvo drivers

5 Volvo and its dealers

6 Volvo dealers and Volvo drivers.

The Oncore and CARE programmes help to ensure consistency across these relationships. Oncore is about the drivers, CARE is about the corporations, but in each case the approach must remain consistent because of the close relationship between the corporations and the drivers (who are employed by the corporations). Currently Volvo still lags behind Mercedes and BMW in terms of numbers of cars sold to corporate clients, but the firm hopes to improve on this over the next few years.

From Volvo's viewpoint, the drivers are of crucial importance even though they do not always make the decision to specify Volvo. The reason for this is that the drivers will have some influence on the decisions (if they do not like the cars or are dissatisfied with Volvo's dealer service they might discourage their firms from specifying Volvo next time). Also, the drivers have families and friends who will see the cars and ride in them and each satisfied driver becomes an ambassador for Volvo.

In the longer term, Volvo seeks to refine both its corporate programme and its driver care programme to provide maximum repeat business. To do this successfully, the company must take account of its input into each of the six relationships identified earlier, and must maintain a clear message and service to its corporate customers and their employees.

(Case contributed by Jim Blythe)

Questions

1 How might Volvo find out why some customers prefer Mercedes or BMW?

2 What types of market research might help Volvo to refine the Oncore programme?

3 What types of market research would help Volvo to refine the CARE programme?

4 How could Volvo find out how to improve each of the six relationships identified earlier?

5 How might Volvo find out how effective the drivers are at acting as ambassadors for the cars?

REFERENCES AND NOTES

1 Cooper, Z (1991) Unpublished MBA dissertation, Department of Management, Keele University, September.

2 McCann, P (1996) Commercial TV audiences rise . . . , *Marketing Week*, 26 April, 15.

3 Reed, D (1996) The data game, *Marketing Week*, 3 May, 47–51.

4 Fry, C (1991) Unpublished MBA dissertation, Department of Management, Keele University, September.

5　Rees, J (1996) PepsiCo needs new strategy for iced tea, *Marketing Week*, 16 April, 23.

6　Smith, A (1992) Opinion polling faces new scrutiny, *Financial Times*, 21 March.

FURTHER READING

Bachman, D, Elfrink, J and Vazzana, G (1996) Tracking the progress of email versus snail-mail, *Marketing Research*, 8, 31–35.

Collins, M (1997) Interviewer variability: a review of the problem, *Journal of the Market Research Society*, 39, 67–84.

Comley, P (2000) Pop-up surveys: what works, what doesn't work and what will work in the future, ESOMAR Net Effects Internet Conference, Dublin, April, http://www.virtualsurveys.com/papers/popup-paper.htm

Craig, C S and Douglas, S P (2001) Conducting international marketing research in the twenty-first century, *International Marketing Review*, 18(1), 80–90.

Davis, G (1997) Are Internet surveys ready for prime time? *Marketing News*, 7 April, 5.

Deming, W E (1950) On errors in surveys, *American Sociological Review*, 9(4).

Dillman, D A (1991) The design and administration of mail surveys, *Annual Review of Sociology*, 17, 225–49.

Dillman, D A and Tortora, R (1998) Principles for constructing respondent-friendly web surveys and their influence on the response, American Statistical Association Meeting, Dallas.

Gubrium, J F and Holstein, J A (2003) *Postmodern Interviewing*, London: Sage.

Kehoe, C, Pitkow, J and Rogers, J (1998) GVU's ninth WWW user survey report, July, http://www.gvu.gatech.edu/user_surveys/survey–1998-04/

Kent, R and Lee, M (1999) Using the Internet for market research: a study of private trading on the Internet, *Journal of the Market Research Society*, 41(4), 377–85.

Mehta, R and Sivadas, E (1995) Comparing response rates and response context in mail vs electronic mail surveys, *Journal of Marketing Research Society*, 37(4), 429–39.

Meuter, M L, Ostrom, A L, Roundtree, R I and Bitner, M J (2000) Self-service technologies: understanding customer satisfaction with technology-based service encounters, *Journal of Marketing*, 64, July, 50–64.

Oppermann, M (1995) E-mail survey – potentials and pitfalls, *Market Research*, 7(3), 29–33.

Ranchhod, A and Zhou, E (2001) Comparing respondents of email and mail surveys: understanding the implications of technology, *Marketing Intelligence and Planning*, 19(4), 254–62.

Ray, N, Griggs, K and Tabor, S (2001) Web-based survey research workshop, WDSI, April, http://telecomm.boisestate.edu/research/

Riche, M F (1990) A bigger role for telephone interviews, *American Demographics*, September, 17.

Rothenberg, R (1989) The trouble with mail interviewing, *New York Times*, 16 August.

Runham, M (1999) Presentation at the IIR Internet Research Conference, December.

Schaefer, R and Dillman, D A (1998) Development of a standard email methodology: results of an experiment, *Public Opinion Quarterly*, 62(3), 378–97.

Schuldt, B A and Totten, J W (1999) Email surveys: what we've learned thus far, *Quirk's Marketing Research Review*, July, www.quirks.com

Sheehan, K B and McMillan, S J (1999) Response variation in e-mail surveys: an exploration, *Journal of Advertising Research*, 39(4), 45–54.

Stanton, J M (1998) An empirical assessment of data collection using the Internet, *Personnel Psychology*, 51(3), 709–26.

Taylor, H (2000) Does Internet research work? Comparing online survey results with telephone survey, *International Journal of Market Research*, 42(1), 51–63.

6 Measurement and scaling

Objectives

After reading this chapter, you should be able to:

- appreciate the basic concepts of measurement and scaling

- distinguish between the various types of measurement scale

- describe and illustrate the comparative types of measurement scale

- distinguish and illustrate the non-comparative types of measurement scale

- appreciate the difference between single-item versus multiple-item scales.

Keywords

attitude scale	projective techniques
comparative scale	Q-sort
graphic scale	ratings
interval scale	ratio scale
Likert scale	scaling
measurement	semantic differential
nominal scale	staple scale
non-comparative scale	Thurstone differential
ordinal scale	

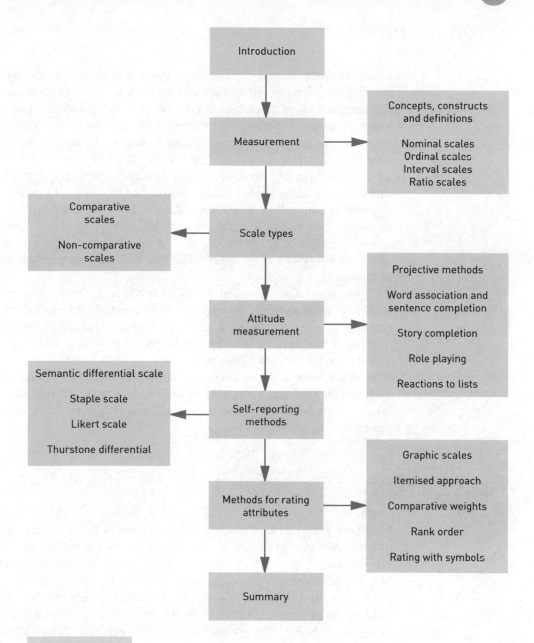

Plan of Chapter 6

INTRODUCTION

In this chapter the basic concepts of **measurement** and **scaling** are introduced and defined, distinguishing between the various types of measurement scale. The chapter goes on to describe and illustrate the comparative types of measurement scale, distinguishing and illustrating non-comparative types of measurement scale. Finally, single-item versus multiple-item scales are discussed.

Measurement is the process by which scores or numbers are assigned to the attributes of people or objects. How this is done is strongly influenced by the sort of information that is being sought. For example, if precise information on cigarette consumption is being sought, it is better to ask people to say how many cigarettes they smoke in a day. By contrast, when trying to collect information on the perceptions of cigarette smokers, it is better to ask people to classify themselves as heavy or light smokers. The two methods produce quite different kinds of measurement.

There are many different kinds of measurement-scaling technique. These scaling techniques often have different properties. It is necessary to understand the correct way to employ a technique because how a characteristic or trait is measured has implications for the interpretation and analysis of the data collected from using the technique.

First we look at some basic concepts of measurement and scaling and then distinguish between **comparative** and **non-comparative scales**. We then illustrate how these different scales are used and finally we compare single-item and multiple-item scales.

MEASUREMENT

Numbers given as answers to questions help in the analysis and interpretation of information that is collected by research. When taking measurements there are rules for assigning numbers to objects to represent the quantities of attributes. The rules apply to the procedure used to assign numbers that reflect the amount of an attribute possessed by an object, a person, etc. Attention must be paid to the objectives of the study, the precise definition of the characteristic to be measured and the correspondence between the measurement rule and the characteristic.

Concepts, constructs and definitions

A concept or construct refers to characteristics that we wish to measure and a definition of the precise meaning of the concept or construct. Many of the constructs measured in typical marketing research studies are directly observable

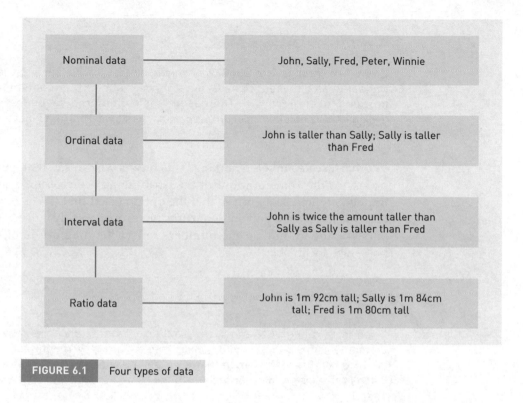

FIGURE 6.1   Four types of data

and many are not. The concepts of sales and market share can be directly linked to observable events. In contrast, the concepts of attitude, product perception or other customer satisfaction factors are measured indirectly.

Depending on the characteristics being measured, the numbers assigned have different properties that affect the kind of statements that can be made about the amount of a characteristic possessed by one individual relative to another. The scales used in these different types of measurement are termed nominal, ordinal, interval and ratio (see Figure 6.1).

Nominal scales allow us to place an object in one and only one of a set of mutually exclusive classes with no implied ordering. For example, a car's registration plate is an example of nominally scaled data. The numbers assigned have no other specific properties other than to identify the car assigned that number. Nominal-scaled variables include examples such as gender, religious denomination and political affiliation. The numbers assigned do not actually reflect the amount of the attribute possessed by the object under scrutiny. Because nominal data do not possess order, distance or origin, only a limited number of statistics are allowable. It is not meaningful, in this case, to compute the mean because it has no significance. However, a nominal variable can be counted: it would, for example, be legitimate to say that 50% of a sample is female. The correct measure of central tendency is the mode, the value that occurs most frequently.

NOMINAL-SCALED DATA

Given three ratings 1, 2 and 3, we cannot say that the distance between 1 and 2 is the same as between 2 and 3, nor can we say that the magnitude of 2 is proportional to both 1 and 3. There is no implied ordered sequence. The numbers assigned have no other specific properties than to identify the object.

Ordinal scales involve ranking. This means we can say that an object has more or less or the same amount of an attribute as some other object. There is an implied ordered sequence so that the option listed first is less or greater than the object listed second and subsequently. No property of distance between the numbers is implied, nor do the numbers reflect the magnitude of a characteristic possessed by an object.

ORDINAL-SCALED DATA

Given three ratings 1, 2 and 3, we cannot say that the distance between 1 and 2 is the same as between 2 and 3, nor can we say that the magnitude of 2 is proportional to both 1 and 3. There *is*, however, an implied ordered sequence so the option listed first is less or greater than the object listed second and subsequently.

An *interval scale* reflects how much more one object has of an attribute than another object. It is possible to tell how far apart two or more objects are with respect to the attribute. Interval data have order and distance properties and the most frequent type of measure of central tendency is the arithmetic mean. The standard deviation is also used to measure dispersion about the mean. Almost the whole range of statistical analysis can be applied to interval measurement scales but interval data do not allow comparisons of the absolute magnitude of the measurements to be made across objects. We cannot say that an object assigned the number 6 has twice as much of the characteristic being measured as the object assigned the number 3. While interval data possess the characteristic of order and distance, there is no absolute origin (zero point). Interval scales are often used in commercial marketing research studies, especially when a researcher collects attitudinal and overall brand rating information.

INTERVAL-SCALED DATA

Given three ratings 1, 2 and 3, we *can* say that the distance between 1 and 2 is the same as between 2 and 3 but we *cannot* say that the magnitude of 2 is proportional to both 1 and 3. There is an implied ordered sequence so the option listed first is less or greater than the object listed second and subsequently.

Ratio scales possess the same kind of properties as interval-scaled data but also possess an absolute or natural origin. Thus, we can say in this case that the number 6 has twice the characteristic being measured as the object assigned the number 3 on a ratio scale. Ratio data are commonly associated with directly observable physical events or entities. Measures of market share, sales, income, etc. possess characteristics that lend themselves to ratio scaling. Ratio scales have all the properties of the other measurement scales, since they possess the characteristics of order, distance and unique origin (zero point).

RATIO-SCALED DATA

Given three ratings 1, 2 and 3, we *can* say that the distance between 1 and 2 is the same as between 2 and 3, and we *can* say that the magnitude of 2 is proportional to both 1 and 3. There is an implied ordered sequence so the option listed first is less or greater than the object listed second and subsequently.

SCALE TYPES

There are two broad classes of measurement scale: comparative and non-comparative scales (see Figure 6.2).

With *comparative scaling* the respondent is asked to compare one set of objects against another. For example, a respondent might be required to compare one brand of butter against the other brands that they consider when making a purchase in a supermarket. Results have to be interpreted in relative terms and have ordinal or rank order properties. The scores obtained indicate that one brand is preferred to another, but not by how much. In the case of this type of scale, relatively small differences among the objectives being compared can be detected.

In *non-comparative scaling* respondents are required to evaluate each object independently of other objects being investigated. Non-comparative scaling is often referred to as *monadic scaling*.

Comparative scales

This type of scaling ensures that all respondents approach the rating task from the same known reference point. There are several variations in the technique used.

Paired comparisons

The respondent is presented with two objects at a time and is required to indicate a preference for one of the two according to some stated criterion. The method yields ordinal scaled data, for example, brand A is better than brand B, or, brand

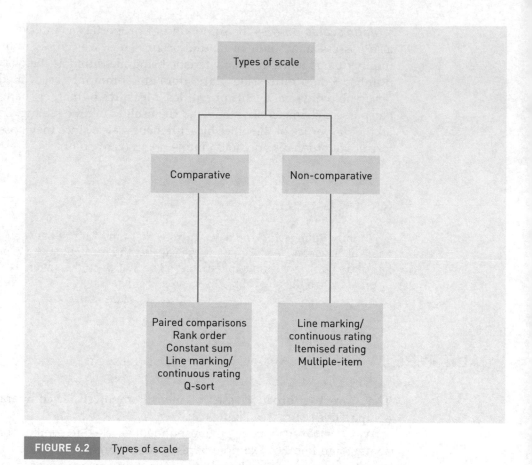

FIGURE 6.2   Types of scale

A is cleaner than brand B and so on. It is often applied in cases where the objects are physical products. One important point about data obtained through **paired comparisons** is that the ordinal data can be readily converted into interval-scaled data.

Rank order scale

In this case, respondents are presented with several objects simultaneously and required to order or rank them.

Constant sum scale

Respondents are asked to allocate a number of points – say, for instance, 100 points – among objects according to some criterion, for example, preference or importance. They are instructed to allocate the points such that if they like brand A twice as much as brand B, they should assign brand A twice as many points.

Line marking/continuous rating comparative scale

This is often used to obtain similarity judgements. Usually, respondents are presented with object pairs and asked to judge their similarity by marking a five-inch line anchored by the phrases 'Exactly the same' and 'Completely different'.

EXAMPLE

Rolex and Longines

Please indicate how similar you believe these two brands of watch to be by placing an X on the line below at the point that approximates your judgement.

Exactly　　　　　　　　　　　　　*Completely*
the same　　　　　　　　　　　　*different*

Q-sort scale

This scale employs a rank order procedure in which objects are sorted into piles based on similarity with respect to some criterion. Respondents are presented with a set of objects (brands, concepts, words or phrases) and are told to sort them into piles, according to some criterion. For instance, a respondent might be given a set of brands and asked to sort them according to which are the most similar to the person's ideal brand.

Once the respondent has completed the **Q-sort**, each item is assigned a rank order. The data are ordinal in nature and can be analysed with statistical procedures that are suitable for these types of data.

Non-comparative scales

The respondent is not instructed to compare the object of interest either against another object or some specified criteria. In rating an object, the respondent assigns the rating based on whatever criteria are appropriate for that individual. In assigning a rating, each respondent must use some criteria of their own: it is not provided by the researcher.

Line marking/continuous rating scale

A line marking or **continuous rating scale** can be used in a non-comparative format. In this case the respondent is required to assign a rating by placing a mark at the appropriate position on a line, usually five inches long, that best describes the subject under study. No standard for comparison is given. The resulting scores are usually analysed as interval data.

Itemised rating scale

Here the respondent is provided with a scale that has numbers and/or a brief description associated with each category. They are asked to select one of the categories, ordered in terms of scale position, that best describes the object under study. The scale can take on various formats reflecting the number of categories used, the nature and degree of verbal description, the number of favourable and unfavourable categories and the presence of the neutral position. This kind of scale can have any number of response categories. However, the controlling factor concerns the respondent's ability to discriminate among categories.

Various types of verbal description and numeric format can be employed and the former do help to ensure that respondents are operating from the same base. However, the presence of verbal descriptions will influence the responses obtained. Pictures and other types of graphics may also be used.

If an equal number of favourable and unfavourable classes are used, a **scale** is **balanced**; otherwise the scale is unbalanced. You might want to use an **unbalanced scale** when the distribution of responses is likely to be skewed. More categories might be used in the direction of the skewness. Unbalanced scales are often used when asking socially threatening questions or in cases where most of the respondents are likely to have positive (or, conversely, negative) opinions about a subject.

When a balanced rating scale is used, there is a choice between using an even or an odd number of scale items. In the case of an odd number of scale items, the middle scale position is usually designated as a neutral point.

Itemised rating scales are often used to measure purchase intentions. Purchase intention scales represent an attempt to measure a respondent's interest in a brand or product.

Multiple-item scale

A multiple-item scale consists of a number of statements to which the respondent must react. For example, a respondent might be asked to indicate how favourable or unfavourable each statement is. An overall score is then determined by combining the reactions to each.

ATTITUDE MEASUREMENT

Attitudes are assumed to be a precursor of behaviour and are considered to express a person's beliefs and, in some sense, to influence the person's ultimate behaviour. Most commercial market research studies contain questions as a means of **attitude measurement**.

People have different notions about what constitutes an attitude but it often involves feelings, emotions and likes or dislikes. Attitudes reflect a person's evaluation of an object based on their beliefs about that object. To some degree, attitudes influence how the person will respond when they encounter the object. An attitude might therefore be looked on as a learned predisposition to respond in a consistently favourable or unfavourable manner to a given object.[1] Such a description assumes that attitudes are learned, that they are a forerunner to behaviour and that they are stable.

There are several types of scaling technique that can be used to measure attitudes. Here we discuss and illustrate some of them.

Projective techniques

The basic premise of **projective techniques** is that the best way to obtain the true feelings and attitudes of people is to enable them to indirectly present data about themselves by speaking through others.

Projective techniques such as sentence, story and picture completion are taken from the domain of abnormal psychology. They were devised in the belief that people have various psychological blockages that prevent them from verbalising their true feelings. The assumption is that normal people, too, experience blockages and that the method is also valuable in these circumstances.

In the case of picture completion or cartoon techniques the respondents are shown a picture of one or more people in a situation related to the subject under study. They are then told to describe what is occurring or to answer a question asked by one or other of the cartoon characters. The characters are usually drawn to be as neutral as possible (no smiles or frowns). Picture frustration (putting one of the cartoon figures in a frustrating position) and thematic apperception tests (depicting more general situations than the frustration method) are the most generally used methods (see Figure 6.3).

Word association and sentence completion

In the case of word association a respondent is given a series of single words and then asked to match each with one of their own. The goal is to elicit quick, unrestrained answers. For example:

Carnation: *perfume*

Flower seller: *anniversary*

Sentence completion follows the same kind of pattern:

The kind of flower I prefer is _____

Men who buy flowers are _____

What do you think is going on?

FIGURE 6.3   Thematic apperception

Story completion, role playing and reactions to lists

Story completion is a longer version of sentence completion in which participants are presented with partial scenarios and asked to complete the story. For example:

> It was a dark day and the headlamps of the cars moved like will-o'-the-wisps in the murky twilight. Candice stepped almost unconsciously into a limousine that stood, door ajar, at the kerb . . .

Role playing

Participants are asked to assume the role of another person and to behave in a manner in which they feel that person would act. For example, to identify people's attitudes towards a particular brand a small group of respondents is asked to provide the conversation they feel would occur in a similar-sized group of consumers discussing their feelings about the brand.

Lists

Lists of various products or activities are shown to participants and they are asked to describe the type of person who would have used such a list. Their answers will shed light on their feelings about the items on the list and what type of people such items appeal to.

LISTS

What kind of shoppers are A and B? Examine the two shopping lists and suggest characteristics for each of the shoppers.

Shopper A	Shopper B
1 tin baked beans (Heinz)	2 kilos new potatoes
2 large cartons of semi-skimmed milk	1 packet of baby corn
6 apples – Coxes	1 box of tea bags (large)
2 packets white sugar	2 cartons of milk (large)
1 jar of Nescafé	1 tub of margarine
2 tins of sardines	1 bottle of aerated water
4 cans of Lager (Skol)	1 packet of Special K cereal
1 tub of chocolate ice-cream (large)	1 tin of tuna chunks
1 packet of PG Tips tea bags (large)	4 yoghurts – organic (fruit)
2 loaves (white – from bakery dept)	6 eggs (medium)
2 packets of pork sausages	

A variation on this method is to have two identical shopping lists, except for one item. The lists are shown to different samples of respondent – i.e. no one person sees both the lists. This helps to spot what people associate with the item that is different on the two lists.

SELF-REPORTING METHODS

Semantic differential scale

The **semantic differential scale** technique was originated by Osgood, Suci and Tannenbaum.[2] The originators of the technique discovered that the perceived meaning of a variety of words and concepts could be decomposed in terms of three components: potency, activity and evaluation. In marketing research, the semantic differential is often used to measure attitudes towards the imagery surrounding products and services. In general, only the evaluative (e.g. good/bad) component is measured.

The scale consists of a number of bipolar adjectival phrases and statements that could be used to describe the objectives being evaluated. In the original work of Osgood et al., only single-word bipolar adjectives, not phrases, were used. However, common practice in marketing research applications is to use adjectival

We would like you to let us know what you think about our restaurant. Below are a number of statements that could be used to describe what we offer. For each pair of adjectival phrases we would like you to mark the category that best describes your feelings about us.

Old-fashioned	___ ¦ ___ ¦ ___ ¦ ___ ¦ ___ ¦ ___ ¦ ___	Modern
Expensive	___ ¦ ___ ¦ ___ ¦ ___ ¦ ___ ¦ ___ ¦ ___	Cheap
Friendly service	___ ¦ ___ ¦ ___ ¦ ___ ¦ ___ ¦ ___ ¦ ___	Unfriendly service
Helpful staff	___ ¦ ___ ¦ ___ ¦ ___ ¦ ___ ¦ ___ ¦ ___	Unhelpful staff
Limited range of menus	___ ¦ ___ ¦ ___ ¦ ___ ¦ ___ ¦ ___ ¦ ___	Wide range of menus
Inviting atmosphere	___ ¦ ___ ¦ ___ ¦ ___ ¦ ___ ¦ ___ ¦ ___	Cold atmosphere
Fast service	___ ¦ ___ ¦ ___ ¦ ___ ¦ ___ ¦ ___ ¦ ___	Slow service
Unattractive decor	___ ¦ ___ ¦ ___ ¦ ___ ¦ ___ ¦ ___ ¦ ___	Attractive decor
Convenient opening hours	___ ¦ ___ ¦ ___ ¦ ___ ¦ ___ ¦ ___ ¦ ___	Inconvenient opening hours

FIGURE 6.4   Semantic differential

phrases as well. An example is shown in Figure 6.4. Each bipolar adjective rating scale consists of seven categories, with neither numerical labels nor category descriptions other than for the anchor categories. To remove any position bias, favourable and unfavourable adjectival phrases are randomly distributed to the left-hand and right-hand anchor positions. The respondent is asked to mark one of the seven categories that best describes their views about the object along the continuum implied by the bipolar object pair. An overall attitude score is computed by summing the responses on each adjective pair. Before computing the overall score, the response categories must be coded. Usually the categories are assigned values from 1 to 7, where 1 is assigned to the unfavourable adjectival phrase and 7 is assigned to the favourable adjectival phrase. Thus, before assigning codes and summing, the researcher must be careful to reverse the individual scale items where necessary so that each attitude continuum ranges from unfavourable to favourable or vice versa.

Ratings on each of the bipolar adjective pairs are often used to provide a profile or image of the objects being investigated. This is achieved by plotting the mean ratings on each of the bipolar adjective pairs for each of the objects. Figure 6.5 shows an example of such profiling. In order to facilitate interpretation of the profile, all the favourable adjectival phrases are positioned on the same side. From this kind of plot, it is possible to obtain an overall impression of people's perceptions of the object.

In Figure 6.5, a comparison is made between two restaurants. Not only does the scale permit such comparisons to be taken in at a glance but it also allows us to see fairly readily where more in-depth research is required. The decor of 'our restaurant', for example, is perceived to be at or about the neutral point. Further research is needed to uncover how it might be improved to the taste of its clientele.

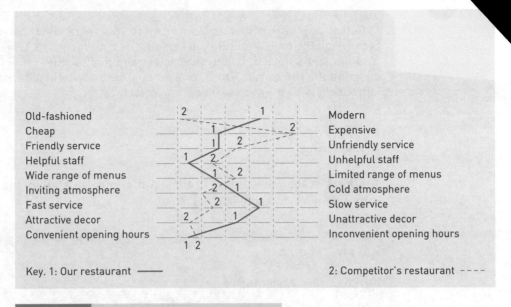

FIGURE 6.5 Semantic differential profile

Staple scale

The **staple scale** technique differs from the semantic differential because it uses just one term and asks the respondent to describe how well that term describes the subject. Circling +5 means that the respondent agrees very strongly that the term is an appropriate description, while circling −4 indicates the reverse. The scores for each respondent can be summed and compared with the total scores of other respondents.

STAPLE SCALE

Our restaurant

+5	+5
+4	+4
+3	+3
+2	+2
+1	+1
Awkward	*Helpful*
−1	−1
−2	−2
−3	−3
−4	−4
−5	−5

Select a plus number for words that you think describe the restaurant accurately. The more accurate you think the description is, the larger should be the plus number selected. Conversely, select a minus number for words that do not describe the restaurant. The less accurate you believe the description to be, the larger should be the minus number you select.

Likert scale

A **Likert scale** measures attitudes and comprise statements with which the respondent has to agree or disagree.

LIKERT SCALE

'Persil washes whiter than white'

Strongly disagree	Disagree	Don't know	Agree	Strongly agree
−2 ☐	−1 ☐	0 ☐	+1 ☐	+2 ☐

In the Likert[3] method, a series of statements is provided and interviewees are required to rate each statement on the basis of the strength of their personal feeling towards it. The numbers assigned to the responses are numerical values associated with each possible answer. When analysing the results, the signs of these numbers are reversed when a statement is unfavourable.

Thurstone differential

When using the **Thurstone differential** method, interviewees are asked to select those statements with which they agree from a list of between 20 and 25 statements. The statements are derived from an original list of 100 to 200 statements that are evaluated by a panel of 15 to 20 judges. Each judge is asked to place those statements in 11 nearly equal piles. These piles represent the judgements of the panel members as to which statements are more favourable and which are least favourable about the subject. The sixth or middle pile is the neutral position.

Mean scores for each of the original 100 to 200 statements are determined on the basis of the piles in which they were placed by the judges. The 20 to 25 statements with the smallest dispersion are chosen to be included in the survey. From this latter list the interviewee is asked to check only those with which they agree, enabling a mean score for each interviewee to be obtained. This score quantifies the attitude of each interviewee towards the subject under study. Many people argue that the scale is an *ordinal* rather than interval scale.

The 20 to 25 statements used in the scale must all deal with the same subject. If attitudes towards a variety of subjects are sought – firm's products, personnel, etc. – a separate list of statements would be required for each subject.

THURSTONE DIFFERENTIAL

Suppose attitudes towards a restaurant are being assessed using a Thurstone scale. An interviewee indicates three statements with which they agree:

Statement	Value assigned by judges
1 The restaurant has a friendly atmosphere	3.0
15 The restaurant offers a good choice of menus	1.5
21 Always rely on the quality of the food	2.7
Average	**2.4**

Some general comments relating to these techniques

When administering these techniques, respondents are provided with a number of choices – words, statements, numbers – and required to select the one that most closely describes their attitude towards the subject. When applying these techniques, the researcher must decide how many choices to include as well as their wording.

There is disagreement on the ideal *number of choices* that should be offered to respondents. Four to eight choices appears to be preferred, with five the number used most often. There is also a lack of consensus on whether there should be an *even or odd number of choices*. An even number of choices compels the respondent to declare a position, whereas an odd number usually provides a middle position for situations where the respondent cannot identify their feelings. The drawback to offering a neutral position is that this choice attracts many respondents who do not have strong feelings on the issue and hence it does not allow the researcher to distinguish between answers.

There is a related issue which is relevant to the point about the 'odd versus even' number of questions: this concerns the provision of a category headed *'don't know'*. There are many situations in which respondents do not have an opinion or are not sufficiently informed on a topic to have an opinion about it. A neutral position and a 'don't know' choice *are not the same thing*. Where both can occur, provision has to be made to record both.

Attention should also be given to the *wording of choices*. There should usually be an equal number of favourable or unfavourable statements. Responses can easily be biased if the majority of choices are either favourable or unfavourable.

An unbalanced set of categories might be preferred, however, when there is prior evidence that, in general, attitudes held are at extreme positions. For example, if all viewpoints are likely to be positive, then more precision may be obtained by offering the categories:

1 outstanding

2 well above average

3 above average

4 average

5 below average.

METHODS FOR RATING ATTRIBUTES

Thus far we have examined techniques that allow respondents to express their feelings on the extent to which an item or topic possesses certain attributes. However, in trying to obtain an overall score for the subject matter under scrutiny, we have assumed equal weighting for all the attributes or statements. It is necessary, however, to measure how important each attribute or statement is for the overall attitude being measured.

Rating scales enable respondents to disclose the intensity of their feelings about certain attributes or about the subject itself.

Graphic scales

Use of a **graphic scale** involves the respondent indicating the intensity of their feelings towards some attribute or object by placing a mark at some point along a continuum that includes all possible ratings.

GRAPHIC SCALE

Please indicate how important each attribute is to you in your selection of a restaurant. Place an X on each line at the position that best reflects your feelings.

Attribute	Not important		Very important
Low prices	_____		
Courteous service	_____		
Varied menu	_____		
Convenient location	_____		

Itemised approach

Here, a list is prepared of the object's attributes and the respondents are asked to identify how important each item is to them in their final attitude towards the object.

ITEMISED APPROACH

Attribute	Very important	Fairly important	Somewhat important	Not important
Price	___	___	X	___
Durability	X	___	___	___
Appearance	___	___	___	X

Comparative weights

Here the respondent is forced to rate the attributes on the basis of their perceived relative importance.

COMPARATIVE WEIGHTS

Price	22
Weight	16
Durability	12
Material	21
Looks	29
Total	**100**

The respondent is asked to divide 100 points among five attributes to denote the relative importance of each attribute.

Rank order

In this case the respondent is asked to arrange a number of objects according to some criterion. This produces strictly ordinal scaling, since no data are presented about the relative difference between any of these objects. The procedure is easy for the respondent to perform if the comparison is limited to six or seven objects.

Multiple-item scales are often used in attitude measurement.

RANK ORDER

Please rank the following restaurants according to the friendliness of their personnel. Place the number 1 beside the restaurant that you feel has the most friendly personnel, 2 by the restaurant with the next most friendly personnel, and so on until all restaurants have been rated.

____   Rembrandt
____   Silver Moon
____   Hole in the Wall
____   Barny's Place
____   Il Seraglio

Rating with symbols

In cases where there may be language or literacy difficulties, an alternative to using words in scales is to use symbols instead. The example in Figure 6.6 illustrates this.

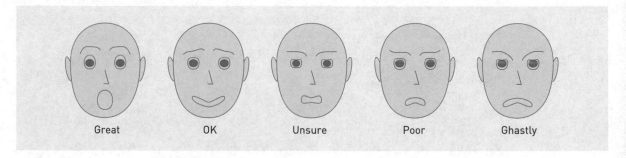

Great	OK	Unsure	Poor	Ghastly

FIGURE 6.6   Example of symbols representing ratings

SUMMARY

This chapter has defined and discussed the basic concepts of measurement and scaling, distinguishing among the various types of measurement scale. A description and illustration of comparative types of measurement scale have been given, as have descriptions and illustrations of non-comparative types of measurement scale. Single-item versus multiple-item scales have been compared and discussed. Various attitude measurement scales have also been examined.

QUESTIONS

1 What do you understand by the term measurement in marketing research?

2 Differentiate between concepts, constructs and definitions.

3 Differentiate between nominal, ordinal, interval and ratio-scaled data and indicate when each might appropriately be used in marketing research.

4 Describe the two main types of scaling.

5 Differentiate between paired comparisons, rank-order scales, constant sum scales, continuous rating, comparative scale or line marking and Q-sort.

CASE STUDY 6.1: SUMMIT MOTORS (1)

Summit Motors' records indicate that less than 40% of its new car buyers remain loyal service customers after the first free service. The dealer is keen to increase the percentage to at least 50%. A number of different attributes have been identified as affecting the patronage of a service facility and the dealer wants to conduct a small survey among new car purchasers who have bought cars during the past two years to assess customer views.

The attributes affecting patronage are considered to be whether or not:

- the job is done first time
- complaints are dealt with speedily
- warranty work is attended to promptly
- the dealer can do any job required
- service is available when required
- the service is friendly and courteous
- a car is ready when promised
- only necessary work on a car is performed
- service prices are low
- the car is cleaned up after service
- the service facility is convenient for home
- the service facility is convenient for work
- courtesy cars are available
- maintenance reminders are posted.

Question

Construct a scale that would be helpful to the dealer and that could be the focal point of the survey.

CASE STUDY 6.2: BARNY'S CAFÉ

Barny's Café is just off the promenade at Eastbourne. It is tucked away down a side street and although it does not enjoy the prominence of many of the cafés in the town, there are a good number of passers-by during the season and many stop for a drink or even a meal. Out of season, however, the café suffers from the usual, perhaps to be expected, seasonal drop in sales. However, Barny has noticed that, unlike many of his competitors, he does not have any regular customers who help to offset the seasonal drop in sales. In the summer, when the town is crowded, it is difficult to get a seat in a café and virtually all the cafés are full to overflowing around lunchtime and in the afternoon. Virtually anyone who can offer a seat and a rest for half an hour can get customers.

Barny sees his problem as one of establishing a customer base – in other words: how to get regular customers and keep them. As far as he can see there does not appear to be anything especially different about the 'more successful' cafés to what he has to offer. One thought that has crossed his mind is the idea of conducting a small survey to find out people's attitudes towards his café and, if possible, their attitudes to other cafés in the town.

Question

Draw up a suitable attitude measurement scale that could help Barny have a better idea of how he might tackle this problem.

CASE STUDY 6.3: LIPTONJUICE (2)

Before making any further decisions, imagine that PepsiCo had decided to undertake an extensive survey of people's attitudes to iced tea in the United States, the United Kingdom, Spain, France, Germany and Italy.

Question

Suggest how PepsiCo might go about measuring people's attitudes to Liptonjuice.

CASE STUDY 6.4: CHINESE IMPORTS

East-West Connections Ltd specialises in the import of novelties and small household products from the Far East, notably from Korea and mainland China. The company's Chinese agents have for some time been suggesting that the firm's range could be extended to include Chinese white goods – washing machines, refrigerators, freezers and so forth – since these were now being produced to high standards and in substantial quantities within the People's Republic. Following in the footsteps of Changhong, the largest TV manufacturer in China (now exporting to the USA), the agents believe that the Western world is ready for Chinese consumer durables.

The directors of East-West are somewhat less enthusiastic. Although they are well aware that firms such as Wuxi Little Swan (washing machine makers) and Qingdao Haier or Guangdon Kelon (refrigerator manufacturers) are seeking opportunities outside China, they feel that the British public still thinks of Chinese goods as being in the 'cheap and nasty' category. For the firm to make the considerable leap from dealing in cheap fans and ceramic ornaments to dealing in consumer durables would require some fairly solid evidence; the capital cost alone could bankrupt the firm if the idea went wrong. Contrariwise, being first to introduce the products into Britain could have very substantial advantages in terms of long-term viability of the firm. After all, there is a limit to how many substandard vases can be sold, and in the long run the firm would need to seek new opportunities.

The obvious answer to the problem was to conduct some research among UK consumers to see what their perception of Chinese goods is. The consultants brought in to do the research decided to begin by using a Q-sort to assess perceptions of Chinese goods against perceptions of 23 other nationalities, including European, American and Far Eastern countries. The perceptions of the countries' goods were assessed across the following criteria: reliability, design quality, durability, price, availability and prestige value. The Q-sort revealed that Chinese goods ranked higher than some countries on price and availability and even ranked higher on design than did a few countries, but in almost all cases China ranked low on durability and reliability.

The country that appeared to be closest to China in terms of public perception of the goods was Korea. Since Korean engineering has become more acceptable in the West over the past 10 to 15 years (with the advent of Korean cars such as Daewoo and Kia), the researchers decided to concentrate further efforts on investigating the relationship between perceptions of China and perceptions of Korea. For this, the researchers decided to use a multidimensional scaling approach so that they could see how great the differences were between China and Korea on the attributes identified.

China was perceived as having a very large advantage on price, a small disadvantage on design, a small disadvantage on prestige and big disadvantages on reliability, durability and availability. For Chinese goods to be successful in the UK, therefore, East-West Connections would need to change the perception of unreliability. In fact, quality testing showed that the Chinese goods were no more unreliable than Korean goods, but the Koreans had the advantage of being able to ride on the back of Japan's reputation for high-quality goods. The Chinese might not have a similar advantage – but without a doubt they were going to be in the market within the next ten years or so.

The directors of East-West Connections were unsure whether the firm would be able to make the substantial changes in public perceptions that appeared necessary; on the other hand, the prospect of being first to market in a potentially huge growth area was very tempting indeed.

(Case contributed by Jim Blythe)

Questions

1 Why might the research team not have used multidimensional scaling across all the comparison countries instead of a Q-sort?

2 What does multidimensional scaling tell us that a Q-sort does not?

3 Draw up a semantic differential scale for assessing attitudes to Chinese goods.

4 What other techniques might have been appropriate to the study?

5 What are the limitations of Q-sort and multidimensional scaling?

REFERENCES AND NOTES

1   Fishbein, M and Azjen, I (1975) *Belief, Attitude, Intention and Behavior*, Reading, MA: Addison-Wesley, 6.

2   Osgood, C, Suci G and Tannenbaum, P (1987) *The Measurement of Meaning*, Urbana, IL: University of Illinois Press.

3   Likert, R (1932) A technique for the measurement of attitudes, *Archives of Psychology*, 140.

FURTHER READING

Churchill, G A (1979) A paradigm for developing better measures of marketing constructs, *Journal of Marketing Research*, 16, February, 64–73.

Foddy, W (1994) *Constructing Questions for Interviews and Questionnaires*, Cambridge: Cambridge University Press.

Gofton, K (1997) If it moves measure it, *Marketing*, 4 September, 17.

Green, P A, Tull, D S and Albaum, G (1988) *Research for Marketing Decisions*, Upper Saddle River, NJ: Prentice-Hall.

Ohanian, R (1990) Construction and validation of a scale to measure celebrity endorsers' perceived expertise, trustworthiness and attractiveness, *Journal of Advertising*, 19(3), 39–52.

Oppenheim, A N (1968, 1969, 1984) *Questionnaire Design and Attitude Measurement*, Oxford: Heinemann.

7   Questionnaires

Objectives

After reading this chapter, you should be able to:

• understand the principles involved in designing and constructing questionnaires

• understand the principles involved in testing and debugging questionnaires.

Keywords

closed-ended questions	questionnaire
dichotomous questions	reliability
layout	response format
multiple-choice questions	scales
open-ended questions	semantic differential
phrasing	sequence
pretesting	survey
projective techniques	validity

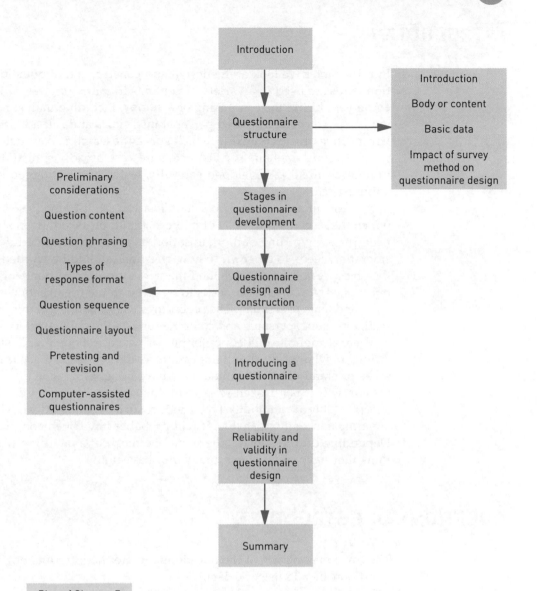

Plan of Chapter 7

INTRODUCTION

In this chapter we look at the design and construction of **questionnaires**. Questionnaires are used in a variety of contexts in marketing research. They can be employed during the conducting of a **survey**, including mail surveys, telephone interviews, formal structured personal interviews and self-administered studies. Irrespective of the context in which survey research is conducted, the ways in which the questionnaire is constructed are very broadly similar. However, questionnaires must be developed carefully, tested and debugged before they are administered.

A questionnaire is a data-collection instrument. It formally sets out the way in which the research questions of interest should be asked. Even simple questions need proper wording and organisation to produce accurate information. Consideration needs to be given to how questions should be worded, in the light of the objectives of the research, and the target group of respondents who are to be questioned. Attention also needs to be given to the organisation of the questionnaire and to its **pretesting**. The procedures recommended in this chapter apply to mail, telephone, personal and computer-assisted telephone interviews.

There are definite guidelines for preparing a questionnaire. First, there are limitations to what a questionnaire can measure. People can accurately report the make or brand of a fashion item they have bought for some time after the actual purchase. If it is a frozen-food item, their memory span will be considerably shorter. If it is a commodity-type product such as salt or sugar, where the brands are almost indistinguishable, it will probably have been completely forgotten. Depending on the subject, there may be recall of something that respondents think they have seen when actually they have not.

QUESTIONNAIRE STRUCTURE

The three major parts of the questionnaire are the introduction, the body of the questionnaire and its basic data.

Introduction

To be successful, the introduction to the questionnaire must achieve two things:

1　It must be persuasive.
2　Usually it must qualify the respondent as someone who belongs in the sample.

The starting point of the questionnaire is self-identification. In a one-to-one interview, the investigator has to explain who they are and name the firm doing the study. The introduction states the topic of the study. If it is a one-to-one survey, the person may have to be qualified to ensure that they really belong in the sample. Possibly only users of a particular type of product or service are wanted.

Body or content

The body or content consists of questions that cover information needed to solve the marketing problem. The range of topics covers facts, knowledge, opinions and attitudes, motives and possible future behaviour. Factual questions include such things as ownership, shopping/buying behaviour and media exposure as well as knowledge possessed by respondents. Questions also attempt to measure opinions and attitudes – feelings about products, firms and advertising. There is also the measurement of motives, still more difficult and uncertain in dependability of results. Finally, there is possible future behaviour. Questioning in this last area must bear in mind that results are an expression of attitude and not an accurate prediction of behaviour. People are often willing to describe their plans, but these may often not be carried out.

DESIGNING THE QUESTIONNAIRE

First, the problem to be tackled by the survey has to be defined. This will enable you to decide what questions to ask. It is always tempting to cover too much in a questionnaire. However, too long a questionnaire can be demoralising for both interviewer and respondent. A questionnaire should only be as long as is absolutely essential for its purpose. Moreover, the aim of the questionnaire should always be borne firmly in mind when constructing it and each question should make contributions to the research objectives.

The information obtained as a result of administering the questionnaire will depend on the respondent's ability and willingness to respond. The aim should be only to ask opinions if the interviewer is reasonably sure that the respondent understands what is involved and is able to give meaningful answers. The interviewer should also aim to ask questions only from those who are able to answer them accurately. It should always be borne in mind that a willingness to respond is not a guarantee of the accuracy of the answers.

Basic data

The last section of the questionnaire is mainly information about the household and the individual. It almost always includes demographics about the household, aspects such as family size, nature and income. Typically, it also covers demographics about the respondent and it may include questions about lifestyle and psychographics.

This section of the questionnaire has three purposes. First, where there are known and dependable statistics about the population from which the sample has been selected, such data provide a rough check on the representativeness of the sampling. Second, through analysis of subgroups, it provides a method for identifying differences of key results in response by subgroups such as gender and age. Third, there is identification material such as the respondent's name, address and telephone number.

Impact of survey method on questionnaire design

Whether survey data are collected through personal interview, telephone, mail or self-administration, they will have an impact on questionnaire design. In a shopping centre interview, for example, there are time limitations that are not encountered in other situations. In the case of a self-administered questionnaire the questions have to be explicit and short. In the case of a telephone interview a rich verbal description of a concept may be necessary to ensure that the respondent understands what is being discussed.

STAGES IN QUESTIONNAIRE DEVELOPMENT

The stages involved in the design of a questionnaire and how they fit in with the general research process are outlined in the following box. This provides an overview of what should have been done prior to the development of the questionnaire. It also examines what is involved in questionnaire development and testing.

STAGES IN THE DEVELOPMENT OF A QUESTIONNAIRE

1 Identification and specification of the research problem/research objectives.

2 Selection of the population to be studied.

3 Choice of data collection: face to face, telephone, mail, computer approach.

4 Ordering of the topics to be addressed.

5 Establishing the required cross-tabulations.

6 Deciding how the topics will be covered – direct/indirect questions, **open-ended questions**, **closed-ended questions** – and how they will be precoded.

7 Questionnaire **layout** and the design of any supporting material, such as showcards.

8 Pretesting of the questionnaire to obtain feedback on the ordering of questions, responses to questions, instructions to interviewers, efficiency of layout and to assess the time taken by the interviewers and the cost of interviews.

QUESTIONNAIRE DESIGN AND CONSTRUCTION

On reaching this stage in conducting a research study it is expected that the research problem has already been expressed in terms of an appropriate set of research questions. These questions have now to be put in a suitable format for the respondents to answer and then arranged into a questionnaire in a valid, logical fashion that will produce meaningful answers. Considerable thought needs to go into the process of constructing a questionnaire: it is not as simple as might appear at first sight. Indeed, the process involves going through the following sequence of steps (see also Figure 7.1):

1 preliminary considerations
2 question content
3 question **phrasing**
4 types of **response format**
5 question **sequence**
6 question layout
7 pretest, revision and final version of the questionnaire.

Preliminary considerations

Attention must be paid to the kind of information that is required, the nature of the respondents who are to be surveyed and the method by which the survey is to be conducted. *The three considerations are interdependent.* For instance, in order to answer questions in a meaningful way, a respondent must have access to relevant information and it must be appropriate for the person concerned to make a response. By way of illustrating the last point, asking the male partner in a household about shopping habits is not appropriate if the female partner does all the shopping.

The questionnaire must address all the data requirements that are specified in the research objectives and attention must be given to ensuring that this is done. It is also important to take account of how the questionnaire is to be tabulated after collection of the data. Each topic should be taken in turn and it should be decided which groups in the survey population warrant individual attention when it comes to discussing this topic.

Question content

When looking at the content of questions, you should ask:

1 *Is the question necessary?* If the answer provided by a question does not contribute to satisfying the research objectives, the question itself should be omitted.

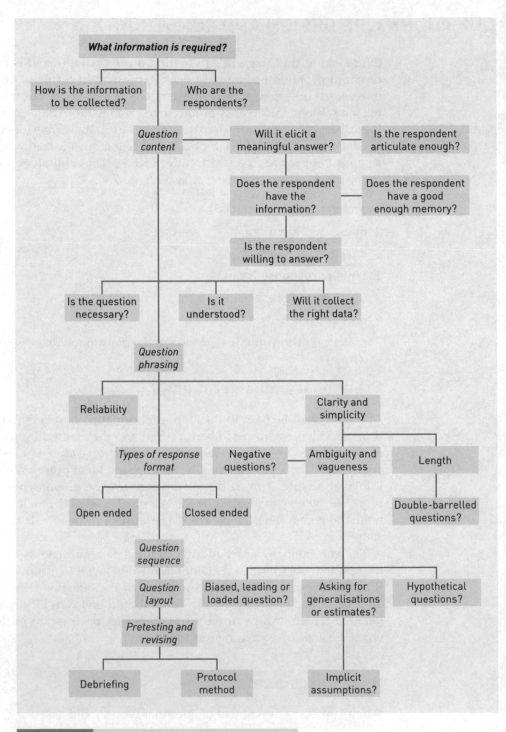

FIGURE 7.1 Questionnaire design and construction

2 *Does the respondent understand the question?* The language of the question should be at the level of the respondent being interviewed.

3 *Will the question suffice to elicit the required data?* Questions may be badly phrased or too ambiguous to produce specific information, for example, 'When do you shop?' Asking the same question, but with the words in a different order, may also produce different answers. For example, asking whether it is right to 'drink and drive' may elicit a different answer to asking whether it is right to 'drive and drink'.

   You should also avoid questions that pose more than one question, for example, 'When and where do you shop?'

4 *Does the respondent have the necessary information to answer the question?* The ability of a respondent to provide a meaningful answer will reflect:
   • *The extent to which the respondent is informed.* Some respondents may not wish to disclose ignorance and may try to bluff their way through certain questions. In constructing and asking questions it is therefore important to ensure that there is no suggestion that the respondent should know the answer.
   • *How good the respondent's memory is.* People forget and need something to jog their memories. It is better to ask people if they recognise something rather than to ask them to recall it.
   • *How articulate the respondent is.* People vary considerably in this respect. Where open-ended questions are being asked it is inevitable that some people will be better than others at getting over the point they wish to make. Closed-ended questions, where an individual has to indicate an option from a prespecified list help to alleviate this particular problem.

5 *Is the respondent willing or able to answer the questions?* Non-response or distorted answers are sometimes made by respondents. Embarrassment or loss of face are strong motivators that influence how a person responds to questions. Ways of alleviating this problem include:
   • removing or redrafting questions that are likely to create these kinds of problem
   • reassuring respondents of the importance of the questions and the confidentiality of the data provided; anonymity of the responses can help.

Question phrasing

Clarity and simplicity

The style of language used should be appropriate for the target population. You should not appear to be condescending, nor should you assume that respondents are as well informed on the subject as the person who asks the questions.

CLARITY AND SIMPLICITY

Don't ask respondents what viscosity of oil they put in their cars. Ask them what grade they use.

Length of questions

Keep the sentences short and to the point.

Ambiguity and vagueness

Ambiguity and vagueness in question wording must be avoided at all costs. If the meaning of a question is unclear, you cannot expect the respondent to provide a clear, unambiguous answer. Avoid confusing words – words that are spelt the same but can have different meanings or words that sound the same but are spelt differently.

AMBIGUITY AND VAGUENESS

The word light can mean both light in weight and light in colour. Using the word on its own can be confusing.

Biased words and leading or **loaded questions**

Biased words have emotional connotations such that the respondent may respond to the word rather than to the question in which it is contained: 'bosses' and 'interference' are two such words. Such words should be avoided. Leading questions are those that either suggest the way in which the respondent should answer or strongly suggest what the questioner's position on the subject is. These too should be avoided.

LEADING QUESTIONS

Avoid leading questions such as: 'Most people believe that advertising puts up the price of goods in the shop. Do you?'

Negative questions

Questions with a negative formulation, with which respondents are asked to agree or disagree, can be confusing. Confusion leads to the respondent guessing and thence to measurement error. Questions phrased in a negative fashion should be avoided.

NEGATIVE QUESTIONS

Questions with the format: 'You don't think . . . do you?' are not only confusing but also leading.

Questions asking for estimates or generalisations

These should be avoided since they are a potential source of error.

ESTIMATES AND GENERALISATIONS

Do not ask people how much they usually spend on their green groceries on average every week. This can be accurately ascertained by keeping consumer diaries.

Hypothetical questions

The words 'would' or 'could' should be avoided in questions since they encourage the respondent to guess and speculate.

HYPOTHETICAL QUESTIONS

Do not ask people if they would purchase something if it were available.

Implicit assumptions

When phrasing questions, do not do so in a manner that assumes that all respondents are well informed and in possession of all the facts. Questions that make an implicit assumption of a respondent's background knowledge will not produce valid, accurate results. Different respondents will make different assumptions, so the questions will not generate useful responses. Indeed, it is advisable, wherever appropriate, to state the essential assumptions on which the question is dependent.

IMPLICIT ASSUMPTIONS

'Would you prefer a holiday in Spain to a holiday in Greece?' is a difficult question to answer unless you know the various assumptions relating to the two holiday venues, for example, that the cost of the holidays is similar.

Response choices should not overlap

This applies to closed-ended questions where a number of answers are provided from which the respondent has to select the most appropriate (see box).

OVERLAPPING RESPONSES

If the categories of response given are in ranges such as:

1 0–5   ☐

2 5–10   ☐

3 10 or more   ☐

then there is clearly overlap between category 1 and category 2, and between category 2 and category 3. Redrafting the categories of response as:

1 less than 5   ☐

2 5 to under 10   ☐

3 10 or more   ☐

removes the problem.

Double-barrelled questions should be avoided

These are questions where two opinions are joined together in the one question.

DOUBLE-BARRELLED QUESTIONS

'Do you think the service provided in the hotel is friendly and efficient?'
   There are really two questions in one here. Is the service friendly? Is the service efficient? Two questions are warranted to avoid confusion in recording and analysing answers.

Reliability and validity of questions

Reliability reflects whether asking the same question of the same person on a subsequent occasion will elicit the same response. **Validity** reflects whether you are ascertaining through a question what you think you are ascertaining. Both are influenced by the respondent's ability to answer a question accurately. If a respondent is not informed on a topic or exhibits poor memory recall relating to the topic, the accuracy of responses will be impeded. Under such circumstances the reliability and validity of the question is in doubt.

QUESTIONNAIRE WORDING

Care has to be taken with how questions are phrased since careful question design can substantially reduce the bias arising from confusion or lack of understanding. It will also help to minimise response bias which is a function of the respondent's perceptions and predispositions. Questions should be simple, intelligible and clear. The tradeoff between the desire to secure a maximum amount of information from a respondent and the need to keep the interview clear has a major bearing on questionnaire design in respect of its length, complexity, layout and wording.

Types of response format

Questions can be open ended, where the respondent may answer in their own way, or closed ended, where all possible answers are prespecified. **Open-ended questions** can reveal more information and are often worthwhile during exploratory work when you want to discover what people think. Closed-ended questions, however, are easier to interpret and tabulate.

There is evidence that respondents react differently to the two types of question. When the same question is put to matched samples of respondents, responses vary with the approach used.[1]

Closed-ended questions

In a **closed-ended question**, the question is followed by a structured response. All possible answers are given with the question. Such questions are easy to use, reduce interviewer bias, reduce the bias exhibited by respondents in answering questions and facilitate coding and tabulation.

Dichotomous question   A **dichotomous question** suggests two answers: usually yes and no. These types of question are excellent where a fact is to be determined and where the views of the respondents are likely to be clear-cut.

DICHOTOMOUS QUESTION

Did you buy your hi-fi on credit terms?

Yes ☐   No ☐

Multiple-choice question   A **multiple-choice question** offers the respondent a list of answers from which to select the one that is closest to their view. This format reduces any bias that can be introduced by the respondent's ability to articulate. It also simplifies the coding of responses. Three or more answers are offered and the respondent usually has to select one of them.

MULTIPLE-CHOICE QUESTION

Which one of the following cities have you visited most often?

| London ☐ | Paris ☐ | New York ☐ | Lisbon ☐ |
| Munich ☐ | Ankara ☐ | Beijing ☐ | Dublin ☐ |

In this same category are **scales**. There is a variety of scales (see Chapter 6):

- Likert scale: measures attitudes
- **semantic differential**: also assesses people's attitudes
- rating scale
- staple scale.

Open-ended questions

Open-ended questions do not suggest an answer and allow people to write whatever they wish. The main purpose of this type of question is to obtain the respondent's own verbalisation of, comprehension of and reaction to stimuli such as advertisements, packages, products and concepts.

Unstructured questions   This type of question allows the respondent to reply in whatever format they prefer:

UNSTRUCTURED QUESTION

'What do you think about Fry's Turkish Delight?'

Projective techniques   **Projective techniques** include word association, sentence completion, story completion and picture completion, all of which are discussed in Chapters 6 and 8.

Question sequence

The sequencing of questions is important. The earlier questions should attempt to create interest in the respondent. The questions should also follow a logical order. Questions about age, salary, etc. should be left until last, except where use is being made of a quota sampling, in which case it is necessary to establish this information at the outset of the interview.

To enhance preparedness to participate in a study, questionnaires should appear logical and carefully thought out. The typical flow in market research surveys involves a progression from evaluative to diagnostic questioning, or vice versa, and then on to classification questions (see the following box).

EXAMPLE OF MOVING FROM EVALUATIVE THROUGH DIAGNOSTIC TO CLASSIFICATION QUESTIONS

Questionnaire concerns consumer opinions of a new product concept.

Evaluative:

- purchase interest or intent

Diagnostic:

- reasoning behind the level of purchase intent or interest
- considered uniqueness of the concept
- considered credibility of the concept
- perceived importance of the main benefit
- anticipated frequency/quantity of purchase/usage
- ratings of the concept with respect to different product benefits

Classification:

- age of respondent
- family size of respondent
- educational attainment of respondent
- occupation of respondent
- income group of respondent

Initial questions should be used to engage interest, to reassure and to give a foretaste of what is to follow. Potentially embarrassing questions should be left until later in the questionnaire. Questions that suggest answers to subsequent questions should be avoided. Overall, the questions should move from the general to the specific and there should be a logical flow from question to question and

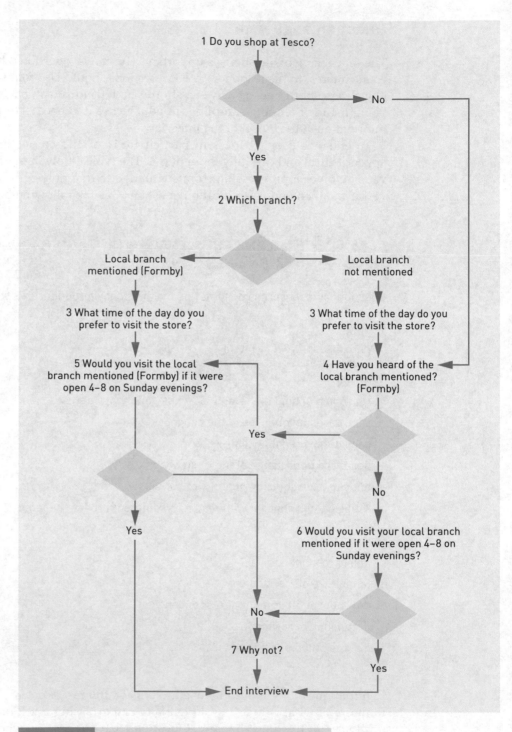

FIGURE 7.2   Flowchart for Sunday shopping questionnaire

from topic to topic. All questions relating to a particular topic should be asked before moving on to another topic, thus making it easy for the respondent to follow and develop a line of thought.

Flowcharts can help to highlight groups of questions that are relevant to some respondents and not to others. They aid in the sequencing and routeing of questions as well as in providing instructions to the interviewer (see Figures 7.2 and 7.3).

Sunday evening shopping

1 Do you shop at Tesco?

Yes ☐

No ☐

(If 'No' go to question 6)

5 Would you visit the local branch mentioned (Formby) if it were open 4–8 on Sunday evenings?

Yes ☐

No ☐

(If 'No' go to question 7

If 'Yes' end interview)

2 Which branch(es) do you use?

(SHOW CARD)

Formby ☐

Other (please state) ☐

_____

_____

_____

6 Would you visit your local store if it were open 4–8 on Sunday evenings?

Yes

No

(If 'Yes' end interview)

3 What time of day do you prefer to visit the store?

Mornings ☐

Lunchtime (12–2) ☐

Afternoons ☐

Evenings ☐

7 Why not?

_____

_____

_____

_____

_____

_____

_____

4 (Only ask this question if Formby is not indicated in the answer to question 2)

Have you heard of the local branch mentioned? (Formby)

No ☐

Yes ☐

(If 'No' go to question 6)

_____

_____

_____

_____

END INTERVIEW

FIGURE 7.3   Flow of questionnaire resulting from Figure 7.2

Funnelling and **inverted funnelling** are also important features of sequencing, although the approach is only really suitable for personal and telephone interviews. A **funnel sequence** is adopted when the respondent is assumed to possess some ideas about a topic. It refers to the procedure of asking the most general questions about the topic first, followed by successively more specific and restricted questions. Such an approach minimises the possibility that early questions will bias responses to later questions. It is a useful approach when the interviewer needs to ascertain the nature of the respondent's frame of reference.

EXAMPLE OF FUNNELLING

Questionnaire relates to assessing customer impressions of a new airline service.

1 What is your overall reaction to the new service we are operating from Manchester to Istanbul?

2 Do you find anything about the new service to your distaste?

3 Do you find the kind of in-flight entertainment to your taste?

Inverted funnelling moves from the specific to the general. Since this approach makes respondents consider certain specific points in reaching their evaluations, it is useful in those instances where the interviewer wishes to ensure that all respondents base their evaluations on similar factors. This approach works best where respondents are questioned about topics about which they have strong feelings.

Questionnaire layout

Questionnaires should be easy to use and encourage the user either to answer questions posed by an interviewer or to self-complete. A questionnaire that is badly presented or printed is likely to cause non-response or measurement error. Design considerations include:

- using good-quality paper
- keeping the body of the questionnaire as trim as possible
- using spacing to break up text and improve its presentation
- using different typefaces to assist reading
- adding colour to promote interest
- using routeing and/or branching instructions to guide a respondent
- making it easy for respondents to answer the questions.

Pretesting and revising a questionnaire

When they are first drafted, questionnaires often contain questions that are ambivalent, cumbersome and vague. Instructions may also be confusing: the questionnaire may be too long and questions that should have been included may have been omitted. The pretest is a means of discovering the faults in a questionnaire before it is administered. To pretest a questionnaire, a small subsample of the intended respondent group is selected: perhaps a dozen or so people. A good range of respondents is needed. The pretest can be run as a **debriefing** session or by using the protocol method.

Debriefing method

Here the questionnaire is presented to respondents in exactly the same manner as it would in a real study. After completing the questionnaire, respondents are asked about their thought processes while they were completing it and whether there were any problems with such items as routeing and branching instructions, understanding questions, and so on.

Protocol method

This involves respondents thinking aloud as the interview proceeds or as they fill in the questionnaire (**protocol analysis**).

In examining the findings of a pretest, particular attention should be given to ensuring that:

- The meaning of the questions is clear.
- The questions are easy to answer.
- The questions flow logically from one to another.
- The routeing/branching instructions are clear.
- The questionnaire is not too long.
- The questionnaire engages and retains the respondent's interest.

There are at least five considerations to be taken into account when conducting a pretest of the questionnaire:

1 All aspects of the questionnaire should be included, most specifically:
   - layout
   - question sequence
   - word meaning
   - question difficulty
   - branching instructions.

2 The pretest should be administered and conducted in an environment and context that is identical to the one to be used in the final survey.

3 The majority of the pretest interviews should be undertaken by regular staff interviewers. This should include experienced and relatively new interviewers.

4 Respondents in the pretest should resemble and be representative of the target population. This means that they should be familiar with the topic and possess similar characteristics, attitudes and opinions to those in the target population.

5 The size of the sample used for pretesting will depend on the variation of the target population. The more heterogeneous the target population, the larger the pretest sample required. And the more complex the questionnaire is, the larger the pretest sample should be.

Computer-assisted questionnaires

Computer-assisted programs can handle long and complicated questionnaires of practically any length and can also accommodate very large samples. They can also be personalised or seem to act in an intelligent manner. In the latter respect, answers from previous questions can be inserted automatically into the text of later questions. For instance, a questionnaire about computers may ask about whether the respondent has used any particular makes recently and ask him or her to name the makes. A later portion of the questionnaire may probe into each such computer experience and the program can be structured so that the name of each computer tried is inserted automatically into the questionnaire at the right point. Another useful feature is that the replies to an open-ended question are available to an interviewer for later access, if required. Any interview temporarily terminated at the respondent's request, for instance a telephone interview, can be rescheduled for completion at a later time.

INTRODUCING A QUESTIONNAIRE

Any questionnaire must be properly introduced to the respondent, whatever method of data collection is employed. Interviewers must introduce themselves to the respondent, indicating the purpose of the study and must establish their credentials. This is also true of postal questionnaires, where either the introductory part of the questionnaire must do this or else an accompanying letter must explain its purpose and benefits.

EXERCISE

Critique the questionnaire in Figure 7.4 relating to cycling in Mudchester and suggest how it might be improved. You should pay attention to the various points about questionnaire design and construction that have already been mentioned.

Mudchester cycle questionnaire

To help us to carry out our policy of improving conditions for cyclists in Mudchester, we should be grateful if you could complete this questionnaire.

A prepaid envelope is attached.

Thank you for your cooperation.

Q1 About you

Q1a What sex are you?   ☐ Male   ☐ Female

Q1b Age   ☐ 0–16   ☐ 17–24   ☐ 25–34

                                                    ☐ 35–44   ☐ 45–59   ☐ 60 plus

Q1c How long have you been cycling regularly in Mudchester?   ☐☐ years

Q1d How long have you been cycling altogether?   ☐☐ years

Q2 About your journey

Q2a How far have you cycled?   ☐ km

Q2b How long did it take you?   ☐ mins

Q2c What is the purpose of your journey?

    1 ☐ Work   2 ☐ Education   3 ☐ Shopping

    4 ☐ Leisure   5 ☐ Other   6 ☐ Not stated

Q2d Other (please specify)   _____

                                       _____

Q2e How many days a week do you cycle? ☐ days

Q3 Your opinion

Q3a Where do you/would you like to park your bicycle?

_____

_____

_____

Q3b What improvements do you think the Mudchester Council should make?

_____

_____

_____

_____

FIGURE 7.4   Mudchester cycle questionnaire

RELIABILITY AND VALIDITY IN QUESTIONNAIRE DESIGN

Reliability refers to the consistency in reaching the same results when the measurement is made over and over again. Validity refers to the degree to which the question measures what it is supposed to be measuring. While a valid measure is always reliable, a reliable measure is not necessarily a valid one. While pretesting, revision and further testing a questionnaire may increase its reliability, it will not necessarily increase its validity. One way to ensure that an instrument really does measure what it is supposed to measure is to compare the results with a 'yardstick' – an external measurement.

KEY POINTS ON QUESTIONNAIRE DESIGN, CONSTRUCTION AND PRETESTING

Preliminary considerations:

- information required
- nature of target respondents
- type of data-collection method required to survey the respondents

Questions:

- reason for asking each and every question
- clarity and conciseness in expression
- exclusivity of response choices
- use of natural, familiar language
- exclusion of bias in phraseology
- avoidance of double-barrelled questions
- alternatives to be stated explicitly
- reliability and validity of questions

Questionnaire construction:

- when to use open-ended as opposed to closed-ended questions
- determination of the appropriate number of response categories and their description in the case of closed-ended questions
- ensuring movement through the questionnaire from evaluative to diagnostic to classification type questions

Pretesting questionnaire

- ensuring all aspects of the questionnaire are tested
- pretesting in an environment and context identical to that which will be used in the final survey
- establishing a debriefing procedure

An assessment of the validity of factual answers usually requires the researcher to consult other sources of information, secondary data or census reports. Nevertheless, while a measure may have excellent validity in the descriptive sense at the time it was taken, it may possess poor validity in terms of its ability to accurately predict an outcome. In the time between the measurement and the actual event, many factors may have had an impact.

SUMMARY

Questionnaire design is a craft. Many factors have to be taken into account when assembling a questionnaire. These include such things as the overall research objectives, the kinds of data analysis that are to be employed, the amount of money that can be spent on the research project and the time in which the research has to be completed. There are no hard and fast rules about designing a questionnaire but there is a set of guidelines that can be followed to help overcome the risk of poor questionnaire design.

In this chapter we have examined issues in questionnaire design and construction. The major activities involved in questionnaire design are:

1 preliminary considerations

2 question content

3 question phrasing

4 types of response format

5 question sequence

6 question layout

7 pretest, revision and final version of the questionnaire.

The discussion emphasised general guidelines and suggested basic principles involved in asking questions. For questionnaire construction, attention was focused on response formats, logical flow and layout considerations. In discussing the pretesting of questionnaires, emphasis was placed on what items should be pretested, the manner in which the pretest should be conducted, who should be the respondents in the pretest and how large a sample is required for the pretest. Finally, attention was paid to establishing the reliability and validity of questionnaires.

QUESTIONS

1 In what contexts are questionnaires used in marketing research?

2 Explain the initial considerations that have to be taken into account before embarking on the construction of a questionnaire.

3 Select from the following list of open-ended questions those that would be better posed as closed-ended questions. Rewrite the ones you choose to make closed ended.

- Exactly how much is the journey going to cost?
- What are your favourite kinds of holiday?
- Where have you been in previous years for your holiday?
- How satisfied are you with your travel agent?
- Which day of the week do you prefer to travel?

4 Describe the two approaches to pretesting and revising a questionnaire. What are the five considerations that should be taken into account when undertaking a pretest?

5 Distinguish between reliability and validity in questionnaire design.

6 Here is a poorly worded set of questions attempting to establish how customers rate and perceive the products and services of a supermarket. The questions have to be answered by someone who has only a few minutes to spare while waiting at the till. Determine what the questions should be trying to elicit, cut down the number of questions asked and see if you can design a shorter questionnaire that will elicit the kind of information being sought.

Hand the completed questionnaire to the cashier as you leave.
Q1   What is your name?
Q2   How old are you?
Q3   Do you come here often?
Q4   What don't you like?

Q5   How much do you have to spend?

Q6   Would you come on Friday nights after 6 o'clock if you thought we were open?

Q7   Have you a car?

Q8   What do you think about the quality of our service?

Q9   Where do you go for your holidays?

Q10   Can you park your car all right?

Q11   Are the trolleys the right size?

Q12   Do you bring your children with you?

Q13   Have you any complaints?

Q14   Do you like our green products?

Q15   Do you not think that we should not close every other Sunday?

Q16   What is your sex?

Q17   How often do you come here?

Q18   Do you think this is a clean shop?

Q19   Do you think we should diversify?

Q20   What promotional offers would you like to see?

CASE STUDY 7.1: CENTRAL TRAINING COLLEGE (2)

In Case study 5.1, a consultant was called in to advise on the viability of opening a recruitment agency in central London. On the basis of initial discussions the consultant produced the following research proposal.

Research proposal

Summary of brief

1 To determine the viability of opening a recruitment agency in central London.

2 To determine if the Central Training College would be a good location.

3 To find out if the name Central Recruitment would be acceptable.

Proposed research objectives

1 Investigate current and future demand for recruitment agencies.

2 Investigate actual intentions to use the service.

3 Discover if the name of the recruitment agency is an important factor in the purchase decision.

4 Investigate student and business attitudes to the provision of such a service.

5 Obtain demographic details of both students and businesses interested in the service.

Proposed research design

Conduct two surveys, one of the students at the college and the other of the employers. Students to be interviewed face to face and the employers will be contacted by post.

Source: Fry[2]

Question

Produce a flowchart and questionnaires that could be used in this research.

CASE STUDY 7.2: THE RHOLAND WATCH COMPANY

Roland believes there is a growing and substantial market for mechanical and automatic wristwatches for both ladies and gentlemen. For the past five years he has produced and marketed watches with quartz movements under the label 'Rholand' using the Greek letter ρ as his trademark.

There is a large and growing market for second-hand mechanical and automatic watches and there is a growing number of 'houses' producing and marketing new models. Most of the major manufacturers now have a token item in their product line – at least as far as the men's wristwatch market is concerned. The new market for mechanical and automatic watches is made up as follows:

Segment 1

Watches usually priced at more than £2500 that do not contain expensive jewellery adornments such as diamonds. This tends to be a specialist market for the connoisseur. Long-established, well-known companies offering watches to this market include Jaeger, Blancpain, Breguet, Patek Philippe, Audemars Piguet, Girard Perregaux and Vacheron Constantin. A number of small, less well-known houses also produce for this market segment. They include Alan Silberstein, Daniel Roth and Frank Muller.

Segment 2

Watches priced between £1000 and £2500. This represents a fairly substantial market and is dominated by Rolex. Other competitors in this price segment include Bretling, which differentiates itself from Rolex by offering mechanical and automatic sports watches. Omega has a range of mechanical and automatic watches in this segment. A relative newcomer to the market, Chronoswiss, offers a range of connoisseur watches to this segment.

Segment 3

Watches priced between £500 and £1000. This represents a popular price range and there are many firms making offerings to this segment, including Eterna, Maurice Lacroix, Oris and Baume & Mercer. Many of the well-known 'mass-production' houses also have at least one offering to this segment. Included in the latter category are Longines and Ebel.

Segment 4

In this segment are found mechanical and automatic watches priced at between £150 and £500. Manufacturers such as Oris, Maurice Lacroix and Michel Herbelin have a presence here.

Segment 5

This segment comprises watches priced between £75 and £150. It has the interest of several small houses, including Claude Helier and Le Cheminant.

Segment 6

This is the cheapest section of the market where watches are priced at less than £75. At the top end of the segment are mechanical and automatic fashion models produced by Swatch along with utility models produced by Seiko. At the ultra cheap end of the market are models by Limit and Sekonda.

Only a few houses manufacture their own mechanical and automatic movements. The majority buy the movements from the Swiss Eta manufacturing company.

Roland would like to start producing and selling mechanical and automatic watches and has decided to survey his dealers and concessionaires for their opinions.

Question

Produce a flowchart and questionnaire that Roland could send to dealers and other intermediaries to help him decide what to do.

CASE STUDY 7.3: RESEARCHING THE SPORTS MARKET

Westbourne Research Consultants is a small market research consultancy based in the west of England. Recently it was approached by the local authority's Leisure and Amenities Department to solve a market research problem.

Leisure and Amenities had decided to conduct a survey of its own to find out the sports in which local people participated most frequently. It had conducted the research outside local sports centres and had come up with some surprising results; for one thing, it appeared that far more local people claimed to participate in sports than could be accounted for by the usage figures obtained from the sports centres themselves. Second, the researchers had the impression that respondents had had real difficulty answering some of the questions. These are the questions that proved problematical:

Q4: Why do you play your favourite sport?

Q8: How can sporting facilities be improved in the area?

Q12: What is your opinion of the Leisure and Amenities Department and why?

Q23: Who do you think should have the most say in deciding which new facilities can be developed?

In fact, the study seemed to be so flawed (and was proving so difficult to analyse) that the Leisure and Amenities Department wanted Westbourne to run a new research project altogether.

Westbourne's research manager asked Leisure and Amenities' management the following questions:

1 What are you hoping to gain from this research?

2 What management decisions will be based on the research?

3 Who are the people whose opinions you wish to canvass?

The managers of the Leisure and Amenities Department explained that the research aim was to improve their knowledge of the needs of the local population in terms of sports provision; they would be basing investment decisions on the results, particularly in the area of sports centre design and playing field provision; and they expected that a representative sample of the local population, including children and the elderly, should be included. In particular, Leisure and Amenities was interested in those people who rarely (or never) took part in sport, since there was a possibility that their needs were not being met at all by the present provisions.

Westbourne Research immediately identified a sampling problem: the original Leisure and Amenities survey had been conducted close to the sports centres and therefore the sample had contained a very high proportion of people who were either entering or leaving the centres. This sampling bias accounted for the very high proportion of people who participated in sport regularly, since clearly people who were entering or leaving the sports centre would be likely to participate in sport.

Leisure and Amenities had not pretested its questionnaire, which possibly accounted for some of the problems, but Westbourne immediately saw a need to redesign the questionnaire somewhat and rerun it. Unfortunately, Leisure and Amenities indicated that it had only very limited funds remaining; having spent considerable staff time on its own questionnaire, the management found it financially embarrassing (and embarrassing from a career viewpoint) to admit that the original study had gone wrong, and asked Westbourne if it could make any use at all of the data already collected.

Overall, Westbourne agreed that the original questionnaire was not entirely useless; apart from the questions already identified, the remainder of the questionnaire seemed to have been reasonably well designed and the researchers had no reason to doubt its worth. They agreed to seek ways to use the information in some way, in order to save costs.

(Case contributed by Jim Blythe)

Questions

1 What should Westbourne do to minimise the sampling bias?

2 How might Westbourne be able to comply with Leisure and Amenities' request to use some of the existing data?

3 What was wrong with the questions that could not be analysed?

4 What are the problems associated with designing a questionnaire to be completed by such a broad range of respondents?

5 What preparatory work should Westbourne do before redesigning the questionnaire?

CASE STUDY 7.4: ATTITUDES OF CAT OWNERS TO CAT FOOD

The following cover letter and questionnaire was made available for self-completion at numerous pet shops throughout the UK. The purpose of the survey was:

1 To identify cat owners' knowledge about the ingredients of cat foods and their cats' dietary requirements.

2 To discover what factors are most important in their choice of cat foods.

Rapid Research
Chester

Dear Cat Owner

This questionnaire is part of a research project on cat foods being conducted to (a) find out more about the feeding procedures followed by cat owners and (b) determine the attitude of cat owners towards existing cat food products. Your cooperation and participation in this study will enable cat food manufacturers to better meet your cat's food requirements. Your name is not required in this study since we are only interested in aggregate replies. Please complete the questionnaire at leisure and place it in the box provided at the checkout next time you visit the shop. Your immediate cooperation in this study will be greatly appreciated.
Sincerely,

Mark Twain
Enclosure

1. Precisely how many cats are there in your household? _____

2. Indicate each cat's breed and estimated value; then indicate the description that most closely describes the cat.

		Description of cat		
Breed	Estimated value	Show cat	Just a pet	Other
[1] _____
[2] _____
[3] _____
[4] _____

3. Indicate the percentage of each type of cat food and frequency with which you feed each type of food to your cat.

	Never 0%	Seldom 1–30%	Frequently 30–70%	Usually 70–90%	Always 90–100%
Table scraps	_____
Canned	_____
Dr	_____

4. Indicate the brands of cat food you presently use [e.g. Tucker's treats, Paws].

5. What is the major health benefit to your cat from each of the following ingredients? [Indicate 'don't know' if applicable.]

Vitamins	[i] Benefit_____	[ii] [ ] Value unknown
Minerals	[i] Benefit_____	[ii] [ ] Value unknown
Fats	[i] Benefit_____	[ii] [ ] Value unknown
Proteins	[i] Benefit_____	[ii] [ ] Value unknown
Carbohydrates	[i] Benefit_____	[ii] [ ] Value unknown

6. Which ingredients do you feel are the most important requirements in your cat's diet?

[ ] Carbohydrates [ ] Vitamins [ ] Minerals [ ] Proteins [ ] Fats [ ] Don't know

7. If you buy canned cat food, indicate how important each of the following factors is in your purchase.

	No influence	Some influence	Important	Very important
Price				
Content [% of meat, etc.]				
Brand name [e.g. Paws]				
Who makes it [e.g. Smith]				
Nutritional value of the cat food				

8. What type of meat do you think is generally used in most canned cat food?

_____ The same as we eat.

_____ Meat that has not been passed for human consumption.

_____ Inedible by-products [e.g. intestines, bones, etc.]

_____ Don't know

_____ Other

9. Do you think canned cat foods satisfy the dietary requirements of your cat?

[ ] Yes [ ] No [ ] Don't know

10. Do you think some breeds of cat require special cat food?

[ ] Yes [ ] No [ ] Don't know

11. Do you supplement your cat's diet with vitamin drops or pills?

[ ] Yes [ ] No [ ] Don't know

12. Who usually purchases your cat food?

_____ Husband

_____ Wife

_____ Children

13. How do you think canned cat food can be improved?

Question

What are the strengths and weaknesses of this questionnaire and cover letter?

REFERENCES AND NOTES

1　Morton-Williams, J and Sykes, W (1984) The use of interaction coding, *Journal of the Market Research Society*, 26(2), April.

2　Fry, C (1991) Unpublished MBA dissertation, Department of Management, Keele University, September.

FURTHER READING

Bolton, R (1991) An exploratory investigation of questionnaire pretesting with verbal protocol analysis, *Advances in Consumer Research*, 18, 558–65.

Booth-Kewley, S, Edwards, J E and Rosenfeld, P (1992) Impression management, social desirability and computer administration of attitude questionnaires: does the computer make a difference? *Journal of Applied Psychology*, 77(4), 562–66.

Churchill, G (1995) *Marketing Research: Methodological foundations* (6th edn), Fort Worth, TX: Dryden.

Foddy, W (1994) *Constructing Questions for Interviews and Questionnaires*, Cambridge: Cambridge University Press.

Hague, P (1987) Good and bad in questionnaire design, *Industrial Marketing Digest*, 12(3), 161–70.

Hague, P (1993) *Questionnaire Design*, London: Kogan Page.

Holtgraves, T, Eck, J and Lasky, B (1997) Face management, question wording and social desirability, *Journal of Applied Social Psychology*, 27(18), 1650–71.

Kalton, G and Schuman, H (1982) The effect of the question on survey responses: a review, *Journal of the Royal Statistical Society*, 145(1), 42–73.

Locander, W, Sudman, S and Bradburn, N M (1976) An investigation of interview method, threat and response distortion, *Journal of American Statistical Association*, 71, 269–75.

Morton-Williams, J (1978) Questionnaire design, in Worcester, R and Downham, J (eds) *Consumer Market Research Handbook*, Wokingham: Van Nostrand Reinhold.

Oppenheim, A N (1968, 1984) *Questionnaire Design and Attitude Measurement*, London: Heinemann.

Payne, S L (1951) *The Art of Asking Questions*, Princeton, NJ: Princeton University Press.

Tull, D S and Hawkins, D I (1990) *Marketing Research: Measurement and method*, New York: Macmillan.

Vinten, G (1997) The threat in the question, *Credit Control* 18(1), 25–31.

Wilkinson, S (1998) Focus group methodology: a review, *International Journal of Social Research Methodology*, 1(3), 181–203.

8 Qualitative research

Objectives

After reading this chapter, you should be able to:

- understand the nature and uses of focus groups

- understand the possible misuse of focus groups

- appreciate the techniques used in moderating group discussions

- understand the difference between focus groups used for consumer product research and those used for industrial research.

Keywords

cartoon test	industrial focus groups
clinical	moderator
depth interview	projective techniques
experiencing	teleconferencing
exploratory	videoconferencing
focus groups	word association
guide	

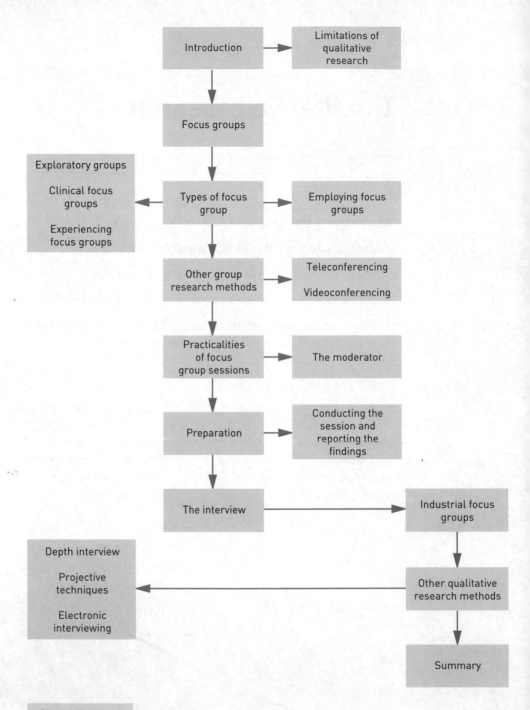

Plan of Chapter 8

INTRODUCTION

This chapter examines the nature and uses of **focus groups**, showing how this method of data collection can obtain information that is largely unavailable through other types of marketing research. Advice is offered about the possible misuse of focus groups, details of the techniques used in moderating group discussions are given and the distinction is made between focus groups used for consumer product research and those used for industrial research. Attention is also drawn to a variety of other qualitative research techniques, notably those relying on projective methods.

Qualitative research is a widely used term for research that does not subject research findings to quantification or quantitative analysis. Qualitative research examines the attitudes, feelings and motivations of product users. The contrast between qualitative research and quantitative research is shown in Table 8.1.

TABLE 8.1   Contrast between qualitative and quantitative research

Comparison dimension	Qualitative research	Quantitative research
Type of questions	Probing *explotary*	Non-probing
Sample size	Small	Large
Information per respondent	Much	Varies
Administration	Requires interviewer with special skills	Fewer special skills required
Type of analysis	Subjective, interpretive	Statistical
Hardware required	Tape recorders, projection devices, video, pictures, discussion guides	
Ease of replication	Difficult	Easy
Researcher training necessary	Psychology, sociology, social psychology, consumer behaviour, marketing, marketing research	Statistics, decision models, decision-support systems, computer programming, marketing, marketing research
Type of research	Exploratory	Descriptive or causal

Qualitative research is characterised by small samples and this has always been the focus of criticism. Executives are reluctant to base important strategy decisions on small-sample research because it relies so much on the subjectivity and interpretation of the researcher. Executives show a preference for a large sample with computer analysis and a summary table of results.

Despite the apparent preferences of executives, qualitative research has grown in popularity, for three reasons. First, it is usually much cheaper than quantitative research. Second, it produces a good mechanism for coming to an understanding of customer attitudes and motivations. Third, it can improve the efficiency of quantitative research.

Qualitative and quantitative research are often combined into a single study or series of studies. The patterns displayed in quantitative research can be enriched with the addition of qualitative information. Qualitative research combines with quantitative measures by providing a thorough understanding of the customer. The techniques of qualitative research involve open-ended questioning and the data are rich and often very revealing.

LIMITATIONS OF QUALITATIVE RESEARCH

Qualitative research does not pick out small differences quite as well as large-scale quantitative research. Nevertheless, qualitative research can detect minor problems that are not apparent in a quantitative study. Another limitation is that qualitative studies do not provide samples that are representative of the target population of the research. In terms of the sort of data produced, small sample size and free-flowing discussion can lead qualitative research projects along many different avenues of thought. Influential or dominant characters within a discussion group can also lead the group off on tangential discussions or bias the 'group view'. There is also the problem of the discussion leader's competence. The usefulness of qualitative research depends very much on the skills of the researcher.

BABY BOOMERS GET THE MESSAGE

Thirty years ago they were listening to the Beatles and enjoying the sixties after growing up in post-war austerity. Now, 45 to 55 year olds in the 'baby boomer' generation are looking at their circumstances and worrying about growing old in an increasingly insecure society.

That general conclusion comes from a study based on qualitative research into the attitudes of this group across 16 markets, including the USA, Japan, Australia, the UK and several countries in continental Europe. It carries strong marketing messages for those seeking to address this group, whose spending power outstrips its numbers. In the UK, for example, it makes up 14% of the population but accounts for almost one-quarter of household expenditure. In France, the 'boomers' account for 20% of spending on goods and services, while in the USA the figure is 17%.

Jane Gwilliam, author of the report, says there is a striking similarity not only in the cares and concerns expressed by the boomers across all the countries where they were questioned but also about the most effective ways to communicate with them.

The prime media for reaching the boomers are television and newspapers. They spend a substantial amount of leisure time at home and although they regard radio as more reliable than TV, the lack of 'grown-up commercial' stations makes it less relevant for advertising.

Most still take at least one newspaper a day, and are more inclined to pay attention to press advertisements than to inserts and flyers. While flyers and 'junk mail' are likely to go straight in the bin, the group seems to have a more positive attitude towards catalogues.

The study concludes that neither cinema nor sponsorship is particularly effective in marketing to boomers. That is partly because they spend so much time at home, but also because they fear their concerns will be ridiculed by the young.

Boomers' attitudes towards brands, as expressed in the study, are in sharp contrast to younger people's views. Gwilliam says that while young people value the brand name itself, and may buy the product without thinking about other brands, for boomers brand names are only as valuable as the goods and services they represent and are likely to have been chosen after other brands have been considered.

The research found that boomers do not like being patronised by advertising. According to Gwilliam, the boomers grew up with television and saw advertising evolve to become more sophisticated. They are therefore more discriminating and more alert to subtly patronising overtones than young people.

'I sometimes wonder whether a 30-year-old account manager really has an understanding of what boomers have gone through.'

Source: Smith[1] (reprinted with permission)

FOCUS GROUPS

A focus group comprises eight to twelve persons who are led by a **moderator** in an in-depth discussion on a particular topic or concept. The aim of focus group research is to learn and understand what people have to say about a topic and understand their arguments. The moderator has to get people to talk about a topic at length and in detail. The purpose is to discover how they feel about a product, concept, idea or organisation and how it forms part of their lives. The moderator wants to discover the amount of emotional involvement people possess with the topic under discussion.

Most marketing research companies use the focus group technique in consumer marketing research. It is often fairly easy to bring together a knowledgeable group of people who can discuss the topic of interest. However, the method is used much less among industrial goods companies: understandably, since the task of getting together executives covering such diverse areas as engineering, sales management or financial management is both costly and time-consuming.

The participants in the group have some common characteristics that relate to the topic discussed in the group. A focus group permits free discussion about a problem or topic and, guided by the moderator, participants' minds can range freely. Interaction with each other can produce ideas and suggestions that exhibit synergy.

A moderator has to keep a discussion alive and guide it towards a conclusion on which all participants can agree. Effective guiding, not leading, is what a good moderator must do. Discussion must be kept to a topic of interest to the sponsor. The sponsoring firm is paying for the exercise and expects relevant results. The

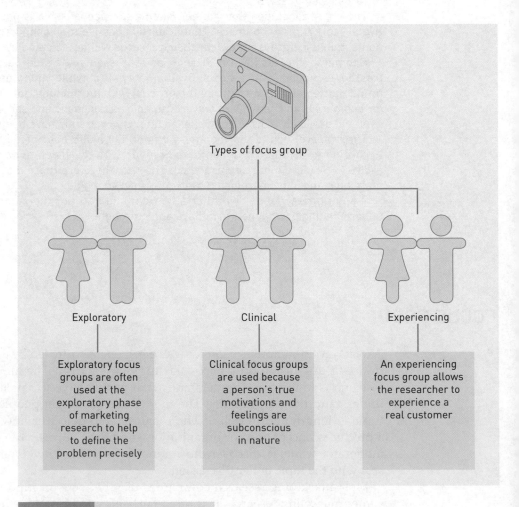

FIGURE 8.1   Types of focus group

moderator must move the group away from irrelevant discussion that is not helpful to the sponsor – and still leave the group free to air valuable new ideas.

Types of focus group

Exploratory groups

Focus groups are often used at the **exploratory** phase of marketing research to help to define the problem precisely (see Figure 8.1). For example, focus groups may be employed to identify the questions to be included in a survey. They may also be used to help generate hypotheses for testing. The various types of focus groups and their applications are summarised in Table 8.2.

Clinical focus groups

Clinical focus groups are used because a person's true motivations and feelings are subconscious. We cannot take at face value what many customers have to say and the research needs to probe beneath the level of consciousness. It is assumed

| TABLE 8.2 | Types of focus group and their characteristics |

Characteristics	Exploratory	Clinical	Experiencing
Experience a real consumer	No	No	Yes
Obtaining a high level of interaction among the group members is essential	No	Yes	Yes
When a homogeneous group of people is required	No	No	Yes
Moderator's interviewing technique is critical	No	Yes	No
Moderator must have scientific credentials	Yes	Yes	No
Observation by management is appropriate	No	No	Yes
Verbatim quotes should be emphasised in the reports	No	No	Yes

that a person's real motives can be uncovered using clinical judgement. The focus group provides data for clinical judgement and the moderator has to be highly skilled to persuade participants to reveal their inner thoughts and feelings.

SOME APPLICATIONS FOR FOCUS GROUPS

New product ideas

Focus groups can give the client firm ideas for new products. A gap in the market may be identified and further research can then seek to identify the true size of the potential gap in the market. If several focus groups should come up with the same idea it may well be worth serious consideration, even though it may have been considered before and rejected. It may be possible to adjust costs, for example, so that profitability is more positive.

Focus groups can indicate the likelihood of success with a new product. It would be possible, for example, to test the concept of a new product for the current market. You would seek answers to questions such as:

- What would be its advantages?
- Would people accept the drawbacks of the product?
- How does the idea compare with other products?
- What is the reaction of the group to various product features?
- What does the group think about the product's performance capabilities?

Problems with decreasing sales

When sales have declined rapidly on certain products, focus groups can help uncover the reasons. The products, for example, might seem to be doing the job they were intended to do, but other problems might become apparent. Minor inadequacies in product design or packaging can cause customers to switch to competitors' products. A focus group can be given several competitors' products to examine (without identification) and their positive and negative comments about the products can then be noted.

Price

In a time of inflation or recession, a producer may be looking for ways to cut costs and lower prices. Unnecessary product features may need to be eliminated. Focus groups can be used to identify these unnecessary features.

Customer attitudes

Focus groups can uncover consumer attitudes towards the sponsoring firm sufficiently to warrant further research that can lead to beneficial and remedial action.

Experiencing focus groups

An **experiencing** focus group allows the researcher to experience a real customer. It gives the researcher an opportunity to experience the emotional framework in which the product is being used. Effectively, the researcher can ascertain all the satisfactions, disatisfactions, rewards and frustrations experienced by the actual customer when the product is used.

Employing focus groups

Focus groups provide data about problems through the mechanism of group dynamics. By talking among themselves and with a moderator, a relatively small group of interested people can produce more valuable thoughts and ideas than if each participant were interviewed separately. Nothing is quite the same as what can happen when a group interested in a topic or a product sit around a table for one to two hours discussing how they feel about it. In terms of bringing out suggestions, an experienced moderator can produce a degree of interaction and cooperation that produce unanticipated ideas.

Focus groups are unique: they can explore customary ways of doing things or customary beliefs and possible reactions to something new. They can try to determine why such conditions and reactions exist and what can be done to change them. Focus groups can highlight attitudes, prejudices, changing ways of using products and changing ways of viewing pricing and distribution.

OTHER GROUP RESEARCH METHODS

While the typical focus group still involves around seven to thirteen participants, a moderator, an agenda for discussion, a room equipped with a one-way mirror in which sponsors may listen and watch, suitable electronic equipment and chalkboards, there have recently been new ideas and new techniques. For example, Option Technologies Inc. offers a system incorporating the following.

A group of people, often a focus group, generates a list of items relevant to the topic under discussion. The list is entered into a computer and the system generates a systematic set of questions about the list that is projected onto a large-screen monitor. This provides a visual stimulus for group members to register their opinions. Participants vote on individual, handheld keypads linked to the computer, which organises the votes into graphics that are fed back to the group by a projection system. Participants orally interpret the meaning of their opinions as projected on the monitor. Group discussion clarifies the issues under research and leads to a systematic and organised basis for further research.[2]

Teleconferencing

Respondents are invited to participate in a group telephone discussion on a specific day, at a specific time. At that time they are contacted at their office or home anywhere in the country over a telephone conference system (hence, **tele-conferencing**). The moderator guides the discussion using techniques designed to create maximum interaction between the participants. The sponsor can give inputs to the moderator's assistant without being heard by the participants. The session lasts for about an hour and a half and provides about as much information as a two-hour face-to-face session.

Videoconferencing

In different locations, usually different parts of the country, groups gathered around tables are asked to sample new or improved products. Video cameras and microphones are installed at the locations (hence, **videoconferencing**). Executives at remote locations are able to watch and hear the groups and can speak to the moderator, sharpening up the direction the group discussion is taking.

All these systems have their strengths and weaknesses. Using the telephone obviously allows hard-to-reach experts to be involved in the research, since they do not have to leave their homes or offices. Each participant can hear all the others and each has a chance to contribute without being identified. The sponsor can listen in on the actual session or later via a tape recording. However, face-to-face groups offer the opportunity for more personal contact – and perhaps the group dynamic works better when all the participants are seated around the table and can see each other. Facial reactions and visible muscular reactions often tell us what the participant is thinking more clearly than words, and other participants can and do react to these signs.

MARKETING RESEARCH AND INNOVATION

There is a danger in relying too heavily on research during the creative process. Hugh Seymour-Davies, a director of Innovation and Development, a new product development company that commissions much marketing research, argues that novel ideas do not come from market research. In his view the consumer can only give a retrospective response about what they use and how it influences their buying decisions. The point is echoed in a slightly different way by John Boult, a director of industrial design company Product First. He argues that research cannot design a new product, but it can act as a catalyst and indicate the direction the innovation should take.

Innovation and Development use two different research techniques to deal with new product innovations. Market researchers are commissioned through Innovation and Development's clients to run consumer discussion groups. During these sessions participants may be 'fooled' into thinking a product idea already exists by being presented with fake newspaper clippings describing it. In this way the researchers discover what consumers like and dislike about the idea.

Discussion groups are also used to prompt representative consumers to fantasise about new products. A skilled discussion leader is required in these situations as eliciting such responses from research consumer groups is an art. It is very easy for such discussion groups to fizzle with embarrassment and awkwardness rather than sizzle with ideas. With an experienced group leader and a productive session, the respondents give the product development specialists clues about possible new product developments.

However, one of the biggest problems in using discussion group feedback is interpreting exactly what consumers mean. When Innovation and Development was working on new product development for Cadbury's chocolate cream liqueur, it included a hint of hazelnut flavouring to give the drink a unique flavour. When the researchers verbally suggested that the liqueur should have this slight flavouring, consumers reacted negatively as they were not used to the idea of mixing the two flavours. However, when taste tests were conducted, without revealing what the extra flavours were, consumers loved the chocolate liqueur laced with hazelnut.

Source: *Marketing*[3]

PRACTICALITIES OF FOCUS GROUP SESSIONS

Seven to twelve participants is ideal. With fewer than seven, there is not enough interplay to provide worthwhile information. It is difficult to work with larger groups, for under such circumstances one or two people tend to dominate the conversation and the discussion is difficult to control.

The group of participants should have enough knowledge of and experience with the type of problem to produce meaningful ideas and reactions.

The participants must feel they are taking part in something that is both worthwhile and interesting, that they are contributing to the solution of the sponsor's problem. Payments to the respondents are perfectly in order and necessary to get a good representative group together.

The moderator

The role of the moderator in a focus session is to get the best and most innovative ideas about the focal problem from the group. The moderator must bring the session to a close with suggestions that will be of value to the sponsor in guiding further research or further thinking.

SUGGESTED CHARACTERISTICS OF A MODERATOR

- Be acceptable to the group as a person with whom they can work easily.

- Have a quick mind capable of noting new ideas that come from the group and pressing for further discussion, even though it may mean leaving the fixed agenda.

- Have a good memory for names. Group dynamics will flourish if each participant can feel the importance of what they are saying and thinking. This is reinforced when participants are known by their names.

- Have the prestige and ability to control a group if it wanders, bringing it back to the topic under discussion without appearing to dominate unduly. The moderator must also be able to recognise the importance of new ideas that were not expected but appear significant.

- Be as neutral as possible.

The moderator should be selected with the particular problem in mind. Selecting a moderator who has no interest in or knowledge of the subject would be pointless: they might easily miss some good ideas that arise unexpectedly from the group.

Preparation

Groups should be carefully screened to get the best people for the problem under discussion. The moderator and the sponsor should manage the choice of participants in the group. The most valuable thoughts and ideas arise when a group is fairly homogeneous. Usually, more than three groups discussing the same problem will add very little, although if there are known or suspected regional differences, for example, more than three may be necessary. It may often be advisable to form the different groups by age and sex.

DISCUSSION GUIDE FOR ACCEPTABILITY OF A NEW PRODUCT CONCEPT

1 *Warm up*

- Explain focus groups.

- No correct opinions – only opinions.

- Need to hear from everyone.

- Associates are watching from behind the mirror. They are very interested in the group's opinions.

- Audiotapes – so notes are not necessary.

- One person to talk at a time. No side discussions or some important comments will be missed.

- No questions to the moderator. What they know is unimportant.

- Participants not to worry if they don't know much about the topic. If there are different views in the group that is also important to know.

- No one will contact participants after the session.

- Any questions?

2 *What comes to mind when this product concept is mentioned?*

- Likes and dislikes?

- Problems?

- Changes you would like to see?

- How do you feel about current brands available?

- What are your likes and dislikes about them?

- How would you change them?

- Do you use more than one brand? What alternatives do you use? Why did you choose those particular brands?

- What factors are important in determining the brands you do use?

3 *Present a description of the new product concept. Ask how the group feels about it*

- How many of you would consider using this product?

- Why do you say that?

- What do you like or dislike about it?

- Do you see any distinct advantages in this product over the brands you are currently using?

- How would you expect this product to be priced?

- Use of product, frequency of purchase, etc. need to be explored next: expand on this example.

4 *Give them the opportunity for final questions and comments*

5 *Thank them for their cooperation*

Preparation of the moderator's **guide** should be a joint effort of the sponsor, the agency (if one is involved) and the moderator. It should contain open, non-leading questions designed to stimulate thinking and discussion. Such questions might not be used verbally at all; rather, they may serve as a reminder to the moderator of matters the sponsor wants to be covered.

The moderator's guide should consider the types of participant in the group – their knowledge and experience. It should not show bias or reflect already formed opinions and should be developed with the counsel of those people who will have to implement the findings of the research study. All interested parties are responsible for making sure that everything pertinent is included in the guide, which should also contain suggestions on the timing of the session.

The client firm should ensure that the moderator understands the problem and the importance of the findings of each session. The moderator should be guided in preparation for the various directions in which the discussion may go. This does not mean that the moderator should prejudge how the discussion should or should not go. The moderator must know enough about the industry and the problem to recognise the unexpected and valuable points that may be aired.

Most professional research firms that offer focus group sessions will have a room dedicated for the purpose. The room will include one-way mirrors so that the client may watch and listen without being seen. It will contain chalkboards, a decent sized table, appropriate television and projection equipment and pads and pencils for taking notes.

Conducting the session and reporting the findings

A useful aid to the moderator is the provision of name cards. Initially, there should be a brief discussion of the ground rules for the session. The moderator tells the group about its purpose, stating that the sponsoring firm looks forward to the group's discussion on this topic as an aid in deciding a crucial matter. The use of a one-way mirror should be explained to the participants. There may be a brief account of who the sponsoring firm is, what it does and why problems such as these make so much difference. Some mention should also be made of how the results of the session will be used. The participants then usually introduce themselves with a few brief remarks.

The moderator's guide should be used to steer participants into discussion of the areas the sponsor wants covered. It should not be necessary for the moderator to spend time merely asking questions and receiving answers. Participants should be encouraged to voice their thoughts without prodding. A well-chosen moderator will be experienced enough to draw out the quiet ones and to quiet the talkative. At the end of the discussion, the moderator should summarise the group's suggestions, ideas and attitudes.

It can be difficult to record informal interviews. Should the interviewer record everything that the respondents say, record only those remarks that are considered relevant or should the respondents' answers be paraphrased? The last two procedures introduce the danger of interviewer bias, so in most cases the verbatim report is probably the best solution.

Tape recording is particularly useful in informal interviews as long as none of the respondents objects. The use of tape recorders permits the recording of everything that respondents say, thus enabling the interviewer to concentrate on the interview. On average it may take two to three times as long to transcribe tapes as it does to record the conversation. Thus an hour-long interview may take two to three hours to transcribe. In transcribing the tapes, everything that the interviewer and the respondents say has to be written down. However, when writing up transcriptions, views, attitudes and factual answers may be put into a logical order for the ease of the reader.

The debriefing and wrap-up should be carried out immediately after the session. Strong points can be emphasised and errors noted while they are fresh in everyone's minds. Debriefing and wrap-up can also come after the conclusion of a number of sessions on the same research problem. Here the emphasis will be on those ideas and attitudes that were common to all groups. There may be a written or video screen report, which should emphasise all the important attitudes and issues expressed by one or more of the groups. The report should also recommend further necessary research.

Formal written reports can take on one of several formats according to the client's needs, the researcher's style and what was formally agreed on in the research proposal. At one extreme, the investigator can prepare a brief impressionistic summary of the main findings, relying mainly on memory. This type of report is often used with experiencing groups, where the main objective is for the clients to experience real customers. The client can retain the tape recordings of the sessions and listen to the groups several times to become immersed in what the customers are saying. At the other extreme, the researcher listens to the tapes, copying down salient quotations and fitting the participants' thoughts into a more general scheme derived from the research objectives and the researcher's training.

A method lying between the two extremes and, indeed, the most common method, is often called the cut-and-paste technique. It lacks the in-depth psychological analysis of the clinical report, but still requires considerable skill and insight on the part of the researcher. The first step is to have the group sessions transcribed. Next, the researcher reviews the transcripts, looking for common threads or trends in response patterns. Similar patterns are then cut out and matched between the groups. The researcher then produces folders containing relevant material by subject matter.

The last step is to write the actual report: the introduction describing the purpose of the research, the major questions the researcher sought to answer, the nature and characteristics of the group members and how they were recruited. This is followed by a two- or three-page summary of findings and recommendations. The report concludes with the main body of findings.

INDUSTRIAL FOCUS GROUPS

Focus groups that deal with industrial research problems are much like those covering consumer products, but with several important differences. First, the moderator must be knowledgeable in the field being discussed. Most moderators know about fast-moving consumer goods or shopping in supermarkets, but not all of them know enough about machine tools to conduct a discussion with a group of technicians and engineers. The screening of possible moderators in industrial areas must be even more thorough than for those in consumer product areas.

Preparing the moderator and the moderator's guide about the industrial problem must also be very thorough. It may be advisable to have an in-house moderator lead the discussion, or at least to have one in the room to help the moderator with difficult technical points. The participants in **industrial focus groups** must also be carefully chosen to make sure that each can speak about the problem. Time considerations are important: a group of people will become impatient if a session runs over time or becomes too wordy and repetitive.

OTHER QUALITATIVE RESEARCH METHODS

Depth interview

Historically, the term **'depth interview'** has meant a relatively **unstructured** one-to-one **interview**. The interviewer is thoroughly trained in the skill of probing and eliciting detailed answers to each question. Sometimes psychologists are used in depth interviews. They use clinical non-directional techniques to uncover hidden motivations.

> ### SOME ADVANTAGES OF DEPTH INTERVIEWS RELATIVE TO FOCUS GROUPS
>
> 1 Group pressure is eliminated so that each respondent reveals more honest feelings.
>
> 2 The personal one-to-one situation gives the respondent the feeling of being the focus of attention, whose personal thoughts and feelings are important and genuinely wanted.
>
> 3 The respondent attains a heightened state of awareness in a personal interview because they are in constant rapport with the interviewer and there are no group members to hide behind.

4 The extra time devoted to individual respondents encourages the revelation of new information.

5 Respondents can be probed at length to reveal the feelings and motivations that underlie their statements.

6 Without the restrictions of cultivating a group process, new directions of questioning can be improvised more easily. Individual interviews allow greater flexibility in exploring casual remarks and tangential issues, which may provide critical insights into the main issue.

7 The closeness of the one-to-one relationship allows the interviewer to become more sensitive to non-verbal feedback.

The direction of the depth interview is guided by the interviewee's response. As the interview progresses, the interviewer thoroughly probes each answer and uses the replies as a basis for further questioning.

The success of any depth interview depends entirely on the interviewer. A second factor that determines the success of depth research is correct interpretation. The unstructured nature of the interview and the clinical nature of the analysis increases its complexity.

Projective techniques

Projective techniques are sometimes incorporated in depth interviews. The origins of projective techniques lie in the field of clinical psychology. In essence, the objective of any projective test is to delve below the surface responses in order to obtain true feelings, meanings or motivations. The rationale behind projective tests comes from knowledge that people are often reluctant to, or cannot, reveal their deepest feelings. In other instances they are unaware of those feelings because of psychological defence mechanisms.

Projective tests are techniques for penetrating a person's defence mechanisms and allowing their true feelings and attitudes to emerge. A subject is usually presented with an unstructured, nebulous situation and asked to respond. Because the situation is ill-defined and has no true meaning, the respondent must use their own frame of reference to answer the question. In theory, the respondent projects their feelings into the unstructured stimulus. Because the subjects are not talking directly about themselves, defence mechanisms are purportedly bypassed. The interviewee is talking about something else or someone else, yet revealing their own inner feelings in the process.

The most commonly applied projective tests used in marketing research are **word association** tests, sentence and story completion, **cartoon tests**, third-person techniques and analogies.

Word association tests

Word association tests are used to select brand names, advertising campaign themes and slogans (see Chapter 6 for an explanation of the test).

Sentence and story completion

These can be used in conjunction with word association tests. The respondent is furnished with an incomplete story or group of sentences and asked to complete them (see Chapter 6 for more information).

Cartoon tests

Cartoon tests create a highly projective mechanism by means of cartoon figures or strips, similar to those in comic books. They can be used to measure the strength of an attitude towards a particular product or brand (see Chapter 6 – thematic apperception test – for more information).

Third-person techniques

Perhaps the easiest projective techniques to apply, other than word association, are third-person techniques. Rather than asking someone directly what they think, it is couched as 'your neighbour' or 'some people' or some other third party. Rather than asking a housewife why she does not typically provide a nutritionally balanced breakfast, a researcher would ask, 'Why don't many housewives provide their families with nutritionally balanced breakfasts?' The third-person technique is often used to avoid issues that might be embarrassing or evoke hostility if answered directly by a respondent.

Analogies

The use of analogies helps us to reveal people's inner feelings. For example, a person may buy a car to suit their personality. Through the purchase, the person is able to express their personality and thereby benefit. The use of the 'personal analogy' technique can sometimes enable researchers to uncover the relationship between people's personalities and potential purchase objects, such as a car.

We all have emotions and feelings. The personal analogy mechanism harnesses the use of our emotions and feelings in order to obtain insights into how people perceive decisions or problems. The idea is to identify ourselves with a non-human object that is the subject of the problem. We have to transfer our own feelings into the entity, imagine how it might feel and act in the problem situation.

For example, we might be asked to imagine what it would feel like to be a new BMW. Answers might be:

- 'I feel powerful.'

- 'I feel extremely fit and raring to go.'

- 'I feel ready for my new executive owner.'

Based on such an analysis it might then be possible to develop advertising themes to aim at specific customer groups. Through such a technique, we can release ourselves from looking at a problem in terms of its previously analysed elements.[4]

Electronic interviewing

Electronic interviewing is a method that can be used for both one-to-one inter-views and focus groups, and offers practical advantages. In the first place it is not constrained by geographical locations or time zones and, second, electronic inter-viewing requires no additional transcription. Not only does this save money but it can also eliminate errors introduced through transcription. Third, electronic interviewing diminishes the problem of interviewer effect. It can also reduce problems caused by dominant or shy participants, particularly in electronic focus groups.

The skills required to conduct online discussions are different skills for both the interviewer and the subject since lack of verbal communication can be a prob-lem. Often tacit information that would be conveyed in a conventional interview situation will be lost in electronic conversations. Non-verbal communication and active listening are essential elements of effective interviewing. No doubt, as tech-nology progresses and videocam equipment becomes commonplace, even some non-verbal communication will be transportable.

SUMMARY

This chapter has examined the nature and uses of focus groups, showing how this method of data collection can obtain information that is largely unavailable through other types of marketing research. Advice has been offered about the possible misuse of focus groups and detail of the techniques used in moderating group discussions has been described. The distinction between focus groups used for consumer product research and those used for industrial research has been made. Attention has also been drawn to a variety of other qualitative research techniques, notably those relying on projective methods. Finally, consideration has been given to a new way of collecting qualitative data through the medium of electronic interviews.

QUESTIONS

1 What are focus groups? What is their purpose? Outline the different types of focus group. Discuss the kind of problems where focus groups may be able to provide useful insights.

2 What is the moderator's guide? What does it contain and how is it used?

3 Indicate the important points that should be made when briefing a moderator.

4 What are the important points to bear in mind about industrial focus groups?

5 What are depth interviews and what is their purpose? What advantages and limitations do they have when compared with focus groups?

6 Explain the nature of projective techniques.

CASE STUDY 8.1: AVON COSMETICS

Some important questions about consumers that need to be answered in the cosmetics industry include:

- Do women buy cosmetics to cover up or to enhance what nature has provided?
- Do women have different wants and needs as far as cosmetics are concerned?
- What kind of advertising gimmicks are likely to be most effective?
- Is there an element of fantasy in buying and using cosmetics?

Glamour appeal in the advertising of cosmetics products to women usually features the faces of attractive celebrities or good-looking young women. Nevertheless, the advertising agency handling Avon's account maintains this is not what women want to see. Avon's group marketing communications manager believes that 'real beauty' comes from the inside and the company is intent on reflecting this in its advertising strategy.

In an attempt to modernise its image, Avon is developing two important themes in its advertising. First, it wants to show that the products it has to offer are for 'real women' and, second, it wants to show that it appreciates the nature of female friendship. After all, many of Avon's 160,000 representatives make most of their sales to friends.

Avon's target audience is essentially women over 25 and under 50, positioned in the mid-market. Its main competitors are Boots and Body Shop. Avon's approach is novel: it challenges the traditionally accepted notions of women's attractiveness. The managing partner of the agency handling the account was quoted as saying that the advertisements spurned the way in which imagery was associated with cosmetic products and, in particular, 'the preying on women's feelings of inadequacy'. He argued that cosmetics were not about hiding inadequacies but rather about making the best of what women have.

In an attempt to bring female friendship and 'real women' into the advertising, one advertisement presents two friends talking about a new romance, along with the 'great for kissing' lipstick with moisturiser. In another advertisement an upset young mother, seeing her child off to school for the first time, is featured. In the latter advertisement a friend offers her a tear-proof mascara. Friendship and 'realness' are also emphasised in press advertisements, where genuine friends are featured talking about each other. The actresses used in sequences have the appearance of 'real women'.

Source: Nicholas[5]

Question

What kind of qualitative research do you think might have been used in this instance?

CASE STUDY 8.2: IBM

'Butterfly was great technology, but very expensive to implement,' according to a Dell spokesman.

IBM's extensively praised Butterfly expandable notebook keyboard design seems ready to die shortly after emerging from its chrysalis and IBM have no plans to replace it. The product was considered an important advance in portable PC design when it appeared in IBM's Think Pad 701C in March 1995 since it offered a reasonable sized keyboard in a sub-A4 system. However, its high price is thought to have reduced anticipated sales and the appearance of larger screens than the 701C's 10.4" display have allowed notebook manufacturers to produce very slim A4 or slightly larger designs which allow more room for keyboard space.

Source: PC Direct[6]

Question

Is marketing research really of any value to a firm such as IBM when it comes to designing new PCs?

 ## CASE STUDY 8.3: MULLER

Muller, a successful German yoghurt brand, established a UK operation in 1987, launching its two brands Muller Fruit Corner and Muller Crunch Corner into the UK market the following year. By 1990 the brand had captured more than 10% of the UK yoghurt market, becoming market leader ahead of the previously domin-ant Ski brand from Eden Vale. In 1993 the brand was the clear market leader with a share of 23%. Sales increased from around £75m in the UK in 1992, to over £100m in 1993.

An important tenet of Muller's success was its adoption of a marketing approach contrary to the style used by existing yoghurt brands in the UK. While many other yoghurt brands emphasised health issues such as low fat, live bacteria and real fruit, Muller brought new momentum to the market with a product that was high in calories and sold as an indulgence product. In 1993 Joanna Lumley was used in the £5m 'pure and sinful' campaign that was seen by industry commentators as a welcome break from the 'squeaky clean' yoghurt marketing campaigns of the past. Muller also sponsors Aston Villa football club.

The rest of the market soon followed Muller's lead: there have been recent launches of 'twin-pot' yoghurt by own-label suppliers and other brands, as well as an increase in yoghurts marketed as indulgence treats rather than as a means of abstaining from calories.

Source: Samways and Whittcome[7]

Question

What kind of marketing research might have led Muller to adopt a strategy that was contrary to the style used by existing yoghurt brands in the UK?

 ## CASE STUDY 8.4: BRAND VALUATION

The brand acts as a focus for all marketing activities; consumers identify with brands and have a mental image of what the brand means not only in terms of its utilitarian values, but also in terms of intangible values such as prestige, value for money or self-image. For example, research shows that in blind taste tests most people prefer Pepsi Cola to Coca-Cola, but when they are able to see the can or bottle (and hence identify the brand) most people prefer the Coke.

For many years, managers have recognised that such brands have a value that is independent of the physical product and most firms have tried (for internal accounting purposes) to place a value on the 'goodwill' generated by the brand itself. Unfortunately, the accounting methods used have varied from one firm to another, which has led to problems when a firm wishes to sell a brand or when the company is being valued for tax purposes or for shareholders' reports.

During 1999 a new accounting standard was introduced in the UK for the valuation of brands. For many years, standards have existed for the valuation of such intangibles as goodwill and patents, but until now no agreed method has been in place for measuring the value of a brand.

For many companies, this is a major breakthrough in asset valuation; it has been estimated that brands and intellectual property make up 96% of the total value of the Coca-Cola Corporation, 95% of the value of Microsoft, and even for heavy industrial corporations such as BP the figure may be as much as 74%.

Shell Oil realises the importance of the brands. Simon Saville, global brand manager for Shell International, says: 'For some years Shell has tracked the health of its brand through market research surveys in key countries. We are extending this to include a tracking of brand value on an annual basis. In order to estimate the Shell brand value, we must first understand how that value is derived: why customers buy our products and services, what they prefer about Shell, and how important this is to them in their purchase decisions.'

Brand value is an important part of franchising and licensing negotiations, and most firms recognise that they are managing an asset which has value. Investment in promoting the brand will increase its value, and having an accounting standard for valuing brands means that marketing managers are better able to argue their case for more investment in the brand, even with the most traditional of finance managers.

For finance managers, the main purpose of brand valuation is to establish a more accurate balance sheet; brands as assets can be included and the finance managers know that other firms are using the same valuation methods. From a marketing management viewpoint, the main purpose of brand valuation is to see the trend over time, rather than to establish an absolute valuation figure. This allows the manager to control what is happening to the brand, perhaps by increasing investment in it or (if the brand's value is low) reducing investment. In the absence of agreed methods for valuing, firms have been operating with a degree of uncertainty, according to many managers.

On the other hand, Alex Batchelor (brand valuation director of consultants Interbrand Newell & Sorrell) says: 'Brand valuation is very much like business valuation with a couple of tweaks. Sure, there are judgements in it but there are judgements in everything. The accounting profession has done a wool-pulling act where people think it's a perfect science when it is not.'

The new accounting standard draws a distinction between intangible assets that have a limited life (for example most patents) and those that have an indefinite life (which would be true of many brands). The standard defines limited life as being less than 20 years. In practice, market research has a major role to play in the valuation of brands, because the consumer's view of the brand will determine not only whether the brand will be purchased during the next few years, but whether the brand is robust enough to survive in the very long term.

Whichever methods marketers use to determine the brand value, it seems that the new accounting standard will not only add more rigour to the estimates, but will also help to focus the minds of managers more keenly on brand management issues.

(Case contributed by Jim Blythe)

Questions

1 How might qualitative research be used to value brands?

2 What methods could be used to determine the most effective routes for investing in brands?

3 What differences in research approach would be needed to meet the differing needs of brand managers and finance managers?

4 How might the robustness of a brand be measured?

5 How might the objectiveness and accuracy of qualitative research into brand valuation be ensured?

CASE STUDY 8.5: HI-FI SYSTEMS

Marketers often seem to be inordinately fond of the word 'new'. Newness appears to be a desirable feature of products, yet the word is difficult to define – is it about freshness or about novelty? Does it refer to something that the particular manufacturer has not made before, does it refer to something that has been brought in from another industry or does it refer to something that the consumer has never seen before? These questions have crucial importance to high-tech industries such as consumer electronics and photography.

Hi-fi purchase involves a substantial investment on the part of the customer. Apart from the obvious monetary cost of buying a top-of-the-range system (which is counted in thousands of pounds rather than hundreds) hi-fi buffs (or audiophiles) are often highly involved in the product purchase. This means that their choice of hi-fi system reflects on them as individuals; they naturally want to be seen with the latest, most technically advanced system as well as have a system that sounds good and lasts.

It appears that the audiophiles' perception of 'newness' of the equipment is a factor and research was conducted by a UK university to find out how consumers judge newness in hi-fi equipment. Several focus groups were invited to examine three hi-fi systems and comment on which was the most innovative and why. The groups were allowed to examine the equipment, play CDs on it and (of course) discuss what they thought about the equipment. The focus groups were recorded on video tape and full transcripts of everything that was said were made; a separate analysis was carried out on the movement and body language of the focus group members and the ways they used the equipment.

The following is a brief extract from the transcripts of one of the focus groups (note that this group was composed entirely of males aged 20 to 25):

Which is the most innovative?

Hard to tell unless, you know, unless you study the brochures.

You'd go for the looks.

But it isn't only looks is it?

But it's innovative design, but like you said earlier, that's been around. You've seen that for absolutely years.

Saying that, that's a new colour, whether it'll take off . . .

The thing is we're not going to find out which is the most innovative unless we read the manuals.

But then I don't understand the jargon they use anyway.

But this one's got this tape thing. I like the tape-to-tape thing.

This one's innovative with the size; they're making them even smaller than that nowadays.

Compared to this one, yeah.

But then you could add to it.

Well, I think I can solve the problem.

This one's more innovative because of the size and because it's more compact and that. They're making them even smaller than that nowadays.

I'm not too sure about these small buttons.

I don't like the small buttons.

The thing is you can't have a small system with really big buttons.

But this has gone too far the other way; with these they're almost pin size.

But with a remote control you just sort of sit there and press that.

But half the time I don't understand the remote control either.

I reckon this one's more innovative, then.

Yeah, but are you going on looks alone?

Yeah, it is swaying me a bit but no. Like the fact that it's more compact and everything, you're going into smaller things now, all your microchips and everything.

That's all we can say really because we don't know about the sound and that.

But if I went into a shop and they, um . . .

That one's more fuddy-duddy, this one's more modern and probably people see that as being more innovative.

There's a record player option on it.

If you go into a shop and they have stacks of stuff there you'd just like listen, I wouldn't know, I wouldn't have a clue which would be the best sound for me really. And the ones that sounded best to me might not be the ones that have the bass and everything on.

I don't like it not being adjustable.

I'd go for this one, I'd go for the adjustable one.

This one looks like the one I've got, five, six or seven years old.

That's quite an old one, isn't it.

Whereas this, this one uses computer interfacing which is quite different.

That's right, yes.

So this one must be more innovative, if it's using digital impulses.

Yeah, very right.

Why, what's the point?

Is it just to cut down . . .

Yeah, that is more innovative.

There are design functions that I like. I like the drawer, I think that's brill, but some of the gimmicks to me are useless, like this search and find a tape thing. I wouldn't use that at all.

It's got a lot of plusses. A lot of it's gimmicks, you've got your sliding out drawer thing which is nice, you've got your buttons which I tend to like, the big ones and your laser display.

Which is the most innovative?

The Denon definitely.

It's the looks.

Which do you think is the most innovative?

Why is it the most innovative?

It's the colour, its image, these sort of little touch controls . . .

This is new.

I agree with what you're saying.

These little touch controls.

Is it really functional, your tape coming out like that? It's quicker just to push a button.

This drawer sliding out and that . . .

It must be a real bummer if your tape gets chewed, I mean how do you manage with head cleaning and that? You sort of take it along to the bloke and say stick your head-cleaning tape in?

I would have thought that came out easily.

This is practical and in a way it hides all its innovations, whereas that one shouts at you this is new, this is Gary Glitter music!

This one doesn't appear to have anything, your stop, your play, your forward. It's programmable, it repeats your scan, it's all standard, maybe it's all inside, whereas that one shouts out what it's got but it doesn't particularly explain why.

There's a thing on – what's that programme called where they test all the cars? *Top Gear* – saying a sports car could be like a cappuccino, looks great but doesn't taste so good, but that sort of tastes good but doesn't look so good.

At the end of the day I'd still stick with that.

But this one's more innovative, just on presentation.

(Case contributed by Jim Blythe)

Questions

1 Using the data in the case study, extract the key issues in judging innovativeness.

2 Build a causal model for the judgement of innovativeness.

3 What other information would be helpful in analysing these data?

4 What other analysis could be undertaken?

5 How might the data be reordered to make analysis easier?

6 What computer software would be available for analysing this type of data?

 ## REFERENCES AND NOTES

1   Smith, A (1997) Baby boomers get the message, *Financial Times*, 26 May.

2   Wheatley, K and Flexmer, W A (1987) Option Technologies, Inc., *Marketing News*, 27 February, 23.

3   Research propels innovation (1994) *Marketing*, 27 January, 33–35.

4   Proctor, T (1992) *Essential Marketing*, London: Collins Educational.

5   Nicholas, R (1994) Avon ads praise the real woman, *Marketing*, 27 January, 6.

6   IBM's Butterfly gets crushed on the wheel (1996) *PC Direct*, May, 57.

7   Samways, A and Whittcome, K (1994) UK brand strategies, *Financial Times* Management Report.

 ## FURTHER READING

Berg, B L (1998) *Qualitative Methods for the Social Sciences*, Boston, MA: Allyn & Bacon.

Berman-Brown, R B and Coverley, R (1999) Succession planning in family businesses: a study from East Anglia, UK, *Journal of Small Business Management*, January, 93–97.

Carson, D, Gilmore, A, Perry, C and Gronhaug, G (2001) *Qualitative Marketing Research*, London: Sage.

Catterall, M and Maclaren, P (1997) Focus group data and qualitative analysis programs: coding the moving picture as well as the snapshots, *Sociological Research Online*, 2(1), 1–11.

Collins, L F (1991) Everything is true, but in a different sense: a new perspective on qualitative research, *Journal of the Market Research Society*, 33, 31–38.

Colwell, J (1990) Qualitative market research: a conceptual analysis and review of practitioner criteria, *Journal of the Market Research Society*, 32.

Denzin, N K (1989) *The Research Act: A theoretical introduction of sociological methods* (3rd edn), Englewood Cliffs, NJ: Prentice-Hall.

Farnham, A (1998) Focus groups fail to reach pin-sharp results, *Sunday Telegraph*, 4 October, 27.

Fontana, A and Frey, J H (1994) Interviewing: the art of science, in Denzin, N K and Freeling, A (1994) Marketing is in a crisis – can marketing research help? *Journal of the Market Research Society*, 36, 97–104.

Gabriel, C (1990) The validity of qualitative market research, *Journal of the Market Research Society*, 32, 507–20.

Gibb, A (1997) Focus groups, *Social Research Update*, 19, Winter, Department of Sociology, University of Surrey, http://www.soc.surrey.ac.uk/sru/sru19.html

Gibb, A (1998) Academic research and the growth of ignorance, Plenary Paper, 21st ISBA National Small Firms Conference, Durham University, November.

Goss, J D (1996) Introduction to focus groups, *Area*, 28(6), 14–115.

Hess, J M (1968) Group interviewing, in Ring, R L (ed.) *New Science of Planning*, Chicago: American Marketing Association, http://www.socresonline.org.uk/socresonline/2/1/6.html.

Hutt, R W (1979) The focus group interview: a technique for counselling small business clients, *Journal of Small Business Management*, 17(1), 15–20.

Kaden, R J (1977) Incomplete use keeps focus groups from producing optimum results, *Marketing News*, 11(4).

Kaushik, M and Sen, A (1990) Semiotics and qualitative research, *Journal of the Market Research Society*, 32, 227–43.

Kitzinger, J (1994) Focus groups: method or madness? in Boulton, M (ed.) *Challenge and Innovation: Methodological advances in social research on HN/ALDS*, London: Taylor & Francis.

Kitzinger, J (1995) Introducing focus groups, *British Medical Journal*, 311, 299–302.

Krueger, R A (1997) Moderating focus groups, *Focus Group Kit* 4, London: Sage.

Krueger, R A (1997) Analyzing and reporting focus group results, *Focus Group Kit* 6, London: Sage.

Lincoln, Y S (ed.) *Handbook of Qualitative Research*, Thousand Oaks, CA: Sage.

Mathews, A (1997) Academic xenophobia and the analysis of focus group data, *Journal of Targeting, Measurement and Analysis for Marketing*, 6(2), 160–71.

Morgan, D L (1998) The focus group guidebook, *Focus Group Kit* 1, London: Sage.

Strauss, A and Corbin, J (1990) *Basics of Qualitative Research*, London: Sage.

Sykes, W (1990) Validity and reliability in qualitative marketing research: a review of the literature, *Journal of the Market Research Society*, 33, 3–12.

Teleconference Network (1990) *The Market Navigator*, Orangeburg, NY: Teleconference Network.

Yin, K R (1994) *Case Study Research – design and methods*, Newbury Park, CA: Sage.

Observation and experiment

Objectives

After reading this chapter, you should be able to:

- understand the role played by observational techniques in marketing research

- appreciate how experimentation can be applied in marketing

- understand the function and limitation of different experimental designs

- understand the different kinds of approaches that can be taken to test marketing.

Keywords

basic designs
consumer-tracking studies
controlled test marketing
experimental design
factorial design
Latin square design
maturation
mortality
psychogalvanator

pupilometer
randomised design
regression effects
scanning
simulated test marketing
statistical designs
test marketing
validity

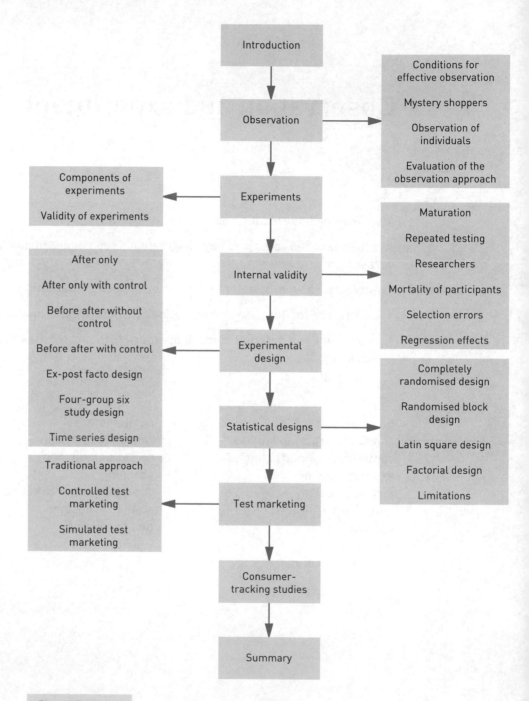

Plan of Chapter 9

INTRODUCTION

This chapter examines a variety of observational methods including those using mechanical means and scanning. It then looks at experimentation as a research method. Different types of **experimental design** are examined, together with a variety of approaches to test marketing.

OBSERVATION

One drawback of the survey method is that much of the information obtained is based on interviewees' statements describing what they have done or expect to do in the future. With respect to past actions, the interviewees can make mistakes in trying to recall what has happened, particularly when some time has elapsed since the event. The same kind of problem also applies to their intended actions, since these may also differ markedly from what actually happens. This is a common occurrence when people are asked about their purchase intentions for such items as cars, homes or major appliances. Many intended purchases never actually take place for a variety of reasons. The observation method does not suffer from these shortcomings since it records events as they actually happen.

Observation involves the personal or mechanical monitoring of selected activities. It records actions as they occur and thus there is no lack of accuracy caused by a respondent's faulty recollection of their past actions or inadequate estimate of future ones.

SHOPPERS UNDER THE MICROSCOPE

The scene is a US convenience store: 'cappuccino devotees' stride confidently towards the coffee dispenser, while 'clandestine consumers' consider a range of snacks after choosing their main purchase and 'explicit treaters' wander in search of something to satisfy a vague desire before selecting the familiar comfort of a chocolate bar.

Clearly, researchers wanting to understand more about consumer habits would learn little about these shoppers merely by analysing how often people visited the store. But by using a technique called observational research – watching how different types of people use goods and services – a fuller picture can be obtained.

By watching what happened in the convenience store, E-Lab, a Chicago-based research consultancy, was able to advise PepsiCo, the international food and soft drinks group, on where and how to position its products in order to get higher sales.

Observing how people behave in different surroundings or how they handle pieces of equipment is valuable in helping a company meet a specified aim, such as entering a new market, and in developing products to meet future needs that consumers have not yet recognised.

▶

Observational research ranges from the distant to the intimate. For some projects, studying footage of people browsing in a shopping mall or negotiating their way through an airport can be appropriate. For others, researchers spend time with subjects as they use the product at home or work.

'It's a matter of trying to get under the skin of real people,' says Tim Brown, European director of Ideo, a product development company. For example, watching a travel agent set up a conference call by arranging a speaker phone for each person and putting the handsets together demonstrated how she equated one phone with one person – an insight Ideo used in its advice on phone software to AT&T, the US telecoms operator. Finding the right people to watch is critical for techniques that involve observation of a few individuals or households. In contrast to conventional market research, where consumers are chosen because they fit squarely in the middle of particular categories, consumers picked for shadowing are intended, as Mr Brown says, to 'hit the edges'.

This might involve selecting people who are 'early adapters' to new technology, and those most resistant to it; or people using the product in an unusual environment.

In the UK the process can still be informal, while in the USA selection is itself a business. 'We use an outside agency – which mainly handles focus groups – to screen and recruit participants,' says Liz Sanders, head of research at Fitch, the design consultancy, in Ohio. One factor driving the growth of observational research is technology. Advances in photography and video recording make it easier to obtain and analyse the observations, increasing the research's value. A second factor, technology, is itself an area where consumers may not be well placed to articulate needs that could be met by a new generation of computers, telephones or other machines.

Fitch used observational research when it was advising Compaq, the computer company, on the design of the Presario personal computer. 'By working with consumers in their homes, we came to the realisation that a computer should be more friendly for home use,' says John Fillingham, director of policy research at Fitch in the UK. 'For example, the Presario's features include a compact disk rack and a great pair of speakers – it looks more like a consumer product.'

He adds, however, that while observation shows researchers what people do, it does not tell them why. 'A combination of observation and what consumers say about what they do gives you an ability to cross-check.'

Dorothy Leonard, writing in the current issue of the *Harvard Business Review*, identifies five types of information available from observation. Apart from needs that consumers have not yet articulated, they are: the triggers that prompt people to use a product or service; how the product relates to the consumer's environment; how consumers customise the product (and so how manufacturers can make those modifications for them); and the intangible qualities consumers value in the product.

Some consultants believe observational techniques can contribute even in the area of brand identity, provided the observations are evaluated properly. This goes well beyond whether packaging is convenient to open or whether a software program is easy to use.

'Every kind of behaviour has a particular framework and theory,' says Rick Robinson of E-Lab. 'It's a matter of finding the meaningful pattern.' Steelcase, the

US office furniture company, wanted to shift from being rooted in manufacturing excellence to being based on understanding work processes. Observational research helped it develop the new identity, and design its showrooms to encourage customers to buy on the basis of that understanding.

Observing how people behave is valuable in helping a company meet a specified aim.

Source: Smith[1] (reprinted with permission)

Conditions required for effective observation

Three conditions usually exist if the observation method is to be effectively carried out:

1 The event must be observable: attitudes, motives and other mental activities are difficult to record with the observation method.

2 The event must occur frequently or be predictable.

3 The event must be completed over a short period of time.

One way in which we can ensure that all three of these conditions are met is to set up an experiment in which all the conditions can be controlled and manipulated. The laboratory environment is often the best setting for observational studies.

Observation is used in shopping studies, especially in stores, when the customer is looking at the shelves and deciding what to buy. It is used to find out how things are done in practice.[2]

TYPES OF OBSERVATION PROCEDURE

- normal versus controlled conditions
- structured versus unstructured observation
- use of mechanical devices to aid observation
- measuring response latency – indicator of certainty of preference

Types of observation procedure

Activities really need to be observed under normal conditions. However, as some activities are not easily observed under normal conditions it is often necessary for the observation to take place in a controlled environment – for example, inviting people into a specially equipped room in order to observe the manner in which they use a product.

When people are aware they are being observed it is argued that they behave in different ways to how they would under normal circumstances where they are not being observed. In some cases this awareness will have little effect on their actions. However, there are many situations in which people change their activities if they know they are being watched. Salespeople in a clothing store may be especially polite to customers if they know their performance is being monitored.

There is also the choice between a structured and an unstructured observation. In a structured situation, the observers are told how and what to observe. Usually a checklist is given to them to record what happens. Structured methods are used where a **hypothesis** is tested. In an unstructured observation, which is most useful in research of an exploratory nature, the observer is given much latitude with respect to what to note.

A variety of mechanical devices are used to observe people's actions or responses. For example, a **psychogalvanator** measures a person's emotional reactions to various stimuli by measuring changes in their perspiration rate. It is used to assess people's reactions to different advertisements. The **pupilometer** measures changes in the size of a person's pupils as they are looking at an advertisement, package or product design. A change in pupil size reflects the person's interest in the object. Eye cameras can monitor a person's eye movements while reading, identifying the parts the reader perceived first, the parts dwelt on and the amount of copy actually read.

One fairly simple observation method is called response latency. It measures the amount of time a respondent takes to answer a question. Quick answers indicate certainty of preference. This observation technique is especially useful in telephone interviews, since latency can be measured with voice-stimulated stopwatches.

Electronic scanning

Electronic scanning is an observation method that is rapidly developing in popularity. Scanners were intended to improve productivity in retail shops, but they have also become valuable tools for researchers. Many retail stores will even sell research firms the data obtained from their own **scanning** records. There are, however, some limitations in scanner data. For example, not all sales data provided by the scanners are accurate. Three conditions must exist for real accuracy: each item must be precoded correctly by the manufacturer; the code must be correctly entered into the retailer's system; and every item must be scanned at the checkout counter.

Scanners are universal in large supermarkets and provide the store and its central office with an immediate record of sales by product (units and value). Data from scanners at checkout counters can be used to assess the impact that a price cut, coupon blitz or store display has on sales and profits. A scanner analysis system allows managers to determine almost instantly how well a promotion is working and what effect price changes, amount of inventory and arrangement on shelves will have on sales. Scanner data can be lined with demographics of areas to guide consumers on what to buy. Foods on supermarket shelves can be tied more closely to the demographics of the particular area. Thus inventory can be matched to local needs and turnover rate can be increased.

Auditing is a method of measuring the amount of movement of merchandise, by category and brand, through a retail outlet. It requires someone to check the amount of goods on hand (both on shelf and in store) at the start of a sales period, the addition to stock during the period (from checking receipts for goods delivered to the store) and the amount of goods on hand again at the end of the sales period.

Observation of the in-store environment

Observations include:

- distribution (and out of stock)
- shelf price
- shelf facings (reported in number and share)
- shelf location
- display activity
- presence of point-of-purchase material.

Results, depending on user needs, can be shown by category, brand and types/sizes. These are reported by total, by individual markets and by major chains. Breaks by sales regions and other special analyses can be provided on order.

Mystery shoppers

Retailers send out employees to shop at competitors' stores. The purpose is to observe fixture layouts, merchandise displays, store traffic and special promotions. Some organisations even send out especially trained staff to pose as customers. In the latter case the interest is in the quality of the customer service. A mystery shopper not only observes a shopping environment but also observes how employees react and behave based on the shopper's actions. It could involve visiting a bank and reporting that one had left at home (many miles away) one's wallet and cheque book and requesting emergency cash. Some large retail organisations employ many part-time mystery shoppers.

Observation of individuals

There are many applications of personal observation techniques. Hand counters were employed for many years in making counts of pedestrians in and around shopping centres. Personal observation is used in most surveys: the interviewer, for example, records observations about gender, age and apparent socioeconomic status. Another personal observation method which has become fashionable is called the 'anthropological' approach.[3] It is almost totally subjective and amounts to an almost live-in approach within a few households or shopping places. It is used to arrive at generalisations about living styles relevant to the specific product.

PERSONAL OBSERVATION AT WORK

A well-known car producer 'discreetly' observed car shoppers as they inspected cars in showrooms. Observations included how shoppers were dressed, whether they appeared confident or timid, whether they kicked the tyres and what questions they asked.

Evaluation of the observation approach

Observation within both households and stores typically requires the setting up of a panel, making it subject to the sampling difficulties and maintaining participation. Another problem is the quality of the data obtained. There may be serious questions about the quality and completeness of store scanner data. Large items may not readily scan and may be incompletely or inaccurately entered by hand; some brands with multiple forms are similarly labelled; and so on.

EXPERIMENTS

In experiments, the researcher manipulates selected **independent variables** and measures the effect of these manipulations on the **dependent variables**. In the survey and observation methods, the information is usually obtained under normal or near normal conditions and the researcher intervenes only to gather data, not to alter the environment. **Causality** means that a relationship exists between two or more events. The first event can be seen as a cause of the second if the occurrence of the first increases the likelihood of the occurrence of the second. The objective is to provide evidence that suggests a high probability of one event leading to another. It does not have to be demonstrated conclusively.

Three types of evidence are used to demonstrate the existence of a causal relationship:

1 *Concomitant variation*, which reflects the extent to which a cause (x) and effect (y) occur together or vary together in some predictable way.

2 *Time order of occurrence of the causal factor* (x), which must either precede or take place simultaneously with the effect (y). This is a logical requirement for a causal relationship, but there are situations where things become confusing because the two factors seem to affect one another.

3 *Absence of other causal factors*, which is the most difficult type of evidence to demonstrate. It states that no other factors could have caused a similar change in the dependent variable (y). This demands extensive testing to eliminate all other possible explanations for the change in x. It accounts for the importance of selecting an appropriate **experimental design**.

As well as these three types of evidence, if a causal relationship is to be useful to management the relationship should be operative in a variety of environments. It should also be a relationship that is stable enough to make future actions by executives worthwhile.

Components of experiments

Experiments should have three components (Figure 9.1):

1 The variable being acted on – variously called the test unit, dependent variable or subject.

2 The change being imposed – the treatment or independent variable.

3 The results related to the change – the effect, outcome or observation.

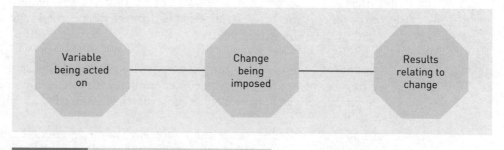

FIGURE 9.1   Three components of experiments

Validity of experiments

Experiments should possess both internal and external **validity**. Internal validity refers to whether the experiment treatment is solely accountable for the changes occurring or whether some extraneous factors were also at work. If there were outside factors as well, then internal validity is affected by the ability to measure their impact. **External validity** is to do with whether the findings can be applied to the real-world situation. Experiments can be conducted either in the field or under controlled laboratory conditions. In the former case the establishment of internal validity can be quite difficult. **Laboratory experiments**, by contrast, may lack external validity because of their controlled environment.

EXTERNAL VALIDITY

It is customary for tests or experiments involving new products to be carried out under laboratory conditions. Unfortunately, because in actual usage the operating conditions for the products may be very different to those in the laboratory, the **external validity** of such tests and experiments is difficult to assess.

Internal validity

Two considerations affect an experiment's internal validity:

1 the influence the treatment had on the actual outcome

2 the influence of extraneous factors.

Extraneous factors can take a number of forms (see Figure 9.2).

History and maturation   The changes associated with the passage of time are described as history and **maturation**. The influence of history is typified by changes in current events external to the experiment but that still may have affected its outcomes. The impact of history becomes greater as the length of the experiments increases. **Maturation** is primarily concerned with changes occurring within the individual subjects.

Repeated testing   This applies in experiments where the same people are tested a number of times. As they become familiar with the testing procedure, their performances may change solely because of this familiarity.

Impact of the researchers themselves   The researchers themselves may cause some of the change. Their very presence may influence the actions of the subjects being observed.

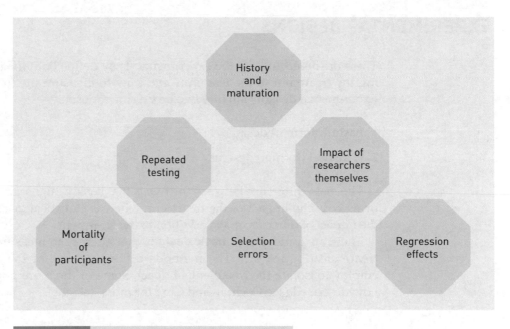

FIGURE 9.2 Extraneous factors influencing validity

Mortality of participants One problem with experiments carried out over a long period is **mortality**, meaning that, for one reason or another, some of the original participants 'drop out'. The problem is often encountered with consumer panels. There is no way of knowing whether the test units lost would have responded similarly to the treatment as those units that remained.

Selection errors The test units may be chosen in a manner that biases the results. They may not be representative of the desired population or the treatments are assigned to them in such a way that they influence the outcome.

Regression effects **Regression effects** occur when test units are chosen on the basis of their extreme score or performance on some earlier test. The outliers, especially those with very low performance, tend to move to a more average position over time.

All these factors represent causes for error in the experiments. Many of them can be controlled if the appropriate experimental design is used. Experiments should be designed primarily to control those extraneous factors most likely to seriously influence the outcome and not try to eliminate all sources of error.

EXPERIMENTAL DESIGNS

These are blueprints for the experiments. They define both the pattern for applying the treatment to the test units and how to measure the treatment's impact. Experimental designs fall into two broad categories:

1 basic (informal) designs

2 statistical (formal) designs.

The main difference between the two is that basic designs concentrate on measuring only the impact of the treatment, whereas statistical designs also measure the impact of other factors in addition to the treatment.

There are a number of **basic designs** that attempt to measure the effect of the treatment (Figure 9.3). The methods differ in terms of the approaches they employ to isolate the treatment's impact. Some of the more popular designs are now described (see Cochran and Cox[4] for more designs).

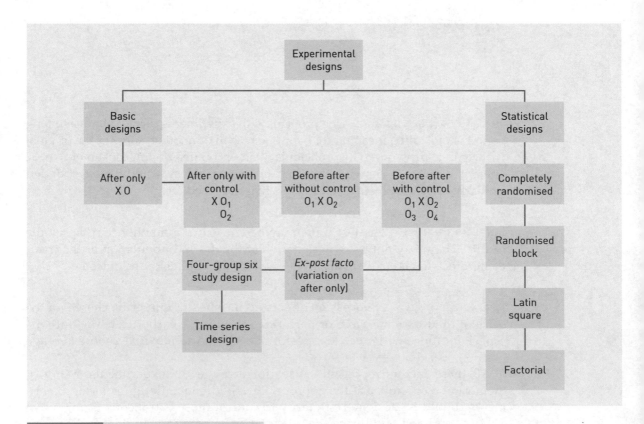

FIGURE 9.3   Types of experimental design

The following symbols are used to help in presenting these designs:

X　=　the period in which the treatment is applied
O　=　the observation periods before and/or after the treatment; subscripts are used to identify the time of each observation
EG　=　the experimental group: the subjects receiving the treatment
OG　=　control group: the subjects matched up with the experimental group, but not receiving the treatment

After only

This is used by researchers who are not overly concerned about the strength of their findings or internal/external validity. Symbolically the design appears as:

$$X \quad O$$

A single group of subjects is exposed to a treatment, and the subjects' responses are recorded once. The subjects are usually selected in a subjective (non-random) manner.

AFTER-ONLY DESIGN

Special pence-off coupons for a shampoo are hand-distributed to women in a shopping mall. The number of these coupons turned in is recorded and a judgement is made of the success of the coupon promotion.

With this form of design, no data exist that can be used to assess the influence of extraneous factors during the period. There is also no evidence about the subject's behaviour before the treatment. The design is simple to use, but its results are not very enlightening. There is no indication, for example, of how the treatment may have changed customer behaviour.

After only with control

This experimental design is the one most commonly used by marketing researchers. It is intended to eliminate the influence of pretesting, so no measurements are taken between either of the groups:

$$EG: \quad X \quad O_1$$
$$O_2$$

A firm wanted to test the success of free gifts as a method of stimulating sales for its detergent product. It posted free sampler packages of its detergent to randomly selected homes in a neighbourhood. A month later it sent coupons offering 25 pence off the purchase of a large package of its detergent to the same group of homes. These coupons were also sent to a control group randomly selected from a comparable neighbourhood but which had not received the free sample. The coupons were coded to enable a count to be made of the number of coupons redeemed by each group. The experimental group redeemed 121 coupons and the control group redeemed 76 coupons. The difference (45 coupons) was felt to be the result of the sampler:

$$\text{Effect of treatment} = O_1 - O_2$$
$$45 = 121 - 76$$

While this design neutralises the impact of pretest, it does not allow any measurement or analysis to be made of the total change that occurred, a situation handled well in the before-after with control design.

Before after without control

This involves measuring the test unit before and after treatment:

$$O_1 \; X \; O_2$$

An example here would be the collecting of sales data for a period of time before the application of, say, a special sales promotion. Let us say that average sales were £450 per day. During the next two weeks a special sales promotion was offered and average daily sales rose to £510 per day:

$$O_1 = £450$$
$$O_2 = £510$$
$$O_2 - O_1 = \text{effect of the treatment}$$
$$£510 - £450 = £60 \text{ per day}$$

It appears that the inclusion of the special sales promotion had a positive effect: daily sales increased by £60. This assumes that any changes in the units sold were caused solely by the introduction of the special promotional offer. Realistically, at least part of the difference could have been caused by extraneous factors such as the unavailability of the main competitor's product during the two weeks in question.

Before after with control

A control group is selected and observed over the entire testing period. This control group is comparable in makeup to the group that will receive the treatment. The major assumption in the design is that both groups are affected in a similar manner by extraneous factors. For this assumption to be correct, the subjects must be randomly selected and the treatments randomly assigned.

The statement of the design is:

$$\text{EG:} \quad O_1 \quad X \quad O_2$$
$$\text{OG:} \quad O_3 \qquad O_4$$
$$\text{Effect of treatment} - (O_2 - O_1) - (O_4 - O_3)$$

A regional bookstore chain wants to determine the effect of new display shelves on the sale of children's books. The shelving is temporarily installed in three of its stores (test stores) and sales are compared with those in three comparable stores in which the old shelving is retained. The following sales occurred in the two sets of stores:

$$O_1 = 290 \text{ books} \quad O_2 = 350 \text{ books}$$
$$O_3 = 285 \text{ books} \quad O_4 = 320 \text{ books}$$
$$\text{Effect of treatment} = (350 - 290) - (320 - 285)$$
$$= 60 - 35$$
$$= 25 \text{ books}$$

The assumption is that the sales increase in the control stores (35 books) was caused by some extraneous factors. Thus, if this impact is to be subtracted from the change in sales in the test stores (60 books) the resulting value of 25 books can be viewed as the direct impact of the treatment (the new shelving).

Ex-post facto design

This is a variation on the after-only design. The difference between the two is that in *ex-post facto* design, neither the experimental nor the control group is chosen until after the treatment is actually applied. This design attempts to create equivalent experimental and control groups but identifies each only after they have been exposed to the experiment.

A group of people who read a certain issue of a particular magazine are contacted. Those who said they read a certain advertisement in the issue are the experimental group; those who did not read the advertisement are the control group. Both are asked about some attribute of different types of the product featured in the advertisement and the difference in the two groups' ratings of the products determines the advertisement's success. The advantage of this design over the after-only study with control design is that the experimental variable will have exerted its influence in a natural setting, enabling the researcher to study a group that, by choice, was exposed to the treatment, rather than having been selected to receive the treatment.

Four-group six study design

This design, also called the Soloman four-group design, is the most sophisticated basic design. It is intended to isolate the effects of various internal validity measures as well as the impact of pretesting. Two experimental and two control groups are randomly selected. The following diagram shows how the design operates:

$$EG_1: O_1 \quad X \quad O_2$$
$$OG_1: O_3 \qquad O_4$$
$$EG_2: \qquad X \quad O_5$$
$$OG_2: \qquad O_6$$

$$\text{Treatment effect} = [O_5 - 1/2(O_1 - O_3)] - [O_6 - 1/2(O_1 - O_3)]$$

Although it is considered the ideal basic design, it is not very often used by researchers because of its expense and the time it requires.

Time series design

This design uses a series of pre- and post-measurements to determine the impact of the experiment. It attempts to measure the impact over a longer period of time than other basic methods.

The time series design appears as follows:

$$O_1 \, O_2 \, O_3 \, O_4 \, X \, O_5 \, O_6 \, O_7 \, O_8$$

It assumes that the researcher will have continual access to the same test units. Consumer panels are prime examples of the application of this type of experimental design. Figure 9.4 shows some possible outcomes from experiments using a time series design.

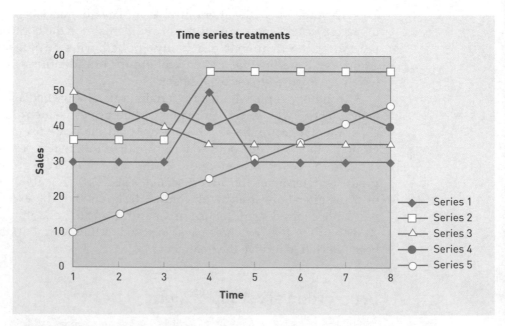

FIGURE 9.4 Time series analysis

Outcome 1: a short-lived positive effect.

Outcome 2: a long-term positive effect – market share increased.

Outcome 3: a positive effect – it halted a decline in sales.

Outcome 4: seems to have no effect – fluctuation continues in the same manner.

Outcome 5: seems to have no effect – growth continues in the same pattern.

Because measurements are made over a longer period of time, such extraneous factors as testing, maturation and regression tend to be neutralised. However, there is always the danger that some other event may have occurred at the same time the experiment took place and this external event could be the real cause of any changes in the observation. The problem of **mortality** – drop out – also increases as the length of the time series increases.

STATISTICAL DESIGNS

Statistical designs provide a framework for statistically testing the impact not only of the treatment but also of other factors. In the case of statistical designs the researcher randomly assigns treatments to randomly chosen test units and the treatments are then systematically applied. The statistical analysis tool often used with these designs is **analysis of variance**. This can help to determine whether one factor (the treatment) significantly affects another factor or whether the observed changes are caused by some other factors or even by chance.

Completely randomised design

In this section we examine statistical designs that are often used with experiments. The design is described, together with the kind of information it can provide.

Treatments are assigned to test units on a random basis and an analysis is then performed to determine whether the treatments caused a significant difference in the test units. The design can only really measure one type of variance – that occurring between treatments, known as the 'treatment effect'.

EXAMPLE

A motorist DIY chain is selling antifreeze in all of its outlets, but it doesn't know the most effective price to charge (see Table 9.1). It tests three different prices per can – £3.89, £4.85, and £5.89 – and records the sales from each. It randomly assigns these prices to nine experimental stores, three using each price.

▶

TABLE 9.1 Antifreeze sales through motorist DIY outlets

Week	Price £3.89	Price £4.85	Price £5.89
1	19	9	15
2	16	13	20
3	22	20	9
4	24	18	12
Total	81	60	56

The analysis would examine the average amount of the product sold at each price. It could disclose whether the difference in sales at the lower price was a significant one or whether it was caused by chance.

It fails, however, to take into consideration the influence of such extraneous factors as weather, size of store or competitors' prices. This design assumes that the extraneous variables have had an equal impact on all the test units, which is also a shortcoming of the basic design. Such an assumption might be acceptable in a laboratory experiment where the researcher controls most of the conditions, but it is an unjustified assumption to make for experiments conducted in a real-world environment. This design is not widely used for field experiments.

Randomised block design

This type of design is used when the researcher is interested in isolating a major source of variation in addition to the treatment's influence. In the example just given, where three different prices were tested, no allowance was made for the different sizes of the stores, a potentially important influence on the actual sales obtained. The randomised block facilitates the isolation of one extraneous factor from the total experimental error, providing a precise picture of the treatment's actual impact (see Table 9.2). This additional variable has to be identified and measured at the time of the experiment.

TABLE 9.2 Antifreeze sales in supermarkets at various prices

Store size £'000	Price £3.89	Price £4.85	Price £5.89
1 100 +	135	100	60
2 50–100	34	26	15
3 20–50	17	12	7
4 < 20	5	2	1
Total	191	140	83

Here we see how the antifreeze example has been expanded to permit the illustration of a **randomised** block **design**. In this case the desire is to control the impact of store size on sales.

Latin square design

This design enables the researcher to isolate the impact of two major extraneous sources as well as measuring the impact of the treatment. It is a complex design and can cost time and money. The additional efficiency it provides must be weighed against the extra costs and the greater expertise needed by the user. It assumes there is no interaction between the factors being measured.

Again expanding on the antifreeze example, this shows how the **Latin square design** can be used to control for the impact of store size and the type of store selling the antifreeze (Table 9.3).

| TABLE 9.3 | Latin square design |

Type of store	Size of outlet (weekly sales)		
	< £5000	£5000–£10,000	> £10,000
Supermarket	Price 2	Price 3	Price 1
Convenience store	Price 1	Price 2	Price 3
Drugstore	Price 3	Price 1	Price 2

In using the Latin square design the number of extraneous variables to be controlled must equal the number of treatments. Thus, in our example, three levels of store size are needed and three different types of store will be involved. The rows and columns of the resulting matrix contain the extraneous variables. The treatment (different prices) is assigned so that each price level occurs only once in each row and column.

Latin square designs are particularly useful in experiments where it is important to establish controls for the effect of store size, the type of store or the time period. The main limitations of the design are:

- It requires equal numbers of rows, columns and treatment levels. This can pose problems when four or five treatments are involved.

- Regardless of the number of treatments, it can still only control two extraneous variables.

- It assumes that the extraneous variables do not interact with one another or even with the treatment: a questionable assumption in many marketing experiments.

| TABLE 9.4 | Latin square design in a supermarket grocery |

	20/6–3/7 Treatment	Sales	Experiment period 4/7–17/7 Treatment	Sales	18/7–31/7 Treatment	Sales
First replication						
Store 1	A	765	B	488	C	410
Store 2	B	330	C	307	A	258
Store 3	C	813	A	579	B	301
Second replication						
Store 1	A	724	C	411	B	308
Store 2	B	366	A	478	C	271
Store 3	C	633	B	366	A	588
Third replication						
Store 1	A	562	B	381	C	322
Store 2	B	308	C	478	A	412
Store 3	C	166	A	233	B	65

Latin square design in a supermarket grocery

The experiment reported in Table 9.4 makes use of a 3 × 3 design. The rows represent three different stores and the columns represent three time periods. Three replications of the 3 × 3 design were included in the experiment, each comprising a different set of three stores. The treatments consisted of three colour ranges of bananas: treatment A – 'highly coloured green', 75–100% good green colour; B – 'partly green', 50–75% good green colour; and C – 'yellow colour', 50–100% good yellow colour. The performance of treatment A (for example, average sales across the nine As) can be thought of as a weighted average, where the weights given to each store and day of the week are equal. Treatment B's performance is based on the same set of weights for stores and days of the week that were used to compute the performance of treatment A. This is also true for the weights used to compute the average performance of treatment C.

The results of the experiment indicate that customers most prefer the highly coloured green bananas and least prefer those in the partly green category.

Factorial design

In the previous designs the assumption was that there were one or two major sources of variation and that the researcher wanted to separate them from the total variance. There was no allowance or even assumption that some factors might interact with one another. Indeed, researchers are often interested in the simultaneous effects of two or more independent variables. In the antifreeze example, the researcher might want to see if outlets serving higher-income clientele have greater success with the higher prices than those outlets serving lower-income clientele. A **factorial design** measures the influence of interacting variables on a dependent variable. In our antifreeze example, improved sales are associated with both the income of an outlet's clientele and any change in the outlet display used. Factorial designs enable researchers to measure the separate effects of each variable as it works alone. The actual design used can be a randomised block or Latin square, but a more complicated form of variance analysis is applied to the results.

Limitations of experiments

Experiments are often limited to assessing short-term response, whereas long-term response is often more relevant to a problem. Moreover, the long-term response to a particular treatment is often quite different to that of the short-term response. As an example, much advertising is well known to be effective over a period of time that is often difficult, if not impossible, to gauge effectively. Thus to measure its effect over a short period of time may be suspect. Also, the longer an experiment is run, the greater is the opportunity for something to occur that will invalidate it – Murphy's Law of 'if anything can go wrong it will go wrong' is almost certain to apply. Moreover, an experiment often cannot be made sufficiently realistic to be useful.

TEST MARKETING: AN INTRODUCTION

Test marketing is about trying something out before making a big commitment to it. It gives the firm producing and marketing the product or service some idea of what is likely to happen should it decide to go ahead with a broader expansion on a regional or national basis. Test marketing aims to provide estimates of sales volume and market share for a new product, a product extension or a new marketing device, such as a modified advertising campaign, varying media mixes or a change in advertising expenditure.

Conceptually it is very much like holding an experiment. The idea is literally to conduct a test or an experiment to arrive at a sales prediction. This may be done by trying things out in a series of balanced markets under normal conditions and this is the format of the traditional test market. In **controlled test marketing**, the research firm forces the distribution of the brand, making sure it is stocked in all selected stores and that stocks are maintained. At another level altogether there is **simulated test marketing** – virtually a laboratory situation, in which real stores are seldom used.

Traditional approach to test marketing

Traditional test marketing is marketing under 'normal' conditions and the company's own salesforce gets retailers to stock the product, give it good shelf position and provide in-store promotion and cooperative advertising. The sales staff also make sure that the shelves remain stocked.

HOMELINK

A new process, Homelink, enables accurate and effective targeting to be achieved in a few hours. The process makes use of a database of over 10,000 adults and is one of the most comprehensive, nationally representative research samples available. It makes use of demographic variables and explores the way in which people live, the products they use and the beliefs they hold.

Thousands of new products are launched every year but many of these initiatives fail to come to fruition. Arguably, by fully researching a target audience in the first place, much waste can be avoided. After all, ensuring that products or services match with customer wants, needs and expectations is a critical element in the new product introduction process. Discussions with potential users of a new product, service or sales campaign is an essential part of getting projects of this type off the ground.

Unfortunately, launchers of new ventures often perceive the research process to be over-complex. They often feel that the more targeted the respondents are, the harder they are to locate and the more complex the process of finding meaningful and manageable market data becomes. With Homelink this type of thinking can be shown to be completely out of date.

In order to ensure that the fullest picture can be drawn from their new market research facility, the designers of Homelink have included a wide range of product and service categories. These include such things as baby products, household equipment, pet food, skincare products, home leisure/entertainment equipment, types of food and much more. This enables people who use specific products and services or who lead particular lifestyles to be identified quickly and cost-effectively. Establishing a baseline from which all aspects of research can be compared is the fundamental question to be answered before the research can begin and Homelink enables this to be done very effectively. Moreover, the framework and database enable information to be gathered from the same respondents over a long period of time which in turn means that sample variability can be reduced. Homelink facilitates the researching of products with both large and small market shares in a cost-effective manner.

Homelink can be used for:

- product or advertisement concept testing
- evaluating market potential for new or revitalised products or services

- testing new or reformulated products to discover how the current users of those products or users of competing brands rate a new or reformulated product
- discovering how products are used in the home environment
- uncovering customer attitudes towards a particular company and its products.

In the case of Homelink, no one remains in the database for more than two years, no one tests more than six concepts or products over the course of a year and no one ever tests more than two products from the same product category.

Source: *Research Plus*[5]

Traditional test marketing rests on the premise that if a few reasonably typical communities throughout the country are selected, and the product or marketing method is tried there, results will pretty well predict what will happen when there is a roll-out on a regional or national basis. Moreover, if a simultaneous series of parallel markets is set up, it will be possible to predict which of two or more product variations, copy approaches or the like will work better. One of the greatest problems is the selection of test areas. The idea is to select test markets not too different from the country as a whole.

Matching local markets with national data on sales may not assure comparability. Change may creep in even without the introduction of any known marketing variables. Matching test cities with one another on the basis of causal variables such as regular price, national advertising, couponing, displays and in-store flyers might help matters.

Other important factors include demographics: per capita income, racial composition, etc. The business nature of the community must also be considered. The area should roughly parallel the business composition nationally, by type of business and, usually, medium-sized cities are selected. The advertising media should be representative. The media should be self-contained: they should not have much coverage beyond the test market.

The duration of a traditional **market test** depends on the nature of the product and the consumers' buying habits. The rule of thumb for packaged goods is an average of three purchases (trial and two repeats). If the product is one with a slow but continuing purchase pattern, the test period has to be long. Competitive pressure also affects the length of the test. A strong competitor means that the marketer must stay in there longer to find out whether it is possible to make inroads into the market.

Competitive action is one of the great risks and uncertainties of the traditional test market. Once a major competitor recognises what is happening, it may decide to make an effort to kill the test by spending heavy marketing funds on advertising and coupons to distort the test results.

Controlled test marketing

This is a test where sales are measured within a controlled store environment. The length and frequency of the checks are set to parallel the real-life elements of expected product movement, the repurchase cycle of the category and purchase seasonality. The research firm conducting the controlled market test obtains distribution of the product in a representative sample of stores within each market selected for the test. It handles 'sell in' and guarantees that this will be 100%. It stocks the product in the stores, handling both warehousing and distribution. The research firm maintains retail inventory levels, handles pricing, shelf conditions and the building and placement of displays.

The approach has several advantages over traditional test marketing. Costs are far lower and the forced test needs only about six months – the whole process is accelerated. The method also makes it more difficult for competitors to recognise what is going on, so there is less chance that a competitor can exert a distortion effect.

Simulated test marketing

Simulated test marketing is really test marketing in a laboratory setting. It applies only to a situation where the product and its packaging, pricing, and advertising and promotion have been developed in finished form. Although there are variations in practice, consumers are usually invited into a central location facility, such as a research centre in a shopping mall. They are given information – usually in the form of advertising – about the test product, then invited to shop from stocked shelves, which include the test product, with provided funds. Following the first purchase, or lack of it, the consumer is later interviewed to determine repeat buying and frequency of purchase of the test product. Then a computer model of customer behaviour provides an estimate of sales volume for the new product or line extension.

CONSUMER-TRACKING STUDIES

Associated with traditional test marketing, **consumer-tracking studies (market-tracking studies)** are diagnostic aids. These studies track what is, or is not, happening as a result of the marketing campaign. They do this by continuing contact with consumers, doing 'waves' of studies, as they are sometimes called, to measure such things as:

- brand awareness
- recall of advertising
- purchase behaviour
- product satisfaction
- intent to repurchase.

Questions about the recall of advertising probe for 'unaided advertising recall'. Typically, the person is first asked about what brands of a product or service they are aware of. The first two brands named are considered by marketers as an indication of probable purchase. Purchase and repurchase behaviour are particularly significant. Overall audit figures report only total sales and market shares. Such reports do not show repurchase behaviour.

Consumer-tracking studies take one of two forms: the one-off study or the panel. Both are carried out in waves, but the one-shot study is conducted with a separate, but comparable, sample of respondents each time. The panel study is conducted with the identical group of people on each wave. Both approaches often make use of the telephone interview method.

Tracking studies must meet rigorous requirements if they are to be useful. Large shifts are rare in tracking studies, so they must be able to measure small differences. Thus the sample design has to include a large and random sample with rigorous controls in execution.

SUMMARY

This chapter has examined a variety of observational methods including those using mechanical means and scanning. It has also looked at experimentation as a research method. Different types of experimental design have been examined, together with a discussion of their limitations, as well as a variety of approaches to test marketing.

QUESTIONS

1 Indicate the different types of observation procedure that may be used. Give examples of when each might be appropriate.

2 What is meant by scanning? What use can be made of information gathered in this way?

3 What are the essential features of an experiment?

4 Distinguish between the different types of experimental design, including statistical designs, indicating the limitations of each one.

5 What is test marketing? What factors should be taken into account when setting up a traditional test market?

6 What are consumer-tracking studies? What is their purpose?

CASE STUDY 9.1: SOAP-SUD

Soap-sud is a washing powder brand name for a product marketed throughout the UK. It is produced by one of the two leading multinational soap powder companies. Soap-sud has been around in slightly different forms for many years and has stood the test of time. Periodically, new ingredients have been added to the powder to produce new benefits for the customer, versions have been introduced that have made it more suitable for automatic washing machines and various packaging designs have been used to keep the image of the product in vogue.

The first non-soap detergents were introduced in 1950 with Tide. This was followed by Surf in 1951 and Daz in 1953. They all promised greater cleanliness and whiteness. But at that time Persil had been proclaiming the importance of whiteness for ten years with its famous slogan 'Persil washes whiter'. In 1956 Persil offered perfume for the first time and other changes followed. A scum-disposal agent was added that gave better performance in hard water, a solid suspension agent to prevent dirt being redeposited and more fluorescers to brighten the wash. Persil was the first brand to be advertised on TV in 1956. In the 1960s the growth of washing-machine sales began to accelerate and in 1964 Persil was reformulated to perform even better with machines. At the end of the decade Ariel exploded onto the market and captured brand leadership but within a year Persil had regained the position. There have been many changes in the market since 1970 but perhaps none so radical as those of the 1950s and 1960s.

Maintaining market share is an important objective for the brand manager in charge of Soap-sud and in a highly competitive industry this is a difficult thing to do. There is also a problem: the company that owns the brand also has two other soap powder brands competing alongside Soap-sud in the marketplace. Bill Carruthers, the brand manager of Soap-sud, is now contemplating a number of changes to the product to give it additional leverage in the market. The changes are as follows:

- The introduction of a special new 'green whitener' ingredient. Tests show that this makes the product even more effective in washing clothes 'whiter than white' and is also environmentally friendly.

- A new television advertising campaign telling users of washing powders of the changes to Soap-sud.

- A brand new package design to promote the idea that the new Soap-sud really is a new product in every way.

Bill is looking for ways of testing out his ideas before making a definite commitment to them.

Question

What advice would you give Bill?

CASE STUDY 9.2: CHEUNG'S CHIPS

Mr Cheung offers a wide range of Chinese food, fried traditional British cuisine, such as fish and chips, and some Italian dishes. Every time he has introduced a new line in the past he has taken a random sample of his customers and asked them whether or not they would be interested in the new line he proposes. If more than 70% of those asked have said they would be interested, he has introduced the new line. Table 9.5 shows his notes on the last five new products he introduced.

TABLE 9.5	Cheung's random sampling technique	
Line	Percentage interested	Weekly average sales turnover (£)
1 Fish and chips	98%	2156
2 Puddings	95%	345
3 Steak pies	94%	213
4 Spaghetti	70%	135
5 Lasagne	71%	123

Mr Cheung wants to set up a method by which he can judge whether it is worthwhile to introduce new lines. He feels that the current method is not very satisfactory and that he may be missing some good opportunities. He also feels that despite the number of people who *say* they would be interested in buying the new lines, in many instances only a few of them actually do.

Someone has suggested that a good research approach would be to use the response latency technique. This measures the amount of time a respondent takes to answer a question and quick answers indicate certainty of preference. The technique is especially useful in telephone interviews since latency can be measured by recording all calls and measuring the time to respond *post facto*.

Question

What advice would you offer Mr Cheung?

CASE STUDY 9.3: THE SAFE 'T' FIREPROOF LETTERBOX

Barry invented the Safe 'T' out of necessity when an aggrieved tenant poured petrol through his letterbox and set fire to it. Being in the locksmith business, he soon realised there was nothing on the market to protect him against further attacks. He began to sketch out the sort of thing he wanted and the Safe 'T' letter-box began to emerge. The letterbox is able to deal with fireworks, lighted newspaper and almost anything of that nature. If someone pours petrol in, it comes out at the bottom straight onto the culprit's feet. Barry feels that his invention has potential since there are some 80,000 reported arson attacks every year in England and Wales alone.

Source: *Business Opportunities World*[6]

Question

Assuming that Barry can find a financial backer to produce and market the invention, how might the idea be tested out among potential customers?

CASE STUDY 9.4: THOMPSON TOYS

Thompson Toys manufactures a range of simple toys for pre-school-age children. The toys are robust, colourful and fun to play with, but also take account of sound educational principles – in toy industry parlance, they have high play value. The company has proved successful, exporting toys throughout Europe and Australia, and acquiring in the process a reputation for quality and durability which has stood them in good stead.

Harry Thompson, the founder of the firm, read in the trade press about the Fisher-Price company's crèche in Chicago. At one time, Fisher-Price ran a free crèche at its headquarters where pre-school children were given the company's toys to play with; observers, behind two-way mirrors, observed how the children played with the toys and which toys were most popular. This had proved invaluable for Fisher-Price when developing and marketing new products.

After reading the article, Harry Thompson decided to set up a similar crèche of his own. The crèche would be free for the children of the company's staff, so Harry let his personnel manager work out the details of setting up the project. Initially the crèche had seven children in it, of ages ranging from one year old to four and a half. The crèche was staffed by a fully trained nursery nurse; two observers were hired, and a room fitted out for the purpose. The main difference between Thompson's crèche and the Fisher-Price one was that Thompson used closed-circuit TV to monitor the children rather than two-way mirrors. This not only turned out to be cheaper, but also allowed the observers to record the children's behaviour for later analysis. A further spin-off of CCTV was that it allowed the observers to take breaks or spend time preparing their reports.

The observers either directly observed or recorded all the children's activities throughout the day, in particular observing their approach to playing with the toys.

Although the costs of running the crèche were high, Thompson thought it worthwhile in terms of new product development; several potentially damaging design problems in toys turned up, and some toys which had seemed promising on the drawing board turned out to be duds with the children. This alone saved the company a fortune in launch costs. The crèche took almost six months to settle down, however, and the researchers detected a number of problems with the set-up.

First, there was a conflict of interest between the nursery nurse's professional training and the needs of the observers. She needed to exercise a degree of control over the children's play, both for educational and nurturing reasons, and also for housekeeping reasons – for example, stopping play when it was time for the children's lunch. The observers, on the other hand, wanted the children to play as freely as possible with the toys. They wanted to observe whether the children spontaneously shared toys with each other, at what point the children became bored with the toys and what happened if another child tried to take a toy away. Also, the nursery nurse was not comfortable about the children playing with prototypes, because she was concerned about the chances of injury from toys that had not yet undergone full safety testing.

Second, the children belonged to the Thompson staff. This meant that most of them were already familiar with the majority of Thompson toys, since staff were allowed to buy toys for their children at very substantial discounts. The observers felt that this might bias the results.

Third, the observers were obtaining so much data from the observations and video tapes that it became impossible to analyse all of them. Choosing which areas should be analysed thoroughly was becoming a nightmare and the observers were reluctant to perform superficial analysis on such rich data.

Finally, the researchers were not confident that good results could be obtained from such a small sample of children.

Despite these difficulties, Harry Thompson still wanted to proceed with the crèche; already, some very useful feedback had been generated and he had high hopes for the future running of the crèche once the initial teething troubles had been overcome. The benefits were already outweighing the difficulties – but all concerned with the project knew that even better results could be obtained.

(Case contributed by Jim Blythe)

Questions

1 How might Thompson Toys resolve the conflicts between the nursery nurse and the researchers?

2 What type of observation would be appropriate in these circumstances?

3 What could be done to overcome the researchers' concerns about sample size?

4 What types of experiment could be substituted for the observation methods used by Thompson?

5 What other factors might affect the validity of the research done at the crèche?

6 How would you design an experiment for Thompson Toys, using the crèche children as experimental subjects?

REFERENCES AND NOTES

1 Smith, A (1997) Shoppers under the microscope, *Financial Times*, 5 December.

2 Hague, P and Jackson, P (1996) *Market Research*, London: Kogan Page.

3 Collins, L F (1991) Everything is true, but in a different sense: a new perspective on qualitative research, *Journal of the Market Research Society*, 33, 31–38.

4 Cochran, W G and Cox, G M (1957) *Experimental Designs* (2nd edn), New York: Wiley.

5 Homelink (1993) *Research Plus*, September, 8–9.

6 Safety letterbox (1996) *Business Opportunities World*, May, 64–65.

FURTHER READING

Adler, P and Adler, P (1994) Observational techniques, in Denzin, N K and Lincoln, Y S, *Handbook of Qualitative Research*, Thousand Oaks, CA: Sage.

Cuba, F (1985) Fourteen things that make or break tracking studies, *Journal of Advertising Research*, 25(1), 21–23.

Eskin, G (1988) *Setting a Forward Agenda for Test Market Modeling*, New York: Advertising Research Foundation, 14–15.

Gibson, R (1992) The fine art of stocking a supermarket's shelves, *Wall Street Journal*, 15 October.

Gibson, R (1993) Broad grocery price cuts may not pay, *Wall Street Journal*, 7 May.

Grove, S J and Fisk, R P (1992) Observational data collection methods for service marketing: an overview, *Journal of the Academy of Marketing Science*, 20(3), 217–24.

Kandathil, J (1985) The advantages of electronic test markets: an advertiser view based on experience, *Journal of Advertising Research*, 25(6), 11–12.

Langbourne, R (1993) How to reach children in stores: marketing tactics grounded in observational research, *Journal of Advertising Research*, 33, November/December, 67–72.

Malhotra, R (1988) *Some Issues and Perspectives on Use of Simulated Test Markets*, New York: Advertising Research Foundation, 57.

Moult, W M (1988) *The Role of Simulated Test Markets and Test Markets*, New York: Advertising Research Foundation, 140.

Robson, C (1993) *Real World Research*, Oxford: Blackwell.

Rosenfeld, J (1985) Speeding up test marketing, *Marketing Communications*, June.

Russo, J (1988) Simulated test markets in the real world, *Pre-Test Market Research*, New York: Advertising Research Foundation, 118–19.

Rydholm, J (1997) Right on cue: mystery shopping makes sure salespeople sing praises of Yamaha digital pianos, *Quirk's Marketing Review*, Article 234, January.

Seaton, A V (1997) Unobtrusive observational measures as a qualitative extension of visitor surveys at festivals and events: mass observation revisited, *Journal of Travel Research*, 35(4), Spring, 25–30.

Test markets: winners and losers (1983) *Advertising Week*, 3 October.

10 Quantitative data analysis

Objectives

After reading this chapter, you should be able to:

- understand how to identify meaningful patterns in research data

- understand how to convert into tables data collected with research instruments

- understand how to code questions

- understand how to analyse data with statistical methods

- appreciate how the computer can be used to transform and facilitate the interpretation of research data.

Keywords

analysis
analysis of variance
averages
chi-square
cluster analysis
coding
conjoint analysis
correlation
editing
factor analysis
hypothesis
interpretation
mean

median
mode
multidimensional scaling
multiple regression
non-parametric
proportion
regression
standard deviation
tabulation
t test
variance
Z test

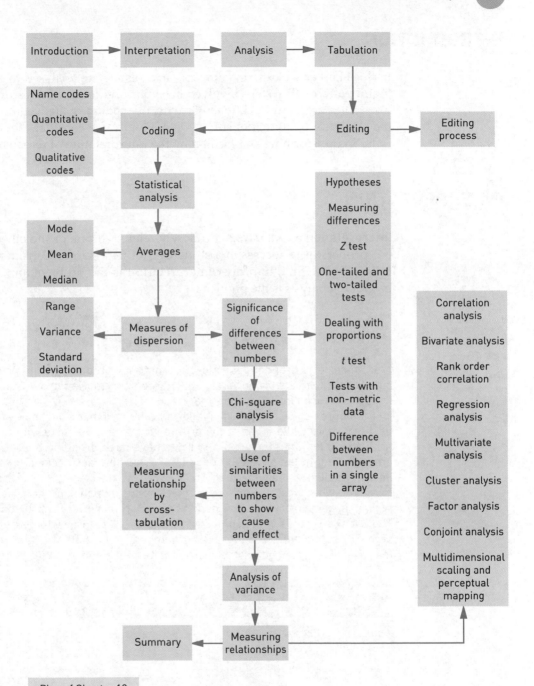

Introduction → Interpretation → Analysis → Tabulation

Name codes
Quantitative codes ← Coding ← Editing → Editing process
Qualitative codes

Coding → Statistical analysis

Mode
Mean ← Averages
Median

Range
Variance ← Measures of dispersion → Significance of differences between numbers →

Hypotheses
Measuring differences
Z test
One-tailed and two-tailed tests
Dealing with proportions
t test
Tests with non-metric data
Difference between numbers in a single array

Correlation analysis
Bivariate analysis
Rank order correlation
Regression analysis
Multivariate analysis
Cluster analysis
Factor analysis
Conjoint analysis
Multidimensional scaling and perceptual mapping

Standard deviation

Chi-square analysis

Measuring relationship by cross-tabulation ← Use of similarities between numbers to show cause and effect

Analysis of variance

Summary ← Measuring relationships

Plan of Chapter 10

INTRODUCTION

In this chapter we examine how research results are analysed to establish meaningful patterns. The steps involved in converting completed research instruments into tables are examined, together with the **coding** of answers to questions and the statistical treatment of survey data. Finally, we consider the role of the computer in transforming and facilitating the interpretation of research data.

INTERPRETATION

Interpretation and **analysis** are closely related. If one or the other is not carried out properly, the success of a study cannot be assured. Consider the cases that follow. In the first, improper interpretation is the problem and, in the second, improper analysis is the problem.

IMPROPER INTERPRETATION

A producer of a branded fast-moving consumer product, which also markets an own-label or private brand version to a large supermarket chain, noted the following sales returns from the supermarket.

The figures show that sales of its own brand have been declining steadily for the past two years while those of the private brand have been steadily increasing. The firm concludes that its own brand sales have been dropping because consumers are switching to the private branded label. The company decided to stop supplying its own product to the supermarket.

In fact, what was happening was that another supplier to the supermarket was making huge gains in terms of market share by running very substantial promotions. The decline in sales of the company's brand was due largely to promotional efforts of the other company. The mistake the company made here was the failure to relate the data it had obtained to other pertinent data – i.e. the activities of its competitor.

		Company brand sales	Private brand sales
1995	1st quarter	151,234	74,340
	2nd quarter	146,530	81,188
	3rd quarter	139,312	83,248
	4th quarter	131,931	91,430
1996	1st quarter	125,245	101,121
	2nd quarter	119,236	110,234
	3rd quarter	111,125	113,122
	4th quarter	102,197	122,008

IMPROPER ANALYSIS

A firm is trying to determine which of three advertisements is most likely to increase sales of its product. It tests out the three advertisements by running each at different times in newspapers in different areas.

Advertisement	Total sales associated with the advertisement
1	39,005 units
2	31,452 units
3	29,438 units

The sales indicated that advertisement 1 was the most successful. The logical result of the research would be to use the advertisement to promote national sales. However, had an analysis of variance been carried out, it would have indicated that the three advertisements did not in fact differ significantly in terms of their impact on sales. Advertisement 1's apparent success was really due to abnormally high demand in area B. Advertisement 1 was not significantly more successful in the other areas.

Advertisment	A	B	C	D	Total
1	7072	16098	8122	7713	39,005
2	7512	7481	7859	8600	31,452
3	7120	7219	9087	6012	29,438

In order to ensure that procedures for analysing the collection of data are given the proper attention, a formal data-analysis plan should be developed in the early stages of the project. Such a plan should identify:

1 major variables to be studied

2 methods used to measure the variables

3 analysis procedures that will be used to give meaning to the collected data.

ANALYSIS

The two major approaches employed in summarising the results of marketing research are **tabulation** and statistical analysis. Tabulation involves laying out data into easy-to-understand summary tables. Tables are the basic way of presenting summary data. Tabulation is the preparation of tables showing the frequency distribution of particular events. Patterns in the data can often be spotted from a cursory examination of data, although when tables themselves are summarised in the form of graphs the patterns are often even more readily discernible. Statistical analysis is undertaken to identify patterns that are not as easy to see in the data. This is often the case when very large amounts of data need analysis.

TABULATION

Three steps are involved in converting completed questionnaires to tables: **editing**, coding and counting. The procedures involved are called data processing and should be planned at the time of the study design. There are at least three good reasons.

First, the researcher has to think ahead about specific potential results. If this is done, it means that plans for specific tables are made as part of the basic study plan. Second, the data-collection method should be designed to provide efficient data processing. This mainly involves the precoding of questionnaires or other research instruments. Precoding is the assignment of codes to various possible responses identified on the research instrument. Whenever possible and reasonable, alternative responses should be identified and listed in advance. Third, if data processing is planned out well, table production is an inexpensive operation.

Editing

Editing is the inspection of data forms to make a modification or correction of responses. This may seem as if the researcher is making sure that results come out as hoped, but this is not the case. The function of editing is to make the best sense out of what is in hand. One intent is to eliminate or minimise errors in the raw data. There are two basic sources of error: interviewer error and respondent error. Interviewers, for example, may check the wrong response category or not ask the proper flow-through questions. Interviewers can also be poor at recording answers to open-ended questions. Respondents may be inconsistent in their replies: at one point they may indicate they do not drink, yet later talk confidently in the manner of people who regularly drink. Editing gets rid of the inconsistencies and improves the quality of the raw data.

Editing process

Editing can be done manually or by computer, depending on the method of data collection. In manual editing, there can be as many as three stages involved: the interviewer, the field editor and the central research office. The computer-editing process starts at the point of data collection. If the respondent or the interviewer enters an inconsistent response, the error must be corrected by the respondent before the next question appears on the screen. The computer is programmed to recognise the acceptable patterns for sequential questions, what to look for in contingent questions and inconsistent replies and how to handle no replies. If definitive action for particular corrections can be identified, the computer also issues instructions accordingly.

Coding

Usually in coding a number is assigned to represent each reply to a question on a questionnaire or some other research instrument. Coding translates the answers or responses into a more readily countable form. However, without considerable care about the coding of inputs, the tables that are produced as a result of analysis may be misleading. Three types of coding are required to handle the three basic kinds of data collected in surveys: names codes, quantitative codes and qualitative codes.

Name codes

Name codes apply to such things as brands or makes of goods, or even to firms. The names in the list are almost always known in advance. Where a product is being researched, it is simple enough to prelist the brand names that will account for the majority of replies and the same applies to a prelisting of retailers or manufacturers.

Quantitative codes

Quantitative codes are used with questions that request replies in terms of numbers. Categories should be mutually exclusive. For example, too often the question about household income shows categories such as:

£20,000–£25,000
£25,000–£30,000

There is no single place to list a £25,000 income.

Both precoding and postcoding can be applied to quantitative questions. Precoding involves a closed-ended list and postcoding has categories that can be set up only after the answers are in hand. Here are examples of the closed-ended type of quantitative question:

- How many times have you driven your car in the past seven days, not including today?

- What size shirt do you wear?

- Do you own your own house? How long have you owned it?

In each case, answer categories can be set up in advance and the range of answers is known in advance.

In the case of open-ended quantitative questions, even though there may be a rough idea of the range of answers, the likely distribution of answers cannot be known in advance. Setting up categories in advance may produce data that destroy the chances to analyse it or, even worse, that actually distort results. Consider the following:

- Where are you intending to go for your holidays?
- Where were you educated?
- What is your favourite TV programme?

Computers take over much of the work in establishing quantitative categories. Each specific response can be entered into the system and totalled for each specific category. These preliminary runs give the researcher or marketer the information needed to set up the quantitative categories that meet all requirements. Appropriate class intervals can be set up and the computer instructed to enter this information for each questionnaire.

Qualitative codes

Qualitative questions usually produce descriptions, explanations and reasons. The question is open ended and answers can range widely. Setting up codes for qualitative answers calls for much thought in terms of what the particular question is intended to contribute by way of information for the specific study.

STATISTICAL ANALYSIS

Numbers resulting from a piece of research seldom provide much meaning by themselves. Using percentages can facilitate our understanding. A figure of 300 pairs of shoes means little, if anything, completely on its own. However, if we ask 'What is the 300 pairs of shoes a part of?', it begins to assume some meaning if we are told that out of 1000 sales of shoes over the past month, 30% have been bought within the last three days. It means even more if we know that this 30% is responding to a special promotional offer that was introduced three days ago.

There are pitfalls in the use of percentages, however. Just because they are an easy-to-understand form of quantifying data does not make them the universal solution to all problems. Percentages from different groups of people should not be averaged unless they are weighted.

AVERAGING PERCENTAGES SHOULD ALWAYS INVOLVE WEIGHTING

The percentage of car owners for three age groups is shown below. We want to determine the percentage of car owners in the first two groups to arrive at a figure showing usage among those aged 18 to 49. Averaging the two percentages gives a figure of 28.4%.

Percentage of car owners among three age groups

	18–29	30–49	50 and over
Total interviews	100.0%	100.0%	100.0%
Car owners	22.0%	34.8%	65.4%
Average of 18–49	28.4%		

However, if a third column is added to show the total for the combined 18–49 group, as shown below, when the two age groups are combined in terms of their real weights in the study, the resultant correct car-ownership figure for the 18–49 group turns out to be 29.1%. While the difference from the average percentage may not appear all that great, the two figures might be of rather different marketing significance in terms of the particular problem. And the difference between an averaged percentage and a weighted one might be far greater.

Number and percentage of car owners among two age groups

	18–29 No.	%	30–49 No.	%	18–49 No.	%
Total interviews	200	100.0	250	100.0	450	100.0
Car owners	44	22.0	87	34.8	131	29.1

Averages

Averages or measures of central tendency come in three forms: the mode, the mean and the median.

Mode

The **mode** represents the point in an array showing the greatest response level. It is not an average used often in marketing research, but it takes on considerable importance when looking at ordinal data.

Mean

The **mean** is a commonly used average in marketing research and is readily understood as the sum total of values divided by the number of cases. However, it has one shortcoming: it is affected by a few large or small numbers (*skewing*), since it is based on all the values in the array. In terms of a product usage-rate study, for instance, the presence of a small number of heavy users in the study could produce mean usage results not truly representative of the typical user in the sample. The mean usage rate is too large to be descriptive of the user.

Median

The **median** is the value of the middle case in an ordered series. There are as many cases on the higher side as on the lower side. The measure offers the advantage of being unaffected by extreme cases at one end or the other. This again is a useful measure when examining ordinal data.

USING AVERAGES – MEASURES OF CENTRAL TENDENCY

The mean, median and mode should first be calculated. If the mean and median are about the same, the mean should be used since the former is the most generally understood. However, if the mean and median are greatly different, the median should probably be used, as it is likely to be a better measure.

Note that it is possible to have more than one modal value in a distribution.

Number of people living in 25 surveyed households

9	7	6	4	3
8	7	6	4	2
8	6	6	3	2
7	6	5	3	1
7	6	5	3	1

Mean 5	Median 6	Mode 6

In marketing research we should use the mean or the median or both. Depending on the nature of the numerical distribution, these may or may not coincide. Taken together they provide a good indication of the average.

Measures of dispersion

The most common methods used to describe the dispersion of data are the range, **variance** and **standard deviation**. Small values for these measures indicate that the data are compact.

Range

This is the interval from the lowest to the highest value in an array of data. In the number of people living in the sampled households example, the range is $9 - 1 = 8$.

Variance

This is an index that indicates the extent to which the values are dispersed. Were every observation in a dataset the same value, the variance would be zero. Variance increases as values differ significantly from the mean. The formula used to calculate variance is:

$$S^2 = \sum_{i=1}^{n}(X_i - \bar{X})^2/(n-1)$$

where X_i is the individual value in an array, $\bar{X}$ is the mean of the array and n is the number of values in an array.

Standard deviation

This is the square root of the variance and is represented by the symbol S.

SIGNIFICANCE OF DIFFERENCES BETWEEN NUMBERS

Hypotheses

The first step in tests of significance is to make a claim which one then has to find evidence against. This statement is called the **null hypothesis**. The test is intended to determine the strength of the evidence against the null hypothesis. Customarily, the null hypothesis is a statement of no difference or no effect. The term null hypothesis is abbreviated as H_0 and is usually stated in terms of some population parameter or parameters. For example, suppose that p_1 is the **proportion** of the whole population of British males who would have been illness free in 1999 had they ridden a bicycle to work each day and let p_2 stand for the illness-free proportion had they gone to work in their cars instead. The null hypothesis is:

$$H_0 : p_1 = p_2$$

because this states that riding a bicycle to work has the same effectiveness as travelling by car. The name given to the statement we hope or suspect is true instead of H_0 is called the **alternative hypothesis**, abbreviated by H_1. The **alternative hypothesis** in this case is that riding a bicycle to work is more effective than travelling by car. In terms of the population parameters this is:

$$H_1 : p_1 > p_2$$

A test of significance assesses the strength of the evidence against the null hypothesis in terms of probability. If the observed outcome is unlikely under the supposition that the null hypothesis is true, but is more probable if the alternative hypothesis is true, that outcome is evidence against H_0 in favour of H_1. The less probable the outcome is, the stronger is the evidence that H_0 is false.

There are many tests of significance appropriate for different types of hypothesis and for different data-collection designs – as well as levels of significance. Some of these are examined later. An outline of what such a test of significance should include is shown in the box.

STEPS IN A TEST OF SIGNIFICANCE

1 Select the null hypothesis H_0 and the alternative hypothesis H_1. The test is designed to assess the strength of the evidence against the null hypothesis. H_1 is a statement of the alternative we will accept if the evidence enables us to reject H_0.

2 Select the level of significance. This states how much evidence against H_0 we will accept as sufficient.

3 Select the test statistic on which the test will be based. This is a statistic that assesses how well the data conform to H_0.

4 Find the probability value that the test statistic would weigh against H_0 at least as strongly as it does for these data, were H_0, in fact, true. If the probability value is less than or equal to the significance level then the test was statistically significant at that level.

Measuring differences

Whenever sample data are being used, we have to compensate for sampling error. Z and t tests are methods used to assess the differences among data while still taking into account the influence that sampling error may have played. The methods are employable when measurement scales are at least interval, observations are independent, only one or two groups are involved, differences between two means are involved and, in the case of the **t test**, where observations are drawn from a normally distributed population.

Provided that these criteria are met, we need to decide which of the two tests is the more appropriate. A **Z test** is used if the sample size is larger than 30. A t test is appropriate when the sample size is less than 30. If the population variance is not known, then the sample variance is assumed to equate to it and is used instead. The t test is usually employed in marketing research.

Z test

One- and two-tailed tests   The tabular value of Z at any level of significance depends on whether a one- or a two-tailed test is involved. Where we are looking for equality between two sets of data, $H_0 : \mu_1 = \mu_2$, a two-tailed test is appropriate.

Where we are looking at a situation that involves evaluating whether something is greater than something else, a one-tailed test is appropriate. The same also applies to situations where we are evaluating whether something is less than something else.

Dealing with proportions If proportions are involved rather than discrete numbers, a different formula is needed – although in other respects the procedure is the same.

The formula used is:

$$Z = (p - P)/\sigma_p$$

where p = sample proportion
  P = population proportion
  $Q = 1 - P$
  $\sigma_p = \sqrt{(P.Q/n)}$ where n is the sample size

t test

The procedures for using the t test are similar to those for using the Z test. However, there are different formulae that are applicable in different situations (see Kress[1]). For example:

$$t = \frac{(\bar{x} - \mu)/s}{\sqrt{(n - 1)}}$$

s = standard deviation of the sample
$\bar{x}$ = sample mean
μ = population mean
n = sample size

When the population data do exist, but the other group is represented by a fairly small sample, this formula should be employed.

Tests with non-metric data

There are several tests that can be used, depending on the nature of the data and the comparisons made. These include:

- *Mann-Whitney U test*: this is used when comparing two groups, but the basis for comparison is data in ordinal form.

- *Wilcoxon or signed rank test*: this is appropriate for situations where two matching (non-independent) samples are being compared using ordinal (**non-parametric**) data.

- *Kruskal-Wallis test*: this is used when more than two independent samples are involved and the data are ordinal.

- *Friedman two-way analysis of data*: this is used when three or more related samples are involved and the data are ordinal.

We have to decide whether the difference between two or more numbers, or sets of numbers, is probably significant, and whether two numbers are causally related.

Difference between numbers in a single array

Suppose that in a survey of 1500, results showed that 64% chose brand X, 24% chose brand Y and the remainder made no choice. Are these real differences? Assuming that this was a probability sample, the answer is yes: the sampling error for 64% is some 2.5% and for 24% it is some 2.2%.

CHI-SQUARE ANALYSIS

Difference between numbers in a series of arrays

In this case a comparison is made between the answers given by people with different sets of characteristics to a particular question. Characteristics of the people include demographics, such as geography, household size, the presence of children, income, sex and age. These are cross-tabulated against such things as awareness or the use of a product category, brand and purchase intent.

EXAMPLE

Question: Are you aware of brand X washing machines? Table 10.1 shows the results.

TABLE 10.1   Awareness results

	Yes	No	Total
Men	50	200	250
Women	150	300	450
Total	**200**	**500**	**700**

Simple inspection of the data would seem to suggest there is a difference between men and women in terms of awareness level. However, we really want to know if the difference observable in cross-tabulating the data is statistically significant: in other words, what the probability is that observed differences could have occurred by chance. In this particular instance we can use the **chi-square** test to see if this is the case (we should, however, consult standard statistical texts to appreciate the suitability of this test and to understand its theoretical underpinning).

The chi-square statistic is calculated by the formula:

$$\chi^2 = \sum_{i=1}^{n} (O_i - E_i)^2 / E_i$$

where O_i = the observed value and E_i = the theoretically expected value, assuming in this case that there is no difference between the occupational backgrounds of respondents (see Table 10.2).

We hypothesise that there is no relationship. However, χ^2 at 2 degrees of freedom at the 5% level = 3.84 and because 13.5 > 3.84 the difference noted in the sample is statistically significant. We must reject the null hypothesis and conclude that the difference in levels of awareness in men and women did not occur by chance.

TABLE 10.2   Breakdown of brand awareness

	Yes	No	Total
Men (O = observed)	50	200	250
	(250 × 200)/700	(250 × 500)/700	
(E = expected)	= 71	= 179	
Women (O = observed)	150	300	450
	(450 × 200)/700	(450 × 500)/700	
(E = expected)	= 129	= 321	
Total	**200**	**500**	**700**

Note: Expected values are rounded off to the nearest whole number.

$$\chi^2 = (50 - 71)^2/71 + (200 - 179)^2/179 + (150 - 129)^2/129 + (300 - 321)^2/321$$
$$= 13.5 \text{ with degrees of freedom } (r - 1)(k - 1) = 1$$

where r = number of rows, k = number of columns

In the example, using a 2 × 2 table, it is usually preferable to use *Fisher's exact test* or include *Yates' correction* where there are a small number of cases. In the latter case the formula is modified to:

$$\chi^2 = \sum_{i=1}^{n} (|O_i - E_i| - 0.5)^2 / E_i$$

Where the sample size is so small that the expected value is less than 5, then chi-square should not be used.

Chi-square is a statistical tool used to evaluate the statistical significance of differences between sets of data. Basically, it compares one or more frequency distributions of data to indicate whether there is a real difference. It compares an actual set of data against a theoretical one to show what would be expected by chance alone.

EXAMPLE

Chi-square

A market researcher has completed a study of soft drinks. The following table shows the brand purchased most often, broken down by male versus female. The researcher wants to know if there is a relationship between the gender of the purchaser and the brand purchased.

Drink	Male	Female
Coke	66	52
Pepsi	67	48
7-Up	35	38
Dr Pepper	34	21
Sprite	32	41
Lilt	33	31
Blackjack	18	25
Tango	34	24

Chi-square 'male' 'female'

Expected counts are printed below observed counts:

	Male	Female	Total
1	66 62.84	52 55.16	118
2	67 61.24	48 53.76	115
3	35 38.88	38 34.12	73
4	34 29.29	21 25.71	55
5	32 38.88	41 34.12	73
6	33 34.08	31 29.92	64
7	18 22.90	25 20.10	43
8	34 30.89	24 27.11	58
Total	**319**	**280**	**599**

$$\chi^2 = -0.159 + 0.181 + 0.541 + 0.616 + 0.387 + 0.440 + 0.757 + 0.863 + 1.216$$
$$+ 1.386 + 0.034 + 0.039 + 1.048 + 1.194 + 0.314 + 0.357$$

$$\chi^2 = 9.533 \quad df = 7$$

The tabular value of χ^2 at 0.05 level of significance and $(8 - 1)(2 - 1) = 7$ degrees of freedom is 14.07. The calculated value (9.533) is lower than the tabular value (14.07). There would not seem to be a significant relationship between gender of the purchaser and the brand purchased.

USE OF SIMILARITIES BETWEEN NUMBERS TO SHOW CAUSE AND EFFECT

Another application of numbers in marketing research is in the analysis and understanding of the similarities between variables. Many surveys try to measure the sales impact of advertising or other marketing efforts. One often-used procedure compares the proportion of purchasers among two groups: those who remember seeing or hearing the advertising and those who do not.

Table 10.3 displays these data, this time ignoring the gender of the respondents. It also shows brand awareness of the washing machine by those who recall the brand's advertising and those who do not. An obvious but incorrect conclusion from the table is that advertising accounted for the 15% difference in the awareness level. However, the results merely show only that there is a **correlation** between advertising awareness and brand awareness. The correlation may be because people become aware of the brand by other means and then notice its advertising.

Interpreting the meaning of cross-tabulations amounts to more than simply taking the figures at face value. There has to be some underlying logical explanation behind the inferences that are drawn from the numbers alone. In this case, there is some evidence to support the argument presented. In the case of higher-priced items, psychologists have found that people pay attention to advertisements after purchase to help reinforce their purchase choice (allaying post-purchase cognitive dissonance).

TABLE 10.3	Brand awareness and advertising recall	
	Those remembering advertising	Those not remembering advertising
Total group	100%	100%
Aware of brand	20%	5%
Not aware of brand	80%	95%

Measuring relationships by cross-tabulation

For data provided by marketing research to be useful in making marketing decisions, it is most important that the cross-tabulation that might help to make
marketing decisions are identified. For example, differences by age groups, or
even concentration on a single age segment, could imply completely different
approaches for each target market.

ANALYSIS OF VARIANCE

Analysis of variance is a method used extensively in evaluating the results
of experiments. The general question involves determining the influence of a
treatment on a dependent variable. The argument is that the total variance that
exists among the data can be apportioned to specific factors by means of formal
mathematical techniques. The amount of variance attributable to each factor is
indicative of the factor's influence on the dependent variable.

EXAMPLE

As part of a new advertising campaign, a firm plans a full-page advertisement in
either a news magazine or a sports magazine. The problem is to decide which
magazine has the lowest ratio of full-page advertisements to the number of pages
in the magazine (see Table 10.4).

TABLE 10.4   Ratio of full-page advertisements to number of pages

Year	News magazine	Sports magazine
1989	0.79	0.60
	0.80	0.46
	0.54	0.38
	0.72	0.42
1991	0.49	0.39
	0.85	0.56
	0.50	0.57
	0.67	0.46
1993	0.36	0.37
	0.65	0.64
	0.47	0.52
	0.68	0.41

Note: The advertisement ratio is calculated by dividing the number of full-
page ads by the number of pages in the issue.

It is also important to establish whether there has been a recent change in this ratio. (See Tables 10.5 and 10.6 for analysis of variance.)

Three hypotheses are to be tested:

H_0: there is no interaction between year and magazine
H_1: there is an interaction between year and magazine
H_0: there is no difference in the average ad ratios for different years
H_1: there is a difference in the average ad ratios for different years
H_0: there is no difference in the average ad ratio when using different magazines
H_1: there is a difference in the average ad ratio when using different magazines.

We reject the hypothesis when the probability is $\leq = 0.05$ (decision rule).

TABLE 10.5   Analysis of variance for advertisement ratio

Source	DF	SS	MS	F	P
Year	2	0.02386	0.01193	0.73	0.494
Magazine	1	0.12615	0.12615	7.76	0.012
Year*Magazine	2	0.03753	0.01876	1.15	0.338
Error	18	0.29265	0.01626		
Total	**23**	**0.48018**			

Produced with the student edition of Minitab.
DF = degrees of freedom; SS = sum of squares; MS = mean square; F = statistic;
P = probability.

TABLE 10.6   Analysis of variance

Test	Effect	F ratio	P-value	Decision
1	Year*Magazine	1.15	0.338	Do not reject H_0: do not conclude there is significant interaction between year and magazine
2	Year	0.73	0.494	Do not reject H_0: the mean ad ratios are probably the same for the three years
3	Magazine	7.76	0.012	Reject H_0: the mean ad ratios are not the same for the two magazines

For further details of analysis of variance, see McKenzie et al.[2]

MEASURING RELATIONSHIPS

Regression and correlation both measure the relationship between a dependent variable and one or more independent variables, but each shows this relationship in a different manner. Regression analysis identifies the nature of the relationship using an equation, whereas correlation analysis describes the strength of relationships between variables by means of an index.

Correlation analysis

A coefficient of determination r^2 is computed and indicates the proportion of change in the dependent variable that is associated with changes in the independent variable. For instance, an r^2 of 0.49 means that 49% of the variation in the dependent variable is associated with changes in the independent variable. The square root of the coefficient of determination is the correlation coefficient r and is an index of association between the two variables.

A strong correlation does not establish causality. There are two major categories of correlation analysis: bivariate and multivariate. Bivariate analysis measures the relationship between two variables whereas multivariate analysis measures the relationship among three or more variables.

Bivariate analysis

EXAMPLE

The first thing we might do before calculating r or r^2 is to produce a scatterplot of the relationship between the two variables. This is shown in Figure 10.1.

From the scatterplot we can see that there is some association between the two sets of data, although it may not be very strong. Were there to be a strong degree of association between the two variables, the graph might have appeared as shown in Figure 10.2. (Table 10.7 shows our data in tabular form.)

Notice that where there is a high degree of association, the points lie along a straight line.

The indices association r and r^2 are calculated according to the formula:

$$r = n(\Sigma YX) - (\Sigma Y)^2 / \sqrt{(n\Sigma X - (\Sigma X)^2)(n\Sigma Y^2 - (\Sigma Y)^2)}$$

r^2 is obtained from r.

In this example correlation of price and alcohol $r = 0.241$.

The significance of r can be tested using the t test:

$$t = r\sqrt{(n-2)/(1-r^2)}$$

$$t = 0.241\sqrt{(14-2)/(1-0.058)} = 0.241 \times \sqrt{(12/0.942)} = 0.86$$

tabular $t = 2.179$ at 0.05 level of significance, 12 degrees of freedom.

Since the computed value is less than the tabular value, the computed value of r indicates no evidence of any association.

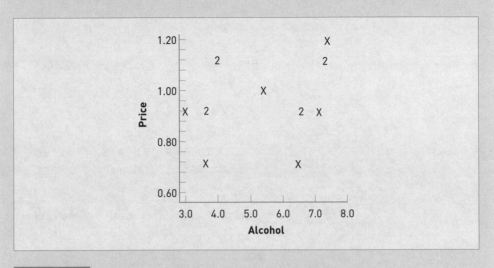

FIGURE 10.1   Price versus alcohol content per glass – low degree of association

TABLE 10.7   Fourteen brands of cider, their price per glass and alcohol content per glass

Brand	Price (£)	Alcohol content (%)
1	1.1	4.2
2	1.1	4.2
3	0.9	4.0
4	0.9	3.0
5	1.2	8.5
6	0.9	8.4
7	0.9	4.0
8	0.7	4.0
9	1.1	8.5
10	1.1	8.5
11	0.9	7.5
12	0.9	7.5
13	0.7	7.6
14	1.0	6.0

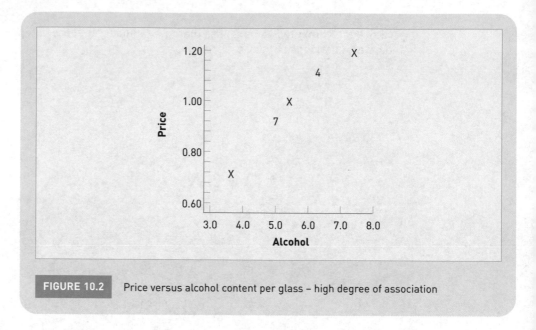

FIGURE 10.2   Price versus alcohol content per glass – high degree of association

Rank order correlation

Where we have ordinal data, it is appropriate to use the *Spearman Rank* correlation method. The formula is:

$$r = 1 - 6\Sigma D^2 / n(n^2 - 1)$$

where D is the absolute difference between rankings and n is the number of observations.

Regression analysis

The first step in regression analysis is to plot the relationships between the dependent and the independent variables on a graph: this is referred to as the scatterplot (as shown in Figures 10.3 to 10.6). This will give some idea of the general kinds of relationship that exist between the data. Once it has been established that a linear relationship exists, it is appropriate to derive values for the equation for fitting a straight line to two variables: $Y = a + b(X)$. Regression analysis fits a line through the data points that minimises the sum of the squared deviations. In order to position the line, two values have to be determined: a, the intercept, and b, the regression coefficient.

Suppose we have the following data about houses for sale:

- price
- area in square feet covered by building
- acres of garden
- number of rooms
- number of bathrooms/toilets.

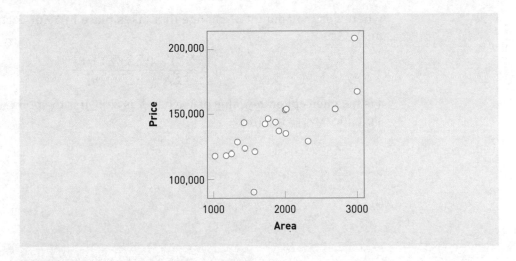

FIGURE 10.3   Scatterplot – price versus area

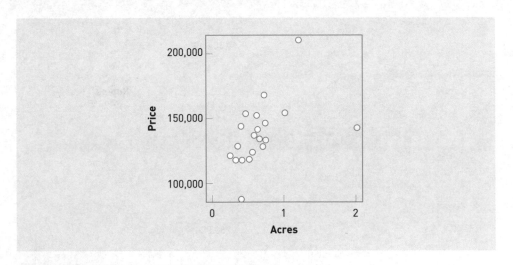

FIGURE 10.4   Scatterplot – price versus acres

Which of the various factors in Table 10.8 that describe the house are most closely associated with the price?

Overall, we see that there appears to be some degree of positive association between each one of the variables and the price. The clustering of data points along a straight line (indicating the goodness of fit) is perhaps best exhibited between area and price, although acres and price also appear to be well associated. We calculate the regression equation for the relationship between one independent variable and one dependent variable by means of the following equation:

$$Y = a + b(X)$$

where b is the amount of change that takes place in Y for each unit of change in X.

$$b = \frac{\Sigma XY - [(\Sigma X)(\Sigma Y)/n]}{\Sigma X^2 - [(\Sigma X^2)/n]}$$

a is the intercept or the value of Y when X is zero. It is the point where the regression line crosses the Y axis.

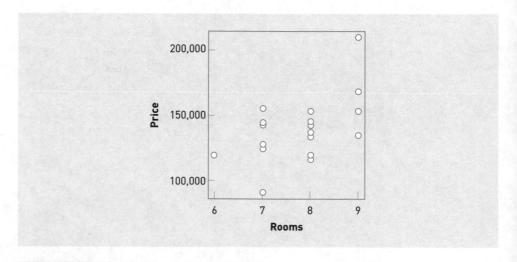

FIGURE 10.5   Scatterplot – price versus rooms

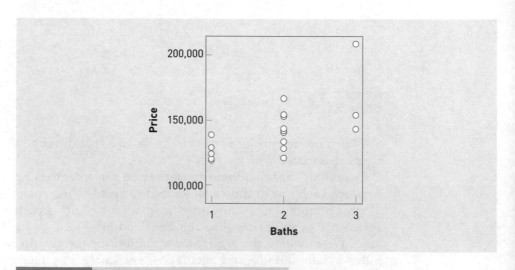

FIGURE 10.6   Scatterplot – price versus bathrooms

TABLE 10.8	Houses for sale			
Price	Area	Acres	Rooms	Baths
£168,500	2990	0.70	9	2
£122,000	1560	0.24	8	2
£136,000	1990	0.65	9	2
£129,000	1320	0.68	7	1
£136,000	1990	0.70	8	2
£154,000	1980	0.45	8	2
£129,000	2300	0.34	7	2
£118,000	1150	0.32	8	1
£144,000	1400	2.00	7	3
£143,000	1700	0.60	8	2
£120,000	1230	0.50	6	1
£155,000	1990	1.00	7	2
£90,000	1550	0.40	7	1
£154,000	2700	0.60	9	3
£125,000	1400	0.55	7	1
£145,000	1850	0.38	7	2
£146,500	1750	0.72	8	2
£118,000	1000	0.40	8	1
£210,000	2950	1.20	9	3
£138,000	1900	0.57	8	1

EXAMPLE

Using Minitab 8.0 for Windows and SPSSPC, the following bivariate regressions are obtained on these data (note that figures may show the effects of rounding off):

where Coef   = regression coefficient
       Stdev   = standard deviation
       t = t-ratio (statistic)
       p = probability of occurrence
       s = standard error of the estimate
       Fit Stdev = fit standard deviation
       St resid = standard residual

▶

1 The regression equation is:

Price = 79312 + 32.6 area

Predictor	Coef	Stdev	t-ratio	p
Constant	79312	12691	6.25	0.000
Area	32.555	6.627	4.91	0.000

s = 16231 R-sq = 57.3% R-sq(adj) = 54.9%

Analysis of variance

Source	DF	SS	MS	F	p
Regression	1	6356522504	6356522504	24.13	0.000
Error	18	4741927496	263440416		
Total	19	11098450000			

Unusual observations

Obs	Area	Price	Fit Stdev	Fit	Residual	St Resid
13	1550	90000	129772	4091	−39772	−2.53R
19	2950	210000	175349	8233	34651	2.48R

R denotes an observation with a large standard residual.

2 The regression equation is:

Price = 119815 + 29593 acres

Predictor	Coef	Stdev	t-ratio	p
Constant	119815	9623	12.45	0.000
Acres	29593	12767	2.32	0.032

s = 21791 R-sq = 23.0% R-sq(adj) = 18.7%

Analysis of variance

Source	DF	SS	MS	F	p
Regression	1	2551202835	2551202835	5.37	0.032
Error	18	8547247165	474847065		
Total	19	11098450000			

Unusual observations

Obs	Acres	Price	Fit Stdev	Fit	Residual	St Resid
9	2.00	144000	179000	17911	−35000	−2.82RX
19	1.20	210000	155326	8547	54674	2.73R

R denotes an observation with a large standard residual.
X denotes an observation whose X value gives it large influence.

3 The regression equation is:

Price = 22518 + 15036 rooms

Predictor	Coef	Stdev	t-ratio	p
Constant	22518	44284	0.51	0.617
Rooms	15036	5682	2.65	0.016

s = 21068 R-sq = 28.0% R-sq(adj) = 24.0%

Analysis of variance

Source	DF	SS	MS	F	p
Regression	1	3108768182	3108768182	7.00	0.016
Error	18	7989681818	443871212		
Total	19	11098450000			

Unusual observations

Obs	Rooms	Price	Fit Stdev	Fit	Residual	St Resid
19	9.00	210000	157845	8523	52155	2.71R

R denotes an observation with a large standard residual.

4 The regression equation is:

Price = 94793 + 24587 baths

Predictor	Coef	Stdev	t-ratio	p
Constant	94793	11123	8.52	0.000
Baths	24587	5782	4.25	0.000

s = 17539 R-sq = 50.1% R-sq(adj) = 47.3%

Analysis of variance

Source	DF	SS	MS	F	p
Regression	1	5561569565	5561569565	18.08	0.000
Error	18	5536880435	307604469		
Total	19	11098450000			

Unusual observations

Obs	Baths	Price	Fit Stdev	Fit	Residual	St Resid
19	3.00	210000	168554	7970	41446	2.65R

R denotes an observation with a large standard residual.

As predicted by the scattergraph the best relationship is that between area and price.

Knowledge of an independent variable, coupled with the appropriate equation, enables an estimate to be made of the dependent variable. Thus knowing the area covered by a house can be used to estimate its likely price.

Multivariate analysis

In the preceding sections, simple regression and correlation have been used to determine the association between two variables. However, it is not usual for one independent variable to play such a major part in explaining the dependent variable. Where an r^2 value between two variables is less than 0.8 it is necessary to search for additional independent variables, which can increase the variation explained by the regression or correlation models.

Multiple regression analysis is usually the preferred way of introducing more than one independent variable into the study. The multiple regression model is an expansion of the simple regression model:

$$Y = a + b_1X_1 + b_2X_2 + \ldots + b_nX_n$$

The number of independent variables used in each model depends on how many are needed to estimate adequately the value of the dependent variable. Most equations usually have fewer than ten independent variables.

A multiple regression model for the house data just examined follows.

Stepwise regression of price on four predictors (rooms, baths, acres and area), with N = 20:

Step	1	2
Constant	79,312	69,085
Area	32.6	30.1
t-ratio	4.91	5.24
Acres		22,800
t-ratio		2.77
S	16,231	13,859
R-SQ	57.27	70.58

We see that only areas and acres are kept in the regression equation. These two independent variables account for more than 70% of the variance in the dependent variable. Since no other independent variables have been included and the total variance accounted for does not come near to 80%, we can only conclude that there must be other factors that are relevant to the house price than those reported here.

For further information on multivariate analysis, see McKenzie et al.[2] and Hair et al.[3]

Cluster analysis

Cluster analysis is the name given to a group of multivariate techniques that identify similar entities from the characteristics possessed by the entities. Objects or variables are identified or classified so that each object is very similar to the others in the cluster with respect to some criteria. The technique examines similarities between observations of entities based on profiles of their scores on a number of measured characteristics. Applications include:

- determining the number and composition of market segments
- facilitating the selection of test markets
- identifying groups of people with common purchasing interests in segmentation studies; this helps to identify target markets and provides information for establishing product **positioning** and developing promotional themes.

EXAMPLE

Various measures of the standard of living in European countries at the end of the 1980s are shown in Table 10.9 and Figure 10.7. On the basis of these measures, countries are clustered according to similarities in the standard of living. The data are standardised and hierarchical clustering using group average linkage is used to obtain clusters.

From the dendrogram a number of clusters are seen, for example: 'Denmark, Sweden and Switzerland', 'France, Netherlands and Norway', and 'Belgium and Spain'. Subsequent clustering obviously depends on what indicators of the standard of living are taken – a different set of indicators could produce different clustering. Another point is that through standardisation of the data in this example, equal weighting to each of the measures is given. It might be desirable to give more weighting to some measures than to others.

For further information on cluster analysis, see Hair et al.[3] and Green et al.[4]

TABLE 10.9   Measures of living standards in Europe

	Private per capita	Per '000 population	Per '000 live births	Per '000 ownership		
	Consumption	Doctors	Infant deaths	TV	Cars	Phones
Austria	7,434	2.1	8.3	323	370	525
Belgium	8,486	3.3	8.6	301	349	478
Denmark	7,705	2.7	7.5	386	321	864
France	8,733	2.6	7.5	332	394	608
Germany	8,120	3.0	7.5	379	457	650
Ireland	5,079	1.5	7.5	216	210	265
Italy	8,577	1.3	8.9	255	408	488
Netherlands	8,133	2.4	6.8	327	348	639
Norway	8,224	2.5	8.3	348	388	622
Spain	6,443	3.7	7.8	322	263	396
Sweden	8,090	3.1	5.8	393	400	890
Switzerland	10,181	2.9	7.3	411	419	856
UK	9,154	1.4	8.4	534	318	524

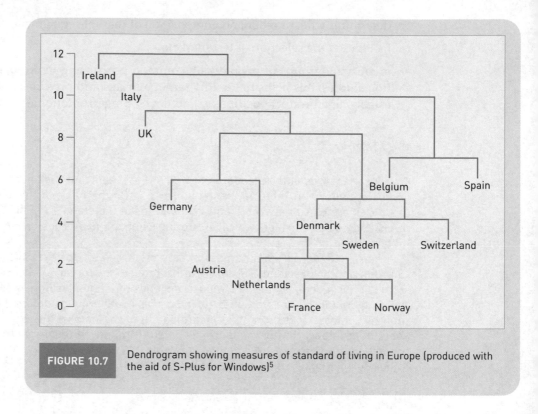

FIGURE 10.7   Dendrogram showing measures of standard of living in Europe (produced with the aid of S-Plus for Windows)[5]

Factor analysis

This is a generic name given to a class of multivariate statistical methods that undertake data reduction and summarisation. The method analyses the inter-relationships among a large number of variables and explains these variables in terms of their common underlying dimensions (factors). For example, a survey questionnaire may consist of 100 questions, but because not all the questions are the same, they do not all measure the basic underlying dimensions to the same extent. **Factor analysis** enables us to identify the separate dimensions being measured by the survey and obtain a factor loading for each variable on each factor.

Factor analysis may be used to discover a set of dimensions that underlie or underpin a set of variables (Figure 10.8).

Applications for factor analysis include:

- uncovering the factors that influence advertising readership
- ascertaining which personal characteristics are associated with preferring one brand of product to another
- uncovering the important dimensions of product/service quality
- uncovering the factors that need to be taken into account in making decisions about such things as product design and promotion.

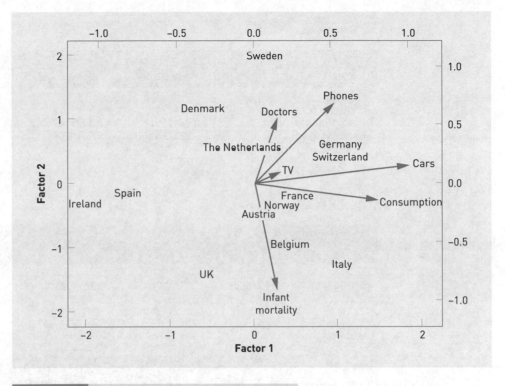

FIGURE 10.8 Scatterplot of standard of living analysis

The example in Table 10.10 shows a factor analysis of the standard of living data just examined. Factor 2 represents the health dimension and Factor 1 the spending power dimension.

For further information on factor analysis, see Hair et al.[3] and Green et al.[4]

Conjoint analysis

Conjoint analysis is a method of portraying consumers' decisions realistically as a tradeoff among multiattribute products or services. Conjoint analysis helps us to understand how people develop preferences for products or services. It is based on the simple notion that consumers evaluate the utility or value of something by combining the separate amounts of utility provided by each attribute.

It is closely related to traditional experimentation. In situations where people are involved we often need to conduct experiments with factors we can control. For example, should a chocolate bar be slightly sweet to the taste or very sweet? Should it be promoted as a Slimmers' product or not? What price should be asked for the product?

In conjoint analysis the use of experimental design in the analysis of consumer decisions has two objectives. First, the experiments may try to assess how the

TABLE 10.10	Importance of factors in standard of living analysis

	Factor 1	Factor 2	Factor 3
SS loadings	1.644996	1.3791295	1.2124108
Proportion variation	0.274166	0.2298549	0.2020685
Cumulative variation	0.274166	0.5040209	0.7060894

The degrees of freedom for the model is 0.

Uniquenesses

Consumption	Doctors	Infant mortality	TV	Cars	Phones
0.08042417	0.7765078	0.3057129	0.3231836	0.1644488	0.1131866

Loadings

	Factor 1	Factor 2	Factor 3
Consumption	0.755		0.588
Doctors	0.108	0.460	
Infant mortality		−0.825	
TV	0.176	0.120	0.795
Cars	0.891	0.161	0.126
Phones	0.481	0.665	0.461

Obtained with the aid of S-Plus for Windows[5] using principal axis method.

sweetness of the chocolate bar contributes to the willingness of the consumer to buy it. It may also seek to assess how much a change in the willingness to buy can be accounted for by differences between levels of sweetness. Second, the experiments may seek to establish a valid model of consumer judgements that is useful in predicting the consumer acceptance of any combination of attributes, even those not originally evaluated by the consumer.

Conjoint analysis has been used in the pharmaceutical industry for product positioning close to launch where the product attributes were not changeable. However, it is now used earlier in product development to help define clinical end-points, and with input into go/no-go decisions.[6]

EXAMPLE

In a furniture polish **concept-testing** experiment, each respondent has been told about the properties of eight dummy cans of polish to rank choices in order of preference for purchase. The responses for two respondents are shown in Table 10.11.

TABLE 10.11 Concept-testing experiment: responses

Size	Properties	Brand	Respondent 1	Respondent 2
Small	A	Alpha	1	1
	A	Beta	2	2
	B	Alpha	5	6
	B	Beta	6	5
Large	A	Alpha	3	4
	A	Beta	4	3
	B	Alpha	7	7
	B	Beta	8	8

For simplicity, in applying the technique we will assume an additive model is appropriate and that the overall preference for a combination of attributes is represented as:

$$\text{Preference sib} = PWs + PWi + PWb$$

where the overall preference for a combination of size, properties and brand (Preference sib) is the sum of PWs, PWi, and PWb, the estimated part-worths for the levels of size, properties and brands, respectively.

In order to calculate the coefficients, we have to specify the composition rules and if the additive rule strictly holds, a simple difference from the mean (ANOVA) should apply. The average rank of the eight combinations is 4.5 and we calculate the impact of each factor. For example, the average ranks for the two levels of size are:

$$\text{Small} = (1 + 2 + 5 + 6)/4 = 3.5$$
$$\text{Large} = (3 + 4 + 7 + 8)/4 = 5.5$$

Figures for properties and brand are similarly calculated. Then, for respondent 1 the average ranks and deviations for each factor from the overall average rank (4.5) are as shown in Table 10.12.

Higher rank and a more preferred stimulus are usually given a smaller number so the next step is to reverse all the signs so that the positive part-worths now indicate higher preference. Coefficients are then calculated using the following method:

TABLE 10.12   Average ranks and deviations for respondent 1

Factor level	Average rank	Deviation
Small	3.5	−1
Large	5.5	+1
A	2.5	−2
B	6.5	+2
Alpha	4.0	−.5
Beta	5.0	+.5

- Square the deviations and find their sum (in this case the total is 10.5).

- Multiply each squared deviation by a standardising value calculated as the number of levels divided by the sum of the squared deviations, in this case (6/10.5) or 0.571.

- Take the square root of the standardised squared deviation to get the actual coefficient.

By way of illustration, for the first level of property (A), the deviation of 2 (reversing the sign!) is squared and then multiplied by 0.571 to obtain 2.284. To calculate the coefficent for this level, we then take the square root of 2.284 to obtain a coefficient of 1.511. This process yields the coefficients for each level, as shown in Table 10.13.

The part-worth estimates are in a common scale, so the relative importance of each factor can be computed directly. The importance of a factor is represented by the range of its levels. The ranges are then standardised by dividing each range by the sum of the ranges. For example, for respondent 1, the ranges are 1.512 and .756. The relative importance for size, properties and brand are calculated as 1.512/5.294, 3.022/5.294, and .756/5.294 or 29%, 57% and 14% respectively.

We can follow the same procedures for the second respondent and calculate the average ranks, deviations and coefficients for each level (Table 10.14).

To examine the ability of the model to predict the actual choices of the respondents, we predict performance order by summing the coefficients for the different

TABLE 10.13   Coefficients for each level

Size		Property		Brand	
Small	Large	A	B	Alpha	Beta
.756	−.756	1.51	−1.51	.378	−.378

TABLE 10.14 Average ranks, deviations and coefficients for respondent 2

Factor level	Average rank	Deviation	Coefficent
Small	3.5	−1	.77
Large	5.5	+1	−.77
A	2.5	−2	1.55
B	6.5	+2	−1.55
Alpha	4.0	−.5	0.0
Beta	5.0	+.5	0.0

TABLE 10.15 Respondent 1: calculations

Product description Size		Properties		Brand		Predicted value Part-worth total	Predicted rank
Small		A		Alpha			
.756	+	1.51	+	.378	=	2.644	1
Small		A		Beta			
.756	+	1.51	+	−.378	=	1.888	2
Small		B		Alpha			
.756	+	−1.51	+	.378	=	−.376	5
Small		B		Beta			
.756	+	−1.51	+	−.378	=	−1.132	6
Large		A		Alpha			
−.756	+	1.51	+	.378	=	1.132	3
Large		A		Beta			
−.756	+	1.51	+	−.378	=	.376	4
Large		B		Alpha			
−.756	+	−1.51	+	.378	=	−1.888	7
Large		B		Beta			
−.756	+	−1.51	+	−.378	=	−2.644	8

combinations of factor levels and rank ordering the resulting scores. The calculations for respondent 1 are shown in Table 10.15.

The predicted preference order can be compared to the respondent's actual preference order for a measure of predictive accuracy. The predictive preference orders for both respondents are shown in Table 10.16.

In the case of respondent 2, since the weights of zero were calculated for the brand name the compositional rule is unable to predict a difference between brands within the ingredient and can size combinations. Brand name may be a

Original rank	Predicted rank order	
	Respondent 1	Respondent 2
1	1	1.5
2	2	1.5
3	3	3.5
4	4	3.5
5	5	5.5
6	6	5.5
7	7	7.5
8	8	7.5

TABLE 10.16   Predictive preference orders: both respondents

random choice, given size and properties. Moreover, when two or more stimuli have equal total-worth predictions, the rank orders are averaged.

The example illustrated assumes an additive model only as the base for the compositional rule. Original rankings assumed that no interaction effect occurs: for example, the respondent prefers Alpha and normally prefers property A over B. If interaction is thought to have a serious effect, steps have to be taken in the analysis to allow for this.

Multidimensional scaling and perceptual mapping

It is easier to understand the relationships between facts, events or objects if we can visualise these relationships spatially. There are a number of techniques that go under the heading of **multidimensional scaling** and perceptual mapping techniques which enable us to do exactly that. They allow us to visualise how users perceive products and services in relationship to one another. There are a variety of perceptual-mapping programs and techniques designed to work with the different kinds of data that have been collected.

EXAMPLE

This example uses Multiscale II.[7] In this case, brands of watch were taken in pairs and respondents were asked to judge how dissimilar the brands were vis-à-vis each other.

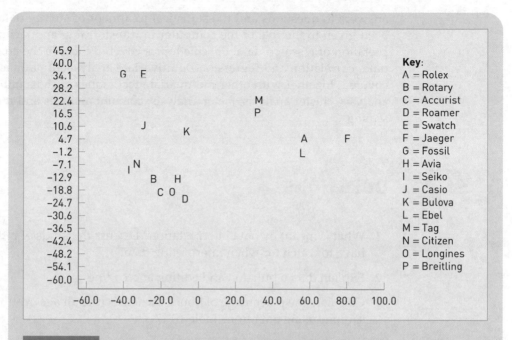

FIGURE 10.9 Configuration plot for dimension 2 (vertical axis) against dimension 1

Judgement-similarity measures between products or brands can be used to create geometric representations in multidimensional spaces called perceptual maps. The brands or products are represented by points in the space, while the dimensions represent the attributes used by the customers in making the similarity judgements. Brands located close to each other are judged to be similar on the attributes and thus form a defined market. In Figure 10.9, information about the competitive sets is obtained by the examination of clusters of points. Products A, F and L (Rolex, Jaeger and Ebel) cluster together, but are separate, for example, from M and P (Tag and Breitling), which form another cluster.

Comparing products at the extreme points of both dimensions gives some idea of the name to give to each of the two axes. On the horizontal axis Jaeger at one extreme contrasts with Fossil at the other – perhaps reflecting the status symbol, high-price dimension – while on the vertical axis, Accurist and Roamer contrast with Swatch and Fossil, reflecting the conservatism, or lack of it, of the brands.

SUMMARY

This chapter has examined how research results can be analysed and interpreted to establish meaningful patterns. The steps involved in converting completed research instruments into tables has been examined, together with the coding of answers to questions and the statistical treatment of survey data. Attention has been given to the role of the computer in transforming and facilitating the interpretation of research data. Specific topics covered include the cross-tabulation of data, correlation and regression. Multivariate analysis of variance has also been covered, together with other multivariate techniques such as multiple regression analysis, cluster analysis, factor analysis, conjoint analysis and multidimensional scaling.

QUESTIONS

1 What is meant by data interpretation? Discuss the kinds of pitfall that we have to watch for when interpreting data.

2 Explain data tabulation and editing and coding.

3 Calculate the percentage of house owners across all age groups for the whole sample, using data from Table 10.17.

TABLE 10.17	Number and percentage of house owners among three age groups		
		Total	
	18–29 (number)	30–49 (number)	50+ (number)
Total interviews	150	230	140
% house owners	36	65	29

4 Calculate the mean, the median and the mode in the case given in Table 10.18.

TABLE 10.18	Cars per household

Number of cars per household in 25 surveyed households				
2	2	4	1	1
1	2	0	1	2
0	1	0	1	2
3	3	0	1	1
2	1	2	2	1

Which average best describes the data?

5 What is the range in the data in Question 4?

6 What is the standard deviation and variance of the data in Question 4?

7 In a survey of 281 consumers, the question asked was: Are you aware of brand X? The tally of responses are shown separately for both men and women in Table 10.19.

TABLE 10.19	Awareness of brand X	
	Yes	No
Men	55	85
Women	65	76

Is there a difference between men and women in terms of their respective levels of awareness of brand X?

8 What are analysis of variance techniques? What do they attempt to measure? In the context of what kinds of problem might they be useful?

9 Data for 14 brands of cider and their price and alcohol content per glass are shown in Table 10.20.

TABLE 10.20	Cider brands, price and alcohol content per glass	
Brand	Price (£)	Alcohol content (%)
1	1.71	3.3
2	1.62	3.2
3	1.94	3.1
4	1.81	3.6
5	1.65	4.3
6	1.67	2.2
7	1.56	3.6
8	1.54	1.8
9	1.76	1.7
10	1.88	2.4
11	1.91	2.1
12	1.93	3.2
13	1.72	3.3
14	1.88	3.1

For the data:

(a) Produce a scattergraph to show the relationship between the two variables.

(b) Calculate the Pearson correlation coefficient to measure the relationship between the two variables.

(c) Calculate the bivariate regression equations (i) using alcohol content as the independent variable and (ii) using the price of cider as the independent variable.

(d) Interpret and comment on the analysis you have undertaken.

10 Table 10.21 is a dataset similar to that in Table 10.8, which refers to a different area of the country. Use multiple regression analysis to analyse the dataset.

TABLE 10.21	Houses for sale in another part of the country			
Price	Area	Acres	Rooms	Baths
£128,500	1220	1.50	6	2
£142,000	1670	0.74	7	2
£146,000	1330	0.25	6	2
£159,000	1560	1.38	8	1
£186,000	1430	0.40	7	1
£174,000	1730	1.95	6	2
£119,000	2210	1.34	8	2
£198,000	1780	0.52	9	1
£134,000	1290	2.30	6	2
£153,000	1340	0.70	7	1
£170,000	1810	1.20	8	1
£185,000	1740	1.90	6	2
£91,000	1330	1.76	6	1
£154,000	2700	0.60	9	3
£125,000	1400	0.55	7	1
£145,000	1850	0.38	7	2
£146,500	1750	0.72	8	2
£118,000	1000	0.40	8	1
£210,000	2950	1.20	9	3
£138,000	1900	0.57	8	1

11 Indicate the possible applications, in marketing research, for:

(a) cluster analysis

(b) factor analysis

(c) conjoint analysis

(d) multidimensional scaling.

CASE STUDY 10.1: LA GAIETÉ PARISIENNE

La Gaieté Parisienne owns four boutiques in and around Paris. Recently it undertook a survey of 1000 customers which, among other things, attempted to ascertain whether there was any association between age and the boutique patronised by respondents. A random sample of 250 customers was taken at each boutique between 12 May and 30 May.

If there were any associations between age and boutique patronage, there might be an argument for changing the mix of items offered for sale at each of the boutiques. Table 10.22 shows the boutiques and the age profile of the respondents interviewed at each boutique.

TABLE 10.22   Boutiques and age profiles

Boutique	Under 18	18–24	25–34	35–44	45 and over
Montparnasse	57	71	61	38	23
St Lazare	48	82	86	20	14
La Fayette	51	66	65	40	28
Madeleine	44	47	54	56	49

Question

What advice would you offer?

CASE STUDY 10.2: SUMMIT MOTORS (2)

Summit Motors' records indicate that less than 40% of its new car buyers remain loyal service customers after the first free service and the dealer is keen to increase the percentage to at least 50%. Some 14 different attributes have been identified as affecting the patronage of a service facility and a small survey has been conducted among new car purchasers who have bought cars during the past two years. Respondents were asked two questions about each of the identified attributes:

1 How important is the attribute?

2 How well did Summit Motors perform in terms of this attribute?

TABLE 10.23   Summit Motors: mean importance and performance ratings

No.	Attribute	Mean importance rating	Mean performance rating
1	Job done first time	3.79	2.68
2	Complaints dealt with speedily	3.61	2.78
3	Warranty work attended to promptly	3.57	3.11
4	Can do any job required	3.59	2.96
5	Service available when required	3.42	3.02
6	Friendly/courteous service	3.36	3.28
7	Car ready when promised	3.33	3.00
8	Only necessary work performed	3.42	3.06
9	Low service prices	3.26	1.95
10	Clean-up after service done	3.22	2.97
11	Convenient for home	2.46	2.21
12	Convenient for work	2.39	2.47
13	Courtesy cars available	2.32	2.33
14	Maintenance reminders posted	1.99	3.38

Note: A five-point rating scale was used in both cases. In terms of importance, the scale ran from extremely important (5) to not important (0). In the case of performance, the scale ran from excellent (5) to poor (0).

Mean importance and performance ratings from some 311 of 682 contacted previous buyers are shown in Table 10.23.

Questions

1 Plot the 28 attribute scores on a two-dimensional graph, the axes being (a) importance of attributes and (b) Summit's performance on the attributes.

2 How might Summit interpret this graphical representation of the data?

CASE STUDY 10.3: MR HUNGRY'S BURGER BAR

Mr Hungry's Burger Bar is a national chain of hamburger restaurants with branches in all major cities of the UK and most large towns. The burger bars typically attract three main categories of customer: teenagers looking for a cheap, filling lunch while cruising shopping malls, parents who take young children to the restaurants for a treat or birthday celebration and office workers and others looking for a quick lunch stop during the day or a pre-cinema snack in the evening.

In an attempt to gauge customer attitudes to the restaurant, each customer is asked to complete a form, which uses a five-point Likert scale to assess responses across a range of issues. The form is shown below.

At Mr Hungry's we are always looking for ways to improve our service to you, the customer. To help us do this, we would be grateful if you could take a few moments to fill out this form.

	):<	):	I:	(:	(:>
Promptness of service from staff					
Quality of food					
Cleanliness of restaurant					
Value for money					
Facilities for children					
Range of choice on menu					
Convenient location					

Thank you for your help. We look forward to seeing you again soon at Mr Hungry's!

Return of the forms tended to be low (less than 10% from most restaurants) but given the very large numbers of customers involved, the firm's customer services department found that it was overwhelmed with forms, with 12,532 useable responses coming in during the first month. A raw tabulation of the forms showed the following pattern.

	):<	):	I:	(:	(:>
Promptness of service from staff	3891	3202	1576	1789	2074
Quality of food	4007	2956	1809	1687	2073
Cleanliness of restaurant	3568	2508	1457	1708	3291
Value for money	4578	3672	1067	1431	1784
Facilities for children	3457	3278	2890	1459	1448
Range of choice on menu	3279	2845	2078	1897	2433
Convenient location	2450	1891	1546	2581	4064

These figures caused some consternation; on the face of it, it seemed that on most measures the restaurants were not doing well. The trend was for customers to be very dissatisfied or dissatisfied with each element of the restaurant, with only the convenience of location coming out well.

Another problem was that the forms could not be segmented; the analysts were unable to tell which sub-category of the firm's target customers had filled in each form. Since the restaurants remained busy, and indeed business seemed to be increasing rather than decreasing, senior management felt that the research must be flawed in some ways. After all, the customers were perfectly capable of voting with their feet by going to any one of half a dozen other hamburger outlets; if the restaurants were obviously all right, and the research said the restaurants were all wrong, then the research had to be at fault. The directors of Mr Hungry's told the researchers to look again at the research design and report back.

(Case contributed by Jim Blythe)

Questions

1 Plot the figures in the form on a graph, using a separate plot for each attribute. What can you deduce from the shape of the lines?

2 How might the respondents be divided so that the researchers could determine whether responses regarding one attribute of the restaurants relate to responses regarding another attribute?

3 Which of the attributes show significant correlations with each other? What might be the reasons for these correlations?

4 What are the sources of bias in data of these types?

5 How might the firm improve the form in order to obtain better quality data?

6 How might you check whether the variation shown in the data is statistically significant?

 REFERENCES AND NOTES

1 Kress, G (1988) *Marketing Research* (3rd edn), Upper Saddle River, NJ: Prentice-Hall, 260–61.

2 McKenzie, J, Schaefer, R L and Farber, E (1995) *The Student Edition of Minitab for Windows*, Reading, MA: Addison-Wesley, Chapter 9.

3 Hair, J F, Anderson, R E, Tatham, R L and Black, W C (1992) *Multivariate Data Analysis*, New York: Macmillan.

4 Green, P E, Tull, D S and Albaum, G (1988) *Research for Marketing Decisions*, Upper Saddle River, NJ: Prentice-Hall.

5 S-Plus for Windows, Statistical Sciences, Inc., 1700 Westlake Av N Suite 500, Seattle, WA 98109.

6 Winters, P (1996) Of mergers, managers, money, mailsters . . . and patients too, *Research Plus*, April.

7 *Multiscale II*, Ramsay, J O, Psychology Department, McGill University.

FURTHER READING

Burdick, R K (1983) Statement of hypothesis in the analysis of variance, *Journal of Marketing Research*, August, 320–24.

Cattin, P and Wittink, D (1982) Commercial use of conjoint analysis: a survey, *Journal of Marketing*, 46, 44–53.

Chakrapani, C (2004) *Statistics in Market Research*, London: Arnold.

Curwin, J and Slater, R (1991) *Quantitative Methods for Business Decisions* (3rd edn), London: Chapman & Hall.

Deal, K (1997) Determining success factors for financial products: a comparative analysis of CART, logit and factor/discrimant analysis, *Service Industries Journal*, 17(3), July, 489–506.

Dolan, C V (1994) Factor analysis of variables with 2, 3, 5 and 7 response categories: a comparison of categorical variable estimaters using simulated data, *British Journal of Mathematical and Statistical Pyschology*, 47, 309–26.

Everitt, B S, Landau, S and Leese, M (2000) *Cluster Analysis* (4th edn), London: Arnold.

Freeman, P (1991) Using computers to extend analysis and reduce data, *Journal of the Market Research Society*, 33(2), 127–36.

Hair, J, Anderson, R, Tatham, R and Black, W (1995) *Multivariate Data Analysis with Readings* (4th edn), New York: Macmillan.

Huberty, C J (1994) *Applied Discriminant Analysis*, New York: Wiley Interscience.

Huff, D (1991) *How to Lie with Statistics*, Harmondsworth: Penguin.

Kaciak, E and Louviere, J (1990) Multiple correspondence analysis of multiple choice experiment data, *Journal of Marketing Research*, 27, 455–65.

Lenell, W and Bissoneau, R (1996) Using causal comparative and correlational designs in conducting market research, *Journal of Professional Services Marketing*, 13(2), 59–69.

Myers, J H (1996) *Segmentation and Positioning for Strategic Marketing Decisions*, Chicago: AMA.

Rogers, K (1996) Correspondence analysis: the big picture, *Quirk's Marketing Research Review*, Article 2, April.

Sawyer, A and Peter, J P (1983) The significance of statistical significance tests in marketing research, *Journal of Marketing Research*, May, 20, 125.

Serious Data Analysis Software (1989), Chicago, IL: SPSS.

Strutton, D and Pelton, L (1994) A multiple correspondence analysis of telephone contact rates, *Mid-Atlantic Journal of Business*, 30(1), 27–39.

Zeisel, H (1985) *Say it with Figures*, New York: Harper & Row.

11 Qualitative data analysis

Objectives

After reading this chapter, you should be able to:

- understand the general overall approach to qualitative analysis

- appreciate the types of computer program that may be used to help in the process of categorisation and other aspects of qualitative research

- understand how to improve data display

- convey meaning in the analysis through the use of matrices, networks and diagrams.

Keywords

categories	KWIC
causal models	matrices
cognitive maps	networks
concordance	taxonomy
index	text segments
keyword in context	transcribing data

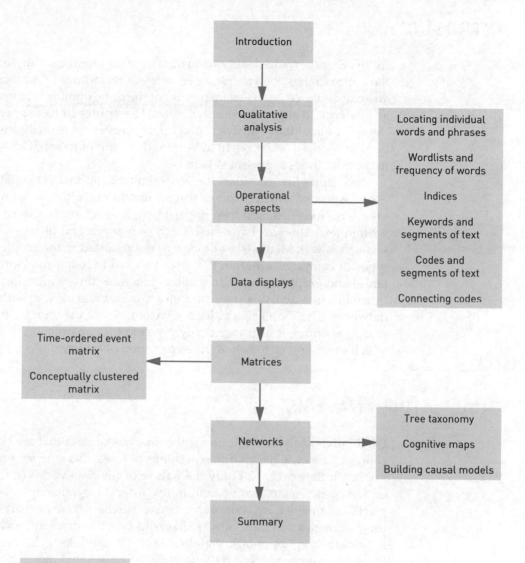

Plan of Chapter 11

INTRODUCTION

In this chapter we look at how qualitative data might be analysed. Traditionally, the approach has been to transcribe notes or recordings of meetings and to make an analysis based on visual inspection of the data, quoting what people have said as evidence to support a point of view. The approach has appeared to lack the rigour of quantitative analysis. Recently, however, more analytical methods have been introduced and brought to bear on this form of research and an introduction to these methods is presented here.

The chapter first considers the general overall approach to qualitative analysis, a key aspect of which involves **transcribing data**, either what has been said or otherwise recorded, and then undertaking a detailed analysis of the transcribed written text. This involves searching for keywords and phrases and categorising sections of text. Methods for doing this are reported in the chapter, together with types of computer program that may be used to help. In quantitative research, tables and graphs are used to display data and convey meaning in the analysis. In qualitative analysis the same effect may be achieved with **matrices** and **networks**. The chapter provides some examples of these tools. In the case of networks, attention is also specifically given to the construction of causal diagrams which can do much to help the interpretation of findings.

QUALITATIVE ANALYSIS

Qualitative analysis is a term for the analysis of data that are not numeric. The concept, however, means different things to researchers, depending on the type of approach they take. Not only the nature of the data varies (responses to open-ended questions, narrative field notes, interview transcripts, personal diaries, public documents, etc.) but even if two researchers were to analyse the same text, their strategies and outcomes are likely to be quite different, each justified in the light of their epistemological and research frameworks. It is necessary, therefore, to take into account the variations in the processes that researchers employ when they set about analysing qualitative data. Moreover, qualitative research tends to lay considerable emphasis on situational and often structural contexts, in contrast to quantitative research, which is often multivariate but weak on context. Qualitative research tends to be weak on cross-comparisons.[1]

Despite many practical variations, the stages in qualitative research follow the lines indicated in Figure 11.1. This may include initial background reading of related documents and formal or informal discussions, followed by focus group or depth interviews, or even open-ended survey questionnaires. Taken together, this constitutes the data-collection stage. The next step involves the subject matter of this chapter: an analysis of transcripts from interviews, discussions and other sources. In the analysis, the data have first to be reduced into a manageable form and from the more manageable form abstractions from the data, usually referred

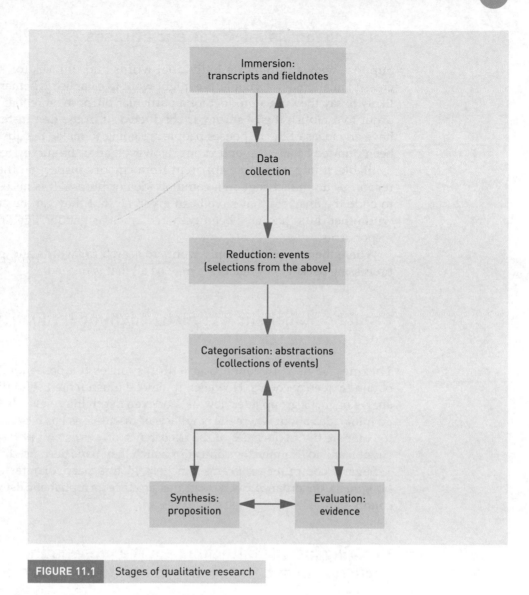

FIGURE 11.1 Stages of qualitative research

to as events, are then categorised. This can then lead to the synthesis of ideas and testable propositions.

OPERATIONAL ASPECTS OF QUALITATIVE RESEARCH

First, we consider the major operations required in qualitative research. The following list is not exhaustive and there may be other operations.

Locating individual words and phrases

Suppose we want to locate individual words and phrases for the purpose of cross-tabulation. For example, we might want to establish whether men are more likely to say they use a product for a particular purpose more than women do. In order to establish this, a survey is conducted. If in the first instance we do not have any ideas of the responses people are going to make, the question will have been phrased as an open-ended one. However, after the survey results are made available, it might be quite apparent from cursory inspection that many of the responses do in fact contain a common idea or phrase. It is necessary therefore to code the answers that have been given so that they can be cross-tabulated with other data that have been gathered, such as gender, age, incomes, etc. of respondents.

Where the researcher simply wants to search for words and phrases, word-processing packages or databases may be all that is needed.

Creating alphabetic wordlists, counting frequency of word occurrence

This may be used in connection with responses to open-ended questions, to obtain frequency counts. However, it may be much more useful in the context of analysing focus group interview data or even depth interviews. In order to obtain an initial idea about where the emphasis of discussions has been, it is often useful to compare the frequencies of the occurrence of words and phrases used in discussion and to examine the context in which they have been used.

Several computer programs can help in this particular task, for example, Longman Concordance. Such programs produce an alphabetic list with frequency counts.

Creating indices (attaching source information to each occurrence) and keyword in context concordance

Where it is important to compare what has been said in one context with what has been said in another context, we could merely compare the frequency of the occurrence of relevant words (content analysis). However, some researchers may prefer to look at a list of locations of each word or phrase. Such a list would be similar to an **index** in the back of a book, but it would provide information on several levels: document name, chapter number, page and perhaps even paragraph number. In this way, not only can the words be compared across texts, but their locations can be found and the context can be taken into consideration. Techniques that are helpful here involve the researcher creating what is commonly called a **keyword in context (KWIC) concordance**. The word is listed and each occurrence is surrounded by a specific range of content.

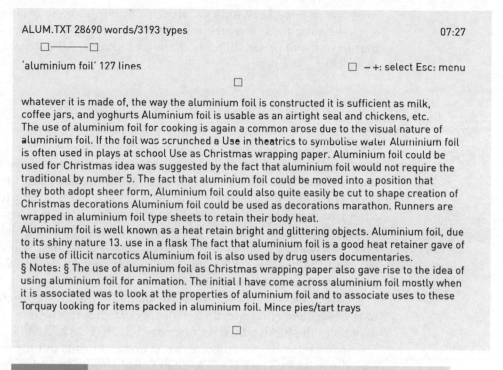

ALUM.TXT 28690 words/3193 types   07:27

☐———☐

'aluminium foil' 127 lines   ☐ — +: select Esc: menu

☐

whatever it is made of, the way the aluminium foil is constructed it is sufficient as milk, coffee jars, and yoghurts Aluminium foil is usable as an airtight seal and chickens, etc. The use of aluminium foil for cooking is again a common arose due to the visual nature of aluminium foil. If the foil was scrunched a Use in theatrics to symbolise water Aluminium foil is often used in plays at school Use as Christmas wrapping paper. Aluminium foil could be used for Christmas idea was suggested by the fact that aluminium foil would not require the traditional by number 5. The fact that aluminium foil could be moved into a position that they both adopt sheer form, Aluminium foil could also quite easily be cut to shape creation of Christmas decorations Aluminium foil could be used as decorations marathon. Runners are wrapped in aluminium foil type sheets to retain their body heat.
Aluminium foil is well known as a heat retain bright and glittering objects. Aluminium foil, due to its shiny nature 13. use in a flask The fact that aluminium foil is a good heat retainer gave of the use of illicit narcotics Aluminium foil is also used by drug users documentaries.
§ Notes: § The use of aluminium foil as Christmas wrapping paper also gave rise to the idea of using aluminium foil for animation. The initial I have come across aluminium foil mostly when it is associated was to look at the properties of aluminium foil and to associate uses to these Torquay looking for items packed in aluminium foil. Mince pies/tart trays

☐

FIGURE 11.2   Output of Longman Concordance program, searching on 'aluminium foil'

Constructing keyword in context is the sole purpose of the KWIC text index. It is a simple, cheap program that makes a list of words in a file or any chunk of it and sorts it alphabetically with reference information. The function is also performed by the Longman Concordance program, an illustration of which is given in Figure 11.2. The keyword that was searched in this case was 'aluminium foil' and a proportion of the 127 abstractions is shown.

Attaching keywords to text segments

In speech or written text, an idea may be verbalised in many ways, without ever using the keyword that precisely defines it (such as talking about our various car-servicing experiences without ever using the word 'garage', or 'dealer' or the phrase 'car-servicing experience'). If the researcher wants to examine a text for topics it is necessary to break the **text** down into **segments** that represent topic units and attach to each the appropriate keyword. All the segments that deal with the same topic can then be brought together or assembled by a keyword and interpreted. This again is something that can well be applied in analysing the transcriptions of focus group discussions.

This kind of data manipulation is only possible if the data do not consist of continuous text, but are structured chunks of information that are put into fields:

then one or more keywords are attached that in some way signify the content of any particular field. A search can then be done using the keyword and all fields that have the appropriate content are reproduced. All database systems provide this facility.

Attaching codes (categorisation symbols) to text segments

The difference between keywords and codes is that keywords are one-word summaries of the content of a text segment, while codes are abbreviations of category names. **Categories** may be thought of as the conceptual equivalent of file folders, each labelled with the name of one aspect of the research project or one topic found in the data. This serves to organise data pieces. These categories may emerge during the analysis, or they may be developed beforehand, or partially both. Keywords are complete normal English words, and there can be as many in the study as there are different topics contained in the text. Codes are abbreviations or other made-up fragments.

QUALPRO[2] is the most basic of the qualitative analysis programs. It invites the user to segment and code, then performs searches for the indicated segments and assembles them. An added refinement of the ETHNOGRAPH is that it allows the researcher to search for co-occurring codes and prints out the segments that were coded with both. The ETHNOGRAPH also permits selective searches. In this case the program does not, as usual, search for a particular code or code combination through all data files, but will automatically select only those that satisfy a certain condition.

Connecting codes (categories)

Many researchers want to go beyond mere classification and explore whether or not the subject under analysis possesses a discernible structure, or whether or not linkages exist between or among particular categories. The purpose is to develop propositional statements or to relate concepts in order to discover the underlying principles – often referred to as the generation of hypotheses. Analysing focus group discussion data in this way can produce questions or hypotheses that might then be answered or tested by large-scale survey work and quantitative analysis.

None of these programs really facilitates 'theory building'. The procedure that theory-building qualitative analysis programs employ is somewhat different to those mentioned previously. Although a code is attached to a particular segment of text, the code 'characterises' the file in which it is present. Codes are therefore thought of as more like 'values' of a variable. For example, if the category or concept is 'relationship with peers' the corresponding codes could be 'competitive', 'cooperative', etc. Any given file will have one of these embedded, perhaps attached to several segments, all of which represent evidence of the

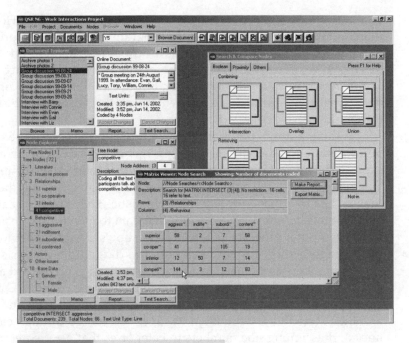

FIGURE 11.3   QSR NUD*IST program

Source: QSR NUD*IST[3] (NUD*IST is developed by QSR International Pty Ltd)

'competitiveness' in the peer relationship, for example. It could also be that among the remaining categories there is one that is concerned with work behaviour. The programs might be used to find that files characterised by competitive relationships with peers are more often than not also characterised by aggressive work behaviour. This might then form the basis of a more formal hypothesis. QSR NUD*IST[3] is a program that facilitates this form of analysis (Figure 11.3). The latest versions of the product are N6 and Nvivo.

NUD*IST stands for non-numerical unstructured data indexing searching and theorising. It is a computer package designed to help users handle non-numerical and unstructured data in qualitative analysis. NUD*IST does this by supporting the processes of indexing, searching and theorising.

NUD*IST handles data such as:

- text – for example, reports or minutes, transcripts of unstructured conversational interviews, evidence transcripts, literary documents, personnel records, fieldnotes, newspaper clippings and abstracts

- non-textual records – for example, photographs, tape recordings, films, maps, plans.

Catterall and Maclaren,[4] in an article examining the use of computers in research, suggest that programs such as NUD*IST take out some of the tedium of exploring qualitative data and therefore help the researcher in this task. However, they also point out that it is important that the program chosen is appropriate to the task in hand and that it remains a tool to assist the researcher and does not become the driving force of the research. They point out that programs such as NUD*IST are sophisticated tools for the researcher, but the intellectual task of conceptualising data remains the researcher's and will reflect their competence and the quality of the data they have collected.

The same authors point out that such programs encourage the researcher to build detailed and complex coding structures that can be an advantage when exploring complex phenomena. However, they warn that the researcher can get 'bogged down' in its complexities. They warn that such procedure can decontextualise data and make procedure mechanistic. They suggest that there is always an advantage in returning to the original data to gain further insights.

The computer program QSR NUD*IST allows the researcher to build up a complex categorisation system to classify the data under analysis. The document system numbers each line of text for you and brings up the text as a window that allows you to explore it and read each interview thoroughly. Using the indexing system, which allows you to tag and code lines of text with an appropriate term and then store this code in an index tree, you can go through each text indexing lines and assigning line numbers to categories that are created as you go along. These categories are changeable and can be revised over time. As new insights are gained, so you are able to create new codes as the data are explored and a better feel for them is experienced. Another advantage is that it is possible to code one piece of text with several codes. Examples of different categories can often be more than one line long, which means that small sections of text can be assigned a number of different codes if they illustrate several different categories. Thus, NUD*IST allows you to multiple code sections of text and, at the same time, to store each code separately in its own category.

USING COMPUTER SOFTWARE IN QUALITATIVE STUDIES

- Making notes in the field.

- Writing up or transcribing fieldnotes or interview proceedings.

- Editing: correcting, extending or revising fieldnotes.

- Coding: attaching a keyword or tags to segments of text to permit later retrieval.

- Storage: keeping text in an organised database.

- Search and retrieval: locating relevant segments of text and making them available for inspection.

- Data 'linking': connecting relevant data segments with each other, forming categories, clusters or networks of information.

- Memoing: writing reflective commentaries on some aspect of the data, as a basis for deeper analysis.

- Content analysis: counting frequencies, sequences of locations of words and phrases.

- Data display: placing selected or reduced data in condensed, organised format, such as a matrix or network for inspection.

- Conclusion drawing and verification: helping the analyst to interpret displayed data and to test or confirm findings.

- Theory building: developing systematic, conceptually coherent explanations of findings; testing hypotheses.

- Graphic mapping: creating diagrams that depict findings or theories.

- Preparing interim and final reports.

Once the first version of categories is completed, you can go back over all the categories, making reports of them using the indexing system in NUD*IST and revising your initial findings. You can then explore the categories created, to try to gain a better understanding of the phenomena they represent and also to work at better conceptual labels to describe them. This can be accomplished by means of the index system in NUD*IST and a separate report of each category can be produced. The reports can contain all the examples of the categories you have tagged in each transcript and, by exploring these reports, you can refine your thinking about the category and shift, add and delete coding as you feel appropriate. This may be important in places where you have coded things wrongly or where a new category has subsequently been created that better describes an example that had previously been assigned to another category. You can also move the position of the categories within the tree structure to represent what feels more appropriate. As a result, the tree may be simplified as the individual categories become more distinctive.

DATA DISPLAYS

In the context of qualitative analysis, a display is a visual format that presents information systematically so that the user can draw valid conclusions and take the required action. In the case of qualitative research the typical mode of display has been extended, unreduced text that the analyst scans through, attaching codes and then extracting code segments and drawing conclusions. The analyst then writes a second form of extended text: a case study report.

Unreduced text by itself is a weak, cumbersome form of display. It makes analysis difficult because data are dispersed over many pages and they are not easy to see as a whole. They are sequential rather than simultaneous, making it difficult to look at two or three variables at once. They are also poorly ordered and can become bulky and monotonously overloading. Making careful comparisons between several extended texts can also be difficult.

Valid analysis requires displays that are focused enough to allow a viewing of a full dataset in the same location and are arranged systematically to answer the research questions at hand. In this sense a full dataset means the condensed, distilled data drawn from a full range of people, events and processes that have been systematically studied. The chances of drawing and verifying valid conclusions are much greater than for extended text: the display is arranged coherently to permit careful comparisons to detect differences in patterns and themes and to spot the trends.

Generating formats to display qualitative data is relatively easy. Formats can be as various as the imagination of the analyst permits. They fall into two major types: *matrices*, with defined rows and columns, and *networks*, with a series of nodes with links between them. The data entries can take on different forms: a short block of text, quotes, phrases, ratings, abbreviations, symbolic figures, labelled lines and so on. The display format and the nature and shape of the entries will depend on what the researcher is trying to understand.

MATRICES

A matrix is effectively the crossing of two lists, set up as rows and columns. A variety of different formats may be of interest to qualitative researchers. The following are illustrative of the kinds of approach that can be taken.

Time-ordered event matrix

Time periods may be defined conceptually and adjusted according to actual happenings. The events may be sorted according to where the event took place or in some other way (Table 11.1).

The display is helpful for understanding the flow, location and connection of events. It can also be easily compared with similar matrices in other studies. With an analysis and commentary attached, it can also provide a good outline of the process of change that may have taken place.

Conceptually clustered matrix

Many studies are designed to answer a string of research questions – and the string often becomes very lengthy. As a consequence, the performance of a separate analysis and case report section for each research question is likely to lead to

TABLE 11.1   Time-ordered event matrix

Place	Time period		
	Morning	Afternoon	Evening
Work		Setting up computer program to analyse results	
Home	Analysis of survey results		Checking all final documentation and overheads

confusion for both the analyst and the reader. The solution is to cluster several research questions so that the meaning can be more easily generated.

A conceptually clustered matrix has its rows and columns arranged so as to bring together items that belong to one another. For example, we may be interested to know whether a relationship exists between people's motives and their attitudes towards purchasing a product. The best way to find out is to cluster the responses to these questions. A format is needed that displays all the relevant responses of all the key informants on one sheet, permits an initial comparison between responses and between informants, lets us see how the data can be analysed further, for multicase studies, lends itself readily to cross-case analysis and will not have to be redone and, for multicase studies, provides some preliminary standardisation. Such a display is shown in Table 11.2.

TABLE 11.2   Research questions

Informants	Motives	Attitude to purchasing/stocking brand
Consumers		
C1	Price	Very positive
C2	Price	Fairly positive
C3	Availability	Neutral
Retailers		
R1	Price margin	Neutral
R2	Consumer advertising	Neutral
R3	Price margin	Fairly positive

The display matrix possesses on one sheet a format that includes all respondents and all responses to the two research questions. It should be noted that comparisons have been set up between different kinds of informants (customers and retailers). Some preliminary scaling or sorting of responses may be required: types of motive or valence of attitude.

NETWORKS

A network is a collection of nodes or points connected by lines. They can be very useful when it is necessary to focus on more than a few variables at a time. Some examples of the use of networks of different kinds are shown here.

Tree taxonomy

To avoid the implication that concepts are always properly sorted into rows and columns, the tree diagram in Figure 11.4 illustrates how they can also be displayed in a network form. This **taxonomy** shows how a respondent might classify motorcars when they are asked the question: 'What kinds of car are there?' As the respondent continues in the interview, they might next be asked: 'What kinds of car do you call luxury sport?' or 'What kinds of car do you call cross-country?' and so on.

Componential analysis may be used as a way to help clarify categories, making it clear why a particular label is assigned to a particular object. We ask for

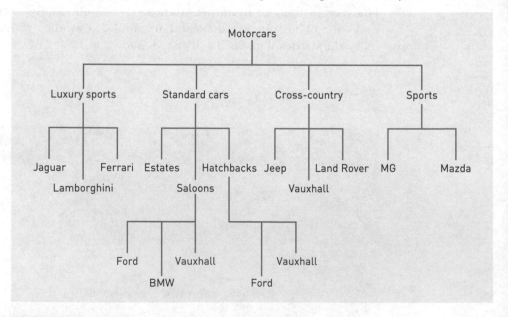

FIGURE 11.4   Taxonomy of cars

	Expensive	Practical	High performance
TABLE 11.3 Smallest group of discriminating features			
Lamborghini	+		+
Ferrari	+		+
Jaguar	+		+
Ford		+	
Vauxhall		+	
Land Rover		+	
MG sports			+
Mazda sports			+

QSR NUD*IST is good at helping to generate taxonomies.

distinctive features of the sort of objects being taxonomised and aim to find the smallest group of features that discriminates them clearly, as shown in Table 11.3.

Cognitive maps

It is useful to have displays that show us the complexities of the person. People's minds are not always organised hierarchically, as we just saw in the taxonomies. They can be well represented in non-hierarchical network form: a collection of nodes attached by links. **Cognitive maps** display the person's representations of concepts about a particular domain, showing the relationships among them.

For example, the cognitive map in Figure 11.5 shows that the respondent thinks a wristwatch needs to be fashionable and how this need to be fashionable is reflected in such things as a good-quality leather strap, having sports features and having a case made from gold or stainless steel.

Building causal models

When we are analysing data we might observe that there are associations between elements in the data. The interest is usually to see whether the associations can be integrated into a meaningful explanatory model. To do this it is necessary to apply some heuristics.

The first heuristic involves ordering the model temporally. The questions to be answered then become:

- Which variables or events of those found relevant occur first in time?

- Which occur along the way during implementation?

- Which might be seen as early and late outcomes?

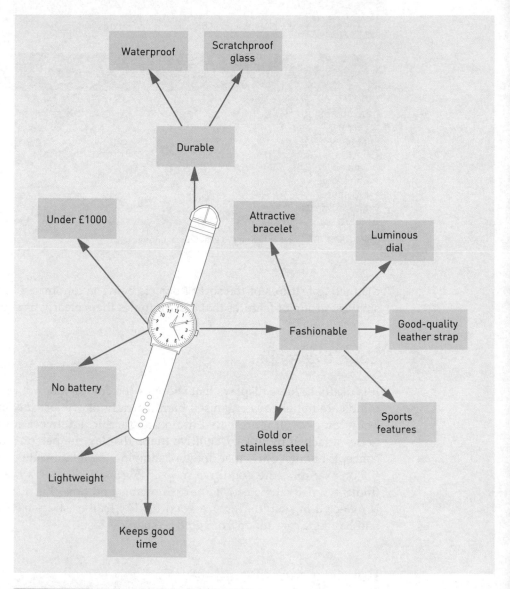

FIGURE 11.5   Requirements of a wristwatch

The second heuristic involves considering which variables might reasonably be expected to have a direct impact on other variables, both preceding them in time and having a plausible direct connection. This rule means that we need to think of the mechanisms that could be involved.

The third rule is to check case informants' explanations. What causal linkages do they claim are present? We need to examine our transcripts and fieldnotes very carefully.

The fourth rule is to consider what available research and theories have to say about causal connections.

Using these rules, we have to play with the data for a while. It can help if we put variables or events on cards and move them around into various configurations, looking at the connections that seem sensible. Graphics packages such as Inspiration[5] can also be helpful. Another special program that can help develop **causal models** is COPE (cognitive policy evaluation).[6] While primarily designed to produce cognitive maps, it enables us to map in two dimensions explanations and consequences of events through a graphic user interface. Since it also has the facility to trace paths throughout the complex network structures that can be constructed, it can also help to establish cause–effect relationships and hence build causal models.

EXAMPLE

Marketing researchers undertaking focus group discussions with groups of patients suffering from a specific disease might discover that in severe cases of loss of appetite, patients are treated in different ways by the GP, depending on whether or not the GP feels they can treat the particular symptom. Where the GP feels confident, a proprietary brand of medicine is prescribed as treatment. Where the GP is unsure, referral is made to the consultant at the hospital, who prescribes a non-proprietary brand. The whole process is captured in Figure 11.6.

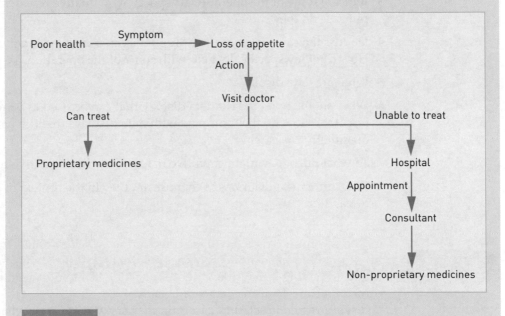

FIGURE 11.6   Causal diagram

SUMMARY

In this chapter, we have examined the general overall approach to qualitative analysis, a key aspect of which involves transcribing what has been said or otherwise recorded and then undertaking a detailed analysis of the transcribed text. This involves searching for keywords and phrases and categorising sections of text. Methods for doing this have been reported in the chapter, together with types of computer program that may be used to help in this process. In quantitative research, tables and graphs are used to display data and convey meaning in the analysis. In qualitative analysis the same effect may be achieved with the use of matrices and networks. The chapter has given some examples of these tools. In the case of networks, attention has also specifically been given to the construction of causal diagrams that can do much to help in the interpretation of findings.

QUESTIONS

1 What do you understand by qualitative analysis? How is it different from quantitative analysis?

2 What are the steps involved in the general process of qualitative research?

3 Indicate some of the operational aspects of qualitative research. What purpose do they serve?

4 Discuss the role that computer programs can play in qualitative research. How can they specifically help with some of the operational aspects?

5 What are data displays?

6 What are the two kinds of data display that can be used in qualitative research? How do they compare with data displays that can be used in quantitative research?

7 To what purposes might cognitive maps be put in qualitative research?

8 What are causal diagrams? What use are they in the context of qualitative research?

CASE STUDY 11.1: CYCLIST SURVEY

A survey was conducted to ascertain cyclists' views on provisions for them in the town. Cyclists were asked what beneficial improvements were needed. The responses to the survey, together with the sex and age of the respondents, can be seen in Table 11.4.

TABLE 11.4   Cyclist survey: results

Sex	Age	Comments
Male	25–34	Improve visibility at A52 junction with Wellington Road
Female	17–24	More space by the library
Male	17–24	More cycle lanes
Male	25–34	More cycle lanes
Male	17–24	More cycle lanes. No motor vehicles on roads in the city centre at certain times
Male	25–34	Why do cycles have to give way to cars on the A52 roundabout when, with no cycle lane, they would have priority!?
Female	25–34	More cycle lanes, particularly in the one-way streets
Male	25–34	Enforcement of town/village traffic speed restrictions
Female	25–34	Very good cycle parking in main streets
Female	17–24	More safe areas for locking bikes – maybe more cycle signs
Male	35–44	More cycle parking racks
Female	25–34	Cycle lanes in and around town and more of them
Male	25–34	Introduce more cycle lanes alongside busy roads and major roundabouts
Male	35–44	More cycle lanes to surrounding towns/villages
Female	35–44	Punishment for those motorists who think the cycle lanes are an extension to the car parks
Female	17–24	Education for drivers. Roads/paths for cycles
Female	25–34	More cycle lanes especially in one-way areas. Control parking outside shops
Female	17–24	More cycle paths
Male	17–24	It would help cyclists if the council were to resurface some of the roads
Female	35–44	More cycle lanes
Male	35–44	Road safety by creating cycle route and traffic lights for cyclists
Female	25–34	Cycle paths for as many streets as possible, in as wide an area as possible
Female	25–34	Cycle *priority* lanes in main areas and roundabouts
Male	17–24	Better edges to roads, as they are too rough and bumpy
Female	25–34	Resurfacing the whole length of the canal lane
Female	35–44	Increase cycle lanes especially around roundabouts where there are two queues of traffic and little or no room for cyclists. I would like to see improved cycle security facilities at the railway station
Male	25–34	Pay and return lock-up facilities
Female	17–24	Cycle bars (sketch here) or thin streetposts (for parking hours etc.) where I can lock my front wheel and frame to the post, neither of which is common in town. Maintain the edges of roads better and avoid putting drains and other obstructions too far out in the road
Male	35–44	More public awareness of bikers' needs

▶

TABLE 11.4   Cyclist survey: results (*continued*)

Sex	Age	Comments
Male	35–44	More cycle lanes
Female	17–24	In city centre with more facilities to lock a cycle to a fixed object. The speed ramps in Sheldon Road and Park Avenue are extremely uncomfortable for cyclists
Male	25–34	Something more safe round the one-way system
Male	35–44	Try and make car drivers more aware of us cyclists
Female	35–44	Cycle lanes
Male	17–24	More cycle lanes
Male	17–24	Cycle lanes are excellent; could these routes be extended?
Female	17–24	Proper cycle racks outside Army & Navy so that you can lock your bike to something solid. On the A529 we need the cycle path lit because at night the place is a deathtrap. If you fell off your bike and broke a leg no one would find you till morning
Female	17–24	More cycle lanes at major roundabouts. College Lane desperately needs a cycle lane and road surface improvements
Male	17–24	Perhaps more parking facilities in town centre
Male	35–44	One-way systems and cycle lanes are unsafe. To cycle in and out of work on the centre of the one-way system is not helped by the cycle lane. Junctions are also dangerous for cyclists
Female	35–44	More cycle pathways
Female	25–34	Add a cycle lane to *all* main roads and sort out the junction at Southern Road/Westwood Avenue
Female	17–24	Better facilities for leaving bikes
Male	25–34	Pedestrian and cycle crossing or bridge over A52 roundabout
Female	35–44	East Street or North Street cycle rack required
Male	35–44	A52 roundabout: design encourages motorists to not signal on leaving roundabout, into North Street/Dale Road and Lavernum Road
Female	35–44	Worst place to leave cycles is at railway station. More cycle lanes
Female	17–24	At the moment it is only a matter of time before there is a fatal accident
Female	35–44	Making sure that vehicles don't keep parking in the cycle lanes
Female	17–24	Cycle-parking facilities that are under cover
Male	35–44	Proper cycle lanes. Get rid of the current system at the Fire Brigade roundabout. Cyclists on the roundabout should be given priority over cars leaving the road, as at any other junction
Female	17–24	More cycle lanes. Promoting more cycle safety
Female	25–34	Somehow, improved safety at roundabouts
Male	25–34	I don't think cycling is a problem in the town. London is different
Male	35–44	Cycle lanes on all main roads. Cycle priority on all roads in city especially A52 roundabout

Sex	Age	Comments
Female	25–34	More bike racks and cycle lanes and, to ease congestion and traffic, develop park and ride schemes for motorists
Female	17–24	More cycle lanes, increase other road users' awareness that bikes have a right to be on the road too
Female	17–24	More cycle lanes please
Male	35–44	New traffic calming humps should have had level gaps in them so that cyclists could ride through them and not up and over
Male	25–34	More secure facilities at station and other places. Better cycleways, particularly in the dangerous one-way systems. Also traffic lights needed at the junction of Redmayne Drive and Haughton Street
Female	25–34	More cycle lanes
Male	35–44	I think there could be more cycle parks in the four main streets of the town
Female	17–24	Make more cycle paths, as we have in Germany
Female	25–34	Cycle lanes on all major roundabouts and one-way systems
Male	35–44	Cycle lanes beside main roads and greater number of road signs. 'Think Bike'
Male	25–34	More cycle racks
Male	35–44	Improve canal towpath cycling. Generally providing better crossing of inner ring road
Male	25–34	More cycle lanes
Female	17–24	In parking facilities, something needed to actually chain bike to
Female	35–44	More cycle lanes and the holes in the roads filled in more often
Male	25–34	Council is lazy and needs to sort town out before it falls apart
Female	17–24	You need cycling lines. Cars do not give enough consideration to cyclists
Male	17–24	More cycle paths in town
Female	25–34	More cycle paths through town
Female	35–44	Cycling around roundabouts needs improvement
Female	17–24	Many more cycle lanes needed for safety
Female	35–44	Various parts of the roadside have potholes or cracks that make cycling both uncomfortable and unsafe
Female	17–24	Supervised parking (preferably sheltered) area near train station
Female	25–34	Make car drivers more aware of cyclists
Female	35–44	Add kerbs to outer cycle lane to prevent drivers encroaching into cycle lanes
Male	17–24	Make car drivers more aware of cyclists on the road
Female	17–24	Everything OK
Female	25–34	*More* cycle parking facilities in town
Male	25–34	Very pleased with cycle route. More of the same would be welcome as, although I have never had an accident, the near misses are countless!

▶

TABLE 11.4 Cyclist survey: results (*continued*)

Sex	Age	Comments
Male	35–44	Prohibition of motor vehicles in and within the town centre
Male	35–44	More cycle lanes especially across the bypass
Male	35–44	More cycle lanes to ring the city and filter lanes for left turns. Additional signs to make motorists aware of cyclists
Female	35–44	A much safer system at A52 roundabout. More cycle lanes on busy roads, which don't suddenly peter out
Female	35–44	Lights or bridge over A52 at roundabout. Cycle lanes on all roads
Female	25–34	Additional cycle space throughout town centre. More cycle routes to and from town areas
Male	17–24	Better cycle lanes and more cycle lanes
Male	17–24	More cycle paths, especially by the main roundabouts
Female	25–34	At the roundabout A52 – experience problems with vehicles as they fail to indicate when turning off or too close to kerb – roundabout making it very dangerous! Trouble with trucks/lorries and pedestrians in town centre
Female	17–24	Cycle lanes are hopeless on roundabouts as no vehicles indicate where they are going
Female	17–24	A lot more spaces in other parts of town
Male	35–44	Allow cyclists to ride through the pedestrianised parts of town
Male	25–34	Do something about A52 roundabout
Male	35–44	I know it's impossible, but all car drivers should be made to cycle regularly and vice versa
Male	25–34	It would be really useful to be able to cycle though town
Female	25–34	Town centre is particularly poorly served for cycle parking. In other places an increase in spaces would be advantageous to combat overcrowding
Female	25–34	Improvement in road surfaces, especially near the edge of carriageway. Improve vehicle driver awareness to cycles
Male	17–24	More cycle lanes
Male	35–44	I have had four near misses from cars pulling across cycle lane on A52
Male	25–34	Perhaps consider a network of cycle lanes or tracks linking up surrounding villages with town centre
Female	35–44	Improve the edges of the roads
Male	17–24	Provide courses for people to know how to ride safely – as most do not know
Male	35–44	Give cycle priority all the way round the roundabout and do away with the dangerous cycle lane
Male	35–44	Educate car drivers to signal their intentions
Female	35–44	Right of way for cyclists at A52 ring road. Also more cycle lanes in other areas

Sex	Age	Comments
Male	25–34	Perhaps a cycle lane on the one-way system
Male	25–34	Cycle lanes exclusively for cyclists, especially on busy main roads
Male	35–44	More cycle lanes
Female	25–34	Improve cycle tracks around town
Male	35–44	The two most hazardous spots to cycle in are at the metropolitan roundabout where cyclists give way to motorists and take a chance to cross
Female	35–44	More cycle lanes around fire station
Male	35–44	Maybe there could be a system of padlocking and paying to lock your bike
Male	35–44	Lockable parking outside library
Female	17–24	Raise driver awareness of cyclists and their problems. More and improved cycle ways *away* from traffic
Female	25–34	Extend cycle lanes and improve awareness of motorists – they don't indicate at roundabouts
Male	35–44	More cycle tracks on country roads especially main roads
Male	17–24	Cycle lanes on one-way system roundabouts
Male	35–44	Cycle lane on all roads around town
Male	35–44	City and district generally desperately need more properly designed cycle lanes

Question

Analyse the responses in the best way you can.

CASE STUDY 11.2: USES OF ALUMINIUM FOIL

Respondents were asked to generate as many ideas as they could for uses of aluminium foil. One of the respondents produced the following list of ideas.

1 Covering roast chicken

2 Wrapping potatoes for baking

3 Covering food for storage in a refrigerator

4 Folding it to make a cup to drink out of

5 Using it as a plate

6 Smoothing it out to make a mirror

7 Reflecting sunlight to attract help/send messages

8 Reflecting a heat source for cooking

9 Lining the wall behind a radiator to reflect heat into a room

10 Wrapping up a flower stem for a buttonhole

11 Making Christmas decorations

12 Making milk bottle tops

13 Stringing small pieces together to make a baby's rattle

14 Making a dish to hold glue

15 Making a dish to hold paint

16 Using under a sleeping bag to stop the cold getting through

17 Wrapping food to cook on a campfire

18 Keeping food fresh without refrigeration

19 Hanging as temporary curtains

20 Sticking on a collage

21 Using to make 'water' for the Brownie Guide pool at Brownie camp

22 Making children's jewellery

23 Wrapping matches to keep them dry

24 Keeping food warm

25 Keeping food cold

26 Screwing it up to make a makeshift ball

27 Making a toy for cats to play with. Foil makes a light but indestructible cat toy

28 Cutting it up into squares to make stepping stones

29 Cutting out fish shapes and having a race to waft them along the hall

30 Cutting a strip to make a bookmark

31 Lining a grill pan to make it easy to clean after use

32 Wrapping up 25th wedding anniversary gifts

33 Wrapping sandwiches for a packed lunch

34 Lining cake-storage tins

Question

Construct a cognitive map showing the respondent's ideas about the possible uses of aluminium foil.

CASE STUDY 11.3: RENAULT CLIO

A researcher was interested to see if there were differences in how males and females interpreted or perceived an advertisement in a magazine for men. The advertisement featured an image of the Renault Clio being driven by a large cat-like creature. Two group discussions were held – one with a group of young men and the other with a group of young women. Both group discussion sessions were taped and the researcher made the following notes on playing back the tape:

The females see the Renault Clio as a male's car that seems to be largely as a result of using the metaphor of the cat. They are being guided that cats are men . . . big cats and speed. The men seem to be divided on it . . . they start by interpreting it by using pronouns such as 'I' and 'we' and 'whatever' but then they get guided off this and one of them says that it's a female's car and so they change. They are not sure. The female group has used the word 'round' in describing the car at one point so perhaps this shows they are moving towards a female interpretation. With the women, however, they think it is a male's car on balance . . . 'men are like animals, men are like wild animals', 'yes, it is going fast' . . . semantic link to speed. 'Like a lad', 'you see them in films don't you, cruising'. They try to fit everything about the car into the narrative that the car is for males . . . Things like used for cruising, etc. The researcher asks whether they think it is a female car . . . and they say, 'well it's got a pretty background to it.' They construct a narrative that this is a male car . . . 'speed'. When they look at potential customer they decide it is a man. Their narrative goes off in this direction . . . they are going to be cool and fast . . . they are going to be a cheetah . . . it is about power . . . all the links here are masculine . . . and then it is about sex . . . Men say that they are wild in bed and stuff . . . 'like to "grrrrr" and get our paws on it'. They are linking it in a masculine way . . . they are not identifying it with themselves. 'The car is female (for the women group) is it?' asks the researcher . . . 'No it's a male car' is the answer from some females in the group . . . so there is some confusion. The cheetah is seen as a male. Then they say that the car will attract 'you a female'. It is stylish (i.e. male) because of the way the cheetah is sitting. But the males also pick up on 'stylish' too . . . indicating they think it is a male car . . . 'one hand on the car', 'relaxed, cruising'. Males see a link between 'cruising' and 'getting your paws on it'; 'cool' and 'fast' denote it is a male car.

Males give different interpretations . . . i.e. cheetah is humour, 'stupid'. They also identify with the cheetah. See themselves in the role. Cheetah has gender differences. Remember the advertisement was aimed at men in the magazine. Would it have a different effect if shown in a female magazine? Females didn't know it was in a male magazine. The males are more informed than the females. City slicker . . . You can go almost anywhere in it. Merging of machinery and grass – semantic links with the countryside through the metaphor of the cheetah. Identify with the cheetah. Using their knowledge to read the picture. 'Hairdresser's car' . . . there is diversity of opinion about the car. They do identify themselves with the cheetah . . . they see themselves in that role. Cheetah has gender differences . . . The car is seen as a woman by the men . . . shows what he thinks a car should look like. When they are constructing the narrative they are drawing on cultural knowledge that they have. Interest and knowledge affect how they construct the narrative . . . males and females constructed the narrative differently . . . Males provide more detail on the car than the females.

Questions

1 Analyse the researcher's notes making use of a cognitive map and data display tables.

2 What differences do you note in terms of male and female interpretations/perceptions of the advertisement?

REFERENCES AND NOTES

1 Strauss, A S (1993) *Qualitative Analysis for Social Scientists*, Cambridge: Cambridge University Press, 2.

2 QUALPRO and ETHNOGRAPH, Qualitative Research Management, 73425 Hilltop Road, Desert Hot Springs, CA.

3 QSR NUD*IST, Qualitative Solutions & Research Pty Ltd, Box 171, La Trobe University Post Office, Victoria, Australia 3083.

4 Catterall, M and Maclaren, P (1995) Using a computer to code qualitative data, in *Proceedings of 1995 Annual Conference of the Marketing Education Group 'Making Marketing Work'*, Bradford University, July.

5 Inspiration, Inspiration Software, Inc., 2920 SW Dolph Court, Suite 3, Portland, Oregon 97219.

6 COPE, Advertising leaflet/working demo, Department of Management Science, University of Strathclyde.

FURTHER READING

Bryman, A and Burgess, R G (1994) Reflections on qualitative data analysis, in Bryman, A and Burgess, R G (eds), *Analysing Qualitative Data*, London: Routledge, 216–26.

Coffey, A, Holbrook, B and Atkinson, P (1996) Qualitative data analysis: technologies and representations, *Sociological Research Online*, 2, http://www.socresonline.org.uk/socresonline/1/1/4.html

Dembhowski, S and Hanmer-Lloyd, S (1995) Computer applications – a new road to qualitative analysis? *European Journal of Marketing*, 29(11), 50–62.

Denzin, N and Lincoln, Y (1993) *Handbook of Qualitative Research*, Newbury Park; CA: Sage.

Fielding, R and Lee, R (eds) (1991) *Using Computers in Qualitative Analysis*, Berkeley; CA: Sage.

Griggs, S (1987) Analysing qualitative data, *Journal of the Market Research Society*, 32, 507–20.

Miles, M B and Huberman, A M (1994) *Qualitative Data Analysis*, London: Sage.

Richards, T and Richards, L (1991) The NUD*IST qualitative data analysis system, *Qualitative Sociology*, 14.

Silverman, D (1993) *Interpreting Qualitative Data*, London: Sage.

Spiggle, S (1994) Analysis and interpretation of qualitative data in consumer research, *Journal of Consumer Research*, 21(3), 491–503.

Stern, B B (ed.) (1998) *Representing Consumers: Voices, views, visions*, London: Routledge.

Strauss, A S (1993) *Qualitative Analysis for Social Scientists*, Cambridge: Cambridge University Press, 2.

Weitzman, E and Miles, M (1995) *Computer Programs for Qualitative Data Analysis*, Thousand Oaks, CA: Sage.

Whipple, Thomas W (1994) Mapping focus group data, *Marketing Research*, 6(1), 16–21.

12 Evaluation, reports and presentation

Objectives

After reading this chapter, you should be able to:

- understand the importance of the presentation to the success of a research study

- appreciate the preparation of different aspects of the presentation

- understand how to use some of the visual and electronic aids that are available to the presenter.

Keywords

executive summary
findings
oral report
outline
presentation

proposal
report
report body
visual aids

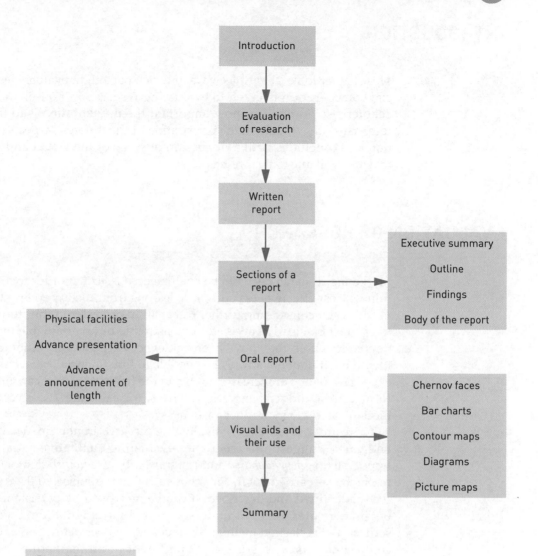

Plan of Chapter 12

INTRODUCTION

This chapter looks at various ways in which one might evaluate research and special consideration is given to evaluating research in non-financial terms. The chapter also emphasises how important the **presentation** is to the success of a research study. It looks at the preparation of the different aspects of the presentation and concludes with a discussion of some of the **visual** and electronic **aids** that are available to the presenter.

EVALUATION OF RESEARCH

Marketing research needs to be evaluated *post-facto* in order to ascertain its usefulness/cost-effectiveness and draw lessons from the experience that may prove useful when considering further research. In order to do this, the research objectives must be clearly specified in measurable or ascertainable terms so that the degree to which they have been achieved, exceeded or underachieved can be identified. It may not always be possible to link financial expectations in terms of expected savings or increased profits to the financial cost of carrying out research. In measuring advertising effectiveness, for example, the objective may be to measure increase in product awareness.

There are several ways of evaluating research in non-financial terms. Lincoln and Guba[1] suggest four criteria for evaluating qualitative research – *credibility, transferability, dependability* and *confirmability*. *Credibility* demonstrates that the research was carried out in a manner such that the subject of the research was correctly identified and described. It can be improved by persistent observation to obtain a greater depth of understanding, by triangulation, by using different sources and collection methods of data and by peer debriefing of colleagues on a continuous basis. This is clearly pertinent to all marketing research studies. *Transferability* is concerned about whether the findings can be applied to another situation that is sufficiently similar to permit generalisation – useful when generating research that may form part of omnibus studies or provide secondary data for other studies. *Dependability* should show that the research processes are systematic, rigorous and well documented. This is an essential foundation on which all marketing research should be based. It permits subsequent users of the research to ascertain how well the research was conducted. *Confirmability* should be used as a criterion where the study has described the research process fully and it is possible to assess whether the findings flow from the data. Again this should be a requirement of a marketing research study. Yet another approach to evaluation involves obtaining *respondent validity* for the analysis. This involves discussing findings from the analysis with those who have participated in the study to obtain their reactions and opinions.

WRITTEN REPORT

The basic requirement is for a **report** and presentation that can be believed and trusted by everyone who will be affected by the research (Figure 12.1). The solution to a particular research problem should produce greater efficiency, lower costs and more benefits for the organisation. The presenter of the research results has to convince the audience that the research findings can be acted on for their own benefit. A written report needs to be put together so that interest and belief develop throughout its reading and the recommended action appears as a natural outcome.

It may be beneficial to delete less important questions in order to emphasise the basic problem. Constant attention to the basic problem and its recommendations will make the study and its presentation more usable and interesting in the minds of the listeners and/or the readers of the final presentation. Presenters

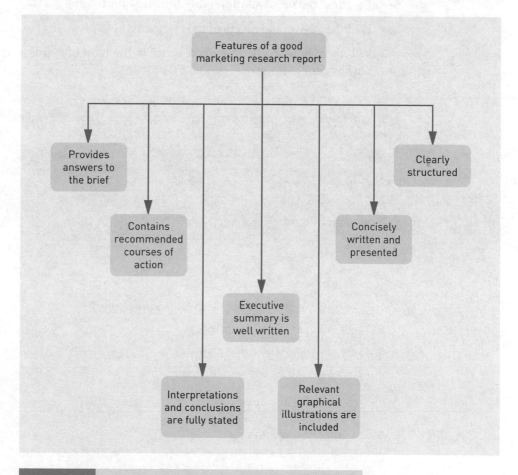

FIGURE 12.1   Characteristics of a good marketing research report

have the best chance of success if they have planned their research well and meet the expectations of their listeners.

A good knowledge and understanding of the audience are essential for good reporting. The presenter of a report should know in advance who will receive copies of the written report or who will be at an oral presentation. The report should address itself directly to these people and their needs.

Anticipating objections from people with known mindsets may alter how a report is written – or even how the research is done.

Research studies sometimes tend to deviate from the original problem and **proposal**. It is often the case that interesting information is uncovered which is peripheral to the study. However, the study should be directed towards the solution of the stated problem and, if research has uncovered another problem that needs looking at, this should be suggested as the basis of another study.

The written or **oral report** must address itself precisely to questions such as:

- Do these recommendations still appear sound?

- Will they affect the needs of the company in the way that was first intended?

- Will the whole study now make sense in the light of conditions when the study was begun?

CONTENTS OF A MARKETING RESEARCH REPORT

Title page

1 Title

2 Client (optional)

3 Research company (optional)

4 Date

Table of contents

1 Section titles and subheadings with page numbers

2 Table of tables: titles and pages

3 Table of figures: titles and pages

4 Appendices: titles and pages

Management or executive summary

1 Statement of objectives

2 Statement of major findings

3 Statement of conclusions and recommendations

4 Other pertinent information such as limitations of the research or background information

Introduction

1 Background to the research undertaken

2 People involved in the research, their positions and roles

3 Acknowledgements

Analysis and findings

1 Analytical approach adopted

2 Tables and figures

3 Explanatory text

Conclusions and recommendations

Research methodology

1 Type of study

2 Purpose of study

3 Definition of population of interest

4 Sampling design and method

5 Data-collection method adopted and justification for method

6 Questionnaire or other data-collection instruments – description and explanation

Limitations

1 Sample size

2 Sample selection

3 Error

Appendices

1 Questionnaire

2 Technical

3 Other

SECTIONS OF A REPORT

Executive summary

This is placed at the beginning of the report and allows executives to quickly and easily grasp what has been learned and what is being recommended. Sometimes the digest is bound separately for executives who will not want to read all the details. Experienced presenters often make use of this technique of the separate **executive summary**.

This executive summary will include:

- action implications backed up by key findings

- discussion of findings for interested middle management

- a short appendix with a few details of procedures, a sample of appropriate materials, a few detailed tabulations, and statistics.

Outline

The **outline** should be as complete as possible, since it will greatly facilitate the writing of the final report. All sources of information should be named and details that might seem so obvious that they need not be put on paper should be entered.

Findings

Key **findings** should stand out, perhaps highlighted by a table, a chart or some other visual aid. The key findings may even form the basis of a separate executive report. Key action recommendations largely stem from the key findings noted.

Details of the procedures followed should be included. These details should include such facts about the study as the research instruments used, sampling methods and the response rate for questionnaires. The procedures should be recorded in enough detail to protect the validity both of the recommendations and of the procedures. This may at some time enable a further study to be made replicating the same procedures so that a comparison can be made with the first study. Once the report has been written up, it can be turned into an oral or a video presentation, or may even become the basis for a small-group seminar.

Body of the report

The **report body** might include the following:

- a statement of the problem, perhaps slightly modified to allow for changes in instructions and changes caused by early findings in the research

- a brief account of how the research was conducted

- a detailed presentation of the findings, but only what is necessary for backing up the recommendations

- a list of the major recommendations

- a statement of the implications of the findings and recommendations for specific departments of the sponsoring company.

Objectivity in report writing is of paramount importance. It is a good idea to list the shortcomings of a study since most studies do in fact have them. Style of writing is most important. A research report needs to be sharp, clear and vivid. Simple words are usually best and jargon should be avoided.

ORAL RESEARCH REPORT

Only rarely will top executives be interested in the minute details of the recommendations. Later they will want to know almost everything that will affect their firm if action is to be taken on the recommendations. At this point the recipients of the report will usually want just the highlights of both findings and recommendations.

Physical facilities

The room must be ready with proper lighting, air-conditioning and a sound system that enables everyone to hear. All possibly distracting noises from outside sources must have been eliminated.

Advance preparation of presentation

The presentation must have been well prepared and all possible interruptions considered. Perhaps several people should participate in the presentation, to relieve the possible boredom of one voice and face.

Advance announcement of length of presentation

Stating how long the presentation will be is a good strategy.

VISUAL AIDS AND THEIR USE

Use of visual aids such as chalkboards, flipboards and overhead transparencies should be made. Too many visuals, however, can become distracting and even boring. They should be used solely to clarify or reinforce a point. It is a mistake to believe that pictures are always better than words. Visual aids should only be used if they serve a real and necessary purpose.

Figure 12.2 illustrates an overhead transparency that can be prepared with a product such as Microsoft PowerPoint. It shows how a graphic presentation can be combined with key points expressed in words.

There is a wide range of graphical illustrations that can be used. The following gives some examples.

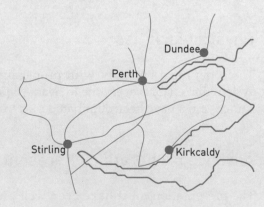

Suggested warehouse locations

Warehouse locations could be sited at:

Dundee, Perth, Kirkcaldy and Stirling

| FIGURE 12.2 | Text and map in an overhead transparency |

Chernov faces

This is a useful way of displaying attitudes to various objects and is more or less self-explanatory. The expression on the faces reflects the attitudes towards the object (Figure 12.3).

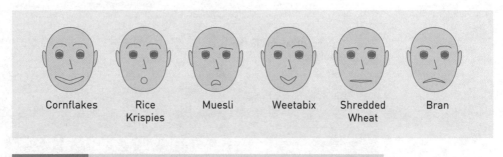

FIGURE 12.3 Chernov faces of attitude towards various brands of cereal

Conventional bar charts

A bar chart is a graph of a frequency distribution (Figure 12.4).

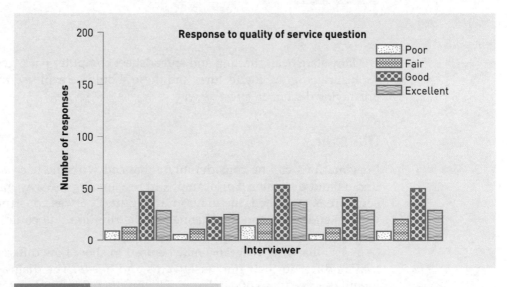

FIGURE 12.4 Conventional bar chart

Contour maps

Where demographic, attitudinal or other data can be shown to vary geographically by region, area or district, and data points are clustered together into fairly homogeneous groupings, contour maps can be used effectively to illustrate how the data are distributed (Figure 12.5).

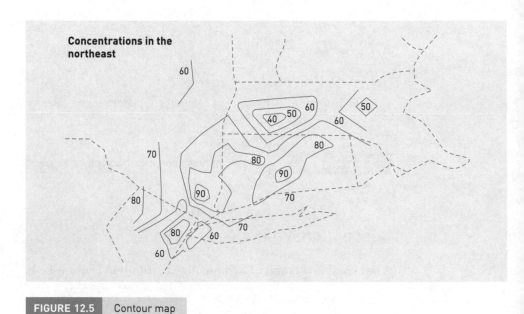

| **FIGURE 12.5** | Contour map |

Many statistical, charting and spreadsheet computer packages now have quite sophisticated graphing features and these should be explored to find methods of portraying data in an effective way.

Diagrams

Presentations can be considerably enhanced with the use of simple, easy-to-understand diagrams. For example, in researching the way in which computer software is marketed, the diagram in Figure 12.6 was constructed to show the various end-users and the channels of distribution that could be used to reach them.

In a similar way, diagrams may be used to show how different groups of customers differ in their purchase wants and needs. The diagram in Figure 12.7 identifies three types of purchaser of bathroom furnishings, together with important, differentiating aspects of their buying behaviour.

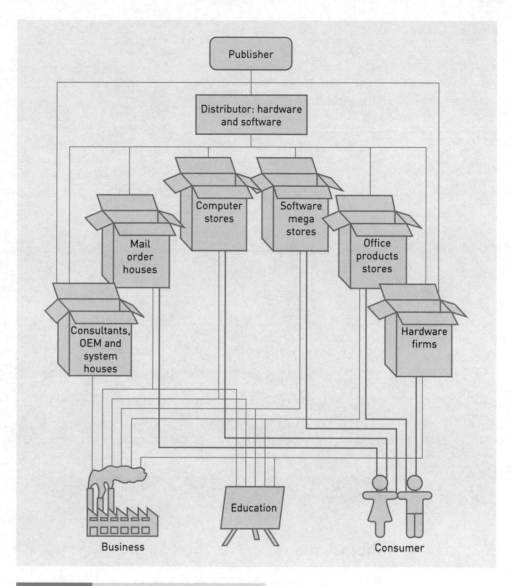

FIGURE 12.6 Use of diagrams in presentation

Sophisticated computer presentation packages now enable combined displays to be produced. These can be used either as a page for incorporation in a report or as an overhead transparency master. The example in Figure 12.8 captures the original spreadsheet data for expenditure on rent and housing, together with expenditure on food and drink, along with the scattergraph showing the relationship between the two. It also shows the distribution of both variables across Europe on a map as well as graphic pictures emphasising the products.

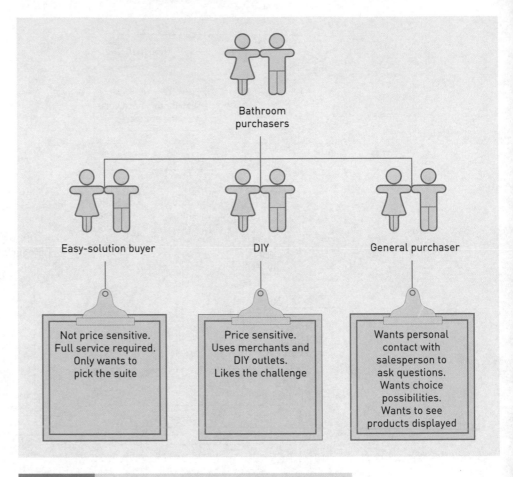

FIGURE 12.7   Three types of purchaser of bathroom furnishings

Picture maps

Picture maps are another way of helping to display information in a readily meaningful way (Figure 12.9).

INSPIRATION[2]

Inspiration is a visual idea development tool for developing ideas and plans. It fully integrates an easy-to-use diagram creator and a powerful outliner. We can use the diagram creator to generate ideas, plan and produce diagrams and the outline view to organise writing. Inspiration's integration of these facilities through different 'views' gives two different perspectives of the same information: a graphic view and

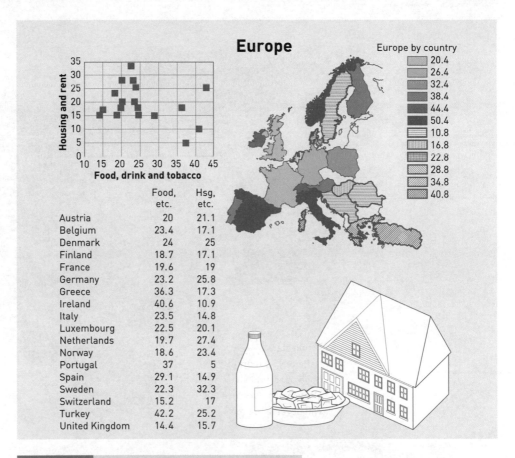

Europe

	Food, etc.	Hsg, etc.
Austria	20	21.1
Belgium	23.4	17.1
Denmark	24	25
Finland	18.7	17.1
France	19.6	19
Germany	23.2	25.8
Greece	36.3	17.3
Ireland	40.6	10.9
Italy	23.5	14.8
Luxembourg	22.5	20.1
Netherlands	19.7	27.4
Norway	18.6	23.4
Portugal	37	5
Spain	29.1	14.9
Sweden	22.3	32.3
Switzerland	15.2	17
Turkey	42.2	25.2
United Kingdom	14.4	15.7

FIGURE 12.8   Multiple items on one page or overhead

a text view. It provides a single tool for idea development and planning and is useful for developing and communicating ideas.

Inspiration makes it easy and fast to create mind maps, cluster diagrams and idea maps as part of your brainstorming and planning process. These are all visual thinking techniques used for generating ideas and clarifying thinking. Visual maps help stimulate thinking and add clarity. They also simplify the process of moving thoughts into words that communicate your ideas. When writing a report, Inspiration saves time because its powerful outliner helps to revise, edit and format work quickly.

Often a picture is the best way to express a concept since it presents its essence instantly. It adds insight by showing the flow of ideas, their relationships and their dependencies. Visual diagrams are a powerful way to communicate an idea or concept, explain a process or procedure, or sell your message.

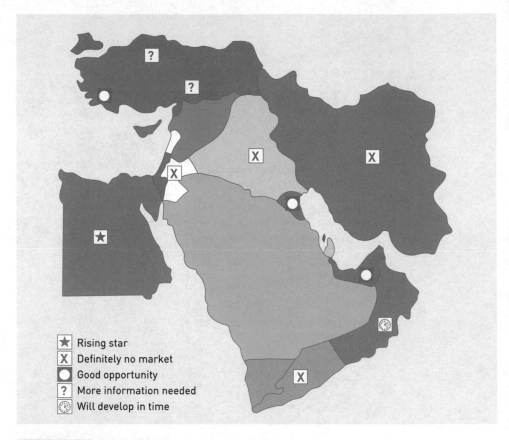

★ Rising star
X Definitely no market
◯ Good opportunity
? More information needed
🕐 Will develop in time

FIGURE 12.9   Picture map

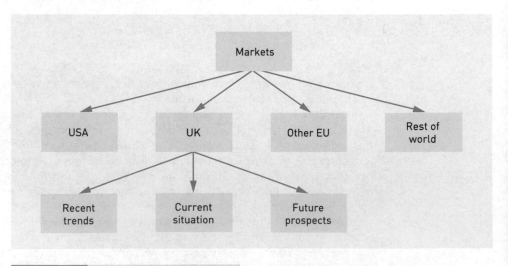

FIGURE 12.10   Diagram view of Inspiration

I Markets
The report will cover the company's progress and prospects in all the markets in which it operates. More specifically: UK, other EU countries, USA and the rest of the world.

II UK
Recent trends In the last three years the company has made sound progress in all its key product markets. Particularly successful have been sales of compound D to dairy farmers.
Current situation Sales to dairy farmers currently make up some 30% of sales to the UK market.
Future prospects Expansion in sales to dairy farmers in the UK is somewhat limited across the whole product range.

III Other EU

IV USA

V Rest of world

FIGURE 12.11   Outline view from Inspiration

Figures 12.10 and 12.11 illustrate Inspiration in use. The diagram in Figure 12.10 shows the various areas that the report is covering. Each of the boxes can be expanded in the outliner view (Figure 12.11).

SUMMARY

This chapter has examined the importance of the presentation to the success of a research study. It looked at the preparation of the different aspects of the presentation and concluded with a discussion of some of the visual and electronic aids that are available to the presenter.

QUESTIONS

1 When preparing a research report, where should you begin? Why?

2 List the various sections that go into making a marketing research report and briefly state what each section includes.

3 How should the oral report differ from the written report?

4 Indicate the types of visual aid that might be used in making an oral presentation.

CASE STUDY 12.1: THE ST HONORÉ DE MAZARIN RESTAURANT, PARIS

A summary of responses to a short questionnaire completed by 24 visitors to the restaurant is shown in Table 12.1. The numbers show the rating given by respondents on a five-point scale (1 is high) on five evaluation criteria.

TABLE 12.1	Responses to questionnaire

Guest	Country of abode	Age	Varied cuisine	Friendly service	Value for money	Quick service	Pleasant surroundings
1	France	<25	2	4	2	2	2
2	England	65+	3	3	2	3	2
3	Germany	25–34	4	4	2	4	2
4	Italy	45–54	3	3	2	2	2
5	France	25–34	4	4	1	3	1
6	Germany	35–44	2	4	2	3	2
7	Italy	65+	3	4	3	3	2
8	France	35–44	4	4	2	2	1
9	France	45–54	3	2	1	1	2
10	Italy	35–44	3	3	2	2	2
11	England	25–34	4	1	1	3	3
12	Germany	45–54	3	3	2	4	2
13	England	55–64	2	2	1	3	2
14	England	<25	3	2	2	2	2
15	Italy	<25	4	3	3	1	3
16	France	55–64	3	4	2	2	2
17	England	45–54	2	3	2	3	3
18	Italy	25–34	3	2	2	2	3
19	Germany	55–64	4	2	1	1	2
20	England	35–44	2	3	2	3	2
21	France	65+	4	4	3	2	1
22	Germany	65+	3	3	2	3	1
23	Germany	<25	2	2	3	3	2
24	Italy	55–64	1	4	2	3	2

Question

Draw up a report based on the summaries shown in the table, paying particular attention to the graphical means of summarising the data.

CASE STUDY 12.2: CENTRAL TRAINING COLLEGE (3)

Two surveys were conducted to find answers to the research questions indicated in the Central Training College (1) case (see Case study 5.1). The first survey was among students and the second was among potential business users. The aim of the research was to establish the viability of setting up a recruitment agency under the aegis of the Central Training College that would be of mutual benefit to students and potential employers. In the first of the surveys, students at the Central College were asked for their opinions, while in the second instance potential employers were asked for their reactions.

The student survey sought answers to a comprehensive list of questions. These were incorporated in a well-designed questionnaire that offered possible answers from which the students might select answers or they could suggest answers of their own. Of students at the 60 colleges contacted, 48.3% returned a completed questionnaire.

The students, 41.4% of them, said that they had used an employment agency before. When asked whether they were satisfied with the service they had been offered, 50% said that they were. Students with experience of using agencies particularly liked a helpful, friendly consultant and career advice. The first factor was mentioned by 50% of students and 16.7% mentioned the second factor. One-third of the students who answered the question complained about agencies' poor communication with students. Consultants would agree to contact a student by a particular time but they would fail to do so and students' costs were therefore increased. Twenty-five per cent of students mentioned the frequency of being sent for an unsuitable position as another source of complaint. Another dislike mentioned by 16.7% of students was being referred to different consultants on each visit. Often, students would have to explain their interests and experience repeatedly to different consultants. Comments written on questionnaires suggested that students felt they were treated very impersonally. Lack of information on pay and holidays supplied by the agencies, the absence of training schemes offered by the agencies to broaden students' skill base and the apparent lack of effort to find the student employment were also cited as shortcomings. However, 37.9% of respondents indicated that they definitely intended using an employment agency in the future and a further 51% said that they would probably do so.

Six people thought that a reputation for being helpful and efficient was the most important consideration when choosing an agency. Five mentioned the need for the chosen agency to have good contacts. Overall reputation, a specialised service for foreign and arts world contacts and a relatively cheap service were each mentioned by four of the respondents. Four thought a personal service, a well-established name and an agency with many branches was important.

Just over half of the students (51.7%) had no idea which agency they intended engaging. Of those who did have some idea, 22.7% stated that they intended to use Kelly, 27.2% said they intended to use Alfred Marks or City Secretaries. Drake and Angela Mortimer each accounted for 9.1% of choices. Also mentioned were Abacus, Angela Pike, Elizabeth Hunt and Pathfinders. Those who indicated that they were not going to use an agency gave high charges as one of the main reasons.

When asked if they thought it was a good idea for a recruitment agency to be opened in the college, 89.6% said that it was. The most frequent reason given for the idea being perceived as a good one was the belief that the service would be specifically designed for the students of the college. It was thought that an agency in the college might have more flexible consulting times. This flexibility would enable the students to meet consultants on a more frequent and regular basis than would be the case with an agency situated several miles away. Of all the respondents, 37.9% said they would definitely use an agency based in the college and 48.3% said they would probably use it. Of the respondents, 10.3% usually lived outside the UK and, of the remainder, 80.8% were resident in London. The majority of respondents (96.5%) were female. There were no respondents over 50 years of age and 34.5% were under 20 years of age. When it came to employment, 51.7% of the students classed themselves as unemployed, 31% were full-time students and 6.9% were self-employed; 34.5% of the respondents with work experience had obtained it in areas where a college agency might find jobs. One-fifth had bookkeeping and accounting experience, two-fifths had experience as secretaries, clerks and receptionists. Just over one-fifth had worked as nannies, waitresses and shop assistants, while 17.2% had teaching experience. A further 17.2% had sales, design or consultant experience, while 10.3% of students had no work experience at all. Most respondents were interested in secretarial work: just over 25% were interested in it. Business administration, receptionist and linguistic work were the next popular choices, each accounting for 13.7% of indicated preference; 3.9% were interested in desktop publishing and bookkeeping. Accounting and spreadsheet analysis were popular with 1.9% of respondents; 19.6% were not interested in office work at all.

As in the case of the student survey, a well-constructed questionnaire was put together for the survey of firms. This time the survey was by post. Only 30 out of 100 questionnaires were returned. Of those that were returned, 30.3% were not completed but were accompanied by a letter stating that the company did not and would not use employment agencies.

Just over half of the respondents said they had never used a recruitment agency in the past. When used, the most frequently sought employees were secretaries (frequency 15), accounting staff (12), receptionists (4), bookkeepers (3) and business administrators (2). Of jobs offered to the agencies, 37.5% were permanent. The most frequent future need was predicted to be for secretaries – 45.4% of respondents indicated this. However, 45.55% of the respondents said they would be using an agency to hire secretaries and accounting staff in the future. Employers said they would not be using agencies to hire desktop publishers, spreadsheet analysts and linguists; 70% said they would not be using agencies to recruit receptionists.

When asked how many recruits they obtained through an agency, most employers indicated this to be less than one per year: 26.3% hired one person per year through an agency; 60% of respondents who said that they had used a recruitment agency indicated they expected no change in the number of people hired per year in this way in the immediate future. While 6.7% expected an increase, 26.7% expected a decrease.

Most firms did not know how many agencies they employed. There appeared to be no predominantly popular agency. Half of the respondents either did not know or said they used various agencies, while 75% said they were satisfied with the service they received.

The feature most liked by the employers was the fact that the ideal person was found. Most employers did not indicate what they disliked about employment agencies. Some, however, mentioned lack of candidate screening and the provision of poor CVs for candidates.

The most common size of firm was 21 to 50 employees – 30.3% of the sample fell into this category; 15.1% employed between 51 and 100 employees and 9.1% employed fewer than six people. Some 6.1% of the sample employed more than 100 employees and 27.3% gave no indication of size.

Source: Fry[3]

Question

Show how you would draw up these findings into a management report and presentation.

CASE STUDY 12.3: SUNRISE HOTELS

Helena Constantine, chief executive of Sunrise Hotels, is keen to ensure that the quality of all hotels in the group is high. As part of a monitoring campaign, 51 completed questionnaires from one of the hotels in the group have recently been returned for her attention. The questionnaire is provided below and the summary responses for each item on the questionnaire are shown in Table 12.2.

SUNRISE HOTELS

At Sunrise Hotels, we want to give guests the best service and facilities. We should like to have your opinions on the service we offer, and would appreciate your thoughts on your stay with us on this visit.
Thank you for choosing Sunrise Hotels and for completing this questionnaire. We look forward to welcoming you back in the near future.

Helena Constantine, Chief Executive

Your name   _____

Your address   _____

_____

_____

From   __/__/__   To   __/__/__

Room number   _____

Your age   ☐ Under 25   ☐ 25–34   ☐ 35–44   ☐ 45–54
             ☐ 55–64   ☐ Over 65

Your sex   ☐ Male   ☐ Female

What was the primary   ☐ Business trip to locality
purpose of your visit?   ☐ Overnight stop en route
                       ☐ Visiting area, sightseeing
                       ☐ Weekend break   ☐ Other

Our general service and facilities

How well did we match with your expectations?	Excellent	Good	Fair	Poor
On reservation				
Accuracy of information provided	1☐	2☐	3☐	4☐
Your welcome				
On arrival at reception	1☐	2☐	3☐	4☐
In reception				
Speed of check-in	1☐	2☐	3☐	4☐
In the bedroom				
Cleanliness of room	1☐	2☐	3☐	4☐
Overall comfort of room	1☐	2☐	3☐	4☐
General maintenance	1☐	2☐	3☐	4☐
In the telephone service				
Staff telephone manner	1☐	2☐	3☐	4☐
Speed of response	1☐	2☐	3☐	4☐

Have you any specific comments you would like to make? If so, please write them in the box below.

Our staff

How would you rate our staff in terms of:

	Excellent	Good	Fair	Poor
Courteousness	1☐	2☐	3☐	4☐
Efficiency	1☐	2☐	3☐	4☐
Reliability	1☐	2☐	3☐	4☐
Anticipating your requirements	1☐	2☐	3☐	4☐
Attending to your requirements	1☐	2☐	3☐	4☐
Ability to deal with problems	1☐	2☐	3☐	4☐

Please mention any member of staff who made your stay especially enjoyable.

```
+--------------------------------------+
|                                      |
+--------------------------------------+
```

Our dining and bar service

How would you rate our service?

In the restaurant

	Excellent	Good	Fair	Poor
Anticipating your requirements	1☐	2☐	3☐	4☐
Range of food and beverages	1☐	2☐	3☐	4☐
Quality of food and beverages	1☐	2☐	3☐	4☐
Quality of service	1☐	2☐	3☐	4☐
Ambiance/decor	1☐	2☐	3☐	4☐

Please write any further comments you may have in the box below.

```
+--------------------------------------+
|                                      |
|                                      |
+--------------------------------------+
```

In the lounge or bar

	Excellent	Good	Fair	Poor
Anticipating your requirements	1☐	2☐	3☐	4☐
Quality of service	1☐	2☐	3☐	4☐
Quality of food and beverages	1☐	2☐	3☐	4☐
Ambiance/decor	1☐	2☐	3☐	4☐

Please write any further comments you may have in the box below.

```
+--------------------------------------+
|                                      |
|                                      |
+--------------------------------------+
```

What do you consider is the hotel's best feature?

```
+-----------------------+
|                       |
+-----------------------+
```

What do you think is the hotel's poorest feature?

```
+-----------------------+
|                       |
+-----------------------+
```

What is your opinion of the hotel in terms of price?

☐ Excellent   ☐ Good
☐ Fair   ☐ Poor

Thank you for taking the time to complete this questionnaire

TABLE 12.2	Sunrise Hotels: questionnaire responses

Name	From	To	Room	Age	Sex	Purpose
Sam Jones	8/3/96	12/3/96	69	25–34	M	Business trip to locality
Janet Mills	5/2/96	7/2/96	123	Over 65	F	Weekend break
Ernest Crabbe	4/2/96	7/2/96	109	Over 65	M	Weekend break
John Plant	17/2/96	18/2/96	15	45–54	M	Overnight stop en route
William Brown	22/1/96	23/1/96	16	45–54	M	Overnight stop en route
Rose Thorne	29/1/96	30/1/96	27	45–54	F	Weekend break
Sam Singleton	9/3/96	10/3/96	6	Under 25	M	Weekend break
John Bright	8/4/96	9/4/96	6	55–64	M	Overnight stop en route
Jim Thickett	24/4/96	27/4/96	11	55–64	M	Not answered
Jolly Forsyte	7/5/96	9/5/96	2	55–64	M	Business trip to locality
Juniper Green	10/11/96	15/11/96	1	Over 65	F	Weekend break
Penelope Snow	7/7/96	21/7/96	123	35–44	F	Visiting area sightseeing
Wallace Arnold	5/3/96	8/3/96	10	35–44	M	Weekend break
William Little	9/9/96	24/9/96	29	45–54	M	Not answered
Claire Charles	12/7/96	17/7/96	140	Over 65	F	Visiting area sightseeing
Cecilia Cardwell	5/4/96	6/4/96	17	45–54	F	Overnight stop en route
Kurt Waldheimer	25/7/96	30/7/96	21	35–44	M	Visiting area sightseeing
Françoise Angouleme	23/8/96	29/8/96	78	25–34	F	Visiting area sightseeing
Peter Pratt	29/4/96	30/4/96	46	45–54	M	Weekend break
René de la Vallière	5/3/96	6/3/96	45	35–44	M	Overnight stop en route
Valerie Carmichael	21/4/96	23/4/96	97	35–44	F	Weekend break
Thomas Thomas	6/6/96	8/6/96	9	35–44	M	Weekend break
Margaret Lemming	21/8/96	24/8/96	1	25–34	F	Weekend break
Duncan Reddish	5/2/96	7/2/96	199	35–44	M	Weekend break
Robert Thompson-Smithers	20/2/96	22/2/96	5	Over 65	M	Other
Arnold Ellis	19/9/96	20/9/96	101	55–64	M	Not answered
Warwick St John-Stevenson	3/4/96	6/4/96	200	45–54	M	Other
Hermione Page	29/1/96	30/1/96	56	25–34	F	Overnight stop en route
Teddie Taylor	21/6/96	28/6/96	17	45–54	M	Weekend break
Ursula Canning	21/12/96	22/12/96	27	Under 25	F	Overnight stop en route
Lionel Clarkson	21/7/96	25/7/96	45	45–54	M	Business trip to locality
Tania Smith	23/1/96	30/1/96	2	Under 25	F	Weekend break
Stella Homer	3/2/96	5/2/96	5	25–34	F	Weekend break
Ronald Leask	2/9/96	5/9/96	4	55–64	M	Visiting area sightseeing
François Morrell	2/4/96	5/4/96	2	45–54	M	Weekend break
Audrey Chapman-Harris-Johnson	9/2/96	11/2/96	20	55–64	F	Weekend break
Robin Rutherford	5/3/96	14/3/96	69	25–34	M	Weekend break

Reservation	Welcome	Check-in	Cleanliness	Comfort	Maintenance	Manner	Response
Good	Fair	Fair	Good	Good	Fair	Fair	Fair
Good	Fair	Fair	Good	Fair	Good	Good	Fair
Good	Good	Fair	Good	Good	Good	Good	Good
Good	Good	Fair	Poor	Fair	Good	Good	Poor
Good	Good	Fair	Good	Good	Fair	Fair	Fair
Good	Good	Good	Fair	Fair	Fair	Good	Good
Good	Good	Excellent	Fair	Good	Fair	Fair	Excellent
Excellent	Fair	Good	Good	Good	Good	Good	Good
Excellent	Good	Good	Good	Excellent	Good	Excellent	Good
Excellent	Good	Excellent	Good	Fair	Good	Good	Fair
Excellent	Excellent	Excellent	Good	Fair	Good	Fair	Excellent
Fair	Good	Poor	Good	Good	Good	Poor	Poor
Excellent	Fair	Fair	Good	Fair	Fair	Good	Fair
Fair	Good	Good	Fair	Good	Fair	Fair	Good
Good	Good	Good	Good	Excellent	Good	Good	Excellent
Poor	Fair	Good	Fair	Poor	Fair	Fair	Good
Good	Good	Good	Fair	Good	Excellent	Fair	Fair
Good	Good	Good	Good	Good	Good	Excellent	Good
Good	Good	Good	Good	Good	Excellent	Good	Good
Excellent	Excellent	Good	Good	Excellent	Excellent	Good	Good
Good	Fair	Fair	Good	Good	Excellent	Good	Fair
Good	Good	Fair	Good	Excellent	Fair	Good	Good
Good	Excellent	Excellent	Good	Excellent	Good	Good	Fair
Fair	Good	Good	Fair	Fair	Fair	Good	Fair
Fair	Good	Excellent	Good	Good	Fair	Good	Good
Excellent	Good	Good	Good	Excellent	Good	Excellent	Good
Poor	Excellent	Good	Fair	Good	Fair	Fair	Good
Poor	Poor	Poor	Fair	Poor	Fair	Fair	Poor
Good	Fair	Fair	Good	Fair	Good	Good	Fair
Fair	Good	Poor	Good	Poor	Good	Poor	Fair
Fair	Good	Poor	Fair	Good	Fair	Fair	Fair
Good	Good	Fair	Fair	Good	Good	Good	Fair
Good	Good	Poor	Good	Fair	Good	Good	Good
Good	Excellent	Fair	Good	Excellent	Fair	Good	Good
Excellent	Poor	Excellent	Fair	Fair	Poor	Good	Excellent
Fair	Good	Poor	Poor	Fair	Fair	Good	Good
Good	Excellent	Fair	Excellent	Excellent	Good	Fair	Good

TABLE 12.2	Sunrise Hotels: questionnaire responses (*continued*)

Name	From	To	Room	Age	Sex	Purpose
Emily Jackson	23/4/96	26/4/96	180	35–44	F	Business trip to locality
Constance Tucker	5/9/96	10/9/96	13	45–54	F	Weekend break
Sandy Sturgeon	4/1/96	11/1/96	73	25–34	F	Weekend break
Morgan Jones	1/4/96	15/4/96	100	55–64	M	Weekend break
David Roberts	24/3/96	26/3/96	1	55–64	M	Visiting area sightseeing
Frederick Cornwallis	24/3/96	26/3/96	4	35–44	M	Not answered
Candice Olsen	24/3/96	25/3/96	16	35–44	F	Overnight stop en route
Owen Tudor-Williams	24/3/96	26/3/96	34	35–44	M	Weekend break
Janice King	24/3/96	26/3/96	131	35–44	F	Weekend break
James Kerr-Jones	24/3/96	26/3/96	77	55–64	M	Not answered
Philip Hardborne	24/3/96	26/3/96	79	35–44	M	Business trip to locality
Rita Davies	22/3/96	23/3/96	79	25–34	M	Overnight stop en route
Walter Pidgeon	8/3/96	12/3/96	88	35–44	M	Visiting area sightseeing

Name	Guests' comment	Courteousness	Efficiency
Sam Jones	Need better chairs in the bedroom	Good	Good
Janet Mills	Chairs in the bedroom uncomfortable; tap drips – needs new washer	Good	Good
Ernest Crabbe	Receptionist too slow	Excellent	Good
John Plant	Receptionist needs training	Good	Good
William Brown	Telephone service is poor	Excellent	Good
Rose Thorne	Chairs are very uncomfortable	Excellent	Excellent
Sam Singleton	Cobwebs in bedroom; leaking tap in bedroom	Excellent	Good
John Bright		Excellent	Good
Jim Thickett	Genial and comfortable	Excellent	Excellent
Jolly Forsyte	Chairs in bedroom uncomfortable	Fair	Good
Juniper Green	Very poor-quality chairs – very uncomfortable	Good	Fair
Penelope Snow		Fair	Fair
Wallace Arnold	Room rather dark and chairs very uncomfortable	Good	Fair
William Little	Wash basin cracked; cobwebs in room and dust under bed	Good	Fair
Claire Charles		Excellent	Excellent
Cecilia Cardwell	Chairs were less comfortable than church pews and the decor was awful	Poor	Fair
Kurt Waldheimer	Cleanliness is poor by German standards	Good	Good
Françoise Angouleme		Excellent	Good

Reservation	Welcome	Check-in	Cleanliness	Comfort	Maintenance	Manner	Response
Excellent	Good	Excellent	Good	Excellent	Good	Fair	Fair
Fair	Good	Poor	Poor	Good	Excellent	Fair	Fair
Good	Good	Excellent	Excellent	Good	Good	Good	Excellent
Poor	Poor	Excellent	Good	Good	Fair	Poor	Fair
Good	Good	Good	Excellent	Fair	Fair	Fair	Good
Good	Good	Fair	Excellent	Good	Fair	Fair	Good
Good	Excellent	Good	Excellent	Fair	Good	Fair	Good
Good	Excellent	Good	Excellent	Excellent	Excellent	Excellent	Good
Good	Excellent	Good	Excellent	Fair	Excellent	Excellent	Good
Good	Good	Good	Excellent	Excellent	Fair	Excellent	Good
Good	Fair	Good	Excellent	Good	Fair	Excellent	Good
Good	Fair	Good	Good	Good	Fair	Excellent	Good
Good	Good	Fair	Good	Fair	Good	Fair	Fair

Reliability	Anticipate need	Attend need	Resolve problems	Special remarks
Good	Fair	Good	Good	Bill the barman
Good	Fair	Good	Fair	Bill the barman: brilliantly funny
Good	Good	Fair	Fair	Sue the chambermaid
Fair	Poor	Fair	Fair	Bill the barman
Good	Good	Excellent	Good	
Excellent	Good	Good	Good	
Excellent	Good	Not answered	Fair	Bill the barman
Good	Good	Fair	Good	
Good	Excellent	Excellent	Excellent	Bill the barman
Excellent	Good	Excellent	Good	Freda the chambermaid
Fair	Good	Fair	Good	
Poor	Poor	Poor	Fair	
Good	Fair	Fair	Good	
Excellent	Good	Fair	Good	
Good	Good	Good	Excellent	
Poor	Fair	Poor	Poor	I wish I could
Good	Good	Good	Good	
Excellent	Good	Excellent	Excellent	

TABLE 12.2 Sunrise Hotels: questionnaire responses (*continued*)

Name	Guests' comment	Courteousness	Efficiency
Peter Pratt		Good	Excellent
René de la Vallière		Excellent	Good
Valerie Carmichael	More staff needed, I think	Good	Good
Thomas Thomas	Tap dripping all night	Good	Good
Margaret Lemming		Excellent	Good
Duncan Reddish	Lack of insulation – draughts	Fair	Fair
Robert Thompson-Smithers	Decor poor	Good	Good
Arnold Ellis		Excellent	Good
Warwick St John-Stevenson		Poor	Good
Hermione Page	Service is very poor and decor is outrageous. Bedroom chairs are hard	Poor	Poor
Teddie Taylor		Good	Good
Ursula Canning	Very uncomfortable bedroom chairs	Good	Poor
Lionel Clarkson		Good	Good
Tania Smith		Excellent	Good
Stella Homer		Good	Good
Ronald Leask		Excellent	Good
François Morrell	Plumbing very noisy: kept me awake all night	Excellent	Excellent
Audrey Chapman-Harris-Johnson		Not answered	Good
Robin Rutherford		Excellent	Good
Emily Jackson		Excellent	Excellent
Constance Tucker	Room was very dusty	Fair	Good
Sandy Sturgeon		Excellent	Excellent
Morgan Jones	I couldn't get the blinds in my room to work	Not answered	Good
David Roberts		Good	Good
Frederick Cornwallis		Not answered	Good
Candice Olsen		Excellent	Good
Owen Tudor-Williams		Excellent	Good
Janice King		Good	Good
James Kerr-Jones		Excellent	Good
Philip Hardborne		Excellent	Good
Rita Davies		Excellent	Good
Walter Pidgeon	Need better chairs in the bedroom	Good	Fair

Reliability	Anticipate need	Attend need	Resolve problems	Special remarks
Excellent	Excellent	Good	Good	
Good	Good	Excellent	Excellent	
Good	Fair	Fair	Good	
Good	Fair	Good	Fair	Bill the barman
Good	Excellent	Good	Good	
Fair	Fair	Fair	Poor	
Good	Fair	Fair	Poor	Couldn't get dripping tap in my room fixed
Good	Excellent	Good	Good	
Poor	Fair	Fair	Poor	Bill the barman
Poor	Fair	Poor	Poor	
Good	Fair	Good	Good	
Good	Poor	Good	Not answered	Staff are poor at giving help when needed
Good	Poor	Good	Not answered	Bill the barman
Good	Excellent	Good	Good	Bill the barman
Good	Fair	Good	Good	
Fair	Excellent	Good	Good	Bill the barman
Good	Good	Good	Excellent	
Good	Fair	Fair	Fair	Bill the barman
Fair	Good	Good	Excellent	Bill the barman
Excellent	Good	Good	Excellent	
Good	Poor	Poor	Fair	No room service provided
Good	Good	Excellent	Excellent	
Fair	Fair	Fair	Poor	No one was able to find the cat in my room
Excellent	Good	Excellent	Good	
Fair	Good	Excellent	Good	Bill the barman – knew him in the army
Excellent	Good	Excellent	Good	Bill the barman
Excellent	Excellent	Excellent	Good	Bill the barman – knew him in the navy
Excellent	Good	Excellent	Good	
Excellent	Excellent	Excellent	Good	
Excellent	Good	Excellent	Good	Bill the barman – knew him in the airforce
Excellent	Good	Good	Good	
Excellent	Fair	Good	Good	Bill the barman

TABLE 12.2 Sunrise Hotels: questionnaire responses (continued)

Name	Anticipation of requirements	Range of food	Quality of food	Quality of service	Restaurant decor	Special remarks	Anticipating in the bar	Bar service	Quality of bar food	Bar decor
Sam Jones	Good	Good	Fair	Good	Good		Fair	Good	Excellent	Good
Janet Mills	Good	Good	Fair	Good	Fair		Good	Good	Good	Excellent
Ernest Crabbe	Good	Good	Good	Fair	Fair		Good	Good	Good	Excellent
John Plant	Good	Fair	Poor	Fair	Fair		Fair	Poor	Fair	Fair
William Brown	Good	Good	Good	Excellent	Good		Fair	Good	Good	Fair
Rose Thorne	Excellent	Excellent	Good	Good	Good		Fair	Fair	Fair	Poor
Sam Singleton	Good	Excellent	Good	Not answered	Fair		Good	Fair	Excellent	Excellent
John Bright	Good	Good	Good	Fair	Good		Excellent	Fair	Excellent	Good
Jim Thickett	Excellent	Good	Excellent	Excellent	Excellent		Good	Excellent	Good	Excellent
Jolly Forsyte	Good	Excellent	Good	Excellent	Good		Good	Good	Excellent	Good
Juniper Green	Fair	Fair	Good	Fair	Good		Good	Fair	Good	Excellent
Penelope Snow	Fair	Poor	Poor	Poor	Fair		Fair	Fair	Fair	Poor
Wallace Arnold	Fair	Good	Fair	Fair	Good		Good	Good	Excellent	Good
William Little	Fair	Excellent	Good	Fair	Good		Fair	Excellent	Good	Excellent
Claire Charles	Excellent	Good	Good	Good	Excellent		Good	Good	Excellent	Fair
Cecilia Cardwell	Fair	Poor	Fair	Poor	Poor	I wish I could	Fair	Poor	Poor	Fair
Kurt Waldheimer	Good	Good	Good	Good	Good		Excellent	Good	Good	Good
Françoise Angouleme	Good	Excellent	Good	Excellent	Excellent		Good	Excellent	Excellent	Excellent
Peter Pratt	Excellent	Excellent	Excellent	Good	Good		Good	Excellent	Excellent	Good
René de la Vallière	Good	Good	Good	Excellent	Excellent		Good	Excellent	Excellent	Excellent
Valerie Carmichael	Good	Good	Fair	Fair	Good		Good	Fair	Good	Fair
Thomas Thomas	Good	Good	Fair	Good	Fair		Excellent	Good	Good	Fair
Margaret Lemming	Good	Good	Excellent	Good	Good		Good	Fair	Excellent	Good
Duncan Reddish	Fair	Fair	Fair	Fair	Poor		Fair	Good	Fair	Fair
Robert Thompson-Smithers	Good	Good	Fair	Fair	Poor	Couldn't get the dripping tap in my room fixed	Good	Excellent	Excellent	Fair

Name						Comments				
Arnold Ellis	Good	Good	Excellent	Good	Good		Good	Excellent	Excellent	Fair
Warwick St John-Stevenson	Good	Poor	Fair	Fair	Poor		Good	Fair	Fair	Good
Hermione Page	Poor	Poor	Fair	Poor	Poor		Fair	Poor	Poor	Poor
Teddie Taylor	Good	Good	Fair	Good	Good		Good	Fair	Good	Fair
Ursula Canning	Poor	Good	Poor	Good	Not answered	Staff are poor at rendering help when needed	Fair	Good	Fair	Fair
Lionel Clarkson	Good	Good	Poor	Good	Not answered		Poor	Good	Fair	Good
Tania Smith	Good	Good	Excellent	Good	Good		Good	Good	Excellent	Excellent
Stella Homer	Good	Good	Fair	Good	Good		Fair	Good	Good	Fair
Ronald Leask	Good	Fair	Excellent	Good	Good		Good	Excellent	Excellent	Good
François Morrell	Excellent	Good	Good	Good	Excellent		Good	Good	Fair	Good
Audrey Chapman-Harris-Johnson	Good	Good	Fair	Fair	Fair		Fair	Good	Fair	Fair
Robin Rutherford	Good	Fair	Good	Good	Excellent		Excellent	Good	Good	Good
Emily Jackson	Excellent	Excellent	Good	Good	Excellent		Excellent	Excellent	Excellent	Good
Constance Tucker	Good	Good	Poor	Poor	Fair	No room service provided	Good	Good	Fair	Fair
Sandy Sturgeon	Excellent	Good	Good	Excellent	Excellent		Good	Excellent	Excellent	Good
Morgan Jones	Good	Fair	Fair	Fair	Poor	No one was able to find the cat in my room	Fair	Good	Good	Fair
David Roberts	Good	Excellent	Good	Excellent	Good		Good	Excellent	Excellent	Good
Frederick Cornwallis	Good	Fair	Good	Excellent	Good		Good	Excellent	Good	Good
Candice Olsen	Good	Excellent	Good	Excellent	Good		Good	Excellent	Excellent	Good
Owen Tudor-Williams	Good	Excellent	Excellent	Excellent	Good		Good	Excellent	Excellent	Excellent
Janice King	Good	Excellent	Good	Excellent	Good		Good	Excellent	Excellent	Excellent
James Kerr-Jones	Good	Excellent	Excellent	Excellent	Good		Good	Excellent	Excellent	Fair
Philip Hardborne	Good	Excellent	Good	Excellent	Good		Good	Excellent	Good	Fair
Rita Davies	Good	Good	Good	Good	Good		Good	Excellent	Good	Good
Walter Pidgeon	Fair	Excellent	Fair	Good	Good		Good	Good	Excellent	Good

▶

| TABLE 12.2 | Sunrise Hotels: questionnaire responses (*continued*) | | | |

Name	Bar comment	Like most	Like least	Value
Sam Jones				Good
Janet Mills	Bill needs some good assistants to help him with the workload			Good
Ernest Crabbe	Poor Bill is overburdened with work – but he is always cheerful	Cheerful staff	Decor	Fair
John Plant	Food poor			Good
William Brown		Mediocrity		Good
Rose Thorne		Price	Restaurant	Excellent
Sam Singleton	More waiters required in bar	Price	Slightly seedy	Excellent
John Bright	Decoration rather gaudy	Price	Homeliness	Good
Jim Thickett		Price	Drabness	Fair
Jolly Forsyte		Price	Lack of good-quality decor	Fair
Juniper Green	More waiters required	Conveniently situated	Rather basic comforts	Fair
Penelope Snow				Fair
Wallace Arnold	Poor range of food			Good
William Little	More staff required	Price	Decor	Good
Claire Charles				Fair
Cecilia Cardwell	I don't drink	None	Everything	Fair
Kurt Waldheimer				Fair
Françoise Angouleme		Price and friendliness	Decor	Good
Peter Pratt				Good
René de la Vallière				Good
Valerie Carmichael		Friendliness		Good
Thomas Thomas		Price	Delays in service	Excellent
Margaret Lemming	Decorations need to be improved	Friendliness	Decor	Good
Duncan Reddish	Decor poor	Price	Poor appearance	Poor
Robert Thompson-Smithers		Price	Decor	Good
Arnold Ellis		Friendliness	Decor	Good
Warwick St John-Stevenson	Poor decor	Price	Decor	Good
Hermione Page	I decided not to eat in the restaurant at all	Has not got one	Everything	Good
Teddie Taylor		Price		Good
Ursula Canning				Good
Lionel Clarkson	Needs a games room	Price	Doesn't cater for vegetarian snooker players	Good

Name	Bar comment	Like most	Like least	Value
Tania Smith				Good
Stella Homer				Fair
Ronald Leask				Poor
François Morrell	Decor not very tasteful	Price		Good
Audrey Chapman-Harris-Johnson				Fair
Robin Rutherford				Excellent
Emily Jackson				Good
Constance Tucker	Decor awful	Price	No room service	Poor
Sandy Sturgeon		Price		Good
Morgan Jones		It is easy to find in the dark	There was a cat in my room	Fair
David Roberts				Excellent
Frederick Cornwallis		Bill the barman	Price	Excellent
Candice Olsen				Excellent
Owen Tudor-Williams		Easy to find		Good
Janice King		Easy to find	Price	Good
James Kerr-Jones		Price	Hard to find	Good
Philip Hardborne		Bill the barman		Good
Rita Davies	Decor rather gaudy	Price	Gaudy decor	Good
Walter Pidgeon		Easy to find	Decor	Good

Question

Produce a report on the findings of this sample survey.

CASE STUDY 12.4: WALLABY TOURS

Wallaby Tours operates a tourist bus link between Adelaide and Melbourne. Instead of taking the inland road, which is the most direct route (taking around 24 hours), the company takes three days to travel along the Great Ocean Highway, stopping off at places of interest on the way – although the cost is considerably higher than the commercial bus route, the passengers see a part of Australia that they would miss if the bus followed the 'boring' route. Each bus carries a maximum of 18 passengers with their luggage; lunch is provided each day, but passengers make their own arrangements for evening meals at the various towns the bus visits. The buses rarely run fully booked, but the service is profitable.

TABLE 12.3   Wallaby Tours: questionnaire responses

Country of origin, age, and gender of passenger	Pleasant driver	Route taken	Accommodation	Quality of lunch	Comfort of bus
Bus 1: Ad. to Mel.					
UK: 27: M	2	1	3	2	3
Aus: 42: F	1	2	4	4	4
Italian: 23: M	4	2	4	4	2
Italian: 23: F	3	3	3	4	2
Swiss: 32: F	3	1	1	2	3
UK: 51: F	2	2	4	1	4
Aus: 26: F	2	1	2	4	2
Aus: 28: M	2	1	2	4	2
UK: 24: M	1	1	1	1	1
Singapore: 22: M	4	1	2	3	2
Singapore: 22: M	5	2	1	2	3
Singapore: 21: F	3	1	2	1	4
UK: 48: F	2	2	4	3	4
Bus 2: Ad. to Mel.					
Aus: 31: F	2	2	4	2	1
Aus: 36: M	1	3	2	2	2
Aus: 24: M	1	2	3	2	2
Aus: 24: M	2	3	2	1	3
Aus: 23: M	2	2	1	2	2
Aus: 24: M	3	2	2	3	1
Irish: 28: F	2	1	3	2	2
Irish: 29: F	1	2	3	2	1
UK: 37: M	2	1	3	3	2
UK: 34: F	2	1	4	4	2
Aus: 26: F	1	1	4	3	3
Dutch: 29: F	1	2	5	3	3
Bus 3: Mel. to Ad.					
Singapore: 25: M	3	2	3	4	1
Singapore: 25: F	3	1	3	4	2
UK: 32: M	1	2	3	2	1
UK: 31: F	1	2	3	2	1
Aus: 26: M	3	1	2	3	2
Aus: 24: M	2	2	2	3	2
Irish: 32: M	1	1	2	2	2
Irish: 37: M	2	1	2	1	2
Bus 4: Mel. to Ad.					
Dutch: 43: M	2	1	4	3	3
Dutch: 37: F	1	1	4	3	2
Aus: 47: M	1	1	2	2	2
Aus: 42: F	2	2	4	3	3
UK: 24: M	1	1	3	2	2
UK: 24: M	2	2	2	1	2

Recently the firm conducted a survey among four groups of passengers – two groups travelling from Adelaide to Melbourne and two travelling the other way. The directors of the company are hoping to use this information to refine the service offered; one of the directors believes that the company should be offering a different service to people of different age groups, since he believes that older people are less prepared to 'rough it' than are the younger ones. The other director is more concerned about gender issues, believing that women have different needs and expectations than men.

The passengers were asked to complete a Likert scale, with 1 as the highest rating and 5 as the lowest. Table 12.3 shows the responses obtained from the passengers.

Ultimately, the directors will be looking to collect feedback from all the passengers on all the buses; this initial survey is intended to show up major gaps in the services, and also to offer ideas for designing future research studies.

(Case contributed by Jim Blythe)

Questions

1 Prepare a report based on the figures in the table.

2 What conclusions can you draw from analysis of the data?

3 What recommendations can you make for Wallaby Tours?

4 How should the report be written in order to meet the needs of the Wallaby Tours directors?

5 What are the key findings of the research?

REFERENCES AND NOTES

1 Lincoln, Y S and Guba, E C (1985) *Naturalistic Inquiry*, Beverly Hills, CA: Sage.

2 Inspiration, Inspiration Software Inc., 2920 SW Dolph Court, Suite 3, Portland, Oregon 97219.

3 Fry, C (1991) Unpublished MBA Dissertation, Department of Management, Keele University, September.

FURTHER READING

Boland, A (1996) Got report-o-phobia? Follow these simple steps to get those ideas on to paper, *Chemical Engineering*, 103(3), March, 131–32.

Britt, S H (1971) The writing of readable research reports, *Journal of Marketing Research*, May, 265.

Carnes, W T (1980) *Effective Meetings for Busy People*, New York: McGraw-Hill.

Dwyer, J (1993) *The Business Communication Handbook* (3rd edn), Erskineville, NSW: Star Printery.

Eagleson, R D (1990) *Writing in Plain English*, Canberra, ACT: AGPS.

Eunson, B (1994) *Writing & Presenting Reports*, Milton, Queensland: Wiley.

Fletcher, W (1984) *Meetings, Meetings*, New York: Morrow.

Hague, P and Roberts, C (1994) *Presentation and Report Writing*, London: Kogan Page.

Haynes, M E (1988) *Effective Meeting Skills*, Los Altos, CA: Crisp Publications.

Hibbins, G M (1990) *Stands to Reason* (4th edn), South Melbourne, Victoria: Macmillan.

Hinkin, S (1995) Charting your course to effective information graphics, *Presentations*, 9(11), November.

Hrisak, D M (1997) Key presentation principles, *Chartered Accountants Journal of New Zealand*, 76(3), April, 24.

Kauder, N B (1996) Pictures worth a thousand words, *American Demographics* (Tools supplement), November, 64–68.

Keys, T (1996) Report writing, *Internal Auditor*, 53(4), August.

Mohn, N C (1989) How to present marketing research results effectively, *Marketing & Research Today*, 17(2), 115–18.

Nutting, J and White, G (1992) *The Business of Communication* (2nd edn), Roseville, CA: McGraw-Hill.

Rawlins, K (1993) *Presentation and Communication Skills: A handbook for practitioners*, London: Emap Healthcare Ltd.

Snell, F (1979) *How to Win the Meeting*, New York: Hawthorn Books.

Sussmans, J (1991) *How to Write Effective Reports*, Aldershot: Gower.

Thomsett, M C (1989) *The Little Black Book of Business Meetings*, New York: American Management Association.

13 Applied marketing research

Objectives

After reading this chapter, you should be able to:

- understand how marketing research may be applied to specific areas of marketing.

Keywords

advertising effectiveness	market segmentation
anthropological studies	memory
attention	monadic testing
blind testing	motivational research
branded testing	new products
cartographying	packaging
consumer product testing	paired comparison
Delphi technique	persuasability
evaluation	product delivery
geographic information system	product testing
ideas for new products	sociological studies

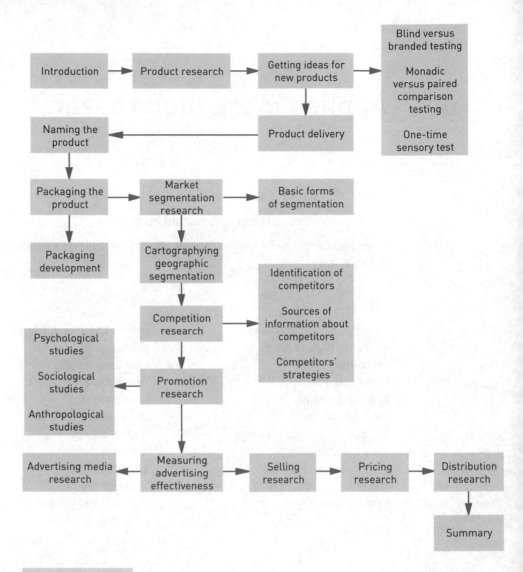

Plan of Chapter 13

INTRODUCTION

This chapter looks at some applied areas of marketing research: product research, segmentation research, promotion research, distribution research and pricing research. These applications of marketing research are substantive enough to warrant specific consideration in their own right. In the case of product research, attention is given to **product** generation and **testing**, **consumer product testing** and **packaging** research. In the case of segmentation research, attention is given to researching ways of segmenting the market. Attention is given to competition research in which understanding the market strategies of competitors is seen as a focal point. The identification of competitors and sources of information about competitors are also seen as key issues. Next, in promotion research, attention is focused on the ways of assessing its effectiveness. This is followed by a discussion of various approaches to pricing research. Finally, aspects of distribution research are considered.

PRODUCT RESEARCH

Most **new products** fail, so the use of research in developing and evaluating products is important since it reduces the risk of failure. Product research covers several different kinds of research. The aim of product research is to provide company management with information about the likely acceptance of a new product, a modified product or an existing product. Product research has three roles to play in this aspect of marketing (Figure 13.1):

1 getting **ideas for new products**

2 **evaluating** new product ideas

3 consumer product testing.

GETTING IDEAS FOR NEW PRODUCTS

Consumers can provide ideas for product improvements and even occasionally identify a new product opportunity in the marketplace. Focus group research may be used to generate product ideas, as it reflects the nature of unsatisfied consumer wants. Through focus group discussion, shortcomings of existing products can be identified as well as desirable new product features (see Chapter 8).

Concept testing means getting reactions to a new product idea or concept and can help eliminate bad ideas. One form of the concept test describes the concept entirely through words. There is a statement about what the product is and does, perhaps listing its major characteristics. Another form is visual, with an illustration

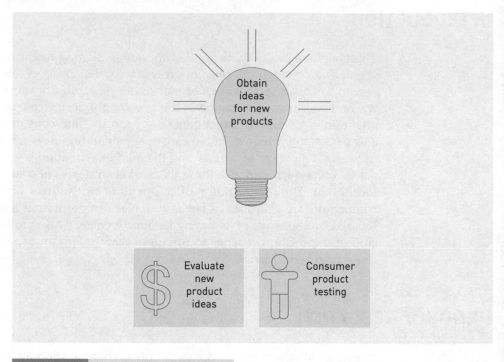

FIGURE 13.1   Scope of product research

(drawing or photograph) presented along with the description. It can even take the form of a draft advertisement, which combines the description and illustration, usually in the form of a print advertisement. A third form of the concept test uses a mock-up of the product. This is something that passes for a prototype, but is really only a dummy product that helps get across the idea of the product.

In the typical concept test, the concept is stated or shown to the consumer and the person is asked about their interest in purchase. It is conducted with a random group of potential consumers and the typical starting sample size is 600. Each respondent is recruited and interviewed at home, then offered the product in a personal call-back interview and for 'real money'. Further sales waves are made by telephone calls and the product is delivered to the homes of purchasers. Sales to the consumer on several occasions over a time period provide an observation of how much the consumer really wants to buy.

MADAME TUSSAUD'S

Each additional waxwork figure, or new theme area that is put into the exhibition, is initially a new product – something the public has not seen before. Ideas for new products originate from several sources. The ideas, which will be for a new figure or theme, come principally from a committee consisting of company executives, totalling about eight people, who meet regularly for brainstorming sessions. The committee also canvasses the opinions of other members of staff and takes into account what the marketing department has discovered through its research. The research team conducts a popularity poll, each year, to find out who are the favourite/least favourite figures and who people would most like to see in the exhibition. These surveys help to overcome the fact that the committee itself is not representative of the people who visit Madame Tussaud's.

The list of possible new figures has to be narrowed down or screened in order to find and drop poor ideas as soon as possible. For Madame Tussaud's it is not so much having to drop poor ideas, as to eliminate the ones that are not practical: for example, the availability of a person, what they look like and what length of life they are likely to have in the exhibition. The question is not so much a monetary one, as one of opportunity cost.

The remaining ideas for figures have to be honed into concepts, because it is these, not the idea, that the consumer will eventually buy. The product concept is what the new product will be and do to satisfy the customers. For Madame Tussaud's concept development consists of deciding where to put the figure, in what pose, in what clothes and whether it will be a 'character' portrayal or not.

Source: Double[1]

Hall tests are used mostly in the context of developing new products. They apply to consumer products and involve displaying and testing products on large numbers of possible purchasers. Often the tests take place in or close to shopping centres or precincts and are located in a hall or other suitable area. People are invited to visit the place where the tests are being held and to try the products for themselves and to register their comments and reactions to the products.

Consumer product testing measures what people think of a new or existing product only after the actual trial of the developed product. The testing does not always predict successful products or failures in the marketplace, for a product may fail because of factors other than the characteristics of the product itself. Even a good product may fail because it lacks the funds to meet the competition or because a competitor has built up so strong a reputation that no amount of spending on advertising and other forms of promotion can make any impression on it. Indeed, a poor or marginal product, as long as it has even a low level of acceptance, may perform acceptably in the marketplace as a result of massive spending on promotional efforts.

The nature of the testing varies according to the product. For a food or drink item, the test may be as simple as a one-time taste test, perhaps conducted at a shopping precinct. For a detergent, a longer term in-home test is required and the brand may be given to people at a shopping centre with a request that they try it at home over an extended time period. In this case, participants in the study are subsequently contacted by telephone to answer questions about the product. You need to decide whether the products in the test are presented on a blind basis (no brand identification) or on a branded basis. Another is whether only a single product is presented to the tester for rating (the **monadic test**), or whether a pair of products is presented (**paired comparison**).

SUGAR-FREE RIBENA: SMITHKLINEBEECHAM

SmithKlineBeecham does a lot of product testing, partly because of the diverse nature of the firm's brands (health, oral care and health drinks) and partly because of the constraints it imposes on methods. The way the company tests Lucozade Sports products reflects the fact that they are specially formulated to taste appropriate for sports activities. The firm tries to test the products in situ, interviewing sports players in leisure centres directly after taking part in a sport (that is, before they can get to a cafeteria or a bar).

The firm is particularly innovative in brand development and extension and a lot of the product research involves concept product testing. A recent example was a concept product test for the firm's new sugar-free Ribena concentrate before its launch. The main aim of the research was to evaluate two formulation options for the concept and to determine which was the better to develop further or even launch. Because the new product would have to live up to the expectations generated by the Ribena name and the quality of other Ribena products, the firm decided to include standard and light formulations in the test for comparison with the sugar-free products. There was some concern about where the volume of sugar free was going to come from and whether the other Ribena concentrate products would be cannibalised.

After discussing these issues with the research agency (RSGB), a recommendation was used to include a technique that would give an indication of the possible volume effects of the launch on the firm's other products. RSGB recommended a constant-sum preference exercise, otherwise known as the 'Chip Game'. The Chip Game asks respondents to score different brands and products (and only those within their present or past repertoire) on the basis of which they would prefer. In this case they were asked to allocate marks out of nine between different pairs of products in their repertoire, one pair at a time. The scoring is such that if a respondent prefers brand A to brand B by quite an extent, they might give brand A six and brand B three marks; and if brand A to brand C by a very large extent, brand A might be awarded eight marks and brand C one mark. In this way a total score is built up for each brand within the market, enabling preference shares and therefore volume share estimates to be calculated for each brand, as shown in the table.

	Brand A	Brand B	Brand C	Total
Brand A	/	6	8	14
Brand B	3	/	5	8
Brand C	1	4	/	5

The exercise can be undertaken twice, once on the current market situation (that is, before the introduction of sugar-free Ribena) and once after the introduction of the new concept, enabling the effects of the launch of sugar-free Ribena on the market and on other brands within the market to be assessed.

The research answered not only the basic objective of product **evaluation** but also many of the other concerns and issues surrounding the project. The final structure of the test was:

Concept stage

1 Basic background information.

2 Chip Game: current situation.

3 Evaluation of sugar-free concept.

4 Sugar-free Chip Game.

Product stage

1 Round Robin product test: four formulations, with each respondent testing two of these.

2 Ranking of sugar-free concept against standard and light concepts.

The research indicated that the concept of the new sugar-free Ribena would be well received and that one of the formulations would be a slightly better option for the launch. It also gave a clear indication of the likely effects on volume share for the other Ribena concentrates, for the brand as a whole and for other brands within the market.

Source: White[2]

Blind versus branded testing

There is almost always a need for **blind testing**, since this really determines how the product, and only the product, is perceived by the tester. It provides basic guidance, when questions about reactions to specific attributes are also asked, as to how the firm can improve its product to make it more acceptable. **Branded testing** also has an important role. The results of such a test provide information about how people react to the product and the brand image. Identified brands typically score higher than blind products, unless the brand is relatively unknown or has a poor image.

Monadic versus paired comparison testing

Monadic testing is the presentation of only one test product at a time, obtaining a rating on that product alone or perhaps against the regular brand used by the consumer. Paired comparison testing means the presentation of two products to be tried, one against the other, and comparative preferences are usually required. In either case, the ratings are not only for overall liking or preference, but usually also cover many attributes or qualities of the product(s).

In conducting the tests, various precautions have to be taken, especially in the case of the paired comparison test. Experience suggests that, all else being equal, the product tried first has a preferred position and may, just because of its sequential position, receive too high a proportion of preferred ratings. The more similar the two products are, the more likely this is to happen. So each product being tested has to be given first position with half of the sample of respondents.

The monadic test reflects the way the real world operates. Consumers rarely make side-by-side choices, although sometimes they do so in a buying situation, particularly with consumer durables. However, experience has shown that the same monadic test may give sharply differing results, probably because those replying have no anchor point on which to base responses. The paired comparison test provides sharper results, because two definite things are being compared. Under some circumstances, however, these results too are not always consistent. Moreover, paired comparison tests are unsuitable for predicting what will happen in the marketplace.

CAUGHT IN THE NEIGHBOURS' TANGLED WEB

Now that everyone in Cyber Street can use a modem and a mouse, it's apparently time to move on to higher things. Microsoft, the software company, has hooked up 30 houses on our north London backwater to the Internet, providing computers, phone lines and plenty of software to let us wander where we will, in an attempt to find out what consumers are going to want from the online revolution.

After just four months of being a market research testbed, everyone is coping with emails, bulletin boards and the Internet.

To refresh the process, the street was invited to a convivial evening's networking at an Islington eaterie to meet our 'Microsoft buddies' – the people who keep in touch with individuals and are available for questions – and to be shown what the company was up to in developing its own output. In common with other big companies, Microsoft hopes that in future people will not just sign up for companies that give them an email address and Internet access.

The people passing round the porc au pixil and Chateau Byte were talking animatedly in TV-speak about 'shows' – a word telly people use about everything from *News at Ten* to *Sunday Night at the London Palladium*. The 'shows' are the extra product the big computer companies want us to buy: similar to television, it is organised in 'channels' including a news and weather service and magazine programmes on everything from cinema, fashion and health to comics.

Over the tables, the street became introspective and the idea seemed to develop that no self-respecting virtual community was complete without its own website.

People thought it might be good to be able to call up pictures of their neighbours and even of their neighbours' pets – it's nice to know whose moggie you're chasing from the back garden. We would trade information on the best restaurants, plumbers, interior decorators and chiropractors. To set it all up, the street's very first online 'chat' was organised, using the 'chat room' that has lain neglected alongside the street's private bulletin board since the start of the project.

A chat room is a sort of online conference call. Instead of speaking and listening, you type in what you want to say in one section of the screen. The names of those taking part are displayed in another panel and the main bit of the screen shows everyone else's writings as they send them. As a means of communication, it ranks somewhere above hiccuping in Morse code. By the time you type your response to one suggestion, five other remarks have been made and your offering comes up behind one of those. So your 'I agree' response to some completely sensible proposal appears on everyone's screens just after some misguided soul has tipped Tottenham for the league.

To make matters worse, the cyber experts have their own language, such as <g>, which is apparently like a slap on the back, but whether this is to approve, say hello, sympathise or dislodge a fishbone from the throat isn't specified. They also like constructing little faces, by typing :-) or :-(to express approval or disapproval respectively. It works really well if you tilt your head through 90°.

The street cantered through its first chat without too much misunderstanding, although this was mainly because there were only seven or eight people online at any one time.

The suggested bits of the website range from the practical – information on shops, restaurants, cinemas and recycling centres – to the avowedly self-indulgent: there was a call for a philosophy column, which isn't a feature of too many other websites.

Only the residents of Cyber Street would have access to the site, although there is apparently a plan to develop an Islington website for general use – the council already has a site about its services, but there was a feeling that something a bit racier would be more helpful.

Not that this is a great time to be creating virtual experiences: the street seems to have gone on holiday en masse, possibly to the same part of Tuscany – this is middle-class Islington, after all – and the bulletin board has gone quiet. However, when everyone returns with their cases of duty-free Chianti, there's renewed enthusiasm for organising a street party, one of the first things suggested on the bulletin board way back in April. There has been a marked increase in contact in the street in recent months – it was never noted for neighbourly contact – but the grand street party is taking a bit of building up to. If it does happen, the online community will become a lot closer to being a real one.

Source: Lynch[3] (reprinted with permission)

One-time sensory test

This form of product test is relatively simple. For example, a flavour test, used to determine which of a product's two flavours is preferred, may require only one central location test, such as in a shopping precinct. In such a high-density traffic location, people can easily be intercepted. Once intercepted interviewers make sure that the respondents are qualified (such as being heavy users of the product category), then they can ask the respondents to sample the product and obtain their reactions to it. Either the monadic or paired comparison presentation of the product(s) can be applied.

PRODUCT DELIVERY

In the discussion that follows, the term 'product' should be construed to mean both product and service. To understand the ways in which marketing research can be helpful in **product delivery**, it is necessary first to talk about symbolism and imagery, for that is what product delivery is all about: the building of an aura around a particular product.

A symbol is something that stands for or represents something else and it helps create an image. Imagery reflects the way we perceive things, how we screen things to arrive at an interpretation of reality. If a brand is perceived as being poor quality, it is difficult for the supplier of that brand to change people's evaluation. Imagery or perception take on great importance in marketing. The name of the product or service, the package and the personalising of product delivery all contribute to imagery. It requires considerable understanding and skill about how to use research to develop and measure the impact of these three areas of product delivery. It is unwise to ask people directly how they like a particular logo or brand name: they will probably give a socially acceptable reply rather than one they really feel.

THE DELPHI TECHNIQUE AND NEW PRODUCT DEVELOPMENT

When a comparison is made between research projects on new products carried out in 1968 and 1980 (Booz, Allen and Hamilton 1983, ESOMAR seminar) with ones carried out in 1993 (EFO Group, *Marketing News*, 21 June 1993), the percentage of failures still remains extremely high. The Achilles heel in the development process of new products is that consumer needs are measured in a static, not dynamic, way. This means that importance is attached to the analysis of the present without giving adequate consideration to the fact that competitive advantages are achieved by satisfying needs that are still embryonic and whose full benefits have yet to come. Consumers are required to judge new products relative to their current needs, which are usually quite well met by existing products. As a result, new products tend to develop from a priority analysis of the present. Products are derived from the analysis of habits rather than from the study of evolving needs. By changing the perspective and the focus of the analysis from current to future needs, a competitive advantage could be achieved by meeting these emerging needs rather than through a better satisfaction of existing needs. This would gain commitment from trendsetters and arouse the interest of the trend followers.

A method that recognises the so-called market weak signals indicating a current change so that the concept of the new product to be developed can then be based on such signals is the **Delphi technique**[4]. It was introduced into Italy in the early 1970s and used for a large number of significant research projects carried out for consumer goods and services. One example of its use was to develop a food product with a long shelf life that did not need cooking or warming up. The research took the following steps:

1 Analysing the Delphi results, mapping out the various evolving consumption opportunities (and their relevant motives) pertaining to the company's business idea. Although food habits are among the slowest to change, the impact caused by the change in working hours and kinds of jobs (less industry and more services), the population's ageing and a greater attention to health-oriented food are causing changes that will not take many years (five to seven) to occur.

2 Defining the possible alternatives of product concepts, in line with the changes expected in the near future.

3 Identifying the weak signals coming from current behaviours by analysing existing research projects on food habits. Sociodemographic research showed that a few behavioural patterns, for which the Delphi technique expected a wide spread during a span of ten years, were already spreading among population classes with less traditional lifestyles.

4 Confirming weak signals and identification of products. Five product lines were found that shared a few basic elements such as recipes, ingredients, and service level with the new line concept. Sales trends among the five products showed they had small markets, but trends were favourable.

5 Defining the contents of the concept to convert it into a briefing for R&D. Elements were separated into these categories: basic ingredients to use; their qualitative features; importance of organoleptic elements (smell, colour, taste); importance of aesthetic aspects; physical elements of packaging; packaging size; product service level; and emotional elements – naturalness, lightness, taste, health.

   Priorities were assigned to the elements because some of them caused technical or economic problems that were not in line with the product budget.

6 Identifying the positioning, which would influence both the recipe and the advertising. Delphi research provided help in determining which food style would be dominant in the years to come and identifying the value system it was based on so that a particular nutritional area could be chosen.

The next steps were the usual ones: elaboration of the recipes, prototypes at experimental cooking level, and the product concept test, which showed an extremely high level of consensus on the concept with respect to the results of similar research projects.

Source: Bolongaro[5]

NAMING THE PRODUCT

There are three stages in naming the product:

1 defining the need

2 developing possible names

3 testing those names.

Definition of the need means that the purpose of the name must be stated in terms of the overall marketing goals and its expected contribution in such terms as imagery or perception of the firm's own name or that of its product or service.

The basic method of developing possible names is brainstorming. Once potential names have been generated, an image or perception test may be the way to determine the best one.

In developing possible names, the first step is to construct a dictionary of verbal terms and symbol fragments (visible and appropriate elements of existing names in the category). These terms are assembled into a word-making pattern that expresses the product category and messages. These may be natural words (apricot) or coined words (NatWest). Each promising name is further modified to emphasise impact, aesthetics, memorability, uniqueness, vocabulary fit, internal or external reference and shelf appeal. The final step is a focus group discussion among the target market group at which the group is exposed to the names and competitive names. They discuss how well each name describes the product and the kind of images each name puts forward.

The symbol associated with the product is also an important ingredient.

PUBLIC PUTS FAITH IN BRAND NAMES

Britain has become a nation that puts more trust in brand names than in traditional institutions, according to a report published today by the Henley Centre, the forecasting organisation.

Research carried out for the report, 'Planning for Social Change 1997', found that four in five people would trust food manufacturers such as Heinz and Kelloggs to be honest and fair.

The comparable figures for the police and the judiciary were three in five and two in five. Only a quarter felt they could trust their local council. When people were asked whether they would trust a multinational company to be honest and fair, only 13% gave a positive response.

However, high street retailers also scored highly, with 83% trusting Marks & Spencer, 74% J Sainsbury and 71% Tesco.

Paul Edwards, chairman of the Henley Centre, said the trust in brand names matched other findings in the research. These showed that people felt both 'in and out of control of their lives', he said. While people felt powerful as consumers, they felt they were not in control in their roles as employees or as members of society.

This perception was associated with the transfer of risk from the state and employers to individuals, leaving people to take responsibility for increasingly complex issues such as financial planning.

Mr Edwards said consumers now trusted certain brands so much that they would welcome their extension into new areas in order to help them to cope with increasing demands on their time.

The research suggests that as retailers moved to develop home shopping services, or even to provide services such as household cleaning, they would find a ready market.

The Henley Centre concludes that: 'Brand management is becoming synonymous with "trust management", demanding strategic attention at the top of the organisation.'

The findings will fuel the debate within the marketing industry about the role of a company's marketing department, and about what type of external adviser – advertising agency or management consultant – should take the lead in giving advice about a company's brand.

Source: Smith[6] (reprinted with permission)

PACKAGING THE PRODUCT

Packaging, particularly for fast-moving consumer goods, has three functions. First, through visibility and appeal, it helps to focus attention on the shelf. Second, it builds an image for the product. Third, it is for the convenience of storage and use by the consumer.

Good packaging can help the chances of the success of the product in the marketplace. In the case of fast-moving consumer goods, package design is important and so specialised that most larger companies use a package designer. The designing of the package must start with a good idea of the imagery desired, the importance of shelf visibility and consumer requirements for storage and use. Marketing research should have preceded this design step.

Packaging development

Discussion with consumers through focus groups in the early stages of package development is useful. The process is similar to that adopted in consumer product research. Drawings or mock-ups of various packages can be shown and discussion in group interviews will produce important points, many of which may not have been previously considered by the firm.

SOFT DRINKS SWITCH TO PET LEAVES INDUSTRY STRUGGLING FT

Aluminium is under attack in its biggest packaging sector – the drinks industry. Put 50 cents into any of the vending machines at the World of Coca-Cola in Atlanta – housing 'the world's largest collection of Coca-Cola memorabilia' – and the soft drink is delivered in a plastic bottle. A year ago the Coke would have been in an aluminium can. The switch from cans to PET (polyethylene terephthalate) for soft drinks in the USA has been so swift and bruising that the aluminium industry is still struggling to come to terms with it.

Aluminium's lightness and flexibility combined with strength, its foldability, good barrier characteristics, non-reactivity in contact with liquids, fats and oils, as well as its abundance and recyclability, all make it a formidable packaging material. Innovative design and effective marketing have enabled it to take share in virtually every type of packaging, in spite of its relatively high price, and growth is continuing in many areas.

Cans represent one of aluminium's most important markets, accounting for 20% of global demand. Cans in the USA alone account for 10% of worldwide sales of the metal. Now this market is under threat, not only from PET in the soft drinks business, but also because glass bottles are back in favour as beer containers.

In the USA the development of microbreweries and the perception that 'premium' beer should be served in glass bottles is having a noticeable impact. Glass's share of the beer package market in the States moved up from 35.8% in 1994 to 38.6% last year while cans slipped from 64.2% to 61.4%.

'Our market research shows that people think glass is classy and that beer tastes better in glass,' says Norman Nieder, group director, packaging technology group at Ansheuser-Busch, the brewing giant. 'A can is a can. It is always the same.'

Robert Budway, president of the US Can Manufacturers' Institute acknowledged the advances glass is making in the beer business but insists that the main threat to the aluminium can is posed by PET bottles in the 'single-serve' soft drinks market, primarily in vending. 'In the US this is a market of 15bn to 18bn units and 80% of all new vending business is going to PET,' he warns.

In 1991 aluminium cans accounted for 55% of US soft drinks packages while PET bottles had 34%. Last year the two were neck and neck at 50% and 47% respectively. While the industry had some time to adjust to the PET threat in North America, it has been startled by the way the aluminium can's progress in Europe has suddenly stalled.

Until 1995 demand for aluminium cans in Europe was growing at 9% a year but since then it has levelled off, not only because of the growth in PET bottles but also because the steel industry, not wanting to see the beverage can market go the same way in the USA – where aluminium had nearly 100% of the market – had fought back spiritedly. Nick Mason, research manager of the aluminium group at the CRU International consultancy, says: 'Until very recently we thought there was scope for the can to penetrate the European beverage packaging mix a little further, even though we recognise the looming threat of PET. But we estimate that, after three years of steady gains, the share of the packaged beer and soft drinks market taken by cans fell very slightly in 1996 to just more than 15%.'

He points out that it is rare for a product to remain at the top for more than ten years and that in the USA and Europe, 'we appear to be at, or close to, the final saturation phase in the life cycle of the can, although I do not believe that precipitate decline is inevitable.'

Another worry for aluminium producers is that the drinks companies, having quickly transferred the PET technology to Europe from the States, might do the same in emerging markets, such as those in Latin America, on which the aluminium industry is heavily relying for future growth in the can business. In soft drinks, for example, two US companies dominate the global business, Coca-Cola, with 47%, and Pepsi with 22.3%. 'One lesson from Europe is that there is a risk, across a whole range of developments in packaging, of a leap to PET,' says Mr Mason. 'Packaging has become a crucial element of brand identity. Over a relatively short period, container and material combinations that offer proprietary distinctiveness have acquired tremendous competitive advantages. 'So far the pace has been set by PET bottles.'

Nevertheless, the can remains an excellent container offering, for example, a 30% cost advantage over glass bottles at the filling stage and, at present, competitiveness with PET in the 'single-serve' container filled in high volumes.

Mr Mason suggests that a 'two-tier market' might emerge, consisting of a high throughput segment in which system economics still dominate – and in which cans retain many advantages – while the other would be the premium part of the market, 'in which the package, as much as the contents, may determine the value of the product to the brand manager'. Ansheuser-Busch's Mr Nieder implies that brewers are still attempting to find a way to win customers by using cans.

'Cans are much more profitable to us than glass bottles,' he points out. His group is experimenting with embossed cans, cans with labels using ten colours, cans with photographs on them, cans that change colour to show whether they are cold or warm, cans with 'touch-off' tops instead of ring pulls and shaped cans.

However, the plastic producers are now developing bottles made of polyethylene naphthalate (PEN) capable of holding beer, so the plastic threat to the aluminium industry could become even more serious.

Source: Gooding[7] (reprinted with permission)

MARKET SEGMENTATION RESEARCH

A segment is a unique group of customers – or potential customers – who share some common characteristics that make them different from other groups. Different segments may have different needs: they may require different versions of the same product; they may pay different prices; they may buy in different places; they may be reached by different media.

In consumer markets, customers and prospective customers can be grouped together, or 'segmented', by: attitude and lifestyle; age, gender or stage in the family life cycle; job types, level of income; and many other relevant variables.

In industrial markets, customers and prospective customers are usually grouped together and slotted into a particular segment depending on customer type, customer size, customer culture and customer location. Customers and prospective customers can be further segmented according to whether they are heavy or light users of a particular product or service and whether they are loyal to a particular competitor.

Segmenting and selecting the optimum market segments is called *target marketing*. This is a vital marketing skill. Target marketing requires an ability to:

- find the key characteristic(s) that break a market into relevant 'actionable' segments
- identify and quantify which customers fall into which segments
- target the segments most likely to give the best results.

Identifying what each segment wants, what it can afford, whether it is loyal to a particular competitor and how it might respond to an offer is vital information. Careful **market segmentation** and accurate targeting keeps a firm close to the market. It reduces waste, finds the best customers and helps to keep them satisfied.

We can segment consumer markets using many different variables, including:

- geographic
- demographic
- geodemographic
- psychographic
- behaviour patterns.

Geographic segments mean location, which can include: streets, towns, cities, regions, countries, continents and trading blocs like the European Union and NAFTA.

Demographics, or social statistics include age, sex, family, life cycle, job type/ socioeconomic and group income level.

Geodemographics mix geographic and demographic data to create categories of house types and locations, for example, people who live in detached houses in exclusive suburbs.

Psychographics attempt to segment according to the psychological profiles of people in terms of their lifestyles, attitudes and personalities, for example, active go-getters.

Behavioural segments address behaviour patterns which include usage (e.g. heavy or light users), and uses: the way a product or service is used – in other words, the benefit enjoyed.

A market can be segmented by the benefits enjoyed: different segments buy the same product for different reasons. Some people use toothpaste for healthy teeth, others to prevent bad breath. Some people buy it for both reasons.

More than one variable can be used when segmenting markets and, indeed, the more variables the better since they help to focus on a tighter target market. Tighter targeting means less waste, more relevant offers to appropriate customers and higher customer satisfaction.

Industrial, organisational or business-to-business markets can also be broken into segments and the most appropriate ones selected as target markets. Different variables are used for these types of markets: customer type; size; location; and how they operate in the corporate culture. Customer type categorises the type of product or service that the customer organisation produces. In the UK, industry type is defined by the Standard Industrial Classification (SIC) code. The size of the customer in terms of sales, number of staff and usage may determine whether or not it is worth targeting. Size of customer is also influenced by whether they are heavy or light users of a particular product or service, and whether they are loyal to a particular competitor.

Basic forms of segmentation

There are three segmentation bases: *consumer*, *business and industrial* and *geographics*.

Consumer segmentation

Consumer segmentation falls into two groups: syndicated and proprietary. Syndicated services use both primary and secondary sources. The information may be pure demographics, an implied mix of psychographics from demographics or pure psychographics. Demographics are vital statistics: age, sex, marital status, ethnicity, family size and composition, nature of housing, occupation, education and other statistical characteristics covered by the census. Psychographics are the psychological attributes that constitute a person's lifestyle and have much to do with the person's self-image and how he or she wants to be perceived. Purely psychographic studies are generally used only in proprietary services, for the sole use of the firm doing the study, because any such study has to be tailored for specific needs and uses. The syndicated sources basically use demographic statistics and embellish them in psychographic terms.

Business segmentation

Business segmentation is the description of areas or customers in terms of various kinds of statistics, such as nature or size of the business. Business segmentation is not as well developed as consumer segmentation. Firms can readily pinpoint business customers and potential customers and then promote directly to them. Moreover, there are few standard sources for such business and economic segmentation information. Some sources provide data on the general business environment and outlook for a particular community and others give more detail about specific kinds of business. On a simple basis, business customers may be segmented by SIC code or by classifications within the Yellow Pages.

Geographics

Many people have difficulty arriving at conclusions by inspecting large tables. It is far easier to look at a coded or coloured map to get rapid and lasting impressions. Where tables show data by area, one can easily use mapping and computer technology has facilitated this. Depending on the data source, maps can be displayed in varying colours or shading patterns with almost unlimited possibilities, according to category, such as proportion of potential or actual customers, per capita spending in a particular product or service group or sales achievement versus potential. Most mapping sources can produce maps on paper, transparency film, slides or colour transparency overlays.

CARTOGRAPHYING GEOGRAPHIC SEGMENTATION

Computer technology has enabled the ready production of maps that display segmentation data effectively, a process known as **cartographying**. Depending on the data source, the maps can be displayed in varying colours or shading patterns with almost unlimited possibilities, according to category, such as proportion of potential or actual customers, per capita spending in a particular product or service group, or sales achievement versus potential. An illustration of how such maps appear with the aid of a spreadsheet package such as Lotus 1–2–3 release 5 is shown in Figure 13.2. Most mapping sources can produce maps on paper, transparency film or slides, and colour transparency overlays are almost always a possibility.

GEOGRAPHIC INFORMATION SYSTEMS

A **geographic information system** (GIS) makes use of graphical map displays on to which various kinds of data, such as business locations or demographic information, can be superimposed. This enables the user to visualise the spatial relationships between the data. A good GIS can be linked to information databases and can make spatial calculations on the data within the maps. This form of analysis helps users to make business decisions about such matters as where to locate a new outlet, by matching customer profiles and population density to actual geographical physical locations.

MapInfo is a leading provider of such systems, and the most recent version of its flagship product, MapInfo Professional (v7.8), has the advantage of being compatible with Microsoft Windows XP and Oracle 10g, both functionally and security-wise. At the same time, the product remains compatible with previous versions of software, such as Oracle 9i, Oracle Locator and Oracle 8.17 as well as Microsoft SQL Server 2000 and IBM Informix 9.4. Aside from database systems, MapInfo

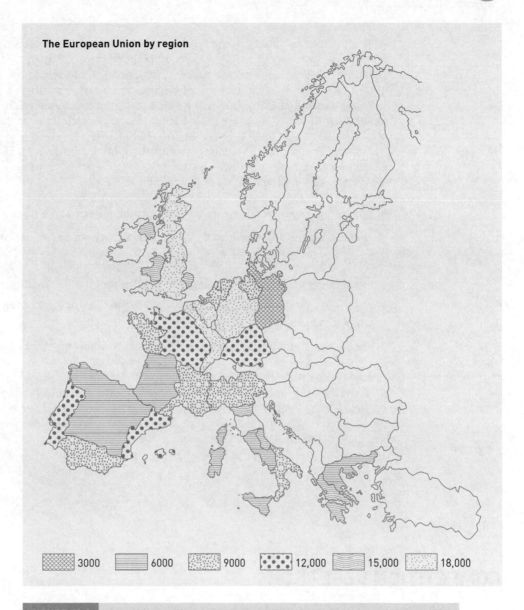

The European Union by region

3000   6000   9000   12,000   15,000   18,000

FIGURE 13.2 Map drawn with the aid of Lotus 1–2–3 showing population figures, 1990

Professional can also access and use information in a variety of commonly used data formats. Supported formats include Microsoft Excel, Microsoft Access, DBF files, delimited ASCII text files, various commonly used drawing data formats (including data from CAD packages and other mapping systems) and data from Web servers.

The product is able to assess the spatial relationship between points of origin and various other locations listed in a table. For example, one can identify a list of sales prospects and the software will automatically find the nearest service centre from a table that lists the location of all available service centres. There is also an extremely useful spider graph feature. If, for example, a supplier company wanted to see how its customers are distributed among its various branches, the spider graph dialog can be used to establish the spatial criteria.

MapInfo Pro enables the user to perform sophisticated and detailed data analysis to increase revenue, lower costs, boost efficiency and improve service with location-based intelligence. Its creators maintain it can:

- create highly detailed maps to enhance presentations and aid in decision making

- reveal patterns and trends in data that may otherwise be impossible to see

- perform sophisticated and extensive data analysis

- enable users to understand customer and marketplace demographics

- facilitate the management of geographically based assets, such as stores, people and property

- enable the planning of logistics and preparations for emergency response.

A very useful feature of the system is the Synchronized Map Window view that enables the user to view the same area with multiple map windows open. As the user zooms or pans within a single map view, all other windows can be synchronised to zoom/pan simultaneously in the same fashion. In this way, map views showing different features (e.g. different thematic maps) of the same area of interest can continue to be studied alongside the principal view of the map currently being used.

Source: MapInfo[8]

COMPETITION RESEARCH

Identifying competitors

The first step is to identify the competition. This may seem a simple question for most firms to answer. For example, at first sight a book publisher's main competitors might appear to be other book publishers. This is, of course, correct. However, product substitution has also to be considered. This involves looking more broadly at the types of business in which the firm operates. If this is done one can identify many producers of goods and services that people use for leisure, education and other informational needs. Many of these products could be potential competition for the publisher. Many of these products could be used instead of the publisher's books – i.e. they can be substituted.

Sources of information about competitors

Decision making can be improved by an adequate supply of relevant information and a knowledge of good sources of information is an important first step. A suitable starting point is to examine what competitors say about themselves and what others say about them. Sources of information fall into four categories:

- public
- trade
- government
- investors.

Public sources

Advertising, promotional materials and press releases are prime sources of information on what competitors have to say about themselves. Articles and newspaper reports provide a good source of information on what others have to say about them. Nonetheless, one does have to be wary of the information gleaned since it may be biased or even distorted.

Trade and professional sources

Courses, seminars, technical papers and manuals prepared by competitors can give detailed insights into their activities. However, it can take a considerable amount of time to distil and analyse this information. Distributors, the trade press and even customers can be good sources of information about what others have to say about competitors.

Government sources

In the UK, companies have to lodge their annual reports at Companies House in London and the contents of these reports provide insights into the operations of competitors. In addition, lawsuits, government ministries and national plans are useful sources of information.

Investors

Annual meetings, annual reports and prospectuses are primary sources of what competitors have to say about themselves. Credit reports and industry studies provide an outsider's viewpoint.

NEWSPAPERS ARE A SOURCE OF INFORMATION ABOUT COMPETITORS

Nike

Is Nike no longer cool? Its shares certainly are not. The sportswear group, a stock-market star for much of the 1990s, has underperformed the S&P 500 by over 70% this year. Even Reebok, its smaller and more fragile rival, has not done quite as badly. The two companies have blamed their recent profit warnings on Asia, and with some justification since the Far East has been an important source of growth in recent years.

More significant, however, are the sudden problems in the USA, which still accounts for over half of sales at both. Some slowing was inevitable. Nike's torrid growth, based on winning market share and ramping up prices in a fundamentally static athletic footwear market, was always going to plateau. But few investors expected footwear sales and orders to start declining, as they did last quarter. That probably reflects resistance to this spring's sharp price increases. Many of Nike's shoes sell for well over $100 a pair, while competitors such as Converse and Adidas have launched ranges at $80 to $100. But the real worry would be if Nike was ever to lose its touch with the notoriously fickle teenagers who set the trends in the sportswear market.

Nike will bounce back. It has a strong balance sheet, a great brand and is branching out into new market segments like golf and soccer. But with no big new product launches until early 1999, and plenty of unwanted stock to unload until then, its comeback will take time.

Source: *Financial Times*[9] (reprinted with permission)

Understanding competitors' marketing strategies

Understanding competition is central to making marketing plans and strategy. A firm has to be regularly comparing its products, prices, channels of distribution and promotional methods with those of its competitors in order to ensure that it is not at a disadvantage. In so doing it can also identify areas where it can gain a competitive advantage.

In order to establish a sustainable competitive advantage in the marketplace it is necessary to know and understand the strategies adopted by competitors. This is more than noting in which markets/segments the competition is operating and their respective market shares and financial performance. In addition, it is important to consider how competition will develop in the future and thus to ascertain the focus of the strategies that competitors are pursuing.

Firms need to monitor competition continually. The main need is for information regarding:

• sales

• market share

- profit margin

- return on investment

- cash flow

- new investment.

In addition, knowledge of competitors' financial performances is useful.

Such information enables firms to gain comprehensive impressions of their rivals that may be useful in predicting short-term strategies to be adopted by competitors. A knowledge of competitors' specific objectives would be very welcome since these would give clues as to future strategies that competitors are likely to pursue. This kind of information may be difficult to obtain but may be inferred from present or past activities.

PROMOTION RESEARCH

Much of promotional research is aimed at the development of advertising appeals. The type of research this requires may be classified as psychological (or motivational), sociological (focus groups) and anthropological (observation).

Psychological (motivational) studies

Motivational research usually employ psychological approaches within the framework of individual interviews. This involves talking with people in depth about what a product may mean to them: products may often evoke strong emotional feelings. Thus it is often possible to discover what a product symbolises.

Sociological (focus group) studies

In Chapter 8 we examined the use of focus group technique. **Sociological studies** may lead to ideas that a single person would be unlikely to generate.

Anthropological studies

Anthropological studies may observe a small number of people in order to understand how a product fits into their lives and what retains their interest in a particular brand. The method has also been used as an in-depth tool to obtain better understanding of consumers. It can provide a way of getting past the level of responses to questions by observing what people actually do, instead of merely listening to what they say.

EFFECTIVENESS OF POSTER ADVERTISING

Some 300 people aged between 18 and 55 were shown ten current posters and asked whether they remembered seeing them before. They were also asked to indicate how much they liked each poster by giving a mark out of ten. More than 80% recognised at least one poster, ranging from 61% for Esso Price-watch to 9% for the National Lottery 'National Heritage' advertisement. Four posters – Esso, Peugeot 406, Silk Cut 'German' and Foster's Lager 'Ambre Solaire' – were recognised by one-third of respondents.

Men were twice as likely as women to have noticed one poster before – but this may have been caused by the rather masculine nature of the products. Male recall was particularly high for the Royal's 'Batman' advertisement and for the Littlewoods FA Cup advertisement for which men make up 70% of the recognisers. Of Channel 4's NBA poster and the Silk Cut and Orange campaigns, the under 25s are similarly important.

The Esso and Royal Insurance poster advertisements tied for top position in the survey, with Esso taking first place among the females and over 35s.

Poster	Liking marks out of 10	Ranking	Recognition % saying	Rank
Royal Insurance	5.4	1	20	8
Esso	5.3	2	61	1
Peugeot	4.9	3	47	2
Silk Cut	4.9	3	47	2
Toyota	4.7	5	22	7
Foster's	4.7	5	35	4
Littlewoods	4.5	7	27	5
Channel 4 NBA	4.5	7	25	6
National Lottery	3.8	9	9	10
Orange	2.8	10	19	9

Source: Poster watch[10]

MEASURING ADVERTISING EFFECTIVENESS

Measurement of **advertising effectiveness** is one of the most difficult aspects of marketing research. Many factors influence sales besides advertising. The other factors include all the elements of the marketing mix, together with the availability of the product and the effect of competition. It is perhaps only when people place orders in response to advertisements, however, that we can be reasonably sure about its effectiveness in terms of producing sales.

Advertising must, however, provide information and it must persuade. Various available copy-testing research services are essentially built around these two premises. Most leading agencies provide services to measure awareness-creation ability, information retention and **persuasability** of advertisements. Another service provides guidance on how the particular advertisement might be modified to be more effective.

Advertising content research tests an advertisement's ability to project the desired message to the target audience. The design and layout of an advertisement are tested together with the basic theme: the copy platform. Different kinds of communication appeal are tested out in this kind of research. Measurements can be taken at two stages: pre-publication and post-publication. At the pretesting phase, emphasis is placed on ideas and methods of publication; at post-testing, the emphasis is on measuring how effectively communication concepts were received by the intended audience.

The pretesting of advertisements can involve the following:

- Direct rating, where a consumer panel is shown different advertisements and asked to rate them on each advertisement's **attention**-getting power, whether it encourages the recipient of the message to listen, watch or read further, the clarity of the message, the effectiveness of the appeal and whether it suggests follow-through action.

- Portfolio tests, where the participant is presented with a collection of advertisements and asked to recall their content. Recalling an advertisement reflects its ability to be understood and remembered.

- Laboratory tests, which are used to measure the consumers' physical reactions to advertisements. Pupil-dilation tests, changes in heartbeat, etc., reflect an advertisement's ability to attract attention.

Post-testing is mainly concerned with the **recognition** and recall of advertisements. Recognition is measured by showing participants an advertisement and asking if they recognise it. Recall can be measured using either unaided or aided recall tests. In unaided recall tests, participants are asked to remember what advertisements they have seen recently, sometimes for a specific product category. In aided recall tests, participants are shown a series of advertisements, including the one you are interested in, and asked which ones they have seen recently and what impact they had.

Advertising campaigns have a number of objectives and advertisers want to know how effective they have been in reaching these objectives. Changing awareness, knowledge and preference about a brand may be the objectives for a campaign. The use of models such as the Lavidge and Steiner[11] hierarchy of effects model may enable researchers to specify the kind of advertising research that is appropriate. Researchers may try to assess how successful an advertising campaign has been in terms of, say, creating awareness of a product or giving people information about a product or service that will move them further up the ladder of purchase intent. Similar measures may be taken for creating a liking, developing a preference, bringing about conviction and, where relevant, actual purchase.

Current thinking about advertising effectiveness suggests that four elements are generally regarded as extremely important:

1 *Awareness.* A variety of studies of assessing awareness point to its importance. Studies by the Dutch organisation NIPO[12] through its brand-monitor system, demonstrate a high correlation between brand loyal buying behaviour scores and aggregate brand awareness. They also found a high correlation with brand awareness and the numbers of people who claim that their next purchase of a durable will be a given brand.

2 *The customer liking an advertisement or finding it appealing.* The Advertising Research Foundation's *Copy Research Validation Study* suggested that the 'like-ability of a commercial was the single best predictor of sales effectiveness'. The use of a likeability scale claims to predict sales winners 97% of the time.[13] Factors such as ingenuity, meaningfulness, energy and warmth were found to underpin likeability. The relative importance of each one of these factors appears to vary across products.

3 *Interest.* Finding an advertisement really interesting is suggested as being even more important than liking the advertisement.[14]

4 *Enjoyment.* The extent to which an advertisement is enjoyed has been found to be a better pretest measure than short-term recall.[15]

These advertising-effectiveness predictors are often used today by market research companies, usually under the direction of the advertising agency. The predictors are linked to the customer's emotional thoughts.

Advertising media research

Research here tries to eliminate waste in advertising by systematically examining the media available for promoting products and services.

Press research

This mainly takes the form of readership surveys, for example, the National Readership Survey, which is based on a stratified random sample of 28,500 adult interviews over a continuous period of 12 months. Businesses making use of this survey obtain breakdowns by demographic characteristics, regional distribution, television viewing, cinema attendance, commercial radio listening and special interests. Average issue readership is provided for each publication, together with a regional analysis. The National Readership Survey is administered by the Joint Industry Committee for National Readership Surveys (JICNARS).

Television advertising research

The Joint Industry Committee for Television Advertising Research (JICTAR) appoints a research organisation to provide a research service based on a television panel of UK households. The service releases information on the size of audiences at different times of the day and week by projecting the viewing patterns of the sample panel. A measure is also taken of the audience appreciation of TV programmes.

Radio research

A Joint Industry Committee for Radio Audience Research (JICRAR) follows the pattern set by JICNAR and JICTAR. The JICRAR survey is based on seven-day diaries distributed among random samples of people aged 15 or more living in private households within a radio station's designated area. The diaries are placed and collected by the interviewers.

Cinema audience research

This is covered mainly by the National Readership Survey administered by JICNARS.

Poster research

The Joint Industry Committee for Poster Advertising Research (JICPAR) commissions a research organisation to estimate both pedestrian and vehicular audiences for all posters. Information is also provided on types of area, shops and commercial characteristics so that posters can be strategically sited.

Television audience measurement

Measuring methods used are diaries, set meters and people meters. A media research diary involves participants keeping records of their television viewing in a structured form. It is usually kept for a week and covers, by day of the week and time of day, station and programme identification. Diaries are on a household basis, with a diary for each household set. Every person 12 years of age or over, or an adult surrogate, is asked to fill in the diary. Viewing of younger children is also recorded.

The set meter is an electronic device attached to the individual television set in the home. It automatically records the time, whether the set is on or off, and the channel to which it is tuned – all reported on a minute-by-minute basis. The data are recorded in a home storage unit and are transferred to the research firm's central computer the next day, through telephone lines. Since the participating home needs an expensive installation, this is operated with a relatively small panel of houses.

The people meter is a special form of the set meter. In this case, each family member pushes buttons on a keypad to indicate viewing and these data are automatically recorded simultaneously with set usage.

Each of the three methods presumes to measure total audience size. The straight set meter measures only whether the set is on or off. Figures showing total audience size and size by nature of household demographics are produced but specific viewers and their demographics cannot be identified. Such measurements are not specific enough to permit an advertiser to pinpoint its desired individual market. Diaries and people meters provide demographic definitions for individual audiences. People meters have added a method of measuring the demographics of the audience to a particular show.

Magazine audience measurement

The method usually used to measure the audience involves taking the person through the book and asking aided recognition questions. The researcher has a deck of cards, each containing the logo of one of the magazines being covered. The deck is handed to the respondent, who is asked to sort the cards into two piles, placing in one pile those he or she might have read or looked into in the past six months and, in the other pile, those the person is sure that he or she has not read or looked into. For each magazine that the respondent 'might have read or looked into,' a stripped issue (containing up to nine articles) is shown. The issue is sufficiently dated to permit time for the magazine to accumulate its total audience. The person is shown each of the articles and then asked whether the particular issue was seen. Then follow other queries such as where the publication was seen and the overall rating the respondent would give. Reports generated show, for each magazine, summaries of audience accumulation and reach, net unduplicated audiences for combinations of magazines, total and in-home audiences by demographics and psychographics, and qualitative measures of readership.

Newspaper audience measurements

Newspaper measurements usually call for two interviews with each respondent, separated by a short time interval, and employ the 'yesterday reading' method. For daily newspapers, respondents are first asked what newspapers they have read or looked into during the past six months. Then, excluding the day of the interview, they are asked when they last looked into an issue of the particular paper and the amount read (but only the replies of those reading yesterday are counted). The same general procedure is followed for Sunday newspapers, with necessary changes. Qualitative questions about place of reading and how the paper was obtained may also be asked.

SELLING RESEARCH

Research into selling is examined by Moutinho and Evans[16] and there are various models reported in the literature that discuss, among other things, how to allocate territories to representatives (see, for example, Lilien et al.[17]). The illustration in the following box, however, shows research in action in terms of the more qualitative dimensions of selling.

GETTING FEEDBACK ON SELLING

Pharmaceutical firms depend primarily on the salesforce as the means of communication with both existing and potential customers. In order to provide information of the effectiveness of representative detailing, 'follow-up research' has developed. The research aims to contact those healthcare professionals who have been visited by the representatives and to question them about their recall of the interview. Research interviews with professionals are usually conducted over the telephone and last 10 to 20 minutes each.

The analysis of the results is usually presented in a series of quantitative measures of various parameters used to assess the effectiveness of the detail. The parameters might include:

- recall of the detail taking place
- recall of the key communication objectives
- reaction to the information provided
- impact on usage.

A wide spread of interviews is obtained by limiting the number of interviews conducted for each representative in the fieldforce. For an average fieldforce of 50 to 60 representatives, a sample of two interviews per representative is a reasonable target. This works well for larger samples and where most of the questions can be precoded. Much more, however, can be learned from a detailed follow-up survey, particularly when interviews are tape recorded. Verbatim transcripts of interviews show the depth and richness of the answers.

Although the results of a detailed follow-up survey are useful in their own right, they are made much more useful when comparisons are made with other detailed follow-up surveys conducted for the same company and with surveys conducted by competitors. Standard norms of performance may be developed for both levels of recall of a product, the number of key communication points that are recalled and the impact on usage. Through the use of these comparisons, an effective measure of the success of the detail can be obtained.

Source: Scott[18]

PRICING RESEARCH

Research into pricing explores pricing approaches both for new products before they are launched and any proposed changes once they have been launched. There are two general approaches to pricing research. The first[19] involves presenting different prices for a product to respondents who are then questioned about whether or not they would buy. A 'buy-response' curve of different prices associated with positive purchase intentions is then constructed. Another approach involves people being shown different sets of brand in the same product category, at different prices. They, too, are then asked which ones they would buy. This latter approach enables competitors' brands to be taken into account by respondents.

Statistical analysis of data is useful for helping to sort out the effects of price versus that of other variables on quantities sold. The main technique used is regression analysis. Data obtained from consumer panels can be analysed with regression analysis to assess the impact of price changes.

Another commonly applied approach is to make use of survey data. A question might be included in a survey such as 'By how much would your sales increase (or decrease) if prices were increased (decreased) to . . . ?' Such a question would be aimed at distributors but similar questions can be put to consumers. But obtaining response curves in this way can be subject to error. Distributors may readily exhibit bias and consumers are usually unable to give reliable answers to questions about how price affects their brand purchase and preferences.

Yet another approach is to make use of laboratory experiments and simulated test markets. This usually involves having a simulated store where prices are altered experimentally and their effects on purchase levels assessed. This is a relatively inexpensive way of estimating the demand for a product at different prices, but getting a sense of reality into the simulation can be difficult and the simulation may not represent the real world at all well.

The standard test market also offers an approach to pricing research.

PRICING PHARMACEUTICALS IN EUROPE

Despite the fact that controllers of drug budgets can exert an influence over what physicians prescribe, the latter have to believe that a product has a 'perceived value' that is commensurate with its price if they are to prescribe it. Some countries are now following the example set by France in requiring firms to examine the volume projections for a new product and using it as a basis for price setting. The danger in this is underlined by the sales history of the antidepressant Prozac. As sales in France exceeded forecast, Lilly was forced into reducing its price. Eventually the price in France was cheaper than that in the UK and other countries and led to parallel importation despite an initial pan-European approach to pricing.

Marketing research is needed to determine the price/volume ratio required to focus as much if not more on the patient's willingness to pay as the physician's willingness to prescribe. In the future, investigations using consumer pricing research techniques, such as the Gabor and Grainger method, will probably become more and more popular. Such studies will also benefit from the 'perceived value pricing' approach developed since 1989 at Martin Hamblin Research. In this latter connection, the adoption in the last two years of choice-based conjoint techniques enables the researcher to examine a variety of scenarios that might affect the market in the future: for example, what happens if important competitors reduce their prices. Choice-based conjoint is a valuable procedure for exploring the potential action that prescribers and buyers would take, given a change in market circumstances. Bowditch and Fitall[20] describe how Janssen used the method when examining a number of alternative line extensions for one of its leading products, enabling the firm to develop a forecasting model. The model not only established the impact on the product and the competitors from the alternatives tested, but also helped to establish the projected profit and loss for each one.

Source: Bowditch[21]

DISTRIBUTION RESEARCH

A variety of research can be conducted to cover distribution. The relevance of such research often reflects whether the sponsors are engaged in business-to-business or consumer marketing. There are many commonalities in terms of requirements. Possibly the main difference reflects the fact that research is required at the retail level – the consumer interface – in the case of consumer-goods marketing.

Research can also be divided or categorised according to whether it is in connection with physical distribution decisions or with channel selection and management. In the case of physical distribution there are obvious overlaps with the broader subject area of operations management and operations research techniques that help to optimise the management process. For example, inventory management may be regarded as part of the distribution system (or part of the production system) depending on whether it is at the factory or at a distribution warehousing facility. The topic of inventory optimisation is well covered in the operational research management literature. Warehouse location and layout for optimal efficiency are also discussed extensively in the operational research literature, as are models to facilitate the optimal transportation of goods policies (see, for example, Taha[22]) although Moutinho and Evans[16] do discuss warehouse location research and retail outlet location research. Lilien et al.[17] provide a good overview of the kind of models and information requirements useful in both physical distribution and channel strategy decisions.

In consumer marketing, Crimp[23] discusses retail audits in general and the use of syndicated trade research in the assessment of performance compared with that of competitors through the retail audit. Retail marketing perhaps offers more opportunities for the traditional market researcher through the medium of shopping surveys. These tend to be restricted to retailing generally and to service marketing where there is a mixing of customers – hotels, restaurants and the like. In these studies, a fieldworker poses as a customer and makes mental notes on aspects of customer service. The shopper may note those aspects of service that were or were not present or they may note the quality or rating of service. Some of the aspects typically covered are:

- product or service quality
- facility quality
- personnel courtesy
- personnel efficiency
- personnel service
- personnel promotion of selected brands, items, features, benefits
- items stocked, offered, on display
- prices.

Such studies are usually handled by an outside specialist firm.

ELECTRONIC REVOLUTION IN THE RETAILING WORLD

More sophisticated sales strategies and strong interest in electronic commerce are fueling a boom in IT use among retailers.

The retail sector is a battleground where the effective deployment of information technology can make the difference between victory and defeat and where recent advances in information systems and the prospects for electronic commerce are bringing about the most rapid changes in retailing for decades.

Meanwhile, in an attempt to differentiate their services and retain customer loyalty, retailers are using IT systems to personalise their offerings and switch from demand-led to customer-focused strategies.

'Consumers have become incredibly demanding,' says Deloitte & Touche Consulting. 'They have high expectations for ever-improving quality, better information, better service at lower real prices – and they are getting it. They are able to enforce these demands because of the information explosion and the increasing competitive alternatives available to them today.' Retailers, already under tremendous pressure on margins, are trying to reduce labour costs, improve customer retention and finetune pricing and inventory. To achieve this, they are deploying a wide range of IT systems ranging from demand forecasting and logistics software, to self-scanners, electronic labelling systems and huge data warehouses.

'There is already a sustained pressure in the retail supply chain to reduce cost and this trend is set to continue,' says IBM, one of the leading suppliers to the retail sector. 'Overall, the strategic trend by the retailer is to move from "product led" to "market led" by improving knowledge of the consumer and consequently increasing margins by more effectively positioning products.'

Demand-chain management software, such as Industri-Matematik's System ESS, is based on the principle that customer 'pull' through the demand chain has primacy over the desire of manufacturers to 'push' products through the supply chain. It is increasingly seen as a key to delivering business benefits such as improved customer service, better financial performance and differentiated products.

According to a recent *Harvard Business Review* study, most retailers estimate the cost of carrying inventory for a year is equivalent to at least a quarter of what they paid for the product. Therefore a two-week inventory reduction represents a cost saving of nearly 1% of sales and a significant boost to profits.

IT systems also help retailers monitor 'customer traffic' using infrared or video-tracking systems to follow shoppers' movements, identify 'cold spots' in the store and help to ensure adequate staffing levels in service-critical areas.

Meanwhile, loyalty cards – increasingly likely to be smartcards – are being used to boost what analysts call 'frequency of shop', especially in the food retailing sector.

Other back-office systems sort out 'customer activity' by hoping to classify shoppers by 'type of purchase' and promoting goods that will appeal to them while in that frame of mind by product positioning or related discount offers.

'Overall, there are two big vectors in retailing,' says Julian David, marketing director for IBM Europe's distribution industry business unit. 'Digitisation, in all its forms, and personalisation.' In spite of reduced market growth expectations, companies in Europe's retail and distribution industries plan to increase their IT investments by up to 10% this year, according to a survey sponsored by IBM. In large companies, IT spending is being driven by the challenges of improving overall infrastructure, cost competitiveness and customer service, with investments focused mainly on supply chain management, targeted marketing and globalisation.

For example, Benetton, the fashion retailer, signed a worldwide agreement with IBM in July, which will eventually link point-of-sale terminals in 7000 shops and five continents. 'Operational management of the business will be simplified and it will be possible to distribute IT services from our central data processing system to the point of sale,' says Bruno Zuccaro, Benetton's computer systems director.

Existing IT investments are also being used differently. When electronic point-of-sale (EPOS) systems were introduced over a decade ago, they were mostly used for stock control and inventory management. Now, however, retailers are using the data they collect in different ways – to identify trends and target individual consumers.

'IT in retailing is moving from being an operational tool, primarily aimed at improving inventory control and front-end technologies, to become an enterprise-wide mechanism for increasing efficiency throughout the supply chain,' says Andy Cummins, retail marketing manager for Siemens Nixdorf in the UK.

'With the merchandise pipeline geared for rapid response, the priority of many retailers is to identify customer requirements and shopping habits using the most recent relational database systems and data mining techniques,' he says.

▶

Retail-based data warehouses manage the records of individual transactions from a variety of processing systems and information sources such as electronic cash registers, inventory systems, weather records and customer demographics. They then enable users such as store managers to query the database. 'Retail is detail,' says Tony Fano, senior vice-president of NCR's Atlanta-based retail group.

NCR, a leading data warehouse provider, says retailers typically begin asking the data warehouse about the company, then about individual stores, followed by inquiries about individual items and prices. They then demand historic data so they can examine trends by season or region. Such information allows retailers to do market-basket analysis, looking at each customer's entire transaction history to design loyalty programmes, determine display space, and judge the effectiveness of promotions. Wal-Mart, which claims to operate the world's largest commercial data warehouse, uses the vast amounts of information stored there to guide its business. It is expanding the warehouse, based on the NCR Teradata system, from 7.5 terabytes to more than 24 terabytes – the equivalent of 6bn pages of text.

'Our business strategy depends on detailed data at every level,' says Randy Mott, senior vice-president in charge of information systems at Wal-Mart. 'Every cost, every item is carefully analysed, enabling better merchandising decisions to be made on a daily basis.'

Among the UK-based stores, Safeway has already deployed its 'Shop and Go' self-scanning service to more than 130 stores and plans to roll it out in another 35 stores by the end of 1997.

Self-scanning systems have been on trial for more than ten years but with mixed results. Analysts believe it is only now as customers become familiar with high-tech systems that the concept seems to have taken off. It has been much the same with multimedia kiosk systems that first appeared in the early 1980s using cumbersome 12-inch video disks.

Numerous schemes have been tested since then and most have failed, but interactive media now seems to be gaining more popular acceptance. Kiosks are seen by many analysts as simply one of a range of channels to market which retailers will deploy in the future. Clearly, the Internet, and the World Wide Web in particular, represents another important and rapidly emerging channel.

Although many early entrants in the home shopping arena, such as Time Warner's Dream Shop, IBM's World Avenue, comprising 20 retail 'shops', and e-Shop Plaza have been slow to take off or have failed, many specialist Internet-based stores are flourishing and most market research firms predict a bright future for electronic commerce. Nevertheless, forecasts for business-to-consumer electronic commerce vary wildly from a conservative $6.6bn in 2000 from Forrester Research to around $200bn from IDC and Input. Despite this, a Cap Gemini sponsored survey of European retailers published in March suggested the greatest uptake of electronic shopping by retailers will come not in the longer term, but over the next two years.

According to the Cap Gemini survey, most retailers outside traditional mail order expect 13% of their sales to be via home shopping within two years, rising to 26% in ten years, yet despite these bullish forecasts, almost 60% said this would not affect their existing store operations. In other words, most retailers hope to run their physical outlets and electronic channels profitably side by side.

Internet shopping in particular is forecast to increase its share of total sales dramatically with 70% of retailers expecting to be receiving customer orders via the Web within two years.

'Over the next decade, Internet shopping will steadily build for traditional store-based retailers to 14% of total sales, and just over half of home shopping sales,' says the Cap Gemini report. 'Television shopping – via both dedicated and interactive channels – is also expected to enjoy major growth after the next two years.'

Source: Taylor[24] (reprinted with permission)

SUMMARY

This chapter has examined several applied areas of marketing research: product research, segmentation research, competition research, promotion research, pricing research and distribution research. In the case of product research, attention has been paid to product generation and testing, consumer product testing and packaging research. In the case of segmentation research, attention has been given to researching ways of segmenting the market. In promotion research, attention has been focused on the ways of assessing its suitability and effectiveness, and various approaches to pricing research were examined. Finally, attention was paid to some aspects of distribution research.

QUESTIONS

1 Explain how marketing research can be used in product generating and testing.

2 What is product delivery? What is the relevance of marketing research to this topic?

3 Discuss the role of the Delphi technique in product research.

4 What is market segmentation research? What actually takes place?

5 Discuss the problems involved in identifying competitors and indicate how firms might obtain information about competitors' strategies and intended strategies.

6 Indicate the different marketing research methods that have been successfully applied in researching the elements of the marketing mix.

CASE STUDY 13.1: TOURISM IN BUKHARA

Central Asia conjures up all kinds of mystic and romantic images for Europeans and others who have no experience of it. Whether it is reading about the expeditions of Marco Polo or listening to the music of Mussorgsky, the image seems quite distinct from that of other parts of the world. Names of places such as Samarkand and Bukhara add to this illusion, bringing into the imagination images of cities glittering with golden palaces and jewel-bedecked rulers.

Some people think that the future of Bukhara in Central Asia lies very much in its past. In the days when the Silk Road was the main highway to the Orient it was crowded with businessmen, merchants, camels and camel drivers. Warehouses full of silk, brocade, cotton, carpets, gold and silverwork were dotted along its route. Today, however, Bukhara still has spectacular buildings in fantastic shape, fitting epitaphs to its illustrious past.

The Lyab-I-Khauz pool is entertaining. It is surrounded by plane trees and is a place where locals and foreigners alike can go to eat *shashlyk* or drink *plov* or tea. On the east side of the pool is the Nadir Divanbegi *madrasa*, built around 1620. Above its main entrance are fantastic mosaics including the sun with a Mongol face, two strange birds and a goat. Such mosaics are not completely contrary to all Muslim teaching, only to Sunni teaching. On the west side of the pool is what was once a *khanaga*, a hostel for wandering dervishes. Today, however, it is an exhibition hall. On the north side of the pool is the Kukeldash *madrasa*, the largest in Bukhara, with over 150 cells, or rooms, and an enormous courtyard inside. In Bukhara there are different bazaars. One such bazaar is the Tag-I-Telpag Furushon where it is possible to purchase quality astrakhan hats and gold-embroidered skullcaps.

In Samani Park one finds the spring of Jacob (or Job, according to some) which is considered by some to possess miraculous powers of healing. Then there is the Ark or Fortress or original Walled City, which contained royal apartments, reception rooms, stables, mosques, a treasury, police department, prison and homes for around 3000 people. It was destroyed time and time again in the 10th, 11th, 13th and 20th centuries.

Bukhara used to be one of the world's most famous religious and trading cities. Some regard it now as simply an overnight stop for package tourists on their way to and from China.

Question

Assume a tourism promotion agency is to be set up in Bukhara. Suggest a research proposal that could be implemented in order to establish how the concepts of *market segmentation*, *targeting* and **positioning** and the *marketing mix* might be profitably applied to re-establish Bukhara as a tourist destination rather than merely an overnight stop in the minds of tourists.

CASE STUDY 13.2: SOUTH AFRICA

The Sotho word, *Gauteng*, translates into English as 'place of gold'. It is the new name given to the Pretoria–Witwatersrand–Vaal triangle, one of the largest industrial regions in the southern hemisphere. In 1886, on a patch of windswept veld, an unemployed miner came across a stone containing traces of gold. From this event came the discovery of the world's richest natural treasurehouse. Speculators, prospectors, fortune seekers and adventurers arrived in the area from all over the world and, in a comparatively short space of time, the pastoral landscape was completely transformed. First, shanty towns sprang up as goldrush fever gripped the area. Then these shanty towns rapidly changed into modern concrete cities. Johannesburg became known as the 'gold capital of the world' and the entire country became the centre of an economic boom. The revenues generated by gold in the world's export markets enabled the country to develop its impressive industrial, commercial and financial strength.

South Africa is home to an extraordinary variety of ethnic groups, cultures, creeds and languages. The background to this human diversity extends over thousands of years to the original inhabitants – the Stone Age hunter–gatherers known as the Bushmen. Black migrants arrived from the north to take their place and they, in turn, were followed by European and Indian immigrants. Gauteng is a dynamic, cosmopolitan kaleidoscope representing most of these different cultural components.

Johannesburg is nouveau riche territory: a modern, cosmopolitan metropolis packed with vitality and verve. In quiet, leafy suburbs, baronial mansions in manicured gardens lined with limousines testify to the fact that the city, at the top of the supertax bracket, is a very affluent society. In the central business district, the astute make daily fortunes on the stock exchange. Skyscrapers tower over chic boutiques, aromatic Indian bazaars and African *muti* (medicine) shops where traditional healers dispense advice and herbal remedies.

Some 50 kilometres north of Johannesburg, Pretoria is well known for its colourful gardens, shrubs and trees. The city developed more slowly than Johannesburg but now boasts high-tech shopping centres, museums, art galleries and multiculinary restaurants. The city has four universities and several scientific institutes, including the Council for Scientific and Industrial Research and the Onderstepoort Veterinary Research Institute, both of which are famous worldwide.

Soweto (South Western Township) is a huge sprawling township, estimated to be inhabited by more than two million people. Homes range from affluent mansions to makeshift shacks. Soweto residents belong to nine ethnic groups, among whom Zulus and Xhosas predominate. The township has the Baragwanath Hospital, which is reputed to be the largest hospital in the southern hemisphere. Here high-quality training and medical standards are provided. The hospital attracts patients not only from the rest of South Africa but also from countries as far north as Nigeria. Despite this, it is estimated that between 80% and 85% of

Soweto residents consult traditional healers. Commercial activities in Soweto are expanding rapidly. New supermarkets, retail chains, banks and shopping complexes are constantly being developed.

In the north of the country lies the Northern Province. The Venda, who inhabit the eastern part of the Soutpansberg, are thought to be descended from chiefs who travelled south from Central Africa towards the end of the 17th century. They are an intensely superstitious people who place great store on rites and rituals. For example, in the python dance, barebreasted teenage girls perform a slow, rhythmic dance to the throb of tribal drums. The drum is central to traditional Venda religious belief.

Scattered throughout the Northern Province are to be found the North Sotho people who live in small settlements with family homesteads clustered around their cattle *kraal*. The most famous member of this tribe was the legendary Rain · Queen, Modjadji, who was believed by many to be immortal. Small numbers of the Tsonga people also inhabit the Northern Province. In rural areas they pursue a leisurely pace, spending time on arts and crafts. Unlike other tribal people, the Tsonga are also keen fishermen. Pietersburg is the commercial and cultural hub of the region, featuring impressive art exhibitions and elegant historical buildings. It also possesses wide streets, jacaranda and coral trees, colourful parks and sparkling fountains. In the vicinity, the countryside is the setting for some of the most prosperous cattle ranches in South Africa.

Mpumalanga (the former Eastern Transvaal) is steeped in the history of pioneers, hunters and fortune seekers and goldrush towns abound. Barberton and Pilgrim's Rest are among the most famous. The Middleveld region is inhabited by the Ndebele people who are renowned for their strikingly attractive dress, characterised by vivid colours, metal rings and beaded hoops. They are also notable for the exceptional quality of their beadwork and the strong geometric designs on the walls of their homes. The capital of the region is Nelspruit and revenues from the extensive fruit growing that has taken place in the region have played a vital role in its development. The town shows the signs of the opulence generated by the natural wealth of the region produced by the fruit growers.

KwaZulu-Natal is the main home of South Africa's Indian population. Languages, especially among the older generation, include Tamil, Telegu, Hindi, Gujarati and Urdu. The strictly regulated patriarchal, extended family is not as evident today as at one time and Indian languages tend to be heard less often. Younger people tend to speak English as a first language and lead an increasingly westernised life. Members of the Indian community are found throughout the upper echelons of commerce, industry and the professions. Durban has good shopping centres where you can buy anything from photographic equipment to couturier clothes and rare antiques. Fleamarkets and craft trails attract leisurely browsers, while discount stores offer quality merchandise at bargain-basement prices. Within a stone's throw of the city centre, oriental bazaars, fragrant with spice and incense, offer silks, saris, unusual jewellery and ornaments. Theatres and concert halls present avant garde and ethnic programmes.

Although most of the South Sotho (Basotho) people live in the kingdom of Lesotho, a self-contained mountain kingdom in the middle of South Africa, many of them live in Qwaqwa and in other parts of the Free State. Marriage customs among traditional South Sotho people involve the exchange of *lobola*, whereby the bridegroom gives a specified number of cattle to the bride's parents. Marriage between relatives is allowed for the simple reason that this keeps wealth within the family. Old tribal traditions still continue in the mountains where the people are fairly isolated. Farmers till the fields with hand-held ox-drawn ploughs. Bloemfontein originated at a spring which at various times was a source of water for Bushman hunters, Sotho farmers, Voortrekkers and enormous herds of game. For many years it remained a tranquil agricultural settlement, but it has recently developed into a prosperous commercial and industrial city – the capital of the Free State and the judicial capital of South Africa. With its stately old buildings dominated by skyscrapers, the city has many facets, ranging from sophisticated up-market shopping centres, restaurants and theatres to vestiges of the gracious Victorian ambience that once prevailed. Surprisingly, for a city that was formerly the capital of a Boer republic, Bloemfontein has many British features – legacies of the Anglo-Boer War when the town was occupied by British forces. In the north of the Free State is the attractive garden-city of Welkom, which lies at the centre of the Freestate goldfields. It has good shopping malls and restaurants, an airport and a thriving theatre. Winburg, steeped in Voortrekker history, is the oldest town and first capital of the former Republic of the Orange Free State. The Voortrekker Monument symbolises five major trekker groups.

In the early days of European settlement in South Africa, groups of Malays were brought to the Cape by the Dutch East India Company. Among the many talents the Malays brought with them were exceptional cooking skills and this has exerted considerable influence over the cuisine of the Western Cape. Over the past 340 years, their lifestyle has become a unique blend of East and West – but much of the mystique remains, as Malay culture is firmly rooted in Islam. Although Malays are found throughout the Western Cape, the area on the lower slopes of Signal Hill, known as the Bo-Kaap, is the place most closely identified with Malay culture. With its majestic Table Mountain backdrop, Cape Town is one of the most magnificent cities in the world. Between high-rise office blocks, Edwardian and Victorian buildings have been meticulously preserved and many outstanding examples of Cape Dutch architecture are to be found. Narrow cobblestone streets and the strongly Islamic ambience of the Bo-Kaap enhance the cosmopolitan sense of the city. Cape Town's shopping provision includes elegant malls, antique shops, craft markets and fleamarkets. Specialist boutiques offer an enticing array of unusual items that are not readily obtainable elsewhere. Gourmets and lovers of fine wines have a treat in store.

The Xhosa are a diversity of Eastern Cape tribes of Nguni origin who moved south across the Kei river from KwaZulu-Natal before the 17th century. While the Xhosa are increasingly moving into towns and adopting the white man's life-style, those who remain on the land cling to their old tribal systems and timeless traditions. Each rural family lives in a group of huts known as a kraal with a cattle byre and a small garden. In every kraal a man lives with his wife and children, together with his married sons and their wives and children. Cattle, sheep and goats play an important role in their social life and its rituals. A man counts his wealth in cattle: his daughters are valuable assets, for their bride price is paid in cattle.

Kimberley is in the Northern Cape and its diamond mines were largely responsible for financing the Witwatersrand goldfields. Today, Kimberley is a modern city with broad, tree-lined streets, attractive parks and gardens, comfortable hotels and busy shopping centres.

Source: South Africa Tourism Board[25]

Question

Discuss the kinds of problem that would be encountered in segmentation research in South African markets.

CASE STUDY 13.3: MUSIC IN MARKETING COMMUNICATIONS

Postmodernism in music originated in the 1980s when up-and-coming composers such as Adams and Corigliano turned to the past for styles, quotations and other points of departure. In terms of compositional philosophy and musical effect, however, there is often little to differentiate their work from that of Stravinsky or Shostakovich in the 1930s. Some essentially modernist composers in the 1930s and 1960s, for example Kagel and Ligeti, have looked with scepticism and humour on the past. It is the idea of looking with scepticism or humour on the past that seems relevant to modern-day marketing communications. Many television advertisements employ popular music tunes to sell cars, jeans, beer and other types of consumer good. For instance, in the USA, if you want to create magic in 2002, it should take the form of a Mercedes-Benz car according to the advertisements of the car company. The message is reinforced by the musical accompaniment of strains of the pop group Lovin' Spoonful's 1966 hit. While it is not clear why this particular combination was featured in the advertisement, two explanations are plausible. It could be that it is targeted at people in their 50s who will have emotionally bonded with the hit at a young age or it may merely be the indulgence of a middle-aged Mercedes executive (or advertising executive) who remembers the tune fondly and assumes that the target audience will respond in a similar manner. Again in the USA, Wrangler sells jeans to Credence Clearwater Revival's 'Fortunate Son'. Other examples include Electric Light Orchestra (ELO), the heavy-string rock band of the early 1970s, which has been revived to sell Volkswagen Beetles. ELO's 'Mr Blue Sky', which was about sunny days and babies joining the human race, now celebrates the rebirth of the classic VW car in the 21st century. In addition there is the Gap, which sells sweaters to the tune of O'Jay's classic, 'Love Train'.

Music is an effective means for triggering mood and communicating non-verbally. In marketing, music has been employed in advertising contexts to influence listeners' emotions, judgements and behaviours. Where messages are generally secondary to the information that a listener or viewer seeks, as is the case in television and radio advertising, music can be used to attract and hold attention or induce a positive mood towards the advertised product or service. In an advertising context, music can operate as a form of non-verbal communication, conveying information in a different way to written and spoken material. However, although music may influence audiences' perceptions, **memory** and persuasion, so far knowledge of exactly when, how, and why music operates as it does seems rather limited.

Classical as well as popular music seems to be a fruitful medium for creating the ambience necessary to reinforce promotional messages. Adrian North and David Hargreaves, for example, have found that classical music prompted the purchase of more expensive wine in an off-licence, compared with when the top 40 was played. Classical music is finding its way into the promotion and advertising of global products. Levi's advertisements have come to be regarded as an indicator of cultural change. Ever since Nick Kamen removed his shirt and pants in a launderette in 1985 to the sound of Marvin Gaye's 'I Heard it Through the Grapevine', the Levi's advertisement has been a quasi-cultural icon, encapsulating the perceptions and aspirations of older teenagers whose attention the advertiser wants to capture. The launderette advertisement was successful not only for Levi but also because it put soul music back on the map. In addition, it put 'Grapevine' to number one in the pop charts. Jonathan Glazer, who devised award-winning surf horses for Guinness and 'Last Orders' for Stella Artois advertisements, has experimented with a musical illustration from the classical repertoire in Levi's recent 'freedom to move ad'. However, the soundtrack for this advertisement is the Sarabande from the Suite in D minor for solo harpsichord by Handel. Classics traditionally evoke nostalgia (brown bread), safety (motor oil), comfort (club class) and perfumes of every kind. Traditionally, the 'mood-generating music' for young people is pop and rock. One could argue that classical music turned the story in the advertisement into a piece of theatre. Apparently, during the research and development of the Levi advertisement, musicologists were called in and many scores were sampled, from Vivaldi to Bartok, before the Sarabande was considered.

We might conjecture that using music in marketing communication advertisements may assist messages and images to achieve specific marketing communications objectives – for example by developing the mood associated with an advertisement. While there is no evidence of effectiveness measurement or how such effectiveness may be defined within the context of marketing communication effectiveness, research does seem to indicate that music can influence attention and the perceived positioning of products and brands and can lend meaning to otherwise unimportant marketing messages. One explanation for this might be the belief that music fills an important need in people's lives. It constitutes consumption for pleasure that is vital to human experience. Music with meaning that represents important social and cultural aspects of a target market can be used as a means of strengthening a message. The greater the relevance of the music to the target market, the better may be the expected results. Measuring the effectiveness of music in marketing communications is clearly an important issue and one that merits attention that it has not to date received. A framework for interpreting and analysing music is a prerequisite. It has been argued that: 'Music that is custom written for a commercial frequently makes little or no sense when heard by itself, away from the context of words and pictures.'

Question

How might one conduct conduct research into the effectiveness of classical and pop music in the context of TV advertising?

CASE STUDY 13.4: BRONCO JEANS

Bronco Jeans distributes its denims direct to retailers. The firm produces and markets a single line of jeans under the brand name Bronco and sells them to retailers at a list price of £8 per pair. Total fixed costs amount to £1000 per week and variable unit costs are £2.00. Various discounts are given to retailers for bulk purchases and the early settlement of debts. Retailers put a 100% mark-up on the list price + VAT. Demand has been quite strong at the retail level and Bronco has been able to sell 1000 pairs of jeans per week. It wants to expand production and at the same time it feels that because it can sell all it produces, it may be pricing itself too low. Most of its competitors' jeans are retailing for around £20 a pair, including VAT at 17.5%.

In an effort to get some hard data to help it reach a decision, the firm has asked the 250 retail outlets it supplies to estimate the impact on demand that various changes in the list price might have. The answers are summarised in Table 13.1.

TABLE 13.1   Bronco Jeans: impact on demand of price changes

Price change (%)	Change in demand mean (%)	Standard deviation (%)
−10	+5	2.1
−5	+2	1.0
+5	0	0.0
+10	−5	1.1
+15	−10	1.5
+20	−25	2.5

Question

On looking at the results of the survey, the firm feels that it should increase its prices by 20%. Do you think this would be a good idea? Explain your reasons.

CASE STUDY 13.5: BRITISH DIVIDED INTO FOUR TYPES

A third of Britons are unhappy with their lot, struggling with life in the modern age, according to market research released yesterday. The group – dubbed *resistors* – makes up 36% of the population. They are offset by *embracers*, the 1990s' successors to the 1980s' yuppies who see new technology as a style statement. Embracers are physically and socially active but decidedly selfish. Only one-third of this group, who make up 27% of the population, believe it is their responsibility to help people worse off than themselves. In the middle are the *pragmatists* – the 'ordinary' men and women who adopt new technology when they believe it offers them proven benefits and are more concerned with the community than a computer – and the *traditionalists*, the smallest group, at 15%. Generally the oldest, generally well off, they are 'a happy self-confident bunch', according to Michael Svennevig, the project's research director.

The classifications come from futura.com, a research project run by Leeds University in partnership with the Independent Television Commission and Ogilvy & Mather and sponsored by a string of big companies including Unilever, IBM, Guinness and Ford as well as the Department of Trade and the Central Office of Information.

Source: Timmins[26] (reprinted with permission)

Question

Discuss how the classifications given in this case study might be used in segmentation research studies.

CASE STUDY 13.6: ŠKODA CARS

Škoda is, by one measure, the third oldest car manufacturer in the world. It is the biggest Czech industrial company and is far and away the biggest employer in the country – some 30% of the Czech workforce are either employed directly by Škoda or owe their jobs to the firm, working for suppliers or firms servicing the company. During the 1930s the company's cars were regarded as prestige auto-mobiles; they were the BMWs of their day and the Škoda company was the flagship of the then-buoyant Czech economy. Czechoslovakia was then the fifth richest country in the world in terms of per-capita wealth and thus had a strong domestic market; unfortunately, the Second World War and the advent of com-munism changed all that.

During the ensuing 40 years of communist rule in Czechoslovakia the com-pany suffered badly from a lack of innovation, from a lowering of quality standards and a poor image elsewhere in the world. The cars acquired a reputa-tion for being unreliable, uncomfortable and hard to resell – in the UK, 'Škoda jokes' became fashionable, with the car as the butt of the humour. The cars could only be sold by being the cheapest available and even then sales were somewhat disappointing.

In 1989 communism collapsed in eastern Europe and in 1991 Volkswagen acquired Škoda and set about changing the firm's products and image. Research showed that the Škoda image was one of unreliability and poor quality; since this was the very opposite of VW's image the company began by stressing the link with VW at every opportunity. Škoda's advertising campaign used the slogan, 'We've changed our cars – can you change your mind?' The target audiences for this campaign were not only the potential buyers for the cars, but also the public at large; the company hoped to stem the flood of Škoda jokes and make Škoda purchase a matter for congratulation rather than ridicule. The next move in the campaign to reinvent Škoda was to invest heavily in the factory, introducing better quality control and modern manufacturing equipment. Škoda's design team were moved from the dingy corner of the factory they had occupied in com-munist days into new offices where they were given the facilities to redesign the cars.

Škoda's UK managing director, Dermot Kelly, said, 'We did image analysis before and after the marketing campaign to assess our progress. While VW is a strong trigger, it doesn't create a strong brand image but it takes away a negative one.'

Currently, the brand is multifaced across Europe; Alfred Rieck, the Dutchman who was appointed as marketing manager of Škoda, aims to create a single brand image across the continent. This will be achieved on the back of the Škoda Octavia, the company's flagship vehicle, which has been well received by motor-ing writers and the general public alike.

The company's greatest accolade might be the influential JD Power Survey, an American research programme that surveys customer satisfaction. The survey canvasses customers' opinions of their cars and the dealerships two years after purchase, and is regarded as highly influential on consumers' decision making. In 1994 Škoda was rated 21st in the survey; in 1995 in came 13th, in 1996 7th, in 1997 it came 6th and finally, in 1998, Škoda was rated first in total overall satisfaction.

So far, Škoda's policies appear to be paying off; in 1994, 170,000 cars were built. This had risen to 357,000 by 1997 and 422,000 by 1999. European demand has been so high the company has been forced to cut deliveries to Asia and the Škoda factory at Mlada Boleslav in Bohemia works 24 hours a day, six days a week, to satisfy demand. Having moved from its 1991 position of having to pay potential customers £10 to induce them to take a test drive, Škoda is now in a position of being unable to meet world demand for the cars. From being the butt of everyone's humour in the 1970s and 1980s, Škoda has again become a force to be reckoned with in the world's automobile markets.

(Case contributed by Jim Blythe)

Questions

1 What role has market research played in the success of Škoda?

2 How might Škoda research a new market, such as China?

3 What techniques might be used to monitor the image of the cars?

4 Although the JD Power Survey has been very positive about Škoda, what are the potential problems with relying on a survey of this kind?

5 What are the market research implications of trying to develop a pan-European image for the cars?

REFERENCES AND NOTES

1 Double, L (1991) Unpublished MBA dissertation, Department of Management, Keele University, September.

2 White, S (1993) Get a helping of the sugar-free chips game, *Research Plus*, September, 3.

3 Lynch, T (1997) Caught in the neighbours' tangled web, *Financial Times*, 15 August.

4 For details of the Delphi technique, see: Goldfisher, K (1992) Modified Delphi: A concept for product forecasting, *Journal of Business Forecasting*, Winter 1992–93; Lindstone, H and Turoff, M (eds) (1975) *The Delphi Method*, Reading, MA: Addison-Wesley – one of the best and most detailed discussions of the Delphi method; McCarthy, K (1992) Comment on the 'Analytic Delphi Method', *International Journal of Production Economics*, May; Mitchell, V-W (1992) Using Delphi to forecast new technology industries, *Marketing Intelligence and Planning*, 10 (2) – contains a broad review of the literature on Delphi and many references to the method and to past studies.

5 Bolongaro, G (1994) Delphi technique can work for new product development, *Marketing News*, 3 January, 11.

6 Smith, A (1997) Public puts faith in brand names, *Financial Times*, 13 October.

7 Gooding, K (1997) Soft drinks switch to PET leaves industry struggling, *Financial Times*, 22 October.

8 www.mapinfo.co.uk/products/software.cfm and company literature, MapInfo, Centennial Court, Easthampstead Road, Bracknell, Berks RG12 1YQ. Tel: 01344 482888.

9   Nike (part of the Lex column) *Financial Times* (1997) 20 December.

10 Poster watch (1996) *Marketing Week*, 26 April, 58.

11 Lavidge, R J and Steiner, G A (1961) A model for predictive measurements of advertising effectiveness, *Journal of Marketing*, 25, October, 59–62.

12 Stapel, J (1990) Monitoring advertising performance, *ADMAP*, July/August.

13 Biel, A (1989) Love the advertisement, buy the product? *ADMAP*, October.

14 Stapel, H (1991) Like the advertisement but does it interest me? *ADMAP*, April.

15 Brown, G (1991) Modelling advertising awareness, *ADMAP*, April.

16 Moutinho, L and Evans, M (1992) *Applied Marketing Research*, Harlow: Addison-Wesley.

17 Lilien, G L, Kotler, P and Moorthy, K S (1992) *Marketing Models*, Upper Saddle River, NJ: Prentice-Hall, Chapter 9.

18 Scott, A (1996) The launch went fine – then the devil's in the detailing, *Research Plus*, April, 14.

19 Gabor, A and Grainger, C (1966) Price as an indicator of quality, *Economics*, 33, 43–70.

20 Bowditch, A J and Fitall, S (1995) Through the looking glass: primary research in multicountry forecasting, *Proceedings of the EphMRA/ESOMAR Pharmaceutical Marketing Research Conference, Geneva*, Amsterdam: ESOMAR, 141–63.

21 Bowditch, A J (1996) In Europe's complex market, check the price is right, *Research Plus*, April, 12–13.

22 Taha, H A (1992) *Operations Research: An introduction* (5th edn), New York: Macmillan.

23 Crimp, M (1990) *The Marketing Research Process* (3rd edn), Hemel Hempstead: Prentice-Hall.

24 Taylor, P (1997) Pressures in the marketplace, *Financial Times*, 3 September.

25 South Africa: A world in one country (1996) South Africa Tourism Board.

26 Timmins, N (1997) British divided into four types, *Financial Times*, 5 September.

FURTHER READING

Brown, S and Turley, D (eds) (1997) *Consumer Research: Postcards from the edge*, London: Routledge.

Brown, G, Copeland, T and Millward, M (1973) Monadic testing of new products – an old problem and some partial solutions, *Journal of the Market Research Society*, (15)2, April, 112–31.

Coffey, A and Atkinson, P (1996) *Making Sense of Qualitative Data*, Thousand Oaks, CA: Sage.

Cooper, L and Nakanishi, M (1988) *Market Share Analysis: Evaluating competitive marketing effectiveness*, Boston, MA: Kluwer Academic Press.

Cox, W E (1979) *Industrial Marketing Research*, New York: Wiley.

Day, E and Stafford, M R (1997) Age-related cues in retail services advertising: their effects on younger consumers, *Journal of Retailing*, 73(2), 211–33.

Douglas, S P and Craig, C S (1983) *International Marketing Research*, Upper Saddle River, NJ: Prentice-Hall.

Geo-Visual Solutions for Today's Business (1990) Mt Olive, NJ: Intelligent Charting.

Gordon, W and Corr, D (1990) The space between words: the application of a new model of communication to quantitative brand image measurement, *Journal of the Market Research Society*, 32(3), 409–35.00

Green, P E and Krieger, A M (1989) Recent contributions to optimal product positioning and buyer segmentation, *European Journal of Operational Research*, 41, 127–41.

Green, P E and Krieger, A M (1992) An application of a product positioning model to pharmaceutical products, *Marketing Science*, 11(2), Spring, 117–32.

Grover, R and Srinivasan, V (1987) A simultaneous approach to market segmentation and market structuring, *Journal of Marketing Research*, 24, May, 139–53.

Gummesson, E (2000) *Qualitative Methods in Management Research*, Thousand Oaks, CA: Sage.

Hammond, K, Ehrenberg, A S C and Goodhart, G J (1996) Market segmentation for competitive brands, *European Journal of Marketing*, 30, 39–49.

Kamakura, W and Russell, G J (1989) A probabilistic choice model for market segmentation, *Journal of Marketing Research*, 26, November, 379–90.

Lewis, P H (1989) When maps are tied to databases, *New York Times*, 28 May, 10.

Lucas, D B (1983) Advertising research and measurement, in *Marketing Manager's Handbook*, Chicago, IL: Dartnell, Chapter 6.

Malhotra, N K (1995) *Marketing Research: An application orientation*, Upper Saddle River NJ: Prentice-Hall.

Marks, A P (1990) The Sinclair C5 – why did it fail? *Management Decision*, 28(4), 9–14.

Mitchell, V (1995) Using astrology in market segmentation, *Management Decision*, 33(1), 48–57.

Moskowitz, H R (1985) *New Directions for Product Testing and Sensory Analysis of Foods*, Westport, CT: Food & Nutrition Press, 171ff.

Moutinho, L and Evans, M (1992) *Applied Marketing Research*, Harlow: Addison-Wesley.

New products (1990) *The Number News*, June, 8.

Newton, S (1993) From hearses to horses: launching the Volvo 850, *Journal of the Market Research Society*, 33, 153–62.

Proctor, S, Papasolomou-Doukakis, I and Proctor, T (2001) What are TV advertisements really trying to tell us? A postmodern perspective, *Journal of Consumer Behaviour*, 1(3), 246–55.

Studies of Media and Markets (1989) New York: Simmons Market Research Bureau.

Uncles, M D, Hammond, K A, Ehrenberg, A S C and Davies, R E (1994) A replication study of two brand-loyalty measures, *European Journal of Operational Research*, 76, 375–84.

Workman, J P (1993), Marketing's limited role in new product development in one computer system firm, *Journal of Marketing Research*, 30, November, 405–21.

14

Marketing research settings: business-to-business, services and internal marketing

Objectives

After reading this chapter, you should be able to:

- understand the differences and similarities between consumer marketing research and business-to-business marketing research

- appreciate how marketing research can be applied to the marketing of services

- understand the concept of internal marketing and the role that can be played by marketing research within such a context.

Keywords

business-to-business markets
internal marketing
service delivery
service quality

service satisfaction
SERVQUAL
shopping surveys
SIC

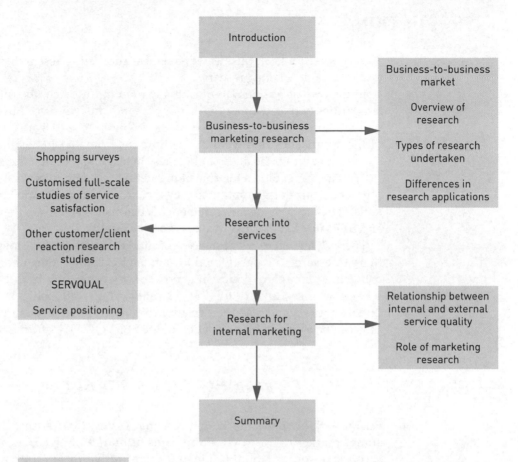

Plan of Chapter 14

INTRODUCTION

This chapter looks at business-to-business marketing research, services research and internal marketing research.

In the case of business-to-business marketing research, the differences and the similarities with consumer marketing research are explored. Business-to-business marketing research has changed considerably in recent years and employs many of the approaches that were at one time the domain of consumer research. The changing nature of business-to-business marketing research is explored further.

The chapter explores the role of marketing research in service marketing, looking specifically at **shopping surveys**, customised, full-scale studies of **service satisfaction** to provide measurement of customer reactions to the **service delivery**, and **SERVQUAL**, designed to assess **service quality**.

The last section looks at the role of marketing research in **internal marketing**. Market research can be adopted to gain feedback for management about working conditions, company policy in general and workers' own understanding about what comprises quality for the customer. The relationship between organisational subunits and also their relationship to top management is also important. This can be assessed by a variation of the SERVQUAL instrument just mentioned.

BUSINESS-TO-BUSINESS MARKETING RESEARCH

Business-to-business marketing research is very similar in many ways to consumer marketing research. Both forms of marketing research use primary and secondary sources, qualitative and quantitative techniques, and internal and external sources of data. Both forms of research use telephone interviews or face-to-face interviews, but organisational marketing research does not use street surveys, door-to-door interviews or hall tests. However, there are some major differences between consumer and **business-to-business markets**. For example, when developing the marketing mix, different strategies are needed for business-to-business customers than for final customers – a difference that significantly affects research activities.

Business-to-business market

Business-to-business markets are composed of those organisations and agencies that purchase goods and services either to aid in the production of other goods and services or for resale purposes. This includes manufacturing firms, government agencies, public utilities and educational institutions as well as intermediaries such as retailers and wholesalers. Consumer markets, by contrast, comprise individuals, families or households who purchase goods and services for their own final consumption.

The demand for business goods is derived from the demand for final consumer goods. If the domestic car market has a bad year the car components industry will also suffer because its sales are closely tied to the demand for cars. Because of this relationship, the demand for business-to-business goods can be very volatile and business-to-business marketing research has therefore to be concerned with general business and economic conditions, levels of inventory and the prices of raw materials.

It is quite common in business-to-business markets to have a small number of customers account for the vast majority of a firm's sales. Often 80% of the business comes from 20% of the customers. Such a relationship influences the type of sampling procedures used in business-to-business markets since a great deal can be learned from surveying only a few large customers.

When trying to determine which factors influence purchase decisions, the business-to-business researcher's task is made more difficult by the fact that more than one person is often involved in making such decisions. It is not possible from one interview in a company to ascertain key buying influences.

Quality of service, availability of supplies and consistent quality of materials are critical factors in the purchase decisions made in the business-to-business market. Businesses-to-business buyers are usually more knowledgeable about their own needs and are swayed less by promotional appeals than are consumers.

Many business-to-business products are engineered or designed specifically for a customer. In these situations the supplier must identify the specific needs of the customer but it also means that there is less need for research of mass markets.

When conducting consumer research, the persons to be surveyed or observed can usually be identified and contacted fairly easily. In business-to-business markets not only are the appropriate respondents hard to identify because of multiple buyers but once identified these people may be difficult to reach directly: many are senior managers and are shielded from would-be interviewers by assistants and secretaries. Senior managers also tend to be less accessible since they travel frequently and possess little uncommitted time. The fact that they are being contacted for their business knowledge usually prevents making such contacts in the evening hours or during weekends.

Most manufacturers of consumer products, especially those in high-tech products, adopt the marketing concept: that is, they attempt to build their product marketing offerings around identified customer needs. The concept, however, is not as prevalent among business-to-business firms primarily because their research activities are strongly influenced by technically oriented people who appear to place more emphasis on distinctive features and technological breakthroughs.

Consumer product firms can purchase information from Nielsen that will afford them a monthly review of how their products, as well as their competitors' products, are doing in terms of unit sales and market share. No similar type of information exists for business-to-business products from either syndicated firms or the firm's own research staff. There appears to be less interest in continuous monitoring of the sales of business-to-business products. This may be due to characteristic sales patterns – infrequent sales – but it could also be due to a difference in outlook of the executives of business-to-business organisations.

Because the costs of developing and producing prototypes of some business-to-business products are quite high, test marketing is not usually an important research tool within business-to-business markets. Some firms also do not like to have proposed products on display in test situations where competitors can observe their operation and usage.

Overview of research

Business-to-business marketing research tends to emphasise the use of internal staff and internal records as a major source of research information. Market intelligence is also a more significant aspect of the marketing information system than in consumer goods marketing. The explanation for this perhaps lies in the fact that business-to-business activity involves being more directly in touch with the market than is usual in the case of consumer goods marketing, where the nature of the distribution system creates a physical separation between the manufacturer and consumers. Close contact with the market makes it advantageous for a business-to-business marketing organisation to maintain a marketing intelligence system that makes use of feedback from the salesforce as a mechanism for reporting customer views.

Desk research has more significance in business-to-business marketing than in consumer marketing. Government publications, trade information, published sources and so on contribute an important part of the data input for marketing planning and decisions. Where the consumer researcher is interested in the census of population, for example, the business-to-business researcher is more likely to be interested in the census of production. As far as syndicated and omnibus research services are concerned these are unlikely to be available in any but the largest and most sophisticated markets.

Business-to-business marketing researchers are more likely to make use of postal research and telephone research in conducting quantitative surveys. Telephone research has traditionally been an important technique for business-to-business marketing researchers and its major advantage over personal interviewing in this case is that a geographically dispersed sample can be more economically contacted and produce better response rates than postal research.

Depth interviews figure predominantly in qualitative research in business-to-business marketing research. It is difficult to get a small group of business executives in the same room at the same time for the purpose of a research group discussion. Nevertheless, group discussions are used and can be useful, but they are the exception rather than the rule. Expert informants in particular fields are valuable for their information, and their participation in depth interviews at the exploratory stage of research study is of particular significance in business-to-business marketing research.

In business-to-business marketing, business directories or even internal customer lists or business mailing lists are often used as sampling frames. Stratification as a sophistication of random sampling and to some extent quota sampling methods are used. In this case the allocation of sample segments might be based on appropriate criteria such as the Standard Industrial Classification (**SIC**) or size of organisation in terms of sales turnover.

One sampling problem, however, concerns who is actually to be asked the questions. The business-to-business marketing researcher has to know which individual in the firm should be asked the questions or to whom a postal or telephone enquiry should be addressed in order to ensure the best chance of getting valid and reliable information.

Types of research undertaken

There is, in fact, a great deal of similarity between the types of research undertaken by consumer product firms and business-to-business product firms. The following similarities and differences should be noted:

1 Consumer product firms are much more involved with all types of research related to advertising.

2 Both groups are heavily involved with economic and sales forecasting.

3 Both groups are heavily involved with most aspects of product research – but business-to-business product firms are less concerned with packaging.

4 Both groups are heavily involved with sales and market analysis.

BALL BEARINGS

A well known ball-bearing firm established its early reputation on an innovative self-aligning ball bearing. The tolerance provided by the bearing permitted rolling bearings to be employed where inaccuracies in the manufacture and assembly methods then used were too destructive for conventional deep-groove bearings.

By the 1980s it was thought that the product might be approaching the end of its life cycle. The market was researched at some length across a wide range of applications using two levels of research team members chosen for their specific knowledge of the specific target sectors. Results indicated that while few firms would admit that their own manufacturing processes were inaccurate or that their assembly was hit and miss, many still were glad of the flexibility that the bearings design permitted. Indeed the concept had proved so valuable that a whole new generation of compact aligning bearings has been developed.

Source: Gorle[1]

Differences in research applications

The market for most business-to-business products is composed largely of other manufacturers or middlemen. Information on these firms is usually contained under Standard Industrial Classification (SIC) headings and includes such information as total shipments, number of employees and size of payroll. In order to put SIC data to good use, the researcher needs to understand the numbering process of the system.

In this classification system all places of business are classified into one of the following sections, covering the entire range of economic activity:

A   Agriculture, hunting and forestry
B   Fishing
C   Mining and quarrying
D   Manufacturing
E   Electricity, gas and water supply
F   Construction
G   Wholesale and retail trade; repair of motor vehicles, motorcycles and personal and household goods
H   Hotels and restaurants
I   Transport, storage and communication
J   Financial intermediation
J   Real estate, renting and business activities
L   Public administration and defence; compulsory social security
M   Education
N   Health and social work
O   Other community, social and personal service activities
P   Private households with employed persons
Q   Extra-territorial organisations and bodies

The principal sections are divided into several major groups, such as printing and publishing or chemicals and allied products, with each major group having assigned to it a two-letter SIC code. Further classification is achieved by subdividing the major groups and adding numbers to the SIC code (see Figure 14.1). By using the SIC system business-to-business markets can be divided into relatively small, medium or large market segments.

Most firms belong to one or more trade associations and the publications of these associations are a major source of statistics about a particular industry. The publications also cover a variety of topics relevant to their member firms.

Many business-to-business firms serve unique markets and for this reason appropriate secondary data may be difficult to obtain. Firms often make use of the services of indexing services, such as *Chemical Abstracts* or *Engineering Index*, to obtain information on unique topics or groups of customers. These agencies search many data sources, such as journals and association publications, to locate articles of possible value to their clients.

SIC code	Description
D	Manufacturing
DA	Manufacture of food products, beverages and tobacco
DA15	Manufacture of food products, beverages
DA15.1	Production, processing and preserving of meat and meat products
DA15.11	Production and preserving of meat
DA15.11/1	Slaughtering of animals other than poultry and rabbits
DA15.11/2	Animal by-product processing
DA15.11/3	Fellmongery

FIGURE 14.1   Some example SIC classifications

Of the methods that may be used to obtain primary data, the survey method is most important for business-to-business researchers. The complexity of the buying process in most business-to-business markets usually precludes the use of either observations or experiments. Personal interviews are favoured on account of the small size and geographical compactness of respondents, the uniqueness of information sought, the frequent need for demonstrations in interviews and the greater amounts of information that can usually be obtained within the time constraints.

Extensive use of probability sampling is not made among business-to-business marketing researchers because most markets are fairly small and can be completely surveyed or the surveys concentrate on the bigger customers in the market. Many business-to-business researchers ignore sampling altogether: they prefer to obtain information through a series of interviews until satisfied that they have obtained an accurate picture of the market. When sampling is used it tends to be judgement sampling.

Since less emphasis is placed on sampling there is less use of sophisticated methods when analysing data. Attitudes merely reflect such conditions as fewer firms in the market, less emphasis on probability sampling, and an emphasis on qualitative data. (See Table 14.1 for a comparison of business-to-business and consumer marketing research.)

CHANGES IN BUSINESS RESEARCH

Business-to-business market research emerged from the protective cloak of consumer market research in the 1960s as being a more appropriate approach to the research needs primarily of business-to-business goods manufacturers. The techniques required for business-to-business markets were very different from those required to measure the brand share of fast-moving consumer goods.

| TABLE 14.1 | Differences between business-to-business and consumer marketing research |

	Consumer	Business to business
Population	Large – usually unlimited	Small
Respondent accessibility	Fairly easy. Can interview at home, in the street, on the telephone or using mail technique	Difficult. Available usually only during working hours at place of work. Usually has other priorities
Respondent cooperation	Has become more and more difficult. Millions still never interviewed	A major concern. Danger of being over-researched
Sample size	Can usually be drawn as large as deemed necessary since the population is so large	Usually much smaller than consumer sample but the statistical confidence is equal due to the relationship of the sample to the total population
Respondent definitions	Usually fairly simple. Users of a brand, demographic characteristics, etc. The ultimate purchaser is also a user for most consumer products and services	Can be difficult. The user and the purchasing decision maker in most cases are not the same
Interviewers	Easily trained. They are familiar with the area under investigation for most categories	Difficult to find good executive interviewers. A working knowledge of the subject being researched is absolutely essential
Research costs	Key factors are sample size and incidence of usage categories (low incidence categories)	Lower incidence levels and difficulties in locating the right respondent are key factors

The rigid separation between business-to-business and consumer research – further enhanced by the Business-to-Business Market Research Association remaining a separate entity from the Market Research Society – continued through the 1970s and early 1980s, when the emergence of the business services sector prompted a fundamental re-examination of which approaches were most relevant to this dynamic sector. By the 1990s the needs of the business-to-business and business services community had moved substantially away from a need to quantify market size and structure to a preoccupation with retaining and satisfying customers. This environment has encouraged a return to a more consumer research-oriented approach. IMRA is no more and the interests of business-to-business market research are now handled by the Business-to-Business Group, a special interest group within the Market Research Society.

Many attempts have been made to quantify the market for business and business-to-business market research. Few are made with much conviction, given the breaking down of boundaries between business and consumer research from an agency perspective and the grey areas of what actually constitutes consumer as opposed to business-to-business research. Some of the most exciting data-capture developments emanate from the business-to-business sector. This is well demonstrated by the development of audiotext as a data-capture tool, the use of predictive diallers in customer satisfaction surveys and cheque-book-sized computers as self-completion tools – all developed and pioneered by leading UK business-to-business agencies. In the field of sampling, data capture and processing – and especially in the larger surveys – consumer research approaches are being used increasingly and are improving efficiency and accuracy for the research customers.

Source: Jamieson[2]

RESEARCH INTO SERVICES

There are many different kinds of service and they demand the full spectrum of research activities. In this section we will consider some of the rather specific kinds of research that are only applicable to services.

Shopping surveys

Shopping surveys are related to retailing and to service marketing where there is a mingling of customers (hotels, motels, restaurants and the like). In a shopping survey, a field worker poses as a customer and, following a list of predefined steps, makes mental notes. The shopper may simply note what aspects of delivery were or were not delivered. In addition, he or she may note the quality or rating of delivery. Major users of such surveys may be retailers such as fast food outlets and hotels. Here are some of the aspects typically covered (both for the organisation and its major competitors):

- product or service quality
- facility quality in various aspects
- personnel courtesy
- personnel efficiency
- personnel service
- personnel promotion of selected brands, items, features, benefits
- items stocked, offered, on display
- prices.

Such studies are generally handled by an outside specialist firm. There are three reasons. First, impartiality: the outside firm has no pre-formed dispositions. Second, skill: it can assist in determining what has to be checked and how to check it. Third, there is much less chance of the shopper being detected by the employees, since it is most unlikely that any employee would know the individual.

Customised, full-scale studies of service satisfaction

Some marketing research firms are offering customised, full-scale studies to provide measurement of customer reactions to the delivery of service. This is a continuing service aimed at firms that have continuing and 'formal' service satisfaction systems (i.e. where consumer reactions funnel into a single central location). It is used to conduct a day-after telephone interview with the customer to measure reaction while the experience is still fresh in the customer's mind. Because of the day-after telephone feature, the service has particular value to utility, financial and healthcare organisations.

Other customer/client reaction research studies

Studies of customer/client reaction are often used by small-scale retailers or service firms as well as by the larger firms. They are typically do-it-yourself research projects.

DECEPTIVE APPEARANCE

There always seems to be at least one moving walkway out of order at London's Heathrow Airport. When I asked Sir John Egan, chief executive of BAA, the owner of Heathrow, why this should be, he said it was because so many people used them. But help was at hand, he said. BAA was empowering its engineers to fix the walkways as they broke down. The night I arrived to catch a flight, the engineers had apparently used their new empowerment to go to the pub. Not only was there a dysfunctional walkway, there was also something unpleasant smeared on the ground outside the airport's third terminal. The check-in area was strewn with litter, while the gents' toilets were flooded and the hand towels needed replacing. The lines of passengers waiting to have their hand luggage X-rayed were long because only a few security machines were in use. The carpet in the security area was dirty.

A short distance away, however, on the other side of the machines, we could see a glittering world of plenty. Swatch and Burberry signs twinkled at us from Heathrow's shops, like a glimpse of cold war West Berlin from the wrong side of the Wall. I am not the only one to have noticed the contrast between the public areas and the shops at the world's busiest international airport. Sir Terence Conran, the retailer and restaurateur, wrote in *The Independent* newspaper last year of a visit to

Heathrow's Terminal One: 'All is glossy and new, clean and tidy in the shopping areas; in the walkways and the departure lounge, however, it's an altogether different story. They are fitted with stained, worn-out carpet held together with odd lengths of black tape, patched plastic tiles, odd wires hanging all over the place, broken chairs with their stuffing hanging out, cigarette burns on table tops, rubbish on the floors. The check-in desks are falling to pieces. Even a third world country would feel disgraced by the squalor and shabbiness.' Before boarding my flight from Terminal Three, I filled in a complaints card and posted it in one of the boxes BAA has put up around the airport. That was over two months ago. I have heard nothing.

Des Wilson, the veteran radical activist who now heads BAA's public relations effort, agreed it was unacceptable that I had had no response. But he strongly contested my view that Heathrow was in danger of becoming a slum. Heathrow's 56m passengers did not feel that way, he said. He sent me to see Stan Maiden, BAA's research director. Before meeting Maiden at Heathrow, I wandered around the terminals. Two moving walkways were out of order, although the empowered engineers were hacking away at one of them. Terminal One's public areas were bright and clean; Terminal Two, largely because it is the oldest, was dark and gloomy; and Terminal Three still looked shabby. Did my complaints, I asked Maiden, really make me one in 56m – or two in 56m, counting Sir Terence? Not quite, he said. Heathrow attracts its share of complaints and tries to act on them. BAA is investing £1m ($1.6m) a day at Heathrow, and its managers' pay is partly tied to what passengers say about the airport. To find out what they think, BAA did a lot of market research, Maiden said. If its activities in this area were a stand-alone operation, BAA would be one of the top 20 market research companies in the UK.

BAA's most basic customer feedback comes from the complaint and comment cards at the airport. Heathrow receives about 7000 complaints a year. The airport's policy, which broke down in my case, is to reply to all of them. Heathrow also receives compliments on the cards, but people were more likely to complain, said Maiden, 'as in any other field'. He uses the cards to identify clusters of complaints, such as a shortage of luggage trolleys or long lines in the security area. The cards are an unsatisfactory form of feedback, however, because they rely on passengers taking the trouble to fill them in. In addition to reading the cards, BAA interviews 26,000 Heathrow customers a year in a range of languages. They are asked to rate everything from flight announcements to public telephones on a scale of one to five, where five is excellent and one is very poor.

He showed me some recent results, which had the airport receiving a score of four in many areas and over 3.5 in almost all. One of the few areas scoring below 3.5 was passengers' perception of the distances they had to walk in the airport. Smokers gave smoking facilities in one part of the airport a mark of only 3.4, but non-smokers judged the same arrangement a 3.7. And Heathrow would rather satisfy the non-smokers? 'Well, there are more of them,' Maiden said. A fairly creditable performance, if BAA's methodology is sound. Maiden insisted it was. Brussels and Vienna airports have asked BAA to implement its survey methods there. The group also carries out market research on specific areas, such as whether customers prefer lifts or escalators. Which do they prefer? 'It rather depends on their age,' Maiden said. BAA also asks passengers to compare Heathrow

▶

with other airports. This gives Heathrow an opportunity to compare itself with competitors such as Amsterdam's Schiphol and Singapore's Changi.

On issues such as availability of trolleys and flight information, Heathrow is somewhere in the middle, below Schiphol and Changi, but above both Paris airports and New York's JFK. Heathrow's cleanliness is rated average, as is seat availability in departure lounges. Heathrow's catering, shops and the attitude of security staff all receive high international ratings. The least critical Heathrow customers are elderly American and British passengers who travel infrequently. And the most critical? 'Regular British business travellers,' Maiden said through clenched teeth. 'People like you.'

Source: Skapinker[3] (reprinted with permission)

SERVQUAL

In 1985 Parasuraman et al.[4] published their now classic article, which led to a revolution in the way that service quality is monitored. The results of their exploratory research included a statement of ten service quality determinants. These represent the basic dimensions that a consumer uses to evaluate a service. In order to improve 'true quality' in a service organisation, the first step is to identify the quality determinants that are most important or relevant to the company's target market[5] and then assess their own and their competitors' performance. This early work formed the basis for the development of SERVQUAL[6] with the ten determinants mapped onto five underlying factors: tangibles, empathy, responsiveness, reliability and assurance.

There are claims that SERVQUAL can be used or adapted to measure service quality in a variety of service settings. However, one should note that there are some who hold reservations about this.[7]

Service positioning

A service organisation is interested in how its image is positioned in the minds of customers and the trade vis-à-vis competition. It wants to know what kinds of people prefer to be its customers and how they compare with non-customers in terms of service perceptions and preferences, benefits sought, lifestyle and demographics. It also wants to know what is happening to its positioning from a more or less dynamic standpoint. For instance, it wants to know from which competitors it is gaining customers and to which competitors it is losing them. Service positioning is of major interest to management and it is here that perceptual maps of how customers see various providers as being similar or different are useful. The maps can help to show what combination of attributes customers prefer in their choice of service.

IN-HOUSE MARKETING RESEARCH IN FIRMS' DISTRICT BANKS

Consumer behaviour research in banks and the financial sector is becoming a focus of interest. Here we will look at some of the more informal and day-to-day marketing research that can be done in-house in banks and other similar types of service organisation that serve a local community.

The most common decisions that bank executives have to make related to customers are simple but at the same time may become complex due to the lack of information to enable the decisions to be made with real confidence. For example, decisions such as:

- Will this advertising convey the information the bank wants the potential customers to have?
- Will the advertising be credible to the potential customers?
- Will an advertising message motivate customers of other banks to visit it?
- How will customers react to a new product?
- Will the interest rates promoted in a particular promotion motivate customers to increase their deposits?
- Why is a branch not attracting enough customers?
- Where are the bank's customers?
- How can the bank best give customers access to services?
- What image should be projected into the customer's mind when positioning the bank as a lender?

The answer to such questions may be obtained through in-house marketing research and information gathered every time the organisation thinks it has doubts about its customers. There are several ways to do this.

The customer's map

It is useful to know where customers live and work. A roadmap of the area served should be covered in transparent foil and mounted on card. The foil is attached to the top of the map with office adhesive tape. Up to four overlay foils can be used on the same map to view four kinds of information simultaneously. For example: customers, competitors, transportation and housing.

On the first overlay of the map you mark with an ink marker, let's say red in colour, a point at the addresses of a sample of customers. The best way to do this sampling is to mark the opening account card in any place in the file and from there on count a set of cards and extract the next. The count quota is established by dividing the total number of customers by the size of the sample. For example, if a branch has 1500 customer cards and you want to make a map with 100 customers, then you will have to extract the residential address of every 15th customer. This produces clusters of points where customers live. This can be repeated with working address. You take the next foil and start the same process with a blue marker. Then you might use another overlay to mark the competitor's and your branches, let's say with a green marker. Finally, you may want to know where the bus stops are. We take the last foil and mark them in black.

Now, if you place the branch and transportation overlays together on the map, you can find opportunities to open branches and place automated teller machines (ATMs) near bus stops. Now if you place the branch foil with the working address foil, you can see how vulnerable your customers can be if they are far from you and near to the competitor's branches.

If you place the residential and working address overlays on the map, then you can see areas where customers are not being served, blockades of natural and man-made obstacles (bridges, rivers, highways, etc.) that make the customers journey in a roundabout way in order to reach the branch. If you have also the approximate population of districts, an overlay with this information on top of the overlay foils will indicate the areas where the bank is not present and a high population density exists. This system works very well for malls, commercial centres, department stores and shops in general.

RESEARCH FOR INTERNAL MARKETING

Internal marketing is based on the idea that every individual in an organisation, particularly a service organisation, should recognise that they have customers to serve. In addition, it implements the philosophy that all internal customers must be convinced about the quality of the service being provided and be content in their work.

Relationship between internal and external service quality

The link between internal service quality and external service quality and hence customer satisfaction, customer loyalty and the profitability of the organisation has been proposed by Heskett et al.[8] They propose that high-quality internal services lead to increased employee satisfaction, which in turn leads to increased service value, leading to increased external customer satisfaction. This is supported by Brooks and Smith,[9] Brooks[10,11] and Davis.[12] Magidson and Polcha[13] also discuss the problem of the inferior quality of many internally produced products and services having a direct relationship with the ability of companies to adjust to changing customer needs and meet competitive challenges. Equally, Azzolini and Shillaber[14] propose that quality service to internal customers converts to quality service to external customers. Furthermore, Hart[15] discusses how internal service is related to external service. In his paper he proposes that internal service guarantees ultimately benefit the (external) customer and the bottom line.

Internal marketing will allow the company to improve the quality of the services and products produced internally and so improve both internal and external customer satisfaction. This assumes that the quality of the internal exchange can be measured.

Role of marketing research

Market research traditionally involves identifying the needs and wants of customers in a systematic manner and monitors the impact of marketing activities on them. The same process can be adopted with employees. Personnel

Instructions

With regard to the following statements there is a six-point answer scale with a brief indication of what the numbers on the scale represent. For each of the statements you are asked to provide an answer for each of the organisational departments or sections with which you come into contact. Fill in as many questionnaires as there are departments or sections.

Name of your department or section

....

Name of the section/department with which you come into contact

....

Scale

Fails altogether to meet our expectations	1
Fails to meet our expectations in many ways	2
Fails to meet our expectations in one way or another	3
Nearly always meets our expectations	4
Meets our expectations in full	5
Surpasses our expectations	6

The way this section/department keeps us informed about progress, problems or changes which affect us.	☐
The ability of this section/department to perform first time and correctly the service we require.	☐
The comprehension this section/department has of our needs and problems along with the constraints we have.	☐
The courtesy shown by members of this section/department towards us.	☐
The speed of this section/department in responding to our requests.	☐
How this section/department is organised so as to be able to meet our requirements.	☐
The condition of work, documents and material which it passes to us for further progressing.	☐
The extent to which it keeps us informed about matters which are of mutual interest.	☐

FIGURE 14.2 Internal customer questionnaire

can be given the opportunity to give feedback to management about working conditions, company policy in general and workers' own understanding about what comprises quality for the customer. The information might be obtained by using questionnaires or focus groups or in-depth interviews with employees. Although surveys of employees need careful handling, they not only provide employees with a measure of satisfaction but can identify early breakdowns in communication.

The relationship between organisational subunits and their relationship to top management are also important since the quality of support they receive from each other impinges on the overall quality of service that is eventually given to the customer. This can be assessed by a variation of the SERVQUAL instrument mentioned earlier, which is constructed to measure the quality of support organisational subunits provide to each other (see Figure 14.2 on p. 445).

In service organisations, those involved in dealing with customers are in a unique position to identify trends and business opportunities. Marketing research or an 'internal marketing' information system can be used to good effect in helping to collect such information and provide it to senior/top management for action.

SUMMARY

The chapter has examined business-to-business marketing research and internal marketing research. In the case of business-to-business marketing research the differences and the similarities with consumer marketing research have been explored. Business-to-business marketing research has changed considerably in recent years and employs many of the approaches that were at one time the domain of consumer research.

Service marketing research includes shopping surveys. In a shopping survey, a field worker poses as a customer and, following a list of predefined steps, makes mental notes. Major users of such surveys are retailers and hotels. Such studies are generally handled by an outside specialist firm. It also makes use of customised, full-scale studies of service satisfaction to provide measurement of customer reactions to the delivery of service. Other customer/client reaction studies are often used by small-scale retailers or service firms as well as by the larger firms.

Parasuraman et al. published their now classic article which led to a revolution in the way that service quality is dealt with. In that paper the results of their exploratory research were presented, including a statement of ten service quality determinants that appeared to be relative. In order to improve 'true quality' in a service organisation the first step is to identify the quality determinants most important or relevant to the company's target market and then assess their own and their competitors' performance. This early work formed the basis for the development of SERVQUAL.

Internal marketing is based on the idea that every individual in an organisation, particularly a service organisation, should recognise that they have customers to serve. There is a positive link between internal service quality and external service quality and hence customer satisfaction, customer loyalty and the profitability of the organisation. Market research can be adopted for use with employees. Personnel can be given the opportunity to give feedback to management about working conditions, company policy in general and workers' own understanding about what comprises quality for the customer. The relationship between organisational subunits and their relationship to top management are also important. This can be assessed by a variation of the SERVQUAL instrument.

QUESTIONS

1   What is business-to-business marketing research? How does it differ from consumer marketing research?

2   Discuss how shopping studies can help decision making in a large retailing organisation.

3   Consider how SERVQUAL might be used in an organisation of your own choice.

4   Discuss the role of marketing research within the context of internal marketing.

5   Examine how marketing research that looks at internal marketing might interface with that which looks at external customers.

6   How can an intranet help manage knowledge?

CASE STUDY 14.1: MANAGEMENT IN THE PUBLIC SECTOR

In recent years one city council has been the object of considerable change. Moreover, following the changes that have occurred, there has been a feeling that what has been left behind results in a disgruntled set of employees whose anger and resentment needs to be assuaged. On being appointed to their posts as executive directors of the city council, the new senior management was faced with their first priority, and that was to find ways of reducing the then currently high level of council tax burden. Staffing levels were an obvious target for savings and became the focus of immediate attention. A thorough analysis of the situation indicated that there appeared to be far too many levels of management – especially at the middle management level. In some cases, the number of levels of management between the chief executive and the ground-floor workers was as many as eight. The executive directors therefore decided to embark on a voluntary redundancy scheme, which had the intention of encouraging middle managers to take early retirement and/or generous redundancy payments on the understanding that they would not be replaced.

While these initiatives were in train the city council decided to commission a study to identify the quality of the communication processes with employees. The senior management of the organisation had felt that there was room for improvement both in terms of communication and management style, but was unsure as to what this should involve. The actions it had taken were a response to these feelings.

Question

Draw up a research proposal for the city council that will specifically address the question of identifying the quality of the communication processes with employees.

CASE STUDY 14.2: ORCHESTRAS AIM TO PASS THE BATON

The lights dim in the concert hall of the Colorado Symphony Orchestra and the audience falls silent. Conductor Martin Alsop raises his baton to direct a piece by composer Scott Bradley and over the performance stage a camera image is projected. Tom and Jerry, the famous duo, scamper across the screen.

What are Tom and Jerry doing at a classical music performance? The symphony orchestra hopes they – and other marketing innovations – will bring in larger and younger audiences.

Symphony orchestra concerts are not the only US entertainment form facing an increasingly grey-haired clientele.

But the demographics of symphonic attendance are striking. A study of concertgoers released last year by the National Endowment for the Arts found audiences declining for every age group under 50. According to the St Paul Chamber Orchestra, only 6% of its audience is under 35.

An ageing audience eventually means more empty seats. Eight symphony orchestras have closed in the USA in the last ten years. Last year alone, the orchestras of San Diego and Sacramento shut down.

What's needed, say observers, is a complete overhaul of marketing strategy. Eugene Carr, president of Culture Finder, a Net information service about the arts, says he realised just how little symphony orchestras have changed when the New York Philharmonic recently presented a concert nearly identical to a performance a century ago.

Previously foreign concepts such as 'building a brand image', 'measuring customer satisfaction' and 'creating name recognition' are finding their way into classical music parlance.

The Oregon Symphony, for instance, has conducted market research to find out what appeals to its viewers. 'Our theory is, the music's not the problem, it's how it's presented,' says Don Roth, director of the orchestra. To attract a younger clientele, the Oregon Symphony has introduced concerts under a new 'brand' name, *Nerve Endings*. 'We did it this way because it lets people know that these concerts will be different from your standard fare,' says Maureen O'Connor, in charge of marketing for the orchestra. Under the auspices of the new brand, the Oregon Symphony is venturing on to new ground. A February concert featured a corpse in the lobby, cordoned off with police tape. The corpse was a dummy of Mozart, a display designed to create a mood for that night's Mozart programme.

Another *Nerve Endings* performance featured a flamenco-inspired classical music programme, complete with dancers, videos of flamenco singers, and discounts to flamenco parties at local night clubs.

Source: Griffith[16] (reprinted with permission)

Question

Suggest a programme of marketing research that could be useful in helping an orchestra develop a good marketing strategy.

CASE STUDY 14.3: DECLINE OF FRILLS

Companies are spending more money on business travel but their employees are gaining little of the benefit as they continue to cut the costs of each trip, Scheherazade Daneshkhu writes.

Euromonitor, the London-based market research group, says that costs are being reduced through shorter trips. Business travellers are also holding back from spending a night in their destination to save on hotel bills. The main reason for the increase in corporate business travel spending is because of the rise in flight costs, according to Euromonitor.

Some companies are continuing to cut the number of trips their employees take as well as trading down the class of air travel. Carlson Wagonlit, the business travel agent, says that 35% of UK companies questioned for its survey in January said that they had changed their policy to allow for a lower class of travel.

The number of companies willing to pay for long-haul business-class travel has been in general decline over the past three years, according to Carlson Wagonlit. There has been a corresponding rise in economy fares. Most of those it questioned said they were prepared to travel on less expensive no-frills flights on short-haul routes, but wanted greater comfort on longer flights.

The latter wish appears not to be granted. The number of those flying in business or first class on long-haul flights dropped compared to last year, while economy-class travel has increased.

But there is some room for optimism. More than two-thirds of the travellers questioned said they expected to make more business trips over the next 12 months – a 36% increase from last year.

Source: Daneshkhu[17] (reprinted with permission)

Question

How might marketing research help the travel business to unravel some of its problems that are as yet unresolved?

CASE STUDY 14.4: JASMINE HOTEL, DUBAI

Jasmine Hotel is located in the Deira district of Dubai in the United Arab Emirates. It is about ten minutes' drive from the airport and within a short walk of the shops. The Gold Souk is a short taxi drive away and the hotel is within walking distance of most of the city on the Deira side of the creek. A complimentary shuttle service operates between the hotel and the public Al Mamzar Beach Park where full beach club and water sports are available for a small fee.

Within the hotel itself there is a good choice of bars and restaurants and there is also a coffee shop. Leisure facilities include a small roof-top swimming pool, a fitness room, sauna and spa. The central atrium is light and spacious and is the focal point of this very recently built hotel.

Dubai enjoys a very hot and dry climate, being subtropical and close to the desert. Temperatures for most of the year exceed 100°F during the daytime and are more than 80°F after sunset. It is not unknown for daytime temperatures to soar to 120°F in July and August. Acclimatisation can take visitors to Dubai a little while to achieve. While locals brave the daytime sun, all-year-round visitors from more temperate climates can find the climate unbearable during the day during July and August.

The accommodation comprises some 250 rooms that are spacious and well furnished with bath and shower, air-conditioning, telephone and television and mini-bar. The hotel has three restaurants: Indian, Thai and Chinese. All are well appointed in traditional style. Guests pay separately for all meals and use of the mini-bar. A typical room costs between 30 and 50 pounds sterling per night, depending on the time of year. The breakfast buffet costs around 12 pounds sterling. Canned soft drinks from the mini-bar cost around 3 pounds sterling a can while beer is around 4 pounds sterling a can. In the neighbourhood there are many good-quality restaurants offering meals at low prices and soft drinks can be bought locally from stores for as little as 10 pence per can.

The hotel employs a large number of staff. These range from several receptionists and doormen to house boys, chambermaids, waiters and cooks. The hotel is keen to improve the level of service it offers to customers and at the same time is also anxious to ensure that it has a fully motivated staff to meet the needs and wants of the wide variety of guests that it entertains. Guests come from all over the world and the hotel also hires out its conference suite on the top floor to both local and foreign clients.

Question

Design a marketing research system that will help the hotel maintain the level of service quality that it is hoping to achieve. Account should be taken of both the hotel's internal and external customers in designing the system.

CASE STUDY 14.5: BANKING IN PORTUGAL

Northern Portugal is the cradle of the nation's entrepreneurial spirit. Businesspeople in the region consider themselves to be the real wheeler-dealers of the Portuguese economy, running mainly small to medium-size businesses, and having a certain air of contempt for their counterparts in Lisbon and further south. According to the northern Portuguese, Lisbonites are mere employees of multinationals who spend their time on politics and parties while the real deals are done in the north.

Of course, in common with most other capital cities, Lisbon is where the power and money gravitates; like the multinationals, banks have a strong presence there. However, the Portuguese have a saying that banks are born in Oporto and die in Lisbon, where deal-making skills become blunted and attention to detail becomes lax. For this reason, Banco Portugues de Investimento (BPI) keeps its headquarters in Oporto.

BPI is an exclusive merchant bank set up in 1981 by Artur Santos Silva; Senhor Silva has, in the meantime, set up or acquired a string of subsidiary banks between Oporto and Lisbon. Two of these, Banco de Fomento e Exterior and Banco Fonsecas & Burnay, have head offices in Lisbon, while a third, Banco Borges & Irmao, remains in Oporto. Borges & Irmao is focused towards northern Portugal, which is where the bulk of its branches are, and Fonsecas & Burnay focuses in the south.

Both subsidiary networks have been briefed to develop consumer lending niches such as credit cards and car purchase loans, segments where BPI claims it has developed key products. The business in the north has the added bonus of using its retail activities to scout for corporate finance – so many of its retail customers are businesspeople running small and medium enterprises. Typically, the banking groups in Portugal divide their markets into three main segments: small and medium enterprises, universal banking, and large corporations. BPI believes that the delivery of tailor-made services to specific segments is the key to success in domestic banking.

Banking executives are painfully aware that there is a lot of work to be done in restructuring the industries of northern Portugal – they talk in terms of identifying products and standardising them, of joint marketing projects, and of pooling companies together for research and testing of projects. Aiding management buy-outs and merger and acquisition deals are seen as ways of ensuring continuity in businesses, and are looking towards cross-border transactions with companies in northern Spain as a way of consolidating businesses.

So far, progress has been slow; the northern business culture is not receptive to involving banks in their activities. The family businesses in the north tend to be mistrustful of banks, are suspicious of marketing ideas and usually employ one graduate to look after the banks – there is a widespread belief that the less the company has to do with the bank, the stronger is the business. Successful firms are perceived as those who neither give nor receive credit, who deal in cash only, and who keep their business dealings close to their chests. There is, fortunately, a growing realisation that these practices might work well for small firms, but will not be effective if the firm is to grow beyond a small family concern. 'Small family companies tend to have opaque accounts which makes risk evaluation very complex; they are also, by definition, very individualistic,' is how one Oporto banking analyst expressed it.

In the near future, the banks are expecting some medium to large firms to emerge in northern Portugal as the merger process accelerates. Better able to compete on a world stage, these firms will probably be engaged in the traditional industries of textiles and leather, but will be better managed and better financed than the present companies. If this is the case, the banks expect to be sharing in their success, and in the growth of northern Portugal as a player on the world business stage.

(Case contributed by Jim Blythe)

Questions

1 What kind of secondary sources might be useful to the banks in identifying business customers?

2 How might banks decide which retail customers are also potential corporate clients?

3 What would be the main difficulties in researching the corporate market in northern Portugal?

4 How might the banks research the market for retail customers?

5 What secondary sources might be useful for the banks in identifying customers within their chosen niche markets of credit cards and car loans?

REFERENCES AND NOTES

1 Gorle, P (1995) The cascade theory that shows practical gains, *Research Plus*, October, 11.

2 Jamieson, D (1995) Now business research is every agency's research, *Research Plus*, October, 4–5.

3 Skapinker, M (1997) Deceptive appearance, *Financial Times*, 3 February.

4 Parasuraman, A, Berry, L L and Zeithaml, V (1985) A conceptual model of service quality and the implications for future research, *Journal of Marketing*, 49, 41–51.

5 Berry, L L, Zeithaml, V A and Parasuraman, A (1985) Quality counts in services, too, *Business Horizons*, May–June, 44–52.

6 Zeithaml, V, Parasuraman, A and Berry, L (1990) *Delivering Quality Service*, New York: Free Press.

7 Buttle, F (1996) *Relationship Marketing*, London: Paul Chapman, 59–60.

8 Heskett, J L, Jones, T O, Loveman, G W, Sasser, W E and Schlesinger, L A (1994) Putting the service profit chain to work, *Harvard Business Review*, March–April, 164–74.

9 Brooks, R F and Smith J V (1993) Service from within, *TQM Journal*, October, 41–45.

10 Brooks, R F (1993) Internal service quality – a manufacturing perspective, *Proceedings of the Marketing Education Group*, Loughborough, 93–94.

11 Brooks, R F (1995) Internal service quality – a theoretical development, *Proceedings of the Marketing Education Group*, Bradford, 80–90.

12 Davis, T R V (1992) Satisfying internal customers: the link to external customer satisfaction, *Planning Review*, 20(1), 34–37.

13 Magidson, D and Polcha, A E (1992) Creating market economies within organisations, a conference on internal markets, *Planning Review*, January–February, 37–40.

14 Azzolini, M and Shillaber, J (1993) Internal service quality: winning from the inside out, *Quality Progress*, November, 75–78.

15 Hart, C W L (1995) The power of internal guarantees, *Harvard Business Review*, January–February, 64–73.

16 Griffiths, V (1997) Orchestras aim to pass the baton, *Financial Times*, 26 May.

17 Daneshkhu, S (1997) The decline of frills, *Financial Times*, 28 April.

FURTHER READING

Anderson, E W (1993) Firm, industry and national indices of customer satisfaction: implications for services, in Swartz, T and Brown, S W (eds), *Advances in Services Marketing Management: Research and practice*, Vol. 2, Greenwich, CT: JAI Press, 87–108.

Anderson, E W, Fornell, C and Rust, R T (1997) Customer satisfaction, productivity, and profitability: differences between goods and services, *Marketing Science*, 16(2), 129–45.

Andreasson, T W (1994) Satisfaction, loyalty and reputation as indicators of customer orientation in the public sector, *International Journal of Public Sector Management*, 7(2), 16–34.

Donnelly, M, Wisniewski, M, Dalrymple, J F and Curry, A (1995) Measuring service quality in local government: the SERVQUAL approach, *International Journal of Public Sector Management*, 8(7), 15–20.

Eklof, J A, Hackl, P and Westlund, A (1999) On measuring interactions between customer satisfaction and financial results, *Total Quality Management*, 10(4–5), 514–22.

Flanagan, T A and Fredericks, J O (1993) Improving company performance through customer satisfaction measurement and management, *National Productivity Review*, Spring, 239–58.

Gronroos, C (1990) *Service Management and Marketing: Managing the moments of truth in service competition*, Lexington, MA: Lexington Books.

Gulledge, L G (1991) Satisfying the internal customer, *Bank Marketing*, 23, 46–48.

Gummesson, E (1993) Quality management in service organizations: an interpretation of the service quality phenomenon and a synthesis of international research, Karlstad, Sweden: International Service Quality Association.

Hague, P (1985) *The Industrial Market Research Handbook* (2nd edn), London: Kogan Page.

Hallowell, R (1996) The relationship of customer satisfaction, customer loyalty and profitability: an empirical study, *International Journal of Service Industry Management*, 7(4), 27–42.

Jobber, D and O'Reilly, D (1996) Industrial mail surveys: techniques for inducing response, *Marketing Intelligence and Planning*, 14(1), 29–34.

Piercy, N (1996) The effects of customer satisfaction measurement: the internal market versus the external market, *Marketing Intelligence and Planning*, 14(4), April, 9.

Piercy, N and Morgan, N (1995) Customer satisfaction measurement and management: a processual analysis, *Journal of Marketing Management*, 11, 817–34.

Schneider, K C and Johnson, J C (1995) Stimulating response to market surveys of business professionals, *Industrial Marketing Management*, 24, 265–76.

Sirkin, A F (1995) Maximizing customer satisfaction, *MLS: Marketing Library Services*, 9(4), June, 3–4.

Smith, A M (1995) Quality aspects of service marketing, *Marketing Intelligence and Planning*, 8(6), 25–32.

Sutherland, K (ed.) (1994) *Researching Business Markets*, London: Kogan Page.

Swindley, D (1992) Retail buying in the United Kingdom, *The Service Industries Journal*, 12, 533–44.

White, D and Abels, Eileen, G (1995) Measuring service quality in special libraries: lessons from service marketing, *Special Libraries*, 86, Winter, 36–45.

Zeithaml, V A, Berry, L L and Parasuraman, A (1996) The behavioral consequences of service quality, *Journal of Marketing*, 60, April, 31–46.

15 Global marketing research

Objectives

After reading this chapter, you should be able to:

- appreciate how marketing research is organised and conducted in global markets

- understand how it may differ from research in the home market.

Keywords

concentration
conceptual equivalence
culture
desk research
developing markets
diversification
ethnic influences

functional equivalence
instrument equivalence
instrument translation
international segmentation
market selection
target market

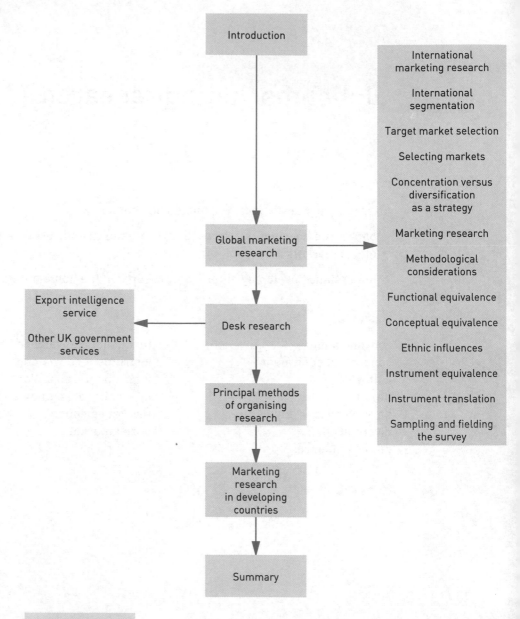

Plan of Chapter 15

INTRODUCTION

This chapter looks at how marketing research is organised and conducted in global markets. Segmentation and targeting are considered along with the selection of markets. Attention is given to methodological considerations when operating in an international context. Desk research is an important source of information and attention is given in the chapter to identifying fruitful sources of information. How marketing research is organised is also covered in the chapter. We then go on to look at the additional difficulties involved in undertaking marketing research in developing countries where the situation is also worsened by a lack of requisite research skills and a poor appreciation of the value of marketing research. Often, few indigenous organisations possess marketing research departments and comparatively few commercial marketing research services exist.

GLOBAL MARKETING RESEARCH

Most firms involved in international marketing activities at least know the destination of their goods. Clearly, this means that such firms really need to understand the foreign marketplace in the same way as they understand the domestic marketplace. It would seem sensible that before undertaking international marketing, firms should undertake analysis of what marketing opportunities exist. A variety of factors should then be taken into account when screening potential international marketing opportunities to enable a sensible decision to be taken about which, if any, of the opportunities should be pursued.

A company engaged in international marketing needs to know foreign government policies about importing the range and type of products it produces, together with information on tariffs and quotas. Because of the complexity of international marketing, knowledge of legal and financial regulations is essential. The marketing and commercial infrastructures of countries differ considerably and it is imperative to understand how these vary from country to country.

As far as consumer behaviour is concerned we can not assume that what applies in the home market will also be applicable in different foreign markets. Life cycle patterns, bases of motivation, cultural values and lifestyles may be very different from what we are used to and require an entirely different marketing approach. Many blunders have been made by firms that have failed to study local customs carefully. In some countries, it is considered unacceptable and even offensive to portray physical contact between the sexes in promotional material. In Thailand, for example, a firm was trying to introduce a mouthwash but was unaware that the foregoing comments were applicable in that country and showed, in its advertisements, a young couple holding hands. This caused offence but by changing the advertisement so that two women were portrayed holding hands the commercials were then considered to be acceptable.[1]

Marketing communication channels must be studied in order to identify how information relating to products and services can be brought effectively to the consumer's attention. Common barriers include those posed by literacy and language and these have to be overcome.

One key factor, however, is the capacity of the market to pay for the goods and services supplied. This is influenced by such things as personal disposable income and government restrictions on the expenditure of foreign currency reserves. In the case of larger items and business-to-business projects, loan terms, interest and capital requirements are also important factors.

International marketing research

Most marketing research work is usually carried out by local researchers but the entire process is directed and coordinated by headquarters staff. Headquarters staff also have to put considerable effort into 'country market screening' – looking at the relative size of each potential market, the size of its purchasing power and its concentration, and the likely rate of future growth. In addition, an assessment of the competitive forces at work in each potential market has to be made.

RISE OF INTERNATIONAL RESEARCH

Consumer marketing has penetrated to most cities in most countries in the world and, along with marketing and advertising, market research is commonplace. Recently, Mary Goodyear sat in a small house in a black township in Cape Town with a group of young men whose prospects seemed limited to casual labour and, possibly, crime. One of the young men chided Mary for showing the group a dull advertisement. 'Surely you must remember AIDA,' he said. 'Attention Interest Desire Action – well I don't see much of interest and desire in that advert.'

Source: Goodyear[2]

TRANSITIONARY MARKETS

Millionaires on the French Riviera are to be expected but it may be surprising to know that there are over 500,000 dollar millionaires in the People's Republic of China and that there is also an emerging middle class in China (those with annual incomes in excess of $15,000 equivalent) that numbers more than 35 million people.

The common view is that China's growing consumer market is tied to its urban population, which represents about 20% to 25% of the nation's 1.2 billion people.

With annual disposable income of about US$465 a head (and much more in purchasing power), urban dwellers reportedly earn about 2.5 times as much as their rural cousins. However, this picture not only undercounts city dwellers but also misses a huge adjunct to the main consumer market: an increasingly affluent suburban economy that has sprouted on the fringes of the cities but is often classified as part of the rural economy. Suburbanites and better off peasants make up some 384 million people and they enjoy average per capita incomes of US$450, almost as much as urbanites. Urban and suburban groups taken together make up some two-thirds of China's population and account for 80% of its gross domestic product. Their purchasing power helps to explain why real retail sales on the mainland continue to grow at 10% per annum despite the nation's recent austerity measures.

Indeed, while European retail sales languish in the doldrums many Asian retail markets are experiencing annual sales growths of more than 10%. Of course, the stage in development of the market may vary considerably from country to country, even within a particular region of the world. Malaysia in 1994 was a buoyant retail economy, but some of its neighbours such as Thailand, Cambodia, Vietnam and Laos did not share the same fortune.

It is possible to characterise the stage of economic development in a country and relate it to levels and types of marketing activity. The following typology is suggested by the Henley Centre:

- The first stage is where the formal cash economy is hardly developed and most consumption is of unbranded commodities.

- At the second stage incomes are in the range $2000 to $3000 per annum; brands consciousness develops and consumption patterns are influenced by a desire to emulate.

- At the third stage consumption is characterised by the demands of an individualistic middle class and people seek to express their individuality. The mass markets that are typical of the second stage are supplemented and even replaced by market niches.

- Stage four sees gender, class, family or caste-based stereotypes disintegrate as individuals act and buy in a way that is alien to the norms of the group to which they have been traditionally affiliated.

- Stage five sees individuals buying brands for occasions. Often more differences exist between the same individual on two different occasions than between two different individuals on the same occasion.

Many of the **developing markets** of Asia appear to be somewhere between stages one and two. However, notable exceptions are Hong Kong and Singapore, where living standards are above those of Ireland and Portugal. Malaysia and Indonesia are developing rapidly and other Pacific Rim countries are likely to develop swiftly as political stability takes root.

Source: Tyrrell[3] and Korents[4]

International segmentation

Market segmentation amounts to dividing markets into groups of consumers with similar buying needs and who are likely to respond, as a group, to specific marketing mixes.

International segmentation helps firms to market their products globally in the most effective ways. It is important to note that all segments should be measurable, accessible and of reasonable size. The international marketing strategist seeks to consolidate numerous small segments across a number of countries into a slice of the global market that is worth serving.

Target market selection

The process involves narrowing down potential country markets to a feasible number of countries and to **target market** segments within them. It is argued that instead of trying to appeal to everyone, firms best make use of their resources by identifying potential markets for entry and expanding selectively over time to those that are considered attractive. The four stages of screening are:

- preliminary screening
- estimation of market potential
- estimation of sales potential
- identification of segments.

Preliminary screening relies on secondary data and in particular indicators of overall buying power in country markets are useful. Estimation of market potential is often undertaken with the aid of secondary data-based analytical techniques that focus on or utilise demand patterns, income elasticity measures etc.

Estimating sales potential involves assessing the market share likely to be achieved. Information on competition, degree of relative product advantage and access to retail outlets must figure predominantly in these assessments.

Selecting markets

It is often the case that opportunities in foreign markets present themselves to would-be exporters/international marketing firms from time to time. In such a case, one has to evaluate each case on its merits. It may also be, however, that a firm is actively searching for such opportunities and in either case it should bear in mind the points that follow.

The kind of information that needs to be obtained before **market selection** occurs should answer questions about the following points:

- approximate size of the market production/imports/exports/consumption
- products that are currently available (how well they satisfy tastes, habits etc.)
- leading competitors, their market shares, promotion methods, services and facilities offered
- channels and costs of distribution
- legal requirements, standards etc.
- tariffs, quotas, import licences – contact the British Overseas Trade Board (BOTB), part of the DTI, for details
- ease of transportation (speed/frequency/costs)
- political/economic stability of the market (BOTB *Hints to Exporters* booklets are a good source)
- growth trends in the market.

Concentration versus diversification as a strategy

A firm's major alternatives are **concentration** on a small number of markets or to achieve growth by **diversification** in a large number of markets in the early stages of international market expansion. The choice of expansion strategy is influenced by market-related, mix-related factors.

NATIONAL ATTITUDES TO ANTIBIOTICS

People were consulted about their beliefs about infections and their problems in taking antibiotics in a large survey of attitudes. The study, conducted in Belgium, France, Italy, Spain, Turkey and the UK, involved some 3610 people. Respondents had taken an antibiotic, or given one to their child, for a respiratory tract infection (RTI), such as colds, sore throats, catarrh, 'flu and earaches in the previous 12 months. Two hundred respondents were drawn from each country in each of three groups: working adults, elderly adults over 55 years and mothers of children under 12 years.

More than 50% of those interviewed thought that antibiotics should be pre-scribed for any respiratory tract infection with the exception of a simple cold. The percentage in France, Spain and Turkey was higher than that in Belgium, Italy and the UK. These differences in expectations were related to patients' perceptions of antibiotics (in particular their fears about their effects) and the extent of their knowledge about antibiotics.

Cultural attitudes underlie individual behaviour and practices in taking courses of antibiotics. Medical opinion strongly advises that a whole course should be used to prevent the development of resistant bacteria and recurrent infection. However, in Spain there was a widespread belief that part of a course could be saved and used for a subsequent illness. Indeed, the proportion of patients who claimed not to have taken the whole of the antibiotic course showed distinct variations across countries. Compliance was high in Belgium, France and the UK, but was lower in Italy and Spain. The main reason for stopping taking the antibiotic before the end of the course was completed was 'feeling better'. In Italy and Spain it had become the norm to stop taking the medicine once you felt better. Differences in the rates of compliance across countries reflect social norms and attitudes and this has profound implications for community health. The research uncovered a natural rhythm in antibiotic taking related to the patient's intrinsic timetable for visiting the doctor, getting antibiotics, then feeling well and consequently stopping the medication.

Ideas about improving antibiotics reflected concern, first, about fewer side-effects (52%) and then improved efficacy (35%) and speed of action (34%). Interest in shorter courses (32%) and fewer daily doses (28%) was also expressed. Interest in reducing the duration of treatment and number of doses was greatest in the UK and Spain but in Italy most were concerned with side-effects.

Nowadays people expect effectiveness and quick results from modern technology. Producers of consumer products, by corresponding closer to patients' lifestyles and the expressed desire for shorter courses of treatment, would not only meet patients' wishes but would also achieve significant medical benefits through improved compliance.

Source: Branthwaite and Bruggemann[5]

Marketing research

Many factors add to the complexity and diversity of conducting marketing research in international markets. They include the following.

Understanding the culture

A thorough understanding of the **culture** is necessary if the researcher is to obtain satisfactory response rates. Quite apart from the problems associated with high rates of illiteracy, in some cultures a woman will not consent to an interview by a stranger, let alone a man. In other cultures men will be reluctant to discuss topics such as personal hygiene or preferences in clothing because they feel that this would be beneath their dignity – and they will definitely not address these issues in the presence of a female interviewer. In addition, it is difficult for respondents to answer questions concerning goods and services that have never been available or are not commonly used in the community, or whose use is not well understood.

Lack of secondary data

The usually large amounts of secondary data that characterise countries such as the USA are in most cases not available in every other country. This is particularly the case in developing or transitional countries. Even if data are available, they will be of variable quality. For instance, population censuses in some countries are frequently made by people who are not professionals and data on income and sales from tax returns can be totally inaccurate in countries where such information is often undeclared or under-reported.

Cost of collecting primary data

One soon discovers, when trying to collect data in international markets, that the cost of collecting it can be considerably higher without a network of established marketing firms. Many countries lack companies that are experienced in collecting information, which means that a sponsoring firm will have to invest in the development of sampling frames and other materials and in the training of interviewers and other necessary personnel.

RESEARCH CAN BE RAINED OFF FOR THE DAY IN INDIA

One of the first things that strikes one about a country such as India is its diversity. It has a population of 900 million people across 26 states, with 16 official languages and over 1600 minor languages and dialects and numerous different religions.

At a general methodological level, there are a number of considerations when conducting marketing research in India. Clearly with such a population and massive regional differences, selecting an appropriate sample of the population in terms of both size and survey centres is a considerable feat to achieve. In addition, with the large number of different languages there is considerable opportunity for misunderstandings or misinterpretations to arise and qualitative research requires executive teams who can speak all of the local languages that may be required.

With respect to data collection methods, postal research in India is a non-starter until the postal system within the country is improved significantly. In addition, because of cultural traditions the telephone is rarely used for lengthy discussions. This being the case, a relatively cheap labour force usually makes face-to-face interviewing the most appropriate method to employ.

There are also other logistical factors to be taken into account. For example, when it rains in India it pours and because research is conducted through personal interviews it makes it impossible to carry on working. Religious festivals also present obstacles that one would not encounter in the West. There are so many of them and the level of devotion practised is so high that scheduling fieldwork requires significant juggling skills.

Source: Bunn[6]

MARKETING RESEARCH IN CENTRAL AND EASTERN EUROPE

Within only five years the countries in central and eastern Europe have moved from state-led command economies to consumer-led demand economies. During this time Western products and services have been actively marketed to the local population. Consumers have had to get used to the new economic situation and its marketing tools: advertising, promotions and branding. The majority have learned to differentiate not only between local and Western brands but also among Western brands. Value for money, an almost unknown concept in 1992, is now part of the everyday vocabulary. Moreover, local brands are increasing in popularity and increasing in quality.

Research existed in the region before the collapse of Communism and most countries have a tradition of government-sponsored research. At the end of the 1980s the value of commercial survey research commissioned by Western companies in the region was probably less than US$100,000 but by 1995 it had risen to more than US$30 million. In the more developed countries some 65% of the commissions are from locally based companies, primarily multinationals. In the less developed areas about 60% of the commissioning companies are based outside the country in which research is undertaken. In the Czech Republic, Hungary, Poland and Russia there are some ten to twenty companies offering full-service qualitative and quantitative research. In addition, there are many others that claim to provide some elements of the marketing research service. There are at least three to five full-service marketing research agencies in each country in the region. In the Czech Republic, Hungary, Poland and Russia major marketing research suppliers are forming associations and considering quality-standard systems for field work. Most major companies are investing in their future by training staff in western Europe and America. In most countries there is at least one viewing facility for qualitative research, one monthly omnibus service, one consumer or specialist panel and one CATI facility. Moreover, several companies in the region are testing or piloting CAPI methods of data collection.

Source: Bartonova[7]

Methodological considerations

A number of methodological considerations affect the construction of questionnaires and other research instruments to be used in international research studies. The problems arise from two sources:

1 the complex cultural differences in the meaning of products and activities

2 the lack of standardised data collection instruments to measure marketing-related variables.

Functional equivalence

The extent to which the same product is used for the same or a similar function in two or more countries is called **functional equivalence**. However, possessions tend to be used for different functions in different societies. In India, for example, the accumulation of jewellery represents less an interest in the display of social status than in security and accumulation of wealth. Refrigerators, used to store food in some countries, are used primarily for chilling water and soft drinks in some other countries.[8] When General Mills entered the UK breakfast cereal market, a box featured a freckled, red-haired, crew-cut kid saying 'Gee kids, it's great.' What General Mills failed to recognise was that the British family is not as child oriented and permissive as the American family to which it was accustomed, and that British parent–child relationships tend to be more authoritarian; consequently, the package had no appeal to the British housewife.[9]

A similar blunder was made by Binoca when it launched a talcum powder advertisement in India. The advertisement showed an attractive, seemingly naked, woman dousing herself with talcum powder. The caption, covering strategic portions of her body, read: 'Don't go wild – just enough is all you need of Binoca talc.' The highly conservative Indian public found the advertisement distasteful and developed strong negative associations with the brand name.[9] To ask proper questions requires that the researchers understand the functional equivalence, or lack of it, of the activities being investigated.

Conceptual equivalence

The extent to which the same concept (e.g. family) has the same meaning in two or more countries is known as **conceptual equivalence**. However, concepts can have totally different meanings in different cultural environments. This requires the careful choice of words used to convey the meaning of what the researcher is attempting to explore. The word 'family', for example, means something different in the USA, where it typically refers to only parents and children, than it does in many other cultures, where it can extend to grandparents, aunts, uncles and other relatives.

Ethnic influences

Researchers need to understand how the cultural values of a society will affect the approach to the research issue of interest. It may be possible to research problems in one culture but not in another because of cultural taboos, different levels of abstraction and other **ethnic influences**. For example, researching attitudes and behaviour concerning personal hygiene products may simply not be possible in some cultures where the norm clearly proscribes public discussion of such issues.

Instrument equivalence

It may not be possible to use the same measuring instrument in every culture, a concept known as **instrument equivalence**. For this reason the researcher may choose to use what are called 'emic' instruments. An **emic instrument** is one that is constructed specifically for investigating an attitude in a specific culture. Closed-ended questions, for example, may not work well in one culture, but because of cultural differences may work well in another. Certain categories may have to be omitted while others may have to be added. Open-ended questions may also pose some problems, especially in countries where the level of literacy is low and where interviewer bias is significant. Other methods of interviewing, such as focus groups and consumer panels, may face problems because of strong social acquiescence tendencies that are the cultural norm in some countries.

In some instances the researcher may construct 'etic' instruments, ones that are transcultural in application, relating to the behavioural analysis of attitudes considered in isolation. This would permit direct comparison of the same variable across cultures. Attempts at developing **etic instruments** have employed non-verbal instruments such as picture completion, TAT instruments and semantic differentials.[8]

Instrument translation

It may seem obvious to suggest that a survey developed in one country be carefully translated into the language of the country where it is going to be administered and assessed (a process known as **instrument translation**). However, mistakes can happen even in the case of literal equivalence: one classic example is a US airline's advertisement of its Boeing 747 'rendezvous lounge' that translated into Portuguese as the 'prostitution chamber'.[9]

Special translation methods have been applied in international research projects:

- *Direct translation*: the survey undergoes a single translation from one language into another by a bilingual translator. This method, however, exposes the instrument to all the problems just mentioned.

- *Back translation*: this is a variation of direct translation that requires the translated survey to be translated back into the original language by another bilingual translator. This lets the translator correct any meaning problems between the original and retranslated instruments. Note that back translation requires that equivalent terms for words or phrases exist in the other language, which may not always be the case.

- *Decentring*: a hybrid of back translation, this method involves a successive iteration process: translation and retranslation of an instrument, each time by a different translator. The back-translated versions in the original language are compared sequentially. If discrepancies occur, the original is modified and the process is repeated until both show the same or similar wordings. Generally each iteration should show more convergence.

Sampling and fielding the survey

In many countries telephone directories, census tract and block data, and detailed socioeconomic characteristics of the target population will not be available or will be outdated. This adversely affects the ability to draw non-probability as well as probability samples and to conduct personal interviews of any variety. For example, lacking age distributions for the target population, it is difficult for a marketing researcher to set representative age quotas. Moreover, in certain cultures, convenience samples are doomed to failure. In Saudi Arabia, for example, because of the seclusion of women, shopping mall interviews produce all-male samples.

Inadequate mailing lists and rudimentary postal and telephone services can make marketing research in some countries extremely difficult. In many countries only a small percentage of the population possesses telephones and an alarmingly large percentage of telephone lines may be out of service at any one time. Mail surveys suffer from similar problems. Delivery delays of weeks are common, and in certain countries, expected response rates are lowered considerably because the questionnaire can be mailed back only at the post office.

The obstacles in conducting international marketing research studies can be formidable. Understanding the cultural environment in which the research is taking place is a necessary condition for success. The researcher must also avoid the tendency to blindly apply conventional research techniques and practices. Designing and implementing international research projects can be done effectively. It just takes effort and sensitivity to asking questions in a manner that increases the likelihood that respondents will provide the desired information.

DESK RESEARCH

Desk research is particularly important in export research. This type of research should be fully explored before considering field research. A great deal of desk research can be conducted in the UK where extremely valuable information is freely available from government and other sources. The British Overseas Trade Board is concerned with giving directions for the development of British export activities and establishing priorities in these areas.

The export marketing information service of the Department of Trade and Industry (1–19 Victoria Street, London SW1H 0ET) has the following resources available:

- *Foreign statistical publications:* produced by both national statistical offices and international organisations, covering a range of topics including trade, production, prices, employment, population and other economic data. The centre can also undertake some searching of selected trade statistics online.

- *Foreign trade directories:* including telephone directories for most countries and specialised directories covering particular sectors of industry.

- *National development plans:* issued by many countries and most are available for loan to exporters.

- *British overseas trade information system:* a database for exporters which contains information on products and markets, overseas contacts, export opportunities and promotional events. This includes:
  1 The product data store – a computerised microfilm database of product and industry information on overseas markets. Sources include unique market reports researched by British embassy staff. Coverage varies from country to country but falls within three broad areas of interest: market size, structure and share.
  2 The Overseas Contacts Service that provides details of potential agents, distributors, importers, retailers and others supplied by British embassies.

Export intelligence service

This service sends export-related information to interested subscribing companies, trade associations and other similar organisations. Its main objective is to secure export orders for British companies by bringing individual export opportunities to their attention. It also supplies market information such as changes in tariff rates and import regulations. Each subscriber is profiled to receive only those notices that are relevant to the organisation – by commodity, overseas market and type of notice.

Other UK government services

There are a number of journals and booklets that provide a wealth of information useful to exporters. These are summarised in Table 15.1.

There are many other sources of data, including:

- National Economic Development Office
- Central Office of Information
- foreign embassies
- British Export Houses Association
- British Standards Institution
- Institute of Export
- London World Trade Centre
- Market Research Society.

TABLE 15.1   UK government services

Source	Content
British Business	Markets, tariff changes, import regulations, overseas trade missions. Special market surveys, details of trade fairs and exhibitions. Covers world markets
CBI overseas reports	
Economic Surveys (HMSO/TSO)	Detailed appraisals of local economic conditions
Euromonitor	
European Union Information Office (8 Storey's Gate, London SW1P 3AT)	
Export and Import Statistics (Statistical Office)	
Hints to Exporters (Department of Trade and Industry)	Booklets that cover all export markets, giving a rapid overview of trading customs, travel facilities, etc.
OECD: Foreign Trade Statistics Bulletin	
Overseas Trade Bulletin (CBI)	

Professional advice on export marketing research is obtainable from organisations such as:

- European Association for Business-to-Business Marketing Research
- Market Research Society
- Business-to-Business Marketing Research Association.

PRINCIPAL METHODS OF ORGANISING RESEARCH

Research for export marketing can be undertaken in a variety of ways, and a brief outline of the principal methods follows.

Use of own staff or importing agents

The first objection to this methodology is lack of objectivity; sales staff are usually incapable of giving an unbiased opinion about the likely success of their product.

The second objection is that agents may have other interests that prevent them from giving an objective assessment of the market.

Research is a specialist's job that requires particular training and expertise and yet, however, this method may be the only feasible way of researching in some markets.

Using research agencies in overseas markets

Selection of these may be difficult and risky and where several markets are involved, multiple agencies may have to be used to cover the whole export pro-gramme. One big advantage is that national research organisations should possess intimate knowledge of their own home market.

Using a UK-based marketing research organisation plus the services of a locally based research firm

This method is rather cumbersome and offers few advantage over the previous method. It could, however, be useful where manufacturers have no trained research staff (as is often the case in smaller companies).

Using the services of a consortium of research agencies

This method is superficially attractive, but member firms can vary considerably in the quality of those services. Closely related to this method is that of an inter-national research organisation linked with advertising agencies over principal markets. This is generally effective.

Several of the larger marketing research companies – e.g. Gallup, BMRB via its associated company MRBI, IFT, and Research Services Ltd – are active in multi-country research.

MARKETING RESEARCH IN DEVELOPING COUNTRIES

There are additional difficulties involved in undertaking marketing research in developing countries. The rapid rate of change occurring in such countries creates problems in maintaining adequate databases. Moreover, as countries develop, there is an increased requirement for both secondary sources of data and primary data-collection research skills. The situation is also worsened by a lack of requisite research skills and a poor appreciation of the value of marketing research.

Often, few indigenous organisations possess marketing research departments and comparatively few commercial marketing research services exist. Government departments make inadequate use of marketing research and are unlikely to be really useful sources of information in this respect. Until adequate documentary detail and data agglomeration infrastructures are set up in such countries, the situation cannot improve.

The overall process of marketing research still applies and with modification to take account of cultural, economic and other environmental considerations, research can produce useful results. Secondary sources are a prime source of data and are used extensively despite their limitations. Field research can be hazardous and there is a propensity to rely on certain methods and techniques in order to obviate sampling and non-sampling errors.

SUMMARY

Emphasis has been placed on how marketing research is organised and conducted in global markets. Desk research is an important source of information and attention has been given in the chapter to identifying fruitful sources of information. There are additional difficulties involved in undertaking marketing research in developing countries and the situation is also worsened by a lack of requisite research skills and a poor appreciation of the value of marketing research. Often, few indigenous organisations possess marketing research departments and comparatively few commercial marketing research services exist.

QUESTIONS

1 How is the majority of international marketing research conducted?

2 Explain international segmentation research.

3 What is involved in selecting target markets in international markets?

4 Compare and contrast concentration and diversification as strategies.

5 What are the main factors to take into account when undertaking international marketing research?

6 Indicate the main sources of desk research material made available by the UK government and the use to which it may be put.

7 What are the principal methods of organising international marketing research?

8 Examine the problems of undertaking marketing research in developing countries.

CASE STUDY 15.1: MICHEL HERBELIN

At the end of the Second World War, a young self-taught watchmaker named Michel Herbelin opened a workshop in Charquemont in the Jura Mountains just across the border from Switzerland. He chose Charquemont principally because his main suppliers were close at hand. Only 15 km away as the crow flies was La Chaux-de-Fonds, centre of Swiss watchmaking for a couple of hundred years and home to some of its most prestigious brands.

To start with he assembled 'private-label' watches for other companies, concentrating particularly on the precision of his manufacture. Very soon, Michel Herbelin gained a reputation for not only the reliability and quality of his products but also for their aesthetic appeal. He longed to have his own brand, however, and in 1968 he launched his first collection under the name Michel Herbelin. These watches were extremely well received and during the course of the 1970s under the direction of his elder son Jean-Claude the brand began to acquire an international reputation. Today it has a presence in 80 countries throughout the five continents and more than 60% of the factory output goes abroad. The majority of sales are to the Middle East and Far East although the brand is well known in Europe. But it is in France that its main success lies. In France it is the leading independent watchmaker and has a 12% share of the under £1000 retail price bracket. Moreover, in each of the past two years it has achieved a 25% increase in sales turnover.

Michel Herbelin retired from active participation in the business in 1993 and the firm is now in the hands of his two sons, Jean-Claude and Pierre-Michel. It employs 80 workers who produce around 120,000 pieces annually of which 90% use quartz movements. The accent has always been on reliability and to this end the firm utilises ETA movements for 80% of its production. The majority are the popular Flatline movements with the Valjoux 7750 automatic chronograph movements in the more complicated models. Quartz movements from France Ebauches, France's largest supplier, are used in certain ladies' models such as the fashionable Chic collection.

The aesthetic appeal of the whole range is the responsibility of a design team under the personal direction of the managing director, Jean-Claude. With a careful eye on fashion trends the team creates two collections a year – rather like their couturier contemporaries in Paris – and works to a distinctive house style notable for its emphasis on softness of line and harmony of dimension enhanced by subtle refinement of detail. The 350 exclusive models of the collection fall into three main ranges. The classic range features traditional styles with simple uncluttered lines. The jewellery range consists of original and elegant designs. The sports range has a strong nautical flavour of ships' wheels and ropes and sea-blue dials and straps.

Jean-Claude's concern for quality ensures that every watch is individually finished by craftsmen and has to undergo 50 quality control procedures during its journey through the factory. Considerable attention is given to protection against moisture penetration, seals being fitted to the crystal, case back and even bezel. Water resistance to 30 metres is standard and verified individually by the routine compression tank immersion and droplet test. Gold plating is another operation where the accent on quality is paramount. Nineteen microns of anti-corrosion alloy are laid over the base metal, followed by five microns of 18ct gold plating which in turn is covered by a one micron layer of 23.7 gold for finish and resistance. The rhodium plating process is equally meticulous.

Michel Herbelin originally entered the UK market in the 1970s but failure to meet the targeted growth led the parent company to withdraw around 1990. It was relaunched under its present sales director, Peter Gauntlett, in 1993, since when it has achieved considerable acceptance by the trade, with some 80 stockists covering the country. Peter Gauntlett indicated that the company had found that a number of go-ahead independent jewellers look on Michel Herbelin as a splendid platform to help them launch their business onwards and upwards. The brand received an encouraging reception at a recent International Jewellery Fair at Earl's Court. Quite a few new accounts were opened and a number of repeat orders were taken.

Source: Edwards[10]

Question

What kind of marketing research do you think would be beneficial to a company such as Michel Herbelin in its attempt to get a strong foothold in the UK market?

CASE STUDY 15.2: CHINA

Before the outbreak of the Second World War, Shanghai was referred to as the 'Paris of the Orient' but after the Communist revolution of 1949 its significance diminished. Today, however, there is talk of it surpassing even Hong Kong in the not too distant future as a capital of enterprise. In the first four months of 1993 business-to-business output surged by more than 20%. American firms such as AT&T, Dupont, Merrill Lynch, Hilton and Sheraton have made their way to Shanghai, joining Volkswagen, Hitachi, Pilkington and many others.

It is on the east side of the city in the Pudong New Area that the business-to-business activity is most in evidence. During the past three years more than 1000 foreign firms have located there and investments have approached nearly $5bn. The Chinese government has chosen Shanghai to become the trade and banking centre not only of Asia but of the whole world by 2010, or at least to surpass Hong Kong as a financial giant. Commercial advertising in Shanghai is gaining in importance. In 1992 advertising appearing on city buses alone sold for more than 10 million yuan. There are some 16 million hoardings on Shanghai's public transport buses every workday.

In Shanghai today, chic young Chinese promenade on the Bund, the waterfront where European, US and Japanese colonial powers built one of the first commercial enclaves in China. Along Nanjing Road a million people pass every day. There the shops are full of foreign luxury items. New businesses in Shanghai are being established at the rate of five an hour. But this growth in the business-to-business and commercial sector has created cost of living rises of around 20% a year. Moreover, the bill for a couple of drinks in a luxury hotel can amount to more than half a month's income for a Chinese peasant.

Chinese women, like their Western counterparts, take a great deal of interest in their appearance and cosmetics are much valued. However, cultural factors have a very strong impact on their tastes, beliefs and attitudes. For example, in 1988 an exhibition in a northern city produced information that revealed that a cosmetic was required that would both moisturise the face and whiten it. To meet this requirement, a new product 'Xiafei Gold Brand Special Whitening Honey' was developed and introduced to the market, breaking the sales record with 20 million items sold in four years.

'Xiafei' and 'Olice' feature among the most well-known brands of cosmetics in China. Both products were introduced to the market by Cao Jianhua, who has just introduced yet another new product, 'Chaotian'. Xiafei's success is attributable to its middle price position and suitability for a wide range of people. Olice was formulated by adapting a product and adding a biological ingredient known as SOD, which was supposed to protect middle-aged women from signs of age. With the name 'Blue Noble', the packaging was given the image of elegance in order to satisfy the customers' desire for fashion and modernity and the product was an immediate success. 'Chaotian Beauty Treasure' was introduced in 1993 into the top ten department stores in Shanghai and this too has been an immediate success.

The brand names, supportive of the positioning strategy adopted, were considered very important to their success. The names sound bright and modern in Chinese – 'Xiafei' means 'the brightening of a colourful morning glow' and names such as 'Whitening Honey', 'Blue Noble' and 'Beauty Treasure' give the impression of safety, nutrition and grace associated with expected levels of product quality.

Source: Xiong[11]

Question

Discuss the kind of marketing research that might well be undertaken with regard to fast-moving consumer and fashion goods in China.

CASE STUDY 15.3: THE FUTURE LIES ABROAD

Over the past year, WPP has started up market research businesses in China, Indonesia and South Korea. We have set up a joint venture in healthcare marketing services in Japan. Earlier this month we bought the largest sales promotion and direct marketing agency in Taiwan.

These initiatives are a sign of our commitment to the so-called 'emerging markets', more aptly named 'fast-growing markets'.

Asia Pacific, Latin America, central and eastern Europe, Africa and the Middle East accounted for about one-fifth of WPP's business last year. This year they will account for almost a quarter, and in five years' time, I would be disappointed if the proportion were not at least one-third.

It seems to me that consumer-driven businesses in the West are preoccupied with the development, or lack of it, of our own markets and so miss out on opportunities elsewhere.

Unilever is a rare exception among multinationals in setting the objective that half of its business comes from Asia Pacific, Latin America, Africa and the Middle East within five years, instead of the one-third currently generated.

It also seems to me that most major multinational businesses are not pursuing global strategies in the way they would have us believe. The average US-based multinational still derives only 20% of its sales from outside the USA. Coca-Cola is the exception not the rule, with 80% of its business outside the USA.

Yet over the next ten years worldwide geographical expansion must be a strategic priority. Many consumer goods and services companies promise growth of 5, 10 or 15% in earnings per share or a similar measure. When the world's population is growing at less than 2% a year on average, this means finding new international opportunities.

As we have seen in the case of Vietnam, with a market of around 75m people, and with South Africa and its market of around 40m people, unprecedented foreign investment flows in as soon as political conditions allow. The same will be true for Burma's 45m people market and Cuba's 11m people. As a result of greater economic stability, more welcoming governments and harder working people, Asia Pacific still retains the lead in terms of interest among multinationals. Latin America is a close second. Within Asia Pacific, only China remains an enigma, with significant revenue growth but limited profitability.

Western businesses should not assume that these markets are simply awaiting their arrival.

Besides the dominant Japanese financial institutions, some of the leading Korean chaebols – conglomerates such as Samsung, Hyundai, LG and Daewoo – have grown as big as or bigger than IBM in a shorter time.

President Foods, one of the world's biggest food companies, based in Taiwan, and San Miguel, the Philippines-based brewing company, are both capable of developing global brands.

Latin America is also witnessing the development of significant global forces. In the media and communications sector, for example, the Azcarraga family, the Marinho family and John Malone of TCI have all collaborated with Rupert Murdoch on pan-regional projects or companies.

Against this background, if we in Western companies don't develop our businesses, products and services in the new, faster growing markets, we will ultimately suffer competitively as the growing forces invade our own backyards.

The author is chief executive of WPP Group.

Source: Sorrell[12] (reprinted with permission)

Question

Discuss the kind of marketing research that might be undertaken in the various markets mentioned in this case study. What kind of problems do you think researchers will encounter in each case?

CASE STUDY 15.4: EUROPEAN LAUNDRY STATISTICS

Detergents are big business, and the world market is dominated by a few very large companies. America's Procter & Gamble and Britain's Unilever are among the biggest. Economies of scale (notably in the construction costs of the huge drying towers used to convert liquid detergents into powders) mean that it is difficult for small firms to enter the powdered detergent market.

It may be a commonly held view that detergents differ very little from one to another, but the fact that differences in washday habits between countries are often very marked means that detergent manufacturers need to take account of these differences if they are to be successful in capturing their share of the global market.

Research conducted on behalf of American detergent manufacturers showed that European clothes-washing practices not only differ from American practices, but also differ between European countries. Procter & Gamble's Walter Lingle had said as early as 1955: 'Washing habits vary widely from country to country. We must tailor products to meet consumer demands in each nation. We cannot simply sell products with US formulas. They won't work – they won't be accepted.'

The main differences revealed by the research were as follows:

1 European washing machines are normally front loading, with a horizontally rotating drum. The typical US washing machine is top loading, with a central agitator.

2 European machines have a smaller water capacity, usually around 3–5 gallons rather than the 12–14 gallons used by American machines.

3 European machines have a 90- to 120-minute wash cycle, whereas US machines cycle in about 20–30 minutes.

4 Water temperatures are much higher in Europe, with 'boil washes' using water hotter than 60°C being commonplace. In some countries, the washing machines do not heat the water, so the powders need to work at lower temperatures and in still other countries hand-washing is common.

5 Americans use more synthetic fabrics than Europeans do and also tend to wash their clothes more often.

6 Although many Europeans do not own a washing machine, those who do tend to use more detergent than Americans use, so that the total detergent consumption in Europe is some 30% above US levels.

The problem for the detergent companies has several aspects. First, the front-loading machines made liquid detergents harder to use. Second, the much slower washing cycle of European machines meant that the washing powders or liquids needed to remain stable in the water for longer. Third, the higher washing temperature meant a different formulation for the product – or a programme of re-educating the consumers to wash at lower temperatures. Fourth, European clothing purchase trends would need to be monitored carefully to see whether there would be an increase in the wearing of synthetics.

Fifth, and in a more positive vein, the European market is clearly an attractive one for US detergent manufacturers since consumption levels are high. The manufacturers were interested in the possibilities of opening up a market for liquid detergents; liquids are much easier to manufacture and the companies were afraid that if they did not establish strong brands in the market fairly quickly, small manufacturers would be able to enter the market and establish a presence. This would create competition in an industry that had previously had very little competitive pressure, due to the high capital costs of establishing plants to manufacture powder detergents. In the meantime, the difficulty of using liquids in European machines was working to the advantage of the major manufacturers.

Although many Americans tend to regard Europe as being one place (in the same way as many Europeans ignore cultural differences between American states), the more sophisticated marketers within the detergent companies realised quickly that separate strategies would need to be worked out for each country and even for regions within each country. This meant that several separate research programmes would need to be carried out, both nationally and regionally. In some cases cultural similarities cross borders; for example, Bavarians often have more in common with Austrians than they do with their fellow countrymen in northern Germany.

Striking a balance between finding economies of scale in manufacture and the need to differentiate the product would prove difficult, but the detergent manufacturers did not see these difficulties as being insuperable. What they needed to do was to identify segments within the European market as a whole, ignoring borders, and develop products that would meet the needs of consumers within those segments.

(Case contributed by Jim Blythe)

Questions

1 What are the main difficulties in designing a research programme for the European detergent market?

2 How would you research the acceptability of low-temperature detergents?

3 What problems might arise when collecting secondary data within Europe?

4 The European market can be segmented by methods other than nationality; in other words, segments exist that cut across national borders. How might you go about identifying thes000e segments?

5 What methods might be available for monitoring pan-European fashion-buying trends?

CASE STUDY 15.5: DELHI DELIGHTS

In Delhi there are many colourful markets that carry a vast and exciting range of handicrafts to attract the money of visitors and tourists in particular. There are also the 'state emporia', run by the government, that have goods at fixed and reasonable prices, and for the well off there are shopping arcades at larger hotels that often have quite exclusive boutiques. However, it is the street stalls and bazaars that reflect the colour of local life and where the bargaining for goods takes place. The shopping experience in Delhi offers a variety of outlets, goods and markets. Shops, bazaars, smart boutiques and department stores offer a variety of goods and produce ranging from food and handicrafts to designer clothes and electronic items. At market locations, stalls sell newspapers, magazines, music cassettes and best-selling books. There are also a large number of book and music shops and some stock a wide variety of books by international publishing houses.

Opening hours for shopping are usually from 10.00 a.m. to 7.30 p.m., although the smaller markets keep longer hours and the government-run emporia close an hour earlier. Shopping centres in the New Delhi area are closed on Sundays but in some other areas the closing days are Monday or Tuesday. Different parts of the city have their own weekly holiday, too.

The larger stores accept international credit cards such as VISA, American Express and Diners and usually display signs prominently within the shop. Bargaining is commonplace when shopping in India and, at the smaller markets, prices are quoted by stallholders on the expectation that customers will haggle. Local shoppers may indulge in long and often acrimonious discussions with shopkeepers about price and quality. The trend, however, seems to be that more retail outlets are labelling their wares with clearly indicated prices.

Questions

1 Indicate the kind of research in consumer behaviour that you feel would be beneficial to an organisation interested in marketing each of the following products:
   (a) tables and chairs
   (b) cookers, refrigerators and washing machines
   (c) cars
   (d) package tours of Europe and America
   (e) wristwatches
   (f) textbooks
   (g) mobile phones.

2 Indicate how you would research the growth in the use of credit cards and the pricing of retail goods in general.

3 How would you research the prime mechanisms used by retailers in the bazaars and the markets to market their goods?

REFERENCES AND NOTES

1 Ricks, D A, Fu, Y C and Arpan, S (1974) *International Business Blunders*, Columbus, OH: Grid.

2 Goodyear, M (1996) The world shrinks, maybe, but there's still the need to travel, *Research Plus*, May, 12.

3 Tyrrell, B (1994) Eastern promise is worth all the pain of red tape, *Marketing*, 3 February, 5.

4 Korents, G (1996) China's other consumers, *Business Week*, 13 May, 11.

5 Branthwaite, A and Bruggemann, J (1996) Why we won't keep taking pills, *Research Plus*, April, 8–9.

6 Bunn, S (1996) Now that India's got GATT, a massive market beckons, *Research Plus*, April, 10–11.

7   Bartonova, M (1996) The markets are emerging – and research is hard on their heels, *Research Plus*, January, 4–5.

8   Choudry, Y A (1986) Pitfalls of international marketing research: are you speaking French like a Spanish cow? *ABER*, 17(4), Winter, 18–28.

9   Ricks, D A, Fu, Y C and Arpan, S (1974) *International Business Blunders*, Columbus, OH: Grid.

10 Edwards, F (1995) The French connection, *International Wrist Watch*, 31, 46–48.

11 Xiong, R (1994) Unpublished MBA dissertation, Department of Management, Keele University, September.

12 Sorrell, M (1997) The future lies abroad, *Financial Times*, 30 June.

FURTHER READING

Brock, S E (1989) Marketing research in Asia: problems, opportunities and lessons, *Marketing Research*, September, 47.

Cateora, P R (1993) *International Marketing* (8th edn), Homewood, IL: Irwin, Chapter 11.

Craig, C S and Douglas, S P (2001) Conducting international marketing research in the twenty-first century, *International Marketing Review*, 18(1), 80–90.

Douglas, S P and Craig, C S (1983) *International Marketing Research*, Upper Saddle River, NJ: Prentice-Hall.

Greenbaum, T L (1996) Understanding focus group research abroad, *Marketing News*, 30(12), June, 3.

Hart, S J, Webb, J R and Jones, M V (1996) Export marketing research and the effect of export experience in industrial SMEs, *International Marketing Review*, 11(6), 4–23.

Johansson, J K and Nonaka, J (1987) Market research the Japanese way, *Harvard Business Review*, May–June, 16–22.

Keillor, B, Owens, D and Pettijohn, C (2001) A cross-cultural/cross-national study of influencing factors and socially desirable response bias, *International Journal of Market Research*, 43(1), 63–84.

Kinsey, J (1988) *Marketing in Developing Countries*, London: Macmillan, Chapter 4.

Malhotra, N K, Agarwal, J and Peterson, M (1996) Cross-cultural marketing research: methodological issues and guidelines, *International Marketing Review*, 13(5), 7–43.

Mattson, J (1990) Measuring inherent product values, *European Journal of Marketing*, 24(9), 25–39.

McKie, A (1996), International research in a relative world, *Journal of the Market Research Society*, 38(1), 7–12.

Munson, J and McIntery, S (1979) Developing practical procedures for measurement of personal values in cross-cultural marketing, *Journal of Marketing Research*, 16.

Pawle, J (1999), Mining the international consumer, *Journal of the Market Research Society*, 41(1), 19–32.

16 Marketing decision-support system

Objectives

After reading this chapter, you should be able to:

- appreciate the nature of marketing decision-support mechanisms

- appreciate, in particular, the use of traditional management science/operational research tools in marketing.

Keywords

assignment model	marketing intelligence
decision-support mechanism	mathematical models
decision trees	Markov analysis
electronic data interchange (EDI)	moving average
expert systems	network models
exponential smoothing	new product
forecasting	queuing theory models
game theory	simulation
inventory models	statistical demand analysis
linear programming	time series analysis
market demand	transportation model

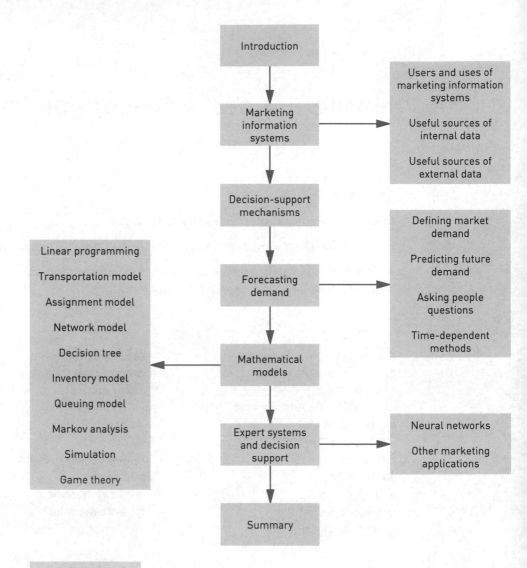

Plan of Chapter 16

INTRODUCTION

This chapter presents the main components of a marketing information system. It covers both objective and subjective approaches to market measurement and **forecasting** and the use of traditional management science/operational research tools in marketing decisions.

First, we take a systematic look at the overall concept of a marketing information system and then explore its various components in more detail. Attention is directed to methods of market measurement and forecasting and then to examining the range of management science and operational research techniques that can be used to help improve our marketing decisions. Finally, we look at the possible uses for **expert systems** as part of the **decision-support mechanism**.

MARKETING INFORMATION SYSTEMS

Marketing information systems exist to help marketing management make good decisions. When the marketing environment is undergoing rapid change, initiative in decision making is necessary. An efficient marketing information system records the relevant changes taking place in the marketplace and prevents management suffering from an overload of redundant information.

A marketing information system supports marketing decisions by facilitating interlinkage and integration between functional departments of the business. Customer perceptions of new products, for example, may be collected by the salesforce and disseminated to product development groups by way of the system. The marketing information system enhances the organisation's ability to respond to a dynamic business environment. For example, as a result of information provided through a link with retail scanners, price changes can be immediately initiated in response to the actions of competitors. A well-designed information system enables the efficient handling, organisation and storage of data and leads to improvements in customer service through increased responsiveness to customer needs (see Figure 16.1).

A marketing information system might comprise the following subsystems:[1]

- An internal reporting system containing data on such things as sales, inventories, cash flows and accounts receivable, all of which can be used to measure current activity and performance.

- A **marketing intelligence** system that collects everyday information about developments in the external environment and, in particular, problems and opportunities.

- A marketing research system that gathers, evaluates and reports information on a specific environmental situation facing a company and provides sufficient information to minimise guesswork.

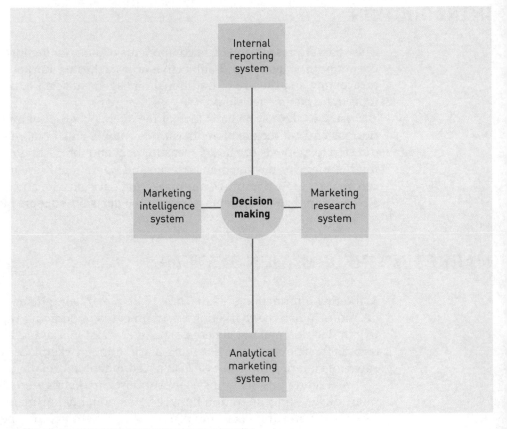

FIGURE 16.1 Marketing information system

- An analytical marketing system that is able to undertake the complex analysis of business problems.

The *analytical marketing system* consists of a set of statistical tools and **mathematical models**. We have already looked at the statistical tools in earlier chapters. The mathematical models help executives to generate better marketing decisions. These tools and models comprise the *decision-support* mechanisms.

Information on competitors' activities and on customers' wants and needs can be obtained from salespersons' reports. These can be entered into the information system in electronic form and this calls for the design of electronic forms which can easily be completed by sales staff. Sales reports tend to be filled in at home at weekends or in hotel bedrooms during the working week. A portable laptop computer directly connected by a modem to the firm's mainframe computer provides an attractive solution to the problem. The communication link is also two way. Information that the company has on the information system can be fed to sales staff in the field. This includes information that is both internal and external to the firm. While internal data are collected as a matter of course as business proceeds, data on the environment and competitive activity can often be bought from consultants and marketing research agencies, which is often already in an electronic form (see Chapter 3 on secondary data).

It is better to store data in a disaggregated form in the database. This allows anyone to manipulate and analyse the data to suit their own particular purposes. Any summary statistical analyses can be kept in a separate file within the database. Having a computer-based information system means that information in the form of reports can quickly be made available to management.

SNAP is a useful computer program, which incorporates questionnaire design, storage of data based on surveys using the questionnaire and data analysis (Figure 16.2). The features of the program are shown in the box overleaf.

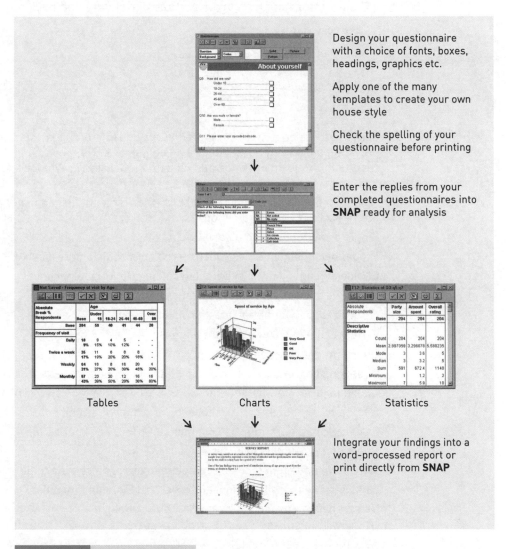

Design your questionnaire with a choice of fonts, boxes, headings, graphics etc.

Apply one of the many templates to create your own house style

Check the spelling of your questionnaire before printing

Enter the replies from your completed questionnaires into **SNAP** ready for analysis

Tables   Charts   Statistics

Integrate your findings into a word-processed report or print directly from **SNAP**

FIGURE 16.2	How SNAP works

Source: SNAP software, Mercator Research Group Ltd

Users and uses of marketing information systems

Sales management is one of the prime users of the marketing information system. The information system can help with the effective allocation of tasks to the salesforce. It also facilitates the assessment of the performance of sales. Sales staff, too, benefit from being able to access the system easily and to get support and information about such things as:

- quantity of the product on hand
- prices and price discounts
- status information on invoices, time of delivery and back orders
- delivery dates
- complete product specifications.

SNAP

SNAP Professional is an integrated survey design and analysis software program providing on-screen questionnaire design, data entry, analysis and presentation of results in the form of tables and charts. It operates in Windows 95, NT, 2000, ME and XP environments.

Questionnaire Design Choice of WYSIWYG on-screen questionnaire design or alternative survey variable definition.

Single or multiple column page layout.

Predefined question styles which are customisable and re-usable.

Choice of Single, Multiple, Date, Literal and Quantity responses.

Up to 250 answer choices per question.

No limit to the number of questions per survey.

Variety of question numbering schemes.

Question renumbering feature.

Questionnaire data view shows completed respondent questionnaires.

Questionnaire analysis view shows counts or percentage survey results.

Bitmap backgrounds can be shown behind questions and notes.

Each code of a question has an optional 'GoTo Q . . .' routing tag.

Questionnaire editing includes a spell-checker.

Style Templates that enable a complete questionnaire style to be saved or loaded.

Links seamlessly with optional Internet and Scanning modules.

Use predefined questions from SNAP surveyPaks.

Use other questions from your own surveys.

Data Entry Up to 100,000 respondents per survey.

Four modes of data entry – Questionnaire, Interview, Prompted and Fast.

Customisable data verification in all modes.

Automatic routing following logic set up through questions.

Configuration of non-response strategy.

Changes may be made to questions even after data entry has begun.

Filtering to select cases for browsing and/or printing reports.

Search and replace feature for data cleaning. Import and export data to/from other SNAP surveys, spreadsheets, databases and other survey software.

Data entry spell-checker.

General Analysis features (applies to both Tabular and Graphical Analysis).

Analyses based on respondents or responses, with or without missing and 'not asked' results.

Unlimited level of filters to tabulate subsets of data.

Weighting capabilities enable weighting by other questions, factors or to targets.

Question responses may be dynamically split, combined and regrouped to construct multi-way analyses. Specification of derived variables to group quantity, date and literal response variables or to combine categories from any number of other single and multiple response variables.

Batch operation to generate large volume reporting in a 'macro' style.

Tables and charts can be saved for future quick reference.

Optional Internet module generates tables for publication on the WWW.

Tabular Analysis Choice of cross-tabulations, frequency tables, grid tables and holecounts.

Predefined table presentation styles which are customisable and re-usable.

Selection of row, column, total per cents, index and expected values, suppress zeros and order rows.

Calculation of score statistics (mean, standard error and confidence) on cross-tabulations and grid tables.

Descriptive statistics: count, sum, mean, mode, median, minimum, maximum, range, standard deviation, variance, standard error, skewness and kurtosis.

Additional statistics on cross-tabulations: Chi square, Cramers V, Phi coefficient, Contingency coefficient. Tables of means, with optional T-test significance results.

Graphical Analysis Choice of 2D and 3D bar, pie, line, area, step, scatter, radar, hi-lo and donut charts. Predefined chart presentation styles which are customisable and re-usable.

Optional inclusion of titles, footnotes, bar and sector labels, values and percentages, coloured backgrounds. Creation of pictograph bar charts using BMP and WMF image files.

Perspective rotation and modification of light source location and intensity on 3D charts.

Source: Mercator Systems[2]

Useful sources of internal data

The information system can help to produce sales forecasts and marketing budgets that form the basis of sales strategies and quotas. The sales forecasts facilitate the planning and control of manufacturing, distribution, advertising and promotion activities (see Figures 16.3–16.5).

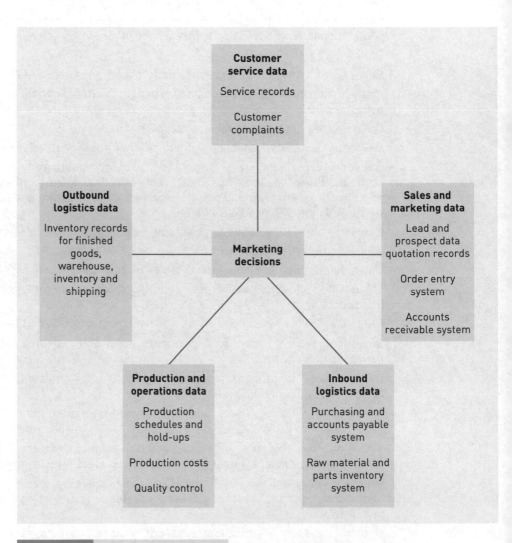

FIGURE 16.3   Sources of internal data

Salesforce performance report

- calls made by sales staff
- calls to sales ratios
- contribution margin on products sold

Customer service report

- purchasing trends
- lost customers
- complaints

Sales performance report

- analysis of total sales volume and sales profitability by:
  1 product line
  2 salesperson
  3 territory
  4 customer groups
  5 comparison with company goals

Promotion report

- media guides for selecting among different media

FIGURE 16.4   Marketing information system reports

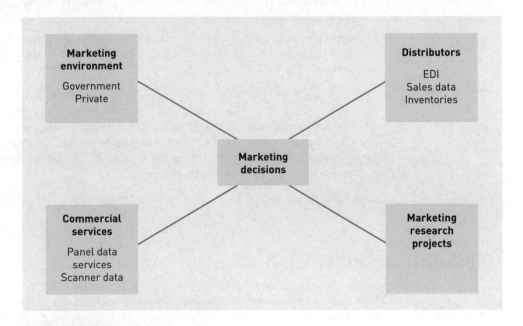

FIGURE 16.5   Sources of external data

ELECTRONIC DATA INTERCHANGE

Electronic data interchange (EDI) improves the process of distribution for both producers and retailers. With the aid of technology a constant communication link is forged between manufacturers and retailers, making the process of supply much more efficient and cost-effective. It means that instead of going through the tiresome and time-consuming process of assessing demand, making an order and waiting for it to be processed, retailers can allow sales information provided by EPOS to be instantly transmitted to suppliers through EDI. This gives the supplier the opportunity to respond immediately to demand, despatching stock as and when required by the retailer.

EDI confers several potential improvements on the process of distribution:

- EDI enables a supplier to use 'real-time' processing as opposed to batch processing. As a result, an order can be despatched when the need is identified, rather than at a regular processing point (usually, the end of the day).

- The system can improve customer service, since goods will be in stock when customers require them.

- EDI reduces operating expenses, since orders are handled more efficiently and more rapidly as there are fewer repetitions involved. Once data is input at the point of sale (via EPOS), there is no need for a re-entry at the supplier end and this reduces costs.

- Where a process is a long one, there is more chance of error. In the case of EDI, there is the need for only one point of data entry and the risk of error is substantially reduced.

EDI can help manufacturers gain a competitive advantage in the market. First, it enables them to gain access to valuable information held by retailers about consumer tastes and behaviour. This in turn helps manufacturers regain some contact with the ultimate consumer – contact that has been lost as a result of growing retailer power. Second, manufacturers are able to use their technical resources as an incentive to attract retailers to stock their brand.

Source: Samways and Whittcome[3]

DECISION-SUPPORT MECHANISMS

Marketing decision-support mechanisms are a collection of tools and techniques, with supporting software and hardware. With it, an organisation gathers and interprets relevant information from business and the environment and turns it into a basis for marketing action. A marketing decision-support system is a computer-based system that helps decision makers deal with problems through direct interaction with databases and software. A decision-support system's computer software allows managers to combine and restructure databases, diagnose relationships, discover patterns, estimate variables, and otherwise analyse the various databases.

Companies can use decision-support systems to provide customer relationship management (CRM). A CRM system might bring together many pieces of information about customers, sales, marketing effectiveness, responsiveness and market trends and describe customer relationships well enough to enable management, salespeople and people providing customer service to know what other products a customer has purchased, and so forth.

Organisations can create their own databases relating to customers and their wants, needs, orders supplied etc. with the aid of off-the-shelf software packages. This kind of customer information will be obtained from the orders placed and enquiries made. Technological developments now allow the combination of cookies or user log-ins and server logging software to enable tracking and recording of a customer's progress through a website, thereby showing interests that would otherwise have gone unnoticed.

Data warehousing involves a centrally stored source of data that have been extracted from various organisational databases and standardised and integrated for use throughout an organisation. They contain a wide variety of data that present a coherent picture of business conditions at a single point in time. Data mining is a class of database applications that look for hidden patterns in a group of data.

The remainder of this chapter examines the various decision-support mechanisms that can be used. The main areas covered are:

1 forecasting tools

2 mathematical models

3 expert systems

4 customer databases.

FORECASTING DEMAND

Forecasting amounts to estimating some future event that is outside the control of the organisation and that provides a basis for managerial planning. The estimates produced often form the basis of production planning, salesforce planning, setting advertising appropriations, estimating cash flow and assessing the need for innovation. Marketing plans are only useful if the size of current and future markets is carefully measured and estimated. Such information is a useful starting point from which to determine how resources should be allocated among markets and products or services.

Defining market demand

Market demand can be measured at several different levels:

- product levels: product item sales, product form sales, product line sales, company sales, industry sales, national sales

- space levels: sales to individual customers, sales by territory, area, country or world sales

- time levels: short-, medium-, long-range sales.

There are many different ways of describing a market. The current number of users of a product or service and the sales volume they generate constitutes the 'penetrated market'. Secondary data sources may provide information on this or it may be necessary to establish this figure by sample survey. This measure does not take account of those people who have an interest in buying the product or service, but who currently do not buy the product. The latter are important, since in looking at future demand they provide a measure of the 'potential market'. A further stipulation is that customers must be able to afford the product or service. In assessing the 'potential market' this too must be established and will lead to a redefinition of the market size. The ability to use a product or service affects the size of the market. If it is not possible to use a product, this will obviously restrict the market size and taking this into account will define the 'available market'. Finally, a firm has only a limited amount of resources at its disposal, so it chooses only certain market segments where it feels it has the capacity to compete effectively and where the market size is sufficiently attractive. This becomes the 'served' or the 'target market'.

Predicting future demand

The following considerations should be borne in mind when choosing the most appropriate forecasting technique:

- *Time horizon*: the technique must be suitable for use over the period of time required.

- *Technical sophistication*: the people doing the forecasting must be comfortable with the technique used and must have the knowledge to understand its use and limitations.

- *Cost*: greater accuracy in forecasting may only be possible at extra cost; we have to assess whether the extra cost of accuracy is worthwhile.

- *The data that can be used*: the extensiveness, currency, accuracy and representativeness of the availability must be assessed before choosing a technique.

Firms can adopt a variety of approaches to sales forecasting but the basic approach is to:

1 Make an environmental forecast about inflation, employment, interest rates, consumer spending and saving, business investment.

2 Make a forecast of sales and profits to be earned by the industry, using the data in 1 together with other information that links industry figures to environmental trends.

3 Make a company sales forecast, using the data in 2 and assuming a given market share.

Often, however, firms may not know the industry sales level. In such cases, sales forecasts are made at the company level at stage 2 and stage 3 is not used.

When forecasting the sales for established products, two approaches are possible, both of which have a number of variants. First, there are methods that rely on asking people questions and, second, there are methods that involve the statistical or mathematical analysis of historical data.

Asking people questions

Surveys of buyers' intentions

Some market research organisations, and even businesses themselves, conduct periodic surveys of buying intentions. Using the results produced by regular sample surveys, predictions of the likely demand for various items or activities can then be made. This method can be applied effectively by producers of many business products and services, particularly industrial plant, machinery and supplies.

Composite of salesforce opinion

The sales team makes contact with the distributors and/or customers in the marketplace and is well positioned to provide estimates on potential sales demand. When making use of estimates produced by the salesforce, account needs to be taken of any bias that may exist. The salesforce may be biased either in the direction of pessimism or of optimism. We also have to remember that the salesforce may not really appreciate the larger economic factors that may influence sales. However, providing we can identify the sources of bias and compensate for them in interpreting predictions, it is possible to make use of these estimates.

Expert opinion

Expert opinion is another method of forecasting. Experts may include dealers, distributors, suppliers, marketing consultants and even trade associations. A key factor that influences patterns of sales in a country is the state of the economy. Various economic experts can provide their opinions and each government produces its own economic forecast.

Analysing past data

Firms tend to base their forecasts on what they have achieved in the past. This approach to forecasting offers few opportunities for mistakes except where there are large variations in sales from one year to the next. There are two basic methods of forecasting, each of which has a number of versions, and these are outlined below.

Time-dependent methods

Classical time series analysis

The first sets of methods are those based on **time series analysis**, which assumes that sales simply vary as a function of time. The time effects are divided into:

- cycle – fluctuations every few years, for example, the effect of trade cycles as various major economies in the world are hit by booms and slumps
- trend – a general upward, downward or static (no trend) pattern, for example, the upward trend of sales of video recorders during the growth phase of the life cycle
- seasonal – systematic variations at certain times of the year, for example, additional sales of swimsuits in the summer months
- erratic – unpredictable or random variations, for example, demand interrupted by an industry-wide strike.

Erratic variation is taken into account when making forecasts, but we do not attempt to predict it exactly. We merely express it as the error we attach to the sales forecast. This method is most suitable for forecasting the sales of products where the unexplained variation is small.

The trend component results from developments in a population, the formation of capital and developments in technology. It is evidenced by a general upward or downward shift in the pattern of sales. If there is no such pattern, there is assumed to be no trend.

The cycle depicts the wavelike flow of sales over a number of years and is most useful when examining data for use in intermediate range forecasts (3–7 years). Traditionally, the cycle represents swings in economic activity.

The seasonal component refers to recurrent sales patterns that may exist within the period of a single year. This will reflect things such as weather factors, holidays and seasonal buying habits.

Erratic variation comprises such things as strikes, fashions and other unforeseen circumstances. These factors are unpredictable and need to be removed from past data in order to inspect the other three elements. Time series analysis consists of decomposing the original sales data into their trend, cyclical, seasonal and erratic components. The series is then recombined to produce a sales forecast.

EXAMPLE

Imagine that Table 16.1 represents quarterly data on shipments of a particular commodity.

More than one way to forecast time series data such as these exist. One method is to use dummy variables and multiple regression analysis. Multiple regression is

TABLE 16.1   Quarterly data on commodity shipments

Period	Year	Sales (tonnes)
1	1993	436
2		291
3		357
4		529
5	1994	386
6		304
7		333
8		471
9	1995	383
10		336
11		365
12		539

a statistical tool that can be applied to past data to discover the most important factors influencing sales and their relative influence. The dummy variables in this particular case represent the factors influencing sales. The approach consists of creating a variable for each of the four quarters and the following equation is then estimated by multiple linear regression analysis (see Table 16.2):

$$\text{Sales} = B_0 + B_1 \text{ Time} + B_2 \text{ Winter} + B_3 \text{ Spring} + B_4 \text{ Summer}$$

TABLE 16.2   Multiple linear regression analysis

Time	Sales	Winter	Spring	Summer	Autumn
1	436	1	0	0	0
2	291	0	1	0	0
3	357	0	0	1	0
4	529	0	0	0	1
5	386	1	0	0	0
6	304	0	1	0	0
7	333	0	0	1	0
8	471	0	0	0	1
9	383	1	0	0	0
10	336	0	1	0	0
11	365	0	0	1	0
12	539	0	0	0	1

One of the dummy variables has to be left out so that the regression can be solved by computer: in this case 'Autumn' is omitted. The values obtained are:

$$B_0 = 510.5 \quad B_1 = 0.3125 \quad B_2 = -110.396 \quad B_3 = -202.042 \quad B_4 = -161.021$$

Substituting values into the equation for subsequent periods enables a forecast of sales to be made. For example:

Period 13 forecast sales $= 510.5 + 0.3125 \times 13 - 110.396 \times 1 = 404$

Moving average

Moving average is one of the simplest methods. Trend, seasonal or cyclical patterns are not usually included in it, although in the more advanced methods it is possible to do so.

The average demand is the arithmetic mean of demand from a number (N) of past periods:

$$A_t = [D_1 + D_2 + \ldots + D_{t-(N+1)}]/N$$

The forecast demand for period t + 1 is a projection of the past average demand. The number of periods included in the average can be increased to give more importance to past demand (referred to as *damping*). In order to finetune the sensitivity of the moving average to certain periods, a weighting factor W_t can be applied to those periods:

$$F_{t+1} = A_t = W_1 D_1 + W_2 D_2 + \ldots + W_N D_{t-(N+1)}$$

where $W_1 + W_2 + \ldots + W_N = 1$

Exponential smoothing

Many businesses produce many hundreds or thousands of products. Notable examples are the firms operating in the pharmaceutical industry. For such firms, a simple forecasting technique is required which requires the minimum of data. In its simplest form **exponential smoothing** requires only three pieces of information:

1 the period's actual sales Q_t

2 the current period's smoothed sales q_t

3 a smoothing parameter a, a value between 0 and 1.

The sales forecast for the next period is given by the formula:

$$q_{t+1} + 1 = aQ_t + (1 - a)q_t$$

Forecasts of this kind are handled by computer. Using an iterative procedure (trial and error), the computer program can regularly determine that value of 'a' which gives the most satisfactory results in making forecasts. The value is the one that gives the best fit to past sales. Once the system has been set up, all we have to do is to add new sales figures to the database as and when they occur. There are a number of more sophisticated variants on this approach, such as double exponential smoothing and exponential smoothing incorporating seasonal and trend components.

Statistical demand analysis

So far, the statistical or mathematical approaches we have considered treat the factors that seem to influence sales as regularly reoccurring phenomena. The difficulty with this approach is that some patterns do not reappear at regular intervals. For example, while there are economic booms and slumps from time to time, their patterns are not so precise as to enable accurate forecasts to be made.

Statistical demand analysis attempts to identify the source of all influences on demand so that more accurate forecasts can be made. The basic statistical method to take account of such factors is multiple regression analysis. Experience indicates that the factors most commonly considered are price, income, population, and marketing promotion.

The first stage in a regression analysis is to build a causal model in which we try to explain sales in terms of a number of independent variables. For example, we might conjecture that industry sales of umbrellas are related to their relative price (P), personal disposable income (I), relative advertising expenditure (A) and the absolute level of rainfall (R). We would express this relationship in the form of an equation:

$$S = a_0 + b_0 P + b_1 I + b_2 A + b_3 R$$

We need to estimate the parameters for a_0, b_1 to b_3 and apply them to quantifications of P, I, A and R for the period of the forecast.

In principle, demand equations of this variety are acquired by fitting the best equations to historical or cross-sectional data. The coefficients of the equation are estimated according to what is called the 'least squares criterion', according to which the best equation is the one that minimises a measure of the error between the actual and the predicted observations. The better the fit, the more useful will be the equation for forecasting purposes.

Although this is a popular technique, it needs to be used with care. There must always be an adequate number of observations: in making annual forecasts, 10–15 years of data are not unreasonable where there are four independent variables. Independent variables can sometimes turn out to influence each other and thus are not independent at all. For example, relative price and relative advertising expenditure may well influence each other, since advertising costs can be reflected in the selling price. There are also other pitfalls to be watched for.

Forecasting sales of new products

To forecast sales of a **new product** we need some initial sales figures with which to work. Given that early sales data are available, it is usually possible, by using one or other of a variety of mathematical models or 'curve-fitting routines' to make some prediction for sales over a specified time period. Alternatively, it may be possible to look at sales histories of similar new products and make predictions by analogy. There are many examples of these models (see, for instance, Kotler and Lilien[4]).

EXAMPLE

The epidemic model of initial sales is a useful tool to have to hand when trying to make a sales prediction for certain kinds of new products. The model developed by Bass,[5] which he specifically tested out on a range of consumer-durable goods, is illustrative:

$$p_t = p + q/M(Y_t)$$

where p_t = probability of purchase given that no previous purchase was made
Y_t = total number who have tried the product
M = total number of potential buyers (saturation level)
q = parameter reflecting the rate of diffusion of the model
p = initial probability of first-time purchase

The model can be estimated by running a regression of current versus past sales (Table 16.3):

$$Sales_t = c_0 + c_1 Y_t + c_2 Y_t^2$$

Analysis of the sales in Table 16.3 gives the forecasting model:

$$Sales_t = 2.06 + 1.016 Y_t - 0.00464 Y_t^2$$

TABLE 16.3   Current versus past sales

Year	$Sales_t$ '000	Y_t '000	Y_t^2 '000
1	1	0	0
2	2	1	1
3	4	3	9
4	10	7	49
5	20	17	289
6	36	37	1,369
7	48	73	5,329
8	58	121	14,641

Forecasting sales of new products in retail outlets

Large retail chains often add new lines to their stock. Most of these retailers have benchmarks against which to judge whether a product is likely to be successful or not. A common practice is to offer the product for sale for a limited period in one of its shops. If the product fails to achieve level of sales within the specified period, it is withdrawn and is not put on sale in other outlets.

APPLICATIONS FOR MATHEMATICAL MODELS IN THE MARKETING DECISION-SUPPORT SYSTEM

Mathematical models are those referred to in the operations research literature. The main models are:

1 Linear programming

2 Transportation model

3 Assignment model

4 Network model

5 Decision tree

6 Inventory model

7 Queuing theory model

8 Markov analysis

9 Simulation

10 Game theory

The various models or techniques have been applied in a wide variety of settings and can help to find solutions to problems in many different areas of marketing. In the following sections, examples are shown (usually omitting calculations) of how these techniques may be applied to marketing problems.

Linear programming

Linear programming helps to determine how to minimise costs or maximise profits (or minimise/maximise some other factors) subject to a set of constraints.

EXAMPLE

A marketing executive has a budget of £5000 and wants to maximise the 'reach' of magazine advertisements. The reach of magazine 1 is 8000 potential customers and that of magazine 2 is 5000 potential customers. The number of potential customers with incomes of less than £10,000 per annum is 1000 and 400, respectively, per column inch advertising seen in each magazine. The cost of an advertisement in magazine 1 is £600 per column inch and £1000 per column inch in the case of 2. The manager would like to reach at most 4500 potential customers whose incomes are less than £10,000 per annum. How many column inches should be bought in each of the magazines in order to maximise profits?

This problem is expressed as follows:

$$\text{Objective: maximise } Z = 8000\,X1 + 5000\,X2$$
$$\text{subject to } X1, X2 \geq 0 \text{ (negative amounts not allowed)}$$
$$\text{and } £600\,X1 + £1000\,X2 \leq £5000 \text{ (budget constraint)}$$
$$\text{and } 1000\,X1 + 400\,X2 \leq 4500 \text{ (reach constraint)}$$

Applying linear programming gives the answer:

3.29 column inches in magazine 1
3.03 column inches in magazine 2
and the number of readers reached is 41,470.

Transportation model

The **transportation model** may be considered a special case of the linear programming model. A special algorithm is developed to solve such problems. Essentially, the idea is to allocate the flow of objects to sources and destinations in such a way as to minimise costs or maximise profits (or some other measure relating to minimisation/maximisation).

EXAMPLE

A company ships goods from three factories to three distribution outlets. The supply capacities of the factories, the demand requirements of the three outlets and the shipping costs (£/tonne) are shown in Table 16.4.

TABLE 16.4 Transportation model

From factory	To distribution outlet			
	1	2	3	Supply (tonnes)
1	12	14	7	160
2	13	6	18	40
3	7	4	5	90
Demand (tonnes)	140	50	100	290

How should supply be equated with demand in order to minimise costs? The solution suggested is shown in Table 16.5.

TABLE 16.5	Transportation model: solution			
		1	2	3	Total
Supply plant	1	60.00	0.00	100.00	160.00
	2	0.00	40.00	0.00	40.00
	3	80.00	10.00	0.00	90.00
Demand		140.00	50.00	100.00	290.00

The solution value = £2260 (cost minimised).

Assignment model

The **assignment model** helps to find the minimum or maximum payoff associated with matching one set of items to a second set. The items may be people, projects, jobs, contracts or territories. For example, we might be concerned with assigning people to jobs, assigning various contracts to people making bids or assigning sales people to territories. An assignment problem is one where only one from a set of items is assigned to only one from a set of other items.

EXAMPLE

This problem involves getting a marketing research project completed in the shortest possible time. A marketing research department has received a request to carry out a study of the market for eight different products. The department manager asks individual members of the department to estimate how long (in days) it would take each of them to complete each of the projects (one for each product). The estimates shown in Table 16.6 were provided.

Entries marked 'M' signify that the person would not have the skills or experience to carry out that particular study.

| TABLE 16.6 | Assignment model |

	Product							
	1	2	3	4	5	6	7	8
John	4	3	4	3	6	3	M	7
Paul	5	4	3	2	5	4	6	7
Bill	3	M	5	4	4	5	7	6
Sam	4	6	6	3	3	2	8	6
Helen	2	7	7	M	5	3	5	7
Mary	4	4	3	6	4	6	6	8
Winifred	5	5	4	5	M	5	5	8
Alice	4	5	5	4	4	M	3	7
Arthur	3	4	M	3	5	3	7	6
Mark	6	3	4	4	6	2	7	4

The objective is to accomplish the task in the shortest possible time. In this case, the firm wants to have only one individual per project since experience indicates that this is usually the quickest way to get things done. In the past the firm has conducted this exercise by assigning tasks according to the shortest available time indicated in each person's product-study column, provided they have not already been previously allocated to one of the other tasks. Thus the assignment made, based on such an heuristic, might be as shown in Table 16.7.

| TABLE 16.7 | Assignment: solution 1 |

Product study	Name	Time
1	Helen	2
2	John	3
3	Mary	3
4	Paul	2
5	Sam	3
6	Mark	2
7	Alice	3
8	Bill	6

This would give a completion time of 24 days. Using the assignment model and minimising the amount of time, the solution indicates that the tasks *can in fact be completed in 23 days* with a different assignment of personnel (Table 16.8).

TABLE 16.8 Assignment: solution 2

Product study	Name	Time
1	Helen	2
2	John	3
3	Mary	3
4	Paul	2
5	Sam	3
6	Arthur	3
7	Alice	3
8	Mark	4
		= 23 days

Network model

There are a variety of different **network models**, including critical path and PERT models. Here we consider a simple type of network.

EXAMPLE

A particular market research study includes ten activities, which have durations and precedences as shown in Table 16.9.

TABLE 16.9 Network model

Activity	Duration (days)	Immediately preceding activities
A		1
B	4	A
C	5	A
D	6	A
E	2	B
F	1	B
G	7	E
H	4	F
I	3	G, H
J	5	G, H, C and D
K	6	D
L	2	I, J and K

Note: Activities D, G and H must be completed before the commencement of J.

The objective is to determine the minimum time that the project would take to complete. This is calculated to be:

A B E G I L 1 + 4 + 2 + 7 + 3 + 2 = 19 days

The minimum time of 19 is on the *critical* path. In order to shorten the time to complete the entire project, an element on this route or *path* has to be shortened. It would be no use shortening C, D or K, for instance (see Figure 16.6).

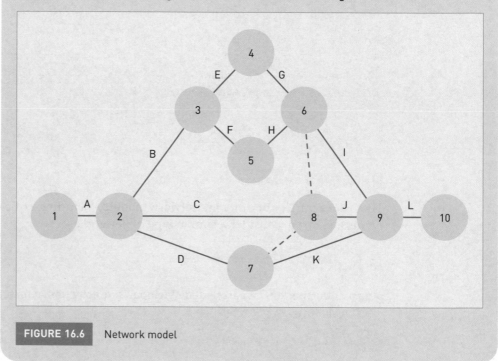

| FIGURE 16.6 | Network model |

Decision tree

Decision trees evaluate the expected payoff of different alternatives. The following example is a simple one and much more complex ones can be built. The expected payoff of the various alternatives are calculated and evaluated.

EXAMPLE

A marketing manager is deciding among a number of alternatives:

1 Launch a new product that has a 0.3 probability of a £5m profit if it is successful and a 0.7 probability of losing £1m if it is unsuccessful.

2 Cut prices temporarily and stimulate market share. This would generate an additional £0.7m.

3 Do nothing for the present, so that there would be neither a gain nor a loss.

Which of these alternatives should be chosen?
The expected values of the three alternatives are:

1 $(0.7 \times -1.0) + (0.3 \times 5.0) = £0.8m$

2 £0.7m

3 £0

Alternative 1 is the best (see Figure 16.7).

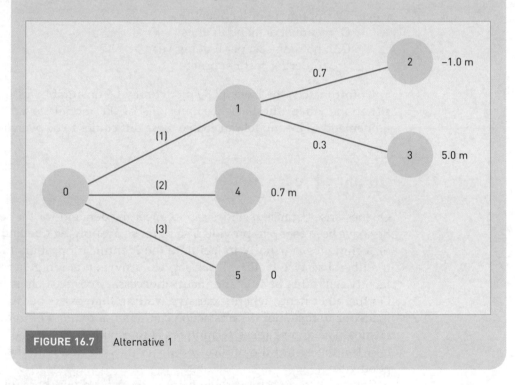

| FIGURE 16.7 | Alternative 1 |

Inventory model

Inventory models are employed to assess the best level of stocks to maintain, the frequency with which to place orders and the quantities to buy. These models provide information on how to minimise the total cost of the inventory system. The total inventory cost is the sum of total ordering costs and shortage costs. Ordering costs refer to the costs connected with placing orders and receiving inventory – salaries in purchasing and accounting departments, wages in the receiving area. Carrying costs are those associated with storage, such as warehouse rent and fuel costs. Shortages are the costs associated with a lost sale and loss of customer goodwill.

Inventory models can be quite complex and take into account a variety of different factors such as quantity discounts, backorders and economic lot sizes. The best-known and the simplest model is the economic order quantity (EOQ) model, the purpose of which is to determine the optimum order quantity. The model assumes a demand pattern that is deterministic and at a constant rate, the instantaneous replenishment of inventory, constant inventory costs and no shortages. The algorithm used is:

$$Q^* = \sqrt{2DC_0/C_h}$$

where Q^* = optimum order quantity
    D = annual demand in units
    C_h = holding cost per unit per year
    C_o = ordering cost per order

Unfortunately, the basic EOQ model may be unsuitable for many real-world situations where the basic assumptions of the model do not apply. Further refinements to the model can enable these difficulties to be overcome.

Queuing theory model

Queues arise because facilities cannot meet the demand for the service the facilities have been set up to provide. The purpose of applying **queuing theory models** or techniques is usually to facilitate the identification of an adequate but not too liberal service facility. If the service provision is too generous, the service facility will often be idle and incur unnecessary costs, such as idle employees. On the other hand, where excessive waiting time exists because the facility is inadequate, customer dissatisfaction can occur and a loss of important goodwill ensues. The aim of these techniques is to establish the economic equilibrium between the cost of the service and the cost associated with the possible loss of goodwill.

Solutions to queuing problems may be determined by common formulae. However, the situations in which they occur are complex and it is often preferable to use simulation methods (see later) to obtain a solution.

Markov analysis

Markov analysis has mainly been restricted to brand-switching behaviour and the impact it has had on market share.

EXAMPLE

Research data show the following probabilities that a person will buy a particular brand of soap, given that they purchased a specific brand on the previous occasion (Table 16.10).

TABLE 16.10   Markov analysis

Transition matrix	Next purchase		
Last purchase	Amy's brand	Bebe's brand	Celia's brand
Amy's brand	0.5	0.2	0.3
Bebe's brand	0.5	0.4	0.1
Celia's brand	0.4	0.3	0.3

The current market shares of the brands is as follows:

Amy's   20%

Bebe's   30%

Celia's   50%

The task is to estimate the long-run market share positions, given that the brand-switching probabilities remain constant. This can be done in several ways. One way is to multiply out the matrices thus:

$$1 \begin{pmatrix} .5 & .5 & .4 \\ .2 & .4 & .3 \\ .3 & .1 & .3 \end{pmatrix} \cdot \begin{pmatrix} .2 \\ .3 \\ .5 \end{pmatrix} = \begin{pmatrix} 0.45 \\ 0.31 \\ 0.24 \end{pmatrix}$$

$$2 \begin{pmatrix} .5 & .5 & .4 \\ .2 & .4 & .3 \\ .3 & .1 & .3 \end{pmatrix} \cdot \begin{pmatrix} 0.45 \\ 0.31 \\ 0.24 \end{pmatrix} = \begin{pmatrix} 0.476 \\ 0.286 \\ 0.238 \end{pmatrix}$$

$$3 \begin{pmatrix} .5 & .5 & .4 \\ .2 & .4 & .3 \\ .3 & .1 & .3 \end{pmatrix} \cdot \begin{pmatrix} 0.476 \\ 0.286 \\ 0.238 \end{pmatrix} = \begin{pmatrix} 0.476 \\ 0.281 \\ 0.243 \end{pmatrix}$$

$$4 \begin{pmatrix} .5 & .5 & .4 \\ .2 & .4 & .3 \\ .3 & .1 & .3 \end{pmatrix} \cdot \begin{pmatrix} 0.476 \\ 0.281 \\ 0.243 \end{pmatrix} = \begin{pmatrix} 0.476 \\ 0.28 \\ 0.244 \end{pmatrix}$$

$$5 \begin{pmatrix} .5 & .5 & .4 \\ .2 & .4 & .3 \\ .3 & .1 & .3 \end{pmatrix} \cdot \begin{pmatrix} 0.476 \\ 0.28 \\ 0.244 \end{pmatrix} = \begin{pmatrix} 0.476 \\ 0.28 \\ 0.244 \end{pmatrix}$$

▶

The solution is:

Amy's = 0.476

Bebe's = 0.28

Celia's = 0.244

The main limitation of the model is the assumption of a stationery transition matrix.

Simulation

The idea behind **simulation** is to find a satisfactory or close-to-best solution to a problem by using a mathematical model of the problem situation and testing it out by varying the various parameters to the model. Simulation does not employ an optimisation algorithm but simply portrays the performance of a particular system, given a set of input parameters. Simulation is usually employed when the problem under study is too complex to be treated by optimisation techniques. A problem may be judged to be too complex when either it cannot be expressed mathematically or the formulation is too involved for economic or practical purposes.

Simulation has been widely used by practitioners because of the degree of realism that can be included in simulation models and the ease with which such models can be explained to non-technical decision makers.[6] In comparison with analytic techniques, such as queuing theory, simulation models do not require the stringent assumptions necessary for tractable solutions. The logic and mathematical relationships are usually more easily understood.

Since simulation models the expected behaviour of a system, the model has to be built from the perspective of the executive who is studying the system. The executive can then experiment with different factors and different scenarios to decide which gives the most satisfactory results. The executive can then experiment with a model rather than interfere with a system in order to understand its behaviour.

The technique of simulation consists of taking random samples from the probability distribution that represents the real-world system under study. Many real-world phenomena are 'normally' distributed and so in many cases probability estimates using the normal curve can be employed. In the case of queues, however, other kinds of distributions may be more appropriate – such as a uniform or a random distribution – and we first need to establish how the events are distributed in reality. The inputs to the model consist of the observed values and the probabilities associated with each event.

Recent software developments for desktop and laptop computers have made it possible for simulations to be developed with comparative ease. An excellent software package is MicroSaint.[7] Illustrations of its use can be found in Proctor.[8, 9]

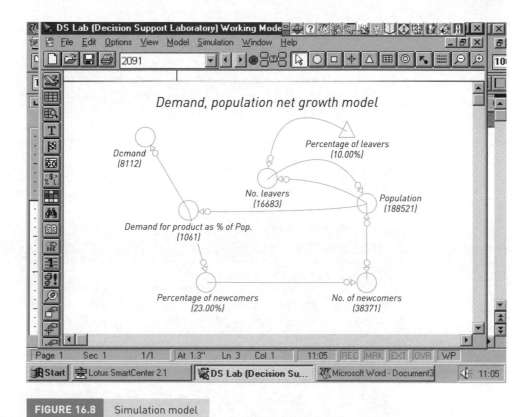

FIGURE 16.8 Simulation model

Source: Screenshot reprinted by permission of Microsoft Corporation

An excellent simulation package is available from Decision Support Laboratory[10] and an illustration of its use is given in Figure 16.8. Here, sales demand for a product is being simulated over a period of time. Decision Support Laboratory is a visual spreadsheet. It provides an easier and faster way to build, edit and explain a spreadsheet model. The basic building block of traditional spreadsheets is a cell. The basic building block of DS Lab is an element. With DS Lab, you define your model in the same way you would think through a problem, using symbols for elements such as inputs, variables, constants, series and tables to define the data with which you work.

DS Lab shows graphically the logic of the model by letting the user represent and manipulate the data with symbols connected by arrows. The symbols (elements) display the data one step at a time, while leaving all the data accessible in an instant with the click of a mouse. The arrows display the relationships between the elements. DS Lab easily manages hundreds of elements over thousands of steps. Time is the parameter most commonly defined for these steps, so DS Lab provides a built-in calendar to define days, weeks, months or years. Steps may be defined as something other than time, such as geography or product type, by simply creating a list of items. The software will then automatically generate the values for each step of the user-defined parameters.

Game theory

Game theory has been found to be useful when considering marketing strategy problems. It helps to determine the best strategy that competing firms can adopt. Games can be constructed for any number of 'players' and the simplest of these to understand is the two-person game.

EXAMPLE

In the model presented here (Table 16.11) there are two players, A and B. Each has three strategies available and it is assumed that full information about the outcome of each possible pair of strategies is available. The two players decide their strategies simultaneously and it is a one-shot game.

The usual way of showing this form of the game is indicated in Table 16.12. The table records the payoffs to A and to B for each possible combination of strategies. For example, the cell containing the payoff 6,4 denotes a payoff of 6 to A and 4 to B.

TABLE 16.11   Game theory

	A	B	C	D	E	F	G	H	I	J	K
1											
2											
3		Payoff				Tables					
4	To A						To B			Row	
5		B1	B2	B3			B1	B2		B3 Max.	
6	A1	6	7	2			4	5		3	5
7	A2	4	2	6			5	4		7	7
8	A3	6	4	2			4	9		3	9
9 Col.											
10 Max.		6	7	6							
11						1 = code number					
12											
13		B1	B2	B3			B1	B2		B3	
14	A1	1	1	0	A1		0	1		0	
15	A2	0	0	1	A2		0	0		1	
16	A3	1	0	0	A3		0	1		0	
17											
18		B1 B2	B3								
19	A1	– NE	–			NE		–	Nash		
20	A2	– –	NE						equilibrium		
21	A3	– –	–						strategies		

TABLE 16.12   Payoff matrix A, B

Strategies	B1	B2	B3
A1	6,4	7,5	2,3
A2	4,5	2,5	6,7
A3	6,4	4,4	2,3

Examination of the payoff table shows, by trial and error, that there are two strategy pairs (A1,B2) and (A2,B3) that satisfy the Nash equilibrium condition that each player's strategy is a best response to the other's. In order to model this game on a spreadsheet, it is necessary to use the data from the payoff matrix to construct two separate payoff tables for A and B, as shown in the main table. Note that the codes used in the following explanation apply to the software used to produce this example – other packages may employ different coding systems.

First, the payoff data for A have to be entered into cells C6 to E8. Next, the payoff data for B have to be inserted into cells I6 to K8. To find A's best response to each of B's strategies, the column maximums for A's payoff table have to be found. Enter @MAX(C6 . . . C8) in cell C10.

This formula should then be copied from C10 to cells D10 and E10. The column maximum signifies the payoff to A when it chooses its best response to B's strategy corresponding to that column. To find B's best response to each of A's strategies, the row maximums for B's payoff table have to be found. Enter @MAX(I6 . . . K6) in cell M6 and then copy the formula to M7 and M8.

The next step is to find out which, if any, pairs of strategies correspond to both a column maximum for A's payoff table and a row maximum for B's payoff table. This is accomplished by first identifying which cells in the payoff tables contain the column and row maximums, respectively, and putting the number 1 in these cells. This identifying code (1) is put in cell G11.

We next create a new set of payoff matrices in rows 14 to 16. In cell C14, enter @IF(C6=C$10,$G$11,$A$11).

This will cause the number 1 (from cell G11) to appear in C14 if C6 equals the column maximum in C10 and 0, from cell A11, if it is not. This formula can now be copied from C14 to C15 and C16 as the row 10 is anchored with the $. In this example the code 1 appears in C16 as strategy A3 is A's best response if B plays B1.

To code A's best response to B2 and B3, copy from the three cells C14 . . . C16 to the column sections commencing D14 and E14. To code B's best response to each of A's strategies it is necessary to indicate which cells in B's payoff matrix correspond to the row maximums in cells M6 to M8. In cell I14, enter @IF(I6=$M6,$G$11,$A$11).

Copy the formula from I14 to J14 and K14, then copy the three cells I14 . . . K14 to the row sections commencing I15 and I16.

Nash equilibrium conditions are satisfied when each player receives the maximum payoff possible, taking into account the other player's strategy. This means that

▶

there will be a 1 in both the coded payoff matrices for this strategy combination. Nash equilibrium pairs in the final matrix can be coded NE in a single matrix of strategy combinations by adding the two matrices already coded and finding cells whose value is 2, i.e. where the strategy combination is both a column maximum for A and a row maximum for B. In cell C1, enter @IF(+C14+I14>G11,H19,I19).

This last entry displays the code NE from cell H19 when the value in C19 is greater than the value 1 in cell G11, i.e. when it equals 2. The dash in I19 is displayed when C19 has the value less than 2. Copy this formula from C19 to the rest of the cells in the matrix C19 . . . C21.

Using the basic principles developed, more complex games can be constructed. Such games might contain payoff tables with larger numbers of rows and columns (see, for example, Rosser 1995[11]). It would also be possible to consider other forms of payoff. For example, the objective may be to minimise the maximum gain of the other player. In such a case a 3,4 strategy would be preferable from A's viewpoint to a 7,8 strategy. Alternatively, minimising the relative gain might be the object, in which case a 7,8 strategy would be preferred to a 2,4 strategy. While the construction of the payoff tables and principles of calculation would be similar in all these cases, the rules to be applied would be different.

EXPERT SYSTEMS AND DECISION SUPPORT

An expert system provides expertise to help problem solving. It can represent the best thinking of the top experts in the field that can lead to solutions to problems that are imaginative, accurate and efficient. An expert system has predictive modelling power and can act as an information-processing model of problem solving in marketing, providing the desired answers for a given problem-solving situation and demonstrating how they would change for new situations.

Expert systems are most appropriately used in the following circumstances:

1 Where the key relationships are logical rather than arithmetical. Generating new ideas is more appropriate for an expert system. Advising on action to be taken in specific situations is another example.

2 Where the problem is semi-structured rather than structured. For structured problems, a traditional algorithm approach will do; for unstructured problems there may not be sufficient knowledge in the knowledge base to provide satisfactory results.

3 Where the knowledge in the domain is incomplete. Expert systems are most applicable in the domains of incomplete knowledge.

4 Where problem solving in the domain requires a direct interface between the manager and the computer system. Situations of decision urgency and online decision support are most appropriate for expert system use.

The three major components of an expert system are:

- a user interface
- a knowledge base
- an inference engine.

The knowledge base includes the definitions of the objects and variables in the system, including data, assumptions, production rules (if–then statements), heuristics and models. The inference engine manipulates the elements in the knowledge base and combines it with information from the user to solve a particular problem.

Expert systems can be used for a variety of purposes. These include:

- *Interpretation*: inferring situation descriptions from sensor data. This is useful in observational market research studies.

- *Prediction*: inferring the likely consequences of given situations. This is useful in forecasting.

- *Planning*: designing actions. Campaign planning or even marketing planning is an area of application.

- *Diagnosis and monitoring*: inferring system malfunctions from observables. This is useful in the context of marketing control, monitoring performance against targets or budgets set.

- *Debugging*: prescribing remedies for malfunctions. Recommending contingency action when plans are not achieved.

- *Design*: configuring objects under constraints. Product design is an area where expert systems can be applied.

- *Repair*: putting contingency plans into action.

Given the wide array of applications for expert systems in marketing, it is not appropriate to discuss or illustrate expert systems in the generic sense. However, there are different commercial packages available that suit specific purposes. A good example is that provided by project-management systems software that incorporates an applications generator capable of facilitating the production of a marketing plan.

In marketing, expert systems have been used to examine single source data for trends, to filter marketing data for quality problems, to develop forecasting models, to set sales quotas, to qualify sales prospects and to train sales personnel.[12, 13]

McCann[14] has described several expert systems that have been useful to consumer packaged goods brand managers.

Neural networks

Whereas expert systems parody experts' thinking processes, neural networks are computer applications that mimic the human brain. One important aspect of neural networks is their ability to learn from their past activities in the sense that records of the system's past performance can influence processing in order to improve future performance. Theoretically, such systems could be self-improving.

The growth of interest in neural networks comes about as a result of the fact that they emulate not only the brain's reasoning but also its learning capabilities. Although neural network applications in marketing are currently sparse, researchers have documented several interesting applications. Kestylyn[15] has studied how neural networks can be used to identify the best sales prospects for a telemarketing operation to call from a list of customers who have not been active recently. Westland[16] has presented systems that save busy executives time by identifying and organising environmental and internal information for them. Proctor[17] has also suggested a potential application of neural networks in evaluating new product opportunities.

BREAKTHROUGHS IN BUSINESS INTELLIGENCE

Neural networks and data-mining software can now mimic human thought when processing vast amounts of sales data, thus allowing large companies to save millions of dollars, enter new markets, retain customers, track fraud and generally become more competitive.

Neural networks and artificial intelligence were among the hot issues in the fast-moving information technology industry in the early 1980s. But when they failed to deliver the instant wins that venture capitalists and others were seeking, neural computing and AI fell out of fashion and out of the high-tech spotlight.

Even Japan's much vaunted Fifth Generation computer project, which was begun in 1982 and was to use parallel processing and AI techniques to develop next-generation 'intelligent' machines, faded from sight.

But in spite of these early setbacks, neural computing, parallel processing and AI techniques have all made substantial advances in recent years aided, in part, by the dramatic advances in microprocessor power.

Although many researchers and high-tech start-ups now shun the AI tag, these advances coupled with more realistic expectations, have ensured that neural computing and AI have not been forgotten. Indeed, many of the technologies pioneered by AI researchers at the Massachusetts Institute of Technology and other laboratories on both sides of the Atlantic have begun to be incorporated into mainstream business applications.

Unlike conventional computing techniques, neural computing is modelled on the biological processes of the human brain and has many human-like qualities.

For example, neural computers can learn from experience and do not need to be programmed with fixed rules or equations. They can analyse vast quantities of complex data and identify patterns from which predictions can be made.

They also tend to be more robust than their conventional counterparts. They have the ability to cope well with incomplete or 'fuzzy' data and can deal with previously unspecified or new situations. As such, they are ideally suited to real-world applications and can provide the solution to a host of currently impossible or commercially impractical problems.

In addition, the time needed to develop a neural application is often less than with a conventional program because there are no algorithms or rules to define. The scope and accuracy of the finished application are also often improved since the neural computer can be exposed to many more examples than can be assimilated by a single human 'expert'. International Business Machines has, for example, integrated neural network and artificial intelligence technology into software applications, such as data-mining packages.

Mr Evangelous Simoudis, a scientist at IBM's Almanden Research Center, says such techniques enable business users to sift through vast quantities of raw data in order to spot hidden trends or anomalies that might otherwise be missed. IBM's business intelligence and data-mining software can mimic human thought when processing information, called the 'verification model', or go beyond human logic to discover correlations between seemingly disparate data, called the 'discovery model'.

The verification model confirms or refutes the hypothesis of a savvy business person while the discovery model reveals patterns that human logic might not see. The classic example was the unexpected connection between beer and nappies discovered during a data-mining experiment on a US supermarket database. The study revealed that the people purchasing nappies on a Friday also tended to buy beer.

Before neural networks and artificial intelligence were used in business intelligence applications, companies lacked the ability to leverage the information they were collecting in data warehouses. They were unable to connect consumer-buying patterns, customise promotions to target a range of customers with different needs or identify potentially fraudulent insurance claims based on past behaviour.

At best, information analysis was done manually, perhaps as much as 90% of analysts' time was spent gathering information, leaving only 10% of the time to digest and analyse the data. With IBM's business intelligence technology, however, customers are now able to save millions of dollars, enter new markets, retain customers, track fraud and generally be more competitive.

Among IBM's customers, Merrill Lynch developed a Trusted Global Advisor (TGA) network that gives up-to-the-minute information on customer portfolios and investments. With access to information in real time, brokers can help customers make better decisions about their financial futures.

Cadbury's saw its market share of the chocolate market slip from 33% to 28%, but an IBM business intelligence solution helped the company focus attention on those product lines that appealed to customers and Cadbury's market share is now back up to 30%.

The Safeway supermarket chain in the UK is improving customer service by **tracking** product purchases – a system created by IBM in only a few weeks. Preferred customers receive marketing information that appeals directly to their individual needs and tastes.

Southern California Edison uses IBM database technology to identify unanticipated opportunities that saved millions of dollars for the United States' second largest utility. One application that looked at credit collection and overdue accounts helped recover more than $8m. The company says its overall return on investment for its databases is 600%.

Neural computing and AI techniques also lie behind many of the sophisticated search engines and intelligent agents found on the Internet and corporate intranets. As Mr Mike Lynch, founder and managing director of Autonomy, the Cambridge-based intelligent agent pioneer, notes: 'In business today, the ability to access the right information at the right time is absolutely critical. The problem is that technologies which promise this ability, namely the Internet and corporate intranets, are flawed in their delivery. Rather than giving users the tools to assimilate the right information into useful knowledge, they are overloading them with too much irrelevant dross.' Autonomy's latest products include server products designed to deliver personalised information to Internet and intranet users in a dynamic fashion. They use the dynamic reasoning engine technology developed by Cambridge Neurodynamics, a recognised world leader in the application of neural network and pattern-recognition technologies.

AI and neural-computing techniques are used in 'case-based reasoning' tools such as those developed by California-based Inference for intelligent problem solving in help desk, customer support and other computer-telephony integration packages.

Other AI and neural computing-based systems are used for credit scoring and to help pinpoint and prevent fraud in areas as diverse as equity trading and cellular telephone networks.

Meanwhile, Neural Technologies, a Hampshire-based start-up has launched a software package called Prospect Explorer. The product, developed in conjunction with Australia's Straits Resources group, is a geological exploration tool with the capacity to analyse a range of different types of raw exploration data and automatically detect and prioritise anomalies. 'Neural computing and other forms of intelligent technology are providing leading edge solutions to complex business problems', says Mr Nick Ryman-Tubb, chief executive of Neural Technologies. 'From manufacturing, banking and finance, defence, telecommunications, pharmaceuticals to the holiday industry, we have already applied neural computing to a wide variety of commercial and industrial applications – particularly those which have, until now, been either impossible or commercially impractical for conventional computing to address,' says Ryman-Tubb.

Nevertheless, even neural computing enthusiasts concede that neural networks will not replace conventional computers. 'Neural computing should not be viewed as a competitor to conventional computing, but rather as a complementary technique,' notes Neural Technologies.

The most successful neural computing applications to date have been those that operate in conjunction with other computing techniques. For example, using a neural network to perform a first pass over a set of incoming data, then passing the results over to a conventional system for subsequent processing.

However, with the growing emphasis on autonomy, intelligence and an increased amount of information required by businesses, traditional computer processing technology can only cope through faster hardware with more complex, bespoke software. With this approach, the question is: how long is it going to take to write this software, how many different versions for each variation and once written, how safe is it from bugs? As Neural Technologies notes in its white paper: 'The problem, growing towards the millennium, is that engineers no longer have the luxury in development to calculate all the algorithms or identify all the rules in these complex systems. In fact, most of these systems are so chaotic that doing so would be futile and prone to failure.

'Neural computers, with their ability to learn from examples, rather than needing to be explicitly programmed, offer a means of making such tasks tractable to a machine.'

Source: Taylor[18]

Other marketing applications

Neuroshell is an expert system shell that can operate in binary or analogue mode. The binary mode enables us to set up an expert system that uses essentially categorical data. Kotler[1] provides an illustration of how a firm might respond to a competitor cutting its price. The conditions and corresponding actions can be set into a decision table (Table 16.13).

The top half of the table shows the various conditions that can occur – the actions that can be undertaken by competitors (inputs). A 'Y' indicates the presence of the condition, whereas an 'N' or a blank space indicates the condition's absence. In the bottom half of the table the reactions (outputs) to the conditions are shown as a 1 in the appropriate column.

The seven cases can then be entered into Neuroshell in its binary mode of operation and the pattern of inputs and outputs learned. After learning has taken place, if we then enter into the program the nature of the competitor's action, the program will respond with the appropriate output – what action should be taken (the lower half of the table).

The ability of neural network shells to work with binary data opens up all kinds of applications for routine strategic decision making.

Further information on neural nets

Eberhart and Dobbins[19] present a comprehensive text on neural network developments and include 'C' source code for several types of neural networking

TABLE 16.13	Decision table showing reaction to a competitor's price cut

Reaction to competitor cutting price	1	2	3	4	5	6	7
Competitor cuts price	N	Y	Y	Y	Y	Y	Y
Competitor's price stable		Y					
Price cut likely to have a significant effect on sales		N	N	Y	Y	Y	Y
Cut is likely to be permanent		N	Y	N	Y	Y	Y
Price has been cut by more than 4%					Y	N	N
Price cut between 2.1% and 4.0%					N	Y	N
Price cut less than 2%					N	N	Y
Drop price to competitor's price					1		
Offer self-liquidating premium to steal limelight from competitor						1	
Run temporary cents off to dilute effect of price cut							1
Hold our prices at present level: continue to watch competitor's price	1	1	1	1			

Source: Kotler, Philip, *Marketing Management*, 11th edition © 2003, p. 499. Reprinted by permission of Pearson Education, Inc., Upper Saddle River, NJ[1]

models. This includes the feed-forward backward propagation model discussed in their article. More material is available from Roy Dobbins on request. McClelland and Rumelhart[20] have also produced a useful handbook that includes source code and diskettes. The work includes material on the backward propagation model and provides tutorial assistance. The major limitation on applications using PC-based neural networking software just now is that imposed by the hardware. The complexities of some types of pattern make it difficult for software to learn the pattern within a reasonable timespan. Ward Systems[21] has tried to overcome this problem with respect to Neuroshell by offering a piece of hardware that accelerates the process. However, it may only be that when parallel programming becomes available on the PC will a step have been taken in the direction of solving this particular limitation.

Statistical tools and decision support

See Chapter 10.

SUMMARY

Marketing information systems exist to help marketing managers get to grips with the volumes of data with which they are constantly bombarded. The marketing information system provides management with a variety of reports to help its decision making.

Marketing planning requires the size of current and potential markets to be carefully measured and estimated. There are several approaches to forecasting. Some methods rely on asking people questions, while others involve the statistical analysis of historical data.

An indication and examples of how management science/operational research techniques and tools can be applied to marketing problems is given. Methods considered include linear programming, transportation models, assignment models, network models, decision trees, inventory models, queuing theory models, Markov analysis, simulation and game theory.

A growing area of interest and importance in the area of decision-support systems are expert systems. There are many opportunities for the implementation of expert systems in marketing.

QUESTIONS

1 How does a marketing information system differ from marketing research? What are marketing decision-support mechanisms? How do they relate to the marketing information system?

2 When forecasting future demand for products or services, what should be the nature of the basic approach?

3 Indicate the kinds of marketing problem to which the following might be usefully applied:
   - linear programming
   - transportation models
   - assignment models
   - network models
   - decision trees
   - inventory models
   - queuing theory
   - Markov analysis
   - simulation
   - game theory.

4 Suggest potential applications for expert systems in marketing management.

5 What type of questions could a manager expect to answer using the company's marketing decision-support system? What makes a decision-support system successful?

CASE STUDY 16.1: DEMAND FOR AGRICULTURAL TRACTORS

Examine Table 16.14 closely, then answer the question that follows.

TABLE 16.14 Demand for agricultural tractors

Average farm size (acres)	Number of farms	AV hp tractors sold	Farms income index	Tractor population	AV price of tractors (units)	Sales of tractors (units)	Average tractor horse power (all producers)	Average big tractor horse power (all producers)	A&B share small tractor sales	A&B share big tractor sales	Year
232	7256	51.2	100	10,425	100	1114	48.0	58.3	12.3	11.5	77
233	7103	51.4	101.5	10,200	100	1108	48.2	59.1	12.5	11.6	78
235	7002	51.7	101.6	10,000	101.5	1196	48.5	60.2	12.8	11.7	79
238	6874	52.4	98.3	9987	101.6	1024	48.8	61.2	13.2	11.8	80
240	6687	52.8	96.2	9915	101.8	1056	49.2	62.3	13.4	11.3	81
246	6502	53.1	95.3	9824	102.1	995	49.4	62.7	13.5	11.8	82
253	6411	54.8	97.2	9810	102.7	1087	49.3	62.8	12.9	12.0	83
258	6301	56.7	96.3	9786	103.5	1056	49.6	63.4	13.2	12.5	84
260	6218	57.5	95.1	9752	104.5	1034	50.1	64.2	13.4	12.8	85
263	6154	58.3	96.5	9664	106.8	1025	50.7	65.3	13.4	12.0	86
268	6058	59.5	97.2	9615	105.6	1048	51.6	66.8	13.6	12.4	87
270	5947	60.5	100.5	9611	105.7	1189	52.3	68.1	13.8	11.8	88
272	5821	61.2	101.2	9588	105.7	1205	54.6	69.0	13.8	12.1	89
275	5714	61.8	102.4	9615	106.4	1314	55.0	69.5	13.9	12.4	90
278	5621	62.4	103.5	9623	108.6	1412	55.1	70.0	13.7	12.5	91
281	5545	62.7	102.0	9625	110.5	1248	55.3	71.2	14.1	12.4	92
284	5432	63.1	100.5	9634	111.5	1232	55.6	72.1	14.0	12.4	93
287	5308	63.8	96.2	9651	112.4	1145	56.1	72.5	13.8	11.8	94
290	5126	64.5	98.5	9667	112.4	1045	56.8	72.8	14.0	12.1	95

Question

Prepare forecasts of sales of all tractor sizes for the next five years.

Hint: Use the regression feature in Lotus 1–2–3, Aseasyas or some other spreadsheet to help with your calculations.

CASE STUDY 16.2: KENBROCK

Kenbrock Timber Finishes Pty Ltd manufactures a range of Cabot's timber treatments. The firm thinks of itself as being one of the smaller national Australian brands, and claims 25% of the total national paint market in Australia. Being in the wood-finishing business, the company reckons its main rivals market paint, wallpaper and other decorative material. It counts on four major competitors, among whom are Dulux and Bristol, both of whom sell Kenbrock's products in their own stores and are important Kenbrock customers. Besides distributing nationally throughout all the states, Kenbrock obtains export orders, mainly from Thailand, which account for roughly 3% to 4% of its total sales volume. In pursuance of its strategy of full market penetration, the company manufactures more than 250 individual products with different features, colours and sizes.

In the past, the company experienced difficulties with its approach to forecasting. Even though the company possessed such a large product range that was distributed nationally, it continued to use a simple, naive 12-month moving average on each product to forecast and schedule production requirements. However, from the analysis of past sales data, a seasonal pattern corresponded closely to the weather conditions observed in each state.

As a result of using a simple moving average method, the company's forecasting system failed to incorporate the seasonal pattern into its forecasting process, which produced misleading forecast results. It was taken for granted that the rolling average was valid, but in the real world some product ranges varied between 25% and 30% either side of the average with the seasonal variations. As the problem existed it led to a combination of increased inventory cost (caused by a build-up of stock) and failure to meet customer demand at peak times. Such a situation impeded the company's market competitiveness.

Source: Waddell and Sohal[22]

Question

Suggest how the firm might have resolved its forecasting difficulties.

CASE STUDY 16.3: RESTAURANT STRATEGIES

Two restaurants, A and B, are positioned at either end of a village and compete with one another for business. Each can adopt one of three strategies with respect to the evening menu and each restaurant has full information about the outcome of each possible pair of strategies available. Both restaurants decide their strategy for the evening meal simultaneously and can only change the strategy for the

TABLE 16.15	Payoff matrix A,B (evening meal sales turnover £'00)		
	b1	b2	b3
a1	2,1	3,2	6,1
a2	4,2	4,2	5,3
a3	4,4	3,4	1,3

next evening meal – it is a one-shot game. Table 16.15 records the payoffs to restaurant A and restaurant B for each possible combination of strategies.

Question

Which strategy leads to each restaurant receiving the maximum possible payoff, taking into account the other restaurant's strategy?

CASE STUDY 16.4: BRAND SWITCHING

Studies indicate the following probabilities that a person will buy a particular brand of jam, given that they purchased a specific brand on the previous occasion, as shown in Table 16.16.

TABLE 16.16	Brand-switching probabilities		
	Next purchase		
Last purchase	A	B	C
A	.6	.1	.3
B	.6	.2	.2
C	.4	.3	.3

Question

Given that the current market shares of the brands are:

A 40%
B 30%
C 30%

estimate the long-run market share position.

CASE STUDY 16.5: SIMON THEODOLOU, HAIRSTYLIST

Simon Theodolou runs two large hairdressing salons in the Midlands. Each salon operates as a separate limited company, with Simon owning half the shares in each one and the salon manager owning the other half. Services such as materials purchase and laundry are provided centrally and economies of scale help ensure that the salons remain highly profitable. The salons' reputation in terms of the quality of the hairdressing is one of the best in Britain, with stylists being regularly entered in competitions, and Simon also operates a training school for his own staff and for hairdressers from other salons.

As a regular routine, each salon collects daily data on the number of clients seen (including a breakdown of the services bought), the daily takings and the takings for each stylist. These figures are aggregated weekly and monthly and comparisons are made with previous months and years. Comparisons are also made between the salons, so Simon and his co-directors can assess whether the individual salons are improving or worsening and whether they are doing better or worse in comparison with each other.

In the short term, the directors are planning to open a third salon in Wolverhampton; in the longer term, the intention is to expand throughout the Midlands, or even nationally. Each director is well aware that expansion of the group will strengthen the individual salons, not only because of the economies of scale in central services, but also because of the greater impact on public perceptions that membership of a large chain would imply. The problem for Simon is that he finds it hard to predict whether a new salon will be a success or not; experience has shown that it takes about a year for business to build up to its permanent level.

Simon also finds it hard to benchmark performances; in other words, he doesn't know whether his salons could be doing even better overall than they are, because he only makes comparisons one with another. Aware that his present systems, although better than most hairdressing salons', are still somewhat naive, he decided to call in a firm of consultants, Midlands Marketing, to re-analyse his figures and come up with some new recommendations. The aggregated figures for the previous 12 months for each salon are shown in Table 16.17.

Simon asked Midlands Marketing to come up with ideas for improving his systems and also to forecast what his businesses will be doing over the next year. He also wants to know how he can predict the performance of the proposed new salon in Wolverhampton and other salons in the future.

(Case contributed by Jim Blythe)

| TABLE 16.17 | Simon Theodolou's two salons: aggregated figures for previous 12 months |

Birmingham (12 stylists)

Month	Perms	Cut & b/dry	Highlights	Tinting	No. of clients	Av. clients per stylist	Takings (£)	Takings per stylist (£)
Oct	75	1002	98	384	1559	130	42,393	3533
Nov	110	1235	97	342	1784	146	49,552	4129
Dec	125	1104	98	374	1701	142	51,730	4311
Jan	62	804	73	205	1144	143	32,432	4054
Feb	77	843	76	227	1223	153	34,966	4371
Mar	84	837	74	229	1224	153	37,430	4679
Apr	79	997	87	260	1423	142.3	40,555	4055
May	93	1055	78	273	1499	149.9	44,970	4497
Jun	104	973	84	285	1446	144.6	46,272	4627
Jul	73	904	78	240	1295	144	34,317	3813
Aug	83	944	72	248	1347	150	36,908	4100
Sept	97	904	70	243	1314	146	39,157	4351

Coventry (8 stylists)

Month	Perms	Cut & b/dry	Highlights	Tinting	No. of clients	Av. clients per stylist	Takings (£)	Takings per stylist (£)
Oct	60	798	75	210	1143	143	32,678	4085
Nov	79	837	78	210	1204	151	34,820	4353
Dec	114	970	92	246	1422	178	45,504	5688
Jan	42	605	54	207	908	114	22,700	2838
Feb	62	698	54	193	1007	126	27,586	3448
Mar	73	620	56	208	957	119	28,953	3619
Apr	82	980	75	241	1378	172	37,895	4737
May	93	995	72	235	1395	174	37,386	4673
Jun	82	825	71	198	1176	147	31,125	3891
Jul	75	807	64	208	1154	144	33,408	4176
Aug	73	798	61	183	1115	139	29,938	3742
Sept	48	809	67	210	1134	142	30,448	3806

Questions

1 Using the figures given in the case study, predict the takings for the next 12 months for each salon.

2 What seasonal trends can be discovered within the data given?

3 If Simon were to open his new salon next March and employ six stylists to begin with, what would be a reasonable expectation for the salon's turnover in the second year?

4 What other information could Simon collect in order to make the predictions more accurate?

5 What differences are apparent between the two salons in terms of the business done?

REFERENCES AND NOTES

1 Kotler, P (2003) *Marketing Management* (11th edn), Upper Saddle River, NJ: Prentice-Hall, 499.

2 SNAP software, Mercator Systems, 5 Mead Court, Bristol B35 3UW. Tel: 44(0) 1454 280800; Fax: 44(0) 1454 281216; http://www.mercator.co.uk

3 Samways, A and Whittcome, K (1994) UK brand strategies, *Financial Times Management Report*, 108.

4 Kotler, P and Lilien, G (1983) *Marketing Decision Making: A model-building approach*, New York: Harper & Row.

5 Bass, F (1969) A new product growth model for consumer durables, *Management Science*, 15 January, 215–27.

6 Hoover, S V and Perry, R F (1989) *Simulation: A problem-solving approach*, New York: Addison-Wesley.

7 MicroSaint: Rapid Data Ltd, Crescent House, Crescent Road, Worthing, West Sussex BN11 5RW (computer software).

8 Proctor, R A (1994) Queues and the power of simulation in helping with business decisions and problems, *Management Decision*, 32(1), 50–55.

9 Proctor, R A (1994) Simulation in management services, *Management Services*, 38(1), January, 18–23.

10 Decision Support Laboratory, *The Visual Spreadsheet*, DS Group, Inc., 474 North Street, Greenwich CT 06830–3449, Version 2.0.

11 Rosser, M (1995) Modelling game theory with spreadsheets, *Cheer*, 9(2), 15–18.

12 Schmitz, J D, Armstrong, G D and Little, J D C (1990) Cover story: automated news findings in marketing, *Marketing Interfaces*, 20(6), November/December, 29–38.

13 Steinberg, M and Planck, R E (1990) Implementing expert systems into business-to-business marketing practice, *Journal of Business and Industrial Marketing*, 5(2), 15–26.

14 McCann, J M (1986) *The Marketing Workbench*, Homewood, IL: Dow-Jones Irwin.

15 Kestylyn, J (1992) Application watch, *AI Expert*, January, 63–64.

16 Westland, J C (1992) Self-organising executive information networks, *Decision Support Systems*, 8, 41–53.

17 Proctor, R A (1992) Marketing decision support systems: a role for neural networking, *Marketing Intelligence and Planning*, 10(1), 21–26.

18 Taylor, P (1997) Breakthroughs in business intelligence, *Financial Times*, 7 May.

19 Eberhart, R C and Dobbins, R W (1990) *Neural Network PC Tools*, London: Academic Press.

20 McClelland, J L and Rumelhart, D E (1988) *Explorations in Parallel Distributed Processing: A handbook of models, programs and exercises*, Cambridge, MA: MIT Press.

21 Ward Systems (1989) *Neuroshell: Neural Network Shell Program*, Ward Systems Inc., 228 W Patrick Street, Frederick, MD 21701.

22 Waddell, D and Sohal, A S (1994) Forecasting: the key to managerial decision making, *Management Decision*, 32(1), 46.

FURTHER READING

Ashill, N and Jobber, D (1999) The impact of environmental uncertainty perceptions, decision-maker characteristics and work environment characteristics on the perceived usefulness of marketing information systems (MkIS): a conceptual framework, *Journal of Marketing Management*, 15(6), 519–40.

Attaran, M (1992) *Management Science Information Systems*, New York: Wiley.

Chakrapani, C (2004) *Statistics in Market Research*, London: Arnold.

Cohen, M A, Jehoshua, E and Teck, H H (1997) An anatomy of a decision support system for developing and launching line extensions, *Journal of Marketing Research*, 34, February, 117–29.

Goff, M (1997) Mapping out markets, *Provider*, 23(10), October, 79–80.

Graver, M S (2002) Using data mining for customer satisfaction research, *Marketing Research*, 14(1), 8–12.

Hoover, S V and Perry, R F (1989) *Simulation: A problem-solving approach*, New York: Addison-Wesley.

Huberty, C J (1994) *Applied Discriminant Analysis*, New York: Wiley Interscience.

Jones, J W and McLeod, R (1986) The structure of executive information systems: an exploratory analysis, *Decision Science*, 17, 220–49.

Kotler, P A (1966) A design for the firm's marketing nerve centre, *Business Horizons*, Fall, 63–74.

Li, E (1997) Perceived importance of information system success factors: a meta analysis of group differences, *Information and Management*, 32, 15–28.

McConagle, J J and Vella, C M (1990) *Outsmarting the Competition*, Naperville, IL: Sourcebooks.

Marshall, K P (1996) *Marketing Information Systems*, Danvers, MA: Boyd & Fraser.

Morris, S (1990) *Using Personal Computers in Marketing*, Oxford: NCC Blackwell.

Orme, B and Huber, J (2000) Improving the value of conjoint simulations, *Marketing Research*, 12, Winter, 12–21.

Ratner, B (2003) *Statistical Modeling and Analysis for Database Marketing*, Boca Raton, FL: Chapman & Hall/CRC.

Watson, H J and Blackstone, J H (1989) *Computer Simulation*, New York: Wiley.

Yava, U (1996) Demand forecasting in a service setting, *Journal of International Marketing and Marketing Research*, 21(1), February, 3–11.

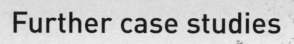

Further case studies

CASE STUDY 1

FT

Noteworthy response

Whenever former Virgin Records managing director Jon Webster has a bad hangover he will lie down and put on a recording of jazz pianist Keith Jarrett's legendary Cologne concert, writes Steve Hemsley.

During a long music industry career this has been Webster's personally prescribed morning-after cure. It exemplifies the power of music to influence the way we feel and act.

Few things stimulate a response as directly as music. It reflects or shapes our mood at the time of listening and our taste for a long time afterwards. The genres we follow when we are young can also make up part of our identity, by connecting us to a particular social group or moment.

Webster runs a music industry consultancy these days. But during his time at Virgin during the 1980s and 1990s he worked with many acts, such as Genesis and Peter Gabriel, whose music had a poignant effect on their fans. 'Brands must never underestimate the impact music has on people's lives,' he says.

Marketers wanting to use music to influence consumer behaviour enter this emotional minefield. Get it right and you can join the advertising hall of fame: Hamlet Cigars (Bach), Levi 501s (1960s soul), Coca-Cola (the New Seekers). Get it wrong and you can end up with Missy Elliott, Madonna and the Gap or the Rolling Stones and Microsoft – combinations that are criticised by the act's fans and end up generating negative, or at least distracting, coverage for the brand.

Whether it is choosing music for a television commercial or a sonic background for customers – British Airways plays birdsong in some terminals to relax travellers – marketers must pay attention to sounds associated with their brands. This is now a question as much for areas such as events sponsorship, product placement and brand extensions as traditional above-the-line advertising.

Music psychology is a growth area. Researchers at the University of Leicester claim that restaurant diners spend about 10% more on food and drink if music is played in the background while they are eating (classical works best, then pop; there are no data for thrash garage).

John Sloboda, a professor at Keele University, says playing German, French or Italian music in the drinks aisles of supermarkets has increased sales of each nation's wines.

'Music is sensory and, as such, is a strong mnemonic. Get it right and music can trigger the right consumer reactions in terms of conjuring up very visual brand images. It is this kind of emotional connection that creates brands rather than just selling products,' says Natasha Kizzie, head of entertainment at Euro RSCG KLP, the marketing agency.

The Jungle Jim consultancy was launched last week to deal with this area. It was set up by Ben Pincus, founder of sponsorship agency The Works London, Mike Kettles, the creator of events such as Tennents in the Park and the V Festivals, music industry lawyer Dave Perez and producer and promoter Jim King.

The consultancy has conducted an online study of 525 14–25 year olds to find their top influences: music, movies, sport, where they grew up or none of these. Eighty-two per cent of respondents said music was one of the top three influences on their lives. Thirty-one per cent said it was more important than any other factor.

How do brands, looking to exploit this appeal, identify the right music partners? As part of its research, Jungle Jim investigated which particular brands attracted which music fans. From a list of 50 lifestyle brands selected by the agency, followers of acts such as Coldplay and Keane rated products from the likes of Vans and Doc Martens as credible. Fans of Justin Timberlake and Britney Spears favoured Levi's and Top Shop. Dance enthusiasts chose Red Bull and Smirnoff. R&B devotees desired clothing from Rocawear, Puma and Lacoste.

Pincus says: 'The challenge for marketers is to navigate their way through what can be a complicated path. You must understand how young people relate to particular music and know who to talk to in the music industry to get deals done. Very few brands have got this area right and this is due in part to the music business's approach to brands as cash cows and its failure to understand what brands can do for the industry in return.'

Music consultancy Frukt also has a seven-step programme called Music Brand Affinity which uses ongoing customer feedback and research to assess the types of music influencing a brand's consumers at a particular time.

'The personal nature of music and the varying tastes people have mean it is as easy to alienate an existing or potential consumer as it is to create a relationship,' warns Frukt's creative director Jack Horner.

Trying to understand how music affects a consumer's attitudes and feelings is clearly enough to give any marketer a headache. The stress remedy, of course, could turn out to be a dose of Keith Jarrett.

Source: Steve Hemsley (2004) *Financial Times*, 26 October. Reprinted with permission.

Question

Discuss how marketing research might be used to try to understand how music affects a consumer's attitudes and feelings.

CASE STUDY 2

Moving images

From tomorrow, Japanese commuters will be able to put away their newspapers and music players and tune in to the world's first commercial multimedia broadcasting service for customers on the move. The service, called Mobaho!, will broadcast seven video channels and 30 music and audio channels from satellite, allowing consumers to watch live video broadcasts on a train, bus or boat. It will charge customers a mix of subscription bundles and à la carte payments.

This is no ordinary start-up. Mobaho! has been launched by the Mobile Broadcasting Corporation (MBCO), which is backed by 85 investors, including some of the giants of the country's consumer electronics and telecommunications sectors – Sharp, Toshiba, Tokyo FM Broadcasting and Nippon Television Network. The Mobaho! service covers all of Japan bar a few outlying islands – although as the signal will not be accessible under tunnels, commuters on Japan's extensive underground system will be unable to use the service.

Hardware for the service is already in the market. Toshiba offers a portable AV device with built-in satellite antenna and LCD screen to receive the channels and next month Sharp launches its version. The handsets retail for just under £400. Sharp's device can also be used as an MP3 player, electronic photo album and electronic book reader.

Other countries will be watching the Japanese launch closely as they trial their own television-on-the-move services. In the UK, Nokia, O_2, NTL and Sony are testing a service from next spring.

But the Japanese platform is the first to go live on such a scale. Its target is to sign up 1.5m customers in three years. One unknown is the level of demand for such offerings and how well Mobaho!'s choice of payment models and content (which does not include any advertising at launch) goes down in Japan. The country already has a sophisticated mobile services market thanks to the launch of 3G, the success of NTT DoCoMo's i-mode interactive service and some 77m mobile phone users.

Mobaho! will offer a bundle of six video channels covering news, sport, entertainment, business, children and music, while a seventh channel, a premium offering, will cover live sports events. The music and audio channels include news, special genre channels (such as jazz and 1980s music), content from US stations, English-language news and English conversation lessons. About 350,000 music tracks will be on the air each month on a 24-hour basis.

There will also be 60 data services offering news, business and cultural information, beamed direct to the portable devices. If the service signs up 1m customers, it believes that it would be realistic to tailor advertising to its customers.

After an initial registration fee of Y2500 (£13), consumers can opt for a package that includes audio, video and data services (excluding the premium channel) at Y2080 per month, or opt for audio-only services for Y1380 per month. Opting for video and data services alone costs the same amount. The premium sports channel is an extra Y1260 per month.

Owners of the new portable AV devices will also be able to use them as home video players. A number of TV sets in Japan can record programmes on to memory cards, and viewers will be able to slip a memory card into their portable AV device and watch the recorded programme.

Worldwide sales of portable video products such as personal DVD players have generally been disappointing. 'I have to admit that I was initially sceptical about whether anyone would want to watch video when they're out of the home, but I've changed my mind,' says Ashley Norris, publisher of Tech-Digest, a consumer electronics information website. 'Video downloading on a mobile phone is a growing activity and you can imagine times when you'd like to watch, say, a live football match when you're on a train.'

But even if there turns out to be a viable market for video on the move, the broadcasters will not able to colonise it. Competition from mobile phone companies looking to increase their revenues and their customer base is likely to be strong.

Japanese consumers can already buy mobile phones with built-in analogue TV tuners. Further, the Japanese digital terrestrial television service has allocated part of the spectrum for mobile television services to mobile phones and other portable devices. Public broadcaster NHK will next year begin mobile TV broadcasts, and Sanyo and NTT DoCoMo have both shown prototype mobile phone handsets with built-in digital tuners at trade shows in Japan.

NTT DoCoMo's handset includes a docking station with a 20GB hard drive that can store up to 80 hours of television programmes.

Mobaho! will not be available for mobile phones, because receiving video services from satellite requires a lot of battery power and today's mobiles would soon run out of juice. However, a new generation of mobile phones that can receive video broadcasts via satellite are under development and are expected to hit the market within the next two years.

If watching video on the move proves as popular as listening to music, expect broadcasters, advertisers and sponsors to pile into this sector.

Source: George Cole (2004) *Financial Times*, 19 October. Reprinted with permission.

Question

Indicate the kind of marketing research that you think might be undertaken before deciding to launch this product into a particular international market.

CASE STUDY 3

Going below the surface

Unilever brand Dove's use of six generously proportioned 'real women' to promote its skin-firming preparations must qualify as one of the most talked-about marketing decisions taken this summer. It was also one of the most successful: since the campaign broke, sales of the firming lotion have gone up 700% in the UK, 300% in Germany and 220% in the Netherlands.

Yet so entrenched is the industry's attachment to the cult of perfection that the idea got off the ground only after Dove's agency, Ogilvy Mather, brought in Susie Orbach, the psychotherapist known for her work on eating disorders, to talk about the benefits of celebrating female forms of all shapes and sizes.

Co-opting academics and clinicians into advertising research is fast becoming a trend, although it raises some ethical questions. Although clinicians use general insights gleaned over the years – rather than confidential individual patient experiences – into groups, some concerns arise about whether such 'white-coat' findings should be used at all for commercial campaigns. The most immediate query from marketers, however, is likely to be 'Does it work?'

Agencies that have used these techniques include Miles Calcraft Briginshaw Duffy and Abbot Mead Vickers BBDO, which brought in psychologists to work for COI Communications and the Departments of Health and Transport.

The Inland Revenue's advertising to promote self-assessment featuring Adam Hart-Davis is an example of a campaign with a psychological foundation. On the advice of expert respondents, MCBD eschewed the hectoring style of the Revenue's earlier campaign and opted instead for an empathetic approach. Among the successes claimed for the campaign are an eightfold increase in electronic submissions and the highest number of forms completed on time since self-assessment began in 1997.

Psychologists and academics from related disciplines such as anthropology are also increasingly in demand with ad agencies looking for deeper explanations of the roles that brands perform in people's lives.

'There's a recognition that we need to ask other questions to avoid being sucked into our own brand mythologies,' says Anthony Tasgal, founder of brand and communications consultancy POV. But it is not just the desire to get back to first principles that is driving brand owners. It has become increasingly common for marketers to question whether consumers can be relied on to express what they feel. 'Often we don't have much self-knowledge; it takes someone else to tell us what's going on,' says Sanjay Nazerali, managing director of brand consultancy The Depot.

To illustrate the point, Nazerali cites work he did for Cacharel which aimed to establish how the company's Anaïs Anaïs brand could be made more relevant to young fragrance wearers. Instead of focus groups, Nazerali interviewed eight clinicians specialising in teen psychology. What the discussions highlighted was that, in a far cry from girl power, teens have a deep-seated, though rarely acknowledged, desire to express their vulnerabilities.

Out of this was born the brand idea of having the confidence to admit your feelings – a theme duly adopted by Cacharel in an integrated global campaign featuring a young woman blowing kisses which turned into petals, under the banner: 'One day, tenderness will move the world.'

Nazerali also undertook a project for United Biscuits, which shed light on the emotional devices that women use to reduce their sense of being separated from their children during the working day.

But what do others in the industry make of such methods? Marco Rimini, director of strategy at J Walter Thompson, believes that talking to psychologists has more to offer than the current fashion of conducting mini-ethnographic studies: 'Half an hour with someone who spends their life talking to teenagers in a profound way will take you further than an evening hanging out with the crowd.'

However, Tasgal thinks there is a danger of trusting implicitly in 'white-coat authority', and Jane Cunningham, planning director at O&M, says that psychologists simply contribute a framework for understanding at a deeper level what consumers have been talking about all along. 'It can help to verify something you think you've spotted and extend your thinking.'

Paying practising psychologists to take part in brand-related research is also not without its critics. While some argue that their input could actually benefit vulnerable groups, others suspect that the whole business is a flagrant attempt to get practitioners from the under-rewarded caring professions to sell what they know about human susceptibilities to brands searching for profits.

Says Nazerali: 'Advertising has always played to people's fears or desires. Talking to psychologists doesn't change the ethical debate. It's just a more intelligent way of working out what's going on in people's minds.'

Source: Alicia Clegg (2004) *Financial Times*, 28 September. Reprinted with permission.

Question

How can psychologists and academics from related disciplines such as anthropology assist ad agencies looking for deeper explanations of the roles that brands perform in people's lives?

CASE STUDY 4

One strike and you're down

'Companies forget that staff have the power to wreck the brand.' This warning comes from Martin Langford, a corporate reputation specialist at PR firm Kissman Langford. But brand owners that probably don't need reminding of this include British Airways, Royal Mail and Jaguar, because of the high profile that staff industrial action, or threats of industrial action, has assumed at all three in recent months.

Management at large organisations do not embark on widespread and risky company restructurings unless they believe their businesses are in straitened financial circumstances. And the potential long-term damage to company branding that can be done if staff and managers clash publicly over plans will almost always take a back seat to other priorities, such as getting the business back into profit.

Nevertheless, brands are a key part of the intangible assets that are playing an increasingly important role on company balance sheets. This means that it can be a serious issue for any business if its brands emerge as tainted in the long term by strikes and other industrial conflicts. If this is the risk, how can corporations or other branded organisations reduce this danger?

Many people believe that mud sticks and it was certainly noticeable that press coverage of the recent talks between unions and management at the now Ford-owned Land Rover plant at Solihull referred to conflicts at the plant as far back as the 1970s and 1980s, when it was part of British Leyland.

Mike Seymour, international director of crisis and issues management for Edelman, describes this trend as the parenthesis factor. 'The negative shadow of previous industrial relations conflicts hang over the current management, which has an undermining effect on the brand,' he says.

Conversely, he points out, the rate of change among senior levels of management is conveniently – and unfairly – forgotten: 'Consumers and the media forget that it is in some cases a different management team which is dealing with the issues today than when the previous problems arose.' This is compounded by the intermittent nature of industrial conflicts and their accompanying media attention.

However, others argue that it is rare for individual incidents to have a significant long-term effect on the fortunes of a company. For this to happen they must be compounded by a flawed strategy.

Risk management company Lippincott Mercer looked at Fortune 1000 companies that had lost at least 25% of their market capitalisation in four weeks or less during the mid- to late-1990s. It found that 58% of those declines were from strategic errors, many of which had affected the brand value.

Langford estimates that about one-third of his clients' problems are caused by the behaviour of their staff, with industrial action and disaffected workers being the most common examples.

John Williamson, board director of brand consultants Wolff Olins, says: 'Poor industrial relations do not come about in isolation. They reflect on the business as a whole and the way in which it is being managed. British Airways management thinks the brand is something that is done by the marketing communications department, which makes for very poor brand strategy.'

There is a particularly acute danger here for service companies. In service businesses, the impression of the brand given to the customer is often dictated by the behaviour of staff at the bottom of the organisation hierarchy. And, in the maelstrom of media activity that goes with major industrial action, the senior management can develop the habit of briefing journalists before their own staff. This has a direct impact on the quality of the service.

Seymour describes this chain of events as a form of self-fulfilling prophesy. 'The people dealing with the public at large service organisations are those way down the management chain, who know least about what is going on,' he says. 'Often these people are getting their information from, and having their opinions shaped by, what they see and hear in the media. This leads to a drop-off in service, which is, of course, the last thing that is needed at such a critical time.'

It follows that the protection of the brand's long-term reputation is also not just a marketing issue. 'People are the primary marketing channel for any service organisation and they should be the first audience for any form of communication,' says Dan Bobby of brand consultancy Dave. 'The best companies start with those staff who are dealing with the public and work back from there.

'The worst thing that can happen is for people to see change management consultants wandering around the workplace without having been briefed as to what needs to be changed,' he says. 'Taken out of context, change means insecurity and job losses.'

'Brands represent the value of the organisation's relationship with its customer. It's the one thing a competitor cannot copy,' says Brenda Banks of insurers Aon, which works with clients on the issue of brand risk. Companies are not able to insure against declines in brand value, but often compound the problem by not managing the risk to their most valuable asset. 'Reputation risk only comes home to roost when things go wrong.'

Source: Richard Gillis (2004) *Financial Times*, 5 October. Reprinted with permission.

Question

How can marketing research inform those people engaged in internal marketing within an organisation on how best to perform their jobs?

CASE STUDY 5

Desmond sizes up shopping

Fancy buying your knickers from a company owned by Richard Desmond? Well, half-owned. Avid readers of the *Daily Express* – and watchers of the newspaper proprietor's Fantasy Channel – will get their chance to do just that from tomorrow, when Desmond launches the Express Shopping Channel.

The joint venture between Northern Shell, his privately owned company, and N Brown Group, the mail order shopping group, will go live on Sky and NTL on Channel 637.

The Express channel will cater to fashion 'for real women', offering lingerie for ladies up to size 48 and bras from B to HH – a cup size so large, one exec joked, that you could 'take three people across the river in it'.

It will also serve up a series of 'lifestyle shows' to highlight its fashion, cooking, DIY and gardening-related offering.

For Desmond, who agreed to invest 'a couple of million quid' to set up the joint venture following a meeting with Lord Alliance, non-executive chairman of N Brown, the combination of Northern Shell's television experience and marketing reach and N Brown's catalogue business represents 'a perfect marriage'.

'I got on with [Lord Alliance], he was telling me about his mail order business, and I've wanted to go into shopping for a few years now,' Desmond says.

Executives involved in the creation of the joint venture say the division of responsibility between the companies has been clearly defined: Northern Shell will provide the joint venture with television expertise, the capacity of its studios and marketing initiatives through its newspapers and N Brown will provide 'back-end' services – the products being sold, the warehouses and call centres.

'I think we're bloody good at front end,' Desmond says.

The channel's shows, including six hours of live broadcasting, will be produced in newly refurbished studios at Northern Shell Tower, in London's Docklands area – the same building where some of Desmond's steamier programmes are edited.

But can the brand that sells Posh and Becks features and stories about women who earn so much 'they can't get a man' really sell frying pans and ladies shoes (which will be offered with up to triple-E-width fittings)?

Desmond, who made headlines earlier this year when he launched a foul-mouthed outburst against executives at the Telegraph group at a board meeting of their West Ferry joint venture, says the Express brand is 'the most reassuring, trustworthy brand' in middle England.

The decision to launch a branded shopping channel represents a new experiment in the expansion of the Express brand name in a market that can be tough for new entrants.

Chris Haslum, a Northern Shell executive who has been named managing director of the shopping channel, says today's home shopping channels have been carried by the trailblazing work done by QVC, the first home-shopping network and market leader.

According to industry folklore, customers watched an average of 50 hours of programming before they started ordering from QVC at the time of its launch nearly two decades ago.

Haslum says it is 'difficult' to avoid adopting a similar model to the QVC one, although he says that the Express channel will offer customers 'more humour, more fun, and more interaction'.

Desmond takes a more direct approach in criticising the market leader, which is owned by Liberty Media, the investment vehicle of US media mogul John Malone.

'I don't think QVC do it very well, to be honest. When you see our channel, the products we've got [are] more relevant and the presentation is better,' he says.

QVC's customers – and the 6.5m viewers who tune in every month – may not agree with Desmond's view. The company's UK arm reported pre-tax profits of £16m on turnover of £226m in 2003.

Dermot Boyd, finance director at QVC UK, says the Express channel's launch is a positive sign for the sector, adding that the group's ability to cross-promote in the Express group's newspapers and magazines would be an advantage that most start-ups lack.

The Express channel is counting, in part, on the experience of Alan White, chief executive of N Brown. As group finance director of Littlewoods in the late 1990s, White shut down Shop!, a television shopping channel the company had set up as a joint venture with Granada.

'I always felt it was an important part of the business. It got to the stage it was doing £40m of turnover. However, it had an expensive infrastructure and there were high costs involved in bringing customers to the channel,' White says.

The N Brown executive says the joint venture expects to break even in two years – in contrast to a flippant remark by Desmond, that he expects to make a profit from the moment the channel airs.

However, Desmond then adds, more seriously: 'It took me seven years on *OK!* [the celebrity monthly mag] to make money, it took five years on the Fantasy Channel, but we've always found a way through. We're winners.'

Perhaps unsurprisingly, White concedes that his initial response was a cautious one: 'Having seen where things can go wrong, I think it is probably fair to say I had some degree of scepticism.' One of his biggest concerns was whether or not the group would be able to create a channel with a low enough cost base to break even in a reasonable amount of time.

Boyd at QVC agrees with the strategy: 'It is a good idea to have the discipline not to invest huge amounts of money and try to get break-even early.'

White says his confidence in the Express channel is based on two key differences from the Littlewoods venture: Express Shopping Channel will have a clearer view on which products work well than Shop! did, and it will benefit from the growth in multichannel viewers. 'We are focusing on customers from middle age and beyond and being a specialist in terms of fittings,' he says.

The extensive range of the group's product offering, including clothes for women sized 12 to 32 and men with 66-inch chests, will be the Express channel's most competitive advantage over the high street.

In the meantime, people hoping to catch a glimpse of Desmond onscreen should not hold their breath. The newspaper owner says he has no plans to be a guest on the channel.

Source: Stephanie Kirchgaessner (2004) *Financial Times*, 19 October. Reprinted with permission.

Question

'The decision to launch a branded shopping channel represents a new experiment in the expansion of the Express brand name in a market that can be tough for new entrants.' Suggest what marketing research might have been undertaken prior to making the decision to go ahead with such a venture.

CASE STUDY 6

Is fizzing up its look enough?

Laurent-Perrier, number three in terms of worldwide sales of champagne, has been getting its house in order. Having bought back Diageo's shareholding, listed on the Paris Stock Exchange in 1999 and finalised its purchase of Chateau Malakoff, a smaller champagne house, earlier this year, Yves Dumont, chairman of L-P's management board, feels he can draw breath.

Which makes this a good time to review L-P's image, particularly among the public. Says Dumont: 'We have been very sales oriented but less focused on the consumer.' In the UK, where alcohol is increasingly bought from supermarkets, that direct connection with the customer is ever more relevant.

L-P wanted a new look for its promotional material, corporate literature including annual reports and press ads. It brought in Paris brand consultancy M Associates, who turned to photographer Jean-Baptiste Huynh. He shot a series of black-and-white images, each intended to express a different variant – a tulip for L-P Brut Non-Vintage, a seashell for Ultra Brut and so on.

The labelling on the bottles has not changed, but from next year the images will appear on material from print ads and point of sale to gift boxes, accompanied by a new brand colour – an earthy hue that L-P calls *terre de champagne*.

The move at L-P, which is majority owned by the Nonancourt family, is a step away from much of the imagery associated with the sector. But then, champagne brands are hardly enthusiastic image updaters. As a glance along any off-licence shelf will prove, champagne is stuck in the design Dark Ages. It's all swirls, crests, gold embossing and italics. The only label that leaps out is Veuve Clicquot – and that's only because it's bright orange or yellow, rather than a pallid cream. Compared with the wine sector, champagne is in a time warp. 'Champagne houses are incredibly conservative – very few brands in this sector stand out,' says John Blackburn of Blackburns, the drinks packaging design specialist.

The champagne companies seem unfazed by this, as sales are going up. Between 1998 and 2002, the UK market value rose by 32% and went up by a further 10% in 2003 to £850m, according to Mintel. Lack of differentiation means that the whole sector exudes brand values that work for all of the members: exclusive, traditional and refined.

Differentiation is instead done through sponsorship, and here the brands are hyperactive. Everyone wants to 'own' an event or a sport, thereby getting the right people to drink their brand in the right environment. So Moët Chandon, major sponsor of London Fashion Week, 'owns fashion', according to David Cunningham, marketing director of Moët Hennessy; Veuve Clicquot, also in the Moët Hennessy portfolio, is the champagne of the 'season', associated with ladies-in-big-hats sporting events. Mumm, on the other hand, is active in the sailing world and its Formula One sponsorship is estimated by Mintel at more than £10m.

So what does this leave L-P to get its teeth into? Dumont says it is focusing on nature and, more recently, design. Hence its regular sponsorship of a garden at the Chelsea Flower Show, and its Eureka design award at this year's London Design Festival.

Unsurprisingly, the vast proportion of champagne houses' marketing spend is on sponsorship rather than advertising or design. L-P doesn't advertise on TV, so sponsorship and event marketing currently account for 90% of its total marketing spend.

L-P hopes that its refocus will help move it from a distant fourth in the UK closer to Veuve Clicquot at number three. The market here is dominated by Moët Chandon, which accounted for 28% of the total market value last year, according to Mintel. Lanson, in second place, accounted for 18%, giving the two top brands together nearly 50% of the market value.

Despite the big volume increases, however, these conservative brands need to watch their backs. The funkier and increasingly credible sparkling wine brigade has the potential to threaten their position, with the UK market growing 27% since 1999, to an estimated value of £1.25bn in 2004.

So new audiences need to be cultivated. Moët Hennessy is doing research with unnamed agencies into who these potential new consumers are. 'Champagne has a lot to learn in targeting new consumers,' says Cunningham, who joined Moët two months ago from Diageo. As this might well mean going for consumers who are less impressed by provenance and heritage and happily slurp cava or prosecco, targeting them will be a challenge.

To do so, Blackburn says, the champagne houses need to do more than tinker at the edges: 'The big threat is the sparkling wines, and tarting up gift boxes to give shelf appeal is not the answer.'

Source: Clare Dowdy (2004) *Financial Times*, 26 October. Reprinted with permission.

Question

Discuss what marketing research might mean to a firm such as this.

CASE STUDY 7

They might just as well be men . . .

Are women who work in marketing making things better for female consumers? Research by FutureBrand suggests not. As part of interviews into women's views on advertising, we talked to 150 women from five, broadly drawn groups. These were: women over size 16; over-50s; lesbians; professional working women; and, separately, women working in advertising, branding, communications or design.

The group that felt most alienated from conventional marketing was lesbians, although the size 16+s felt almost as disconnected. It's noteworthy that the latter group, which constitutes around half of all UK women, should feel almost as negative as a group that comprises an estimated 5%.

By contrast, the audience that felt most adequately represented was the marketers. Some 67% of this group felt that ads were aimed at women like them, compared to an average among the four other groups of 49%. It is startling that, while one in 10 lesbians and women size 16+, and one in 12 professional working women thought that none of the ads they saw was targeted at them, not a single woman in marketing we interviewed felt that way.

Only 29% of marketing women believe the industry is misogynistic, but 64% of them feel it is their responsibility to change attitudes. Is it not curious that as female marketers we are willing to help change things, even if we don't really think there's a problem in the first place? So, in what ways are marketers failing to connect with female audiences?

Overall, women professionals felt represented in ads. But when they were asked to name brands that spoke to them as business women, they could not do so. They felt less able than their male counterparts to compartmentalise their lives. Men, they said, were much more able to disengage from the home when they were in the office and could view the weekend as pure leisure time. By contrast, professional women talked about the reality of ordering groceries online while talking to a client on the phone or using weekends to catch up on household chores.

To these professional women, it felt as if business-to-business brands were marketing to the whole man in his office environment, but only to part of a woman in the same setting. As one woman put it: 'I am all four characters of *Sex and the City* rolled into one, plus a bit of Dawn French, Carol Vorderman, Mo Mowlam and Anita Roddick.' B2B brands are not marketing to that woman in all her facets.

For lesbians, there was the perennial issue of being part of a minority. By definition, mainstream marketing almost never deals with feelings of exclusion. Most branding is about conformity, in a world where sexuality is almost always heterosexuality and on-screen families are of a highly conventional variety.

For women over 50, the disconnect between advertising and the reality of their lives is improving. Brands such as Saga have targeted this group, and our research showed the approach was resonating well. (As an aside, only 4% of the women marketers we interviewed described themselves as aged over 40 – a reflection, perhaps, of a wider ageism in the industry)

For women over size 16 the disconnect is clear. More than half of size 16+ women took the view that fashion brands and their use of super-thin models undermined women's self-confidence. This issue was highlighted by all groups bar the female marketers, where only 35% agreed. And whereas 36% of size 16+ women said fashion brands contributed to anorexia, only 11% of the marketers thought so.

Drill down and there appears to be another discrepancy of view. Some 93% of women in marketing feel shops cater for women their size. This is not surprising given that 76% of women in marketing describe themselves as a size 12 or less, and not one described herself as over size 16. Remember, 47% of UK women are a size 16 or more. And the discrepancy between women in the marketing fields and our other groups came through in their brand preferences, too.

Overall, there were only two brands that all women asked associated with enhanced self-esteem: The Body Shop and Dove.

As women in marketing, we are not only out of touch but we are too aware of the tactics of marketers to think like consumers. Even if women in marketing saw the need for change – which they do not – and even if they were willing to help bring it about – which they generally are – it could be argued that they would still not be able to change on the basis of personal experience alone.

For once, women's intuition won't work. We need to approach marketing to women as we might approach marketing to men: by admitting that we don't understand them, aren't very much like them, want to get inside their heads and need to connect with them better. Brands should see this as a major opportunity. The playing field is wide open for brands to capture women's hearts by promoting – rather than plundering – their self-esteem.

Source: Jasmine Montgomery (2004) *Financial Times*, 5 October. Reprinted with permission.

Question

Imagine you are a buyer working for a large department store that sells ranges of women's clothes. What use could you make of the information contained in this study? How might you pass on such information to sales staff in the store so that they are better equipped to deal with customers?

CASE STUDY 8

Now interacting with lots of new partners

It would be unfair to describe Nivea consumers as diet-obsessed, chain-smoking single women with little success with men. Yet many of the consumers which the personal care brand wants to target do seem to have a fascination with the struggles experienced by Helen Fielding's character Bridget Jones.

In fact, more than 6m women in the UK within Nivea's core demographic are predicted to watch the movie *Bridget Jones: The Edge of Reason* when it opens in UK cinemas on 12 November. This is why Nivea is placing the film at the centre of a new integrated marketing campaign which starts this week.

Nivea's marketing manager, Samantha Wright, is one of a growing number of marketers demanding her media planners think differently and work more closely with above- and below-the-line agencies to engage consumers and bring a brand story to life.

The term 'media neutrality' has been bandied around for a while within marketing circles, but for many marketers it is becoming reality. To hit the target these days, brands need a thorough understanding of how and where their consumers are likely to interact with them. The traditional media planning ideal of shouting the loudest to reach the greatest number of people is no longer enough.

And planners need to do more than simply demonstrate that they can allocate funds to different media without overloading the audience or busting the budget. Today, the role is much more about building a media schedule around a consumer's interests and tastes, making the brand more relevant.

'Clever media planning is a way for marketers to extend their thinking. Today's planners must be able to take a conventional media schedule and then ask the right questions so different ideas can be bolted on,' says Alison Hoad, planning partner at Campbell Doyle Dye and a convenor of judges for this year's IPA Effectiveness Awards.

Carat Media is project managing the Nivea campaign, but Wright briefed all her agencies at the same time, including the creative teams at TBWA and FCB London, making sure that everyone had bought into the integrated concept. Red Baron Media, a creative partnership agency, helped Nivea's owner, Beiersdorf, to sign up the brand as one of Universal Studios' official marketing partners for the movie.

Initially, Nivea wanted product placement in the film, but research revealed its consumers would not see this as a credible link for the brand. Instead, consumers will see promotions and traditional advertising linked to the movie through various touch points, including at retail outlets, on the Web and via mobile-based promotions to complement the glossy magazines and outdoor ads.

Carat's communications planner, Ciaran Challis, accepts media planners must be multifaceted these days. 'Planners must look at the bigger picture and understand the value of other disciplines, such as PR, and know how to use them. It is essential to develop media opportunities around the interests of the target market. If consumers like going to the movies, then that is where we need to talk to them,' he says.

Media fragmentation is adding to the pressure on media planners to think smarter. Take the music and dance phenomenon created by Bartle Bogle Hegarty for Lever Fabergé's toiletries brand Lynx Pulse. As well as booking traditional media, the plan involved releasing the single 'Make Luv' by Room 5 featuring Oliver Cheatham, which topped the singles chart for four weeks selling 325,000 copies. The campaign included an interactive element with a website and screensaver, while events such as Pulse parties were held in clubs.

Planning agency Naked was established on the belief that brand owners must move away from the old media planning model and that planners need to understand how to build excitement around a brand by focusing on a consumer's preferences. Naked helped boost awareness of directory inquiries brand 118 118 by getting its runners to interact with the public and through guerrilla tactics.

'We are at the beginning of a restructuring of the communications industry. Media is increasingly being seen as a place to showcase your creative message and demonstrate how your brand interacts with consumers. It is no longer just about having a single grandstanding piece of creative work or a factory producing TV commercials,' says Naked partner Will Collin.

Indeed, advertising agencies that have traditionally insisted on being guardians of the brands they represent are accepting that they must work more closely with other marketing services companies. They realise that it is as important to reach consumers when they are shopping or in the pub, as when they are watching *Coronation Street*.

The British Heart Foundation's fatty cigarette campaign has been one of the most memorable of the year. The activity is being managed by advertising agency Euro RSCG London, which wanted to ensure that the image of how a person's arteries clog up and ooze with fat every time they smoke is in their mind when they are having a cigarette. As well as booking outdoor and television space the BHF worked with different agencies to produce beer mats for pubs and to create a micro website carrying advice on how to give up.

During the first burst of activity in January, the BHF helpline received almost 13,000 calls and the website attracted more than 250,000 visitors. It is estimated that around half that number will go on to give up the habit.

BHF launched the second phase of its campaign last week, with new elements such as text and email support, interactive TV and a Tetris-style computer game, Fatris, which can be played on a mobile phone or the BHF website.

Says Malcolm White, executive planning director at Euro RSCG: 'This is an example of where the client is providing the integrated glue for all the marketing agencies to stick together. Clients are becoming reluctant to buy all their media services from one group and are preferring to purchase the best facilities from different places, so that they can be the force that ensures that everyone works together in a way that brings the most benefit to the brand.'

Source: Steve Hemsley (2004) *Financial Times*, 12 October. Reprinted with permission.

Question

'To hit the target these days, brands need a thorough understanding of how and where their consumers are likely to interact with them.' How can marketing research help firms to get to grips with this problem?

CASE STUDY 9

Lake Lucerne Navigation Company (SGV)

The Lake Lucerne Navigation Company (SGV) is Switzerland's largest steam and motor ship operator. Its fleet of five nostalgic paddle steamers and 15 elegant motor ships transports 2.3 million passengers a year. The ships have been carrying both tourists and local people over beautiful Lake Lucerne since 1835. The lake offers a varied landscape ranging from the fertile shores of the lowlands and the steep slopes of the Alpine foothills to the vertical rock faces of the towering Alps surrounding Lake Uri.

It is 170 years since businessman Friedrich Knörr, from Alsace, realised his dream and founded a 'limited company for the purpose of the establishment of a steam ship on Lake Lucerne'. This limited company is now known as the Lake Lucerne Navigation Company (SGV) and has become the largest shipping company in Switzerland. However, this beautiful lake in Central Switzerland still retains something from those pioneering days. Out of a total fleet of 20 ships, five are genuine paddle steamers from the early years of the last century.

A versatile company

The core business of the Lake Lucerne Navigation Company is timetable and special cruises. In addition it runs restaurants and arranges entertainment, as well as running its own shipyard where it builds its own ships and boats for other people. In addition to all this, working with Auto AG Schwyz (AAGS) the SGV runs the Riviera bus service between Küssnacht am Rigi and Schwyz. In Lucerne, Brunnen and Flüelen, Navirag, a subsidiary, runs three bistros and a newspaper stand. Add in the Weggis Travel Centre, which specialises in the sale of freight cruises, and it is clear that the SGV is also an innovative company in the outgoing sector.

Catering services on the boats are run by a leasing company, Schiffsgastronomie AG.

A modern employer

The Lake Lucerne Navigation Company is an important and popular employer in central Switzerland. After the SBB (Federal Swiss Railways) it is one of the most important transport companies in the heart of Switzerland and possesses the largest shipyard in the country. The company employs 160 people a year, on average, as well as 13 apprentices. The typical SGV employee is multitalented and very flexible. In summer employees work on the boats, be it as controller-sailor or captain, while in winter the majority of staff work in the company's shipyard in their other professional capacity, such as electrician, welder or carpenter.

Imposing figures

Even the company's figures are impressive. Every year, 2.3 million passengers travel 380,000 km in 20 boats. In other words, the Lake Lucerne Navigation Company transports the population of Paris nine times around the world! The fleet has a capacity for 13,000 passengers and 3,200 restaurant seats.

Without taking Schiffsgastronomie AG into account, the Lake Lucerne Navigation Company has an income of 26 million francs, 20 million of which come from cruises. The main markets are Switzerland and Germany, plus the more distant markets of Asia and America. A rough calculation shows that 70% of passengers are Swiss and 30% are foreign tourists.

Beautiful landscape and attractive range of services

The Lucerne/Lake Lucerne region is one of Switzerland's tourist centres. A ride on a ship, over a beautiful lake, is an unforgettable highlight. With its 35 boat landings spread along the shores of the lake, the Lake Lucerne Navigation Company is able to offer passengers from near and far an unbeatable range of cruises. These can be combined with a trip into the mountains or a walk along the lakeshore, or can simply be a pleasant round trip on a ship; the Lake Lucerne Navigation Company has something for everyone, all year round.

Special cruises

The Lake Lucerne Navigation Company also offers special cruises and runs these as professionally as ever. With its 600 special cruises a year, the company has acquired a lot of know-how in this area. Be it a wedding, a company jubilee, a banquet or a business meeting, the SGV, with its 20 boats in various sizes and its 3,200 restaurant seats, is well-equipped for any situation.

The Lake Lucerne Navigation Company and its partners offer an infinite range of attractive services. The following gives a brief – but incomplete – overview. If you require more detailed information, or wish to make a reservation, the company would be happy to be of service at any time.

Timetable cruises

Departures are scheduled approximately every hour on these main routes:

- Lucerne – Weggis – Vitznau – Beckenried – Gersau – Brunnen – Rütli – Flüelen

- Lucerne – Kehrsiten (– Bürgenstock) – Stansstad – Alpnachstad

Visitors are offered an attractive choice of cruises lasting between one and six hours. Between spring and autumn the Lake Lucerne Navigation Company operates five nostalgic paddle steamers in addition to its numerous motor ships. In Lucerne, Brunnen, Flüelen and Alpnachstad, the lake is connected to the Swiss and European railways and fully integrated in their system of schedules and fares. Around the lake you will find ideal parking for cars and coaches.

On-board gastronomy

On all main routes, the company offers refined service for breakfast, lunch, coffee/cakes and dinner. In addition, working with Schiffsgastronomie AG, the company offers a wide range of speciality cuisine

- breakfast cruise (Zmorge-Schiff)

- brunch cruise with childcare on board

- year-round lunch cruise

- lunch cruise with departure from Brunnen

- SUSHIP – the sushi ship

- Indian buffet

- cruise with Chinese fondue.

Evening cruises

For that unforgettable moment on Lake Lucerne, the largest navigation company in Switzerland also has a wide range of thematic round trips on offer for the evening:

- sunset dinner cruise
- evening cruises with music and gastronomy
- Irish cruise
- night boat (Swiss folklore).

Family-friendly Lake Lucerne cruises

With the Junior Card, children aged from 6 to 16 can travel free when accompanied by one parent. Thanks to the new Grandchild Card, even grandparents can introduce their grandchildren to the beautiful region of Lake Lucerne and the fascinating world of ship cruises. The SGV strives to be family-friendly – which is why it also offers junior menus and issues the travel brochure *Walking Trails for Baby Carriages*.

Lucerne Concert Hall accessible by boat

The new Lucerne Concert Hall (KKL) was inaugurated in 1998. Some of the SGV landing stages by the main railway station are located directly under architect Jean Nouvel's spectacular projecting roof. The proximity of the landing stage to the KKL offers a range of attractive combinations (side programmes, exhibitions, various events, transfers etc.).

Cast off and find time for hiking, walking and biking

Twenty ships bring excursionists and people who want to relax into the nature arena of Lake Lucerne, year-round, rain or shine. Many guests seek that special positive feeling attained through physical activity and enjoying a ride. The SGV offers those guests a wide range of possibilities:

- **Hiking and strolling**: detailed description of routes for the Swiss Path and 15 other lakeside paths are available, free.
- **Guided hiking tours, baby-stroller and wheelchair friendly hiking paths**: suggested routes for all generations available in two free brochures.
- **Bike and lake**: delightful panoramic routes for bikers and inline skaters. Children's bikes are transported free of charge.

- **Walking and Nordic walking**: wide lakeside paths for athletic walking, an ideal sport for your health, with or without special Nordic walking sticks. And to freshen up there are **numerous swimming opportunities** in the clean lake on public or natural beaches.

The Swiss Path

Fourteen years ago, the scenic Swiss Path walking trail was opened. The Swiss Path is a joint cantonal effort in commemoration of Switzerland's 700th anniversary (1291 to 1991). It starts at Rütli Meadow, birthplace of the Confederation, and ends in Brunnen. Each canton designed one segment of the trail (there are 5mm of trail for each citizen). The sponsoring cantons are making sure that their gift will retain its value by financing and ensuring its continuity. The trail is accessible via nine ship landings, three railway stations, a funicular railway and four bus lines.

Combination lake and mountain trips

All mountain cable and rail systems can be reached quickly and conveniently by our ships:

- **Rigi cogwheel railway**: Lucerne – Vitznau, approx. 60 minutes
- **Pilatus cogwheel railway**: Lucerne – Alpnachstad, approx. 80 minutes
- **Klewenalp aerial cable car**: Lucerne – Beckenried, approx. 90 minutes
- **Seelisberg funicular**: Lucerne – Treib, approx. 110 minutes
- **Bürgenstock funicular**: Lucerne – Kehrsiten, approx. 40 minutes
- **Stanserhorn and Titlis lifts**: Lucerne – Stansstad, approx. 60 minutes
- **Seebodenalp aerial cable car**: Lucerne – Küssnacht am Rigi, approx. 60 minutes.

Ideal combination options for round trips and walks. Bargain package rates including ship fare, lift fare and snack are available for trips to Bürgenstock/ Felsenweg, Seebodenalp, Rigi and Klewenalp.

Lake Uri

The beautiful, historic and unique cultural region of Lake Uri is well worth a visit. Good public transport connections and adequate parking are available near Brunnen and Flüelen landing stages.

Top price–performance ratio

- **Villas and castles cruise**: particularly good-value round trips in the Bay of Lucerne and in Lake Küssnacht. Pleasant cruises along the shoreline, past villas and castles.

- **Group discount**: groups of ten or more people receive attractive reduced prices on all boats.

- **Price reductions**: the following are recognised by the SGV: Half-fare Card, Annual General Season Ticket (GA) and Swiss Travel Cards, Swiss Boat Pass, Swiss Family Boat Pass and the Tell Pass of Central Switzerland.

- **Children**: children under 5 and children aged between 6 and 16 with a Junior Card or a Grandchild Card travel free.

- **Day cards**: both summer and winter, the SGV offers day cards at attractive prices and gives you total freedom of movement on Lake Lucerne.

- **Winter Fun GA**: the super-value winter general season ticket.

William Tell Express: the only alpine express by boat and train

The William Tell Express is a top tourist attraction connecting two of the most fascinating Swiss regions – Central Switzerland and Ticino. On board the paddle steamer, your journey takes you over Lake Lucerne, from Lucerne to Flüelen, where you transfer to a train on the world-famous Gotthardt Railway and ride past steep gorges, over innumerable bridges and through sinuous tunnels, to Lugano or Locarno. Now there are two new connections per day from Central Switzerland to Tessin, and vice versa. Taking approximately five hours, the William Tell Express can easily be incorporated in many travel programmes, for example in combination with the Bernina or Glacier Express.

Lake Lucerne is in season all year round!

During the winter months, the SGV daily offers six lake cruises leaving Lucerne for Hertenstein, Weggis, Vitznau (Rigi), Beckenried (Klewenalp), Gersau, Treib (Seelisberg), Brunnen and Rütli. On Sundays and public holidays additional landing stages on Lake Uri will also be in operation. The following offers are especially attractive:

- lunch cruise
- fondue cruise

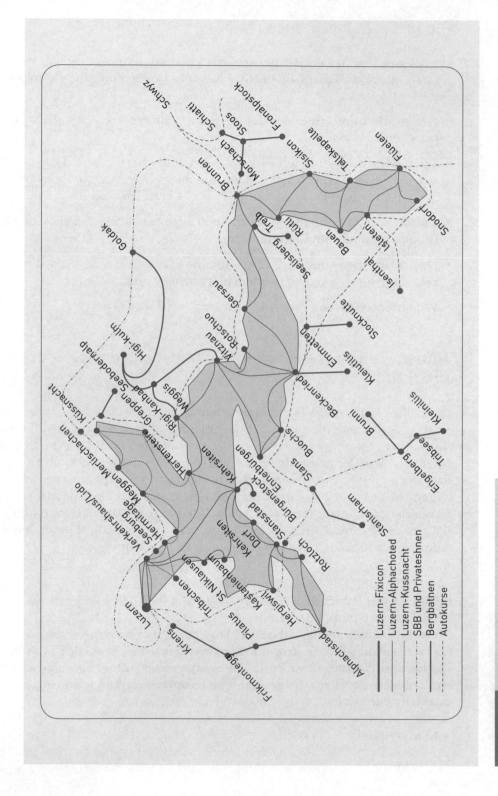

FIGURE CS9.1   Lake Lucerne Navigation Company map

- Chinese fondue cruise
- gateau boat
- Sunday breakfast boat
- brunch boat.

Lakeview for all: www.lakelucerne.ch

The Lake Lucerne Navigation Company's up-to-date website will enthrall you with its many ideas. The live-cam on landing stage 3 in Lucerne delivers live pictures of main landing stages 1 and 2 every 30 seconds, thus boats on cruise and the schedules can be followed on screen. Current weather and temperature forecasts for Lucerne and Flüelen also come in very handy.

Source: Lake Lucerne Navigation Company, Switzerland (2005).

Question

The marketing manager is keen to find out visitor attitudes and opinions about what the company presently provides. Outline a number of research studies that might provide the company with useful information in this respect.

CASE STUDY 10

Gondolas for Liverpool

Liverpool is a big city but like most cities its centre is relatively small. The only problem with Liverpool is that the centre is on two sites: the old centre around Lime Street, the James Centre and the City (as far as the Town Hall) and the new centre on the waterfront around the Pier Head and the Albert Dock. For the new centre there have been several recent proposals for expansion, including a vast shopping complex and a new site for Everton football stadium. In addition, the new centre has an industrial complex and residential up-beat apartments built in what were once the old dockland buildings.

Liverpool has an underground railway system that traverses the River Mersey but there are only four underground stations on the Liverpool side of the Mersey – James Street, Moorfields, Lime Street and Central. The last two are in the heart of the old shopping area. During the 19th century Liverpool was among the foremost cities in Britain in terms of innovation of travel around the city. The city's network of tramcars rivalled that of modern-day San Francisco while its overhead railway, which ran the length of the docklands, rivalled that of modern-day New York. Sadly, both of these systems of transportation are no more. Buses and taxis ply their trade where once these transport systems ruled supreme.

Recently, on a visit to Switzerland, Liverpool City Councillor Dan Smith encountered the gondola transportation system in operation at the foot of Mount Pilatus near Krienz next to Lucerne. The red gondolas are an impressive sight as they continually ply their way from the terminus station at Krienz, through an intermediate dropping off point, to the higher station some 4500 feet above sea level (an ascent of some 3500 feet) two-thirds of the way up Mount Pilatus. The journey covers several miles and takes around half an hour to complete. Dan was not able to count the number of gondolas on the continuous belt system but he reckoned it to be several hundred. Each gondola could carry four people so that the whole system must have been able to carry at least 1000 people at any one time. A gondola is a bit like a four-seater bubble car that is suspended from a cable that runs in a continuous loop-over circuit and is supported from pylons. The gondolas at Krienz can be up to 100 feet above the ground, although more often the distance is 20 to 30 feet.

Dan felt that perhaps a gondola transportation system might be the answer to what Liverpool really needed. Such a system would be highly innovative in the UK and be an attraction that would outperform the new tram systems in either Sheffield or Manchester. He felt an obvious first route would be from Lime Street to the Pier Head with maybe an intermediate station in the city close to the Town Hall. The system might also be extended to other parts of the city in due course, e.g. Anfield and the Liverpool football ground, the Liverpool University and John Moores University campuses.

Dan mulled these ideas over and decided that perhaps some sort of feasibility study would be required. At the next meeting of the City Council he put forward his ideas and suggested that perhaps a feasibility study would be worthwhile. His colleagues were quite interested in the idea but pointed out that they could not really waste ratepayers' money on a 'pie in the sky' scheme. Dan said he thought it might be worthwhile to find out ratepayers' attitudes to such a scheme in the first place. If these were positive, he argued, then his idea would have some support and it would be worthwhile taking the scheme on to the next stage where one might assess its costs and benefits.

Questions

1 Is Dan right in suggesting one should assess customer attitudes to such a scheme prior to undertaking a cost–benefit analysis? Explain.

2 Draw up a research proposal indicating how you would set about measuring ratepayers' attitudes as Dan suggests.

3 In making a decision about this project, what information is required? What role would marketing research play in providing the relevant information – i.e. what further information is required?

Glossary

aided questions Questions that provide clues to help respondents recall more accurately.

aided recall Respondents are asked if they remember an advertisement for a particular brand.

alternative hypothesis A competing hypothesis to the null.

analysis of variance A method of testing hypotheses of no differences among means for more than two independent samples.

attitude A learned predisposition to act in a consistent manner with respect to a given object.

audit A formal examination of the movement of goods at the retail level or in and out of stock in warehouses.

balanced scale Scale employing an equal number of favourable and unfavourable categories.

blind testing Tests where the brand name of the product under test is not disclosed.

branded testing Test where the name of a product is made known.

causality The effect of one variable creating change in another.

census A complete enumeration of the pre-specified group.

chi-square test statistic Measures the goodness of fit between the numbers observed in the sample and the numbers that should have been evident in a sample were the null hypothesis true.

cluster sampling Design where one first selects a sample of clusters and next decides on which sampling unit to include.

coding Involves the assignment of an alphanumeric symbol or a numerical value to represent a specific response to a question. It also includes the column position that the designated code occupies on a data record.

comparative scaling Sometimes called non-metric scaling, it requires the respondent to compare a set of stimulus objects directly against one another.

concept Something intended to satisfy customers' wants and needs.

concept evaluation test A test for screening new product ideas or alternative end benefits for products.

concept tests Data on purchase intentions, attribute ratings and likes/dislikes with respect to ideas for new products or repositioning of existing ones.

construct validity Assessment of whether the variables measured in a study adequately represent the intended theoretical constructs.

content validity Assessment of whether scale items adequately reflect the entire spectrum of the construct under examination.

continuous rating scale Involves the respondent indicating a rating by placing a mark at an appropriate position on a line.

continuous tracking A study whereby the measurements are taken during the entire length of the campaign.

copy recall The number (percentage) of respondents who can recall the copy in an advertisement being tested.

copy testing Advertising effectiveness research.

cross-sectional surveys Data obtained by survey from a number of different respondents at a single point in time.

debriefing Respondents' explanation of answers to questions, interpretation of meanings and nature of problems encountered during the conduct of a study.

dependent variable The response measure which is being studied in a research exercise.

depth interview A one-to-one interview in which feelings and opinions are discussed. Usually intended to uncover motivations, prejudices and attitudes.

diary panels Households that agree to give information regularly for an extended period of time. Respondents record events as they occur, e.g. purchases.

double-barrelled questions Requests for information that simultaneously try to elicit answers to two questions.

electronic scanner services Services that record information on purchases made with the aid of electronic optical checkout devices.

emic instrument An instrument that investigates a cultural construct.

ethnography Systematic recording of human cultures.

etic instrument An instrument to make comparisons of the same variable across different cultures.

experimental design The particular approach adopted in an experiment to minimise the effect of different sources of error.

exploratory analysis No prior assumptions are made and the data themselves allow for the findings that are obtained.

extended-use product test In-home tests where a product is tried out for an extended period of time.

external validity The extent to which research findings can be generalised to and across populations of interest in different situations and at different times.

filter questions Questions posed to determine the route to be followed through a questionnaire.

follow-up Means of contacting respondents from time to time after an initial contact.

funnel sequence In an interview or questionnaire, the process of asking questions of a general nature followed by questions of a more precise and pointed nature that refer to the topic being explored.

hypothesis An assumption a researcher is making about a characteristic of, or a relationship in, a population of interest.

independent variable A factor that has influence on the values adopted by the dependent variable in a phenomenon being explored.

inverted funnel sequence Moving from the specific to the general when exploring a topic in a questionnaire or interview.

itemised questions (closed ended) Questionnaire format in which the respondent is allowed a number of predetermined descriptions and requested to select the one he or she prefers.

judgemental data Data reflecting perceptions or preferences.

judgemental sampling A sample selected for study because it is considered to be representative of the population of interest or because it fits with the requirements of the research study.

laboratory experiment Experimentation under artificially created conditions in which the experimenter has direct control over most of the factors that influence the outcome of the experiment.

latent theoretical construct A construct that is not directly observable.

loaded questions Questions that suggest what the answer might be or express the researcher's own position on the matter.

longitudinal design A research design in which time is an important variable.

longitudinal surveys A survey in which respondents are questioned at different points in time.

market testing Test designed to assess the impact of a change in a marketing mix element.

market tracking studies Provide performance benchmarks by examining performance of competitors.

maturation The changes that take place in the dependent variable under study in research with the passage of time and that are unrelated to the influence of the independent variable.

monadic product tests Product tests undertaken without comparison to other products as benchmarks.

mortality Drop out or loss of respondents in the course of a longitudinal research project.

multicollinearity The correlations that exist among independent variables, which make it difficult to assess the true impact of individual independent variables on the dependent variable.

multiple-item formats Attitude scaling measures requiring the subject to respond to several items (usually statements) of belief, feeling and intention.

non-comparative scaling (monadic scaling) A scaling method in which the respondent is asked to evaluate each object on a scale independently of the other objects being evaluated.

non-probability samples A sample where there is no way of assessing what the probability is of selecting any particular element or unit into the sample.

non-response error Error that is introduced because not all the respondents included in a sample do, in fact, respond. It reflects the possibility that the responses of non-respondents may well be different to those of people who actually respond and hence the results produced are not representative of the whole population of interest.

null hypothesis The hypothesis being tested.

open-ended questions Questions that allow respondents freedom to express their answers in whatever format they choose.

optical scanning Direct machine reading of numerical values or alphanumeric codes and transcription into electronic storage devices.

order bias A condition whereby responses to stimuli (questions, pictures, objects etc.) is influenced by the order in which they are shown.

paired comparison scale A scale that presents the respondents with objects two at a time requesting the respondent to select one or other of them according to some criterion.

positioning A means of determining how to set the marketing-mix elements so as to maximise the appeal of a particular product in the minds of a specific target population.

protocol analysis A procedure in which the subject in the research verbalises his or her thoughts while answering questions.

qualitative research Methods of research, usually involving small samples, that attempt to elicit descriptive information about the thoughts and feeling of respondents on a topic of interest to the research.

quantitative research methods An approach usually involving large samples that are designed to generate data that can be projected onto the whole population.

random sampling error Error produced because the selected sample is not a perfect representation of the overall population.

recall A measure of the number of people who can remember having seen an advertisement.

recognition A measure of whether respondents can recognise the name of a particular brand.

reliability The extent to which measures are free from random error and give consistent results.

response error Error occurring as a result of inaccurate or wrongly recorded answers.

response rates The percentage of people who respond positively to requests to participate in the research.

sampling frame List of members of the population of interest who are eligible for inclusion in a sample.

sampling unit Elements that make up a population.

spurious association Inappropriate assumption that a causal relationship exists between observed events.

structured interview Method of interviewing where the questions are entirely predetermined.

syndicated research services Suppliers of market research data which are collected on a regular basis through standardised procedures. The data are sold to individual clients.

target population The set of people, products or objects that possesses the information of interest to the researcher.

tracking System that permits the assessment of key sales components of customer awareness and trial and repeat purchases.

treatment Refers to manipulation of the independent variable – especially in experiments.

Type I error A situation where the null hypothesis is true but it is rejected on the basis of the sample data.

Type II error A situation where the null hypothesis is not rejected when, in fact, the alternative hypothesis is true.

unaided questions Questions that do not provide any clues as to the answer.

unbalanced scale A scale that uses an unequal number of unfavourable or favourable scale categories.

unstructured interview An interview wherein questions are not entirely pre-determined and the interviewer can probe for details and underlying thoughts.

validity The extent to which instruments measure that which they are intended to measure or research findings reflect reality as we might know it.

verification Procedures aimed at ensuring the accurate transcription of research data.

Bibliography

Abdel-Ghany, M and Sharpe, D L (1997) Consumption patterns among the young-old and old-old, *Journal of Consumer Affairs*, 31(1), Summer, 90–112.

Abraham, M and Lodish, L (1990) Getting the most out of advertising and promotion, *Harvard Business Review*, 68, 3.

Achrol, R S and Stern, L W (1988) Environmental determinants of decision making uncertainty in marketing channels, *Journal of Marketing Research*, 25, 36–50.

Adcock, C J (1997) Sample size determination – a review, *Statistician*, 46(2), 261–83.

Adler, P and Adler, P (1994) Observational techniques, in Denzin, N K and Lincoln, Y S (eds), *Handbook of Qualitative Research*, Thousand Oaks, CA: Sage.

Advertising Association (published annually) *Marketing Pocket Book*, The Advertising Association in conjunction with NTC Publications, Farm Road, Henley-on-Thames, Oxfordshire RG9 1EJ. Also the *Lifestyle Pocket Book*, the *Media Pocket Book* and the *Regional Marketing Pocket Book*.

Albaum, G (1987) Do source and anonymity affect mail survey results? *Journal of the Academy of Marketing Science*, 15, 74–81.

Albaum, G and Strandskow, J (1989) Participation in a mail survey of international marketers: effects of pre-contact and detailed project explanation, *Journal of Global Marketing*, 2(4), 7–23.

Albrecht, T L, Johnson, G M and Walther, J B (1993) Understanding communication processes in focus groups, in Morgan, D L (ed.), *Successful Focus Groups: Advancing the state of the art*, Newbury Park, CA: Sage.

Allison, B, O'Sullivan, T, Owen, A, Rice, J, Rothwell, A and Saunders, C (1996) *Research Skills for Students: Transferable and learning skills*, London: Kogan Page.

AMA (1987) New marketing research definition approved, *Marketing News*, 21, 6–8.

Anderson, E W (1993) Firm, industry and national indices of customer satisfaction: implications for services, in Swartz, T and Brown, S W (eds), *Advances in Services Marketing Management: Research and practice* vol. 2, Greenwich, CT: JAI Press.

Anderson, E W, Fornell, C and Rust, R T (1997) Customer satisfaction, productivity, and profitability: differences between goods and services, *Marketing Science*, 16(2), 129–45.

Anderson, P F (1983) Marketing, scientific progress, and scientific method, *Journal of Marketing*, 47(4), 18–31.

Andreasen, A (1983) Cost-conscious marketing research, *Harvard Business Review*, 61, 4.

Andreasson, T W (1994) Satisfaction, loyalty and reputation as indicators of personal values in cross-cultural marketing, *Journal of Marketing Research*, 7(2).

Arnett, R (1990) Mail panel research in the 1990s, *Applied Marketing Research*, 30(2), 8–10.

Aschenbaum, A A (1993) The future challenge to market research, *Marketing Research: A magazine of management and application*, 5(2), 12–18.

Ashill, N and Jobber, D (1999) The impact of environmental uncertainty perceptions, decision-maker characteristics and work environment characteristics on the perceived usefulness of marketing information systems (MkIS): a conceptual framework, *Journal of Marketing Management*, 15(6), 519–40.

Attaran, M (1992) *Management Science Information System*, New York: Wiley.

Azzolini, M and Shillaber, J (1993) Internal service quality: winning from the inside out, *Quality Progress*, November, 75–78.

Bachmann, D P (1987) Cover letter appeals and sponsorship effects on mail survey response rates, *Journal of Marketing Education*, 9, 45–51.

Bachman, D P, Elfrink, J and Vazzana, G (1996) Tracking the progress of email versus snail-mail, *Marketing Research*, 8, 31–35.

Bailar, B A (1997) Does sampling work? *Business Economics*, 32(1), January, 47–53.

Baker, K (1989) Using geodemographics in market research, *Journal of the Market Research Society*, 31, 37–44.

Barrie, C (1996) Second rescue for spluttering Reliant, *Guardian*, 6 April, 2.

Bartonova, M (1996) The markets are emerging – and research is hard on their heels, *Research Plus*, January, 4–5.

Bass, F (1969) A new product growth model for consumer durables, *Management Science*, 15, January, 215–27.

Bates, B (1996) Quality will mark the route to deeper client relationships, *Research Plus*, March, 9, 14.

Bekesi, J (1997) Gruppe Phänomenologie. Society for the Advancement of the Critical Development of Phenomenology and its Impulses, http://gpn.freezope.org

Berg, B L (1998) *Qualitative Methods for the Social Sciences*, Boston, MA: Allyn & Bacon.

Berry, L L, Zeithaml, V A and Parasuraman, A (1985) Quality counts in services, too, *Business Horizons*, May–June, 44–52.

Berry, L L, Zeithaml, V A and Parasuraman, A (1989) Five imperatives for improving service quality, *Sloan Management Review*, 31–32, 89–91.

Bhaduri, M, de Souza, M and Sweeney, T (1993) International qualitative research: a critical review of different approaches, *Marketing and Research Today*, 21(3), 171–78.

Biel, A (1989) Love the advertisement, buy the product? *ADMAP*, October.

Blattberg, R and Deighton, J (1991) Interactive marketing: exploiting the age of addressability, *Sloan Management Review*, 33, 1.

Blattberg, R and Hoch, S (1990) Database models and managerial intuition: 50% model + 50% manager, *Management Science*, 36(8), 887–99.

Blum, G and Law, K (1984) Making focus groups even more effective, *Agri Marketing*, March, 24ff.

Bogda, P and Meyers, G C (1991) Grab a partner for more effective research, *Marketing News*, 7 January, 2ff.

Boland, A (1996) Got report-o-phobia? Follow these simple steps to get those ideas on to paper, *Chemical Engineering*, 103(3), March, 131–32.

Bolongaro, G (1994) Delphi technique can work for new product development, *Marketing News*, 3 January, 11.

Bolton, R N (1991) An exploratory investigation of questionnaire pretesting with verbal protocol analysis, *Advances in Consumer Research*, 18, 558–65.

Bolton, R N (1994) Covering the market, *Marketing Research: A magazine of management and application*, 6(3), 30–35.

Booth-Kewley, S, Edwards, J E and Rosenfeld, P (1992) Impression management, social desirability and computer administration of attitude questionnaires: does the computer make a difference? *Journal of Applied Psychology*, 77(4), 562–66.

Bowditch, A J (1996) In Europe's complex market, check the price is right, *Research Plus*, April, 12–13.

Bowditch, A J and Fitall, S (1995) Through the looking glass: primary research in multicountry forecasting, *Proceedings of the EphMRA/ESOMAR Pharmaceutical Marketing Research Conference*, Geneva, Amsterdam: ESOMAR, 141–63.

Branthwaite, A and Bruggemann, J (1996) Why we won't keep taking pills, *Research Plus*, April.

Britt, S H (1971) The writing of readable research reports, *Journal of Marketing Research*, May, 265.

Brock, S E (1989) Marketing research in Asia: problems, opportunities and lessons, *Marketing Research*, September, 47.

Brooks, R F (1993) Internal service quality – a manufacturing perspective, *Proceedings of the Marketing Education Group*, Loughborough, 93–94.

Brooks, R F (1995) Internal service quality – a theoretical development, *Proceedings of the Marketing Education Group*, Bradford, 80–90.

Brooks, R F and Smith, J V (1993) Service from within, *TQM Journal*, October, 41–45.

Brown, G (1991) Big stable brands and advertisements' effects, *ADMAP*, May.

Brown, G (1991) Modelling advertising awareness, *ADMAP*, April.

Brown, G, Copeland, T and Millward, M (1973) Monadic testing of new products – an old problem and some partial solutions, *Journal of the Market Research Society*, 15(2), 112–31.

Brown, S (1996) Art or science? Fifty years of marketing debate, *Journal of Marketing Management*, 12(4), 243–67.

Brown, S and Turley, D (eds) (1997) *Consumer Research: Postcards from the edge*, London: Routledge.

Bryman, A and Burgess, R G (1994) Reflections on qualitative data analysis, in Bryman, A and Burgess, R G (eds), *Analysing Qualitative Data*, London: Routledge.

Bunn, S (1996) Now that India's got GATT, a massive market beckons, *Research Plus*, April, 10–11.

Burdick, R K (1983) Statement of hypotheses in the analysis of variance, *Journal of Marketing Research*, August, 320–24.

Burns, T (1997) Saffron revivalists turn to genetic engineering, *Financial Times*, 15 January.

Butcher, B (1994) Sampling methods – an overview and review, *Survey Methods Centre Newsletter*, 15, 4–8.

Butler, P (1994) Marketing problems: from analysis to decision, *Marketing Intelligence and Planning*, 2(2), 4–13.

Buttle, F (1996) *Relationship Marketing*, London: Paul Chapman.

Byers, P Y and Wilcox, J R (1991) Focus groups: a qualitative opportunity for researchers, *Journal of Business Communication*, 28(1), 63–78.

CACI (1989) *Market Analysis*, London: CACI.

Cahill, D (1998) When to use qualitative marketing research: how about at the midpoint? *Marketing News*, 32(1), 5 January, 15, 17.

Campbell, S (1997) Management: marketing wake-up, *Financial Times*, 3 June.

Carnes, W T (1980) *Effective Meetings for Busy People*, New York: McGraw-Hill.

Carson, D, Gilmore, A, Perry, C and Gronhaug, G (2001) *Qualitative Marketing Research*, London: Sage.

Cateora, P R (1993) *International Marketing* (8th edn), Homewood, IL: Irwin.

Catterall, M and Maclaren, P (1995) Using a computer to code qualitative data, in *Proceedings of 1995 Annual Conference of the Marketing Education Group* 'Making Marketing Work', Bradford University, July.

Catterall, M and Maclaren, P (1997) Focus group data and qualitative analysis programs: coding the moving picture as well as the snapshots, *Sociological Research Online*, 2(1), 1–11.

Cattin, P and Wittink, D (1982) Commercial use of conjoint analysis: a survey, *Journal of Marketing*, 46, 44–53.

Chakrapani, C (2004) *Statistics in Market Research*, London: Arnold.

Chapman, R G (1989) Problem definition in marketing research studies, *Journal of Services Marketing*, 3(3), 51–59.

Chisnall, P M (1992) *Marketing Research* (4th edn), Maidenhead: McGraw-Hill.

Choudry, Y A (1986) Pitfalls of international marketing research: are you speaking French like a Spanish cow? *ABER*, 17(4), Winter, 18–28.

Churchill, G A (1979) A paradigm for developing better measures of marketing constructs, *Journal of Marketing Research*, 16, February, 64–73.

Churchill, G A (1995) *Marketing Research: Methodological foundations* (6th edn), Fort Worth, TX: Dryden.

Churchill, V B (1988) How good is mail panel research? *Address before Advertising Research Foundation Conference*.

Churchill, V B (1988) Learning to live with continuing household panels, *Telenation Reports*, Summer, 1–2.

Clark, L G (1986) Focus groups are a phone call away, *Marketing News*, 3 January.

Cochran, W G and Cox, G M (1957) *Experimental Designs* (2nd edn), New York: Wiley.

Coffey, A and Atkinson, P (1996) *Making Sense of Qualitative Data*, Thousand Oaks, CA: Sage.

Coffey A, Holbrook, B and Atkinson, P (1996) Qualitative data analysis: technologies and representations, *Sociological Research Online*, 2, http://www.socresonline.org.uk/socresonline/1/1/4.html

Cohen, M A, Jehoshua, E and Teck, H H (1997) An anatomy of a decision support system for developing and launching line extensions, *Journal of Marketing Research*, 34, February, 117–29.

Collins, L F (1991) Everything is true, but in a different sense: a new perspective on qualitative research, *Journal of the Market Research Society*, 33, 31–38.

Collins, M (1997) Interviewer variability: a review of the problem, *Journal of the Market Research Society*, 39, 67–84.

Colwell, J (1990) Qualitative market research: a conceptual analysis and review of practitioner criteria, *Journal of the Market Research Society*, 32.

Comley, P (2000) Pop-up surveys: what works, what doesn't work and what will work in the future. *ESOMAR Net Effects Internet Conference*, Dublin, April, http://www.virtualsurveys.com/papers/popup-paper.htm

Cooper, L and Nakanishi, M (1988) *Market Share Analysis: Evaluating competitive marketing effectiveness*, Boston, MA: Kluwer Academic.

Cowan, C D (1991) Using multiple sample frames to improve survey coverage, quality and costs, *Marketing Research: A magazine of management and applications*, 3(4), 66–69.

Cowan, D (1994) Good information, *Journal of the Market Research Society*, 36(2), 105–14.

Cox, W E (1979) *Industrial Marketing Research*, New York: Wiley.

Craig, C S and Douglas, S P (2001) Conducting international marketing research in the twenty-first century, *International Marketing Review*, 18(1), 80–90.

Cresswell, J W (1994) *Research Design: Qualitative and quantitative approaches*, London: Sage.

Crimp, M (1990) *The Marketing Research Process* (3rd edn), Hemel Hempstead: Prentice-Hall.

Crouch, S (1985) *Marketing Research for Managers*, London: Pan.

Cuba, F (1985) Fourteen things that make or break tracking studies, *Journal of Advertising Research*, 25(1), 21–23.

Curwin, J and Slater, R (1991) *Quantitative Methods for Business Decisions* (3rd edn), London: Chapman & Hall.

Daneshkhu, S (1997) The decline and fall of frills, *Financial Times*, 28 April.

Davis, G (1997) Are Internet surveys ready for prime time? *Marketing News*, 7 April, 5.

Davis, T R V (1992) Satisfying internal customers: the link to external customer satisfaction, *Planning Review*, 20(1), 34–37.

Day, E (1998) Know consumers through qualitative research, *Marketing News*, 32(1), 5 January, 14.

Day, E and Stafford, M R (1997) Age-related cues in retail services advertising: their effects on younger consumers, *Journal of Retailing*, 73(2), 211–33.

De Bono, E (1992) in Peter, T, *Liberation Management*, New York: Macmillan.

Deal, K (1997) Determining success factors for financial products: a comparative analysis of CART, Logit and factor/discriminant analysis, *Service Industries Journal*, 17(3), July, 489–506.

Dembhowski, S and Hanmer-Lloyd, S (1995) Computer applications – a new road to qualitative analysis? *European Journal of Marketing*, 29(11), 50–62.

Deming, W E (1950) On errors in surveys, *American Sociological Review*, 9(4).

Dent, T (1992) How to design for a more reliable customer sample, *Business Marketing*, 17(2), 73–76.

Denzin, N and Lincoln, Y (1993) *Handbook of Qualitative Research*, Newbury Park, CA: Sage.

Dillman, D A (1978) *Mail and Telephone Surveys: The total design method*, New York: Wiley Interscience.

Dillman, D A (1991) The design and administration of mail surveys, *Annual Review of Sociology*, 17, 225–49.

Dillman, D A and Tortora, R (1998) Principles for constructing respondent-friendly web surveys and their influence on the response, American Statistical Association Meeting, Dallas.

Dillman, D A, Singer, E, Clark, J R and Treat, J B (1996) Effects of benefits appeals and variations in statements of confidentiality on completion rates for census questionnaires, *Public Opinion Quarterly*, 60(3).

Dolan, C V (1994) Factor analysis of variables with 2, 3, 5 and 7 response categories: a comparison of categorical variable estimators using simulated data, *British Journal of Mathematical and Statistical Psychology*, 47, 309–26.

Donnelly, M, Wisniewski, M, Dalrymple, J F and Curry, A (1995) Measuring service quality in local government: the SERVQUAL approach, *International Journal of Public Sector Management*, 8(7), 15–20.

Douglas, S P and Craig, C S (1983) *International Marketing Research*, Upper Saddle River, NJ: Prentice-Hall.

Dutka, S and Frankel, L R (1988) *Techniques for the Cost-Efficient Sampling of Small or Rare Populations*, New York: Audits and Surveys.

Dwyer, J (1993) *The Business Communication Handbook* (3rd edn), Erskineville, NSW: Star Printery.

Eagleson, R D (1990) *Writing in Plain English*, Canberra, ACT: AGPS.

Eames, A (1997) When time means money, *Financial Times*, 24 May.

Easterby-Smith, M, Thorpe, R and Lowe, A (1991) *Management Research: An introduction*, London: Sage.

Eberhart, R C and Dobbins, R W (1990) *Neural Network PC Tools*, London: Academic Press.

Edwards, F (1995) The French connection, *International Wrist Watch*, 31, 46–48.

EFO Group (1993) *Marketing News*, 21 June.

Eklof, J A, Hackl, P and Westlund, A (1999) On measuring interactions between customer satisfaction and financial results, *Total Quality Management*, 10(4–5), 514–22.

Embree, L (1997) What is phenomenology? Center For Advanced Research in Phenomenology, http://www.phenomenologycenter.org/phenom.htm

Eskin, G (1988) *Setting a Forward Agenda for Test Market Modeling*, New York: Advertising Research Foundation.

Eunson, B (1994) *Writing and Presenting Reports*, Milton, Queensland: Wiley.

Everitt, B S, Landau, S and Leese, M (2000) *Cluster Analysis* (4th edn), London: Arnold.

Farnham, A (1998) Focus groups fail to reach pin-sharp results, *Sunday Telegraph*, 4 October, 27.

Fazey, I H (1997) Watching paint fly, *Financial Times*, 25 September.

Fielding, R and Lee, R (eds) (1991) *Using Computers in Qualitative Analysis*, Berkeley, CA: Sage.

Fishbein, M and Azjen, I (1975) *Belief, Attitude, Intention and Behavior*, Reading, MA: Addison-Wesley.

Flanagan, T A and Fredericks, J O (1993) Improving company performance through customer satisfaction measurement and management, *National Productivity Review*, Spring, 239–58.

Fletcher, K (1995) Jump on the omnibus, *Marketing*, 15 June, 25–28.

Fletcher, W (1984) *Meetings, Meetings*, New York: Morrow.

Fletcher, W (1997) Why researchers are so jittery, *Financial Times*, 3 March.

Foddy, W (1994) *Constructing Questions for Interviews and Questionnaires*, Cambridge: Cambridge University Press.

Fontana, A and Frey, J H (1994) Interviewing: the art of science, in Denzin, N K and Freeling, A (1994), Marketing is in a crisis – can marketing research help? *Journal of the Market Research Society*, 36, 97–104.

Freeman, P (1991) Using computers to extend analysis and reduce data, *Journal of the Market Research Society*, 33(2), 127–36.

Gabor, A and Grainger, C (1966) Price as an indicator of quality, *Economics*, 33, 43–70.

Gabriel, C (1990) The validity of qualitative marketing research, *Journal of the Market Research Society*, 32, October, 507–19.

Geo-Visual Solutions for Today's Business (1990) Mt Olive, NJ: Intelligent Charting.

Gibb, A (1997) Focus groups, *Social Research Update*, 19, Winter, Department of Sociology, University of Surrey, http://www.soc.surrey.ac.uk/sru/sru19.html

Gibson, R (1992) The fine art of stocking a supermarket's shelves, *Wall Street Journal*, 15 October.

Gibson, R (1993) Broad grocery price cuts may not pay, *Wall Street Journal*, 7 May.

Goff, M (1997) Mapping out markets, *Provider*, 23(10), October, 79–80.

Gofton, K (1997) If it moves measure it, *Marketing*, 4 September, 17.

Gold, L N (1996) Do it yourself interviewing, *Marketing Research: A magazine of management and applications*, 8(2), Summer, 40–41.

Goldfisher, K (1992) Modified Delphi: A concept for product forecasting, *Journal of Business Forecasting*, Winter 1992–93.

Gooding, K (1997) Soft drinks switch to PET leaves industry struggling, *Financial Times*, 22 October.

Goodyear, M (1996) The world shrinks, maybe, but there's still the need to travel, *Research Plus*, May, 12.

Gordon, W and Corr, D (1990) The space between words: the application of a new model of communication to quantitative brand image measurement, *Journal of the Market Research Society*, 32(3), 409–35.

Gorle, P (1995) The cascade theory that shows practical gains, *Research Plus*, October, 11.

Goss, J D (1996) Introduction to focus groups, *Area*, 28(6), 14–115.

Government Statistics: A brief guide to sources, London: Office for National Statistics.

Graver, M S (2002) Using data mining for customer satisfaction research, *Marketing Research*, 14(1), 8–12.

Green, P A, Tull, D S and Albaum, G (1988) *Research for Marketing Decisions*, Upper Saddle River, NJ: Prentice-Hall.

Green, P E and Krieger, A M (1989) Recent contributions to optimal product positioning and buyer segmentation, *European Journal of Operational Research*, 41, 127–41.

Green, P E and Krieger, A M (1992) An application of a product positioning model to pharmaceutical products, *Marketing Science*, 11(2), 117–32.

Greenbaum, T L (1984) Keys to improving the effectiveness of focus group research, *Marketing Review*, June–July, 23.

Greenbaum, T L (1988) *The Practical Handbook and Guide to Focus Group Research*, Lexington, MA: Heath.

Greenbaum, T L (1996) Understanding focus group research abroad, *Marketing News*, 30(12), 3 June.

Griffiths, J (1997) World tyre industry may face shake out, *Financial Times*, 14 May.

Griffiths, V (1997) Orchestras aim to pass the baton, *Financial Times*, 20 May.

Griggs, S (1987) Analysing qualitative data, *Journal of the Market Research Society*, 32, 507–20.

Gronroos, C (1990) *Service Management and Marketing: Managing the moments of truth in service competition*, Lexington, MA: Lexington Books.

Grove, S J and Fisk, R P (1992) Observational data collection methods for service marketing: an overview, *Journal of the Academy of Marketing Science*, 20(3), 217–24.

Grover, R and Srinivasan, V (1987) A simultaneous approach to market segmentation and market structuring, *Journal of Marketing Research*, 24, 139–53.

Gubrium, J F and Holstein, J A (2003) *Postmodern Interviewing*, London: Sage.

Gulledge, L G (1991) Satisfying the internal customer, *Bank Marketing*, 23, 46–48.

Gummesson, E (1990) *Qualitative Methods in Management Research*, London: Sage.

Gummesson, E (1993) Quality management in service organizations: an interpretation of the service quality phenomenon and a synthesis of international research, International Service Quality Association, Karlstad, Sweden.

Gummesson, E (2000) *Qualitative Methods in Management Research*, Thousand Oaks, CA: Sage.

Hague, P (1985) *The Industrial Market Research Handbook* (2nd edn), London: Kogan Page.

Hague, P (1987) Good and bad in questionnaire design, *Industrial Marketing Digest*, 12(3), 161–70.

Hague, P (1993) *Questionnaire Design*, London: Kogan Page.

Hague, P and Jackson, P (1996) *Market Research*, London: Kogan Page.

Hague, P and Roberts, C (1994) *Presentation and Report Writing*, London: Kogan Page.

Hahlo, G (1992) Examining the validity of re-interviewing respondents for quantitative surveys, *Journal of the Market Research Society*, 34, 99–118.

Hair, J F, Anderson, R E, Tatham, R L and Black, W C (1992) *Multivariate Data Analysis*, New York: Macmillan.

Hair, J F, Anderson, R E, Tatham, R L and Black, W C (1995) *Multivariate Data Analysis with Readings* (4th edn), New York: Macmillan.

Hallowell, R (1996) The relationship of customer satisfaction, customer loyalty and profitability: an empirical study, *International Journal of Service Industry Management*, 7(4), 27–42.

Hammond, K, Ehrenberg, A S C and Goodhart, G J (1996) Market segmentation for competitive brands, *European Journal of Marketing*, 30, 39–49.

Hammond, M (1986) Creative focus groups: uses and misuses, *Marketing and Media Decisions*, July, 154–55.

Hannabuss, S (1995) Approaches to research, *Aslib Proceedings*, 47, January, 3–11.

Harding, J (1997) China's future dragons, *Financial Times*, 14 August.

Hart, C W L (1995) The power of internal guarantee, *Harvard Business Review*, January–February, 64–73.

Hart, S J, Webb, J R and Jones, M V (1994) Export marketing research and the effect of export experience in industrial SMEs, *International Marketing Review*, 11(6), 4–23.

Haynes, M E (1988) *Effective Meeting Skills*, Los Altos, CA: Crisp.

Heskett, J L, Jones, T O, Loveman, G W, Sasser, W E and Schlesinger, L A (1994) Putting the service profit chain to work, *Harvard Business Review*, March–April, 164–74.

Hess, J M (1968) Group interviewing, in Ring, R L (ed.) *New Science of Planning*, Chicago: American Marketing Association, http://www.socresonline.org.uk/socresonline/2/1/6.html

Hibbins, G M (1990) *Stands to Reason* (4th edn), South Melbourne, Victoria: Macmillan.

Hill, A, Roberts, H, Ewings, P and Gunnell, D (1997) Nonresponse bias in a lifestyle survey, *Journal of Public Health Medicine*, 19(2), June, 203–7.

Hinkin, S (1995) Charting your course to effective information graphics, *Presentations*, 9(11), November.

Hirschman, E C (1986) Humanistic inquiry in marketing research: philosophy, method and criteria, *Journal of Marketing Research*, 23, 237–49.

Hoinville, G, Jowell, R and Associates (eds) (1978) *Survey Research Practice*, London: Heinemann.

Holtgraves, T, Eck, J and Lasky, B (1997) Face management, question wording and social desirability, *Journal of Applied Social Psychology*, 27(18), 1650–71.

Homelink (1993) *Research Plus*, September, 8–9.

Hoover, S V and Perry, R F (1989) *Simulation: A problem-solving approach*, New York: Addison-Wesley.

Hrisak, D M (1997) Key presentation principles, *Chartered Accountants Journal of New Zealand*, 76(3), April, 24.

Huberty, C J (1994) *Applied Discriminant Analysis*, New York: Wiley Interscience.

Huff, D (1991) *How to Lie with Statistics*, Harmondsworth: Penguin.

Hutt, R W (1979) The focus group interview: a technique for counselling small business clients, *Journal of Small Business Management*, 17(1), 15–20.

Hutton, R (1994) Best of the bunch, *Scottish Business Insider*, March, 662–63.

IBM's Butterfly gets crushed on the wheel (1996) *PC Direct*, May, 57.

Jack, A (1997) Canal satellite disappoints, *Financial Times*, 12 September.

Jackson, P (1994) *Buying Market Research*, London: Kogan Page.

Jackson, P (1994) *Desk Research*, London: Kogan Page.

Jamieson, D (1995) Now business research is every agency's research, *Research Plus*, October.

Jick, T D (1979) Mixing qualitative and quantitative methods: triangulation in action, *Administrative Science Quarterly*, 24, 602–11.

JICNARS (1981) *National Readership Survey*, London: JICNARS.

Jobber, D and O'Reilly, D (1996) Industrial mail surveys: techniques for inducing response, *Marketing Intelligence and Planning*, 14(1), 29–34.

Johansson, J K and Nonaka, J (1987) Market research the Japanese way, *Harvard Business Review*, May–June, 16–22.

Jones, J W and McLeod, R (1986) The structure of executive information systems: an exploratory analysis, *Decision Science*, 17, 220–49.

Kaciak, E and Louviere, J (1990) Multiple correspondence analysis of multiple choice experiment data, *Journal of Marketing Research*, 27, 455–65.

Kalton, G and Schuman, H (1982) The effect of the question on survey responses: a review, *Journal of the Royal Statistical Society*, 145, Part 1, 42–73.

Kamakura, W A and Russell, G J (1989) A probabilistic choice model for market segmentation, *Journal of Marketing Research*, 26, 379–90.

Kamakura, W A and Wedel, M (1997) Statistical data fusion for cross-tabulation, *Journal of Marketing Research*, 34(4), November, 485–98.

Kandathil, J (1985) The advantages of electronic test markets: an advertiser view based on experience, *Journal of Advertising Research*, 25(6), 11–12.

Kauder, N B (1996) Pictures worth a thousand words, *American Demographics* (Tools supplement), November, 64–68.

Kaushik, M and Sen, A (1990) Semiotics and qualitative research, *Journal of the Market Research Society*, 32, 227–43.

Keillor, B, Owens, D and Pettijohn, C (2001) A cross-cultural/cross-national study of influencing factors and socially desirable response bias, *International Journal of Market Research*, 43(1), 63–84.

Kent, R and Lee, M (1999) Using the Internet for market research: a study of private trading on the Internet, *Journal of the Market Research Society*, 41(4), 377–85.

Kerlinger, F (1973) *Foundations of Behavioral Research*, New York: Holt, Rinehart & Winston.

Kestylyn, J (1992) Application watch, *AI Expert*, January, 63–64.

Keys, T (1996) Report writing, *Internal Auditor*, 53(4), August.

Kinsey, J (1988) *Marketing in Developing Countries*, London: Macmillan.

Kitzinger, J (1995) Introducing focus groups, *British Medical Journal*, 311, 299–302.

Korents, G (1996) China's other consumers, *Business Week*, 13 May, 11.

Kotler, P (1966) A design for the firm's marketing nerve centre, *Business Horizons*, Fall, 63–74.

Kotler, P (1988) *Marketing Management: Planning, analysis and control* (6th edn), Upper Saddle River, NJ: Prentice-Hall.

Kotler, P and Lilien, G (1983) *Marketing Decision Making: A model-building approach*, New York: Harper & Row.

Kress, G (1988) *Marketing Research* (3rd edn), Upper Saddle River, NJ: Prentice-Hall.

Krueger, R A (1997) *Analyzing and Reporting Focus Group Results: Focus group kit 6*, London: Sage.

Krueger, R A (1997) *Moderating Focus Groups: Focus group kit 4*, London: Sage.

Lafferty, F (1997) Management: the English Bear Company – partners, *Financial Times*, 28 April.

Langbourne, R (1993) How to reach children in stores: marketing tactics grounded in observational research, *Journal of Advertising Research*, 33, November/December, 67–72.

Larson, E (1992) Watching Americans watch TV, *The Atlantic Monthly*, March.

Lautenschlager, G and Flaherty, V L (1990) Computer administration of questions: more desirable or more social desirability? *Journal of Applied Psychology*, 75, 310–14.

Lavidge, R J and Steiner, G A (1961) A model for predictive measurements of advertising effectiveness, *Journal of Marketing*, 25, October, 59–62.

Lenell, W and Bissoneau, R (1996) Using causal comparative and correlational designs in conducting market research, *Journal of Professional Services Marketing*, 13(2), 59–69.

Levitas, R and Guy, W (eds) (1996) *Interpreting Official Statistics*, London: Routledge.

Lewis, D B (1983) Advertising research and measurement, in *Marketing Manager's Handbook*, Chicago, IL: Dartnell.

Lewis, P H (1989) When maps are tied to data bases, *New York Times*, 28, May, F10.

Li, E (1997) Perceived importance of information system success factors: a meta analysis of group differences, *Information and Management*, 32, 15–28.

Likert, R (1932) A technique for the measurements of attitudes, *Archives of Psychology*, 140.

Lilien, G L, Kotler, P and Moorthy, K S (1992) *Marketing Models*, Upper Saddle River, NJ: Prentice-Hall.

Lincoln, Y S and Guba, E G (1985) *Naturalistic Inquiry*, Beverly Hills, CA: Sage.

Lindstone, H and Turoff, M (eds) (1975) *The Delphi Method*, Reading, MA: Addison-Wesley.

Locander, W, Sudman, S and Bradburn, N M (1976) An investigation of interview method, threat and response distortion, *Journal of the American Statistical Association*, 71, 269–75.

Lynch, T (1997) Caught in the neighbours' tangled web, *Financial Times*, 15 August.

Macht, J (1999) The new market research, *Inc*, 20(10), 86–94.

Magidson, D and Polcha, A E (1992) Creating market economies within organisations, a conference on internal markets, *Planning Review*, January–February, 37–40.

Malhotra, N K (1995) *Marketing Research: An application orientation*, Upper Saddle River, NJ: Prentice-Hall.

Malhotra, N K, Agarwal, J and Peterson, M (1996) Cross-cultural marketing research: methodological issues and guidelines, *International Marketing Review*, 13(5), 7–43.

Malhotra, R (1988) *Some Issues and Perspectives on Use of Simulated Test Markets*, New York: Advertising Research Foundation.

Marek, D (1998) We all need to address declining respondent co-operation, http://www.mra-net.org.

Markland, R E (1983) *Topics in Management Science*, New York: Wiley.

Marks, A P (1990) The Sinclair 5 – why did it fail? *Management Decision*, 28(4), 9–14.

Marsh, C and Scarborough, C (1990) Testing nine hypotheses about quota sampling, *Journal of the Market Research Society*, 32, October, 485–506.

Marsh, P (1997) The growing business: same aims, different strategies, *Financial Times*, 23 December.

Marshall, K P (1996) *Marketing Information Systems*, Danvers, MA: Boyd & Fraser.

Mathews, A (1997) Academic xenophobia and the analysis of focus group data, *Journal of Targeting, Measurement and Analysis for Marketing*, 6(2), 160–71.

Mattson, J (1990) Measuring inherent product values, *European Journal of Marketing*, 24(9), 25–39.

Mayer, M (1990) Scanning the future, *Forbes*, 15 October.

Mazzella, G F (1997) Show and tell focus groups reveal core boomer values, *Marketing News*, 3(12), H8.

McCann, J M (1986) *The Marketing Workbench*, Homewood, IL: Dow-Jones Irwin.

McCann, P (1996) Commercial TV audiences rise . . . , *Marketing Week*, 26 April, 15.

McCarthy, K (1992) Comment on the 'Analytic Delphi Method', *International Journal of Production Economics*, May.

McClelland, J L and Rumelhart, D E (1988) *Explorations in Parallel Distributed Processing: A handbook of models, programs and exercises*, Cambridge, MA: MIT Press.

McConagle, J J and Vella, C M (1990) *Outsmarting the Competition*, Naperville, IL: Sourcebooks.

McCullough, D (1999) Why marketing research is a waste of money (and what you can do about it), *Marcom Today*, November.

McDaniel, C and Gates, R (2002) *Marketing Research: The impact of the internet* (5th edn), Cincinnati, OH: South-Western.

McDonald, W (1993) Focus groups research dynamics, *Journal of the Academy of Marketing Science*, 21(2), 161–68.

McKenzie, J (1988) Study of characteristics of ex-directory telephone owners, *Market Research Newsletter*, December.

McKenzie J, Schaefer, R L and Farber, E (1995) *The Student Edition of Minitab for Windows*, Reading, MA: Addison-Wesley.

McKie, A (1996) International research in a relative world, *Journal of the Market Research Society*, 38(1), 7–12.

Mchta, R and Sivadas, E (1995) Comparing response rates and response context in mail vs electronic mail surveys, *Journal of Marketing Research Society*, 37(4), 429–39.

Miles, M B and Huberman, A M (1994) *Qualitative Data Analysis*, London: Sage.

Mitchell, V (1995) Using astrology in market segmentation, *Management Decision*, 33(1), 48–57.

Mitchell, V-W (1992) Using Delphi to forecast new technology industries, *Marketing Intelligence and Planning*, 10(2).

Mohanty, R P and Deshmukh, S G (1997) Evolution of a decision support system for human resource planning in a petroleum company, *International Journal of Production Economics*, 51(3), September, 251–61.

Mohn, N C (1989) How to present marketing research results effectively, *Marketing & Research Today*, 17(2), 115–18.

Morgan, D L (1998) *The Focus Group Guidebook: Focus group kit 1*, London: Sage.

Morris, S (1990) *Using Personal Computers in Marketing*, Oxford: NCC Blackwell.

Morton-Williams, J (1978) Questionnaire design, in Worcester, R and Downham, J (eds), *Consumer Market Research Handbook*, Wokingham: Van Nostrand Reinhold.

Morton-Williams, J and Sykes, W (1984) The use of interaction coding, *Journal of the Market Research Society*, 26(2), April.

Moskowitz, H R (1985) *New Directions for Product Testing and Sensory Analysis of Foods*, Westport, CT: Food and Nutrition Press.

Moult, W M (1988) *The Role of Simulated Test Markets and Test Markets*, New York: Advertising Research Foundation.

Mouncey, P (1996) With growing demands for data, will purity prove only theoretical? *Research Plus*, May, 9.

Moutinho, L and Evans, M (1992) *Applied Marketing Research*, Harlow: Addison-Wesley.

Munson, J and McIntery, S (1979) Developing practical procedures for measurement of personal values in cross-cultural marketing, *Journal of Marketing Research*, 16.

Murray, P J (1997) Using virtual focus groups in qualitative research, *Qualitative Health Research*, 7(4), 542–49.

Myers, J H (1996) *Segmentation and Positioning for Strategic Marketing Decisions*, Chicago: AMA.

Nairn, G (1997) Golden nuggets on a long and winding road, *Financial Times*, 3 December.

Newton, S (1993) From hearses to horses: launching the Volvo 850, *Journal of the Market Research Society*, 33, 153–62.

Nicholas, R (1994) Avon ads praise the real woman, *Marketing*, 27 January, 6.

Number News (1990) New products, June, 8.

Nuttall, C (1996) Research needs more creativity, *Marketing Week*, 29 April, 32.

Nutting, J and White, G (1992) *The Business of Communication* (2nd edn), Roseville, CA: McGraw-Hill.

Ohanian, R (1990) Construction and validation of a scale to measure celebrity endorsers' perceived expertise, trustworthiness and attractiveness, *Journal of Advertising*, 19(3), 39–52.

Oppenheim, A N (1984) *Question Design and Attitude Measurement*, London: Heinemann.

Oppermann, M (1995) E-mail survey – potentials and pitfalls, *Market Research*, 7(3), 29–33.

Orme, B and Huber, J (2000) Improving the value of conjoint simulations, *Marketing Research*, 12, Winter, 12–21.

Osgood, C, Suci, G and Tannenbaum, P (1987) *The Measurement of Meaning*, Urbana, IL: University of Illinois Press.

Parasuraman, A, Berry, L L and Zeithaml, V (1985) A conceptual model of service quality and the implications for future research, *Journal of Marketing*, 49, 41–51.

Parker, L (1992) Collecting data the e-mail way, *Training and Development*, 52–54.

Pawle, J (1999) Mining the international consumer, *Journal of the Market Research Society*, 41(1), 19–32.

Payne, S L (1951) *The Art of Asking Questions*, Princeton, NJ: Princeton University Press.

Pereira, R E (1999) Factors influencing consumer perceptions of web-based decision support systems, *Logistics Information Management*, 12(1/2), 157–81.

Perrott, N (1995) Research that becomes part of a company's strategy, *Research Plus*, October, 6ff.

Perry C, Reige, A and Brown, L (1999) Realism's role among scientific paradigms in marketing research, *Irish Marketing Review*, 12(2), 16–23.

Peter, P J and Olson, C (1989) The relativist/constructionist perspective on scientific knowledge and consumer research, in Hirschman, E (ed.), *Interpretive Consumer Research*, Provo, UT: ACR.

Piercy, N (1996) The effects of customer satisfaction measurement: the internal market versus the external market, *Marketing Intelligence and Planning*, 14(4), 9.

Piercy, N and Evans, M (1993) *Managing Marketing Information*, London: Croom Helm.

Piercy, N and Morgan, N (1995) Customer satisfaction measurement and management: a processual analysis, *Journal of Marketing Management*, 11, 817–34.

Poster watch (1996) *Marketing Week*, 26 April, 58.

Proctor, R A (1992) Marketing decision support systems: a role for neural networking, *Marketing Intelligence and Planning*, 10(1), 21–26.

Proctor, R A (1994) Queues and the power of simulation in helping with business decisions and problems, *Management Decision*, 32(1), 50–55.

Proctor, R A (1994) Simulation in management services, *Management Services*, 38(1), January, 18–23.

Proctor, S, Papasolomou-Doukakis, I and Proctor, T (2001) What are TV advertisements really trying to tell us? A postmodern perspective, *Journal of Consumer Behaviour*, 1(3), 246–55.

Proctor, T (1992) *Essential Marketing*, London: Collins Educational.

Proctor, T (1999) *Creative Problem Solving for Managers*, London: Routledge.

Ranchhod, A and Zhou, E (2001) Comparing respondents of email and mail surveys: understanding the implications of technology, *Marketing Intelligence and Planning*, 19(4), 254–62.

Ratner, B (2003) *Statistical Modeling and Analysis for Database Marketing*, London and Boca Raton, FL: Chapman & Hall/CRC.

Raudsepp, T (1987) Establishing a creative climate, *Training and Development Journal*, April, 50–53.

Rawlins, K (1993) *Presentation and Communication Skills: A handbook for practitioners*, London: Emap Healthcare Ltd.

Rebondir (1996) Un restaurant de gambas ouvrir un commerce, 12, 35.

Reed, D (1996) The data game, *Marketing Week*, 3 May, 47–51.

Rees, J (1996) PepsiCo needs new strategy for iced tea, *Marketing Week*, 16 April, 23.

Research propels innovation (1994) *Marketing*, 27 January, 33–35.

Richards, T and Richards, L (1991) The NUD*IST qualitative data analysis system, *Qualitative Sociology*, 14.

Riche, M F (1990) A bigger role for telephone interviews, *American Demographics*, September, 17.

Rickards, T (1974) *Problem Solving through Creative Analysis*, Aldershot: Gower.

Rickards, T (1988) Creativity and innovation: a transatlantic perspective, *Creativity and Innovation Yearbook*, Manchester: Manchester Business School.

Ricks, D A, Fu, Y C and Arpan, S (1974) *International Business Blunders*, Columbus, OH: Grid.

Robson, C (1993) *Real World Research*, Oxford: Blackwell.

Robson, S (1991) Ethics: informed consent or misinformed compliance? *Journal of the Market Research Society*, 33, 19–28.

Rogers, K (1996) Correspondence analysis: the big picture, *Quirk's Marketing Research Review*, Article 2, April.

Rosenfeld, J (1985) Speeding up test marketing, *Marketing Communications*, June.

Rosser, M (1995) Modelling game theory with spreadsheets, *Cheer*, 9(2), 15–18.

Rothenberg, R (1989) The trouble with mail interviewing, *New York Times*, 16 August.

Rowland, M L and Forthofer, R N (1993) Adjusting for non-response bias in a health examination survey, *Public Health Reports*, 108(3), May–June, 380–86.

Russo, J (1988) Simulated test markets in the real world, *Pre-Test Market Research*, New York: Advertising Research Foundation, 118–19.

Rydholm, J (1997) Right on cue: mystery shopping makes sure salespeople sing praises of Yamaha digital pianos, *Quirk's Marketing Review*, Article 234, January.

Safety letterbox (1996) *Business Opportunities World*, May, 64–65.

Samways, A and Whittcome, K (1994) UK brand strategies, *Financial Times Management Report*.

Sanderson, T (1996) How a spoonful of research helps the medicine go down, *Research Plus*, April, 6–8.

Sawyer, A and Peter, J P (1983) The significance of statistical significance tests in marketing research, *Journal of Marketing Research*, 20, May, 125.

Schindler, R M (1992) The real lesson of New Coke: the value of focus groups for predicting the effects of social influence, *Marketing Research: A magazine of management and applications*, December, 22–27.

Schmitz, J D, Armstrong, G D and Little, J D C (1990) Cover story: automated news findings, *Marketing Interfaces*, 20(6), 29–38.

Schneider, K C and Johnson, J C (1995) Stimulating response to market surveys of business professionals, *Industrial Marketing Management*, 24, 265–76.

Schuldt, B A and Totten, J W (1999) Email surveys: what we've learned thus far, *Quirk's Marketing Research Review*, July, www.quirks.com.

Scott, A (1996) The launch went fine – then the devil's in the detailing, *Research Plus*, April, 14.

Seaton, A V (1997) Unobtrusive observational measures as a qualitative extension of visitor surveys at festivals and events: mass observation revisited, *Journal of Travel Research*, 35(4), Spring, 25–30.

Semon, T T (1994) A good sample of accounts may not always be a good sample of your customers, *Marketing News*, 28(9), 8–11.

Semon, T T (1994) Save a few bucks on sample size, risk millions in opportunity loss, *Marketing News*, 28(1), 19.

Shait, D I (1994) Report writing, *HR Focus*, 71(2), 20.

Shea, C Z and LeBourveau, C (2000) Jumping the hurdles of marketing research, *Marketing Research*, 12(3), 22–30.

Sheehan, K B and McMillan, S J (1999) Response variation in e-mail surveys: an exploration, *Journal of Advertising Research*, 39(4), 45–54.

Silverman, D (1993) *Interpreting Qualitative Data*, London: Sage.

Singer, E, Von Thurn, D R and Miller, E R (1995) Confidentiality assurances and response. A quantitative review of the experimental literature, *Public Opinion Quarterly*, 59(1), 67–77.

Sirkin, A F (1995) Maximizing customer satisfaction, *MLS: Marketing Library Services*, 9(4), 3–4.

Skapinker, M (1997) Deceptive appearance, *Financial Times*, 3 February.

Smith, A (1995) Quality aspects of service marketing, *Marketing Intelligence and Planning*, 8(6), 25–32.

Smith, A (1997) Baby boomers get the message, *Financial Times*, 26 May.

Smith, A (1997) Opinion polling faces new scrutiny, *Financial Times*, 21 March.

Smith, A (1997) Public puts faith in brand names, *Financial Times*, 13 October.

Smith, A (1997) Shoppers under the microscope, *Financial Times*, 5 December.

Smith, L A and Gupta, S (1985) Project management software in P & IM, *P & IM Review and APICS News*, June, 66–68.

Snell, F (1979) *How to Win the Meeting*, New York: Hawthorn.

Soroczynski, P (1999) *Technical Communication Handbook*, Darwin, NT: NTU Press.

Sorrell, M (1997) The future lies abroad, *Financial Times*, 30 June.

South Africa: a world in one country (1996) South Africa Tourism Board.

Spiggle, S (1994) Analysis and interpretation of qualitative data in consumer research, *Journal of Consumer Research*, 21, December, 491–503.

Stanton, J M (1998) An empirical assessment of data collection using the Internet, *Personnel Psychology*, 51(3), 709–26.

Stapel, H (1991) Like the advertisement but does it interest me? *ADMAP*, April.

Stapel, J (1990) Monitoring advertising performance, *ADMAP*, July/August.

Steinberg, M and Planck, R E (1990) Implementing expert systems into business-to-business marketing practice, *Journal of Business and Industrial Marketing*, 5(2), 15–26.

Stern, B B (ed.) (1998) *Representing Consumers: Voices, views, visions*, London: Routledge.

Strauss, A S (1993) *Qualitative Analysis for Social Scientists*, Cambridge: Cambridge University Press.

Strauss, A S and Corbin, J (1990) *Basics of Qualitative Research*, London: Sage.

Strutton, D and Pelton, L (1994) A multiple correspondence analysis of telephone contact rates, *Mid-Atlantic Journal of Business*, 30(1), 27–39.

Studies of Media and Markets (1989) New York: Simmons Market Research Bureau.

Sussmans, J (1991) *How to Write Effective Reports*, Aldershot: Gower.

Sutherland, K (ed.) (1994) *Researching Business Markets*, London: Kogan Page.

Swindley, D (1992) Retail buying in the United Kingdom, *The Service Industries Journal*, 12, 533–44.

Sykes, W (1990) Validity and reliability in qualitative marketing research: a review of the literature, *Journal of the Market Research Society*, 33, 3–12.

Sylvester, S (1993) Don't ask consumers to supply your answers, *Research Plus*, November, 8.

Synodinos, N E and Brennan, J E (1988) Computer interactive interviewing in survey research, *Psychology and Marketing*, 5, Summer, 115–38.

Taha, H A (1992) *Operations Research: An introduction* (5th edn), New York: Macmillan.

Taylor, H (2000) Does Internet research work? Comparing online survey results with telephone survey, *International Journal of Market Research*, 42(1), 51–63.

Taylor, P (1997) Breakthroughs in business intelligence, *Financial Times*, 7 May.

Taylor, P (1997) Electronic revolution in the retailing world, *Financial Times*, 3 September.

Teleconference Network (1990) Orangeburg, NY: The Market Navigator.

Test markets: winners and losers (1983) *Advertising Week*, 3 October.

Thomsett, C (1989) *The Little Black Book of Business Meetings*, New York: American Management Association.

Tillet, L S (2000) A 24-hour focus group – sites dig into search queries to learn consumer preferences, *Internet Week*, 808, 10 April, 170.

Timmins, N (1997) British divided into four types, *Financial Times*, 5 September.

Tse, C B, Tse, K C, Yin, C H, Ting, C B, Yi, K W, Yee, K P and Hong, W C (1995) Comparing two methods of sending out questionnaires: e-mail vs mail, *Journal of the Market Research Society*, 37(4).

Tull, D S and Hawkins, D I (1990) *Marketing Research: Measurement and method*, New York: Macmillan.

Tyrrell, B (1994) Eastern promise is worth all the pain of red tape, *Marketing*, 3 February, 5.

Uncles, M D, Hammond, K A, Ehrenberg, A S C and Davies, R E (1994) A replication study of two brand-loyalty measures, *European Journal of Operational Research*, 76, 375–84.

Vinten, G (1997) The threat in the question, *Credit Control*, 18(1), 25–31.

Waddell, D and Sohal, A S (1994) Forecasting: the key to managerial decision making, *Management Decision*, 32(1), 46.

Warner, S L (1965) Randomised response: a survey technique for eliminating evasive answer bias, *Journal of the American Statistical Association*, 60, 63–69.

Watson, H J and Blackstone, J H (1989) *Computer Simulation*, New York: Wiley.

Watson, M A (1992) Researching minorities, *Journal of the Market Research Society*, 34(4), 337–44.

Weible, R and Wallace, J (1998) Cyber research: the impact of the Internet on data collection, *Market Research*, 10(3), 19–27.

Weinman, C (1991) It's not an 'art', but marketing research can be creative, *Marketing News*, 25(8), 9–24.

Weitzman, E and Miles, M (1995) *Computer Programs for Qualitative Data Analysis*, Thousand Oaks, CA: Sage.

West, C (1995) Marketing research, in Baker, M J (ed.) *Companion Encyclopaedia of Marketing*, London: Routledge.

Westland, J C (1992) Self-organising executive information networks, *Decision Support Systems*, 8, 41–53.

Wheatley, K and Flexmer, W A (1987) Option Technologies, Inc., *Marketing News*, 27 February, 23.

Whipple, T W (1994) Mapping focus group data, *Marketing Research*, 6(1), 16–21.

White, D M and Abels, E G (1995) Measuring service quality in special libraries: lessons from service marketing, *Special Libraries*, 86, Winter, 36–45.

White, S (1993) Get a helping of the sugar-free chips game, *Research Plus*, September, 3.

Wilkinson, S (1998) Focus group methodology: a review, *International Journal of Social Research Methodology*, 1(3), 181–203.

Winters, P (1996) Of mergers, managers, money, mailsters . . . and patients too, *Research Plus*, April.

Workman, J P (1993) Marketing's limited role in new product development in one computer system firm, *Journal of Marketing Research*, 30, November, 405–21.

Yava, U (1996) Demand forecasting in a service setting, *Journal of International Marketing and Marketing Research*, 21(1), February, 3–11.

Yin, K R (1994) *Case Study Research – Design and Methods*, Newbury Park CA: Sage.

Zeisel, H (1985) *Say It with Figures*, New York: Harper & Row.

Zeithaml, V A, Berry, L L and Parasuraman, A (1993) The nature and determinants of customer expectations of a service, *Journal of the Academy of Marketing Science*, 21(1), 1–12.

Zeithaml, V A, Berry, L L and Parasuraman, A (1996) The behavioral consequences of service quality, *Journal of Marketing*, 60, April, 31–46.

Zeithaml, V A, Parasuraman, A and Berry, L L (1990) *Delivering Quality Service*, New York: Free Press.

Zemke, R (1978) How market research techniques can pay off for trainers, *Training*, 15(12).

Index

Numbers in **bold** indicate glossary entries.